HISTORICAL TIME LINE

Korean War, during which amphetamines are distributed to soldiers	1950–1953	
		1973	Drug Enforcement Administration (DEA) established
Boggs Act increases penalties for drug law violations	1951	
		1976	President Jimmy Carter campaigns to decriminalize marijuana
Narcotic Control Act further increases penalties for drug law violations	1956	
		1977	Popularity of cocaine reflected in glamorous media portrayals
Widespread use of amphetamines as a diet aid	1950s–60s	
		1978	"Cocaine wars" in Florida between rival Colombian groups
Attitudes toward recreational drug use change; LSD becomes popular; medical profession re-asserts itself on the issue of drug abuse—there is a new focus on treatment, including the use of methadone	1960s	
		1980s	New "drug scare"; crack cocaine becomes popular; smokable form of amphetamine, *ice*, appears; Mexico becomes a major transshipment point for Colombian cocaine
		1981	Rise of the Medellin cartel
California establishes a civil commitment program to treat drug addicts	1961	
		1982	FBI given concurrent jurisdiction with the DEA for drug law enforcement
Several states decriminalize possession of marijuana for personal use	1970s	
		1986	College basketball star Len Bias dies of a cocaine overdose
Legislation representing a new legal approach to federal drug policy predicated, not on the constitutional power to tax, but on federal authority over interstate commerce; Comprehensive Drug Abuse Prevention and Control Act consolidates previous drug laws and reduces penalties for marijuana possession	1970	
		1988	Office of National Drug Control Strategy established
		1990s	Remarkable for the lack of political interest in drug abuse
		1993	Pablo Escobar is killed by Colombian police
		1995	Crack use declines
At a press conference President Richard Nixon says drug abuse is public enemy number one in the United States—during his administration, the majority of funding goes towards treatment rather than law enforcement	1971	
		2000	Absence of drugs as a political issue
		2001	Ecstasy use becomes more prevalent and heroin (for smoking) makes a comeback
National Commission on Marijuana and Drug Abuse recommends possession of marijuana for personal use be decriminalized; French Connection between Corsican gangsters and the American Mafia is broken and heroin shortage ensues	1972	
		2004	Methamphetamine use increases, particularly in more rural parts of the country
		2005	A new prescription painkiller, OxyContin, becomes an important drug of abuse
		2006	Afghanistan becomes the world's leading source of heroin

Drug Use and Abuse

Drug Use and Abuse

A Comprehensive Introduction

SIXTH EDITION

Howard Abadinsky
St. John's University

THOMSON ™
WADSWORTH

Australia • Brazil • Canada • Mexico • Singapore • Spain
United Kingdom • United States

THOMSON

WADSWORTH

Drug Use and Abuse: A Comprehensive Introduction, **Sixth Edition**
Howard Abadinsky

Senior Acquisitions Editor, Criminal Justice:
   Carolyn Henderson Meier
Assistant Editor: Rebecca Johnson
Editorial Assistant: Beth McMurray
Marketing Manager: Terra Schultz
Marketing Assistant: Emily Elrod
Marketing Communications Manager: Tami Schultz
Project Manager, Editorial Production: Jennie Redwitz
Creative Director: Rob Hugel
Art Director: Vernon Boes
Print Buyer: Judy Inouye

Permissions Editor: Bobbie Broyer
Production Service: Antima Gupta, ICC Macmillan Inc.
Photo Researcher: Billie Porter
Copy Editor: Barbara Willette
Cover Designer: Yvo Riezebos Design
Cover Image: Top left: Photodisc Red/Getty Images;
   top right: istockphoto.com; bottom: John Still/Photographer's
   Choice/Getty Images
Compositor: ICC Macmillan Inc.
Text and Cover Printer: Thomson West

Library of Congress Control Number: 2007921613

ISBN-13: 978-0-495-09339-8
ISBN-10: 0-495-09339-4

Thomson Higher Education
10 Davis Drive
Belmont, CA 94002-3098
USA

For more information about our products, contact us at:
Thomson Learning Academic Resource Center
1-800-423-0563
For permission to use material from this text or product,
submit a request online at
http://www.thomsonrights.com.
Any additional questions about permissions can be
submitted by e-mail to
thomsonrights@thomson.com.

Photo Credits

p. 2: © Richard Hutchings/PhotoEdit
p. 18: © AP Photo/The Herald Leader, Pablo Alcala
p. 33: © Bettmann/Corbis
p. 41: © Bettmann/Corbis
p. 97: © AP Photo/CP, Stephen Thorne
p. 101: © VCG/Getty Images
p. 130: © J. Pickerell/The Image Works
p. 134: © Janine Wiedel Photolibrary/Alamy
p. 168: © Brand X Pictures/Alamy
p. 177: © AP Photo/David Zalubowski
p. 187: © Michael Jang/Getty Images
p. 212: © Imagesource/Photolibrary

p. 230: © AP Images
p. 243: © AP Photo/Lee Mariner
p. 273: © Index Stock Imagery
p. 292: © Greg Smith/Corbis
p. 309: © Francoise de Mulder/Corbis
p. 348: © Amy C. Etra/PhotoEdit
p. 381: © Owen Franken/Getty Images
p. 382: © Tony Freeman/PhotoEdit
p. 407: © A. Ramey/PhotoEdit
p. 415: © Fiora Leeuwenberg/Corbis

Brief Contents

Contents

CHAPTER 10   Drug Abuse Prevention   269

Preface

While there are numerous texts on drug abuse, most focus on a particular aspect or aspects of the issue: pharmacology, psychology, sociology, treatment, the business of drugs, prevention, laws and law enforcement, or policy. This book is different. Rather than focusing on a single aspect of drug abuse, this text provides the reader with a thorough understanding of drug abuse, examining drug history, the biological, psychological, and sociological explanations of drug abuse, the various types of treatment and prevention programs, the business of drugs, and drug laws and law enforcement. Without an understanding of these topics, an informed discussion of drug abuse policy is not possible. And without an understanding of the dynamics of drug abuse, a discussion of the problem becomes an exercise equivalent to the proverbial blind men attempting to describe an elephant—each can accurately portray only that part he or she can touch. Hence the logic for the comprehensive nature of this book.

Because the subject of drugs transcends so many disciplines—history, law, neuropharmacology, political science, social work, counseling, psychology, and sociology—the literature is massive and diverse, and putting together all aspects of drug abuse in a single book is a daunting task. This Sixth Edition nonetheless maintains the comprehensive approach the book is known for, updating and adding information on pharmacology, inhalants, herbal stimulants, "club drugs," the changing nature of the drug business, and recent developments in policy. Other updates include:

- Chapter 1: Updated and expanded material on estimates of the extent of drug use.
- Chapter 2: Extended and updated coverage of drug use history and legislation.
- Chapters 3, 4, 5, 6: Updated research findings on drugs of abuse.
- Chapter 6: New coverage of the controversy surrounding medical use of marijuana; expanded coverage of "club drugs" such as Ecstasy; and new coverage of the problem of prescription drug abuse.
- Chapter 9: Expanded coverage of drug abuse treatment and research results.
- Chapter 10: Expanded coverage of the efforts at drug abuse prevention.
- Chapter 11: Expanded and updated coverage of the business of drugs.
- Chapters 12, 13, 14: Expanded coverage of drug use policy issues with an extensive international focus.

ORGANIZATION

Drug Use and Abuse: A Comprehensive Introduction is organized into 14 chapters using a syllabus format for ease of classroom presentation.

- *Chapter 1* explores the drug use continuum from abstinence to dependence and the slippery term *drug abuse*. Categories of drugs and methods for estimating their prevalence are explained, as well as the relationship between drugs, crime, and violence.
- *Chapter 2* presents a history of the drugs of abuse, beginning with the temperance movement and Prohibition, the patent medicine problem, and the intertwining of foreign affairs in the Opium Wars and the Harrison Act. The chapter reviews the opiates, the erratic popularity of cocaine in its various forms, the marijuana saga, the history of artificial depressants and stimulants, and natural and artificial hallucinogens. There is an examination of United States policy as it moved from indifference to the "war on drugs."
- *Chapter 3* explores the complex world of neurology—but explanatory diagrams and easily understood prose reveal that it is "science for poets." This prepares the student for examining how each of the drugs of abuse manipulates the organism to produce its effects in Chapters 4, 5, and 6. This chapter examines the disease model, arousal theory, and genetic predisposition, as well as the roles of setting and expectations in producing a drug's effects.
- *Chapter 4* focuses on depressants, from opiates to alcohol and sedatives to inhalants. It identifies the role of neurotransmitters, which while they can produce profound positive effects—euphoria, stress inhibition, pain reduction—can also result in dependence, addiction, and death.

- *Chapter 5* focuses on stimulants ranging from caffeine and nicotine to cocaine and amphetamines. Here as well neurotransmitters play a major role, both in producing positive effects such as euphoria, increased energy levels, enhanced mood, and lessening of depression, can also lead to dependence, damage to critical organs, and death.

- *Chapter 6* examines hallucinogens and marijuana, which has depressing, stimulating, and hallucinogenic characteristics. So-called *psychedelics* overwhelm the nervous system's ability to modulate sensory input, and produce altered perceptions of reality, sensory illusions, and hallucinations. These substances range from those used in religious ceremonies by Native Americans, to LSD, PCP, and the so-called "club drugs" MDA and MDMA/ecstasy.

- *Chapter 7* examines sociological studies and theories that consider psychoactive drugs in their social context, characterizes their stages, and suggests explanations for their abuse. Combined with the biological views of Chapters 3 to 6, this chapter and the psychological views expressed in Chapter 8 provide the full range of knowledge critical to an informed view of the causes of drug abuse.

- *Chapter 8* moves the study of drug abuse to the field of psychology. It examines the two major branches of that discipline, one based on psychoanalytic theory, the other on behavior/learning theory, and their explanations for drug abuse.

- *Chapter 9* reviews the various treatment approaches to drug abuse, reflecting drug abuse causes explored in Chapters 3 through 8. Programs ranging from methadone to mandatory, private and public, in- and outpatient, twelve-step, and the therapeutic community are described and their theoretical underpinnings discussed. There is an analysis of the difficulty of evaluating drug program effectiveness and the lack of research support for much of what is offered as substance abuse treatment.

- *Chapter 10* explores the relatively new and often illusory field of drug abuse prevention through a critique of basic premises and a description of the leading programs. Research on prevention is analyzed and the alternative harm reduction approach discussed.

- *Chapter 11* provides a tour of the drug economy as characterized by freewheeling capitalism that responds only to market conditions of supply and demand, and as influenced by competitive violence and law enforcement efforts. There is an examination of the business of drugs, a world filled with private armies and violence, from its highest (international) levels down through mid-level wholesalers and finally to the retail (street) level. The chapter ends with a discussion of a critical element in the wholesale drug business: the various methods used to launder money.

- *Chapter 12* looks at the law enforcement response to the business of drugs as constrained by the U.S. Constitution and jurisdictional limitations. There is an examination of the various statutes used to investigate and prosecute drug offenders, such as conspiracy, RICO, tax, and money-laundering laws, as well as the investigative agencies and the techniques of drug law enforcement. The chapter concludes with an analysis of these techniques.

- *Chapter 13* ties together all of the previous chapters with an examination and critical analysis of U.S. policy with respect to drug abuse.
- *Chapter 14* extends the drug policy issue beyond our borders by examining the approach taken in Great Britain and the European alternative referred to as *harm reduction*. The chapter concludes with a comparative critique of drug decriminalization/legalization.
- Because the language of drugs and drug abuse can be confusing, an extensive *glossary* is presented after Chapter 14.

SUPPLEMENTS

An extensive package of supplemental aids accompanies this edition of *Drug Use and Abuse: An Introduction*. They are available to qualified adopters. Please consult your local sales representative for details.

Instructor Resources

Instructor's Resource Manual   The already extensive *Instructor's Resource Manual*, which is available in both print and electronic formats, has been completely revised and updated for this edition by Gordon Armstrong. The instructor's resources include learning objectives, detailed chapter outlines, key terms and definitions, class exercises, and discussion questions for each chapter of the text. The *Instructor's Resource Manual* also features a full test bank containing approximately 60 multiple choice, true-false, fill-in-the-blank, and essay questions for each chapter, accompanied by a full answer key.

The Wadsworth Criminal Justice Resource Center www.thomsonedu. com/criminaljustice   Designed with the instructor in mind, this website features information about Thomson Wadsworth's technology and teaching solutions, as well as several features created specifically for today's criminal justice student. Supreme Court updates, timelines, and hot-topic polling can all be used to supplement in-class assignments and discussions. You'll also find a wealth of links to careers and news in criminal justice, book-specific sites, and much more.

The Wadsworth Criminal Justice Video Library   So many exciting, new videos—so many great ways to enrich your lectures and spark discussion of the material in this text. View our full video offerings and download clip lists with running times at **www.thomsonedu.com/criminaljustice/media_center/index.html**. Your Thomson Wadsworth representative will be happy to provide details on our video policy by adoption size. The library includes these selections and many others:

- *ABC® Videos*: Feature short, high-interest clips from current news events as well as historic raw footage going back 40 years. Perfect for discussion starters or to enrich your lectures and generate interest in the material in the text, these brief videos provide students with a new lens through which to view the past and present, one that will greatly enhance their knowledge and understanding of significant events and open up to them new dimensions in learning. Clips are drawn from such programs as *World News Tonight*, *Good Morning America*, *This Week*, *PrimeTime Live*, *20/20*, and *Nightline*, as well as numerous ABC News specials and material from the Associated Press Television News and British Movietone News collections. Your Thomson Wadsworth representative will be happy to provide a complete listing of videos and policies.

- *60 Minutes DVD*: Featuring 12-minute clips from CBS's *60 Minutes* news program, this DVD will give you a way to explore a topic in more depth with your students without taking up a full class session. Topics include the Green River Killer, the reliability of DNA testing, and California's Three Strikes Law. Produced by Wadsworth, CBS, and Films for the Humanities.
- *The Wadsworth Custom Videos for Criminal Justice*: Produced by Wadsworth and Films for the Humanities, these videos include short five- to ten-minute segments that encourage classroom discussion. Topics include white-collar crime, domestic violence, forensics, suicide and the police officer, the court process, the history of corrections, prison society, and juvenile justice.
- *Oral History Project*: Developed in association with the American Society of Criminology, the Academy of Criminal Justice Society, and the National Institute of Justice, these videos will help you introduce your students to the scholars who have developed the criminal justice discipline. Compiled over the last several years, each video features a set of Guest Lecturers— scholars whose thinking has helped to build the foundation of present ideas in the discipline. Vol. 1: Moments in Time; Vol. 2: Great Moments in Criminological Theory; Vol. 3: Research Methods.
- *Court TV*: One-hour videos presenting seminal and high-profile cases, such as the interrogation of Michael Crowe and serial killer Ted Bundy, as well as crucial and current issues such as cyber crime, double jeopardy, and the management of the prison on Riker's Island.
- *A & E American Justice*: Forty videos to choose from on topics such as deadly force, women on death row, juvenile justice, strange defenses, and Alcatraz.
- *Films for the Humanities*: Nearly 200 videos to choose from on a variety of topics such as elder abuse, supermax prisons, suicide and the police officer, the making of an FBI agent, domestic violence, and more.

Student Resources

Wadsworth's Guide to Careers in Criminal Justice, Third Edition This handy guide, compiled by Caridad Sanchez-Leguelinel of John Jay College of Criminal Justice, gives students information on a wide variety of career paths, including requirements, salaries, training, contact information for key agencies, and employment outlooks.

Careers in Criminal Justice Website www.thomsonedu.com/login This unique website helps students investigate the criminal justice career choices that are right for them with the help of several important tools:

- *Career Profiles:* Video testimonials from a variety of practicing professionals in the field as well as information on many criminal justice careers, including job descriptions, requirements, training, salary and benefits, and the application process.
- *Interest Assessment:* Self-assessment tool to help students decide which careers suit their personalities and interests.
- *Career Planner:* Résumé-writing tips and worksheets, interviewing techniques, and successful job search strategies.
- *Links for Reference:* Direct links to federal, state, and local agencies where students can get contact information and learn more about current job opportunities.

ACKNOWLEDGMENTS

I would like to thank Carolyn Henderson Meier, senior editor at Wadsworth, for her confidence in me; and Jennie Redwitz, production manager, and Antima Gupta, production editor, for their interest and careful attention to detail. Thanks also to copy editor Barbara Willette and proofreader Martha Williams, as well as the many people who submitted suggestions for this edition.

Howard Abadinsky

About the Author

Howard Abadinsky is professor of criminal justice at St. John's University, Jamaica, NY. He was an inspector for the Cook County (IL) Sheriff's Office for eight years and a New York State parole officer and senior parole officer for 15 years. He holds a B.A. from Queens College of the City University of New York, an M.S.W. from Fordham University, and a Ph.D. from New York University. He is the author of several books, including *Probation and Parole*, Ninth Edition, *Organized Crime*, Eighth Edition, and *Law and Justice*, Sixth Edition.

Dr. Abadinsky can be reached at abadinsh@stjohns.edu and encourages comments about his work.

An Introduction to Drug Abuse

Our society makes artificial distinctions among addictive drugs. We foster the false impression that because nicotine and alcohol are legal, they must be less dangerous and less addictive than the illicit drugs.

Avram Goldstein (2001: 4)

The legal distinction between licit and illicit drugs is sometimes treated as if it had pharmacological significance. Vendors of licit drugs and proponents of a "drug-free society" share an interest in convincing tobacco smokers and alcohol drinkers that smoking and drinking are radically different than "drug abuse." But a nicotine addict can be just as hooked as a heroin addict, and the victim of an alcohol overdose is just as dead as the victim of a cocaine overdose.

Mark A. R. Kleiman (1992: 7)

Nicotine addiction is the largest cause of preventable mortality in the world.

Andrew R. Tapper et al. (2004: 1029)

Study behavior you regard as pathological and you will find pathological motivations. We should not be asking, "Why do people use drugs?" Rather, we should ask, "How do some people maintain healthy relationships with drugs, and how do some develop unhealthy relationships?"

Kevin W. Whiteacre and Hal Pepinsky (2002: 26)

Advances in science are rapidly dispelling both popular and clinical myths about drug abuse and addiction and what to do about them [although] scientific understanding has not yet totally displaced the moralizing that continues to shadow any discussion on this topic.

Alan I. Leshner (1999a: 1)

Nicotine Dependence/Addiction

Nicotine dependence is the most common substance use disorder in the United States. Approximately 60 percent to 80 percent of current smokers fulfill classic criteria for drug dependence; for example, they have difficulty stopping, have symptoms of withdrawal when they stop, show increasing tolerance levels, and continue despite knowledge of personal harm. Nicotine appears to have a dependence potential at least equal to that of other drugs. For example, among people who experiment with alcohol, 10 to 15 percent will meet criteria for alcohol dependence at some point in their life. Among people who experiment with cigarettes, 20 to 30 percent will meet criteria for nicotine dependence in their lifetime (American Psychiatric Association 1995). If addiction is defined as compulsive drug-seeking behavior, even in the face of negative health consequences, than tobacco use is certainly addiction (National Institute on Drug Abuse 2001d).

Hookin' 'em good!
The Massachusetts Department of Public Health discovered that between 1988 and 2004 tobacco companies increased the amount of nicotine delivered to the average smoker by 10 percent ("Raising Nicotine Doses, on the Sly" 2006).

This book is concerned with psychoactive drugs that have the potential to harm their users, who might in turn harm others, such as occurs when people drive while intoxicated. While statutes distinguish between lawful drugs such as nicotine and alcohol and illegal drugs such as heroin and cocaine, biology recognizes no such distinction. Nicotine is a drug that meets the rigorous criteria for abuse liability and dependence potential, and "cigarettes are one of the major drugs of addiction in the United States and in the world and are responsible for more premature deaths than all of the other drugs of abuse combined" (Schuster 1993: 40).

According to scientific and pharmacological data used to classify dangerous substances for the protection of society, **alcohol** should be a Schedule II

Suspected of being intoxicated, a teenager attempts to walk a straight line for law enforcement. Statistics prove that youth who experiment with alcohol are most likely to use marijuana and other drugs later on.

The Gateway to Illegal Drug Abuse

"Both tobacco and alcohol share a role as 'gateway drugs' that presage use of other psychoactive drugs; in other words, alcohol and/or tobacco use precedes most subsequent use of marijuana and cocaine" (Shiffman and Balabanis 1995: 18). Thus, "there is a fairly consistent progression of adolescent substance use beginning with the licit drugs alcohol and/or cigarettes, moving on to illicit substances initiating with marijuana and progressing to cocaine and 'harder,' more problematic drugs" (P. Johnson, Boles, and Kleber 2000: 79).

"Each day, more than 3,000 young persons smoke their first cigarette, and the likelihood of becoming addicted to nicotine is higher for these young smokers than for those who begin later in life" (Zickler 2002: 7). Nearly one in four high school seniors smokes every day, and more than one in eight smokes a half-pack or more each day (National Institute on Drug Abuse 2000). "Young people age twelve to seventeen who smoke are about twelve times more likely to use illegal drugs and sixteen times more likely to drink heavily than youths who did not smoke. Young people use alcohol more than illegal drugs and the younger a person is when alcohol use begins, the greater the risk of developing alcohol abuse or dependence later in life. . . . Alcohol use among the young strongly correlates with adult drug use. For example, adults who started drinking at early ages are nearly eight times more likely to use cocaine than adults who did not drink as children" (Office of National Drug Control Policy 2000: 10).

narcotic, a Drug Enforcement Administration (DEA) category referring to a substance that is highly addictive and available only with a government narcotic registry number. The cost of alcohol abuse is twice the social cost of all illegal drug abuse. Alcohol is reputed to be the direct cause of 80,000 to 100,000 deaths annually, and alcohol-related auto accidents are the leading cause of death for teenagers (Wicker 1987; Li, Smith, and Baker 1994). But alcohol for recreational use is permitted to be legally manufactured, imported, sold, and possessed. Because of this reality, while it has been associated with a myriad of social problems, since the repeal of Prohibition in 1933 trafficking in alcohol has not been associated with rampant violence and corruption. Indeed, the repeal of Prohibition resulted in a dramatic decrease in the murder rate in the United States, which began to increase in the 1960s along with the prevalence of illicit drug use (Myers 1995).

Distinctions between alcohol and other psychoactive drugs reflect neither reality nor science (N. Miller 1995). Indeed, heroin users have typically used marijuana and alcohol while adolescents, and from-heavy-alcohol-use-to-injecting-heroin is a typical sequence for most addicts (Inciardi, McBride, and Surratt 1998).

With these incongruities serving as a backdrop, this opening chapter will begin by describing the problems inherent in defining terms such as *drugs* and *drug abuse*, the drug use continuum from abstinence to dependency, measuring the extent of drug use, and the connection between drugs and crime.

Perspectives

Not a Happy New Year
The 17-year-old high school student in Lake County, Illinois, joined a group of friends celebrating New Year's Eve. Over a three-hour period he consumed almost a quart of vodka. He subsequently passed out and died before paramedics arrived (Santana 1996).

But They're Not Using Pot
Each weekend, three to ten students at the University of Virginia drink so much that they need medical treatment (Winerip 1998).

An Illegal Drug (for Adolescents)
The Missouri Division of Alcohol and Drug Abuse (1999) reports that in their state 86 percent of adolescents have used alcohol by the time they have reached the twelfth grade.

Alcohol and the Average College Day
"On an average day . . . 4 college students die in accidents involving alcohol. An additional 1,370 suffer injuries tied to drinking . . . and an estimated 192 are raped by their dates or sexually assaulted after drinking"[1] (Schemo 2003: 16).

Danger to Others
Alcohol disturbs behavior in a way that "threatens the safety of others even when used occasionally and not compulsively" (Goldstein 2001: 5).

DRUGS: REACHING A DEFINITION

Binging in the Boondocks

A federal government survey revealed that residents of the Dakotas, Montana, and Wyoming drink to excess at very early ages, well above the national average. An earlier survey found that rural youths were twice as likely to abuse alcohol as urban youngsters (Egan 2006).

The term *drug* is derived from the fourteenth century French word *drogue*, meaning a dry substance—most pharmaceuticals at that time were prepared from dried herbs (Palfai and Jankiewicz 1991). There is no completely satisfying way of delineating what is and what is not a drug—for example, the differences between water, vitamin supplements, and penicillin (Goode 1989). Therefore, some feel it appropriate to refer to chemical or **substance abuse**. Imprecision in the use of the term *drug* has had serious social consequences.

Because alcohol is excluded from most people's definition of what is a drug, the public is conditioned to regard a martini as something fundamentally different from a marijuana cigarette, a barbiturate capsule, or a bag of heroin. Similarly, because the meaning of the word *drug* differs so widely in therapeutic and social contexts, the public is conditioned to believe that "street" drugs act according to entirely different principles than "medical" drugs, alcohol, and nicotine do, with the result that the risks of the former are exaggerated and the risks of the latter are overlooked (Uelmen and Haddox 1983).

"In contemporary society the word drug has two connotations—one positive, explaining its crucial role in medicine, and one negative, reflecting, not the natural and synthetic makeup of these chemicals, but the self-destruction and socially deleterious patterns of misuse" (K. Jones, Shainberg, and Byer 1979: 1). In this book the term *drug* will refer to substances that have mood-altering,

---

[1] For a review of the research on college drinking, see Baer (2002).

Perspectives

Alcohol?

"Drug abuse and related crime permeate every corner of our society, afflicting inner cities,affluent suburbs, and rural communities. Drugs affect the rich and poor, educated and uneducated, professionals and blue-collar workers, young and old" (Office of National Drug Control Policy 2001: 3).

Hypocrisy?

In England the government notes that "drug prevention policies which ignore licit drugs [alcohol and tobacco] lack credibility" (Advisory Council on the Misuse of Drugs 1998: xi). In 1999 the U.S. Congress defeated an administration plan to include antidrinking messages in federal efforts to keep youngsters from using illicit drugs. There are an estimated 14 million people in the United States who are addicted to alcohol; that is, they suffer from Jellinek's disease (Ynclan 2002).

Adolescent Drug Problem

Monitoring the Future (discussed later in the chapter) revealed that in 2004 nearly half of high school seniors reported that they had drunk more than a few sips of alcohol in the past month.

psychotropic (or psychoactive) effects. This definition includes caffeine, nicotine, and alcohol, as well as illegal chemicals such as marijuana and heroin.

DRUG ABUSE AND ADDICTION

Drug abuse implies the misuse of certain substances; it is a moral, not a scientific, term: "An unstandardized, value-laden, and highly relative term used with a great deal of imprecision and confusion, generally implying drug use that is excessive, dangerous, or undesirable to the individual or community and that ought to be modified" (Nelson et al. 1982: 33). Drug abuse "implies willful, improper use due to an underlying disorder or a quest for hedonistic or immoral pleasure" (N. Miller 1995: 10). Numerous definitions of drug abuse reflect social values, not scientific insight: "One reason for the prevalence of definitions of drug abuse that are neither logical nor scientific is the strength of Puritan moralism in American culture which frowns on the pleasure and recreation provided by intoxicants" (Zinberg 1984: 33). Such definitions typically refer to:

1. the nonmedical use of a substance
2. to alter the mental state
3. in a manner that is detrimental to the individual or the community and/or
4. that is illegal.

For example, the American Social Health Association (1972: 1) defines drug abuse as the "use of mood modifying chemicals outside of medical supervision, and in a manner which is harmful to the person and the community." Other definitions, such as those offered by the World Health Organization and the American Medical Association, include references to physical and/or psychological dependency (Zinberg 1984).

The *Diagnostic and Statistical Manual of Mental Disorders, Fourth Edition* (DSM-IV), published by the American Psychiatric Association (1994: 182), refers to substance abuse as a "maladaptive pattern of substance use manifested by recurrent and significant adverse consequences related to the repeated use of substances. There may be repeated failure to fulfill major role obligations, repeated use in situations in which it is physically hazardous [such as driving while intoxicated], multiple legal problems, and recurrent social and interpersonal problems."

In fact drug abuse may be defined from a number of perspectives: "The legal definition equates drug use with the mere act of using a proscribed drug or using a drug under proscribed conditions. The moral definition is similar, but greater emphasis is placed on the motivation or purpose for which the drug is used. The medical model opposes unsupervised usage but emphasizes the physical and mental consequences for the user, and the social definition stresses social responsibility and adverse effects on others" (Balter 1974: 5).

DRUG ABUSE CONTINUUM

The *use* of psychoactive chemicals, licit or illicit, can objectively be labeled drug *abuse* only when the user becomes dysfunctional as a consequence, for example, is unable to maintain employment, has impaired social relationships, exhibits dangerous—reckless or aggressive—behavior, and/or significantly endangers his or her health. Thus, drug *use*, as opposed to drug *abuse*, can be viewed as a continuum, as shown in Figure 1.1. At one end is the nonuser who has never used prohibited or abused lawful psychoactive drugs. Along the continuum are experimental use and culturally endorsed use, which includes the use of drugs—wine or **peyote**, for example—in religious ceremonies. "Regardless of the duration of use, such people tend not to escalate their use to uncontrollable amounts."[2] For example, "long-term cocaine users have found that recreational patterns can be maintained for a decade or more without loss of control. Such use tends to occur in weekly or biweekly episodes and users perceive that the effects facilitate social functioning" (Siegel 1989: 222–223). At the far end of the drug use continuum is the drug-dependent, compulsive user whose life often revolves around obtaining, maintaining, and using a supply of drugs. For the compulsive user, failure to ingest an adequate supply of the desired drug results in psychological stress and discomfort, and there may also be physical **withdrawal** symptoms.

Understanding the use of psychoactive substances as a continuum allows the issue of drugs to be placed in its proper perspective: There is nothing inherently either evil or virtuous about the use of psychoactive substances. For some—actually many—people, they make life more enjoyable; hence the widespread use of **tobacco** and alcohol without serious unpleasant effects. For others drugs become a burden as dependence brings dysfunction. In between these two extremes are a variety of drug *users*, such as the underage adolescent using tobacco or alcohol on occasion, as is very common in our society. Adults may experiment with illegal drugs—marijuana and cocaine, for example—without moving up to more frequent, that is, recreational use. The recreational user enjoys some beer or cocktails on a regular basis or ingests cocaine or heroin

Figure 1.1
Drug Use
Continuum

Nonuse

Experimental use

Culturally endorsed use

Recreational use

Compulsive use

---

[2] For the story of a recreational heroin user who was not dysfunctional, see Marlowe (1999).

Perspectives

Cocaine for Recreational Use

"The justification for outlawing cocaine was mainly the supposed psychological and physiological consequences of prolonged use. But the law does not distinguish, as we must, between moderate and excessive doses. The more spectacular consequences of cocaine abuse are not typical of the drug's effects as it is normally used any more than the phenomena associated with alcoholism are typical of the ordinary consumption of that drug" (Grinspoon and Bakalar 1976: 119).

Healthy Drug Use?

"Acknowledging potentially healthy relationships with drugs allows us to better identify unhealthy ones. This may sound heretical to the professionals who readily categorize all illicit drug use as abuse. But the refusal to recognize healthy relationships with stigmatized drugs hinders our understanding of drug-related problems and healthy relationships with them. This refusal can even increase negative drug use by failing to consider broader circumstances such as poverty, exclusion, and marginalization itself, which may influence one's relationship with drugs" (Whiteacre and Pepinsky 2002: 27).

just before or at social events, during which the drug eases social interaction for this actor. Outside of this specific social setting, the recreational user abstains and thereby is in control of his or her use of drugs. Thus, even for cocaine, a very addictive drug, only 15–16 percent of people become addicted within ten years of first use (T. Robinson and Berridge 2003). For some, recreational use crosses into compulsive use marked by a preoccupation with securing and using drugs in the face of negative consequences, losing a job, severe disruption of social relationships, and/or involvement with the criminal justice system.

What we know about those who use psychoactive drugs is skewed toward compulsive users, particularly with respect to illegal drugs: Noncompulsive users have received very little research attention because they are hard to find: "Much data on users are gathered from treatment, law enforcement, and correctional institutions, and from other institutions allied with them. Naturally these data sources provide a highly selected sample of users: those who have encountered significant personal, medical, social, or legal problems in conjunction with their drug use, and thus represent the pathological end of the using spectrum" (Zinberg et al. 1978: 13). Such data "cannot be used to support a causal interpretation because of the absence of information on individuals who may have ingested a drug but had minimal or no negative consequences" (Newcomb and Bentler 1988: 13), such as the recreational user.

ADDICTION

Norman Miller (1995) avoids use of the term *drug abuse* and opts instead for **addiction**[3] characterized by:

1. *Preoccupation*: The addict assigns a high priority to acquiring drugs. Social relationships and employment are jeopardized in the quest for drugs and the consequences of use.

---

[3] *Addiction* is from the Latin verb *addicere*, meaning "to bind a person to one thing or another."

Perspectives

Addiction

Often used interchangeably with the term *dependence*, *addiction* denotes a complex illness characterized by repeated, compulsive, at times uncontrollable behavior that persists even in the face of adverse social, psychological, and/or physical consequences. For many people addiction becomes chronic, with relapse possible even after years of abstinence. The elements are the same no matter whether the addiction is to alcohol, tobacco, controlled substances, or sex: compulsion and continuation despite adverse consequences.

Drug Addiction

"Drug addiction is defined as having lost control over drug taking, even in the face of adverse physical, personal, or social consequences" (Society for Neuroscience 2002: 33).

2. *Compulsion*: The addict continues to use drugs despite serious adverse consequences. He or she will often deny the connection between the adverse consequences and the use of drugs.
3. *Relapse*: In the face of adverse consequences, addicts discontinue drugs but subsequently return to abnormal use.

Dennis Donovan (1988: 6) conceives of addiction as a "complex, progressive behavior pattern having biological, psychological, sociological, and behavioral components. What sets this behavior apart from others is the individual's overwhelmingly pathological involvement in or attachment to it, subjective compulsion to continue it, and reduced ability to exert personal control over it. . . . The behavior pattern continues despite its negative impact on the physical, psychological, and social function of the individual."

DEFINITION DETERMINES RESPONSE

A variety of lawful substances are addicting and have been abused by any number of "respectable persons," including top government officials, not to mention people in sports, entertainment, and the popular media. Social expectations and definitions determine what kind of drug-taking is appropriate and the social situations that are approved and disapproved for drug use. The use of drugs is neither inherently bad nor inherently good—these are socially determined values (Goode 1989). Thus, Mormons and Christian Scientists consider use of tea and coffee "abusive," while Moslems and some Protestant denominations have the same view of alcohol, although they permit tobacco smoking. The National Commission on Marijuana and Drug Abuse (1973: 13) argues that the term *drug abuse* "must be deleted from official pronouncements and public policy dialogue" because the "term has no functional utility and has become no more than an arbitrary code-word for that drug use which is presently considered wrong." As the history in Chapter 2 informs us, moderate use of a drug will be defined as *abuse* (and illegal) or it will be considered socially acceptable (and lawful) as society determines, regardless of the actual relative danger inherent in the substance. In other words, how society *defines* drug abuse determines how society *responds to* drug use.

Social Conventions

Those who use cocaine or heroin are labeled "drug abusers"; those who use alcohol and nicotine escape even the label of "drug user."

DRUGS OF ABUSE

In this book we will examine psychoactive drugs in each of three categories according to their primary effect on the central nervous system (CNS): depressants, stimulants, and hallucinogens. (Some chemicals, such as cannabis and MDMA, also known as ecstasy, have a combination of these characteristics.) A drug can have at least three different names: chemical, generic, and trade; and drugs that have a legitimate medical use may be marketed under a variety of trade names. Trade names begin with a capital letter, while chemical or generic names are in lowercase (see Table 1.1).

Depressants

Depressants depress the CNS and can reduce pain. The most frequently used drug in this category is alcohol; the most frequently used illegal drug is the **opiate** derivative **heroin**. Other depressants, all of which have some medical use, include **morphine**, codeine, **methadone, barbiturates**, methaqualone, and **tranquilizers**. These substances can cause physical and psychological dependence—a craving—and withdrawal results in physical and psychological stress. Opiate derivatives (heroin, morphine, and codeine) and opiumlike drugs such as methadone are often referred to as **narcotics**. The depressant category also includes inhalants, a variety of readily available products routinely kept in the home, such as glue, paint thinner, hair spray, and nail polish remover. They produce vapors that, when inhaled, can cause an intoxication similar to that of alcohol.

Stimulants

Stimulants elevate mood—produce feelings of well-being—by stimulating the CNS. The most frequently used drugs in this category are **caffeine** and **nicotine**; the most frequently used illegal stimulant is **cocaine**, which, along with **amphetamines**, has some limited medical use.

Hallucinogens, "Club Drugs," Marijuana/Cannabis, and Inhalants

Hallucinogens alter perceptual functions. The term *hallucinogen* rather than, for example, *psychoactive* or *psychedelic*, is a value-laden one. The most frequently used hallucinogens are **LSD** (lysergic acid diethylamide) and **PCP** (**phencyclidine**); both are produced chemically, and neither has any legitimate medical use. There are also organic hallucinogens, such as **mescaline**, which is found in the peyote cactus. The lawful use of peyote is limited to the religious ceremonies of the Native American Church, which some, but not all, states exempt from their controlled substances statutes.

Club drugs is a term used to characterize psychoactive substances associated with dance parties or *raves*, in particular **MDMA**, known as **ecstasy**.

Table 1.1 | Commonly Abused Drugs

Substances: Category and Name	Examples of *Commercial* and Street Names	DEA Schedule/ How Administered	*Intoxication Effects*/Potential Health Consequences
Cannabinoids			*euphoria, slowed thinking and reaction time, confusion, impaired balance and coordination*/cough, frequent respiratory infections; impaired memory and learning; increased heart rate, anxiety, panic attacks; tolerance, addiction
hashish	boom, chronic, gangster, hash, hash oil, hemp	I/swallowed, smoked	
marijuana	blunt, dope, ganja, grass, herb, joints, Mary Jane, pot, reefer, sinsemilla, skunk, weed	I/swallowed, smoked	
Depressants			*reduced anxiety; feeling of well-being; lowered inhibitions; slowed pulse and breathing; lowered blood pressure; poor concentration*/fatigue; confusion; impaired coordination, memory, judgment; addiction; respiratory depression and arrest; death
barbiturates	*Amytal, Nembutal, Seconal, Phenobarbital:* barbs, reds, red birds, phennies, tooies, yellows, yellow jackets	II, III, V/injected, swallowed	
benzodiazepines (other than flunitrazepam)	*Ativan, Halcion, Librium, Valium, Xanax:* candy, downers, sleeping pills, tranks	IV/swallowed, injected	Also, for *barbiturates—sedation, drowsiness/depression, unusual excitement, fever, irritability, poor judgment, slurred speech, dizziness, life-threatening withdrawal*
flunitrazepam	*Rohypnol:* forget-me pill, Mexican Valium, R2, Roche, roofies, roofinol, rope, rophies	IV/swallowed, snorted	*for benzodiazepines—sedation, drowsiness/dizziness*
GHB	*gamma-hydroxybutyrate:* G, Georgia home boy, grievous bodily harm, liquid ecstasy	I/swallowed	*for flunitrazepam—visual and gastrointestinal disturbances, urinary retention, memory loss for the time under the drug's effects*
methaqualone	*Quaalude, Sopor, Parest:* ludes, mandrex, quad, quay	I/injected, swallowed	*for GHB—drowsiness, nausea/vomiting, headache, loss of consciousness, loss of reflexes, seizures, coma, death* *for methaqualone—euphoria/depression, poor reflexes, slurred speech, coma*
Dissociative Anesthetics			*increased heart rate and blood pressure, impaired motor function*/memory loss; numbness; nausea/vomiting
ketamine	*Ketalar SV:* cat Valiums, K, Special K, vitamin K	III/injected, snorted, smoked	Also, for *ketamine—at high doses, delirium, depression, respiratory depression and arrest*
PCP and analogs	*phencyclidine:* angel dust, boat, hog, love boat, peace pill	I, II/injected, swallowed, smoked	*for PCP and analogs—possible decrease in blood pressure and heart rate, panic, aggression, violence*/loss of appetite, depression
Hallucinogens			*altered states of perception and feeling; nausea; persisting perception disorder (flashbacks)*
LSD	*lysergic acid diethylamide:* acid, blotter, boomers, cubes, microdot, yellow sunshines	I/swallowed, absorbed through mouth tissues	Also, for *LSD and mescaline—increased body temperature, heart rate, blood pressure; loss of appetite, sleeplessness, numbness, weakness, tremors*
mescaline	buttons, cactus, mesc, peyote	I/swallowed, smoked	*for LSD—persistent mental disorders*
psilocybin	magic mushroom, purple passion, shrooms	I/swallowed	*for psilocybin—nervousness, paranoia*
Opioids and Morphine Derivatives			*pain relief, euphoria, drowsiness*/nausea, constipation, confusion, sedation, respiratory depression and arrest, tolerance, addiction, unconsciousness, coma, death
codeine	*Empirin with Codeine, Fiorinal with Codeine, Robitussin A-C, Tylenol with Codeine:* Captain	II, III, IV, V/injected, swallowed	

	Cody, Cody, schoolboy; (with glutethimide) doors & fours, loads, pancakes and syrup		*Also, for codeine—less analgesia, sedation, and respiratory depression than morphine*
fentanyl and fentanyl analogs	*Actiq, Duragesic, Sublimaze:* Apache, China girl, China white, dance fever, friend, goodfella, jackpot, murder 8, TNT, Tango and Cash	I, II/injected, smoked, snorted	
heroin	*diacetylmorphine:* brown sugar, dope, H, horse, junk, skag, skunk, smack, white horse	I/injected, smoked, snorted	*for heroin—staggering gait*
morphine	*Roxanol, Duramorph:* M, Miss Emma, monkey, white stuff	II, III/injected, swallowed, smoked	
opium	*laudanum, paregoric:* big O, black stuff, block, gum, hop	II, III, V/swallowed, smoked	
oxycodone HCL	*OxyContin:* Oxy, O.C., killer	II/swallowed, snorted, injected	
hydrocodone bitartrate, acetaminophen	*Vicodin:* vike, Watson-387	II/swallowed	
Stimulants amphetamine	*Biphetamine, Dexedrine:* bennies, black beauties, crosses, hearts, LA turnaround, speed, truck drivers, uppers	II/injected, swallowed, smoked, snorted	*increased heart rate, blood pressure, metabolism; feelings of exhilaration, energy, increased mental alertness/rapid or irregular heart beat; reduced appetite, weight loss, heart failure, nervousness, insomnia*
cocaine	*Cocaine hydrochloride:* blow, bump, C, candy, Charlie, coke, crack, flake, rock, snow, toot	II/injected, smoked, snorted	*Also, for amphetamine—rapid breathing/tremor, loss of coordination; irritability, anxiousness, restlessness, delirium, panic, paranoia, impulsive behavior, aggressiveness, tolerance, addiction, psychosis*
MDMA (methylenedioxymethamphetamine)	Adam, clarity, ecstasy, Eve, lover's speed, peace, STP, X, XTC	I/swallowed	*for cocaine—increased temperature/chest pain, respiratory failure, nausea, abdominal pain, strokes, seizures, headaches, malnutrition, panic attacks*
methamphetamine	*Desoxyn:* chalk, crank, crystal, fire, glass, go fast, ice, meth, speed	II/injected, swallowed, smoked, snorted	*for MDMA—mild hallucinogenic effects, increased tactile sensitivity, empathic feelings/impaired memory and learning, hyperthermia, cardiac toxicity, renal failure, liver toxicity*
methylphenidate (safe and effective for treatment of ADHD)	*Ritalin:* JIF, MPH, R-ball, Skippy, the smart drug, vitamin R	II/injected, swallowed, snorted	*for methamphetamine—aggression, violence, psychotic behavior/memory loss, cardiac and neurological damage; impaired memory and learning, tolerance, addiction*
nicotine	cigarettes, cigars, smokeless tobacco, snuff, spit tobacco, bidis, chew	not scheduled/smoked, snorted, taken in snuff and spit tobacco	*for nicotine—additional effects attributable to tobacco exposure: adverse pregnancy outcomes; chronic lung disease, cardiovascular disease, stroke, cancer; tolerance, addiction*
Other Compounds inhalants	*Solvents* (paint thinners, gasoline, glues), *gases* (butane, propane, aerosol propellants, nitrous oxide), *nitrites* (isoamyl, isobutyl, cyclohexyl): laughing gas, poppers, snappers, whippets	not scheduled/inhaled through nose or mouth	*stimulation, loss of inhibition; headache; nausea or vomiting; slurred speech, loss of motor coordination; wheezing/unconsciousness, cramps, weight loss, muscle weakness, depression, memory impairment, damage to cardiovascular and nervous systems, sudden death*

Source: National Institute on Drug Abuse.

Wonder Drugs

If currently outlawed psychoactive substances were legal, given how these substances can affect people, it would be easy to conceive of an advertising campaign (Fields 2001: 18):

"Feeling down and depressed? Lack the energy to do even the most basic things? Suffer from lowered sex drive, sleep disturbances, or have difficulty with interpersonal relationships? Not making the kind of money you would like to, need a vacation, a general lift? Wondering what life is all about what or if it is even worth it." Be happy, feel satisfied, and do not worry about the problems of life.

Cannabis, frequently used in the form of marijuana, exhibits some of the characteristics of hallucinogens, depressants, and even stimulants. Its lawful use (in the liquid form of **tetrahydrocannabinol**, or **THC**, its psychoactive ingredient) is limited to the treatment of glaucoma and to reduce some of the side effects of cancer chemotherapy.

Inhalants are substances produced for commercial nondrug purposes, such as glue and nail polish remover, that when inhaled can cause a psychoactive response.

ESTIMATING THE EXTENT OF THE DRUG PROBLEM

Information on the drug problem in the United States is derived from five indicators, each providing a different perspective on the problem, and they complement one another. Although the indicators have recognized limitations and deficiencies that affect the quality of information, the agencies that prepare them believe the data can reliably portray general trends. Richard Rosenfeld and Scott Decker (1999) found a high correlation between drug use measurements that rely on the criminal justice system (Arrestee Drug Abuse Monitoring) and those based on reports from hospitals and medical examiners (Drug Abuse Warning Network). The fact that these two different indicators tell basically the same story raises confidence in their validity. Those indicators using self-reports (National Survey on Drug Use and Health) raise questions, since they have been found to be least valid for the more stigmatized drugs such as heroin and cocaine (General Accounting Office 1998).

Efforts to determine the prevalence of heroin use have a long history, with precise estimates remaining difficult to determine. Standard methods of measuring prevalence such as household surveys are not adequate; for instance, heroin use is rare in the general population, so only a small number of users would be included in a household survey. Survey-based estimates substantially underestimate prevalence because of difficulties in locating heroin abusers (many of them are not living in stable households). In addition, because heroin use is an illegal activity, heroin users might not accurately report their use. Despite the shortcomings in data reliability, in 2003 the DEA stated that since the 1970s overall illegal drug use is down "by more than a third" (2003: 4), with about 123,000 Americans who use heroin at least once a month and 1.7 million who use cocaine at least once a month. By way of comparison, the DEA noted 109 million using alcohol and about 66 million using tobacco at least once month. Of course, smokers and drinkers are easy to find and more likely to be forthcoming about their use of these substances. For example, I am one of those consuming alcohol at least once a month—actually, a glass of wine once a week—but I do not use tobacco.

National Survey on Drug Use and Health

Called the National Household Survey on Drug Abuse (NHSDA) before 2002, the National Survey on Drug Use and Health (NSDUH) is funded by the Substance Abuse and Mental Health Services Administration of the U.S. Department of Health and Human Services. NHSDA was conducted every two or three years between 1972 and 1990 and has been conducted annually since 1990. The survey provides data on incidence, prevalence, and trends of drug use for individuals age 12 and older living in households. Results are based on about 9,000 interviews with people randomly selected from the household population, who record their responses on self-administered answer sheets. The NHSDA sample was increased to more than 30,000 interviews in 1991 and to 70,000 interviews in 1999.

The resulting data are used in conjunction with Monitoring the Future survey data (discussed below) to describe levels of drug use in specific segments of the population. The NSDUH data may also be used in conjunction with DAWN data (discussed below) to describe long-term trends in drug abuse. In the past, self-report surveys on drug use have been found to be reasonably trustworthy (Oetting and Beauvais 1990), but more recently, questions have been raised (General Accounting Office 1998) about their accuracy.

Survey limitations include the fact that the homeless and people living in military installations, dormitories, and institutions such as jails, prisons, and hospitals are not covered, although the survey attempts to approximate these populations by using a controversial "imputation" procedure (General Accounting Office 1993). Also, some people refuse to participate. Because the survey is voluntary and the questionnaires are self-administered, the results may be biased (and probably understate the scope of the drug problem). Concern has also been expressed over privacy and comprehension issues. During the interviews of 25–30 percent of respondents ages 12 to 17 at the time the survey was administered, a third person was present. And any numbers of people have difficulty with English or with understanding the drug use jargon employed by the survey (General Accounting Office 1993). One observer (Whiteacre 2005: 7) is skeptical of respondent veracity: "It seems quite unlikely that wealthy 'respectable' community members, having more to lose, would come forward about their drug use when surveyed" by the NHSDA.

Monitoring the Future

The Monitoring the Future (MTF) study is conducted by the Institute for Social Research at the University of Michigan for the National Institute of Drug Abuse. Annual surveys of high school seniors began in 1975, and eighth- and tenth-grade students were added in 1991. The survey population is chosen to be representative of all students in U.S. public and private schools. About 50,000 students located in more than 400 public and private schools complete questionnaires in their classrooms every spring.

Primary uses of the data include (1) assessing the prevalence and trends of drug use among high school seniors and (2) gaining a better understanding of the lifestyles and value orientations associated with patterns of drug use and monitoring how these orientations are shifting over time. Follow-up surveys of representative subsamples of the original graduates that have been conducted for over a decade provide data on young adults and college students.

The survey has several limitations. High school dropouts (about 30 percent of students), who are associated with higher rates of drug use, are not part of the sampled universe. Chronic absentees, who may also have higher rates of abuse, are less likely to be surveyed (L. Liu 1994). In Texas, for example, youths entering that state's detention facilities are nearly twelve times as likely to have used cocaine as are youngsters in school (Fredlund et al. 1990). Conscious or unconscious distortions in self-reporting information can also bias results. In addition, new trends in drug abuse, such as the use of crack, might not be initially detected because the survey is designed to measure only drugs that are abused at significant levels. Questions about crack were asked for the first time in the 1986 survey, and questions about ecstasy (MDMA) were first asked in 1996. There is also concern over the lack of anonymity: The name, address, and telephone number of the respondent appear on the questionnaire's cover sheet to facilitate follow-up surveys.

Drug Abuse Warning Network

Drug Abuse Warning Network (DAWN), which was initiated in 1972 and is funded by the National Institute of Drug Abuse, is a large-scale drug abuse data collection system designed as an early-warning indicator of the nation's drug abuse problem. An episode report is submitted for each drug abuse patient who visits the emergency room of a hospital participating in DAWN and for each drug abuse death encountered by a participating medical examiner or coroner. In a single emergency room episode, a patient might mention having ingested more than one drug. DAWN records each drug a patient reports having used within four days before the hospital visit and relays the information to the DEA. Data are collected from a nonrandom sample in about twenty selected metropolitan areas throughout the country, representing approximately one third of the U.S. population.

While standard definitions and data collection procedures exist, variations among individual reporters may occur. Incomplete reporting, turnover of reporting facilities and personnel, and reporting delays of up to one year (primarily for medical examiner data) are some of the system's limitations. For hospital emergencies the National Narcotics Intelligence Consumers Committee (NNICC), in its last two publications, has used data from the DAWN Consistent Panel rather than data from the Total Panel. The Consistent Panel includes only hospitals that report on a consistent basis (specifically, 90 percent or more of each year). Data representing the total DAWN system were not used for trend analysis by NNICC because of reporting fluctuations. While data from medical examiners and coroners are not subject to the same inconsistencies, these reports are so small in comparison with the total DAWN system that they are not considered a valid trend indicator. (For a discussion of the uses and abuses of DAWN data, see Caulkins, Ebener, and McCaffrey 1995.)

NNICC Narcotics Intelligence Estimates

The NNICC is a federal interagency mechanism for coordinating drug intelligence collection requirements and producing joint intelligence estimates. NNICC issues periodic reports on the worldwide illicit drug situation. The report contains estimates of illegal drug production and availability and discusses four major drug categories: marijuana, cocaine, opiates, and synthetic drugs. The report also contains information on drug-trafficking routes and methods and on the flow of drug-related money. Estimates of illegal drug quantities are very difficult to make because little reliable data exist. NNICC obtains drug production data for individual countries from host country records, local contacts, informants, and sophisticated intelligence-gathering techniques. It derives drug availability and consumption estimates from sample surveys, drug seizures, drug price and purity data, drug-related hospital emergencies, and other data.

The price and purity levels of illegal drugs at the retail (consumer) level are key values in the NNICC estimating process. The DEA gathers these data, which are used as an indicator of drug availability. Drug prices are derived from a computerized database containing reports on purchases of, and negotiations to purchase, illegal drugs by undercover federal, state, and local law enforcement officers. Purity levels for heroin and cocaine are determined through laboratory analysis. (Purity levels are not applicable to marijuana and most synthetic drugs.) The limited number of reports and lack of randomness are problems that have plagued these indicators in the past (Comptroller General 1988). In addition, the price paid by undercover officers is affected by quantity discounts, thus underestimating the actual per dose retail price; or the officers might pay a premium price because they are not known to their dealers and new customers are typically charged more (Caulkins 1994).

Pulse Check

Since 1992 the Office of National Drug Control Policy (ONDCP) has been providing information on illegal drug use and drug markets in twenty-five major U.S. cities as derived from the perceptions of researchers, treatment providers, and law enforcement officials. According to the ONDCP, *Pulse Check* "provides a comprehensive snapshot of drug abuse patterns in communities across the country" (Office of National Drug Control Policy 2004a: 2). While *Pulse Check* offers "a rich picture of the changing drug abuse situation," it is "not intended as a quantitative measure of the prevalence of drug abuse or its consequences" (Office of National Drug Control Policy 2004a: 1).

The most recent report provides answers to a number of concerns, such as:

How difficult is it for undercover police and users to buy drugs?

What are the prices and purity levels?

How have marketing innovations such as packaging, and tools such as use of the Internet complicated law enforcement efforts?

Have there been any changes in sellers and users?

On a scale of 0 to 100, how serious is the perceived drug problem?

How has the perceived drug problem changed: no; somewhat worse; much worse?

How available are treatment programs?

What are the most serious drug problems?

Arrestee Drug Abuse Monitoring

Arrestee Drug Abuse Monitoring (ADAM) began in New York City in 1987, and by 1990 twenty-five of the largest cities in the United States were involved. By 2000 there were more than thirty-nine, most of them large urban areas. ADAM measured the extent of drug use in the high-risk population of people who had been arrested. Demographic, drug use and purchase, housing, method of support, and health insurance data were collected in central police booking facilities in each city. For approximately fourteen consecutive evenings each quarter, staff members obtained voluntary and anonymous urine specimens and interviews from a new sample of arrestees. In each site approximately 225 males were sampled. All female arrestees, regardless of charge, were included in the sample because of the small number of female arrestees available. Responses were consistently high: Over 90 percent agreed to be interviewed, and more than 80 percent of those interviewed provided urine specimens.

To obtain samples with a sufficient distribution of arrest charges, the number of male arrestees in each sample who were charged with drug-related offenses (sale or possession) was limited—one out of five such individuals were most likely to be using drugs at the time of their arrest and thus were undersampled. ADAM statistics were minimum estimates of drug use of male arrestees.

Urine samples were analyzed for ten drugs: cocaine, opiates, marijuana, PCP, methadone, benzodiazepine (Valium), methaqualone, propoxyphene (Darvon), barbiturates, and amphetamines. Except for marijuana and PCP, which can be detected several weeks after use, urine tests detect use in the previous two to three days. The ADAM data revealed that cocaine continued to be the substance of choice of a majority of those arrested, with heroin remaining important but far less popular. Amphetamines were detected in fewer than 10 percent of the arrestees and were most likely to be found in Western states.

A number of validation issues arose with respect to ADAM. Central booking facilities, where the samples were selected, served different areas of a city or county. This made generalizing to the wider population of arrestees unreliable. The busy, if not frantic, pace of most central booking facilities made respondent selection procedures difficult, leading to questions about sampling techniques. And a study by the General Accounting Office (1993) revealed that ADAM standards in selecting arrestees had not been applied uniformly across sites. Further, the nature of lockups in booking facilities made confidentiality difficult to achieve.

Peter Reuter (1999: 18) concluded that each of the four drug use indicators provides useful information: "Monitoring the Future provided early indications of the cocaine epidemic, while ADAM did a good job in tracking its later stages. DAWN has shown that drug problems can increase even as the rate of drug use in the population stabilizes and has provided compelling evidence that drug problems are disproportionately borne by poor and urban minority populations. The National Household Survey on Drug Abuse has provided an essential measure of the decline in drug use in the general population through the 1980s."

Despite its obvious importance as a measure of drug use, ADAM was discontinued in 2004 because of a lack of funds—about $8 million annually.

DRUG USE: HOW MANY, HOW MUCH?

What do these indicators reveal? About 19 million Americans use illegal drugs, primarily marijuana. There are an estimated 230,000 "casual" and 500,000 "heavy" users of heroin, while about 3 million individuals have used heroin at least once in their lifetime. An estimated 1.8 million Americans age 12 and older are users of cocaine; cocaine use reached a peak of 5.7 million in 1985. About 9 million people have tried methamphetamine at least once.

The numbers for alcohol have remained the same for years: More than half of the U.S. population age 12 and older use alcohol, while 55 million admit to binge drinking (drinking five or more drinks on the same occasion on at least one day in the past thirty days). More than 11 percent of pregnant women reported alcohol use, while drinking and driving remained a serious problem, with more than 32 million individuals reporting have been behind the wheel while intoxicated.

Nicotine-smoking rates in the United States have remained virtually unchanged for more than a decade. In 2004 there were more than 70 million people using tobacco. The highest rate of tobacco use (about 40 percent) continued to be among those aged 18 to 25. The end of the twentieth century and beginning of the twenty-first saw a significant decline in teenage smoking. By 2005 the downward trend had stopped, with about one in four adolescents smoking cigarettes. Adults who live below the poverty line are more likely to smoke than are those living above the poverty line, and high school dropouts are three times more likely to smoke than are college graduates. About 44.5 million adults describe themselves as smokers who had quit.

Adolescent drug use began increasing dramatically in the late 1960s, peaked in 1979, and then fell through the 1980s, hitting a low in 1991 and 1992 before beginning to climb again. By the end of the 1990s it remained steady, with only minor fluctuations. The year 2001 marked the fifth year in a row that drug and alcohol use among eighth, ninth, and twelfth graders remained stable or, in some cases such as cigarette smoking, decreased. In 2002, for the first time, smoking, drinking, and the use of illegal drugs among adolescents fell simultaneously. The use of MDMA (ecstasy) also showed statistically significant declines for the first time. The only significant increases in drug use were crack use by tenth graders and use of sedatives by twelfth graders. From 2001 to 2005 there was almost a 20 percent decline in teen drug use, and while the decline in smoking had leveled off, it was at the lowest rate in the thirty years of the survey. The 2006 statistics revealed that while the decline in drug—mostly marijuana—and alcohol use was continuing, the decrease in daily cigarette smoking ended, and an increase in the misuse of prescription drugs such as OxyContin and Vicodin was continuing.

The "good news" found in these indicators contrasts markedly with data on drug-related deaths that increased 400 percent in two decades, reaching 28,000 in 2004, a year when there were 940,000 drug-related hospital emergency cases (Males 2006).

PRESCRIPTION DRUG ABUSE

The estimates given in the preceding section might not account for the abuse of prescription drugs—painkillers and sedatives—typically by white people of at least middle class status. For these people such drugs are easier to acquire than their illegal street counterparts. And they are cheaper than street drugs such as heroin and cocaine. The cost of an evening's worth of cocaine or heroin can run

According to the National Institute on Drug Abuse, an estimated 48 million people over age 12 have used prescription drugs for nonmedical reasons in their lifetime. Prescription drugs are easier to acquire and cheaper than their illegal street counterparts. Here, Jennifer Shearer (left) of the Kentucky Bureau of Investigation addresses the media after agents from the KBI seized about 60 packages containing prescription drugs in a March 2006 crackdown on companies that sell pharmaceuticals via the Internet.

©AP Photo/The Herald Leader, Pablo Alcala

Most Commonly Abused Prescription Drug Categories

Although many prescription drugs can be abused or misused, there are three classes of prescription drugs that are most commonly abused:

> *Painkillers* such as OxyContin, Percodan, morphine, Vicodin, Lortab, Lorcet, Darvocet, Darvon, and Tylenol with codeine
>
> *CNS depressants* used to treat anxiety and sleep disorders, including barbiturates such as Mebaral and Nembutal and benzodiazepines such as Valium, Librium, Xanax, Ativan, and Restoril
>
> *Stimulants* prescribed to treat the sleep disorder narcolepsy, attention-deficit hyperactivity disorder, and obesity, such as Dexedrine and Ritalin

Source: National Institute on Drug Abuse.

into the hundreds of dollars, whereas in Miami, dealers sell Vicodin, Valium, Xanax, and OxyContin, a painkiller often given to cancer patients, for as little as three to four dollars a pill.

In addition, these drugs are popular because even without a doctor's prescription, access is increasing. Restocking trips are often taken to Mexico, where the black market continues to grow. It is estimated that Tijuana alone has about 1,700 pharmacies, many of which sell controlled substances illegally over the counter. And in some instances, doctors in Mexico sell prescriptions (Kirsebbaum 2002). Diversion from lawful sources, often the result of "doctor shopping" or overprescribing, has gained more attention in recent years (Querna 2005). One aspect of this problem is trafficking in the synthetic opiate **OxyContin,** particularly in rural areas of the United States that have not heretofore had a drug problem. In the rural Appalachian region, which has many miners with injuries and a shortage of doctors, prescribing of the drug has often been indiscriminate. A similar situation has occurred among injured steelworkers in eastern Ohio. The result has been diversion to the black market. In these areas, a number of doctors have been convicted for over prescribing (Bowman 2005).

One physician set up a pain management practice in Portsmith, Ohio. At about the same time police noticed a startling rise in drug-related crime. Undercover agents were dispatched to the pain clinic. With little or no physical examination each paid $200 and was given a prescription for OxyContin, the powerful synthetic opiate. In a subsequent raid agents found almost $500,000 in cash and passbooks for offshore accounts ("'Poor Man's Heroin'" 2001). In 2002 a 55-year-old Florida medical doctor received a sentence of sixty-two years in prison after a manslaughter conviction that involved running an OxyContin "pill mill" that was linked to several overdose deaths (Associated Press 2002).

According to the Substance Abuse and Mental Health Services Administration, the prevalence of nonmedical use of prescription psychotherapeutic drugs generally remained stable from 2002 through 2004. This pattern of stable rates generally held as well for specific categories of prescription psychotherapeutic drugs.

The National Institute on Drug Abuse estimates that 48 million Americans over age 12 have used prescription drugs for nonmedical reasons in their lifetime. About 10 percent of high school students report nonmedical use of prescription drugs. "The elderly are among those most vulnerable to prescription abuse or misuse because they are prescribed more medications than their younger counterparts" (National Institute on Drug Abuse 2005: 1).

In 2003 it was revealed that methadone, often prescribed for treating chronic pain, is being diverted to the black market and abused by recreational drug users, often with deadly consequences. There has been an alarming number of methadone overdose fatalities, which since 1997 have surpassed those from heroin. Methadone is usually taken when the drug of choice, heroin or OxyContin, is not readily available (Belluck 2003).

In 2005 people who used prescription drugs nonmedically were asked how they obtained the drugs they used most recently. Almost 60 percent got the drugs from "a friend" for free; about 17 percent were prescribed the drugs by a doctor; about 4 percent purchased them from a dealer or other stranger; and about 1 percent bought them over the Internet (*SAMHSA News* 2006).

A related issue is the abuse, usually by adolescents, of over-the-counter medications, in particular cough medicines containing **dextromethorphan** (DXM). Although DXM is generally recognized as safe when used appropriately, when taken in large amounts, it produces hallucinations and a "high" similar to that of PCP. Side effects include blurred vision, loss of coordination, abdominal pain, and rapid heartbeat.

CONNECTION BETWEEN DRUGS AND CRIME

A great deal of the concern over drugs is their connection to crime. The traditional way of considering the question of drugs and crime is the tripartite model offered by Paul Goldstein (1985):

1. *Pharmacological*: offenses that are psychopharmacology induced, that is, the result of a response to the intoxicating effects of a drug, including biological features discussed in Chapter 3
2. *Economic-compulsive*: crime driven by a need to buy drugs
3. *Systemic*: drug use as part of a pattern of criminal behaviors but not driven by or the result of drug use, for example, violence associated with the business of drugs

The outlawing of certain drugs creates criminal opportunity for those daring enough to enter this market (discussed in Chapter 11). They become part of a business that has no mechanisms for resolving disputes except violence. The outlawing of certain drugs also makes the people who use these chemicals (actually, the crime is "possession" of the drugs) criminals while substantially inflating the cost of the substances to the consumer. To secure their preferred substance, abusers of illegal drugs typically target salable property but will also commit robbery and/or sell drugs. There is a criminal population whose nondrug law violations are based only on their desire to secure drugs. However, it is also clear that an unknown percentage, perhaps a majority, of drug abusers, particularly those addicted to heroin, were criminals whose drug abuse is simply part of a pattern of hedonistic and antisocial behavior. George Vaillant (1970: 488) reports that no matter what their class origins, most people who use narcotics "have a greater tendency than their socioeconomic peers to be delinquent," and even drug-abusing physicians "are relatively irresponsible before drug addiction."[4] In a study of drug addicts in a treatment (DATOS) program, drug use played an earlier role than it did in offender-based studies. But among the general population, other forms of deviance or criminality precede the onset of illicit drug use. However, "those who began committing crimes after initiating regular drug use were much less likely to engage in predatory (relative to victimless) crime than those for whom criminality preceded regular drug use" (Farabee, Joshi, and Anglin 2001: 217).

Research on Adolescents

Research has determined that "youngsters who have conduct problems are more likely than others to be exposed to illicit drugs" (Swan n.d.: 1). Adolescents with emotional and behavioral problems are more likely to abuse alcohol, tobacco, and illicit drugs, according to a study by the Substance Abuse and Mental Health Services Administration (1999). The study found that adolescents who were inclined toward substance abuse admitted to delinquent behaviors such as stealing, cutting classes or skipping school, and hanging around with others who get into trouble. They also reported poor peer and parental relations and such problems as difficulty concentrating in school or focusing attention on tasks at home, at part-time work, or even when involved in sports.

When compared to adolescents having fewer or less serious behavioral problems, adolescents who repeatedly stole, showed physical aggression, or ran away from home were seven times as likely to be dependent on alcohol or illicit drugs. They were more than four times as likely to have used marijuana in the past month and seven times more likely to have used other illicit drugs. They were nearly three times as likely to have used alcohol in the past month, three times as likely to have smoked cigarettes in the past month, and nearly nine times as likely to need treatment for drug abuse. According to the 2001 National Household Survey on Drug Abuse (discussed earlier), youths who engaged in violent behaviors during the past year were more likely to report past month alcohol and illicit drug use than were youths who did not engage in violent behaviors during the past year.

---

[4] Concern over the abuse of morphine by medical doctors dates back to at least the latter part of the nineteenth century (Mattison 1883), and in 1961 Charles Winick wrote of the physician addict, a loner who does not knowingly associate with other addicts. In fact, drug abuse is a significant problem for the medical profession, with the addiction rate for physicians estimated at anywhere from 30 to 100 times that for the population at large (Grosswirth 1982; Kennedy 1995; McDougal 2006).

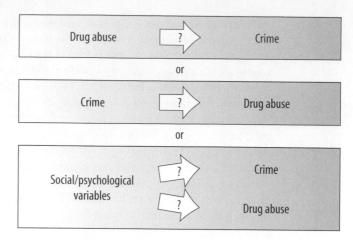

Figure 1.2 | Relationship Between Drugs and Crime: Three Possibilities

A study of male adolescent ninth- and tenth-graders in Washington, D.C., found that for about half of those who used drugs (mostly marijuana), criminal behavior preceded use; for the other half criminal behavior followed drug use. However, "those both using and selling drugs were more than twice as likely to have started using drugs before committing crimes as were those using but not selling drugs" (Brounstein et al. 1990: 3–4). In fact, we cannot be sure whether drug abuse leads to crime or criminals tend to abuse drugs (or perhaps neither); there are variables that lead to drug abuse, and the same variables lead to crime (see Figure 1.2) (McBride and McCoy 1981; see also Speckart and Anglin 1985, 1987). Indeed, areas with high levels of delinquency and crime also have high levels of drug usage, while the reverse is also true. In their study, Cheryl Carpenter and her colleagues (1988) found that the most seriously delinquent adolescents also abused drugs, but crime and drug use appeared to be independent of one another, both apparently being related to other causal variables. In fact, extensive research informs us that a relatively small segment of youths commit a disproportionate amount of juvenile crime, and "the majority of serious crimes committed by youths are concentrated among serious delinquents who are also heavy users of alcohol and other drugs" (B.D. Johnson et al. 1991: 206). For these individuals both drug use and crime appear to be part of a troubled lifestyle.

Research on Adults

There is undoubtedly a high correlation between drug use and nondrug crime (e.g., Gandossy et al. 1980; B. D. Johnson et al. 1985; Nurco et al. 1985; Inciardi 1986; Wish and Johnson 1986). One study found that more than half of the men arrested in twelve major cities tested positive for recent use of illicit drugs (Kerr 1988). "A strong consensus has emerged in the research literature that the most frequent, serious offenders are also the heaviest drug users" (Visher 1990: 330). However, is it drug use that leads to criminal behavior?

The question of whether crime is a predrug use or postdrug use phenomenon is actually an oversimplification, and James Inciardi (1981: 59) argues that "the pursuit of some simple cause-and-effect relationship may be futile." His data found, for example, that

> [a]mong the males there seems to be a clear progression from alcohol to crime, to drug abuse, to arrest and then to heroin use. But on closer inspection the pattern is not altogether clear. At one level, for example, criminal activity can be viewed as predating one's drug-using career, because the median point of the first crime is slightly below that of first drug abuse and is considerably before the onset of heroin use. But at the same time, if alcohol intoxication at a median age of 13.3 years were to be considered substance abuse, then crime is clearly a phenomenon that succeeds substance abuse. Among the females the description is even more complex. In the population of female heroin users criminal activity occurred after both alcohol and other drug abuse and marijuana use but before involvement with the more debilitating barbiturates and heroin.

A study of heroin addicts in Wilmington, Delaware, revealed criminal and drug careers that were rather independent of one another, the two merging as the use of heroin become overarching (Faupel and Klockars 1987).

This issue has serious policy implications. If drug abusers simply continue in crime after they have given up drug abuse, efforts to reduce crime by reducing drug abuse are doomed to fail. As James Q. Wilson (1975: 137) points out, perhaps "some addicts who steal to support their habit come to regard crime as more profitable than normal employment. They would probably continue to steal to provide themselves with an income even after they no longer needed to use part of that income to buy heroin" or any other illegal substance. M. Douglas Anglin and George Speckart (1988: 223) found, however, "that levels of criminality after the addiction career [is over] are near zero, a finding that is compatible with data presented by other authors and is illustrative of the 'maturing out' phase of the addiction career 'life cycle.'"

In fact, the sequence of drug use and crime has produced contradictory findings (Huizinga, Menard, and Elliott 1989). For example, James Vorenberg and Irving Lukoff (1973) found that the criminal careers of a substantial segment of the heroin addicts they studied antedated the onset of heroin use. Furthermore, they found that those whose criminality preceded heroin use tended to be more involved in violent criminal behavior. Anglin and Speckart (1988) report that between 60 and 75 percent of the addicts in their samples had arrest histories that preceded addiction. Paul Cushman (1974: 43) found, however, that the heroin addicts he studied were predominantly noncriminal before addiction and experienced "progressively increased rates of annual arrests after addiction started." (Of course, this finding could be the result of addicts being less adept at crime.) Whatever the relationship—drug abuse leading to crime or criminals becoming drug abusers—some researchers (McGlothlin, Anglin, and Wilson 1978; Ball et al. 1979; B. D. Johnson, Lipton, and Wish 1986a) have found that the amount of criminality tends to be sharply reduced when people who have been narcotic addicts are no longer addicted. Furthermore, Bruce Johnson and his colleagues (1985, 1989) and Anglin and Speckart (1988) found that the more frequent the drug use, the more serious the types of crime committed, for example, burglary and robbery instead of shoplifting and other larcenies. (For a summary of research findings on this issue, see Chaiken and Chaiken 1990.)

The question of the relationship between crime and drug abuse has typically been related to the abuse of heroin, not cocaine. During the time that this writer was a parole officer in New York (1964–1978), offenders who had used cocaine were rare, while studies by the New York State Division of Parole indicated that those who had used heroin were a substantial majority of parole clientele in the New York City area. Almost four decades ago, Troy Duster (1970: 42) was able to state that "cocaine usage is rare in the United States." However, during the 1980s the abuse of cocaine dramatically increased in the same populations that have traditionally been the major consumers of heroin. During these years cocaine use crossed social class lines, and the age of onset dropped considerably. Furthermore,

> [u]ntil recently, it has been assumed that cocaine was not a criminogenic force toward income-generating crime because cocaine does not have the physiological addictive power of heroin and because cocaine users were viewed as unlikely to come from population groups with high crime rates. Cocaine was thought to be a drug of the middle and upper classes. These assumptions appear to be unjustified. Weekly and daily cocaine use is associated with high levels of illegal income. (J. Collins, Hubbard, and Rachel 1985: 759)

During the 1980s cocaine (in the smokable form known as crack), not heroin, became the "in" drug among 18- to 25-year-old young adults in the low-income areas of New York City. This was a dramatic change from the drug scene of the late 1960s and 1970s, when heroin was the major problem. Furthermore, heroin abusers typically use cocaine, many as frequently as they do heroin, in a combination known as a speedball. The use of these substances, David Smith (1986) notes, is part of a lifestyle that also includes abuse of alcohol, marijuana, barbiturates, and amphetamines—and crime. In one study of 105 drug abusers, cocaine was the primary drug of choice, and 50 percent also abused alcohol (B.D. Johnson, Anderson, and Wish 1989). And one study found that the business of crack is crime-intensive in that it "leads serious delinquents to become even more seriously involved in crime" (Inciardi and Pottieger 1991: 268). It appears that crack intensifies the criminal behaviors in which users were actively involved before initiation into crack use, except for women; they moved from property crimes to prostitution (Chin and Fagan 1990). Indeed, the significant drop in homicides in some major cities, New York in particular, is, at least in part, attributed to the decline in crack use by young people.

The National Institute of Justice concludes: "Assessing the nature and extent of the influence of drugs on crime requires that reliable information about the offense and the offender be available, and that definitions be consistent. In face of problematic evidence, it is impossible to say quantitatively how much drugs influence the occurrence of crime" (1995a: 3). While "there is a generally consistent overall pattern of positive and sometimes quite strong associations between illegal drug use and criminal behavior of other types," research has not been able to validate a causal link between drug use and criminal behavior (Anthony and Forman 2000: 27). While many different data sources establish a raw correlation between drug use and criminal offenses, correlation does not equal causation. Thus, drug use might cause (promote or encourage) crime, or criminality might cause (promote or encourage) drug use, and/or both may be caused (promoted or encouraged) by other variables—environmental, situational, and/or biological (MacCoun, Kilmer, and Reuter 2002).

DRUGS AND VIOLENCE

More than three decades ago, Edwin Schur (1965) argued that narcotic addiction in the United States seems to reduce the inclination to engage in violent crime. However, a more recent research effort found that heroin users (not necessarily addicts) are at least as violent as, and perhaps more violent than, their non-drug-using or non-heroin-using criminal counterparts (B.D. Johnson, Lipton, and Wish 1986a), which is consistent with the writer's experience as a parole officer. In fact, the researchers report, "About half of the most violent criminals are heroin abusers" (B.D. Johnson, Lipton, and Wish 1986b: 3). It is difficult to determine whether this is simply a problem of changing definitions or one of a changing drug population. While there is no evidence that crime results from the direct effects of heroin itself—indeed, the substance appears to have a pacifying effect—the irritability resulting from withdrawal symptoms has been known to lead to violence (P. Goldstein 1985).

This writer dealt with heroin addicts for fourteen years and found many, if not most, to be quite capable of committing violent acts, including homicide—they were frequently convicted of violent crimes. In addition, as we shall discuss in Chapter 11, the heroin distribution subculture at every level—from wholesaling to street sale—is permeated with extreme levels of violence. And, as was noted earlier, many drug abusers use more than one psychoactive chemical (polydrug abuse), thus expanding the possible behavioral effects of the different combinations. If the additional substance is alcohol, which is relatively inexpensive, the drug-crime nexus is mitigated, at least for income-generating crimes; a great deal of violent noneconomic crime is known to be linked to alcohol intoxication. Crimes against persons and violence by drug users are often related to their use of alcohol (Dembo et al. 1991; P. Goldstein et al. 1991). And a Canadian study found that alcohol-dependent prison inmates were twice as likely to have committed violent crimes as their most serious crime compared with prisoners who were dependent on drugs ("Canadian study quantifies link between substance abuse and crime: alcohol abuse associated with violent offenses" 2002).

Similar findings were reported by Susan Martin and her colleagues (2004), who found that while cocaine was not associated with violent crime, alcohol was. While violence associated with cocaine involved dealing, alcohol-related violence was usually the result of interpersonal disputes—insults and arguments involving intoxicated offenders.

Alcohol is an important element in a great deal of crime: Drunk driving is the cause of about 16,000 deaths annually; more than 60 percent of homicides involve alcohol use by both offender and victim; and about 65 percent of aggressive sexual acts against women involve alcohol use by the offender. Research has revealed that the pharmacological effects of alcohol can cause aggression in some people and that alcohol is a factor in nearly half of the murders, suicides, and accidental deaths in the United States; it is a factor in nearly 40 percent of violent crimes ("Coming to Grips with Alcohol" 1987; Chermack and Taylor 1995; Associated Press 1998, 1999a; Greenfeld 1998).

More than 20 percent of prison inmates incarcerated for violent crimes were under the influence of alcohol when they committed their crime (National Center on Addiction and Substance Abuse 1998). But is there a causal link: Would the crimes have been committed in the absence of alcohol? Was alcohol used to provide "courage" for an act that was already being planned? We know that alcohol consumption can lead to disinhibition, but what distinguishes "the life of the party" from the felonious assailant? Alcohol can also impair the processing of information and judgment, thus causing a misinterpretation of events or the behavior of others, resulting, for example, in assault and/or aggressive sexual behavior (e.g., "date rape").

Other drugs (e.g., PCP and cocaine) may involve otherwise normal people in violent behavior. The Detroit medical examiner's office reported that 37 percent of that city's homicide victims had cocaine in their blood samples (Franklin 1987), indicating that cocaine users either engage in dangerous behavior or expose themselves to places or situations in which violence is likely to occur. And people who are intent on committing violent crimes, such as robbery, may ingest alcohol or stimulants for courage—alcohol in small doses acts as a stimulant (W.A. Hunt 1983). "The relationship between drugs and violence has been consistently documented in both the popular press and in social scientific research" (P. Goldstein 1985: 494).

Research has found that crack users are more likely to commit crimes against persons than against property. Crack sellers also appear to be more violent than other drug sellers, and their violence is not limited to drug transactions (Belenko and Chin 1989; Fagan and Chin 1991). There was a surge in children beaten and killed by their crack-abusing parents (Kerr 1988). However, a study in Kansas City, Missouri, of almost 1,500 arrestees, about half of whom abused cocaine, found "no reason to believe that drug using offenders, especially those characterized by heavy or addictive use, are more likely to be arrested for serious or violent offenses than nondrug using offenders. At the very least, it appears that nondrug using offenders commit a relatively higher rate of violent and predatory crimes" (Whitlock, Collings, and Burnett 1990: 21).

SUMMARY

While the drug use continuum ranges from nonuse to dysfunctional use, what we know about those who use psychoactive drugs is skewed toward compulsive users. The term *drug use continuum* helps in defining the slippery term *drug abuse*, but the important point is that how society defines drug abuse determines how society responds to drug use. While statutes distinguish between lawful drugs such as nicotine and alcohol and illegal drugs such as heroin and cocaine, biology recognizes no such distinction. They all have abuse potential, and nicotine and alcohol are responsible for serious behavior health problems. The terms *drug* and *abuse* lack precision, a problem that is compounded by a tendency to moralize and politicize pressing social issues.

Drugs can be grouped into one of three categories—depressants, stimulants, and hallucinogens—depending on their effect on the central nervous system, although some, such as cannabis and MDMA, have more than one effect. There is no definitive way to measure the amount of drug use, which is complicated by polydrug use. Information on the drug problem in the United States is derived from five indicators (a sixth method, Arrestee Drug Abuse Monitoring, was discontinued in 2004):

1. National Survey on Drug Use and Health (NSDUH)
2. Monitoring the Future (MTF)
3. Drug Abuse Warning Network (DAWN)
4. National Narcotics Intelligence Consumers Committee Narcotics Intelligence Estimates
5. *Pulse Check*

The connection between drugs and crime can be pharmacologically driven, particularly with respect to alcohol, or based on the need to secure drugs; or crime and drugs might not be connected—criminals simply also use drugs. The sequence of drugs and crime—which came first—is not clear, and if alcohol is included even more unclear.

Now that we have introduced the topic, in Chapter 2 we will examine the history of drugs and drug abuse.

REVIEW QUESTIONS

1. Why is *drug abuse* not a scientific term?
2. What are the four variables that typically enter into a definition of drug abuse?
3. What are the three categories of drugs of abuse?
4. Why have noncompulsive drug users received little research attention?
5. What factors determine whether the moderate use of a psychoactive substance will be defined as drug abuse?
6. What is the difference between drug abuse and drug addiction?

7. What are the methods used to estimate the amount of drug use in the United States?
8. What are the shortcomings of these efforts?
9. How does polydrug use make the issue of drug abuse more complicated?
10. What are the three possible relationships between drugs and criminal behavior?
11. What has research determined with respect to adolescent drug use?
12. What is the relationship between drugs and violence?
13. What policy implications flow from the relationship between drugs and criminal behavior?

Drug Use and Legislation: A History

The United States of America during the nineteenth century could quite properly be described as a dope fiend's paradise.

Edward M. Brecher (1972: 3)

American concern with narcotics is more than a medical or legal problem—it is in the fullest sense a political problem. The energy that has given impetus to drug control and prohibition came from profound tensions among socioeconomic groups, ethnic minorities, and generations— as well as the psychological attraction of certain drugs. The form of this control has been shaped by the gradual evolution of federal police powers. The bad results of drug use and the number of drug users have often been exaggerated for partisan advantage. Public demand for action against drug abuse has led to regulative decisions that lack a true regard for the reality of drug use.

David Musto (1973: 244)

If anything has been learned about taking drugs in the United States, it is that fads and fashions come and go in the drugs of abuse. Epidemics and pandemics emerge of brews both familiar and strange, and from one decade to the next any variety of venerable and ignoble psychoactive compounds are pursued, rediscovered, and reformulated.

James A. Inciardi (2002: 69)

The history of drug use and attempts at its control provide insight into the complexity of more contemporary control, enforcement, and social issues on this subject.[1] As with many attempts at historical analyses, we are handicapped by the lack of adequate data on a number of items, particularly the extent of drug abuse at earlier periods in our history and of alcohol use during Prohibition. Providing an empirically based analysis of changing policies with respect to drugs is difficult without the ability to measure the effect of these changes, and in fact, we cannot provide such measurements. Even today the number of people abusing various substances, from alcohol to heroin, is the subject of debate.

Policy decisions, as we shall see in this chapter, have frequently been based on perceptions, beliefs, and attitudes with little empirical foundation. They have often reflected popular prejudices against a variety of racial and ethnic groups: "What we think about addiction very much depends on who is addicted" (Courtwright 1982: 3). And sometimes policy has reflected concern over issues of international, rather than domestic, politics. Because the earliest drug prohibitions in the United States reflected a concern with alcohol, we will begin our examination with a history of that substance.

ALCOHOL AND THE TEMPERANCE MOVEMENT

Drinking alcoholic beverages for recreational purposes has an ancient history, with records of such use dating back more than 5,000 years. The Bible records that Noah planted a vineyard and drank of the wine "and was drunken" (*Genesis* 9: 21). Later we are told that the daughters of Lot made their father drunk with wine to trick him into propagating the family line (*Genesis* 19: 32–36). This unseemly use of alcohol could certainly serve as an object lesson against its use, but the practice of drinking alcoholic beverages appears near universal.

The citizens of the United States have traditionally consumed large quantities of alcohol. "Early Americans drank alcohol at home and at work, and alcohol was ever-present in colonial social life" (W. L. White 1998: 1). When he retired from politics, George Washington started a whiskey business. In 1785 Dr. Benjamin Rush, the Surgeon General of the Continental Army and a signer of the Declaration of Independence, authored a pamphlet decrying the use of high-proof alcohol, which he claimed caused, among other maladies, moral degeneration, poverty, and crime. This helped to fuel the move toward prohibition and inspired the establishment in 1808 of the Union Temperance Society, the first of many such organizations (Musto 1998). The Society was superseded by the American Temperance Union in 1836, and the work of the Union was supported by Protestant churches throughout the country. But the movement was divided over appropriate goals and strategies: Should moderation be preached, or should abstinence be forced through prohibition? "Between 1825 and 1850, the tide turned toward abstinence as a goal and legal alcohol prohibition as the means" (W. L. White 1998: 5).

---

[1] For an excellent history of global drug use, see Davenport-Hines (2002).

Bad—and Therefore to be Banned—for All

"The temperance ideology differed from the modern alcoholism movement in that it maintained that alcohol is inevitably dangerous for everyone. That is, some people might believe they can drink moderately, but it is only a matter of time before they encounter increasing problems and completely lose control of their drinking. As strange as it seems to us today, the temperance message thus was that alcohol is inevitably addicting, in the same way that we now think of narcotics" (Peele 1995: 37).

U.S. opposition to alcohol was often intertwined with **nativism**, and efforts against alcohol and other psychoactive drugs were often a thinly veiled reaction to minority groups. (The early temperance movement, however, was strongly abolitionist.) Prohibitionists were typically rural, white Protestants antagonistic to urban Roman Catholics, particularly the Irish, who used the social world of the saloon to gain political power in large cities such as New York and Chicago (Abadinsky 2007a).

The temperance movement made great progress everywhere in the country, and it often coincided with the anti-immigrant sentiment that swept over the United States during the 1840s and early 1850s. In 1843 this led to the formation in New York of the American Republican Party, which spread nationally as the Native American Party, or the "Know-Nothings." (Many clubs were secret, and when outsiders inquired about the group, they were met with the response "I know nothing.") Allied with a faction of the Whig Party, the Know-Nothings almost captured New York in 1854, and they did succeed in carrying Delaware and Massachusetts. They also won important victories in Pennsylvania, Rhode Island, New Hampshire, Connecticut, Maryland, Kentucky, and California. In 1855 the city of Chicago elected a Know-Nothing mayor, and prohibition legislation was enacted in the Illinois legislature (but was defeated in a public referendum that same year [Asbury 1950]). By 1855 about a third of the United States had prohibition laws, and other states were considering their enactment (Musto 1998). Slavery and abolition and the ensuing Civil War subsequently took the place of temperance as the day's most pressing issue (Buchanan 1992).

In 1869 the Prohibition Party attempted, with only limited success, to make alcohol a national issue. In 1874 the Women's Christian Temperance Union was established. Issues of temperance and nativism arose again strongly during the 1880s, leading to the formation of the American Protective Association, a rural-based organization that was strongly anti-Catholic and anti-Semitic. (For an excellent history of nativism in the United States, see Bennett 1988.) In 1893 the Anti-Saloon League was organized.

Around the turn of the century, these groups moved from efforts to change individual behavior to a campaign for national prohibition. After a period of dormancy, the prohibition movement was revived in the years 1907–1919

(Humphries and Greenberg 1981). By 1910 the Anti-Saloon League had become one of the most effective political action groups in U.S. history; it had mobilized Protestant churches behind a single purpose: to enact national prohibition (Tindall 1988). In 1915 nativism and prohibitionism fueled the rise of the Ku Klux Klan, and this time the KKK spread into Northern states and exerted a great deal of political influence. During World War I an additional element, anti-German xenophobia, was added because brewing and distilling were associated with German immigrants (Cashman 1981).

Big business was also interested in prohibition. Alcohol contributed to industrial inefficiency, labor strife, and the saloon, which served the interests of machine politics:

> Around 1908, just as the Anti-Saloon League was preparing for a broad state-by-state drive toward national prohibition, a number of businessmen contributed the funds essential for an effective campaign. The series of quick successes that followed coincided with an equally impressive number of wealthy converts, so that as the movement entered its final stage after 1913, it employed not only ample financing but a sudden urban respectability as well. Substantial citizens now spoke about a new discipline with the disappearance of the saloon and the rampaging drunk. Significantly, prominent Southerners with one eye to the Negro and another to the poorer whites were using exactly the same arguments. (Wiebe 1967: 290–291)

Workmen's compensation laws also helped to stimulate business support for temperance. Between 1911 and 1920 forty-one states had enacted workmen's compensation laws, and Sean Cashman (1981: 6) points out: "By making employers compensate workers for industrial accidents the law obligated them to campaign for safety through sobriety. In 1914 the National Safety Council adopted a resolution condemning alcohol as a cause of industrial accidents."

NATIONAL PROHIBITION

The acrimony between rural and urban America, between Protestants and Catholics, between Republicans and (non-southern) Democrats, between "native" Americans and more recent immigrants, and between business and labor reached a pinnacle with the ratification in 1919 of the Eighteenth Amendment. According to William Chambliss (1973: 10), **Prohibition** was accomplished by the political efforts of an economically declining segment of the American middle class: "By effort and some good luck this class was able to impose its will on the majority of the population through rather dramatic changes in the law." Andrew Sinclair (1962: 163) points out that "in fact, national prohibition was a measure passed by village America against urban America." We could add that it was also passed by much of Protestant America against Catholic (and, to a lesser extent, Jewish) America: "Thousands of Protestant churches held thanksgiving prayer meetings. To many of the people

The first significant piece of prohibitionary drug legislation in the United States was enacted by the city of San Francisco in 1875; the ordinance prohibited the operation of opium dens, commercial establishments for the smoking of opium.

©Bettmann/Corbis

who attended, prohibition represented the triumph of America's towns and rural districts over the sinful cities" (Sinclair 1962; Gusfield 1963; Coffey 1975: 7).

The Eighteenth Amendment to the Constitution was ratified by the thirty-sixth state, Nebraska, on January 16, 1919. According to its own terms, the amendment became effective on January 16, 1920. Ten months after ratification, over a veto by President Woodrow Wilson, Congress passed the National Prohibition Act, usually referred to as the **Volstead Act** after its sponsor, Congressman Andrew Volstead of Minnesota. The Volstead Act strengthened the language of the amendment and defined as intoxicating all beverages containing more than 0.5 percent alcohol; it also provided for federal enforcement. Thus, the Prohibition Bureau, an arm of the Treasury Department, was created, soon becoming notorious for employing agents on the basis of political patronage.

In addition to being inept and corrupt, bureau agents were a public menace. By 1930, 86 federal agents and 200 civilians had been killed, many of them innocent women and children. Prohibition agents set up illegal roadblocks and searched cars; drivers who protested were in danger of being shot. Agents who killed innocent civilians were rarely brought to justice; when they were indicted by local grand juries, the cases were simply transferred, and the agents escaped punishment (Woodiwiss 1988). The bureau was viewed as a training school for bootleggers because agents frequently left the service to join their wealthy adversaries.

The response of a large segment of the American population also proved to be a problem. People do not necessarily acquiesce to new criminal prohibitions, and general resistance can be fatal to the new norm (Packer 1968). Moreover, primary resistance or opposition to a new law such as Prohibition can result, secondarily, in disregard for laws in general—negative contagion. During Prohibition, notes Sinclair (1962: 292), a "general tolerance of the bootlegger and a disrespect for federal law were translated into a widespread contempt for the process and duties of democracy." This was exemplified by the general lawlessness that reigned in Chicago:

> Banks all over Chicago were robbed in broad daylight by bandits who scorned to wear masks. Desk sergeants at police stations grew weary of recording holdups—from one hundred to two hundred were reported every night. Burglars marked out sections of the city as their own and embarked upon a course of systematic plundering, going from house to house night after night without hindrance. . . . Payroll robberies were a weekly occurrence and necessitated the introduction of armored cars and armed guards for the delivery of money from banks to business houses. Automobiles were stolen by the thousands. Motorists were forced to the curbs on busy streets and boldly robbed. Women who displayed jewelry in nightclubs or at the theater were followed and held up. Wealthy women seldom left their homes unless accompanied by armed escorts. (Asbury 1950: 339)

The murder rate in the United States went from 6.8 per 100,000 persons in 1920 to 9.7 in 1933, the year Prohibition was repealed (Chapman 1991c), after which it began to decline. And while the United States had local organized crime before Prohibition, there were no large crime syndicates (King 1969). Pre-Prohibition crime, insofar as it was organized, centered on corrupt political machines, vice entrepreneurs, and, at the bottom, gangs. The "Great Experiment" of Prohibition provided an opportunity for organized crime, especially violent forms, to blossom into an important force. Prohibition acted as a catalyst for the mobilization of criminal elements in an unprecedented manner, unleashing a heightened level of competitive violence and reversing the order between the criminal gangs and the politicians. It also led to an unparalleled level of criminal organization (Abadinsky 2007a). When the repeal of Prohibition left a critical void in their business portfolios, these criminal organizations turned to the drug trade.

OPIUM: A LONG HISTORY

The earliest "war against drugs" (other than alcohol) in the United States was a response to **opium**, a depressant and pain reliever. Opium is the gum from the partially ripe seedpod of the opium **poppy**. There is no agreement on where the plant originated, and a great deal of debate surrounds its earliest use as a drug, which might date back to the Stone Age. The young leaves of the plant have been used as an herb for cooking and as a salad vegetable, and its small, oily seeds, which are high in nutritional value, can be eaten, pressed to make an edible oil, baked into poppy seed cakes, ground into poppy flour, or used as lamp oil. As a vegetal fat source "the seed oil could have been a major factor attracting early human groups to the opium poppy" (Merlin 1984: 89). Archaeologists have discovered ancient art relics that may depict opium use in Egyptian religious rituals as early as 3500 B.C.E. (Inverarity, Lauderdale, and

Field 1983). By 1500 B.C.E. the Egyptians had definitely discovered the medical uses of opium: It is listed as a pain reliever in the Ebers Papyrus (Burkholz 1987). From Egypt its use spread to Greece (R. O'Brien and Cohen 1984). Opium is discussed by Homer's works, the *Iliad* and the *Odyssey* (circa 700 B.C.E.), and the term **opium** is derived from the Greek word *opion*, meaning the juice of the poppy (Bresler 1980). Hippocrates (460–357 B.C.E.), the "father of medicine," recommended drinking the juice of the white poppy mixed with the seed of the nettle.

Opium was used by doctors in classical Greece and ancient Rome, and Arab traders brought it to China for use in medicine. Later, the Crusaders picked it up from Arab physicians and brought it back to Europe, where it became a standard medicine. Opium is mentioned by Shakespeare in *Othello* and by Chaucer, Sir Thomas Browne, and Robert Burton. In the early sixteenth century the physician Paracelsus made a tincture of opium—powdered opium dissolved in alcohol—that he called *laudanum*, and until the end of the nineteenth century it proved to be a popular medication (R. O'Brien and Cohen 1984). De Quincey (1952) noted that opium was often cheaper than alcohol.

Two centuries ago, opium was generally available as a cure for everything. It was like aspirin; every household had some, usually in the form of laudanum. Naturally, the general availability of opium and the medical profession's enthusiasm for it helped to create addicts, some of them very famous; Samuel Taylor Coleridge (1772–1834) and Thomas De Quincy (1785–1859) are the best known. At the time medicine was primitive, doctors had no concept of addiction, and opium became the essential ingredient of innumerable remedies dispensed in Europe and America for the treatment of diarrhea, dysentery, asthma, rheumatism, diabetes, malaria, cholera, fevers, bronchitis, insomnia, and pain of any kind (Fay 1975). There was nothing to alert patients to the dangers of the patent medicines they were prescribed or to prepare them for the side effects. As a result no more stigma was attached to the opium habit than to alcoholism; it was an unfortunate weakness, not a vice. Wherever it was known, opium use was both medicinal and recreational (Alvarez 2001).

In explaining the popularity of opium, Charles Terry and Mildred Pellens (1928: 58) state: "When we realize that the chief end of medicine up to the beginning of the [nineteenth] century was to relieve pain, that therapeutic agents were directed at symptoms rather than cause, it is not difficult to understand the wide popularity of a drug which either singly or combined so eminently was suited to the needs of so many medical situations."

Opium is a labor-intensive product. To produce an appreciable quantity requires repeated incisions of a great number of poppy capsules: about 18,000 capsules—one acre—to yield 20 pounds of opium (Fay 1975). Accordingly, supplies of opium were rather limited in Europe until the eighteenth century, when improvements in plantation farming increased opium production. Attempts to produce domestic opium in the United States were not successful. While the poppy could be grown in many sections of the United States, particularly the South, Southwest, and California, labor costs and an opium gum that proved low in potency led to a reliance on imported opium (H. W. Morgan 1981).

As the primary ingredient in many "**patent medicines**" (actually secret formulas that carried no patent at all) opiates were readily available in the United States until 1914, and quacks prescribed and promoted them for general symptoms as well as for specific diseases. People who were not really ill were frightened into the patent medicine habit (Young 1961). Patients who were actually sick received the false impression that they were on the road to recovery. Of course, because there was often little or no scientific medical treatment for even the mildest of diseases, a feeling of well-being was at least psychologically, and perhaps by extension physiologically, beneficial. However, babies born to opiate-using mothers were often small and experienced the distress of withdrawal. Harried mothers often responded by relieving them with infant remedies that contained opium.

The smoking of opium was popularized by Chinese immigrants, who brought the habit with them to the United States. During the latter part of the nineteenth and early twentieth centuries they also operated commercial opium dens that often attracted the attention of the police, "not because of the use of narcotics but because they became gathering places for thieves, footpads [highwaymen] and gangsters." In fact, "opium dens were regarded as in a class with saloons and, for many years, were no more illegal" (Katcher 1959: 287).

MORPHINE AND HEROIN

At the end of the eighteenth century (Latimer and Goldberg 1981) or early in the nineteenth (Bresler 1980; Nelson et al. 1982; Merlin 1984; Musto 1987) a German pharmacist poured liquid ammonia over opium and obtained an alkaloid, a white powder that he found to be many times more powerful than opium. Friedrich W. Serturner named the substance *morphium* after Morpheus, the Greek god of sleep and dreams; ten parts of opium can be refined into one part of morphine (Bresler 1980). It was not until 1817, however, that articles published in scientific journals popularized the new drug, resulting in widespread use by doctors. Quite incorrectly, as it turned out, the medical profession viewed morphine as an opiate without negative side effects.

By the 1850s morphine tablets and a variety of morphine products were readily available without prescription. In 1856 the hypodermic method of injecting morphine directly into the bloodstream was introduced to U.S. medicine. The popularity of morphine rose during the Civil War, when the intravenous use of the drug to treat battlefield casualties was rather indiscriminate (Terry and Pellens 1928). Following the war, morphine use among ex-soldiers was so common as to give rise to the term *army disease*. Nevertheless, "Medical journals were replete with glowing descriptions of the effectiveness of the drug during wartime and its obvious advantages for peacetime medical practice" (Cloyd 1982: 21). Hypodermic kits became widely available, and the use of unsterile needles by many doctors and laypersons led to abscesses or disease (H. W. Morgan 1981).

In the 1870s morphine was exceedingly cheap, cheaper than alcohol, and pharmacies and general stores carried preparations that appealed to a wide segment of the population, whatever the individual emotional quirk or physical ailment. Anyone who visited nearly any physician for any complaint, from a toothache to consumption, would be prescribed morphine (Latimer and Goldberg 1981), and the substance was widely abused by physicians themselves. Morphine abuse in the latter part of the nineteenth century was apparently widespread in rural America (Terry and Pellens 1928).

Starting in the 1870s, doctors injected women with morphine to numb the pain of "female troubles" or to turn the "willful hysteric" into a manageable invalid. By the 1890s, when the first drug epidemic peaked, female medical addicts made up almost half of all addicts in the United States. In the twentieth century the drug scene shifted to underworld elements of urban America, the disreputable "sporting class": prostitutes, pimps, thieves, gamblers, gangsters, entertainers, active homosexuals, and youths who admired the sporting men and women (Stearns 1998).

In 1874 a British chemist experimenting with morphine synthesized diacetylmorphine, and the most powerful of opiates came into being: "Commercial promotion of the new drug had to wait until 1898 when the highly respected German pharmaceutical combine Bayer, in perfectly good faith but perhaps without sufficient prior care, launched upon an unsuspecting world public this new substance, for which they coined the trade name 'heroin' and which they marketed as—of all things—a 'sedative for coughs'" (Bresler 1980: 11). Jack Nelson and his colleagues (1982) state that heroin was actually isolated in 1898 in Germany by Heinrich Dreser, who was searching for a non-habit-forming pain reliever to take the place of morphine. Dreser named it after the German word *heroisch*, meaning large and powerful.

Opiates, including morphine and heroin, were readily available in the United States until 1914. In 1900, 628,177 pounds of opiates were imported into the United States (Bonnie and Whitebread 1970). The President's Commission on Organized Crime (1986) notes that between the Civil War and 1914 there was a substantial increase in the number of people using opiates. This was the consequence of a number of factors:

- The spread of opium smoking from Chinese immigrants into the wider community
- An increase in morphine addiction as a result of its indiscriminate use to treat battlefield casualties during the Civil War
- The widespread administration of morphine by hypodermic syringe
- The widespread use of opium derivatives by the U.S. patent medicine industry
- Beginning in 1898, the marketing of heroin as a safe, powerful, and non-addictive substitute for the opium derivatives morphine and codeine

CHINA AND THE OPIUM WARS

Until the sixteenth century, China was a military power whose naval fleet surpassed any that the world had ever known. A fifteenth century power struggle ultimately led to a regime dominated by Confucian scholars; in 1525 they ordered the destruction of all oceangoing ships and set China on a course that would lead to poverty, defeat, and decline (Kristoff 1999).

In 1626 a British warship appeared off the coast of China, and its captain imposed his will on Canton (now Guangzhou) with a bombardment. In response to the danger posed by British ships the Emperor opened the city of Canton to trade, and Britain granted the British East India Company a monopoly over the China trade. Particularly important to this trade was the shipping of tea to England. By the 1820s the trade situation between England and China paralleled trade between the United States and Japan. Although British consumers had an insatiable appetite for Chinese tea, the Chinese desired few English goods. The British attempted to introduce alcohol, but a large percentage of Asians have enzyme systems that make drinking alcohol extremely unpleasant. Opium was different (Beeching 1975). Poppy cultivation was an important source of revenue for the Mughal emperors (Muslim rulers of India between 1526 and 1857). When the Mughal Empire fell apart, the British East India Company salvaged and improved the system of state control of opium. In addition to the domestic market, the British supplied Indian opium to China.

Opium was first prohibited by the Chinese government in Peking (Beijing) in 1729, when only small amounts of the substance were reaching China. Ninety years earlier, tobacco had been similarly banned as a pernicious foreign article. Opium use was strongly condemned in China as a violation of Confucian principles, and for many years the imperial decree against opium was generally supported by the population (Beeching 1975). In 1782 a British merchant ship's attempt to sell 1,601 chests of opium in China resulted in a total loss, as no purchasers could be found. By 1799, however, a growing traffic in opium led to an imperial decree condemning the trade. Dean Latimer and Jeff Goldberg (1981) doubt that opium addiction was extensive or particularly harmful to China as a whole. The poorer classes, the authors note, could afford only adulterated opium, which was unlikely to produce addiction. "Just why the Chinese chose to obtain their supplies from India," states Peter Fay (1975: 11–12), "is no clearer than why, having obtained it, they smoked it instead of ate it." In the end, he notes, the Chinese came to prefer the Indian product to their own. However, because the preference was to smoke opium, it had to be specially prepared by being boiled in water, filtered, and boiled again until it reached the consistency of molasses, thereby becoming "smoking opium."

Like the ban on tobacco, the one on opium was not successful (official corruption was endemic in China). As consumption of imported opium increased and the method of ingestion shifted from eating to smoking, official declarations against opium increased, and so did smuggling. "When opium left Calcutta, stored in the holds of country ships and consigned to agents in Canton, it was an entirely legitimate article. It remained an entirely legitimate article all the way up to the China Sea. But the instant it reached the coast of China it became something different. It became contraband" (Fay 1975: 45). In fact, the actual shipping of opium to China was accomplished by independent British or Parsee merchants. Thus, notes Beeching, "the Honourable East India Company was able to wash its hands of all formal responsibility for the illegal drug trade" (1975: 26).

Opium furnished the British with the silver needed to buy tea. Because opium was illegal in China, however, its importation—smuggling—brought China no tariff revenue. Before 1830 opium was transported to the coast of China, where it was offloaded and smuggled by the Chinese themselves. The outlawing of opium by the Chinese government led to the development of an organized underworld; gangs became secret societies—triads—that still move heroin out of the Far East to destinations all over the world (Latimer and Goldberg 1981). (This will be discussed in Chapter 11.) The armed opium ships were safe from Chinese government intervention, and the British were able to remain aloof from the smuggling itself.

In the 1830s the shippers grew bolder and entered Chinese territorial waters with their opium cargo. The British East India Company, now in competition with other opium merchants, sought to flood China with cheap opium and drive out the competition (Beeching 1975). In 1837 the emperor ordered his officials to move against opium smugglers, but the campaign was a failure, and the smugglers grew even bolder. The following year the emperor changed his strategy and moved against Chinese traffickers and drug abusers, as only a total despot could do, helping to dry up the market for opium. As a result, the price fell significantly (Hanes and Sanello 2005).

The First Opium War

In 1839, in dramatic fashion, Chinese authorities laid siege to the port city of Canton, confiscating and destroying all opium awaiting offloading from foreign ships. The merchantmen agreed to stop importing opium into China, and the siege was lifted. The British merchants petitioned their own government for compensation and retribution. The reigning Parliamentary Whig majority was very weak, however, and compensating the opium merchants was not politically or financially feasible. Instead, the cabinet, without Parliamentary approval, decided on a war that would result in the seizure of Chinese property (Fay 1975).

In 1840 a British expedition attacked the poorly armed and poorly organized Chinese forces. In the rout that followed, the Emperor was forced to pay $6 million for the opium his officials had seized and $12 million as compensation for the war. Hong Kong became a Crown colony, and the ports of Canton, Amoy (Xiamen), Foochow (Fuzhou), Ningpo, and Shanghai were opened to British trade. Opium was not mentioned in the peace (surrender) treaty, but the trade resumed with new vigor. In a remarkable reversal of the balance of trade, by the mid-1840s China had an opium debt of about 2 million pounds sterling (Latimer and Goldberg 1981). In the wake of the First Opium War, China was laid open to extensive missionary efforts by Protestant evangelicals, who, although they opposed the opium trade, viewed saving souls as their primary goal. Christianity, they believed, would save China from opium (Fay 1975). Unfortunately, morphine was actively promoted by Catholic and Protestant missionaries as an agent for detoxifying opium addicts (Latimer and Goldberg 1981).

The Second Opium War

The Second Opium War began in 1856, when the balance of payments once again favored China. In that year a minor incident between the British and Chinese governments was used as an excuse to force China into making further treaty concessions. This time the foreign powers seeking to exploit a militarily weak China included Russia, the United States, and particularly France, which was jealous of the British success. Canton was sacked, and a combined fleet of British and French warships sailed right up the Grand Canal to Peking and proceeded to sack and burn the imperial summer palace, 200 buildings spread over eighty square miles of carefully landscaped parkland with extensive libraries and priceless works of art (Hanes and Sanello 2005).

The Emperor was forced to indemnify the British 20,000 pounds sterling, more than enough to offset the balance of trade which was the real cause of the war. A commission was appointed to legalize and regulate the opium trade (Latimer and Goldberg 1981) that increased from less than 59,000 chests a year in 1860 to more than 105,000 by 1880 (Beeching 1975). Until 1946 the British permitted the use of opiates in its Crown colony of Hong Kong, first under an official monopoly and, after 1913, directly by the government (Lamour and Lamberti 1974). During Japan's occupation of China, which began a few years before its attack on Pearl Harbor, large amounts of heroin were trafficked by the Japanese army's "special services branch," which helped to finance the cost of the occupation (Karch 1998).

THE CHINESE PROBLEM AND THE AMERICAN RESPONSE

Chinese laborers were originally brought into the United States after 1848 to work in the gold fields, particularly in those aspects of mining that were most dangerous because few white men were willing to engage in blasting shafts, placing beams, and laying track lines in the gold mines. Chinese immigrants also helped to build the Western railroad lines at pay few whites would accept—known as "coolie wages." After their work was completed, the Chinese were often banned from the rural counties; by the 1860s they were clustering in cities on the Pacific coast, where they established Chinatowns—and where many of them smoked opium.

The British opium monopoly in China was challenged in the 1870s by opium imported from Persia and cultivated in China itself. In response, British colonial authorities, heavily dependent on a profitable opium trade, increased the output of Indian opium, causing a price decline that was aimed at driving

Prohibition authorities Izzy Einstein and Moe Smith with a still they captured in a cellar in New York City. In addition to being inept and corrupt, Prohibition Bureau agents were a public menace. Prohibition agents set up illegal roadblocks and searched cars; drivers who protested were in danger of being shot. Agents who killed innocent civilians were rarely brought to justice.

©Bettmann/Corbis

the competition out of business. The resulting oversupply increased the amount of opium entering the United States for the Chinese population.

Beginning in 1875, there was an economic depression in California. As a result, the first significant piece of prohibitionary drug legislation in the United States was enacted by the city of San Francisco. "The primary event that precipitated the campaign against the Chinese and against opium was the sudden onset of economic depression, high unemployment levels, and the disintegration of working-class standards of living" (Helmer 1975: 32). The San Francisco ordinance prohibited the operation of opium dens, commercial establishments for the smoking of opium, "not because of health concerns as such, but because it was believed that the drug stimulated coolies into working harder than non-smoking whites" (Latimer and Goldberg 1981: 208).

Depressed economic conditions and xenophobia led one Western state after another to follow San Francisco's lead and enact anti-Chinese legislation that often included prohibiting the smoking of opium. The anti-Chinese nature of the legislation was noted in some early court decisions. In 1886 an Oregon district court, responding to a petition for habeas corpus filed by Yung Jon, who had been convicted of opium violations, stated: "Smoking opium is not our vice, and therefore it may be that this legislation proceeds more from a desire to vex and annoy the 'Heathen Chinese' in this respect, than to protect the people from the evil habit. But the motives of legislators cannot be the subject of judicial investigation for the purpose of affecting the validity of their acts" (Bonnie and Whitebread 1970: 997).

"After 1870 a new type of addict began to emerge, the white opium smoker drawn primarily from the underworld of pimps and prostitutes, gamblers, and thieves" (Courtwright 1982: 64). During the 1890s Chicago's Chinatown was located in the notorious First Ward, whose politicians grew powerful and wealthy by protecting almost every vice known to humanity. But First Ward alderman John "Bathhouse" Coughlin "couldn't stomach" opium smokers and threatened to raid the dens himself if necessary. There was constant police harassment, and in 1894 the city enacted an antiopium ordinance. By 1895 the last of the dens had been raided out of business (Sawyers 1988).

Anti-Chinese efforts were supported and advanced by Samuel Gompers (1850–1924) as part of his effort to establish the American Federation of Labor. The Chinese served as scapegoats for organized labor that depicted the "yellow devils" as undercutting wages and breaking strikes. Anti-opium legislation was also fostered by stories of white women being seduced by Chinese white slavers through the use of opium.[2] In 1882 the Chinese Exclusion Act banned the entry of Chinese laborers into the United States. (It was not until 1943, when the United States was allied with China in a war against Japan, that citizenship rights were extended to Chinese immigrants, and China was then permitted an annual immigration of 105 individuals.)

In 1883 Congress raised the tariff on the importation of smoking opium. In 1887, apparently in response to obligations imposed on the United States by a Chinese-American commercial treaty negotiated in 1880 and becoming effective in 1887, Congress banned the importation of smoking opium by Chinese subjects. Americans, however, were still permitted to import the substance, and many did so, selling it to both Chinese and American citizens (President's Commission on Organized Crime 1986). The Tariff Act of 1890 increased the tariff rate on smoking opium to $12 per pound, resulting in a substantial increase in opium smuggling and the diversion of medicinal opium for manufacture into smoking opium. In response, in 1897 the tariff was reduced to $6 per pound (President's Commission on Organized Crime 1986).

During the nineteenth century opiates were not associated with crime in the public mind. While some people may have frowned on opium use as immoral, employees were not fired for addiction. Wives did not divorce their addicted husbands or husbands their addicted wives. Children were not taken from their homes and lodged in foster homes or institutions because one or both parents were addicted. Addicts continued to participate fully in the life of the community. Addicted children and young people continued to go to school, Sunday School, and college. Thus, the nineteenth century avoided one of the most disastrous effects of current narcotics laws and attitudes: the rise of a deviant addict subculture, cut off from respectable society and without a road back to respectability. (Brecher 1972: 6–7)

---

[2] Similar anti-Chinese hysteria, especially the diatribe that they used opium to seduce white women, led to anti-opium legislation in Australia at the end of the nineteenth century (Manderson 1999).

TWENTIETH-CENTURY EFFORTS AND LEGISLATION
The Pure Food and Drug Act

National efforts against opiates (and cocaine) were part of a larger campaign to regulate drugs and the contents of food substances; in 1879 a bill was introduced in Congress to accomplish national food and drug regulation. These efforts were opposed by the Proprietary Association of America, which represented the patent medicine industry. The medical profession was more interested in dealing with quacks within the profession than with quack medicines, and the American Pharmaceutical Association was of mixed mind: Its members, in addition to being scientists, were merchants who found the sale of proprietary remedies bulking large in their gross income (J. H. Young 1961). Toward the end of the nineteenth century the campaign for drug regulation was assisted by agricultural chemists who decried the use of chemicals to defraud consumers into buying spoiled canned and packaged food. In 1884 state-employed chemists formed the Association of Official Agricultural Chemists to combat this widespread practice. They began to expand their efforts into non-foodstuffs, including patent medicines.

The nation's newspapers and magazines made a considerable amount of money from advertising patent medicines. Toward the turn of the century, however, a few periodicals, in particular *Ladies Home Journal* and *Collier's*, began vigorous investigations and denunciations of patent medicines. Eventually, the American Medical Association (AMA, founded in 1847), which was a rather weak organization at the close of the nineteenth century because the vast majority of doctors were not members (Musto 1973), began to campaign in earnest for drug regulation.

U.S. Senate hearings on the pure food issue gained a great deal of newspaper coverage and aroused the public (J. H. Young 1961). The dramatic event that quickly led to the adoption of the Pure Food and Drug Act, however, was the 1906 publication of Upton Sinclair's *The Jungle* (1981/1906). Sinclair, in a novelistic description of the meat industry in Chicago, exposed the filthy, unsanitary, and unsafe conditions under which food reached the consumer. Sales of meat fell by almost 50 percent, and President Theodore Roosevelt dispatched two investigators to Chicago to check on Sinclair's charges. Their "report not only confirmed Sinclair's allegations, but added additional ones. Congress was forced by public opinion to consider a strong bill" (Ihde 1982: 42). The result was the Pure Food and Drug Act, passed later that same year, which required medicines to list certain drugs and their amounts, including alcohol and opiates.

China and the International Opium Conference

The international U.S. response to drugs in the twentieth century is directly related to its trade with China. To increase its influence in China and thus improve its trade position, the United States supported the International Reform Bureau (IRB), a temperance organization representing over thirty missionary societies in the Far East, which was seeking a ban on opiates. As a result, in 1901 Congress enacted the Native Races Act, which prohibited the sale of alcohol and opium to "aboriginal tribes and uncivilized races." The provisions of the act were later expanded to include "uncivilized elements" in the United States proper: Indians, Eskimos, and Chinese (Latimer and Goldberg 1981).

As a result of the Spanish-American War in 1898, the Philippines were ceded to the United States. At the time of Spanish colonialism opium smoking was widespread among Chinese workers on the islands. Canadian-born Reverend Charles Henry Brent (1862–1929), a supporter of the IRB, arrived in the Philippines as the Episcopal bishop during a cholera epidemic that began in 1902 and that reportedly had led to an increase in the use of opium. As a result of his efforts, in 1905 Congress enacted a ban against sales of opium to Filipino natives except for medicinal purposes. Three years later the ban was extended to all residents of the Philippines. It appears that the legislation was ineffective, and smoking opium remained widely available (Musto 1973). "Reformers attributed to drugs much of the appalling poverty, ignorance, and debilitation they encountered in the Orient. Opium was strongly identified with the problems afflicting an apparently moribund China. Eradication of drug abuse was part of America's white man's burden and a way to demonstrate the New World's superiority" (H. W. Morgan 1974: 32).

Bishop Brent proposed the formation of an international opium commission, to meet in Shanghai in 1909. This plan was supported by President Theodore Roosevelt, who saw it as a way of assuaging Chinese anger at the passage of the Chinese Exclusionary Act (Latimer and Goldberg 1981). The International Opium Commission, chaired by Brent and consisting of representatives from thirteen nations, convened in Shanghai on February 1. Brent was successful in rallying the conferees around the U.S. position that opium was evil and had no nonmedical use. The commission unanimously adopted a number of vague resolutions, the most important being (Terry and Pellens 1928):

1. That each government take action to suppress the smoking of opium at home and in overseas possessions and settlements
2. That opium has no use outside of medicine and, accordingly, that each country should move toward increasingly stringent regulations concerning opiates
3. That measures should be taken to prevent the exporting of opium and its derivatives to countries that prohibit its importation

Only the United States and China, however, were eager for future conferences, and legislative efforts against opium following the conference were generally unsuccessful. Southerners were distrustful of federal enforcement, and the drug industry was opposed. Efforts to gain Southern support for antidrug legislation focused on the alleged abuse of cocaine by African Americans—the substance was reputed to make them uncontrollable. Although tariff legislation with respect to opium already existed, Terry and Pellens (1928) note that its purpose was to generate income. The first federal legislation to control the domestic use of opium was passed in 1909 as a result of the Shanghai conference.

"An Act to prohibit the importation and use of opium for other than medicinal purposes" failed to regulate domestic opium production and manufacture, nor did it control the interstate shipment of opium products, which continued to be widely available through retail and mail order outlets (President's Commission on Organized Crime 1986).

A second conference was held in the Hague in 1912, with the United States, Turkey, Great Britain, France, Portugal, Japan, Russia, Italy, Germany, Persia, the Netherlands, and China in attendance. A number of problems stood in the way of an international agreement: Germany wished to protect her burgeoning pharmaceuticals industry and insisted on a unanimous vote before any action could be agreed upon; Portugal insisted on retaining the Macao opium trade; the Dutch demanded to maintain their opium trade in the West Indies; and Persia and Russia wanted to keep on growing opium poppies. Righteous U.S. appeals to the delegates were rebuffed with allusions to domestic usage and the lack of laws in the United States (Latimer and Goldberg 1981). Nevertheless, the conference managed to put together a patchwork of agreements known as the International Opium Convention, which was ratified by Congress on October 18, 1913. The signatories committed themselves to enacting laws aimed at suppressing the abuse of opium, morphine, and cocaine as well as drugs prepared or derived from these substances (President's Commission on Organized Crime 1986). On December 17, 1914, the Harrison Act, which represented this country's attempt to carry out the provisions of the Hague Convention, was approved by President Woodrow Wilson.

The Harrison Act

The Harrison Act provided that any person who was in the business of dealing in drugs covered by the act, including the opium derivatives morphine and heroin, as well as cocaine, was required to register annually and to pay a special annual tax of $1. The statute made it illegal to sell or give away opium or opium derivatives and coca or its derivatives without a written order on a form issued by the commissioner of revenue. People who were not registered were prohibited from engaging in interstate traffic in the drugs, and no one could possess any of the drugs who had not registered and paid the special tax, under a penalty of up to five years imprisonment and a fine of no more than $2000. Rules promulgated by the Treasury Department permitted only medical professionals to register, and they had to maintain records of the drugs they dispensed. Within the first year more than 200,000 medical professionals registered, and the small staff of Treasury agents could not scrutinize the number of prescription records that were generated (Musto 1973).

It was concern with federalism—constitutional limitation on the police powers of the central government—that led Congress to use the taxing authority of the federal government to control drugs. While few people today would question the Drug Enforcement Administration's right to register physicians and pharmacists and control what drugs they can prescribe and dispense, at the

Revisionist History or Historical Ignorance?
"Addictive drugs were criminalized because they were harmful; they are not harmful because they were criminalized" (Office of National Drug Control Policy 2001: 56).

beginning of the twentieth century federal authority to regulate narcotics and the prescription practices of physicians was generally thought to be unconstitutional (Musto 1998). In 1919 use of taxing authority to regulate drugs was upheld by the Supreme Court (*United States* v. *Doremus* 249 U.S. 86):

> If the legislation enacted has some reasonable relation to the exercise of the taxing authority conferred by the Constitution, it cannot be invalidated because of the supposed motives which induced it. . . . The Act may not be declared unconstitutional because its effect may be to accomplish another purpose as well as the raising of revenue. If the legislation is within the taxing authority of Congress—that is sufficient to sustain it.

The Harrison Act was enacted with the support of the AMA and the American Pharmaceutical Association, both of which had grown more powerful and influential in the first two decades of the twentieth century, since the medical profession had been granted a monopoly on dispensing opiates and cocaine. The Harrison Act also had the effect of imposing a stamp of illegitimacy on the use of most narcotics, fostering an image of the immoral and degenerate "dope fiend" (Bonnie and Whitebread 1970). At this time, according to Courtwright's (1982) estimates, there were about 300,000 opiate addicts in the United States. But, he notes, the addict population was already changing. The medical profession had, by and large, abandoned its liberal use of opiates—imports of medicinal opiates declined dramatically during the first decade of the twentieth century—and the public mind, as well as that of much of the medical profession, came to associate heroin with urban vice and crime. In contrast with opiate addicts of the nineteenth century, opiate users of the twentieth century were increasingly male habitués of pool halls and bowling alleys, denizens of the underworld, and they typically used heroin (Kinlock, Hanlon, and Nurco 1998; Acker 2002). As in the case of minority groups, this marginal population was an easy target of drug laws and drug law enforcement.

The commissioner of the Internal Revenue Service was placed in charge of upholding the Harrison Act, and in 1915, 162 collectors and agents of the Miscellaneous Division of the Internal Revenue Service were given the responsibility for enforcing drug laws. In 1919 the Narcotics Division was created within the Bureau of Prohibition with a staff of 170 agents and an appropriation of $270,000. The Narcotics Division, however, was tainted by its association with the notoriously inept and corrupt Prohibition Bureau and suffered from a corruption scandal of its own: "The public dissatisfaction intensified because of a scandal involving falsification of arrest records and charges relating to payoffs by, and collusion with, drug dealers" (President's Commission on Organized Crime 1986: 204). In response, in 1930 Congress removed drug enforcement from the Bureau of Prohibition and established the Federal Bureau of Narcotics (FBN) as a separate agency within the Department of the Treasury. "Although the FBN was primarily responsible for the enforcement of the Harrison Act and related drug laws, the task of preventing and interdicting the illegal importation and smuggling of drugs remained with the Bureau of Customs" (President's Commission on Organized Crime 1986: 205).

Case Law Results

In 1916 the Supreme Court ruled in favor of a physician (Dr. Moy) who had provided maintenance doses of morphine to an addict (*United States* v. *Jin Fuey Moy* 241 U.S. 394). In 1919, however, the Court ruled (*Webb* v. *United States* 249 U.S. 96) that a prescription for morphine issued to a habitual user not under a physician's care that was intended not to cure but to maintain the habit is not a prescription and thus violates the Harrison Act. However, private physicians found it impossible to handle the large drug clientele that was suddenly created; they could do nothing "more than sign prescriptions" (Duster 1970: 16).

In *United States* v. *Behrman* (258 U.S. 280, 289, 1922) the Court ruled that a physician was not entitled to prescribe large doses of proscribed drugs for self-administration even if the addict was under the physician's care. The Court stated: "Prescriptions in the regular course of practice did not include the indiscriminate doling out of narcotics in such quantity as charged in the indictments." In 1925 the Court limited the application of *Behrman* when it found that a physician who had prescribed small doses of drugs for the relief of an addict did not violate the Harrison Act (*Linder* v. *United States* 268 U.S. 5). In reversing the physician's conviction the Court distinguished between *Linder* and excesses shown in the case of *Behrman*:

> The enormous quantities of drugs ordered, considered in connection with the recipient's character, without explanation, seemed enough to show prohibited sales and to exclude the idea of *bona fide* professional activity. The opinion [in *Behrman*] cannot be accepted as authority for holding that a physician, who acts *fide bona* and according to fair medical standards, may never give an addict moderate amounts of drugs for self-administration in order to relieve conditions incident to addiction. Enforcement of the tax demands no such drastic rule, and if the Act had such scope it would certainly encounter grave constitutional guarantees.

In fact, the powers of the Narcotics Division were clear and limited to the enforcement of registration and record-keeping regulations. "The large number of addicts who secured their drugs from physicians were excluded from the Division's jurisdiction. Furthermore, the public's attitude toward drug use," notes Donald Dickson (1977: 39), "had not much changed with the passage of the Act—there was some opposition to drug use, some support of it, and a great many who did not care one way or the other. The Harrison Act was actually passed with very little publicity or news coverage."

Richard Bonnie and Charles Whitebread (1970: 976) note the similarities between the temperance and antinarcotics movements: "Both were first directed against the evils of large scale use and only later against all use. Most of the rhetoric was the same: These euphoriants produced crime, pauperism and insanity." However, "the temperance movement was a matter of vigorous public debate; the anti-narcotics movement was not. Temperance legislation was the product of a highly organized nationwide lobby; narcotics legislation was largely ad hoc. Temperance legislation was designed to eradicate known evils resulting from alcohol abuse; narcotics legislation was largely anticipatory." In fact, notes

H. Wayne Morgan (1981), comparisons between alcohol and opiates—until the nature of addiction became clear—were often favorable to opium. It was not public sentiment that led to antidrug legislation; nevertheless, the result of such legislation was an increasing public perception of the dangerousness of certain drugs (Bonnie and Whitehead 1970). As we will see, this perception was fanned by officials of the federal drug enforcement agency.

NARCOTICS CLINICS AND ENFORCEMENT

Writing in 1916, Pearce Bailey (1974: 173–174) noted that the passage of the Act "spread dismay among the heroin takers":

> They saw in advance the increased difficulty and expense of obtaining heroin as a result of this law; then the drug stores shut down, and the purveyors who sell heroin on the street corners and in doorways became terrified, and for a time illicit trade in the drug almost ceased. . . . Once the law was established the traffic was resumed, but under very different circumstances. The price of heroin soared [900 percent, and was sold in adulterated form]. This put it beyond the easy reach of the majority of adherents, most of whom do not earn more than twelve or fourteen dollars a week. Being no longer able to procure it with any money that they could lay their hands on honestly, many were forced to apply for treatment for illness brought about by result of arrest for violation of the law.

Beginning in 1918, narcotics clinics opened in almost every major city. Information about them is sketchy (Duster 1970), and there is a great deal of controversy over their operations. While they were never very popular with the general public, most clinics were well run under medical supervision (H. W. Morgan 1981). While some clinics were guilty of a variety of abuses, the good ones enabled addicts to continue their normal lives without being drawn into the black market in drugs (Duster 1970). The troubled clinics, however, such as those in New York, where the number of patients overwhelmed the medical staff, generated a great deal of newspaper coverage, resulting in an outraged public.

Following World War I and the Bolshevik Revolution, xenophobia and prohibitionism began to sweep the nation. The United States severely restricted immigration, and alcohol and drug use was increasingly associated with an alien population. In 1922 federal narcotics agents closed the drug clinics and began to arrest physicians and pharmacists who provided drugs for maintenance. At issue was Section 8 of the Harrison Act, which permitted the possession of controlled substances if prescribed "in good faith" by a registered physician, dentist, or veterinarian in accord with "professional practice." The law did not define "good faith" or "professional practice." Under a policy developed by the federal narcotics agency, thousands of people, including many physicians—more than 25,000 between 1914 and 1938 (W. L. White 1998)[3]—were charged with violations: "Whether conviction followed or not

---

[3] There continues to be a stigma within the medical profession attached to physicians who treat drug abusers (S. Gilbert 1996).

mattered little as the effects of press publicity dealing with what were supposedly willful violations of a beneficent law were most disastrous to those concerned" (Terry and Pellens 1928: 90). "Once a strict antidrug policy had been established, both the public's and policymakers' curiosity about the details of a drug's biological effects faded. Federal scientists also feared their research findings might conflict with official policies, so they avoided some areas of investigation" (Musto 1998: 62).

The medical profession withdrew from dispensing drugs to addicts, forcing them to look to illicit sources and giving rise to an enormous illegal business in drugs. People who were addicted to opium smoking eventually found their favorite drug unavailable—the bulky smoking opium was difficult to smuggle—and turned to the more readily available heroin that was prepared for intravenous use and would produce a more intense effect (Courtwright 1982). The criminal syndicates that resulted from Prohibition added heroin trafficking to their business portfolios. When Prohibition was repealed in 1933, profits from bootlegging disappeared accordingly, but drug trafficking remained as an important source of revenue for organized criminal groups. (The business of drugs is discussed in Chapter 11.) Law enforcement efforts against drugs have proven as ineffectual as efforts against alcohol during Prohibition, with similar problems of corruption.

The federal government shaped vague and conflicting court decisions into definitive pronouncements reflecting the drug enforcement agency's own version of its proper role: "American administrative regulations took on the force of ruling law" (Trebach 1982: 132). The drug agency also embarked on a vigorous campaign to convince the public and Congress of the dangers of drugs and thereby to justify its approach to the problem of drug abuse. According to Bonnie and Whitebread (1970: 990), the existence of a separate federal narcotics bureau "anxious to fulfill its role as crusader against the evils of narcotics" has been the single major factor in the legislative history of drug control in the United States since 1930.

The actions of the federal government toward drug use must be understood within the context of the times. The years immediately following World War I were characterized by pervasive attitudes of nationalism and nativism and by a fear of anarchy and communism. The Bolshevik Revolution in Russia, a police strike in Boston (see Russell 1975), and widespread labor unrest and violence were the backdrop for the infamous Palmer Raids of 1919, in which Attorney General A. Mitchel Palmer, disregarding a host of constitutional protections, ordered the arrest of thousands of "radicals." That same year the Prohibition Amendment was ratified, and soon legislation ended large-scale (legal) immigration. Drug addiction—morphinism/heroinism—was added to the un-American "isms" of alcoholism, anarchism, and communism (Musto 1973). In 1918 there were only 888 federal arrests for narcotics law violations; in 1920 there were 3,477. In 1925, the year the clinics were closed, there were 10,297 (Cloyd 1982). "During the 1920s and 1930s," notes Susan Speaker, "newspaper and magazine accounts of narcotics problems, and the propaganda of various anti-narcotics organizations used certain stock ideas and images to construct an intensely fearful public rhetoric about drugs. Authors routinely described drugs, users, and sellers as 'evil,' described sinister conspiracies to undermine American society and values, credited drugs with immense power to corrupt users, and called for complete eradication of the problem" (Speaker 2001: 1).

According to William White (1998: 113), Treasury Department opposition to prescribing drugs for addicts was based on a belief in the prevailing propaganda of the day with respect to alcohol treatment. "The Treasury Department opposed ambulatory treatment because, for many patients, it turned into sustained maintenance, and also because the remaining inebriate hospitals and asylums of the day were still boasting 95% success rates. After all, leaders of the Treasury Department argued, why should someone be maintained on morphine when all he or she had to do was to take the cure? It was through such misrepresentation of success rates that the inebriate asylums and private treatment sanitariums contributed inadvertently to the criminalization of narcotic addiction in the U.S."

In 1923 legislation was introduced to curtail the importation of opium for the manufacture of heroin, resulting in a virtual ban on heroin in the United States. (In 1956 Congress declared all heroin to be contraband.) Among the few witnesses who testified before Congress, all supported the legislation. The AMA had already condemned the use of heroin by physicians, and the substance was described as the most dangerous of all habit-forming drugs, some witnesses arguing that the psychological effects of heroin use serve as a stimulus to crime. Much of the medical testimony, in light of what is now known about heroin, was erroneous, but the law won easy passage in 1924 (Musto 1973). A pamphlet published the same year by the prestigious Foreign Policy Association summarized contemporary thinking about heroin (cited in Trebach 1982: 48):

- It is unnecessary in the practice of medicine.
- It destroys all sense of moral responsibility.
- It is the drug of the criminal.
- It recruits its army among youths.

The use of opiates, except for narrow medical purposes, was now thoroughly criminalized, both in law and in practice. The law defined drug users as criminals, and the public viewed heroin use as the behavior of a deviant criminal class.

THE UNIFORM DRUG ACT

Until 1930 efforts against drugs were primarily federal. Only a few states had drug control statutes, and these were generally ineffective (Musto 1973). At the urging of federal authorities, many states enacted their own antidrug legislation. By 1931 every state restricted the sale of cocaine, and all but two restricted the sale of opiates. State statutes, however, were far from uniform. As early as 1927, this lack of uniformity, combined with the growing hysteria about dope fiends and criminality, resulted in several requests for a uniform state narcotics law. The diversity of state drug statutes was not an anachronism. The need for greater uniformity in state statutes was recognized in the first half of the nineteenth century, when a prominent New York attorney, David Dudley Field (1805–1894), campaigned for a uniform code of procedure for both civil and criminal matters. During the 1890s the American Bar Association set up the National Conference of Commissioners on Uniform State Laws, whose efforts resulted in a variety of uniform codes that were adopted by virtually all jurisdictions (Abadinsky 2007b).

A uniform drug act for the states was the goal of both the Committee on the Uniform Narcotic Act and representatives of the AMA because doctors wanted uniformity of legal obligations. Their first two drafts copied a 1927 New York statute that listed coca, opium, and cannabis products as habit-forming drugs to be regulated or prohibited. Because of opposition to its inclusion on the habit-forming list, cannabis was dropped from later drafts with a note indicating that each state was free to include cannabis or not in its own legislation without affecting the rest of the act. The final draft also used the 1927 New York statute as a model and included suggestions from the newly appointed commissioner of the FBN, Harry Anslinger. The draft was adopted overwhelmingly by the National Conference of Commissioners on Uniform State Laws, to which each governor had appointed two representatives. By 1937 thirty-five states had enacted the Uniform Drug Act, and every state had enacted statutes relating to marijuana. Despite propagandizing efforts by the FBN, "The laws went unnoticed by legal commentators, the press and the public at large" (Bonnie and Whitebread 1970: 1034).

The lack of public concern is related to the demographics of drug abuse, which was concentrated in minority, lower-class areas and the criminal subculture. Before the Harrison Act there was considerable use in rural areas; the South, where drugs often substituted for alcohol in dry areas, used more opiates than other parts of the country. After the Harrison Act addicts in rural areas were attended to quietly by sympathetic doctors. Heroin was heavily concentrated in urban areas of poverty. For example, during the early decades of the twentieth century heroin use in New York was heaviest in the Jewish and Italian areas of the Lower East Side. As these two groups climbed up the economic ladder and moved out, they were replaced by African Americans looking for affordable housing; this group then became the basis of the addict population (Helmer 1975). Demographics intensified the problem; African Americans had a higher birthrate than Jews and Italians, and an extraordinary number of youngsters were 16 years old, the age of highest risk for addiction. After World War II the white ethnic population became increasingly suburban, and the inner city became increasingly black and Hispanic—a new vulnerable population in a drug-infested environment.

Pointing to the similarities between the prohibition against alcohol and that against other drugs, David Courtwright (1982: 144) asks why, since both reform efforts had ended in failure, did the public withdraw its support for one and increase its support of the other? "One factor (in addition to economic and political considerations) must have been that alcohol use was relatively wide-spread and cut across class lines. It seemed unreasonable for the government to deny a broad spectrum of otherwise normal persons access to drink. By 1930 opiate addiction, by contrast, was perceived to be concentrated in a small criminal subculture; it did not seem unreasonable for that same government to deny the morbid cravings of a deviant group."

World War II had a dramatic impact on the supply of heroin in the United States. The Japanese invasion of China interrupted supplies from that country, while the disruption of shipping routes by German submarines and attack battleships reduced the amount of heroin moving from Turkey to Marseilles to the United States. When the United States entered the war, security measures "designed to prevent infiltration of foreign spies and sabotage to naval installations made smuggling into the United States virtually impossible." As a result, "at the end of World War II, there was an excellent chance that heroin addiction could be eliminated in the United States" (A. W. McCoy 1972: 15). Obviously, this did not happen (the reasons will be discussed later and in Chapter 11), and "by the 1980s, an estimated 500,000 Americans used illicit opioids (mainly heroin), mostly poor young minority men and women in the inner cities" (Batki et al. 2005: 13).

COCAINE: FROM COCA TO CRACK

Cocaine is a stimulant, an alkaloid found in significant quantities only in the leaves of two species of coca shrub that are indigenous to certain sections of South America, though they have been grown elsewhere.[4] "For over 4,000 years among the native Andean population the coca leaf has been used in ancient rituals and for everyday gift giving. Holding spiritual, economic, and cultural significance, coca is seen as an important medium for social integration and human solidarity in the face of adverse conditions" (Wheat and Green 1999: 42). To the Incas the plant was of divine origin and was reserved for those who believed themselves descendants of the gods. In Bolivia it is drunk as *mate* (coca tea), and the leaves are chewed for hours by farmers and miners along with an alkaloid that helps to release the active ingredients. "The result is similar to a prolonged caffeine or tobacco buzz. But it is more than that. It improves stamina, is a sacred symbol central to community life and provides essential nutrients" (Wheat and Green 1999: 43).

European experience with chewing coca coincided with Spanish exploration of the New World. While the early Spanish explorers, obsessed with gold, referred to coca leaf chewing with scorn, later reports about the effects of coca on Indians were more enthusiastic. Nevertheless, the chewing of coca leaves was not adopted by Europeans until the nineteenth century (Grinspoon and Bakalar 1976). A "mixture of ignorance and moral hauteur played an important role in the long delay between the time Europeans first became acquainted

---

[4]During the 1920s, Indonesia exported more coca leaf than did Latin America (Karch 1996).

with cocaine—in the form of coca—and the time they began to use it" (Ashley 1975: 3). The coca leaves tasted bitter and were favored by pagans—Peruvian Indians—"an obviously inferior lot who had allowed their great Inca Empire to be conquered by Pizarro and fewer than two hundred Spaniards." Early records indicate that the effects of coca—stamina and energy—were ascribed not to the drug but to a pact the Indians had made with the devil or simply to delusion— the Indian is sustained by the *belief* that chewing coca gives him extra strength.

Nineteenth-Century Use

The Best-Known "User" of Cocaine

"Save for the occasional use of cocaine, [Sherlock Holmes] had no vices, and he only turned to the drug as a protest against the monotony of existence when cases were scanty and the papers uninteresting." Sir Arthur Conan Doyle (1899: 29). Doyle, an ophthalmologist, was familiar with cocaine's use in eye surgery (Karch 1998).

Alkaloidal cocaine was isolated from the coca leaf by German scientists in the decade before the American Civil War, and the German chemical manufacturer Merck began to produce small amounts (Karch 1998). Scientists experimenting with the substance noted that it showed promise as a local anesthetic and had an effect opposite that caused by morphine. Indeed, at first cocaine was used to treat morphine addiction, but the result was often a morphine addict who was also dependent on cocaine (Van Dyke and Byck 1982). Enthusiasm for cocaine spread across the United States, and by the late 1880s a feel-good pharmacology based on the coca plant and its derivative cocaine emerged, as the substance was hawked for everything from headaches to hysteria. "Catarrh powders for sinus trouble and headaches—a few were nearly pure cocaine— introduced the concept of snorting" (Gomez 1984: 58). Patent medicines frequently contained significant amounts of cocaine.

One very popular product was the coca wine *Vin Mariani*, which contained two ounces of fresh coca leaves in a pint of Bordeaux wine; another, *Peruvian Wine of Coca*, was available for $1 a bottle through the 1902 Sears, Roebuck catalog. The most famous beverage containing coca, however, was first bottled in 1894, and an advertisement for Coca-Cola in *Scientific American* in 1906 publicized the use of coca as an important tonic in this "healthful drink" (May 1988b: 29). A 1908 government report listed more than forty brands of soft drinks containing cocaine (Helmer 1975). In contrast to the patent medicines, however, these beverages, including wine and Coca-Cola, contained only small, typically trivial, amounts of cocaine (Karch 1998).

In 1884 Sigmund Freud began taking cocaine and soon afterward began to treat his friend Ernst von Fleischl-Marxow, who had become a morphine addict, with cocaine. The following year, von Fleischl-Marxow suffered from toxic psychosis as a result of taking increasing amounts of cocaine by subcutaneous injection, and Freud wrote that the misuse of the substance had hastened his friend's death. Although Freud continued the recreational use of cocaine as late as 1895, his enthusiasm for its therapeutic value waned (Byck 1974).

After the flush of enthusiasm for cocaine in the 1880s its direct use declined. Cocaine continued to be used in a variety of potions and tonics, but unlike morphine and heroin, it did not develop a separate appeal (H. W. Morgan 1981). Indeed, it gained a reputation for inducing bizarre and unpredictable behavior.

| ## Doctor, Heal Thyself

Influenced by the writings of Sigmund Freud on cocaine, William Stewart Halstead, surgeon-in-chief at Johns Hopkins Hospital and the "father of American surgery," began experimenting with the substance in 1884. When he died in 1922 at age 70, Dr. Halstead was still addicted to cocaine despite numerous attempts at curing himself (W. L. White 1998).

Cocaine in the Twentieth Century

After the turn of the century, cocaine, like heroin, became identified with the urban underworld and, in the South, with African Americans. "As with Chinese opium, southern blacks became a target for class conflict, and drug use became one point of tension in this larger sociopolitical struggle" (Cloyd 1982: 35). The campaign against cocaine took on bizarre aspects aimed at winning support for antidrug legislation among Southern politicians, who traditionally resisted federal efforts that interfered with their concept of states' rights. Without any research support, a spate of articles alleged widespread abuse of cocaine by African Americans, often associating such abuse with violence and the rape of white women (Helmer 1975). Ultimately, notes Jerald Cloyd (1982: 54), "Southerners were more afraid of African-Americans than of increased federal power to regulate these drugs." At the time of the Harrison Act there was considerable discussion—but no evidence—of substantial cocaine use by blacks in Northern cities (H. W. Morgan 1981).

As with opiates, the legal use of cocaine was affected by the Pure Food and Drug Act of 1906 and finally by the Harrison Act in 1914. Before this federal legislation many states passed laws restricting the sale of cocaine, beginning with Oregon in 1887. By 1914 forty-six states had such laws, while only twenty-nine had similar laws with respect to opiates (Grinspoon and Bakalar 1976). With its dangers well known, by the end of World War I the medical community had largely lost interest in cocaine (Karch 1998), and in 1922 Congress officially defined cocaine as a narcotic and prohibited the importation of most cocaine and coca leaves. This caused an increase in law enforcement efforts, and the price of cocaine increased accordingly. In 1932 amphetamines became available, and this cheap, legal stimulant helped to further decrease user interest in cocaine (Cintron 1986).

In the United States, from 1930 until the 1960s there was limited demand for cocaine and, accordingly, only limited supply.[5] Cocaine use was associated with deviants at the fringes of society—jazz musicians and the denizens of underworld—and sources were typically diverted from medical supplies. During the late 1960s and early 1970s attitudes toward recreational drug use became more liberal because of the wide acceptance of marijuana. Cocaine was

---

[5] This was not the case in Europe and the Far East, where major drug firms provided cocaine—often surreptitiously—for sale in the drug black market (Karch 1998).

Drug Hysteria

According to Steven Belenko (1993: 24), all drug scares have four common elements:

1. The scope of the problem is never as great as originally portrayed in the media.
2. Despite the media portrayals, compulsive use and addiction are not inevitable consequences of using the drug.
3. The violent behavior associated with the use of the drug is not as common as initially believed, nor is it necessarily caused by the drug.
4. The popularity of the particular drug waxes and wanes over time, and prevalence rates do not continue to increase.

no longer associated with deviants, and the media played a significant role in shaping public attitudes:

> By publicizing and glamorizing the lifestyle of affluent, upper-class drug dealers and the use of cocaine by celebrities and athletes, all forms of mass media created an effective advertising campaign for cocaine, and many people were taught to perceive cocaine as chic, exclusive, daring, and nonaddicting. In television specials about cocaine abuse, scientists talked about the intense euphoria produced by cocaine and the compulsive craving that people (and animals) develop for it. Thus, an image of cocaine as being extraordinarily powerful, and a (therefore desirable) euphoriant was promoted. (Wesson and Smith 1985: 193)

Cocaine soon became associated with a privileged elite, and the new demand was sufficient to generate new sources. Refining and marketing networks outside of medical channels (Grinspoon and Bakalar 1976) led to the development of the criminal organizations discussed in Chapter 11.

During the 1980s a new form of cocaine-called **crack**-became popular in a number of cities, particularly New York. Its popularity dramatically altered the drug market at the consumer level: Both users and sellers were much younger than was typical in the heroin business. Younger retailers and a competitive market increased the level of violence associated with the drug business. The appearance of this new form of cocaine, which is smoked, set off a frenzy of media interest. Elected officials responded by increasing penalties for this form of the substance as opposed to the powdered form, which is typically sniffed.

By 1987 the rapid expansion of crack use stopped, and by 1989 its popularity began to diminish. The hysteria with which the media and public officials had greeted this "new scourge" was subjected to research and reflection: "Crack itself was never instantly addictive or totally devastating as asserted by the media, political speeches, and statements of public policy. In particular, it did not draw the naive and young in droves into this new and dangerous lifestyle." Indeed, crack use was centered in those populations in which drug abuse has always been endemic: the urban underclass (B. D. Johnson, Golub, and Fagan 1995: 291).

Cocaine has very limited medical use as a local anesthetic for ear, nose, and throat surgery. Its early use, however, led to the development of procaine (Novocain), which in 1905 was introduced into medicine and continues to be used today, particularly in dentistry (Snyder 1986). Novocain and other synthetic drugs have, for the most part, replaced cocaine as a local anesthetic. Coca leaves are legally imported into the United States by a single chemical company, which extracts the cocaine for pharmaceutical purposes. The remaining leaf material, which contains no psychoactive agents, is prepared as a flavoring for Coca-Cola.

MARIJUANA: FROM IMMIGRANTS TO THE COUNTERCULTURE

Cannabis sativa L., the hemp plant from which marijuana and **hashish** are derived, grows wild throughout most tropical and temperate regions of the world; it has been cultivated for at least 5,000 years for a variety of purposes including the manufacture of rope and paint. There is a great deal of interest in the cultivation of hemp for its fiber, particularly in the American apparel and paper industries (Mintz 1997).

Marijuana's use as an intoxicant was brought to Africa by Arab traders, and the plant was introduced into Brazil through the slave trade in the 1600s. The word **marijuana** (sometimes spelled "marihuana") is derived from the Spanish term for any substance that produces intoxication: *maraguano*. Until the early 1900s recreational use of marijuana was popular chiefly among Mexican laborers in the Southwest and certain fringe groups such as jazz musicians (Weisheit 1990).

When the dried leaves of the marijuana plant are smoked like tobacco, perceptual changes occur that vary widely according to the strength of the substance, the person smoking the marijuana, and the environmental conditions. In the past most of the cannabis growing wild in the United States derived from plants originally cultivated for their fiber rather than their drug content, so their psychoactive potency was quite weak (Peterson 1980). In more recent years entrepreneurial horticulturists in the United States began producing more powerful strains of the plant.

Early Marijuana Legislation and Literature

As has already been discussed in this chapter, race, religion, and ethnicity have been closely identified with the reaction to drugs in the United States: the Irish and alcohol; the Chinese and opium; African-Americans and cocaine; and, finally, Mexicans and marijuana. Bonnie and Whitebread (1970) state that the most prominent influence in marijuana legislation was racism: State laws against marijuana, they argue, were often part of a reaction to Mexican immigration. Before 1930 sixteen states with relatively large Mexican populations had enacted anti-marijuana legislation. "Chicanos in the Southwest were believed to be incited to violence by smoking it" (Musto 1973: 65). Jerome Himmelstein (1983: 29) argues, however, that the "crucial link between Mexicans and federal marihuana policy was not locally based political pressure from the Southwest, but a specific image of marihuana that emerged from the context of marihuana use by Mexicans and was used to justify anti-marihuana legislation. Because Mexican laborers and other lower-class groups were identified as typical marihuana users, the drug was believed to cause the kinds of antisocial behavior associated with those groups, especially violent crime." Because of marijuana's association with suspect marginal groups—Mexicans, artists, intellectuals, jazz musicians, bohemians, and petty criminals—it became an easy target for regulation (Morgan 1981). In the eastern United States marijuana was erroneously believed to be addictive and there was fear that it would serve as a substitute for narcotics that were outlawed by the Harrison Act.

In light of more contemporary research into marijuana (which will be reviewed in Chapter 6), the hysterical anti-marijuana literature that was produced during the 1930s can often seem amusing. Earle Rowell and Robert Rowell (1939: 49) wrote, for example, that marijuana "seems to superimpose upon the user's character and personality a devilish form. He is one individual when normal, and an entirely different one after using marijuana." According to these authors, marijuana "has led to some of the most revolting cases of sadistic rape and murder of modern times." In 1936 the FBN presented a summary of cases that illustrate "the homicidal tendencies and the generally debasing effects which arise from the use of marijuana" (Uelmen and Haddox 1983: 1–11). The 1936 motion picture *Reefer Madness* showed a horrifying portrait of the marijuana user.

"It is clear," note Bonnie and Whitebread (1970: 1021–1022), "that no state undertook any empirical or scientific study of the effects of the drug. Instead they relied on lurid and often unfounded accounts of marijuana's dangers as presented in what little newspaper coverage the drug received." By 1931 twenty-two states had marijuana legislation that was often part of a general-purpose statute against narcotics (Bonnie and Whitebread 1970). Despite its being outlawed, marijuana was never an important issue in the United States until the 1960s: "It hardly ever made headlines or became the subject of highly publicized hearings and reports. Few persons knew or cared about it, and marihuana laws were passed with minimal attention" (Himmelstein 1983: 38).

The FBN, operating on a Depression era budget, was reluctant to take on the additional responsibilities that would result from outlawing marijuana at the federal level. Harry J. Anslinger, FBN commissioner from 1930 until his retirement in 1962, hoped that the states would act against marijuana, leaving the bureau free to concentrate on heroin and cocaine. To get the states to act, the FBN dramatized the dangers of marijuana. But in such trying economic times, the states were reluctant to take on additional work, and the FBN's own propaganda forced it to act (Himmelstein 1983).

At the urging of Anslinger, Congress passed the Marijuana Tax Act of 1937. Because of uncertainty about the federal government's ability to outlaw marijuana, the act placed an exorbitant tax on cannabis—$100 an ounce—rather than prohibiting the substance outright. This tax act was a result of three days of congressional hearings that Bonnie and Whitebread (1970: 1054) characterize as "a case study in legislative carelessness." Commissioner Anslinger was able to orchestrate an undocumented and hysterical presentation before the House Ways and Means Committee on the dangers of marijuana, and the floor debate on the bill, Bonnie and Whitebread argue, represented a near-comic example of dereliction of legislative responsibility. Anslinger (with Tompkins 1953: 20–21) maintained that marijuana was "a scourge which undermines its victims and degrades them mentally, morally, and physically." The AMA's opposition to the bill was ridiculed by members of the Ways and Means Committee. Marijuana was being treated as just another narcotic (Bonnie and Whitebread 1970). The states followed the federal lead and increased their penalties for drug violations, including marijuana. In 1951 penalties for possession and trafficking in marijuana were substantially increased—along with those for other controlled substances—with the passage of the Boggs Act (discussed below).

Counterculture Use and Changing Laws

During the 1960s public attitudes toward marijuana underwent considerable change. A nonconformist counterculture, whose members were often from the white middle class, emerged. The rebellious nature of the hippies encouraged greater experimentation with sex and drugs, marijuana in particular. In fact, note Charles Lidz and Andrew Walker (1980), marijuana use helped to tie together diverse interests: civil rights, antiwar, and antiestablishment groups and individuals. Its primary importance was as a membership ritual for an otherwise very diffuse and disorganized culture. No longer confined to minority or subcultural groups—Chicanos, African Americans, beatniks, musicians—marijuana soon found widespread acceptance among people of the middle and upper classes. This led to significant scientific inquiry into the effects of marijuana, and toward the latter part of the 1960s it became clear that whatever its dangers might be, the substance was simply not in the same class as heroin or cocaine on any important pharmacological dimension. Young, white, middle-class users, however, like their ghetto counterparts, were being subjected to the significant penalties that obtained for heroin and cocaine.

The rise of middle-class marijuana users offered the public a new view of the phenomenon in *Life* magazine's October 31, 1969, issue. Marijuana was the lead story, and the magazine presented photographs of white, middle-class people enjoying marijuana in a variety of congenial social settings. Also included was an in-depth story of a young man from Nashville, Tennessee, a long-distance runner and prep school graduate attending the University of Virginia on an athletic scholarship. He was arrested for possession of three pounds of marijuana and in a Virginia state court received a sentence of twenty years in prison. The same issue of *Life* contains an article by the former director of the U.S. Food and Drug Administration, James L. Goddard, who stated: "Our laws governing marijuana are a mixture of bad science and poor understanding of the role of law as a deterrent force. They are unenforceable, excessively severe, scientifically incorrect and revealing our ignorance of human behavior" (1969: p. 34). The following year Robert Kennedy, Jr. and R. Sargent Shriver III, juveniles at the time, were arrested for possession of marijuana. Public pressure soon caused legislators to reconsider state and federal penalties for marijuana.

"As of 1965, marihuana laws still bore the mark of the harsh legislation of the 1950s. Simple possession carried penalties of two years for the first offense, five for the second, and ten for the third" (Himmelstein 1983: 103). By the end of the 1960s penalties on the state level had been significantly reduced. However, the Comprehensive Drug Abuse Prevention and Control Act of 1970 established five schedules for controlled substances, and marijuana, along with heroin, was placed in the highest category, Schedule I, which has the following features:

1. The drug or other substance has a high potential for abuse.
2. The drug or other substance has no currently accepted medical use in treatment in the United States.
3. There is a lack of accepted safety for the use of the drug or other substance under medical supervision.

While the penalties remained as high as imprisonment for five years for nonnarcotic drugs (i.e., marijuana), such sentences are reserved for possession of large amounts with intent to sell—for wholesale traffickers, the only type of offender traditionally of interest to federal drug law enforcement. Simple possession was made into a misdemeanor, a crime punishable by imprisonment for not more than one year. The major elements of the federal law were copied by most states.

In 1972 the presidentially appointed National Commission on Marijuana and Drug Abuse recommended that possession of marijuana for personal use or noncommercial distribution be decriminalized. The following year Oregon became the first state to abolish criminal penalties for the possession of one ounce or less of marijuana, replacing incarceration with relatively small fines. In 1975 California made possession of one ounce or less of marijuana a citable misdemeanor with a maximum penalty of $100, and there were no increased penalties for recidivists. By 1978 eleven states had decriminalized marijuana, a position supported by President Jimmy Carter (Himmelstein 1983) but opposed by the President's Commission on Organized Crime (1986), which was appointed by President Ronald Reagan. As a result of a ballot initiative in 1990, Alaska, after fifteen years, has made marijuana possession illegal again.

In more recent years there has been some medical use of the active ingredient in marijuana—but not marijuana itself—to control the side effects of chemotherapy and to treat glaucoma. Despite vigorous opposition at the federal level, in 1997 voters in California and Arizona passed referenda authorizing physicians to prescribe marijuana. Maine voters did the same in 1999.

For the Birds

In 1998, Canada declared hemp a legal crop, joining several European nations that also have commercial hemp industries. When a Canadian producer of birdseed shipped nearly twenty tons of his product to the United States, it was seized by U.S. Customs agents because the shipment consisted of sterilized seeds produced from industrial hemp (Wren 1999b).

AMPHETAMINES: SPEED AND ICE

First synthesized in 1887, amphetamine was introduced into clinical use in the 1930s and was eventually offered as a "cure-all" for just about every ailment. Between 1932 and 1946 there were thirty-nine generally accepted medical uses for amphetamines, including the treatment of schizophrenia, morphine addiction, low blood pressure, and caffeine and tobacco dependence (D. E. Smith 1979). Manufactured under the trade name Benzedrine, in 1932 amphetamine was marketed as an inhalant for use as a nasal decongestant. "Amphetamines were unique: never before had a powerful psychoactive drug been introduced in such quantities in so short a period of time, and never before had a drug with such a high addictive potential and capability of causing long-term or irreversible physical and psychological damage been so enthusiastically embraced by the medical profession as a panacea or so extravagantly promoted by the drug industry" (Grinspoon and Hedblom 1975: 13).

By the end of the decade, as their stimulating properties became widely known, amphetamines were used primarily as analeptics—stimulating drugs. Many amphetamine-based inhalants appeared on the market and were widely available without prescription. These quickly became the subject of widespread abuse. During World War II, British, German, and Japanese governments issued amphetamines to soldiers to elevate mood and to counteract fatigue and pain, and U.S. military personnel were exposed to their use through contact with the British military. During the Korean conflict the United States authorized the distribution of amphetamines to military personnel. The first major wave of abuse appeared when American servicemen in Korea and Japan mixed the substance with heroin to create "speedballs," which were taken intravenously (Grinspoon and Hedblom 1975).

Dextroamphetamine, a more potent version of Benzedrine, was marketed as Dexedrine. **Methamphetamine**, manufactured under the trade name Methadrine, is an even more potent analeptic. Currently the drug of choice for street abusers, who refer to it by the brand name Methadrine or as "meth," **"crank,"** **"speed,"** or "ice," methamphetamine is injected, snorted, or smoked. Reports of its abuse by businessmen and athletes appeared as early as 1940, and a black market in the substance—"pep pills"—began to develop. It was (and perhaps still is) particularly popular among long-distance truck drivers and college students trying to stay awake. Amphetamines were widely prescribed in the 1950s and 1960s as an aid in dieting, leading to abuse by housewives taking "diet pills."

In the 1960s the Food and Drug Administration launched a widespread anti-amphetamine campaign with the slogan "Speed Kills" (R. O'Brien and Cohen 1984), and in 1971 federal laws restricted the conditions under which amphetamines could be prescribed. During the late 1980s the smokable crystal methamphetamine called *ice* appeared on the drug scene. Media and political concern over the possible spread of this new form of drug led to a new drug scare. Widespread abuse continues, particularly in more rural parts of the country where the drug is often manufactured.

BARBITURATES

Barbiturates are sedating drugs synthesized from barbituric acid. Barbituric acid was first synthesized in Germany in 1863 by Nobel Prize–winning chemist Adolf von Baeyer. The first barbiturate was synthesized in 1882 but not marketed until 1903 (McKim 1991). Accounts vary as to how barbituric acid acquired its name. In 1903 it was released under the trade name Veronal, a name derived from the Italian city of Verona. It is known generically in the United States as barbital (Wesson and Smith 1977).

Barbiturates were used to induce sleep, replacing other aids such as alcohol and opiates. Since the appearance of phenobarbital in 1912, thousands of barbituric acid derivatives have been synthesized, although only about a dozen are commonly used; these are marketed under a variety of brand names. Barbiturates were widely prescribed in the United States during the 1930s, when their toxic effects were not fully understood. By 1942 there were campaigns against the nonmedical use of barbiturates, and by the 1950s barbiturates were one of the major drugs of abuse among adults in the United States. In the 1960s barbiturate abuse quickly spread to the youth population (R. O'Brien and Cohen 1984). Nonmedical abuse of barbiturates is usually the result of diverting licit supplies through theft or burglary, forged prescriptions, or illegal manufacture in other countries, particularly Mexico. Supplies diverted from licit sources may be repackaged in nondescript capsules, thus disguising their source (Wesson and Smith 1977).

TRANQUILIZERS AND SEDATIVES

Along with amphetamines and barbiturates, many doctors in the 1960s routinely prescribed a variety of substances to reduce anxiety. Tranquilizers or **sedatives** such as Miltown and Valium enabled millions of housewives to "get by with a little help from their friends." These substances were the subject of heavy advertising, much of it depicting women in need of relief from tension and anxiety, by drug companies that offered their products as aids in coping with the normal problems of life. Consumers often became so dependent on these substances that they could not function without them, having lost the ability to deal with normal levels of stress. As a result of unfavorable attention by health and consumer organizations and a congressional hearing in 1979, the manufacturers of Valium and other tranquilizers shifted their focus to promote these substances' ability to ease the stress of modern living. In 1980 the Food and Drug Administration required tranquilizers to be labeled as generally not appropriate for anxiety or tension associated with the stress of everyday life. Nevertheless, they continue to be widely prescribed for patients experiencing "troubling times."

HALLUCINOGENS

Hallucinogens such as LSD became popular during the 1960s, particularly among rebellious college students and people who identified themselves as antiestablishment. Lester Grinspoon (1979: 57) states: "It is impossible to write an adequate history of such an amorphous phenomenon [LSD] without discussing the whole cultural rebellion of the 1960s." LSD was first synthesized in Switzerland in 1938, but its hallucinogenic qualities did not become apparent until its discoverer took his first "trip" in 1943. During the 1950s the U.S. Army and the Central Intelligence Agency conducted LSD experiments on soldiers and civilians, without their knowledge or consent, to test its suitability for chemical warfare and its utility as a "truth serum" (Henderson 1994a).

Although LSD arrived in the United States from Europe in 1949 for experimental use in treating psychiatric disorders (Stevens 1987), it was virtually unknown before 1962 except to a small number of psychiatrists and psychologists (Brecher 1972). Two psychologists, Timothy Leary and Richard Alpert of Harvard College, were experimenting with the hallucinogenic mushroom **psilocybin**. While the "Psilo-cybin Project" began as a scientific endeavor, it ended as casual use of the drug by many friends and acquaintances, including a small clique of psychedelic enthusiasts such as the authors Aldous Huxley (*Brave New World*) and Ken Kesey (*One Flew Over the Cuckoo's Nest*) and the poet Allen Ginsberg (see Wolfe [1968] for a look at Kesey and his Merry Pranksters' psychedelic world). Experiments that Leary and Alpert conducted on inmates at Concord State Prison suggested that aggressive and hardened inmates became introspective and caring under the influence of psilocybin. Leary began encouraging his psychology students to use psilocybin. Word of their activities spread beyond the Harvard community when it was picked up by newspapers as a result of a story in the *Harvard Crimson*. Federal agencies began making inquiries. School officials were anxious to rid themselves of Leary and Alpert, so their research and control over psilocybin were placed under a faculty committee while the school awaited the expiration of Leary and Alpert's teaching contracts. No matter, they had been introduced to LSD.

"In a major city like Los Angeles," notes Jay Stevens (1987: 171), "it was as easy to go on an LSD trip as it was to visit Disneyland. Interested parties could either contact the growing number of therapists who were using LSD in practice, or they could offer themselves as guinea pigs to any of the dozens of research projects that were under way at places like UCLA." Therapists were using LSD "to heighten the traditional psychotherapeutic values of recall, abreaction, and emotional release," in most cases with apparent success and without negative side effects (Stevens 1987: 180). However, the reaction of mainstream, establishment medicine and psychiatry toward LSD was generally negative, particularly when it was used by nonphysicians such as psychologists. Stevens refers to the resulting conflict as a turf war between medically trained practitioners and all other therapists. LSD was also widely used without the guise of any therapeutic milieu, such as at the "LSD colony" in Hollywood, where, according to Leary (R. Rosenbaum 1988: 135), "Cary Grant was the high cardinal."

In 1962 Congress enacted legislation that gave the Food and Drug Administration control over all new investigational drugs. Although aimed at amphetamines, the legislation also applied to LSD (Stevens 1987). That same year Leary, Alpert, and thirty-five disciples moved to Zihuatanejo, Mexico, where they used LSD freely. The two psychologists established the International Foundation for Internal Freedom and "Freedom Center" at a small hotel in Zihuatanejo. A second headquarters was opened in Newton, Massachusetts, just outside of Boston. Their goal was to "turn on America." Leary popularized the use of LSD, and as a result of his Harvard connection, LSD gained the attention of the mass media (Grinspoon 1979). As a self-appointed High Priest of LSD (the title of Leary's book), he traveled widely and lectured on the virtues of using acid to "turn on, tune in, and drop out." Acid rock songs such as "White Rabbit" by the Jefferson Airplane, "Sunshine Superman" by Donovan, and the Beatles' "Magical Mystery Tour" and "Lucy in the Sky with Diamonds" became top hits. The books of Nobel Prize winner Hermann Hesse (1877–1962) were very popular among the youth of the1960s, and his work helped to popularize the "psychedelic" experience (Engel 1974). Psychedelic jargon and colors became fashionable, and the media reported on the activities of hippies in New York's Greenwich Village and San Francisco's Haight-Ashbury district. LSD use became part of the counterculture and the antiwar movement.

In 1963 an editorial attacking LSD appeared in the *Journal of the American Medical Association*, and in 1965 LSD was outlawed in the United States. In 1963 Leary and Alpert were discharged from Harvard. That same year, the Mexican authorities closed down Freedom Center, and Leary was deported. In 1965 Leary was returning to the United States from a trip to Mexico with three other people, one of whom had secreted marijuana in her undergarments. When the drug was discovered during a strip search, Leary blurted out, "I'll take responsibility for the marijuana." At the time possession of marijuana was a serious crime in Texas. Despite his defense that the use of drugs was part of his religious liberty, Leary was convicted and sentenced to thirty years in prison. Leary appealed; in the meantime his harassment by law enforcement agencies resulted in numerous arrests. In 1969 the U.S. Supreme Court ordered Leary's marijuana case to be retried. In 1970 he was convicted again and sentenced to ten years. Leary appealed, but several weeks later he was convicted of another drug-related charge in California, where he received a one- to ten-year sentence. He was immediately remanded to a minimum-security prison.

Facing further trials in other states, later that year the forty-nine-year-old Leary escaped from prison and subsequently reappeared in Algeria, where he found refuge with the Black Panthers. After being placed under house arrest for purposes of "revolutionary discipline," Leary fled again, this time to Switzerland. Eventually, he made his way to Afghanistan, where he was captured by U.S. drug enforcement agents. Leary wound up in the maximum-security prison at Folsom, California. After reportedly agreeing to provide information to the government, Leary was released in 1976 (R. Rosenbaum 1988). For a number of years he was popular on the collegiate lecture circuit, often appearing with G. Gordon Liddy, of Watergate fame, who was responsible for much of the harassment to which Leary had been subjected (Stevens 1987). In 1996, at age 75, Leary died of prostate cancer (Mansnerus 1996).

GOVERNMENT ACTION AFTER WORLD WAR II

In the years immediately before World War II the FBN seemed to have the drug problem well under control. Commissioner Anslinger released statistics indicating a significant drop in the addict population. Then came the war. Opiate smuggling dwindled, and Americans of an age most susceptible to drug use were in Europe and Asia. Drug use was viewed as unpatriotic as well as illegal. Alcohol, barbiturates, and amphetamines were the substances most widely abused during the war years, when the price of opiates increased dramatically. The addict population appeared to reach an all-time low.

At the end of the war there was fear of an epidemic of drug use as U.S. soldiers began to return from Far Eastern locations where opiate use was endemic. The epidemic failed to materialize. The FBN became a victim of its own propaganda and apparent success, and Congress would not increase the drug-fighting budget (H. W. Morgan 1981). Then in 1950 and 1951 a spate of news stories on drug abuse reported that the use of heroin was spilling out of the ghetto and into middle-class environs, where it was poisoning the minds and bodies of America's (white) youth. Musto (1973) points out a parallel between the periods following World War I and World War II: Both were characterized by an atmosphere of hostility to radicals and Communists, and both led to punitive sanctions against drug addicts. Any expression of tolerance for radical political ideas or drug addicts was un-American. In a timely stroke of political genius the FBN linked heroin trafficking to Red China.

Anslinger accused the People's Republic of China of selling opium and heroin to the free nations of the world to finance overseas ambitions (Cloyd 1982). As we shall see in Chapter 11, Far Eastern heroin was, and continues to be, the business of Chinese Nationalists, triads, Thais, and Burmese insurgents— not the People's Republic, which routinely executes drug traffickers. Indeed, "at the time of the Communist takeover in 1949, China was the world's largest producer and consumer of narcotic drugs" (Lee 1995: 194).

On the basis of statistics showing that between 1946 and 1950 there had been a 100 percent increase in the number of arrests related to narcotics laws and that over a five-year period the average age of people committed to Public Health Service hospitals had declined from 37.5 to 26.7 years, Congress concluded that drug addiction was increasing and that penalties for drug trafficking were inadequate. In 1951 Congress passed the Boggs Act, which increased penalties for violations of drug laws. Once again, using rather dubious statistical data, Congress concluded that the increased penalties of the Boggs Act had been quite successful in reducing drug trafficking. As a result, in 1956 Congress passed the Narcotic Control Act, which further increased the penalties for drug violations, for example, the sale of heroin to individuals under 18 years of age was made a capital offense; the Act also increased the authority of the FBN and agents of the Customs Bureau (President's Commission on Organized Crime 1986). State legislatures, responding to the federal initiative, significantly increased penalties for drug violations.

"Public concern over the problem of drug abuse, which had been relatively dormant during the 1940s and 1950s, flared again during the 1960s. The intensification of national concern resulted in increasing pressure for federal initiatives in the area. In response to this development, a White House Conference on Narcotics and Drug Abuse was convened in 1962, which resulted in the establishment of the President's Advisory Commission on Narcotics and Drug Abuse (Prettyman Commission) on January 15, 1963" (President's Commission on Organized Crime 1986: 215). The commission recommended discarding the antiquated legal notion that drug control was simply a taxing measure, and they suggested that the responsibilities of the FBN be transferred to the Department of Justice. On the other hand, the commission recommended that the regulation of marijuana and lawful narcotic drugs be transferred from the FBN to the Department of Health, Education, and Welfare (HEW). It also recommended increasing the number of federal drug agents and enacting legislation for the strict control of nonnarcotic drugs capable of producing psychotoxic effects when abused.

In the 1960s concern increased over the diversion of dangerous drugs from licit sources. As a result, Congress passed the Drug Abuse Control Amendments of 1965, which, among other things, mandated record-keeping and inspection requirements for depressant and stimulant drugs throughout the chain of distribution, from the basic manufacturer to (but not including) the consumer. Enforcement of the 1965 legislation was left to a newly created agency within HEW's Food and Drug Administration: the Bureau of Drug Abuse Control. The Treasury Department's monopoly over drug enforcement had ended (President's Commission on Organized Crime 1986).

A TURN TOWARD TREATMENT

During the 1960s the medical profession began to reassert itself on the issue of drug abuse in both treatment and research. Treating disciplines—psychology and social work—and researchers in sociology and public health began to focus on the drug issue as a social problem, not simply a law enforcement problem. The social activism of the 1960s also influenced the perspective on drug abuse (H. W. Morgan 1981), and a new strategic approach was implemented: reducing demand by rehabilitating large numbers of drug addicts. Arnold Trebach (1982: 226) argues that this approach was facilitated by the resignation of Harry Anslinger as commissioner of the FBN ("which had been accomplished with the active encouragement of the Kennedy brothers"). Anslinger was replaced by Harry Giordano, a pharmacist, and the pendulum of drug policy began to shift away from a law enforcement model toward a treatment model. The 1963 Prettyman Commission recommended the relaxation of mandatory prison sentences for drug convictions, greater research, and the dismantling of the FBN, whose functions were to be divided between HEW (prevention and treatment), and the Department of Justice (law enforcement).

In 1961 California established a civil commitment program in which drug addicts were taken into custody and committed—like mentally ill people in need of hospitalization—to a nonpunitive period of confinement and drug treatment. Confinement was followed by a period of aftercare (parole supervision). In 1966 New York established the Narcotic Addiction Control Commission, a large-scale effort whose goal was to confine as many drug addicts as possible under civil commitment statutes. As in California, whose lead New York was following, confinement was followed by a period of parole supervision. (This writer was employed briefly as a senior narcotics parole officer for the Narcotic Addiction Control Commission. This agency, which expended billions of dollars, was dismantled during the 1970s as a very costly failure.) In 1966 Congress passed the Narcotic Addict Rehabilitation Act, which in lieu of prosecution authorized federal district courts to order the voluntary and involuntary civil commitment of certain defendants who were found to be drug addicts and mandated the Surgeon General to establish rehabilitation and posthospitalization care programs for drug addicts. The legislation also authorized the financing of state efforts to treat addicts.

Between 1969 and 1974 the number of federally funded drug rehabilitation programs dramatically increased from 16 at the beginning of 1969 to 926 in 1974. Federal expenditures on drug treatment rose from about $80 million to about $800 million during that period. About half of the 80,000 clients in these programs were being maintained on methadone (Moss 1977), a synthetic opiate. During the 1960s a pilot program of methadone maintenance was initiated at Rockefeller University in New York. The drug, which was taken orally, prevented withdrawal symptoms in heroin addicts who were maintained with daily doses. Trebach (1982: 227) refers to this approach to heroin addiction as the "greatest theoretical and practical departure in American rehabilitation strategies and clinical attitudes since the early 1920s." While the program was successful in aiding the rehabilitation of certain kinds of drug users, methadone when ingested intravenously produces a heroinlike euphoria, and by the early 1970s large quantities had been diverted to the illegal street market. In response, Congress passed the Narcotic Treatment Act in 1974, which required annual registration by practitioners dispensing narcotic drugs and imposed new standards for the legal dispensing of dangerous drugs (President's Commission on Organized Crime 1986).

The 1960s and 1970s also experienced a rise in the popularity of the therapeutic-community approach to treating addiction, the best known being Synanon in California and Daytop Village in New York. Operated by recovered addicts, these drug-free centers use a variety of talking and confrontational therapies mixed with aspects of behavior modification. (Methadone, therapeutic communities, and other approaches to the treatment of drug abusers will be discussed in Chapter 9.)

COMPREHENSIVE DRUG ABUSE PREVENTION AND CONTROL ACT OF 1970

As the turn of the decade approached, alarming statistics (of dubious validity) about drug abuse were publicized. The drug problem was quickly becoming a major political issue. In 1968 President Lyndon Johnson decried the fragmented approach to drug law enforcement. With congressional approval the President abolished the FBN and the Bureau of Drug Abuse Control and transferred their responsibilities to a newly created agency, the Bureau of Narcotics and Dangerous Drugs (BNDD), in the Department of Justice. Revenue and importation aspects of drug trafficking remained within the Treasury Department's Internal Revenue Service and Bureau of Customs. In 1970 President Richard Nixon clarified the responsibilities of the federal agencies involved in drug control, announcing that BNDD "controls all investigations involving violations of the laws of the United States relating to narcotics, marijuana and dangerous drugs, both within the United States and beyond its borders." Several months later guidelines were promulgated that provided increased authority for customs officials at ports and borders.

The two-pronged approach to dealing with drug abuse—*reducing availability* by investigating and prosecuting traffickers and *reducing demand* by preventing addiction and treating addicts—was now firm policy. The Comprehensive Drug Abuse Prevention and Control Act of 1970 authorized HEW to increase its efforts at prevention and rehabilitation through a program of grants to special projects and made the HEW National Institute on Drug Abuse, the agency with primary responsibility for drug education and prevention activities. The legislation also established five schedules into which all controlled substances could be placed according to their potential for abuse (discussed in Chapter 12); imposed additional reporting requirements for manufacturers, distributors, and dispensers; promulgated new regulations for the importation of controlled substances; and established the Commission on Marijuana and Drug Abuse. BNDD was authorized to increase its strength by 300 agents.

The 1970 legislation represented a new legal approach to federal drug policy. It was predicated not on the constitutional power to tax, but on federal authority over interstate commerce. The President's Commission on Organized Crime (1986: 228) notes that this shift had enormous implications for the way in which the federal government would approach drug enforcement in the future. The act "set the stage for an innovation in federal drug law enforcement techniques. That innovation was the assigning of large numbers of federal narcotic agents to work in local communities. No longer was it necessary to demonstrate interstate traffic to justify federal participation in combating illegal drug use." The new approach was upheld by decisions of the Supreme Court, and the National Conference of Commissioners on Uniform State Laws drafted a model act based on the 1970 statutes, which has been adopted by most states.

A 1973 reorganization plan led to the creation of the Drug Enforcement Administration (DEA) within the Department of Justice. All investigative and enforcement responsibilities for drug control, except those related to ports of entry and borders, were given over to the new agency. In 1982 the Federal Bureau of Investigation (FBI) was given concurrent jurisdiction with the DEA for drug investigation and law enforcement. In addition, the DEA director was required to report to the director of the FBI, who was given responsibility for supervising drug law enforcement efforts and policies. That same year the Department of Defense Authorization Act contained a provision outlining military cooperation with civilian authorities. This provision was aimed at improving the level of cooperation by delineating precisely what assistance military commanders could provide. It also permits military personnel to operate military equipment that had been loaned to civilian drug enforcement agencies (President's Commission on Organized Crime 1986). (In 1988 the military's role in drug law enforcement was substantially increased; this is discussed in Chapter 12.)

THE DRUG SCARE OF THE 1980s

As 1980 approached, the lack of public interest in and even tolerance of drug use began to shift as grassroots parent groups began to influence the political landscape. A mother "who later presided over the National Federation of Parents for Drug-Free Youth, attended a rock concert in 1978 with her two young children and discovered rampant drug use all around them. Her anger, shared by others she contacted, apparently was a major factor in the defeat of her Congressman, . . . who had sponsored a bill favoring the decriminalization of an ounce of marijuana. That a broad base of parents were antagonistic to drugs and that they were now organizing their political power had been demonstrated" (Musto 1987: 271). With encouragement from Dr. Robert L. DuPont, then director of the National Institute on Drug Abuse, an "antipot" handbook for parents was published. The antidrug theme was soon picked up by the Reagan Administration.

The issue of drug abuse is politically safe and useful because no one is in favor of it. During the presidency of Ronald Reagan drugs again became a major political issue. On June 19, 1986, Len Bias, a basketball star from the University of Maryland, died of a cocaine overdose; on June 27, Don Rogers, a defensive back for the Cleveland Browns, also died of a cocaine overdose. These widely reported incidents, occurring within a short time of each other and less than five months before congressional elections, led to an intensification of antidrug efforts, a widespread public relations effort utilizing sports and entertainment personalities whose message to television viewers was "Just Say No!" (to drugs). Not to be outdone, Congress responded with huge allocations to combat this scourge, and politicians scrambled for partisan advantage. "Len Bias' death brought together the political and human aspects of drug abuse. His death accentuated that attention placed on drugs after the announcement of the 'war on drugs.' Although consensus about the need to 'do something' was generally accepted, politicians continued to argue over the best approach" (Merriam 1989: 25). With the elections over and Congress in the hands of the Democrats, the President significantly scaled back the allocations.

The fight against drugs and drug abuse was an important issue in the presidential campaign of 1988. The heat of the national campaign led to the enactment of an omnibus drug bill (the Anti-Drug Abuse Act of 1988) in the final days of the 100th Congress. The legislation states: "It is the declared policy of the United States Government to create a Drug-Free America by 1995." The bipartisan measure, which was approved overwhelmingly, increased antidrug spending, earmarking 50 percent for treatment, a figure that was to increase to 60 percent over the next few years. On both federal and state levels penalty distinctions between marijuana and drugs such as heroin and cocaine have been erased—"zero tolerance" (Pollan 1993).

The statute mandated greater controls over **precursor** chemicals and devices used to manufacture drugs, such as encapsulating machinery. It also created a complex and extensive body of civil penalties aimed at casual users, including fines and ineligibility for federal benefits such as educational loans and mortgage guarantees and/or the loss of a maritime, pilot, or stockbroker license for a number of years. Penalties were enhanced for selling drugs to minors, and a judge was empowered to impose the death penalty for murders committed as part of a continuing criminal enterprise or for the murder of a law enforcement officer during an arrest for a drug-related felony.

The legislation also established the Office of National Drug Control Policy headed by a director ("drug czar") appointed by the President. The director is charged with coordinating federal drug supply reduction efforts, including international control, intelligence, interdiction, domestic drug law enforcement, treatment, education, and research, and serves as a liaison between the federal government and state and local drug control efforts. The first director was William J. Bennett, who served as drug czar for twenty-two months, using the position primarily as a rhetorical platform to focus attention on the issue of drug abuse as seen by the administration. His approach attracted extensive media attention, but the powers of the director are so circumscribed that he accomplished little else.

INTO THE TWENTY-FIRST CENTURY

The 1990s began a remarkable period of a lack of political interest in drug abuse. Indeed, as officials began to recognize the extent of prison overcrowding resulting from state and federal drug policies, statutory and administrative remedies were formulated that placed more drug offenders in diversion or drug treatment programs, on probation, and on parole. Laws providing significantly greater prison sentences for the sellers of crack cocaine than for sellers of powdered cocaine came under fire because the former substance is more likely to be used by minorities, the latter by middle-class whites. There is a mandatory five-year minimum for selling 5 grams of crack or 500 grams of powdered cocaine and ten years for selling 50 grams of crack or 5,000 grams of powdered cocaine.

The cocaine market was affected by crack, because many crack users were purchasing the powdered form (cocaine hydrochloride) in large doses and converting it to crack themselves, reducing the demand for street-level crack, which many users believed inferior to what they could produce themselves. The use of methamphetamine increased, with new supplies coming from Mexico. In some areas methamphetamine was almost as popular as cocaine. Marijuana remained readily available, and both its use and sale transcend ethnic, racial, and gender boundaries. Users of marijuana tend to be under 20 years old (Office of National Drug Control Policy 1995).

While cocaine remained the dominant (illegal) drug of abuse, heroin, prepared for smoking and snorting, made a comeback, particularly outside its typical core clientele, the urban poor. This revival, which was fueled by the availability of high-grade heroin, particularly from Colombia, is following a pattern set by cocaine in the 1970s. The abundance of heroin is reflected in the purity levels found at the retail level.

The twenty-first century has experienced a rise in the use of methamphetamine in rural parts of the United States, while in urban areas crack use has ceased to be an epidemic. Concern over the nonmedical use of prescription medicine has led the government to focus on that problem.

In sum, this country has moved from a century of permissiveness to draconian sanctions as the result of foreign affairs, the policy of a single federal agency, and a volatile mix of racism and politics. This has led to two drug problems in the United States:

1. The drug problem of the affluent: "It is by no means insignificant, and it has caused more than its share of personal tragedies. But it is a *manageable* problem, and it has been steadily decreasing for several years, for reasons unrelated to the war on drugs" (Currie 1993: 3).
2. The drug problem of America's have-nots: "That problem has grown malignantly in the face of the drug war—and it is much further from solution than it was when that war began" (Currie 1993: 3).

SUMMARY

Policy decisions have frequently been based on perceptions, beliefs, and attitudes with little empirical foundation, and they have often reflected popular prejudices against a variety of racial and ethnic groups. U.S. opposition to alcohol was often intertwined with nativism, and efforts against alcohol and other psychoactive drugs were often a thinly veiled reaction to minority groups.

The 1905 Pure Food and Drug Act effectively ended the patent medicine problem, but federal antidrug legislation—the Harrison Act—was the result of U.S. efforts at improving our trade relationship with China. Implementation of the Harrison Act was given to the Treasury Department that shaped U.S. drug policy in favor of a strict enforcement approach to the problem of drugs.

At the end of World War II there was fear of an epidemic of drug use as U.S. soldiers began to return from Far Eastern locations where opiate use was endemic. The epidemic failed to materialize. In 1950 and 1951 a spate of news stories on drug abuse reported that the use of heroin was spilling out of the ghetto and into middle-class environs, where it was poisoning the minds and bodies of America's (white) youth. New federal laws increased penalties, and drug enforcement was given over to the Justice Department. At the same time rehabilitation of addicts gained momentum. Prominent among the new approaches was the use of methadone and the therapeutic community.

During the late 1960s and early 1970s attitudes toward recreational drug use became more liberal because of the wide acceptance of marijuana. Cocaine soon became associated with a privileged elite, and the new demand was sufficient to generate new sources, leading to the development of major international cocaine organizations.

The drug scare of the 1980s brought the issue back into the political arena with a "war on drugs" and creation of the Office of National Drug Control Policy. The 1990s saw an absence of drugs as a political issue along with increased penalties for crack cocaine and the rising use of methamphetamine.

Now that we have completed our review of the evolution of the problem of drug abuse in the United States, in the next chapter we will examine the neurology of psychoactive substances.

REVIEW QUESTIONS

1. What was the relationship between nativism and Prohibition?
2. How can Prohibition be explained in terms of rural versus urban America?
3. Why did the end of Prohibition lead to an increase in drug trafficking?
4. Why can the United States during the nineteenth century be described as a "dope fiend's paradise"?
5. How was recreational use of opium popularized in Europe during the late eighteenth and early nineteenth centuries?
6. How did the primitive state of medicine explain the popularity of opium into the nineteenth century?
7. Why was the production of opium unsuccessful in the United States?
8. What was the patent medicine problem?
9. What was the relationship between the Civil War and the popularity of morphine?
10. What was the primary cause of the Opium Wars?
11. What was the relationship between the Chinese immigrants and legislation controlling opiates at state and local levels in the United States?
12. What international events led to the enactment of the Harrison Act?
13. What were the important events that led to the passage of the Pure Food and Drug Act?
14. How can the efforts of the temperance movement and the U.S. response to drugs be explained, at least in part, in terms of racial prejudice?
15. What were the major provisions of the Harrison Act?
16. What was the relationship between the development of the Harrison Act and a concern for federalism?
17. After the Harrison Act was passed, what was the Supreme Court's attitude toward physicians who dispensed opiates?

18. What was the role of federal drug enforcement officials in determining the U.S. policy toward drugs?
19. What was the relationship between prevailing political attitudes after World War I and our reaction to drug users?
20. What led to the development of the Uniform Drug Act?
21. What accounted for the general lack of public concern about drug abuse before World War II?
22. How did World War II affect drug use in the United States?
23. Why did Spanish explorers have a negative view of coca chewing?
24. What was the relationship between the campaign against cocaine and African Americans in the South?
25. What led to the sudden popularity of cocaine beginning in the 1960s?
26. Why has the domestic cannabis crop in the United States until recently been unattractive to potential smokers?
27. What has made domestic cannabis more appealing to potential smokers?
28. What was the relationship between racial and ethnic prejudice and efforts to outlaw marijuana?
29. What was the relationship between the military and the promotion of amphetamines?
30. Why are the properties of amphetamines popular among some students and truck drivers?
31. What was the connection between Timothy Leary and the popularizing of LSD?
32. What was the relationship between public attitudes in the post–World War II era and the U.S. response to drugs?
33. What led to the turn toward treatment of drug abuse during the 1960s?
34. What is the purpose of the Office of National Drug Control Policy (the "drug czar")?
35. Why has the issue of drugs proven so popular with politicians?
36. What distinguishes the 1980s from the 1990s with respect to the problem of drug abuse?
37. What distinguishes the issue of drug abuse in the twenty-first century from that in the twentieth century?

Drugs and the Nervous System

Even though psychological and social factors predominate in the presentation and diagnosis of addiction, the disease is at its core biological; changes that a physical substance (drug) causes in vulnerable body tissue (brain).

Eric J. Nestler (2005: 9)

Virtually all drugs of abuse have common effects, either directly or indirectly, on a single pathway deep within the brain—the mesolimbic reward system. Activation of this system appears to be a common element in what keeps users taking drugs. This activity is not unique to any one drug; all addictive substances affect this circuit.

Alan I. Leshner (1997: 46)

Neurobiological research findings show that tobacco, marihuana and other drugs all seem to apply to the same neurotransmitters in the brain. This proposes a chain of causation between the use of cigarettes, alcohol, and the subsequent use of cannabis and other drugs.

S. E. Baumeister and P. Tossmann (2005: 97)

Distinctions between the neurology and pharmacology (discussed in Chapters 3, 4, 5, and 6) of drug use, the sociology (Chapter 7) of drug use, and the psychology (Chapter 8) of drug use are quite artificial (Peele 1985). Although the explanatory value of each by itself is limited, the interaction of these three dimensions can explain drug use. Their separation into different chapters is therefore for pedagogical rather than scientific purposes. (The neurology of drug abuse also has important treatment and policy implications—topics of subsequent chapters.) In this chapter we will examine how psychoactive drugs affect the central nervous system. In subsequent chapters we will apply this information to specific drugs—depressants, stimulants, hallucinogens, club drugs, and marijuana.

NEUROLOGICAL THEORIES OF DRUG ABUSE

A theory helps us to explain events. It organizes events so that they can be placed in perspective; explains the causes of past events; and predicts when, where, and how future events will occur. "A theory consists of a set of assumptions; concepts regarding events, situations, individuals, and groups; and propositions that describe the interrelationships among the various assumptions and concepts" (Binder and Geis 1983: 3). Theory is the basic building block for the advancement of human knowledge. In the physical sciences, such as chemistry and physics, theory can usually be subjected to rigorous testing and replication. However, testing neurological theories of drug abuse is limited to working with laboratory animals and observing and examining current users. We could not give non-drug-using human beings varying doses of drugs to find out how their central nervous system responds (which might also require an autopsy).

THE DISEASE MODEL

Drug abuse is often discussed in terms such as "overpowering desire," "compulsion," or even "enslavement," as if the substance had a power all its own to "hook" people foolish enough to ingest it. Such theories emphasize the involuntary nature of drug use—use based on a craving—that has found some support in laboratory experiments with animals. Indeed, with the exception of marijuana and hallucinogens, animals will abuse the same chemicals that humans do (Friedman 1993). According to this approach, sometimes referred to as the **disease model**, the drug-dependent person is a victim of forces beyond his or her control. This theoretical approach has treatment implications. For example, it would support two very different approaches to substance abuse: the use of methadone detoxification and maintenance and the Alcoholics Anonymous (AA) chemical-free approach that emphasizes a need for total abstinence. (Methadone and AA will be discussed in Chapter 9.)

Scientists have discovered reward pathways located in the mesolimbic area of the brain that are activated by a variety of psychoactive substances. Drugs

Drug Effects

The effects of any drug depend on the:

- amount taken
- user's past drug experience
- manner in which the drug is taken
- circumstances under which the drug is taken (the place, the user's psychological and emotional stability, the presence of other people, the simultaneous use of alcohol or other drugs)

Source: Alcoholism and Drug Addiction Research Foundation, Toronto.

such as heroin, nicotine, cocaine, and amphetamines appear to affect these pathways through the release of the neurotransmitter dopamine (discussed later), a common element in continued use. "Dopamine effects in the reward pathway are enhanced not only by cocaine, amphetamines, and opiates, but also by nicotine and alcohol." The "stimulation of a dopaminergic reward pathway is what makes a drug addictive" (A. Goldstein 2001: 66). Sudden cessation of drug use causes dopamine neurotransmission to drop below normal levels for several days, resulting in withdrawal (Robinson and Berridge 2003).

Some psychoactive chemicals alter the central nervous system, creating what appears to be a compulsion to use the drug to restore a sense of well-being. Prolonged opiate use, for example, causes pervasive changes in brain function that persist long after the individual stops taking the drug. Heroin addicts themselves state that they take the drug to "feel normal." Thus, to the heroin addict, notes John Irwin (1970: 19), "it is the fix that cures the sickness, and it is the fix that is central to the whole dope life." After a period of abstinence an addict who returns to heroin use is likely to make statements such as "'It makes me feel normal again'—that is, it relieves the ex-addict's chronic triad of anxiety, depression, and craving" (Brecher 1972: 14). While drug use might begin through experimentation, dependence would be the inevitable result of these physiological changes. In sum, drugs that were taken initially to achieve pleasurable effects ("highs") are taken after addiction to avoid withdrawal ("lows"). However, craving for the pleasurable effects appears to be a better motivator, since addicts often relapse after being free of withdrawal (Robinson and Berridge 2003).

AROUSAL THEORY

Some neurological theories describe the drug abuser as a person whose body is malfunctioning with respect to the production of crucial neurotransmitters, making drug use self-medicating. According to this view, the user's choice of drug is the result of an interaction between its pharmacological properties and the primary feeling state experienced. Thus, according to **arousal theory**, those whose central nervous system quickly habituates to incoming stimuli owing to a neurotransmitter malfunction are most apt to be reinforced for engaging in antisocial behavior and less likely to learn alternative behavior patterns. Subjectively, such people regard many ordinary environments as boring and unpleasant and would therefore be more motivated than most people to seek novel and/or intense sensory stimulation. The behavior of such people would include impulsivity, risk taking, and an inclination to use psychoactive substances (Ellis 1990). While social factors may determine whether a person is exposed to drugs, genetics may help to explain why only some of those who are exposed become drug dependent.

GENETIC PREDISPOSITION

Genetics and Addiction

"What makes certain individuals particularly vulnerable to addiction and others relatively resistant?" Extensive epidemiological studies reveal that roughly half of a person's risk for addiction is genetic. "This degree of heritability exceeds that of many other conditions that are considered highly heritable, such as type 2 (non-insulin dependent) diabetes, hypertension, and breast cancer" (Nestler 2005: 8–9).

More than a century ago, genetic explanations were proposed to explain addiction: The addict inherits a nervous system that has more energy or perhaps more actual nerve fiber. Drugs provide such nervous systems with a substance that is necessary but deficient; when the user finds that a drug satisfies this deficiency, repeated drug use naturally follows. A complementary theory views drug users as having an inherited predisposition to "nervous weakness," for which the use of drugs compensates. Other observers conceived of a lack of hereditary endowments that leaves some people ill equipped to deal with the fast pace of societal change; for them drug use provides chemical compensation.

In more contemporary times the National Institute on Drug Abuse (NIDA) has been funding studies on this issue, and evidence uncovered reveals that an individual's genetic makeup is a major factor in vulnerability to drug abuse (Volkow 2006). NIDA-funded researchers found that although family and social environmental factors determine whether an individual will begin using drugs, progression from use to dependence was largely dependent on genetic factors, particularly for males, and the genetic influence for heroin addiction surpassed that of any other drug (Zickler 1999). While drug abuse is the result of a complex interplay of environmental, social, psychological, and biochemical factors, genetic factors play an important role in the vulnerability to drug abuse: The more severe the abuse, the greater is the role of genetic factors (Comings 1996; Crabbe 2002). Interaction between genetics and the environment is complex, since "environmental factors can alter the expression of genes involved with the way the brain works and responds to the environment, thus influencing the behavior of the individual" (Volkow 2006: 70).

LIMITATIONS IN THE NEUROLOGICAL STUDY OF DRUG ABUSE

Our discussion of the neurology of psychoactive drugs will necessarily have limitations, since there is a great deal that is not known about the details of how these drugs actually affect the nervous system. There is evidence, for example,

The Complexities of Drug Effects

"Drug effects are strongly influenced by the amount taken, how much has been taken before, what the user wants and expects to happen, the surroundings in which it is taken, and the reactions of other people. All of these influences are themselves tied up with social and cultural attitudes and beliefs about drugs as well as more general social conditions. Even the same person will react differently at different times" (Institute for the Study of Drug Dependence 1987: 1).

that the same substance can have a different impact on different people. The social context (the setting in which the drug is ingested) and the user's expectations can influence a drug's effects (Becker 1967, 1977; Schnoll 1979). Whether a person will interpret the effect of a drug such as marijuana, LSD, or an opiate, especially the first few times he or she takes it, as euphoria or pleasure depends very much on the setting and other complex psychological and social conditions (Grinspoon and Hedblom 1975). In other words, use of the substances discussed in this book is not automatically pleasurable. Many, if not most, people who have been exposed to morphine or heroin, for example, find the initial experience distinctly unpleasant: "not everyone responds to the analgesic experience the same way. Some people find a narcosis tremendously alluring, while others report that the sensations of helplessness are disturbing and distinctly unappealing" (Peele 1980: 143). Thus, "one person's dysphoria may be another person's euphoria" (Schnoll 1979: 256). Some people get "high" from dangerous pursuits, others from chemicals; still others seek to avoid both.

Laboratory studies, which form the basis for much of our knowledge of psychoactive drugs, fail to reproduce social context, and their results are accordingly limited. The dependence potential of various drugs is typically based on laboratory studies with monkeys and rats, although research has discovered that there are interspecies differences in the effects of cocaine on the brains of rodents and primates. The discrepancy in findings between rodents and primate studies illustrates the limitations of animal models of drug abuse (Bolla, Cadet, and London 1998). Furthermore, in experimental environments these animals can also become addicted to stinging electric shocks delivered to the tail or the paws (Bennett 1988). Indeed, researchers have discovered that with animals "almost any environmental stimulus can serve as a reinforcer or punisher under the right environmental conditions" (Dworkin and Pitts 1994: 106).

Experimentation on human subjects is obviously limited by ethical considerations. Thus, with respect to alcohol, a lawful drug, "because of ethical considerations, prospective studies of ethanol reactivity in children and young adolescents (before they have initiated regular drinking) have not been conducted" (Sher 1991: 86). And laboratory studies also cannot actually replicate street use in which any of the substances under discussion may be abused with alcohol or in some other combination. This leads to our next topic.

POLYDRUG USE

Understanding the neurology of psychoactive drugs is also complicated by the phenomenon of **polydrug use**—abusers consuming more than one type of psychoactive chemical. Research shows overwhelmingly that compulsive users use more than one drug, so this is a major difficulty in studying drug abuse. Heroin addicts are very often polydrug users abusing alcohol and other drugs (Vaillant 1970; B. D. Johnson, Lipton, and Wish 1986b; McFarland 1989). Bruce Johnson and his colleagues (1985) found that 90 percent of the heroin addicts they studied also abused alcohol and cocaine (Johnson, Lipton, and Wish 1986b). A large proportion of heroin users also use heroin in combination with other drugs, especially cocaine and alcohol (Epstein and Gfroerer 1997). In a study of heroin addicts in San Antonio it was discovered that 100 percent used alcohol, almost half on a daily basis (Maddux and Desmond 1981). Almost 19 percent of the people admitted for heroin abuse treatment in Colorado also reported the use of cocaine (Colorado Alcohol and Drug Abuse Division 1987). Mark Gold and his colleagues (1986: 55) found that "most cocaine abusers are concurrently abusing alcohol or other sedative-hypnotics to alleviate the unpleasant side effects of cocaine." Crack users frequently "administer heroin because it enhances the euphoric effect while ameliorating the intense stimulant effects of cocaine" (Drug Enforcement Administration 1994b: 1), and alcohol is frequently used to moderate the effects of cocaine. In Colorado more than 35 percent of cocaine users admitted for treatment report the use of alcohol (Mendelson and Harrison 1989).

The New York State Division of Substance Abuse Services (1986: 14–15) reported that the "use of more than one substance continues to be the predominant pattern of abuse. Both heroin and cocaine are commonly used with one drug ameliorating the undesired effects of the other; PCP is used by some heroin abusers to heighten the effect of heroin. Alcohol use is almost always involved." In San Antonio, Texas, approximately two thirds of substance-related deaths have involved both cocaine and heroin (Spence 1989). In Minnesota polydrug use, which includes alcohol, is widespread among that state's chemical-abusing population (Minnesota Department of Human Services 1987). With respect to methadone patients, thirty years ago most abused only heroin. "In New York today, approximately 30 percent abuse other substances as well, including alcohol, cocaine, methamphetamine, benzodiazepines, and marijuana" (Marion 2005: 26).

Criss-crossing (alternately inhaling lines of cocaine and heroin) is popular among drug enthusiasts, and some users are snorting heroin and smoking crack in combination. The primary drug in this combination is believed to be crack, heroin being used to ease the agitation associated with crack. Finally, drug users who are unable to secure their preferred substance because of insufficient funds or connections when the supply is scarce often seek available substitutes.

The neurological effects of mixing drugs can be (Schnoll 1979):

1. **Additive:** Two drugs that have similar actions are ingested, and the effect is cumulative (1 + 1 = 2).

2. **Synergistic:** Two drugs that have similar actions are ingested, but the effect of their joint action is more than cumulative (1 + 1 = 3).
3. **Potentiating:** Two drugs have different actions, but when they are taken together, one enhances the effects of the other (1 + 1 = 4).
4. **Antagonistic:** Two or more drugs are taken together, and one counteracts the effects of the other(s) (1 + 1 = 0).

Drugs that are prepared for street sale are typically impure or a mixture of psychoactive chemicals. "The users of illegally purchased drugs are often totally unaware of the actual chemical substance, the dose being purchased, and the contaminants that may be present in the sample." Many of these contaminants can produce toxic reactions in their own right (Schnoll 1979: 257).

PSYCHOACTIVE SUBSTANCES AND THE CENTRAL NERVOUS SYSTEM

All of the substances we are interested in affect the central nervous system: depressants, stimulants, hallucinogens, and cannabis, the last of which produces all three effects. The body consists of cells organized into tissues, and specialized cells along the surface of the body receive information about the environment that is translated into electrochemical signals that we experience as sight, sound, smell, and touch. Information from the internal and external environment—collectively known as stimuli—is received by the **central nervous system (CNS)**, consisting of the brain and the spinal cord, whose cells—neurons—send information to a specific processing center of the brain. Three brain circuits are especially important in initiating and maintaining drug abuse:

1. stress pathways
2. reward pathways
3. obsessive-compulsive pathways

Distinct but interrelated, they are linked directly or indirectly to other parts of the brain, such as regions involved in cognition, sensory perception, and emotion. Each pathway releases, and is influenced by, a plethora of neurotransmitters (discussed later). They exert differential roles as a person moves from controlled drug use to addiction. Controlled use activates reward pathways in a region of the brain called the **mesolimbic system. Reward** pathways influence motivation and some types of learning. During learning, the brain undergoes *plastic* changes, that is, the way the neurons connect is altered, allowing us to adapt to and learn from environmental changes. Addictive drugs induce plastic changes that are hardwired into the brain, which might be one reason why drug use tends to persist. As dependence begins to emerge, the reward system becomes more active. However, continued use also activates stress pathways that contribute to negative emotions, such as depression and anxiety, which are persistent among drug abusers. As full-blown addiction emerges, drug use strongly activates the stress and obsessive-compulsive pathways, and the reward system becomes less important ("Pharmacy Update" 2003).

THE BRAIN

The brain, a dense mass weighing about 3 pounds and consisting of 10 billion to 50 billion anatomically independent but functionally interrelated neurons, is connected to the spinal cord by fibers and cells (the **peripheral nervous system**) that carry sensory information and muscle commands to the rest of the body (Fig. 3.1). "This single organ controls all body activities, ranging from heart rate and sexual function to emotion, learning and memory" (Society for Neuroscience 2002: 5). After receiving and processing information, the brain sends commands to muscles and glands through three processes:

1. **Behavior processes**, which include voluntary movements such as walking and talking, and the autonomic bodily functions (such as those of the heart,

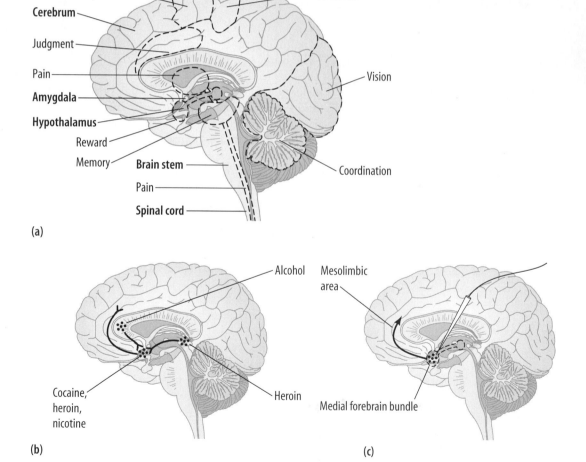

(a)

(b)

(c)

Figure 3.1   The Brain: (a) Parts and functions of the human brain; (b) Activation of the reward pathway of the brain by addictive drugs; (c) Effects of electric stimulation on the brain

Drugs and the Brain's Reward System

"Almost all abused drugs produce pleasure by activating a specific network of neurons called the brain reward system. The circuit is normally involved in an important type of learning that helps us to stay alive. It is activated when we fulfill survival functions, such as eating when we are hungry or drinking when we are thirsty. In turn, our brain rewards us with pleasurable feelings that teach us to repeat the task. Because the drugs inappropriately turn on this reward circuit, people want to repeat drug use" (Society for Neuroscience 2002: 33).

lungs, and digestive system) are involuntary functions that are regulated by the **autonomic nervous system**, which in turn has two divisions that have opposite effects:

(a) The **sympathetic nervous system** acts (actually, it reacts) to mobilize the organism for action—for example, for "fight" or "flight." The release of the neurotransmitter **norepinephrine** into the blood system or of drugs that mimic norepinephrine (stimulants such as cocaine) activates the sympathetic nervous system.

(b) The **parasympathetic nervous system** is concerned with the digestive system and acts to conserve bodily resources. The effects of various psychoactive drugs on the digestive system are related to this nervous system.

2. **Affective processes** govern mood, feelings, and emotions.

3. **Thought processes** involve the ability to reason, categorize, organize, abstract, and pay attention.

The brain contains areas that produce pleasurable sensations—reward pathways. The pharmacological activation of brain reward systems is largely responsible for producing a psychoactive chemical's potent addictive properties. Direct electrical stimulation of the **medial forebrain bundle** produces intensely rewarding effects, while stimulants and depressants can activate this reward system by their pharmacological actions.

NEURONS

A neuron is the basic working unit of the central nervous system, a specialized cell designed to transmit information from the brain to other nerve cells or to muscle or gland cells. **Neurons** come in many sizes and shapes and form chains of specialized and excitable cells. They differ from other body cells in that they can conduct information in the form of electrical impulses over long distances. There are over 100 billion neurons in the body and across them, from neuron to neuron, move signals or impulses—information in the form of electrical activity. A neuron consists of a **cell body (soma)** containing the nucleus and an electricity-conducting fiber; the **axon**, which also gives rise to many smaller axon branches before ending at nerve terminals; **synapses**, contact points where one neuron communicates with another; and **dendrites**, which appear as

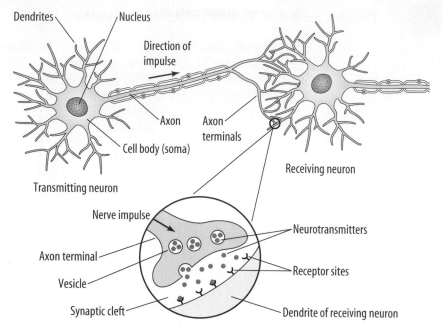

Figure 3.2 | Neuron, Showing Synapse, Neurotransmitters, and Receptor Sites

branches of a tree and extend from the neuron cell body and receive messages from other neurons (see Fig. 3.2). "The dendrites and cell body are covered with synapses formed by the ends of axons of other neurons" (Society for Neuroscience 2002: 7). Each neuron has multiple dendrites that form structural networks for receiving information from another neuron or from the environment in the form of light, sound, smell, and so on and converting it (through transduction) into electrical activity that is transmitted to the axon.

Axons may be long or short. Neurons in the brain stem have axons that extend down into the spinal cord, where they divide into thousands of branches, making contact with different receiving neurons. The axon conducts ("fires") electrical impulses to terminals, which react by releasing neurotransmitters that are stored in synaptic buttons, which are vesicles at the end of the axon. These neurotransmitters move across the synaptic gap to receptor sites on the dendrites on the other side, triggering activity—the release of secondary messengers—in the next neuron. Through this mechanism an impulse is directed to the spinal cord and into the proper circuit for transmission to the brain.

Neurons do not interlock but instead are separated by synapses, fluid-filled microscopic gaps (0.0002 mm) that provide a chemical bridge for signals in the form of charged particles or ions from one neuron to another. A neuron may have over 10,000 synapses. There are two functional types of synapses: (1) *excitatory* synapses, which enhance electrical impulses, and (2) *inhibitory* synapses, which retard electrical impulses. Depressants reduce synaptic transmission by inhibiting

Nerve Cell Communication

"Nerve signals often travel over long distances in the body. For example, if you step barefooted on a sharp object, the sensory information is relayed from your foot all the way to the brain; from there, nerve signals travel back to the leg muscles and cause them to contract, drawing back the foot. Dozens of neurons can be involved in such a circuit, necessitating a sophisticated communication system to rapidly convey signals between cells. Also, because individual neurons can be up to three feet long, a rapid-relay mechanism within the neurons themselves is required to transmit each signal from the site where it is received to the site where it is passed on to a neighboring cell. Two mechanisms have evolved to transmit nerve signals. First, within cells, electrical signals are conveyed along the cell membrane. Second, for communication between cells, the electrical signals generally are converted into chemical signals conveyed by small messenger molecules called neurotransmitters" ("Principles of Nerve Cell Communication" 1997: 107).

nerve impulse conduction at synapses; this causes a reduction in sensory pain signals received by the brain (Tortora 1983). Stimulants facilitate synaptic transmission. A large concentration of positively charged particles entering a receiving neuron tells the neuron to pass on the message. On the other hand, a large concentration of negatively charged particles entering the neuron will inhibit it from passing on the message (Society for Neuroscience 2002).

NEUROTRANSMITTERS

Central nervous system information is carried by **neurotransmitters**, chemicals (drugs) released from sacs (vesicles) clustered in the synaptic terminals at the end of axons of neurons. On reaching the ends of an axon, these voltage changes trigger the release of neurotransmitters, chemical messengers. Neurotransmitters are released at nerve ending terminals and bind to receptors on the surface of the target neuron (Society for Neuroscience 2002).

Neurotransmitters inhibit or enhance the release of **ions**, electrical charges similar to those of a battery, and communication occurs when a sufficient number of synapses are activated by these electrical impulses. About 100 neurotransmitters are found in the central nervous system; some (the **catecholamines**: dopamine, epinephrine, norepinephrine) excite (speed firing), and others (such as **endorphins**) inhibit (slow firing). The body uses these chemicals to trigger such effects as anger or to regulate the operation of different organs. Each neurotransmitter has a receptor site—a protein located on the surface of a nerve cell—designed to receive it, and the ensuing reaction may cause the stimulation or inhibition of a specific function. "Of greatest interest for addiction would be the presence of a neurotransmitter in the midbrain reward pathway, where dopamine neurons are thought to play a key role in mediating pleasurable (hedonic) effects" (A. Goldstein 2001: 33).

Dopamine, one of a number of neurotransmitters found in the central nervous system, has received special attention from psychopharmacologists because of its apparent role in the regulation of mood and affect and because of its role in motivation and reward processes. Studies have revealed that the reinforcing effects of psychoactive drugs in humans are associated with increases in brain dopamine (Volkow et al. 1999b). "Although drugs affect a variety of neurotransmitters, virtually all of them increase the levels of dopamine in the brain's mesolimbic region, which is involved in pleasure, reward and motivation" (L. Carroll 2000: D6). Although there are several dopamine systems in the brain, the mesolimbic dopamine system appears to be the most important for motivational processes. Some addictive drugs produce their potent effects on behavior by enhancing mesolimbic dopamine activity.

Dopamine is necessary to sustain life. This neurotransmitter "acts as a pacesetter for many nerve cells throughout the brain. At every moment of our lives, dopamine is responsible for keeping those cells operating at the appropriate levels of activity to accomplish our needs and aims. Whenever we need to mobilize our muscles or mind to work harder or faster, dopamine drives some of the involved brain cells to step up to the challenge" (Nestler 2005: 5).

A dopamine deficiency is believed to cause **Parkinson's disease;**[1] an excess is believed to cause Tourette syndrome.[2] The brains of schizophrenics are high in dopamine, and antischizophrenic (neuroleptic) drugs work because of their ability to block dopamine (Snyder 1986). Cocaine and the dopamine agonist amphetamine can cause schizophrenic symptoms because these substances interfere with the reuptake of dopamine (Palfai and Jankiewicz 1991; Bloom 1993). The failure of the reuptake system increases the concentration of dopamine in the brain, particularly within pleasure centers. Ecopipam, a potent antagonist of dopamine D_1 and D_5 receptors, is able to block stimulant and reinforcing properties of cocaine and might play a potential role in treatment of cocaine dependence (Romach et al. 1999).

Cells in the mesolimbic dopamine system are spontaneously active, releasing small amounts of dopamine into the synaptic cleft (Fig. 3.3). The levels of dopamine that are produced when the cells are active at this low rate might be responsible for maintaining normal affective tone and mood. "To keep the receiving cells in each brain region functioning at appropriate intensities for current demands—neither too high or too low—the dopaminergic cells continuously increase and decrease the number of dopamine molecules they launch" (Nestler 2005: 5). Neurotransmitter level is controlled by chemicals in the presynaptic terminal known as **monoamine oxidases (MAO).**

---

[1] Clinical studies of cocaine users in their thirties show an increase in symptoms of Parkinson's disease—tremors or stiffness, apparently the result of a decrease of dopamine receptors (Hartel 1993). Flupentixol, a drug that blocks dopamine, reduces the effects of cocaine but cannot be used for drug treatment because it also produces symptoms of Parkinson's disease (Bloom 1993).

[2] Tourette syndrome is an incurable genetic affliction whose symptoms can range from mild tics to coprolalia—periodic outbursts of foul language (Brody 1995).

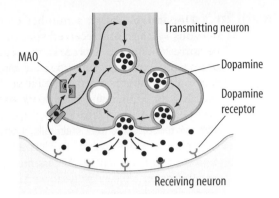

Figure 3.3 | Dopamine's Normal Action

Scientists speculate that some forms of clinical depression may result from unusually low dopamine levels.

It has also been revealed that pathological obesity and drug addiction often share a common element: a brain deficient in nerve cell (D^2) receptors, which dopamine activates to stimulate pleasurable feelings. This deficiency "may contribute to continued overeating to compensate for reduced stimulation of their brain reward circuits" (Mahias 2001: 13).

Repeated use of psychomotor stimulants such as cocaine and depressants such as heroin produces changes in the mesolimbic dopamine system. Specifically, repeated use of cocaine or heroin can deplete dopamine from this system. These dopamine depletions may cause normal rewards to lose their motivational significance. At the same time the mesolimbic dopamine system becomes even more sensitive to pharmacological activation by psychoactive substances (Addiction Research Unit 1998).

Abstinence from cocaine or from morphine after repeated administration may decrease dopamine levels in this brain system, and this diminished dopamine function may be related to the intense craving associated with withdrawal in drug-dependent humans. The subjective experience of craving is related to relapse into drug-taking behavior following abstinence and therefore is an important factor in drug addiction.

Serotonin is found in many tissues, including the lining of the digestive tract and the brain. Serotonin is involved in sleep, mood, depression, and anxiety. It serves to moderate primitive drives, such as aggression, sex, and food-seeking, while improving the ability to interact socially. The medically prescribed antidepressant Prozac (fluoxetine) inhibits the reuptake of serotonin. Norepinephrine governs arousal reactions and appears to play a role in elevating mood; norepinephrine agonists such as cocaine and amphetamine produce a "high."

Receptor sites consist of large molecules on the surface of cells where neurotransmitters attach, creating a lock-and-key effect and causing chemical substances to interact and produce pharmacological actions. Receptors are sensory-specific and distinguish between substances. Upon receiving the correct substance

It's All in Your Mind

The desire for drugs is largely a desire to reexperience the intense pleasure recalled from past episodes of drug use. The **nucleus accumbens** region of the brain includes important memory centers that enable people to recall actions that led to the pleasures associated with dopamine release, such as sexual orgasm or a drug high. Chronic drug abusers often avoid acting on their drug-seeking urge for long periods of time. If their resolve to abstain fails, it often does so when they encounter something or someone they associate with past drug taking. Research suggests that, like drugs themselves, such encounters produce surges in dopamine levels and that these surges push the individual toward active drug seeking and drug taking. In drug abuse, as in other parts of life, however, there is a difference between desiring something and actually taking steps to achieve it (Zickler 2004; Nestler 2005).

(creating a chemical fit), they transmit signals that bring about pharmacological action in the target tissue. Many psychoactive drugs (**agonists**—substances that stimulate receptor sites) mimic the action of neurotransmitters and "fool" the receptor into accepting it. Competing drugs (**antagonists**—substances that inhibit the action of a receptor site) can counteract the effect of an agonist by their ability to occupy receptor sites without triggering activity, providing a basis for using chemicals to deal with drug abuse. Low levels of the dopamine D_2 receptors have been found to predispose people to enjoy the effects of stimulating drugs that might compensate for this receptor deficiency by increasing the activation of reward circuits (Volkow et al. 1999a).[3]

Drugs exert their principal effects on individual cells in the brain, where receptor sites controlling particular organs have an affinity for certain psychoactive substances. Opiates, for example, will lock into brain receptor sites that control such autonomic functions as breathing and blood pressure.

Once they have performed their assigned task—conveying messages to nearby neurons—neurotransmitters are recycled by the sending neuron in a process called **reuptake**. This process conserves the neurotransmitters by bringing them back into the presynaptic terminal for storage so that they can be used again. Proteins called **transporters**, located on the surface of the sending neurons, latch onto the neurotransmitters and transport them back inside for use at a later time. Psychoactive substances not only cause the release of neurotransmitters, but also may inhibit the transporters from performing their reuptake task so that the neurotransmitters continue to stimulate the receiving neuron.

After being released into the synapse, dopamine attaches to receptor sites on the receiving neuron. Then the dopamine is either quickly recycled by a transporter or broken down by MAO.

---

[3] It should be noted that this predisposition alone is not sufficient to explain drug use; the experimental subjects who found stimulants rewarding were not drug users.

The entire volume of human blood—11.6 pints for an average-sized adult male, 9.5 pints for an average-sized adult female—makes a complete circulation about every sixty seconds. Psychoactive drugs are absorbed into the bloodstream and quickly carried to the central nervous system. Eventually, they pass through the **blood-brain barrier**, causing the release of neurotransmitters in the brain. The barrier acts as a gatekeeper, preventing certain substances from entering brain tissue, for example, penicillin (because it would cause convulsions), but readily admits psychoactive substances (and general anesthetics). Since their blood-brain barrier has not matured, infants are particularly vulnerable to the effects of psychoactive chemicals.[4]

DRUG INGESTION

Drugs enter the bloodstream in one of three ways, and the route of administration affects how fast the substance will enter the brain and thus assert a psychoactive response:

1. *Oral ingestion*: The substance is swallowed and enters the bloodstream through the gastrointestinal tract, the slowest route of administration.
2. *Inhalation*: The substance is sniffed and rapidly reaches the bloodstream through mucous membranes of the nose or sinus cavities, or it is smoked and quickly absorbed through the linings of the lungs, which are surrounded by capillaries.
3. *Injection*: The substance is injected into a vein (**intravenous**), and all of the drug enters the bloodstream. Some is carried directly to the brain, producing an effect within seconds. Injecting a drug under the skin (**subcutaneous**) increases the time required for the substance to enter the bloodstream and thus produces a delayed and reduced effect.

Some drugs can be ingested in a number of ways; for example, different forms of heroin and cocaine can be sniffed, smoked, or injected. Other drugs can be taken in only one way; for example, marijuana must be smoked.

A drug that is taken intravenously is carried to the right chamber of the heart, where it mixes with blood returning from the rest of the body, and it is then pumped through the lungs, returns to the heart, and is then delivered to the brain. This takes about sixteen seconds, and when the drug arrives at the brain, it is greatly diluted. A substance that is smoked results in some passing directly into the bloodstream through membranes of the mouth. With deep inhalations, however, most of the drug will spread though the fine membranes of the lungs (all of the blood in the body moves through the lungs) and pass directly into the blood, carrying drug molecules to the left side of the heart, where it is pumped directly to the brain without dilution; this takes

---

[4] A fetus is also vulnerable because the placental barrier is more permeable than the blood-brain barrier is. Infants also lack a fully functioning liver and therefore cannot readily deactivate and eliminate psychoactive chemicals.

about three seconds. Each breath produces an immediate drug spike in the brain, an immediate euphoric effect that is more powerful than the intravenous route. Inhalation also avoids the danger of overdose. Oral ingestion results in slow **absorption** from stomach and intestine and is the method least favored by drug users (A. Goldstein 2001).

The amount of time it takes for the substance to be eliminated from the body is measured in terms of **half-life**, the time it takes for one half of the drug to be eliminated through the liver[5] and primarily into the kidneys for urination. The half-life of some drugs may be as short as a few minutes, while traces of other drugs may remain in the system for several weeks. Drugs that are lipid-soluble will be absorbed by body fat and subsequently released into the bloodstream in small doses over a relatively longer period of time, thus having a greater half-life. This explains why the percentage of body fat is a factor in the effect of drugs. The greater the half-life, the less severe are the withdrawal symptoms after use of the drug has been discontinued. The longer a drug remains in the bloodstream, the less likely it is that tolerance will occur.

TOLERANCE

The continued use of certain drugs, particularly depressants, produces **tolerance**, "a progressive increase in the ability of the body to adapt to the effects of a drug that is used at regular and frequent intervals. It is manifested in two ways: (1) progressively larger doses must be administered to produce the same effects; and (2) eventually as much as ten or more times the original lethal dose can be safely taken" as the metabolism adapts to the substance (Ausubel 1978: 14).

> Tolerance develops as the body becomes progressively immune to the chemical effects of the drug at the cellular level. Should usage continue, a physiological dependence on the narcotic will occur as the affected tissues and cells accommodate the chemically induced processes that result from the introduction of the drug. The *homeostatic* processes of the body adjust to the narcotic and bring about a new physiological equilibrium. If the equilibrium and normal functioning are to be maintained at the physiological level, regular and stable amounts of the drug [or a similar drug—**cross-tolerance**[6]] must be taken. (Biernacki 1986: 9; italics added)

Homeostasis refers a state of equilibrium achieved through the self-adjusting characteristics of the body. Through homeostasis complex organisms adapt themselves to changes in the environment by means of, for example, changes in body temperature, blood sugar level, and heart rate. The physiology and biochemistry of the body change according to information received and processed by the nervous system, particularly the central nervous system, and the endocrine system (glands such as the thyroid and adrenal). With respect to both neurotransmitters and receptors, the brain behaves as if trying to maintain

---

[5] Advanced alcoholism may impair the liver's ability to deactivate and eliminate alcohol.

[6] Cross-tolerance refers to the ability of one drug (an agonist) to substitute for another.

all its operating systems on an even keel. Psychoactive substances upset this normal balance (A. Goldstein 2001).

The toxicity of a drug is affected by tolerance. Thus, an alcoholic—someone addicted to alcohol—can ingest quantities of alcohol that would be potentially fatal for an occasional user. Some psychoactive drugs do not produce tolerance (marijuana), while others may produce various degrees of tolerance, from hardly perceptible to severe. There is also **selective tolerance**; for example, tolerance to the "nod" experienced by heroin users develops rapidly, while the "rush" will always be experienced by heroin users no matter how high their level of tolerance. There is also some evidence of **reverse tolerance**, referred to as *kindling*, to certain drugs: becoming more sensitive to the same or a lesser dosage over time. Pharmacologists use the term **sensitization** to refer to this increase in a drug's effect with repeated administration, the change being in the opposite direction of tolerance (Robinson and Berridge 2003).

When tolerance develops, the failure to ingest enough of a drug on a timely basis will disrupt homeostasis and cause the onset of withdrawal symptoms. These symptoms can manifest themselves in a number of ways, all of them unpleasant to the person being subjected to them, usually taking the form of being directly opposite of the effects produced by the drug, an overactivity of a system that was originally suppressed. Thus, chronic heroin use can induce constipation, whereas in withdrawal, in direct contrast to the initial condition, the addict suffers stomach cramps and diarrhea. "During withdrawal from alcohol, delirium tremens may develop into convulsions owing to over activity of the central nervous system" (Taylor 2002: 138). While in withdrawal, the addict may experience extreme anxiety, hyperactivity, shaking, cold sweat, and severe depression.

DRUG CUES AND SEXUAL DYSFUNCTION

Brain imaging and other modern technologies show that the addicted brain is distinctly different from the nonaddictive brain; the differences are manifested by changes in brain metabolic activity, receptor availability, gene expression, and responsiveness to environmental cues. It appears that the intensity of the drug euphoria burns emotional memories into brain circuits, making that person vulnerable to the appearance of drug cues. These memories are encoded into a part of the brain—the **amygdala**—that operates outside of conscious control to cause intense cravings for re-creating the euphoric experience. Research has discovered a connection between cues and reversion to drug use (Childress et al. 1999). Even tolerance and withdrawal symptoms in laboratory animals are affected by environmental cues (Hinson 1985; Bloom 1993). Indeed, a person who has been removed from his or her drug-seeking environment to treat addiction but then is returned to the former environment gets secondary associations that can induce the person to go back to using drugs (Bloom 1993).

In approximately two thirds of cocaine-dependent subjects in a laboratory setting, drug cues increased craving for cocaine (Avants et al. 1995). In another research effort cocaine users who viewed items related to their drug use, such as a glass crack pipe, a mirror, razor blade, a straw, a rolled $20 bill, lactose powder, and simulated crack rocks, elicited a higher degree of craving, as measured by brain scans, than had been previously reported, and while it involved the amygdala, the activity extended to other parts of the brain (Bonson et al. 2002). In alcoholics, alcohol-associated cues can trigger craving for that substance (Heinz et al. 2003).

Drug abuse is characterized by a pattern of sexual dysfunction. Drugs can substitute for sexual activity through corresponding stimulation of pleasure regions of the brain. "Cocaine abusers may experience a powerful urge to take the drug when they encounter environmental cues such as people, places, or paraphernalia that they associate with drug use. This cue-induced behavior may be accompanied by physical sensations—light-headedness, increased heart rate, or mild drug like 'high'—like those produced by cocaine" (Zickler 2001: 1). These same brain regions that are activated by these cocaine cues are also activated by sexual activity through corresponding stimulation of pleasure regions of the brain. There is also a disruption of hormonal balance in the hypothalamus and pituitary glands.

The **hypothalamus**, a small gland located near the base of the brain, integrates information from many sources and is the control center for the autonomic nervous system. It is also the primary point of contact between the nervous system and the endocrine system, sending messages in the form of impulses to appropriate control centers to restore normal levels of blood chemicals in line with the homeostatic needs of the body.

Many drugs enter the brain in high concentrations at the blood-rich hypothalamus, creating initial autonomic effects on consciousness and mood. The hypothalamus controls such basic drives as sexual activity. It regulates the release of hormones from the pituitary gland, located directly below. These hormones act directly on the adrenal glands, testes, and ovaries. Disruptions in the normal flow of hormones from the pituitary can adversely affect sexual function, and chronic drug use upsets hormonal balance by decreasing dopamine secretion from the hypothalamus ("Sexual Dysfunction and Addiction Treatment" 2000).

If addiction is, at its core, a consequence of fundamental changes in brain function, a goal of treatment must be to either reverse or compensate for those brain changes (J. Cooper 1998). Although drug addicts might not be able to control their cravings, through behavior therapy (discussed in Chapter 9) they may be able to control the way they respond to the cravings (Grady 1998).

SUMMARY

According to the disease model, a drug-dependent person is a victim of forces beyond his or her control. Some neurological theories describe the drug abuser as a person whose body is malfunctioning with respect to the production of crucial neurotransmitters, making drug use self-medicating. Drugs are not automatically pleasurable, and not everyone responds to the experience in the same way. An individual's genetic makeup is a major factor in vulnerability to drug abuse. Our ability to research the effect of drugs on humans is limited by legal and ethical considerations. It is further confounded by the phenomenon of polydrug use.

By definition all psychoactive substances affect the central nervous system. Reward pathways located in the brain are activated by a variety of psychoactive substances through the release of the neurotransmitter dopamine, a common element in continued use. Some psychoactive chemicals alter the central nervous system, creating what appears to be a compulsion to use the drug to restore a sense of well-being.

A neuron is the basic working unit of the central nervous system, a specialized cell designed to transmit information from the brain to other nerve cells, muscle, or gland cells Communication is by way of neurotransmitters, each having its own specific receptor site. After their impact, neurotransmitters are subject to reuptake, a mechanism with which drugs often interfere.

The continued use of certain drugs, particularly depressants, produces tolerance; and with some drugs there is cross-tolerance that is linked to withdrawal symptoms. Addicted individuals are influenced by drug cues, which can help to explain reversion to drugs after abstinence.

Now that we have examined the neurology of drug abuse, in the next chapter we will apply this dimension to depressants.

REVIEW QUESTIONS

1. Besides dosage, what variables determine a drug's impact on an individual?
2. Why is laboratory testing of drugs on humans of limited value in determining the impact of these substances on actual substance abusers?
3. Why can't the findings of laboratory studies on animals be generalized to humans?
4. What are neurotransmitters?
5. What are receptor sites in the brain?
6. What is the relationship between drug abuse and the pleasure centers of the brain?
7. What are transporters and reuptake?
8. What is the blood-brain barrier?
9. What is the relationship between homeostasis and tolerance?
10. What is reverse tolerance?
11. How does body fat affect half-life?
12. What is meant by drug cues?

4

Depressants

In determination of a drug's status, more than abuse potential should be considered. What are the toxicities of the drug? What are the chances of becoming dependent on the drug? Is dependency on a drug necessarily bad? Sometimes these questions are difficult to answer. Certainly, two of the most toxic drugs we know are alcohol and tobacco (nicotine). These drugs are sold legally. . . . Dependency to both of these drugs develops, as it does to caffeine. . . . Why are we so concerned about dependency on opiates and not caffeine? Heroin, if given in pure form for long periods of time, has few toxic effects.

Sidney H. Schnoll (1979: 255)

This category of drugs—depressants—includes alcohol, barbiturates, sedatives/ tranquilizers, and the narcotics. The latter may be natural (opium derivatives such as morphine and codeine), semisynthetic (such as heroin), or synthetic (such as methadone and Demerol).[1] Depressants are typically addicting, and studies have indicated the possibility of a relationship between certain chemical deficiencies and the propensity for addiction to depressants.

ENDORPHINS

During the 1970s a number of scientists, working independently, discovered material and analgesics in brain and body tissues generally referred to as *endorphins*, a contraction of the term *endogenous morphine*. Three families of endorphins (enkephalins, dynorphins, and beta-endorphins) have many of the characteristics of morphine, and the body contains receptor sites that are programmed to receive these neurotransmitters. When they reach the receptor sites in the central nervous system (CNS), endorphins relieve pain. Pain is the result of a trauma experienced by the body, information about which is detected by sensors that send impulses along the nervous system, through neurons and across synapses as they move toward the brain. The subsequent release of endorphins in the brain inhibits pain impulses. Eventually, endorphins are destroyed by enzymes.

When people stub a toe or injure a finger, they usually grit their teeth and clench their fists, activities that apparently cause the release of these naturally occurring opiates that reduce sensations of pain. The athlete's ability to overcome pain during competition and the soldier's ability to perform heroic feats while severely wounded can be explained by the endorphin-receptor phenomenon, as can success in treating pain with acupuncture (Snyder 1977, 1989; Davis 1984; J. Goldberg 1988).[2] These receptor sites are programmed to receive endorphins, but they are also receptive to external chemicals such as opiates.

These opioid receptors are found in the brain's reward pathways and are distributed widely throughout the nervous system and in the nerves that supply the extremities, the skin, the blood vessels, and most internal organs. These receptors are found along pain pathways and, when activated, interrupt the pain pathway to the brain, diminishing the perception of pain (A. Goldstein 2001).

Endorphins also enable the organism (including many animals) to deal with psychological stress by curbing an autonomic overreaction and producing calm: They slow breathing, reduce blood pressure, and lower the level of motor

---

[1] In contrast to depressants, which act centrally on the brain, analgesics such as acetaminophen (e.g., Tylenol, Panadol, Anacin-3), ibuprofen (e.g., Nuprin, Mediprin, Advil), and aspirin relieve pain via localized action. They are not addictive (Brody 1988).

[2] In one study, treating drug abusers with acupuncture was not found to be beneficial (Latessa and Moon 1992). Another study found it effective in detoxification treatment (Brewington, Smith, and Lipton 1994).

activity (Davis 1984). A "deficiency in an endorphin system that ordinarily would support feelings of pleasure and reinforcement might lead to feelings of inadequacy and sadness" (Levinthal 1988: 149), a phenomenon that would make the use of depressants essentially a form of self-medication.[3] As was noted in Chapter 3, the use of psychoactive substances does not automatically produce a pleasurable response. However, people who are at risk for addiction may suffer from an endorphin deficiency. For such people, addiction would be the result of a genetically acquired deficiency or of a temporary or permanent impairment of the body's ability to produce endorphins. "This point of view would help account for the puzzling variability from individual to individual in the addictive power of opiate drugs. If an endorphin deficiency exists, however, the question would still remain as to what precipitating circumstances would lead to such a deficiency and whether these circumstances were environmental, inherited genetically, or a product of both" (Levinthal 1988: 154).

The ingestion of large amounts of heroin or some other opiate can also cause this deficiency (Snyder 1977). Thus, an abstaining addict would be unusually sensitive to feelings of pain or stress and would be inclined to use narcotic drugs again. In other words, receptors become increasingly dependent on external depressants, which in turn further reduce the production of endorphins, leaving the receptors increasingly dependent on substances from the outside. "If the opiate drug is later withdrawn, the receptors are now left without a supply from any source at all, and the symptoms of withdrawal are a consequence of this physiological dilemma" (Levinthal 1988: 156).

STRESS AND ADDICTION

Depressants such as heroin inhibit stress hormones (such as cortisol and adrenalin) and stress-related neurotransmitters. A person who is having difficulties dealing with stress and is exposed to opiates is likely to find them rewarding and thus become addicted. In the absence of stress, many people who take heroin over long periods of time do so without becoming addicted, and hospital patients who self-administer morphine for pain do not increase their intake over time, nor do they suffer from a morphine craving when the pain subsides and they no longer have access to the drug (Peele 1985; E. Rosenthal 1993). One study found that only four out of more than 12,000 patients who were given opioids for acute pain became addicted to the drugs. Even long-term morphine use has limited potential for addiction. In a study of thirty-eight chronic pain patients, most of whom received opioids for four to seven years, only two patients actually became addicted, and both had a prior history of drug abuse (National Institute on Drug Abuse data).

Drug addicts who are trying to remain off drugs can often resist the cravings brought on by seeing reminders (cues) of their former drug life. For months they can walk past the street corner where they used to buy drugs and

---

[3] Mark Gold (1994) disputes the self-medication thesis.

not succumb. But then there is a sudden relapse that addicts explain with statements such as "Well, things weren't going well at my job" or "I broke up with my girlfriend." Sometimes the problem is as simple as a delayed welfare check. That they often relapse, apparently in response to what most people would consider mild stressors, suggests that addicts are perhaps more sensitive than nonaddicts to stress. This hypersensitivity "may exist before drug abusers start taking drugs and may contribute to their initial drug use, or it could result from the effects of chronic drug use on the brain, or its existence could be due to a combination of both" (Jeanne Kreek quoted in Stocker 1999: 12). Chronic use of heroin, however, may increase hypersensitivity to stress and trigger a cycle of continued drug use when the effects of heroin wear off.

Research has shown that during withdrawal the level of stress hormones rises in the blood, and stress-related neurotransmitters are released in the brain. These chemicals trigger emotions that are perceived as highly unpleasant, driving the addict to take more drugs. Because the effects of heroin last only four to six hours, addicts often experience withdrawal three or four times a day. This constant switching on and off of the stress systems of the body heightens whatever hypersensitivity these systems might have had before the person started taking drugs. The result is that these stress chemicals are on a sort of hair-trigger release, surging at the slightest provocation (Kreek in Stocker 1999).

The body reacts to stress by secreting two types of chemical messengers: hormones in the blood and neurotransmitters in the brain. Some of the hormones travel throughout the body, altering the metabolism of food so that the brain and muscles have sufficient stores of metabolic fuel for activities, such as fighting or fleeing, that help the person to cope with the source of the stress. In the brain the neurotransmitters trigger emotions, such as aggression or anxiety, that prompt the person to take action.

Normally, stress hormones are released in small amounts throughout the day, but when the body is under stress, the level of these hormones increases dramatically. Endorphins inhibit these stress hormones, thereby inhibiting stressful emotions. Heroin and morphine inhibit the stress hormone cycle and presumably the release of stress-related neurotransmitters just as endorphins do. Thus, when people take heroin or morphine, the drugs add to the inhibition already being provided by the endorphins.

HEROIN

The opium poppy,[4] *Papaver somniferum*, requires a hot, dry climate and very careful cultivation (Wishart 1974). It grows best in loamy soil that retains moisture and nutrients. To grow opium poppies, the seeds are scattered across

---

[4] Sale of poppy seeds for cultivation has been illegal in the United States since 1970. (Sale for culinary use is legal; poppy seeds often appear on bagels.) The Drug Enforcement Administration has been conducting an ineffectual campaign against the cultivation of the pretty red poppy flower, which looks elegant when dried (Vest 1997).

the surface of freshly cultivated fields. Three months later, when the poppy is mature, the green stem is topped by a brightly colored flower. Gradually, the flower petals fall, off leaving a seedpod about the size of a small egg. Incisions are made in the seedpod just after the petals have fallen but before it is fully ripe, a labor-intensive process. A milky-white fluid oozes out and hardens on the surface into a dark brown gum, which is raw opium. It is collected by scraping the pod with a flat, dull knife, another labor-intensive process. "Because the yield per acre is small and because laborious care is required in collecting the juice, it can only be grown profitably where both land and labor are cheap" (Ausubel 1978: 9). Because the plant matures only one time, that is, it does not regenerate, new seed must be planted each season.

Raw or cooked opium contains more than thirty-five different alkaloids, including morphine and codeine. In the mainland countries of Southeast Asia, the morphine alkaloid alone accounts for approximately 10 percent of the total weight of opium. Heroin manufacturers must first extract the morphine from the opium before converting the morphine to heroin. The extraction is a simple process, requiring only a few chemicals and a supply of water. Morphine is sometimes extracted from opium in small clandestine laboratories, which are typically set up near the opium poppy fields. Because the morphine base has about one tenth the weight and volume of raw opium, it is desirable to reduce the opium to morphine before transporting the product from the field to a heroin laboratory.

The process of extracting morphine from opium involves dissolving opium in boiling water; adding lime (calcium oxide), slaked lime (calcium hydroxide), or limestone (calcium carbonate) to precipitate nonmorphine alkaloids; and then pouring off the morphine in solution. Ammonium chloride is then added to the solution to precipitate morphine from the solution. The chemicals that are used to process opium to morphine have a number of legitimate purposes and are widely available on the open market. An empty oil drum, some cooking pots, and filter cloths or filter paper are also needed.

The conversion of morphine to heroin base is a relatively simple and inexpensive procedure. The necessary chemicals for conversion to heroin are commonly available as industrial chemicals. The equipment is very basic and quite portable. Heroin conversion laboratories are generally located in isolated, rural areas because of the telltale odors of the laboratory's chemicals. Acetic anhydride, in particular, is a key chemical with a very pungent odor resembling that of vinegar. Thai speakers in the Golden Triangle Area commonly refer to acetic anhydride as *nam-som* (vinegar).

Heroin synthesis from morphine (either morphine base or morphine hydrochloride) is a two-step process that requires between four and six hours to complete. Heroin base is the intermediate product. Typically, morphine hydrochloride bricks are pulverized, and the dried powder is then placed in an enamel pot. Acetic anhydride is added, which then reacts with the morphine to form heroin acetate. (This acetylation process will work with either morphine hydrochloride or morphine base.) The pot lid is tied or clamped on, using a damp towel for a gasket. The pot is carefully heated for about two hours, below

Incisions are made in the opium poppy seed-pod just after the petals have fallen but before it is fully ripe. A milky-white fluid oozes out and hardens on the surface into a dark brown gum—raw opium. The raw opium is collected by scraping the pod with a flat, dull knife, a labor-intensive process. Heroin manufacturers must first extract the morphine from the opium before converting the morphine to heroin.

©AP Photo/CP, Stephen Thorne

boiling, at a constant temperature of 185° Fahrenheit. It is never allowed to boil or to become so hot as to vent fumes into the room. The mixture is agitated by tilting and rotation until all of the morphine has dissolved. When cooking is completed, the pot is cooled and opened. During this step, morphine and the anhydride become chemically bonded, creating an impure form of diacetylmorphine (heroin).

Water is added to the thick, soupy mixture, and the mixture is stirred as the heroin dissolves in the solution. Sodium carbonate (a crystalline powder) is dissolved in hot water and then added slowly to the heroin solution until effervescence stops. This precipitates heroin base, which is then filtered and dried by heating in a steam bath. For each kilogram of morphine, 685–937 grams of crude heroin base is formed, depending on the quantity of morphine.

The tan-colored heroin base (about 70 percent pure heroin) may be dried, packed, and transported to a heroin-refining laboratory, or it may be purified further before conversion to heroin hydrochloride (a water-soluble salt form of heroin) at the same site. In the mainland countries of Southeast Asia, heroin base is an intermediate product that can be further converted to either "smoking heroin" (heroin no. 3) or "injectable heroin" (heroin no. 4), a powder that is between 80 and 99 percent pure.

Lawfully produced morphine is usually harvested by the more modern industrial poppy straw process of extracting alkaloid from the mature dried plant. The extract may be either liquid, solid, or powder (Drug Enforcement Administration 1989). In equivalent doses, heroin is about two and a half times as potent as morphine because heroin more easily penetrates the blood-brain barrier. Once heroin reaches the brain, however, it is converted back into morphine (Royal College of Psychiatrists 1987). The Drug Enforcement

Morphine: Uses and Effects

Classification: Narcotic

CSA Schedule: Schedule II

Trade or Other Names: Duramorph, MS-Contin, Roxanol, Oramorph SR

Medical Uses: Analgesic

Physical Dependence: High for nonmedical use, low for medical patients in pain

Psychological Dependence: High

Tolerance: Yes

Duration (hours): 3–6

Usual Method: Oral, smoked, injected

Possible Effects: Euphoria, drowsiness, respiratory depression, constricted pupils, nausea

Effects of Overdose: Slow and shallow breathing, clammy skin, convulsions, coma, possible death

Withdrawal Syndrome: Watery eyes, runny nose, yawning, loss of appetite, irritability, tremors, panic, cramps, nausea, chills, and sweating

Source: U.S. Drug Enforcement Administration.

Administration (DEA) reports that more than 400 tons of opium or its equivalent in poppy straw concentrate are legally imported each year into the United States. Part of this quantity is used to extract codeine (an opiate alkaloid that is about 20 percent as potent as morphine), an ingredient used in many cough medicines.

Pure heroin is a white powder with a bitter taste and little odor, but street heroin comes in many different forms, depending on how it was made and what has been added to it. Street heroin can be white, tan, brown, gray, or black. It can be a fine, fluffy powder; coarse like sand; chunky; or a solid mass that is either gummy or rock hard (black tar heroin). It can smell like vinegar, vitamins, or medicine—or have no smell. No matter what its color or form, all heroin is either heroin salt or heroin base. Heroin salt dissolves easily in water, so it is easy to inject or sniff. Heroin base (like cocaine base) is easy to smoke but needs to be mixed with an acid such as vitamin C to dissolve. White powder and black tar heroin are usually heroin salt, and brown heroin is usually heroin base. The term *white powder* refers to heroin salt, which is mostly snorted or injected (China White, Number 4). The term *brown base* refers to heroin base (Persian, Brown Sugar, Pakistani), which can be smoked but needs to be heated in a solution of water and mild acid to inject. The term *black tar* refers to the black, sticky, gumlike form of heroin (Chiva, Mexican Tar, or Black Tar Heroin), mostly smoked or injected (Harm Reduction Coalition 1998).

Codeine: Uses and Effects

Classification: Narcotic

CSA Schedule: Schedule II, III, V

Trade or Other Names: Tylenol w/Codeine, Empirin w/Codeine, Robitussin A-C, Fiorinal w/Codeine, APAP w/Codeine

Medical Uses: Analgesic, antitussive (cough suppressant)

Physical Dependence: Moderate

Psychological Dependence: Moderate

Tolerance: Yes

Duration (hours): 3–6

Usual Method: Oral; injected

Possible Effects: Euphoria, drowsiness, respiratory depression, constricted pupils, nausea

Effects of Overdose: Slow and shallow breathing, clammy skin, convulsions, coma, possible death

Withdrawal Syndrome: Watery eyes, runny nose, yawning, loss of appetite, irritability, tremors, panic, cramps, nausea, chills, and sweating

Source: U.S. Drug Enforcement Administration.

For street sale heroin is typically diluted ("stepped on" or "cut") with any powdery substance that dissolves when heated, such as lactose, quinine, flour, or cornstarch. Until the 1990s consumer-available heroin prepared for intravenous use usually had a purity of less than 5 percent.[5] In recent years the purity level of retail heroin sold in New York City has averaged above 60 percent, revealing that heroin is being subjected to little cutting before it reaches the consumer. Increased purity makes smoking and sniffing feasible; the substance prepared for sniffing or smoking is generally 40 percent heroin. The increased purity and the concern about AIDS may be causing the shift from injecting to smoking and sniffing among heroin users (Epstein and Gfroerer 1997; Adrade, Sifaneck, and Neaigus 1999). Numerous reports have suggested a rise in heroin use in recent years, attributed to young people who are smoking or sniffing rather than injecting.

Effects of Heroin

Heroin has analgesic and euphoric properties. Although brief, sharp, localized (phasic) pain is poorly relieved by opiates, they do effectively relieve duller, more chronic, and less localized (tonic) pain (Snyder 1977; R. Melzack 1990).

---

[5] A low purity level does not necessarily indicate diluting ("cutting") but might simply be the result of processing. Thus, a sample with a purity level of 50 percent heroin might be devoid of any adulterants but contain many by-products of heroin manufacture (Coomber 1999).

The Adolescent Brain and Drugs

Different regions of the brain develop on different timetables. One of the last parts of the brain to mature deals with the ability to make sound judgments and calm unruly emotions. Along with surges in testosterone at puberty, this could account for the rise in aggressiveness and irritability seen in adolescents. On the other hand, the developing adolescent brain drives an interest in novelty that vastly exceeds that of children or adults. The choice of "novelty" often depends on the youngster's environment: Middle-class youths are more likely to have access to activities such as skiing and scuba diving, while for many others, crime, sex, and drugs are the most viable outlets (Brownlee 1999).

As with all opiates, heroin "acts chiefly on the central and autonomic nervous systems and, to some extent, directly on smooth muscles. Effects on the central nervous system are primarily depressant, although larger doses may bring out stimulant properties, especially at the spinal level of reaction. . . . The depressant actions include analgesia (relief of pain, sedation, freedom from anxiety, muscular relaxation, decreased motor activity), hypnosis (drowsiness and lethargy), and euphoria (a sense of well-being and contentment). Unlike anesthetics, opiates are able to produce marked analgesia without excessive drowsiness, muscular weakness, confusion, or loss of consciousness" (Ausubel 1978: 11).[6]

Heroin is typically ingested intravenously, a method that has a ten-second onset, although some users inject it just under the skin ("skin-popping"), a method that has a delayed onset of five to eight minutes. To be prepared for injection, powdered heroin is placed in a "cooker"—usually a spoon or bottle cap. A small amount of water is added, and the mixture is heated with a match or lighter until the heroin is dissolved. The mixture is drawn up into a hypodermic needle and inserted into a vein that has been distended by being tied with a tourniquet (or under the skin). The intravenous heroin user might bring blood back into the hypodermic, where it can mix with the heroin, a process known as "booting." Heroin can also be sniffed like cocaine and even smoked. When smoked ("chasing the dragon"), heroin is heated and the fumes are inhaled, usually through a small tube; the effects peak in ten to fifteen minutes.

Michael Agar (1973) points out that the heroin user can experience four different effects from ingesting heroin:

1. *The rush.* Heroin produces euphoria, referred to as the "rush": "About 10 seconds after the beginning of an injection of heroin the subjects had a

---

[6] The effects of opiates vary with species; for instance, in cats and horses morphine produces intense stimulation and is sometimes used (illegally) to "dope" race horses for a better performance (Harris 1993).

Heroin users come in all types, including adolescents from upper-middle-class homes. Psychologists say that immature drug-dependent personalities ignore long-term negative consequences of behavior and opt for the short-term positive reinforcement that drugs provide.

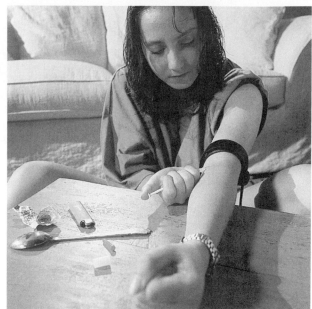

© VCG/Getty Images

typical narcotic 'rush,' including a wave of euphoric feelings, visceral sensations, a facial flush and a deepening of the voice" (Dole 1980: 146). Heroin and cocaine activate brain systems that are responsible for the reinforcing properties of such natural rewards as food and sex; male and female users describe the euphoric rush produced by heroin and cocaine as similar to, but several times stronger than, sexual orgasm (National Institute of Drug Abuse 1997b). Agar (1973) notes that while heroin is believed to have no effect on an addict after his or her tolerance builds up, heroin users actually experience the rush no matter how addicted they are. Addicts frequently describe the rush in sexual terms: "I felt like I died and went to heaven. My whole body was like one giant fucking incredible orgasm" (Inciardi 1986: 61). Indeed, heroin use substitutes for sex, in which the addict usually has little or no interest. Typically, the onset of heroin-using behavior coincides with adolescence, and remission usually occurs, with or without treatment, as the sex drive diminishes with age; there are few heroin addicts among people older than forty years of age, including the elderly.

2. *The high.* Described by addicts as a feeling of general well-being, the high decreases with increased tolerance; thus, increasing dosages are required to achieve the high. Whereas the rush is experienced over a period of seconds, the high can last for several hours.

3. *The nod.* This is described by addicts as being "out of it," in a state of unawareness, oblivious to one's surroundings—an escape from reality. The nod ranges from a slight dropping of the eyelids and jaw to complete

Heroin

Like other opiates, heroin:

1. Depresses breathing by changing neurochemical activity in the brain stem, where autonomic body functions are controlled
2. Changes the limbic system, which controls emotions, increasing feelings of pleasure
3. Blocks pain messages transmitted from the body through the spinal cord

unconsciousness: "they become calm, contented, and detached. They appeared to be quite uninterested in external events" (Dole 1980: 146). One addict provides this description: "It just knocks you completely into another dimension. The nod is like—you know, it's not describable. There's not words to express the feeling. The feeling is *that* good. So good that once hooked you never really live the feeling down" (Rettig, Torres, and Garrett 1977: 35). Tolerance affects the nod dramatically, and doses greater than that required for the high are needed to sustain the nod.

4. *Being straight.* This is how addicts describe their condition when they are not sick, that is, not suffering the onset of withdrawal symptoms; that is, when their bodies are homeostatic. Unless tricked into buying a "blank," addicts will get a rush and get straight, although they will not necessarily experience a high or the nod (Agar 1973).

Heroin impairs homeostatic body functions. There is a slight decrease in body temperature, although dilation of blood vessels gives the user a feeling of warmth. The body retains fluids. There is also a decrease in the secretion of digestive fluids, and a depression of bowel activity, and the user suffers from constipation. Heroin also causes a dilation of the pupils, which explains why addicts frequently wear sunglasses. At relatively high doses, the sedating effects cause a semistuporous, lethargic, and dreamy state ("nodding"), in which there is a feeling of extreme contentment. Unlike alcohol, heroin depresses aggression. It also stimulates the brain area that controls nausea and vomiting, and instead of euphoria, some initial users experience nausea and vomiting: "I got such a bad pain in my head that I thought I was fucking brain damaged. I puked my guts out" (Inciardi 1986: 61). However, the vomiting caused by opiates "is not accompanied by the usual adverse feelings that nausea and vomiting produce in most people" (Harris 1993: 87).

A very dangerous side effect of heroin is that it depresses the respiratory centers in the brain. Thus, an overdose can result in respiratory arrest and death from lack of oxygen to the brain. (Physicians use the antagonist Naloxone to undo the heroin-induced depressed respiration rate.) It is believed that there are millions of occasional users of heroin—*chippers* or *weekenders*, whose use parallels that of people who drink heavily only on weekends or at parties; they appear to avoid addiction.

| ## Withdrawal: The Voice of Experience

"The first twenty-four hours are totally fine; you feel like you're getting a cold. The next day is fucking terrible—constantly shitting, pissing, spitting, everything just flowing out of you. You feel achy, twitchy. You can't focus and the restlessness is intolerable. Every nerve ending is flared up; everything feels raw. You're consumed with this one idea: You need to get drugs because this isn't working" (Anonymous 2006: 126 [edited]).

Tolerance for Heroin

Tolerance to some aspects of heroin use, in particular the high, requires an increase in the dosage in order to gain the same level of response. In other words, a maintenance dose of morphine or some other narcotic will prevent physical withdrawal symptoms. Those seeking the high, however, must keep increasing the dosage until it is no longer feasible (that is, economically possible) to do so. They might then seek some way to reduce the level of tolerance, possibly by entering a drug rehabilitation program. With a lowered level of tolerance, the addict can resume low-dose usage and gain the sought-after response. There is also cross-tolerance; that is, tolerance to heroin carries over to other narcotic drugs, such as morphine and methadone (which will be discussed in Chapter 9), but not to other depressants, such as alcohol or barbiturates. (But because of cross-tolerance, alcohol withdrawal symptoms— delirium tremens, convulsions, and hallucinations—can be relieved by barbiturates or sedatives.) However, as was mentioned earlier, rapid physical tolerance does not develop in medical patients who take morphine for physical pain (Melzack 1990).

Heroin Withdrawal

The neuroadaptation that we refer to as *tolerance* often results in *rebounding* when the substance is withdrawn; that is, the withdrawal symptoms tend to be the opposite of effects produced by the drug. "Thus, withdrawal from a depressant drug will give rise to brain excitation as adrenergic neurons that have been unnaturally inhibited by a drug such as heroin in its absence become hyperactive and cause anxiety, shaking, and cold sweat" (Royal College of Psychiatrists 1987: 34) and sometimes spontaneous orgasm. Heroin depletes the neurotransmitter dopamine, and in withdrawal the dramatic increase in dopamine activity intensifies other unpleasant symptoms (Fishbein and Pease 1990). Physicians often use clonidine, a nonaddicting drug (discussed in Chapter 9), to slow down these neurons and thereby relieve withdrawal symptoms (Davis 1984). Withdrawal symptoms, as David Ausubel (1978: 16) notes, while undoubtedly uncomfortable, "are seldom more severe than a bad case of gastrointestinal influenza." Symptoms peak in twenty-four to

Signs and Symptoms of Opioid Withdrawal

The signs and symptoms of withdrawal from opioid drugs, in temporal order of appearance, are as follows (Ginzburg 1985):

1. Several hours after last use: anxiety, restlessness, irritability, drug craving
2. Eight to fifteen hours since last use: yawning, perspiration
3. Sixteen to twenty-four hours since last use: sneezing, sniffles, anorexia (severe appetite loss), vomiting, abdominal cramps, bone pains, tremors, weakness, insomnia, goose flesh, convulsions (very rarely), cardiovascular collapse

forty-eight hours and subside in about a week, although the psychological symptoms may persist indefinitely. While never fatal to otherwise healthy adults, heroin withdrawal can cause the death of the fetus in a pregnant addict (National Institute of Drug Abuse 2005b).

Children born to addicted mothers, in addition to having a host of other physical problems, such as small size, anemia, heart disease, hepatitis, and pneumonia, also suffer from withdrawal symptoms (O'Brien and Cohen 1984). The National Institute on Drug Abuse reports that infants who are born to heroin-abusing mothers frequently suffer from neonatal abstinence syndrome—withdrawal symptoms that may require medication. This view has been challenged by Stanton Peele (1985), who argues that the symptoms exhibited by the newborn of heroin addicts—undue crying and ineffective feeding, followed cyclically by restless periods of sleep—are not symptoms of heroin withdrawal but result from the cumulative effects of the mother's unhealthy lifestyle.

Medical Use of Heroin

Since 1924 heroin has been virtually banned in the United States, even for medical use as an analgesic. The prohibition against the use of heroin under any circumstances, even to alleviate the intractable pain experienced by some cancer patients, is controversial. Arnold Trebach (1982: 79) argues that heroin should be made available under such circumstances. "For some patients, heroin is superior to other medicines for the control of pain, anxiety, and related conditions." John Kaplan (1983b) states that while most patients cannot tell the difference between heroin and morphine in equivalent doses, patients in England, where such use is legal, who take the drug intravenously tend to prefer heroin. The greater euphoric effect of intravenous heroin appears to provide some relief for terminal patients whose painful existence is often measured in weeks, days, or hours. However, heroin is not the most powerful of the narcotics. The synthetic chemical etorphine is 5,000–10,000 times more potent than morphine. Because of its potency, etorphine is usually used only by

Heroin: Uses and Effects

Classification: Narcotic

CSA Schedule: Schedule I

Trade or Other Names: Diacetylmorphine, horse, smack

Medical Uses: None in United States, analgesic, antitussive

Physical Dependence: High

Psychological Dependence: High

Tolerance: Yes

Duration (hours): 3–6

Usual Method: Injected, sniffed, smoked

Possible Effects: Euphoria, drowsiness, respiratory depression, dilated pupils, nausea

Effects of Overdose: Slow and shallow breathing, clammy skin, convulsions, coma, possible death

Withdrawal Syndrome: Watery eyes, runny nose, yawning, loss of appetite, irritability, tremors, panic, cramps, nausea, chills, and sweating

Source: U.S. Drug Enforcement Administration.

veterinarians to immobilize large wild animals (Snyder 1977; Drug Enforcement Administration 1989).

Dangers of Heroin Use

Ingesting heroin that is significantly more pure than the user's level of tolerance leads to overdose reactions that can include respiratory arrest and death. And because heroin is illegal, there is no way for the user to determine the level of purity. Indeed, the "hot shot"—a dose of heroin pure enough to be fatal—is used as a relatively easy way of eliminating addicts who have become police informers. Another danger is that heroin cut for street sale might contain adulterants that can be harmful to the user. Even if the heroin is not adulterated, the user might mix it with other drugs, such as the stimulants cocaine and amphetamine, to enhance the euphoric reaction (potentiating effect); such combinations can be fatal.

Users also face the dangers associated with diseases that are transmitted by shared hypodermic needles, particularly hepatitis and AIDS. In New York City, where there are believed to be about 200,000 heroin addicts, as many as 60 percent of them might be infected with the AIDS virus, and addicts are the leading cause of the spread of AIDS. In addition to transmission by shared needles, infected addicts spread the disease through sexual relations with nonaddicts.

OXYCODONE

Oxycodone, a synthetic version of morphine, is a DEA Schedule II drug that was first introduced in December 1995 and marketed under the trade name of OxyContin. In 2005 a federal appeals court ruled that the patent for Oxy-Contin is invalid, opening the door for generic versions. Oxycodone is sold in tablets that contain 40–160 milligrams in a time-released formulation. The 160-milligram tablet is intended to work for up to twelve hours (Clines and Meier 2001). This powerful depressant is prescribed and very effective for severe and chronic pain but has been linked to numerous overdose fatalities, the result of diversion to the substance abuse market. Produced by Purdue Pharma of Connecticut, OxyContin is a time-release medication. But abusers crush the pills and swallow, inhale, or inject the powder to produce an immediate and intense reaction (Meier 2001; Meier and Peterson 2001). The most famous abuser of OxyContin has been conservative talk radio host Rush Limbaugh, who reportedly took as many as thirty pills a day (Adler 2003).

BARBITURATES

There are about 2,500 derivatives of barbituric acid and dozens of brand names. Lawfully produced barbiturates are found in tablet or capsule form; illegal barbiturates may be found in liquid form for intravenous use because barbiturates are poorly soluble in water. Classified as sedative/hypnotics, they include amobarbital (e.g., Amytal), pentobarbital (e.g., Nembutal), pheno-barbital (e.g., Luminal), secobarbital (e.g., Seconal), and the combination amobarbital-secobarbital (e.g., Tuinal).

Effects of Barbiturates

"Barbiturates depress the sensory cortex, decrease motor activity, alter cer-ebellar function, and produce drowsiness, sedation, and hypnosis" (*Physicians Desk Reference* 1987: 1163). They inhibit seizure activity and can induce unconsciousness in the form of sleep or surgical anesthesia. Unlike opiates, barbiturates do not decrease reaction to pain and may actually increase it. They can produce a variety of alterations in the CNS, ranging from mild sedation to hypnosis and deep coma. In high enough dosage they can induce anesthesia, and an overdose can be fatal. Although they are CNS depressants, in some people they produce excitation (*Physicians Desk Reference* 1988). The user's expectations can have a marked influence on the drug's effect: "For instance, the person who takes 200 mg of secobarbital and expects to fall asleep will usually sleep, if provided with a suitable environment. Another individual, who takes the same amount of secobarbital and expects to have a good time in a stimulating environment, may experience a state of paradoxical stimulation or disinhibition euphoria" (Wesson and Smith 1977: 28).

Barbiturates are often used for their intoxicating effects. Some people take them in addition to alcohol or as a substitute. Heavy users of other drugs

Barbiturates: Uses and Effects

Classification: Depressant

CSA Schedule: Schedule II, III, IV

Trade or Other Names: Amytal, Florinal, Nembutal, Seconal, Tuinal, phenobarbital, pentobarbital

Medical Uses: Anesthetic, anticonvulsant, sedative, hypnotic, veterinary euthanasia agent

Physical Dependence: High to moderate

Psychological Dependence: High to moderate

Tolerance: Yes

Duration (hours): 5–8

Usual Method: Oral, injected

Possible Effects: Slurred speech, disorientation, drunken behavior without odor of alcohol

Effects of Overdose: Shallow respiration, clammy skin, dilated pupils, weak and rapid pulse, coma, possible death

Withdrawal Syndrome: Anxiety, insomnia, tremors, delirium, convulsions, possible death

Source: U.S. Drug Enforcement Administration.

sometimes turn to them if their usual drugs are not available or to counteract the effects of large doses of stimulants such as amphetamines or cocaine. Barbiturates are known generally on the street as "downers" or "barbs." Many are named for the colors of their brand-name versions: blues or blue heavens (Amytal), yellow jackets (Nembutal), red birds or red devils (Seconal), and rainbows or reds and blues (Tuinal).

A small dose (e.g., 50 mg or less) may relieve anxiety and tension. A somewhat larger dose (e.g., 100 to 200 mg) will, in a tranquil setting, usually induce sleep. An equivalent dose in a social setting, however, can produce effects similar to those of drunkenness—a "high" feeling, slurred speech, staggering, slowed reactions, loss of inhibition, and intense emotions often expressed in an extreme and unpredictable manner. High doses characteristically produce slow, shallow, and irregular breathing and can result in death from respiratory arrest. Barbiturate use during pregnancy has been associated with birth defects.

Barbiturates are classified according to the speed with which they are metabolized (broken down chemically) in the liver and eliminated by the kidneys: slow, intermediate, fast, and ultrafast. In low doses, barbiturates may actually increase the reaction to painful stimuli. The fast-acting barbiturates, particularly Nembutal (pentobarbital sodium), Amytal (amobarbital sodium), Seconal (secobarbital sodium), and Tuinal (secobarbital sodium and amobarbital sodium combined), are most likely to be abused (O'Brien and Cohen 1984). Exactly how barbiturates cause their neurophysiological effects is not fully understood, but the substance impairs the postsynaptic action of excitatory neurotransmitters (McKim 1991). Barbiturates serve as a positive reinforcer for laboratory animals.

Tolerance for Barbiturates

As with opiates, tolerance develops to barbiturates; but in contrast to opiates there is a fatal dosage level, and the margin between an intoxicating dosage and a fatal dosage becomes smaller with continued use. "Tolerance to a fatal dosage, however, does not increase more than twofold. As this occurs, the margin between an intoxicating dosage and a fatal dosage becomes smaller" (*Physicians Desk Reference* 1988: 537). Drinking alcohol can further reduce that margin because alcohol "enhances the absorption and produces an additive CNS depression." When under the influence of small amounts of barbiturates or a combination of alcohol and barbiturates, a "person may 'forget' that he has already taken barbiturates and continue to ingest them until he reaches a lethal dose." Such overdoses often appear, incorrectly, to be suicidal (Wesson and Smith 1977: 24).

Barbiturate Withdrawal

Withdrawal symptoms range from the mild—muscle twitching, tremors, weakness, dizziness, visual distortion, nausea, vomiting, and insomnia—to the major—delirium, convulsions, and possibly death (*Physicians Desk Reference* 1987).

Medical Use of Barbiturates

Barbiturates are used primarily as sedatives for the treatment of insomnia and as anticonvulsants to help prevent or mitigate epileptic seizures. The ultrafast barbiturates—the best-known being sodium pentothal—are used to induce unconsciousness in a few minutes. At relatively high dosages, they are used as anesthetics for minor surgery and to induce anesthesia before the administration of slow-acting barbiturates.

Because of the risks associated with barbiturate abuse and because new and safer drugs such as the tranquilizers/benzodiazepines are now available, barbiturates are less frequently prescribed than in the past. Nonetheless, they are still available both by prescription and illegally.

Dangers of Barbiturate Use

The disinhibition euphoria that can follow intake is what makes barbiturates appealing as intoxicants (Wesson and Smith 1977). Intoxication results in slurred speech, unsteady gait, confusion, poor judgment, and a marked impairment of motor skills. Unlike opiates, barbiturates make it dangerous to operate a motor vehicle. With continuous intoxication at high doses the user typically neglects his or her appearance, bathing infrequently and becoming unkempt and dirty as well as irritable and aggressive (McKim 1991). Like opiates, barbiturates are addicting, with both psychological and physiological dependence. High doses characteristically produce slow, shallow, and irregular breathing and can result in death from respiratory arrest. "Following a large overdose of secobarbital or phenobarbital (short-acting barbiturates), an individual may be in coma for several days" (Wesson and Smith 1977: 20).

Taking barbiturates with other CNS depressants, for example, alcohol; tranquilizers such opioids as heroin, morphine, meperidine (Demerol), codeine, or methadone; or antihistamines (found in cold, cough, and allergy remedies), can be extremely dangerous, even lethal. Over the long term, high dosage produces chronic inebriation; the impairment of memory and judgment; hostility, depression, or mood swings; chronic fatigue; and stimulation of preexisting emotional disorders, which can result in paranoia or thoughts of suicide. The prescribing of barbiturates has declined notably since the safer benzodiazepine tranquilizers (discussed below) were introduced.

BENZODIAZEPINES

Benzodiazepines (ben-zo-di-az-a-pins), which are minor tranquilizers or **sedatives**—referred to pharmacologically as *sedative-hypnotics*—are among the most widely prescribed of all drugs. One of earliest, Valium (diazepam), was approved by the Food and Drug Administration in 1963 to treat anxiety. Others now include Librium (chlordiazepoxide) and Equanil and Miltown (meprobamate). Prozac is a more recent and more widely prescribed selective serotonin reuptake inhibitor (SSRI), and the newer and longer-acting Klonopin is believed to have fewer withdrawal problems because it is metabolized more slowly and leaves the body gradually. The full extent of the nonmedical use of sedatives is not known, although it appears that their abuse often occurs in combination with other controlled substances. They produce effects that are subjectively similar to those of alcohol and barbiturates, but unlike these other depressants, benzodiazepines have few effects outside the CNS (McKim 1991). Major or antipsychotic tranquilizers such as Thorazine (chlorpromazine) do not produce euphoria and therefore are rarely used nonmedically.

Effects of Tranquilizers

Minor tranquilizers or SSRIs are absorbed into the bloodstream and affect the CNS, slowing down physical, mental and emotional responses. The CNS contains benzodiazepine receptors that (through a complex process involving GABA receptors) inhibit the brain's limbic system, which regulates emotions (Smith and Wesson 1994). Although it has yet to be discovered, scientists believe that the body produces its own benzodiazepine-like substance that controls anxiety.

Benzodiazepines: Uses and Effects

Classification: Depressant

CSA Schedule: Schedule IV

Trade or Other Names: Ativan, Dalmane, Diazepam, Librium, Xanax, Serax, Valium, Tranxene, Verstran, Versed, Halcion, Paxpam, Restoril

Medical Uses: Antianxiety, sedative, anticonvulsant, hypnotic

Physical Dependence: Low

Psychological Dependence: Low

Tolerance: Yes

Duration (hours): 4–8

Usual Method: Oral, injected

Possible Effects: Slurred speech, disorientation, drunken behavior without odor of alcohol

Effects of Overdose: Shallow respiration, clammy skin, dilated pupils, weak and rapid pulse, coma, possible death

Withdrawal Syndrome: Anxiety, insomnia, tremors, delirium, convulsions, possible death

Source: U.S. Drug Enforcement Administration.

Medical Use of Benzodiazepines

Minor tranquilizers are usually prescribed for anxiety or sleep problems. They can be used to treat panic disorders and muscle spasms. Sometimes referred to as "sleeping pills," these CNS depressants have largely replaced barbiturates, which reportedly have a significantly greater potential for abuse and risk for fatal overdose. In laboratory animals benzodiazepines have proven to be less effective reinforcers than barbiturates (National Institute on Drug Abuse 1991). Benzodiazepines have an upper limit of effectiveness; after a certain point, increasing the dosage will not increase the effect, and overdoses are rarely fatal (McKim 1991): "Even when a benzodiazepine is taken in an overdose of 50–100 times the usual therapeutic dose, fatalities from repertory depression is rare" (Smith and Wesson 1994: 180).

Valium is often prescribed to relieve stress, because it produces a sense of calm and well-being. It is also addictive. Benzodiazepines are not effective for treating anxiety beyond four months, and Valium can generate intense and severe secondary anxiety. Therefore, if the underlying cause of the anxiety is not treated, benzodiazepines may worsen the condition and increase the risk of suicide (Miller and Gold 1990). Valium has a very long half-life (twenty-four to forty-eight hours), which means that even after it is discontinued, it stays in the system, metabolizing slowly (Bluhm 1987). A benzodiazepine known as Versed is ten times more potent than Valium and is used to induce "twilight sleep" for surgery patients who need to be relaxed but conscious.

Tolerance for Benzodiazepines

When benzodiazepines are used as sleeping pills, tolerance develops rapidly, and effectiveness may wear off after three nights. Because of tolerance, even if the dosage is increased, benzodiazepines are not effective for treating anxiety beyond four months.

Withdrawal from Benzodiazepines

Repeated use leads to dependence, and discontinuing tranquilizers can produce withdrawal symptoms, although it is unclear in what proportion of users. Symptoms include anxiety, insomnia, agitation, anorexia, tremor, muscle twitching, nausea/vomiting, hypersensitivity to sensory stimuli and other perceptual disturbances, and depersonalization. Discontinuing use after prolonged exposure to high doses can produce hallucinations, delirium, grand mal convulsions, and, on rare occasions, death (National Institute on Drug Abuse 1987; Smith and Wesson 1994). Valium withdrawal symptoms may first appear after seven to ten days and may be quite serious and even life-threatening (Bluhm 1987). Someone using minor tranquilizers under medical supervision for more than two or three weeks is usually withdrawn gradually over a period of months.

Dangers of Tranquilizer Use

Common short-term effects of tranquilizer use include drowsiness, dizziness, confusion, and mood swings. Common long-term effects include lethargy, irritability, nausea, loss of sexual interest, increased appetite, and weight gain. Regular use of minor tranquilizers can produce both psychological and physical dependence. Combining minor tranquilizers with alcohol, painkillers, or drugs containing antihistamines, such as cough, cold, and allergy medications, can result in unconsciousness and failure to breathe. A life-endangering CNS depression can result when benzodiazepines are used in conjunction with alcohol. In some people benzodiazepines can induce hostility and even aggression (McKim 1991). Valium overdose is the second leading cause of drug-related emergency room admissions in the United States. Some tranquilizers block receptors for the neurotransmitter dopamine, which can lead to symptoms of Parkinson's disease. In 2005 it was revealed that babies born to women who take SSRIs late in pregnancy often exhibit jitteriness, irritability, and serious respiratory problems. Although the symptoms were generally mild, some babies required hospitalization and intensive care (Associated Press 2005).

METHAQUALONE

Such drugs as glutethimide (Doriden), methyprylon (Noludar), ethchlorvynol (Placidyl), and methaqualone (found in Mandrax) were introduced as barbiturate substitutes in the belief that they would be safer. It was soon found, however, that they shared problems similar to those of barbiturates, including abuse leading to overdose and interaction with other CNS depressants. The caution that is necessary in using barbiturates therefore applies to these other sedative/hypnotics as well.

Methaqualone was first synthesized in 1951 in India, where it was introduced as an antimalarial drug but proved to be ineffective. At the same time its sedating effects caused it to be introduced in Great Britain as a safe, non-barbiturate "sleeping pill." The substance subsequently found its way into street abuse, and similar patterns occurred in Germany and Japan. In 1965 methaqualone was introduced into the United States as the prescription drugs Sopors and Quaalude without any restrictions—it was not listed as a scheduled (controlled) drug. By the early 1970s "ludes" and "sopors" were part of the drug culture. Physicians were overprescribing the drugs for anxiety and insomnia, believing that they were safer than barbiturates. Street sales were primarily diversions from legitimate sources.

Eight years after methaqualone was first introduced into the United States, the drug's serious dangers had become evident, and in 1973 it was placed on the DEA's Schedule II list. Although the drug is chemically unrelated to barbiturates, methaqualone intoxication is similar to barbiturate intoxication. Addiction develops rapidly, and an overdose can be fatal. However, though similar to barbiturates in its effect, methaqualone produces an even greater loss of motor coordination, which is why it is sometimes referred to as a "wall-banger." Methaqualone is now illegally manufactured in Colombia and smuggled into the United States.

ALCOHOL

Alcohol is a potentially dangerous drug that is used by mainstream religions such as Judaism and Catholicism (though alcohol consumption is prohibited by Islam and several Protestant denominations) and whose recreational use in moderation is an accepted part of American culture: Two out of every three adult Americans consume alcohol.[7]

Alcohols are compounds that are used in perfumes, paints, and many other products. Ethyl alcohol (ethanol) is used as a beverage. A natural substance, ethyl alcohol is formed by the **fermentation** that occurs when sugar reacts with yeast. It can be made by distillation or by fermenting fruits, vegetables, or grains. In pure form, the substance is colorless and has a bitter taste. Although some people apparently enjoy the taste of beverages that contain alcohol, many others ingest the drug *despite* its taste. The substance can produce feelings

---

[7]Unless otherwise noted, information in this section is from the Office of Substance Abuse Studies, University of Maryland; Missouri Division of Alcohol and Drug Abuse; Alcoholism and Drug Addiction Research Foundation, Toronto, Canada; Canadian Centre on Substance Abuse, Ottawa, Canada; and the Centre for Education and Information on Drugs and Alcohol in New South Wales, Australia.

of well-being, sedation, intoxication, or unconsciousness, depending on the amount and the manner in which it is consumed.

Extensive research indicates that alcohol taken in moderate amounts—more than 5 grams but not more than thirty grams of pure alcohol[8] (Burros 1996)—can help to protect against heart disease by raising the level of high-density lipoproteins (so-called good cholesterol) that help to cleanse the arteries of fatty deposits (Angier 1991).[9] More recent research has revealed that as little as a single glass of wine or beer per week can significantly reduce the risk of ischemic stroke, which is the most common type of stroke and is caused by clots that reduce blood flow to the brain. An estimated 600,000 people in the United States suffer a stroke each year (Greenberg 1999).

Alcohol is a *regulated* substance rather than *controlled* substance; that is, it can be purchased and possessed with only a few restrictions. There are three major classes of alcoholic beverage:

1. *Beer*. Beer is produced by the fermentation (brewing) of barley malt or other grains. It is usually flavored with hops or other aromatic bitters. In the United States beer generally contains no more than 5 percent alcohol (10 proof), although some "ice" beers contain closer to 6 percent and some (mostly foreign) brews contain 7 percent.[10] A variant of beer known as "malt liquor" can contain 8 percent alcohol (16 proof). There are also "light" beers (about 3 percent alcohol) and nonalcoholic beers (about 0.05 percent alcohol).

2. *Wine*. Wine is obtained from the fermentation of the juice of grapes (and sometimes other fruits). It usually contains 6–14 percent alcohol (12–28 proof). Wine coolers, mixtures of wine and fruit juice, range from 5 percent to 8 percent alcohol. There are also fortified wines that have had additional alcohol added. Port and sherry wines are examples of high-quality fortified wines. Low-priced fortified wines are produced by adding grain alcohol to low-grade wine; these are often sold in screw-top bottles and are favorites of low-income alcoholics and of youths, since these wines produce more intoxication at less cost than other types of alcoholic beverage.

3. *Liquor*. When alcohol produced by fermentation (of corn, malt, other grains, molasses, or potatoes) reaches about 15 percent, it kills the alcohol-producing yeast cells. To obtain higher concentrations of alcohol, **distillation** is necessary: The mix is heated—alcohol has a lower boiling point than the other liquids—and its cooling vapors are collected. After several distillations nearly pure alcohol can be obtained. The colorless liquid is usually mixed with water, coloring, and flavoring agents. It contains at least 25 percent alcohol (50 proof) but may be as high as 50 percent alcohol

---

[8] A six-ounce glass of wine has about eleven grams of alcohol; a twelve-ounce can of beer has about thirteen grams; and a one-ounce shot of liquor has about fifteen grams.

[9] For a review of this issue, see the Spring 1994 edition of *Contemporary Drug Problems*.

[10] In 1935, fearing that beer manufacturers would attempt to lure customers by raising the amount of alcohol in their brews, Congress enacted legislation that prohibited the listing of alcohol content on beer labels. In 1995 the Supreme Court ruled that law unconstitutional.

The Basics of Bourbon

In 1776 Virginia named its western frontier Kentucky County. After the American Revolution, the county was divided, and one part was named Bourbon County in honor of France's help in the war. Later, the state of Kentucky was formed largely from what had been Bourbon County. One of the chief products of Kentucky was corn whiskey, which became popularly known as bourbon. Bourbon, which by law must be derived from at least 51 percent corn—as distinct from rye whiskey—receives its color and almost all of its taste from the charred barrels in which it is stored for at least two years. For the substance to be labeled *bourbon*, according to U.S. law, the barrels can be used only once. Bourbon whiskey's cousin, Tennessee whiskey, sold under the brand names Jack Daniel's and George Dickel, is the result of slow filtering over the course of several days through maple charcoal (Allen 1998).

Scotch whiskey is aged for three years in used barrels, mostly bourbon barrels imported from Kentucky (Allen 1998; Kummer 1999).

(100 proof). This category includes whiskey (including the Kentucky version known as bourbon and the Scottish version known as Scotch as well as Tennessee, Irish, Canadian, and rye whiskeys), brandy, rum, gin, and vodka.

Alcohol is absorbed primarily through the small intestine. The rate of absorption depends on the type and amount of foods in the stomach, if any; foods, especially solid and fatty foods, slow the absorption process. Body weight and gender also influence the effects of alcohol: Heavier people have more bodily fluids and thus dilute more of the substance; women have less gastric acid and will absorb about 30 percent more alcohol than men. Once absorbed into the bloodstream, alcohol moves to wherever there is water in the body, including inside cells of the CNS.

Effects of Alcohol

Alcohol and Tobacco
"Alcohol and tobacco seem to go together. Consumers of one drug are likely to consume the other. Moreover, alcohol and tobacco often are used at the same time" (Shiffman and Balabanis 1995: 17).

Alcohol is a psychoactive (mind-altering) chemical that, like heroin and tranquilizers, depresses the CNS. It is an efficient tranquilizer with the ability to reduce short-term anxiety (Willoughby 1988). However, alcohol first affects the part of the brain that controls inhibitions: Drinkers talk more, exude self-confidence, and may get foolish or even rowdy; there is a general loss of self-restraint (Valenzuela 1997).

The mechanism by which alcohol does this involves two receptors: GABA receptors restrain neuron activity so that chaotic communication is avoided; NMDA receptors promote communication necessary to encode memories, generate thoughts, and make decisions. Alcohol reinforces GABA activity while reducing NMDA activity, thereby slowing communication between neurons (Kotulak 2002b). As the dose increases, so do the effects, the brain experiencing greater difficulty communicating with nerves and muscles. This results in

Binge Drinking

A common problem among college students, binge drinking is defined as having at least five drinks (for men) or four drinks (for women) in a two-hour period. This causes a rapid rise in the blood alcohol level, placing the person at risk for experiencing a blackout during which he or she might engage in potentially dangerous behavior such as driving and unprotected sex that the inebriated person might not remember (National Institute on Alcohol Abuse and Alcoholism 2004).

slurred speech, staggering, and a loss of emotional control. Further ingestion can lead to stupor from which arousal is difficult, severe respiratory depression, coma, and possibly death.

Alcohol is a complex substance that affects a number of neurotransmitter and receptor systems in the brain: endorphin, dopamine, serotonin, and glutamine. When alcoholics imbibe, their brains release elevated levels of endorphins, triggering rewarding sensations that entice the person to drink more. However, at low doses, alcohol acts as a stimulant, and initially, the user of alcohol often experiences it as an energizer with euphoric effects (Bukstein, Brent, and Kaminer 1989). As with most other psychoactive substances, this is the result of alcohol stimulating the dopaminergic reward pathway in the brain (Dettling et al. 1995).

As with other drugs the influence of alcohol is mediated through setting and expectations. Imbibers at a funeral will act differently than they would if they imbibed at a wedding or other happy occasion. The two effects—stimulation and sedation—appear to be influenced by the degree of excitability of the CNS at the time of ingestion, which depends on the setting in which alcohol is used as well as the personality of the user. In a quiet environment the excitatory influence may be impaired, and alcohol produces sedation and drowsiness. If the environment is loud and lively, the drinker demonstrates excitement.

Similar reactions have been found with respect to alcohol and sexual arousal. Increasing doses of alcohol suppress physiological arousal for both men and women. But subjective sexual arousal is affected not only by blood alcohol concentration, but also by a person's beliefs about the effects of alcohol. Thus, in men, but not women, the culturally transmitted connection between sex and alcohol enhances arousal. Culturally transmitted beliefs and expectations exert a powerful influence over sexuality in drinking situations. That is, expectations about the relationship between alcohol and sex generated by the culture influence how a person believes he or she will respond to sexual stimuli while under the influence of alcohol (George and Norris n.d.).

Regular use of moderate daily amounts of alcohol can produce psychological dependence, the lack of alcohol resulting in anxiety and mild panic attacks. Prolonged or chronic drinking produces both psychological and physical dependence. The stronger depressant effect lasts about two hours, while a weaker stimulation of the CNS lasts about six times as long. As the time

Alcohol and Sex
Except at very low doses, alcohol makes it more difficult for males to maintain an erection sufficient for intercourse and retards their ability to achieve orgasm. These effects increase with increased alcohol consumption (George and Stoner 2000).

Alcohol and Aging

At age 65 the body's ability to respond to alcohol is quite different from that at age 45. Thus, older adults can get into trouble after drinking an amount of alcohol that would not be considered immoderate at a younger age. As people age, they lose muscle, bone, and lean body mass and acquire a greater percentage of body fat. As a result, there is a decrease in body water, in which alcohol is soluble, replaced by fat, in which alcohol is not soluble. Aging also results in a decline in a stomach enzyme that breaks down alcohol before it reaches the bloodstream. As a result, there is greater burden on the liver, where most alcohol metabolism takes place. Advancing age also causes a decline in the blood flow through the liver, so alcohol is eliminated more slowly from the blood. Thus, blood alcohol levels in older people are 30–40 percent higher than those in younger people (Wald 2002).

Alcohol and Violence

As was noted in Chapter 1, alcohol is associated with a great deal of violence and crime. Alcohol causes some people to become very aggressive. Males under the influence of alcohol are more easily provoked and more likely to react in a violent manner than are males who are not under influence of alcohol (Hoaken, Campbell, Stewart, and Phil 2003).

since the last drink increases, the longer-lasting stimulating effect becomes dominant, and the drinker becomes agitated—the "morning-after hangover." This is the start of the drinker's withdrawal syndrome. Because of alcohol's primary depressant effect, calm can be temporarily restored by more drinking. For the alcoholic the morning drink has a calming effect that is part of a vicious cycle of continued alcohol use.

Asians often carry a gene that makes them physically ill and flushed before they can consume an addicting amount of alcohol (Brody 2003).

Blood Alcohol Level   Almost all alcohol is burned as fuel. Unlike other drugs of abuse, alcohol provides calories and is technically a food with some eliminated through the lungs and in urine. Breathalyzer tests measure the **blood alcohol level**—the amount of alcohol in the blood—because alcohol in the air exhaled closely parallels concentrations in the blood. In most states, a blood alcohol level of 0.10 is the legal standard for intoxication, although a number of states have lowered the level to 0.08. Tables 4.1a and 4.1b show the degrees of impairment at different blood alcohol levels for men and women, respectively, and the numbers of drinks typically required to reach these levels. Alcohol use produces tolerance, and people with high levels of alcohol

Table 4.1a | Alcohol Impairment Chart, Men

	Approximate Blood Alcohol Percentage[1]								
Body Weight[2]	100	120	140	160	180	200	220	240	
Drinks[3] 0	.00	.00	.00	.00	.00	.00	.00	.00	Only safe driving limit
1	.04	.03	.03	.02	.02	.02	.02	.02	Impairment begins
2	.08	.06	.05	.05	.04	.04	.03	.03	Driving skills significantly affected
3	.11	.09	.08	.07	.06	.06	.05	.05	
4	.15	.12	.11	.09	.08	.08	.07	.06	Possible criminal penalties
5	.19	.16	.13	.12	.11	.09	.09	.08	
6	.23	.19	.16	.14	.13	.11	.10	.09	
7	.26	.22	.19	.16	.15	.13	.12	.11	Legally intoxicated
8	.30	.25	.21	.19	.17	.15	.14	.13	
9	.34	.28	.24	.21	.19	.17	.15	.14	Criminal penalties
10	.38	.31	.27	.23	.21	.19	.17	.16	

Table 4.1b | Alcohol Impairment Chart, Women

	Approximate Blood Alcohol Percentage[1]									
Body Weight[2]	90	100	120	140	160	180	200	220	240	
Drinks[3] 0	.00	.00	.00	.00	.00	.00	.00	.00	00	Only safe driving limit
1	.05	.05	.04	.03	.03	.03	.02	.02	.02	Impairment begins
2	.10	.09	.08	.07	.06	.05	.05	.04	.04	Driving skills significantly affected
3	.15	.14	.11	.10	.09	.08	.07	.06	.06	
4	.20	.18	.15	.13	.11	.10	.09	.08	.08	Possible criminal penalties
5	.25	.23	.19	.16	.14	.13	.11	.10	.09	
6	.30	.27	.23	.19	.17	.15	.14	.12	.11	Legally intoxicated
7	.38	.32	.27	.23	.20	.18	.16	.14	.13	
8	.40	.36	.30	.26	.23	.20	.18	.17	.15	Criminal penalties
9	.45	.41	.34	.29	.26	.23	.20	.19	17	
10	.51	.45	.38	.32	.28	.25	.23	.21	19	

[1] Subtract .01% for each 40 minutes of drinking.

[2] In pounds.

[3] One drink is 1.25 ounces of 80 proof liquor, 12 ounces of beer, or 5 ounces of table wine.

Source: Data supplied by the Pennsylvania Liquor Control Board.

Alcohol and Gender

Alcoholic women are more vulnerable than alcoholic men to many of the medical consequences of alcohol use. Alcoholic women develop cirrhosis of the liver, alcohol-induced damage of the heart muscle (cardiomyopathy), and nerve damage (peripheral neuropathy) after fewer years of heavy drinking than do alcoholic men (National Institute on Alcohol Abuse and Alcoholism 2004).

tolerance can perform tasks with a blood alcohol level that would render a nontolerant person a "falling-down drunk." Alcohol has a cross-tolerance with barbiturates and benzodiazepines. It appears to act on the CNS in the same manner as benzodiazepines; that is, it acts on benzodiazepine receptors, which are inhibitory.

Genetic Influence on Alcohol Use   A wide variety of studies clearly indicate that genetic factors influence the development of alcoholism, but the studies differ in their estimate of the degree of genetic influence. Although genes (segments of chromosomes that code for the production of specific proteins) are important in the control of behavior, they do not directly cause a person to become alcoholic or drug-dependent, although genes are believed to produce a tendency or predisposition to respond to drugs (including alcohol) in a certain manner. "If you are the son of a male alcoholic who began his alcoholism in early adolescence or early adulthood, the chance of your becoming an alcoholic is 7 to 10 times greater than that of the average population. If you are the twin of a male alcoholic, the chance of your becoming an alcoholic is about 70 percent. This means there is some factor, or factors, passed to the male offspring that make them more vulnerable to the actions of alcoholism" (Bloom 1993: 24). Research that compared fraternal and identical male twins supports the role of genetic factors in alcoholism. The researchers also found that environmental factors had little influence on the development of alcoholism (Prescott and Kendler 1999).

In the Genes

"Research has shown conclusively that familial transmission of alcoholism risk is at least in part genetic and not just the result of family environment" (National Institute on Alcohol Abuse and Alcoholism 2003: 1).

Studies have revealed that some people with particular inherited characteristics are at greater risk for addiction than are people without these characteristics. "Researchers have identified as important influences such inherited characteristics as how an individual metabolizes alcohol, hormonal and behavioral effects of alcohol and tolerance of high levels of alcohol in the blood" (Brody 1987: 14; also see Tarter, Alterman, and Edwards [1985] and Tarter [1988] for a review of research on behavioral traits and predisposition to substance abuse). Studies have shown that first-degree relatives of alcoholics are more likely to be alcoholics than are close blood relatives of nonalcoholics. Adopted children with alcoholic natural parents are more likely to become alcoholics than are adopted children with nonalcoholic natural parents (Schuckit 1985). Identical twins are about twice as likely as fraternal twins to

Under the Influence

After one drink, a person weighing 120 pounds has a blood alcohol level of about .04; a person weighing 140 pounds has a blood alcohol level of about .03; and a person weighing 240 pounds has a blood alcohol level of about .02. Following are the effects of alcohol at different blood levels:

.02–.03: Slight euphoria and loss of inhibition

.04–.06: Feeling of well-being and relaxation, sensation of warmth, minor impairment of reasoning and lowering of caution

.07–.09: Slight impairment of balance, motor coordination, vision, and self-control; slurred speech

.10–.12: Significant impairment of motor coordination, balance, vision, and reaction time; loss of good judgment

.30–.40: Loss of consciousness and possible death from respiratory arrest

resemble each other in terms of the presence of alcoholism (National Institute on Alcohol Abuse and Alcoholism 2003).

Research reveals that the genetic component of alcoholism appears to be related to an abnormality of a dopamine receptor gene (Blum et al. 1990). People who have this defect are at potentially greater risk for the disease than is the general population. While another study (Gelernter, Goldman, and Risch 1993) disputes the findings of Blum and colleagues,[11] subsequent research identified a specific genetic (dopamine-related) abnormality associated with susceptibility for alcoholism (Dettling et al. 1995; Guardia et al. 2000). It has been shown that another stimulating neurotransmitter, serotonin, also influences drinking behavior (Gulley et al. 1995), and a deficiency in serotonin or serotonin receptors has been linked to a predisposition to alcoholism (Goleman 1990). The ability of alcohol to produce both depressant and stimulant effects may be related to the fact that, in contrast to other psychoactive substances, alcohol can affect many different parts of the CNS (Kotulak 1997).

Alcohol Tolerance and Withdrawal

Although tolerance does not develop to alcohol's rewarding effects, people who drink on a regular basis become tolerant to many of the unpleasant effects of alcohol and are thus able to drink more before suffering these effects (National Institute on Alcohol Abuse and Alcoholism 1997). Even with increased consumption many such drinkers do not appear intoxicated.

In the liver, alcohol is converted to acetaldehyde, which in high levels causes permanent liver damage. In the alcoholic—though not in people who are

---

[11] "Individuals who become alcoholic or severely alcoholic probably do so for a variety of different reasons, and for the majority of alcoholics the causation may not even be primarily genetic" (Gelernter et al. 1993: 1677).

not addicted to alcohol—acetaldehyde builds up and is transported through the blood-brain barrier, where it combines with neurotransmitters to produce tetrahydroisoquinolines (TIQs). TIQs attach to CNS receptors to produce a feeling of well-being similar to that produced by morphine. This activity causes brain cell membranes to become abnormally thickened and to require a constant supply of alcohol. Thus, the brain cells have become addicted to alcohol. In its absence, membranes function poorly, and the alcoholic experiences withdrawal symptoms (Catanzarite 1992; Kotulak 2002b).

A physically dependent alcoholic who abruptly stops drinking will experience a withdrawal syndrome that can range from very mild to life threatening. If large amounts of alcohol are consumed for a long time, withdrawal symptoms will often be severe and far more dangerous than withdrawal from heroin. By contrast, the morning-after hangover—nausea, shakiness, and headache—may result from a single bout of alcohol abuse.

In the typical course of withdrawal, symptoms begin within the first twenty-four hours after the last drink, reach their peak intensity within two or three days, and disappear within one or two weeks. As the blood alcohol level begins to drop, the person may experience headaches, anxiety, involuntary twitching of muscles, tremor of hands, weakness, insomnia, nausea, anxiety, rapid heart rate, and increased blood pressure. At this point the alcoholic usually craves alcohol. The second stage of alcohol withdrawal includes hallucinations; these are usually visual but may include auditory or olfactory as well. If hallucinations develop, they may persist for hours, days, or even weeks.

The third stage occurs during the next forty-eight hours as symptoms become progressively more intense. There may be a fall in blood pressure; fever; delirium characterized by disorientation, delusions, and visual hallucinations; and convulsions similar to those exhibited in grand mal epileptic seizures. The fever, delirium, and convulsions are the most serious symptoms and can be fatal.

If the person remains untreated, the syndrome may progress to **delirium tremens** (DTs): profound confusion, disorientation, hallucinations, hyperactivity, and extreme cardiovascular disturbances. Without close medical management the person may harm himself or herself or others or could die from the medical complications. Prevention of the DTs involves the use of sedatives such as Valium, since once the DTs begin, no known medical treatment is able to stop them. If left untreated, DTs can be fatal.

Dangers of Alcohol Use

Alcohol has a pervasive effect on the body's gastrointestinal tract, liver, bloodstream, brain and nervous system, heart, muscles, and endocrine system. Some harmful consequences are primary; that is, they result directly from prolonged exposure to alcohol's toxic effects (such as heart and liver disease or inflammation of the stomach). Others are secondary, indirectly related to chronic alcohol abuse; these include loss of appetite, vitamin deficiencies, infections, and sexual impotence or menstrual irregularities. Because alcohol can be utilized as a source of energy, this supply of calories often suppresses appetite, leading to dietary deficiencies that may be responsible in part for the pathologic conditions that are seen in chronic alcoholism. The risk of serious disease increases with the amount of alcohol consumed:

- Loss of control of eye muscles
- Hypoglycemia (low level of glucose in the blood)
- Gastritis (chronic inflammation of the stomach)
- Increased susceptibility to infections
- Cardiac arrhythmia (irregularity)
- Anemia (red blood cell deficiency)
- Neuritis (nerve inflammation)
- Pancreatitis (inflammation of the pancreas)
- Increased blood pressure
- Cardiomyopathy (heart muscle disorder)
- Cancer of the tongue, mouth, pharynx, hypopharynx, esophagus, and liver
- Decreased white blood cells
- Weakened immune system
- Depletion of vitamins and minerals
- Lowered hormone levels, leading to sexual dysfunction

Wernicke-Korsakoff Syndrome   Most long-term alcoholics suffer from Wernicke-Korsakoff syndrome, a deficiency in thiamine (vitamin B1), an essential nutrient required by all tissues, including the brain. Wernicke-Korsakoff syndrome consists of two separate syndromes, a short-lived and severe condition called Wernicke's encephalopathy and a long-lasting and debilitating condition known as Korsakoff's psychosis. The symptoms of Wernicke's encephalopathy include mental confusion, paralysis of the nerves that move the eyes (oculomotor disturbances), and difficulty with muscle coordination. Victims might be too confused to find their way out of a room or might not even be able to walk.

About 80 to 90 percent of alcoholics with Wernicke's encephalopathy also develop Korsakoff's psychosis, a chronic and debilitating disease characterized by persistent learning and memory problems, being forgetful and quickly frustrated, and having difficulty with walking and coordination. Although these patients have problems remembering old information (retrograde amnesia), it is their difficulty in "laying down" new information (anterograde amnesia) that is the most striking. For example, these patients can discuss in detail an event in their lives, but an hour later they might not remember ever having the conversation (National Institute on Alcohol Abuse and Alcoholism 2004).

Liver and Brain Damage   About one out of five heavy drinkers develop fatty liver (steatosis), which usually produces no clinical symptoms except an enlarged liver. Although the condition can be reversed if alcohol consumption is significantly reduced, it can eventually be fatal. Heavy drinkers may also suffer from alcoholic hepatitis, the symptoms of which include a swollen liver, nausea, vomiting, and abdominal pain. They may also experience jaundice, bleeding, and liver failure. If severe drinking continues, there is about a 50 percent chance of mortality, or the person will probably develop cirrhosis.

Cirrhosis results in scar tissue replacing normal liver tissue, causing a disruption of blood flow through the liver, preventing it from working properly. Symptoms include redness of the palms caused by capillary dilation, shortening of muscles in the fingers caused by toxic effects or fibrous changes, white nails, thickening and widening of the fingers and nails, liver enlargement or inflammation, and abnormal accumulation of fat in normal liver cells. About 10–15 percent of people with alcoholism develop cirrhosis, but many survive it. Many are unaware that they have it; about 30– 40 percent of cirrhosis cases are discovered at autopsy. When late-stage cirrhosis develops, that is, when jaundice, accumulation of fluid in the abdomen, or gastrointestinal bleeding has occurred, the survival rate is only 60 percent for those who stop drinking and 35 percent for those who do not (Mann, Smart, and Govoni 2004).

Prolonged liver dysfunction, such as liver cirrhosis, can also harm the brain, leading to a serious and potentially fatal brain disorder known as hepatic encephalopathy (Tuma and Casey 2004). Research has found serious brain deficits in alcoholics, but there is no conclusive evidence that can link this to any one variable. The most plausible explanation is some combination of prolonged use of alcohol and individual vulnerability to some forms of brain damage (Oscar-Berman and Marinkovic 2004).

Fetal Alcohol Spectrum Disorders   Fetal alcohol spectrum disorders are a variety of conditions that result from a mother who drinks during pregnancy. Foremost among them is fetal alcohol syndrome (FAS). The serious effects of FAS include mental retardation, growth deficiency, head and facial deformities, joint and limb abnormalities, and heart defects. (When the symptoms of FAS are present without the characteristic facial features, the disorder is referred to as *fetal alcohol effects*.) When a FAS baby is born, he or she may experience withdrawal from alcohol, exhibiting tremors, irritability, fits, and a bloated stomach. Why some pregnant women who drink heavily give birth to normal babies while others have babies who are severely damaged is not known. But there are an unknown number of babies who, while affected by their mother's drinking, appear relatively normal but subsequently develop behavioral and learning problems (Carroll 2003). Whether an individual child will have FAS appears to depend on a number of factors in addition to alcohol, including parental health, other drug use, lifestyle, and other socioeconomic factors. Some of the factors contributing to FAS may be male-mediated. This influence may occur biologically through damage to the sperm or physically and psychologically through violence or other abuse to the mother before and during pregnancy.

Alcohol-related birth defects include malformations in the skeletal and major organ systems, while alcohol-related neurodevelopmental disorder involves CNS deficits (Substance Abuse and Mental Health Services Administration 2004). Researchers have discovered that even moderate drinking by a pregnant woman can impair the child's intellectual ability in school (Goleman 1989), and alcohol has been linked to a tenfold increased risk of developing leukemia during infancy ("New Hazard of Drinking in Pregnancy Is Found" 1996). Because alcohol affects so many parts of the brain, it is viewed as the most harmful drug of abuse that a pregnant mother can use. Indeed, much of the damage ascribed to cocaine, particularly crack, appears to be primarily the result of the mother using alcohol as well (Carroll 2003).

The fetus is at greatest risk of harm during the first three months of pregnancy, as the major organs and limbs are starting to form during that time. Research indicates that ethanol induces the destruction of large numbers of neurons from several regions of the developing brain (Ikonomidou et al. 2000). A 2004 study indicates that just two cocktails consumed by a pregnant woman can kill developing brain cells in a fetus and thus can lead to a lifetime of neurological problems (Associated Press 2004b).

ANALOGS AND DESIGNER DRUGS

Many chemical variations, or **analogs**, of the drugs discussed in this chapter have been found or developed. These include semisynthetic opiates such as hydromorphine, oxycodone, etorphine, and diprenorphine and synthetic opiates such as pethidine, methadone, and propoxyphene (Darvon). The synthetic drug **fentanyl** citrate, which is often used intravenously in major surgery, works exactly like the opiates: It kills pain and produces euphoria and, if abused, leads to addiction. The substance is easily produced by people who are skilled in chemistry. Fentanyl compounds are often sold as "China White," the street name for the finest Southeast Asian heroin, to addicts who cannot tell the difference. Those who know the difference may actually prefer fentanyl because it is usually cheaper than heroin and more readily available, and some users believe that it contains fewer adulterants than heroin (Roberton 1986; K. Johnson 2006). However, fentanyl compounds are quite potent and difficult for street dealers to cut properly, a situation that can lead to overdose and death. One derivative, 3-methyl fentanyl, is extremely potent (approximately 3,000 times as potent as morphine) and is thought to have been responsible for a number of overdose deaths. In 1988 3-methyl fentanyl led to the death of eighteen people in the Pittsburgh area. A local chemist without a criminal record was found to be the source; he apparently got the idea from a television news report. In 1991 the drug killed ten people in one weekend in four Northeastern cities (Nieves 1991). In 2006 fentanyl mixed with and sold as heroin was responsible for killing hundreds of people in cities from Chicago to Philadelphia (Associated Press 2006; K. Johnson 2006). Some of the victims had snorted the drug (Santora 2006). Fentanyl has been used (illegally) to "dope" racehorses because the substance is very difficult to detect in urine or blood.

Analogs designed by underground chemists (**designer drugs**) to mimic controlled substances are an emerging problem: "These chemists change the

Alcohol and Adolescents

In 1999 Congress allocated $195 million for a media campaign to dissuade youngsters from using illegal drugs, but nothing was appropriated to warn about the dangers of alcohol. The alcoholic beverage industry spends $3 million a year promoting its products (Wren 1999a).

Fentanyl: Uses and Effects

Classification: Narcotic

CSA Schedule: Schedule I, II

Trade or Other Names: Innovar, Sublimaze, Alfenta, Sufenta, Duragesic

Medical Uses: Analgesic, adjunct to anesthesia, anesthetic

Physical Dependence: High

Psychological Dependence: High

Tolerance: Yes

Duration (hours): 10–72

Usual Method: Injected, transdermal patch

Possible Effects: Euphoria, drowsiness, respiratory depression, dilated pupils, nausea

Effects of Overdose: Slow and shallow breathing, clammy skin, convulsions, coma, possible death

Withdrawal Syndrome: Watery eyes, runny nose, yawning, loss of appetite, irritability, tremors, panic. cramps, nausea, chills, and sweating

Source: U.S. Drug Enforcement Administration.

molecular structure of a drug and thus make the drug legally unrestricted. Since the passage of the Anti-Drug Abuse Act of 1986 all analogs of controlled substances have themselves become controlled substances. The changes in chemical structure may also change its potency, length of action, euphoric effects, and toxicity" (National Institute on Drug Abuse 1987: 27).

SUMMARY

The central nervous system contains endorphins, neurotransmitters that have the characteristics of morphine. An endorphin deficiency would place a person at risk for drug abuse, as would difficulties dealing with stress.

Morphine and heroin have analgesic and euphoric properties. Heroin users experience different effects: the rush, the high, and the nod. Tolerance develops to the high but not to the rush.

Heroin has no lawful uses in the United States, but the heroin analogs fentanyl and oxycodone are available for medical use. Heroin depresses the respiratory centers in the brain, and an overdose can result in respiratory arrest and death from lack of oxygen to the brain. Withdrawal from heroin is similar to a bad case of the flu, and symptoms subside in about a week.

Barbiturates have limited medical use, and although they produce euphoria, they do not ease pain. Tolerance develops, and in contrast to opiates, there is a fatal dosage level. In medicine barbiturates have largely been replaced by benzodiazepines.

Alcohol is a depressant that initially acts as a stimulant and affects the part of the brain that controls inhibitions. In addition to the dangers imposed by alcohol itself—such as cirrhosis of the liver and damage to the heart muscle—behavior problems that result from ingestion include violence and impaired driving. Alcohol produces tolerance, and withdrawal symptoms range from the morning-after hangover to life-threatening delirium tremens.

REVIEW QUESTIONS

1. What is the relationship between pain and endorphins?
2. How can a deficiency in endorphins explain heroin use?
3. How does heroin affect the user?
4. How does the concept of tolerance help to explain addiction?
5. Why would heroin addicts who do not intend to abandon the use of heroin enter a drug treatment program without being coerced?
6. For heroin users, what are the differences between the rush, the high, and the nod?
7. How does heroin impair homeostatic body functions?
8. Why is a heroin overdose life-threatening?
9. What is the effect of barbiturates on the user?
10. How are the different barbiturates classified?
11. How does methaqualone affect the user?
12. What are the medical uses of sedatives?
13. Why have benzodiazepines largely replaced barbiturates in medicine?
14. Why is alcohol considered a food?
15. What are the three classes of alcohol?
16. Why is alcohol referred to as a regulated drug?
17. How is alcohol similar to heroin?
18. How does alcohol differ from heroin?
19. What are the dangers of alcohol abuse?
20. What are designer drugs?

5 CHAPTER | **Stimulants**

Stimulants produce profound subjective well-being with alertness. Normal pleasures are magnified and anxiety is decreased. Self-confidence and self-perceptions of mastery increase. Social inhibitions are reduced and interpersonal communication is facilitated. All aspects of the personal environment take on intensified qualities but without hallucinatory perceptual distortions. Emotionality and sexual feelings are enhanced.

Frank H. Gawin, M. Elena Khalsa, and Everett Ellinwood, Jr. (1994: 113)

As the term *stimulant* indicates, substances in this category stimulate the central nervous system (CNS). In moderation they enhance mood, increase alertness, and relieve fatigue. Two commonly used stimulants are nicotine, which is found in tobacco products, and caffeine, an active ingredient in coffee, tea, and some soft drinks. Used in moderation, these substances tend to relieve malaise and increase alertness.

More powerful stimulants, such as cocaine and amphetamines, are taken orally, sniffed, smoked, or injected. Smoking, snorting, or injecting stimulants produces a sudden sensation known as a "rush" or a "flash." Abuse is often associated with a pattern of binge use, that is, consuming large doses of stimulants sporadically. Heavy users might inject themselves every few hours, continuing until they have depleted their drug supply or reached a point of delirium, psychosis, and physical exhaustion. During this period of heavy use, all other interests become secondary to re-creating the initial euphoric rush. Tolerance can develop rapidly, and both physical dependence and psychological dependence occur. Abrupt cessation, even after a weekend binge, is commonly followed by depression, anxiety, drug craving, and extreme fatigue ("crash").

It has been hypothesized that stimulants such as cocaine and amphetamine compensate for a deficiency in three neurotransmitters—dopamine, norepinephrine, which acts with epinephrine (adrenaline), and serotonin—that can otherwise result in apathy and depression (Khantzian 1985; Nunes and Rosecan 1987), bolstering the theory of drug use as being self-medication.

As was discussed in Chapter 3, in the presynaptic terminals of normal people, monoamine oxidases (MAO) control the level of neurotransmitters. In some individuals an excess of MAO lowers the amount of dopamine, norepinephrine, and serotonin, which results in depression (Sunderwirth 1985). Indeed, MAO-inhibiting drugs such as Nardil (phenelzine) are medically prescribed to treat depression. The use of powerful stimulants by some people and not others, given that both groups have equal access to these drugs, can be explained by physiological deficiencies, much as the use of insulin by diabetics can be explained: Nondiabetics will not find the ingestion of insulin a positive experience. The users of stimulants, according to this view, are attempting to reduce inner tension and increase energy and activity levels (see, e.g., Fishbein, Lozovsky, and Jaffe 1989).

At the other extreme, in people who are highly extroverted, perhaps even manic, stimulants make more dopamine available to the brain and are thus highly rewarding even in small doses, making such people susceptible to addiction (Goleman 1990). In 1995 a variant of the dopamine receptor D^4 was found to be associated with novelty seeking; people with this genetic factor tend to be extroverted, quick-tempered, impulsive, and easily bored (Angier 1995). Several teams of researchers working independently have reported that such people possess a gene that makes them especially responsive to dopamine, and this is believed to be related to participation in extreme sports such as skydiving and ice climbing, as well as drug use (Koerber 1997).

Scientists have also discovered a mechanism that appears to account for the different levels of euphoria people experience when they take a stimulant. People who have lower levels of dopamine D^2 receptors in their brains were found to be more inclined to like the effects of a mild stimulant than were those who have higher levels of these receptors, who were found to dislike the drug's effects (National Institute on Drug Abuse 1999f). Dopamine deficiencies in the brain cannot be remedied by introducing corrective substances because the blood-brain barrier prevents most substances from reaching it.

COCAINE

Coca is a flowering bush or shrub (*Erythroxylon coca*) that in cultivation stands three to six feet high and yields at most four ounces of waxy, elliptical leaves that are about 1 percent cocaine by weight. Conversion into cocaine hydrochloride—powdered cocaine—requires several steps. Immediately after being harvested, the leaves are pulverized, soaked, and shaken in a mixture of alcohol and benzene (a coal tar derivative) for about three days. After the liquid has been drained, sulfuric or hydrochloric acid, depending on the alkaloid content of the leaves, is added, and the solution is again shaken. Sodium carbonate is added, forming a precipitate, which is washed with kerosene and chilled, leaving behind crystals of crude cocaine known as **coca paste**, which is allowed to dry.

Between 200 and 500 kilograms of coca leaves are required to make one kilo of paste; two and one-half kilos of coca paste are converted into one kilo of cocaine base—a malodorous, rough, greenish yellow powder of more than 66 percent purity—and finally into cocaine hydrochloride by being treated with ether, acetone, and hydrochloric acid. One kilo of cocaine base is synthesized into one kilo of cocaine hydrochloride, a white crystalline powder that is about 95 percent pure. Those who process the substance are exposed to noxious fumes and the real danger of an explosion.

In the United States cocaine hydrochloride is "cut" (diluted) for street sale by adding sugars (such as lactose, inositol, and mannitol) or talcum powder, borax, or other neutral substances, as well as local anesthetics such as procaine hydrochloride (Novocain) or lidocaine hydrochloride. (Novocain is sometimes mixed with mannitol or lactose and sold as cocaine.) After cutting, cocaine typically has a consumer sale purity of less than 20 percent, although huge increases in the availability of cocaine can result in a level as high as 50 percent and a concomitant increase in the number of emergency room admissions for cocaine overdoses.

Effects of Cocaine

Cocaine typically enters the bloodstream by being snorted into the nostrils through a straw or rolled paper or from a "coke spoon." "Because cocaine is a vasoconstrictor, it inhibits its own absorption, and the time it takes to reach

■ | ## Cocaine: Uses and Effects

Classification: Stimulant

CSA Schedule: Schedule II

Trade or Other Names: Coke, flake, snow, crack

Medical Uses: Local anesthetic

Physical Dependence: Possible

Psychological Dependence: High

Tolerance: Yes

Duration (hours): 1–2

Usual Method: Sniffed, smoked, injected

Possible Effects: Increased alertness, excitation, euphoria, increased pulse rate and blood pressure, insomnia, loss of appetite

Effects of Overdose: Agitation, increased body temperature, hallucinations, convulsions, possible death

Withdrawal Syndrome: Apathy, long periods of sleep, irritability, depression, disorientation

Source: U.S. Drug Enforcement Administration.

peak concentration gets longer as the dose gets larger" (Karch 1996: 19). Some abusers will take it intravenously, which is the only way to ingest 100 percent of the drug. Because this is a more efficient method, users with limited funds sometimes buy and inject cocaine as a group, a method that can spread HIV/ AIDS. Cocaine can also be absorbed through genital or rectal application, during which its anesthetic properties prolong vaginal intercourse or suppress the discomfort of anal intercourse. This extremely dangerous practice can lead to seizure, coma, and death (Karch 1998). When the drug is inhaled, its effects peak in fifteen to twenty minutes and disappear in sixty to ninety minutes. Intravenous use results in an intense feeling of euphoria that crests in three to five minutes and wanes in thirty to forty minutes. (Smoking crack cocaine is discussed later in the chapter.)

Neurological Effects   "Smoked, snorted, or injected, cocaine rapidly enters the bloodstream and penetrates the brain. The drug achieves its main imme- diate psychological effect—the high—by causing a buildup of the neuro- chemical dopamine" (Nestler 2005: 5). The drug binds to specific receptor sites on brain membranes and triggers the release of dopamine but also serotonin and norepinephrine. These neurotransmitters enhance mood and, at high enough doses, produce feelings of euphoria by activating the sympathetic nervous system, giving rise to increased heart rate, blood pressure, breathing rate, body temperature, and blood sugar (Washton 1989). A deficiency in serotonin was found to be linked to a desire for cocaine, and genetically altered mice continued to find cocaine rewarding even when it failed to

When inhaled, the effects of cocaine peak in about 20 minutes but disappear within 90 minutes. Users have an initial sense of euphoria, with illusions of increased mental alertness. When the drug wears off, depression usually follows.

©J. Pickerel/The Image Works

increase their (already high) levels of dopamine (Blakeslee 1998; Parsons, Weiss, and Koob 1998; Rocha et al. 1998; National Institute on Drug Abuse 1999e). The substance also acts on the hypothalamus to decrease appetite and reduces the need for sleep by inducing the release of stimulant neurotransmitters.

In addition to stimulating their release, cocaine blocks or inhibits the reabsorption of dopamine, norepinephrine, and serotonin by the discharging neurons by preventing a reuptake transporter from performing its usual function (Fig. 5.1).[1] As a result, neurotransmitters continue to bombard their receptor sites. The neurons remain in a state of excitement, the brain is stimulated accordingly, and euphoria increases (Sunderwirth 1985; Holloway 1991). This "initial, short-term effect—a buildup of the neurochemical dopamine—gives rise to euphoria and a desire to take the drug again" (Nestler 2005: 4).

As the supply of dopamine depletes, however, depression sets in. Research has discovered that cocaine-dependent people have fewer dopamine receptors than do normal controls, which also helps to explain why they feel depressed when not on cocaine (Holloway 1991). Depletion of both dopamine and serotonin in specific brain regions that control drive and affect may contribute to the craving and depression that are evident in the aftermath of cocaine abuse, "but when cocaine is readministered, frontal brain regions may be reactivated, again contributing to the compulsion to use cocaine" (Bolla, Cadet, and

---

[1] A strain of mice bred for the absence of the dopamine transporter is impervious to cocaine; these mice are also highly active, fail to eat, and often die from exhaustion (Grady 1996).

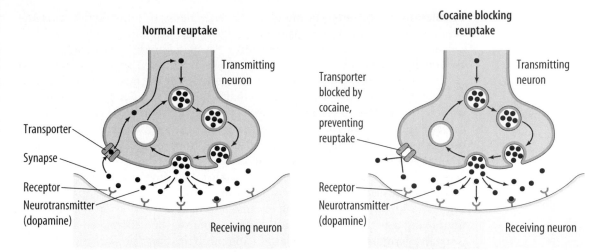

Figure 5.1 | Cocaine Blocking Reuptake of Neurotransmitters. Blocked neurotransmitters can include dopamine, norepinephrine, and serotonin. This results in their accumulation in the synapse, stimulating the receiving neuron.

London 1998: 281). Although the case for dopamine's centrality remains airtight, another neurotransmitter, glutamate (or mGluR5), appears to play an independent role in the rewarding qualities of cocaine. Indeed, research in Geneva, Switzerland, reveals that glutamate's role in cocaine dependence is even more central than dopamine's (Hollon 2002).

There are regions within the brain that, when stimulated, produce feelings of pleasure. One neural system that appears to be most affected by cocaine originates in such a region (the **ventral tegmental area**, or **VTA**), located deep within the brain. Cocaine short-circuits the reward pathways of the brain (Dunwiddie 1988), and in laboratory animals cocaine has usurped other rewards, such as food and sex. In laboratory tests, monkeys pressed a bar as many as 12,800 times for an infusion of 0.5 milligram of cocaine. "No other drug, including opiates and amphetamine, has been reported to be more potent than cocaine in such tests" (Geary 1987: 31). The ultimate consequence of unlimited access to cocaine is death. Without unlimited access, however, monkeys are able to self-regulate their cocaine use (Siegel 1989).

Would monkeys in the wild succumb to the allure of unlimited amounts of cocaine? Laboratory conditions do not replicate the animals' natural environment, nor are the results of such experiments readily generalizable to humans, who have such species-exclusive traits as a sense of values and a desire for self-control (Peele 1985). Some dopamine agonists are self-administered by and rewarding to animals but do not produce euphoria in humans (Rothman 1994). Furthermore, we know that the use of cocaine is related to behavioral stress (National Institute on Drug Abuse 1997b), and monkeys in the laboratory setting are under considerable stress.

Physiological Effects In small doses cocaine will bring about extreme euphoria and indifference to pain, along with illusions of increased mental and sensory alertness and physical strength: "A few hundredths of a gram of cocaine hydrochloride, chopped finely and arranged on a smooth surface into several lines, or rows of powder, can be snorted into the nose through a rolled piece of paper in a few seconds. The inhalation shortly gives rise to feelings of elation and a sense of clarity or power of thought, feelings that pass away for most people in about half an hour" (Van Dyke and Byck 1982: 128). At higher doses, however, the drug has the potential "to produce megalomania and feelings of omnipotence in most individuals" (Gold et al. 1986: 44). Cocaine causes the body to feel as if there were an impending threat, a response to stimuli that causes the release of stimulating neurotransmitters (dopamine and norepinephrine): "In essence the cocaine stimulated reactions in the body are mimicking a natural physiological stress response; the generalized adrenergic discharge stimulates the energy producing mechanisms to prepare the CNS and skeletal muscles for 'fight' or 'flight.' The body feels the chemistry of fright, tension and anxiety but the brain gives the message that everything is better than fine" (Gold et al. 1986: 38).

Studies suggest that cocaine actually heightens the body's sensitivity to stress, although the user fails to recognize that this is occurring. Cocaine activates stress systems, much like what occurs when an opiate addict goes into withdrawal, but the person perceives this as part of the cocaine rush because cocaine is also stimulating the parts of the brain that are involved in feeling pleasure. When cocaine's effects wear off and the addict goes into withdrawal, the stress systems are again activated. This time, the cocaine addict perceives the activation as unpleasant because cocaine is no longer stimulating the pleasure circuits in the brain. Because cocaine switches on the stress systems both when it is active and during withdrawal, these systems rapidly become hypersensitive (Kreek 1997).

Chemically similar substances such as lidocaine (Xylocaine) and procaine (Novocain), as dental patients recognize, eliminate all feeling when applied topically or subcutaneously. Single small doses of procaine, when taken intranasally or smoked, produce the same euphoric response as does cocaine in experienced cocaine users. Users cannot distinguish between the two substances, and tests indicate that laboratory animals will work as hard for procaine as they will for cocaine (Van Dyke and Byck 1982). In laboratory tests with animals, however, while procaine served as a reinforcer similar to cocaine, lidocaine did not (Balster 1988).

Coca Paste and Cocaine Combinations

Versions of the drug other than cocaine hydrochloride have become popular among certain abusers. Coca paste, which is typically smoked with either tobacco or marijuana products, is used extensively in cocaine-processing countries. Because it requires less processing than cocaine, coca paste—called *bazuco*—is popular among low-income groups in these countries and has become a major abuse problem in Colombia. In the late 1980s the substance made its way into the United States, where it became known as "bubble gum" to young abusers because of the phonetic association of the word *bazuco* with Bazooka bubble gum. The substance usually results from an error in the water/sulfuric acid ratio. The paste has at least traces of a host of dangerous chemicals used in its production, including kerosene, sulfuric acid, leaded gasoline, and potassium permanganate, which can cause irreversible damage to the liver, lungs, and brain.

Some intravenous abusers combine cocaine with heroin—a practice known as "speedballing." This was the combination that led to the death of comedian John Belushi in 1982. It appears that heroin enhances the subjective effects of cocaine, although the neurobiology of the interaction is unclear. Because heroin and cocaine work on different parts of the mesolimbic dopamine neurons, they can be combined to produce even more intense dopamine activation. The heroin increases cell firing and dopamine release, while the cocaine keeps the released dopamine in the synaptic cleft longer, thereby intensifying and prolonging its effects. Users show very rapid psychological and physiological deterioration. Although speedball use produces extremely intense activation of brain reward systems, it is often short-lived because this drug combination is associated with a very high fatality rate. The combination of cocaine and heroin is perhaps the most dangerous form of illicit substance use (Addiction Research Unit 1998). Some cocaine users also ingest heroin to soften and prolong the impact of cocaine.

Some users mix cocaine and alcohol consumption, a combination that increases the euphoric effects.

Crack

Crack, the drug abuser's answer to fast food, became popular among young men and women during the 1980s.[2] The drug is relatively cheap, five to ten dollars a "rock," although users hooked on crack report spending between $100 and $200 a day on the substance. Crack is generally sold on the street in small glass vials or tiny plastic bags. Versions of crack may contain any combination of freebase residue, concentrated caffeine, or different amphetamines.

Although cocaine hydrochloride cannot easily be smoked—the melting and vaporization point is very high (195° Celsius)—freeing the alkaloid from the hydrochloride attachment (**freebase**) will produce purified crystals of cocaine base that readily vaporize at 98 degrees Celsius. Cocaine cooked in a mixture of sodium bicarbonate (baking soda) and water becomes hard when heat-dried and is called **crack**. The soaplike substance is then cut into bars or chips (sometimes called quarter rocks) and smoked. This freebase cocaine can be crushed and smoked in a special glass pipe or sprinkled on a

---

[2] For a thorough examination of the different facets of crack, see Chitwood, Rivera, and Inciardi (1996).

Cocaine cooked in a mixture of sodium bicarbonate (baking soda) and water becomes hard when heat-dried, and is called crack. The soap-like substance is then cut into bars or chips. This freebase cocaine can be crushed and smoked in a special glass pipe or sprinkled on a tobacco or mari-juana product. The term crack refers to the crackling sound heard when the mixture is smoked (heated).

©Janine Wiedel Photolibrary/Alamy

tobacco or marijuana product. The term *crack* refers to the crackling sound heard when the mixture is smoked (heated), presumably from the sodium bicarbonate.

Dennis Watlington (1987), a former crack user, states that crack is typi-cally smoked in a glass pipe about five inches long and a quarter inch in diameter with a metal screen at the top to hold a small clump of the substance. When lit, the substance melts and clings to the screen; some of it oozes down inside the stem where it dries and forms a hard residue that can later be scraped off and smoked. "The most satisfying way to smoke crack," Watlington notes, "is to insert this stem into a glass bowl the size of an espresso cup. Through a second pipe inserted into the side of the bowl, the smoker pulls the smoke after it collects in quantity in the bowl" (1987: 150).

Because crack is inhaled directly into the lungs, bypassing much of the circulatory system en route to the brain, it takes about five seconds to take effect—even faster than intravenous ingestion. When "crack is heated, the drug crosses the blood-brain barrier in only a few seconds, providing a virtually instantaneous 'high' and intense gratification, often described as a 'sexual euphoria,' or orgasm" (McCoy, Miles, and Inciardi 1995: 172). "Crack can excite sexual desires while inhibiting the ability to achieve orgasm, creating sexual encounters that are prolonged and more conducive to the spread of AIDS" (Drug Enforcement Administration 1994a: 3).

The vapors first produce a potent **rush**: "This 'rush' lasts a few seconds, and is replaced by a euphoric excitation that lasts for several minutes. A five to twenty minute period of less pleasurable hyperexcitability follows. Then the 'ultimate high' degenerates into the ultimate low" (National Institute on Drug

Abuse 1986: 4). "After smoking crack repeatedly, the user develops an intense craving for more. Although it can take months or even years for a nasal cocaine user to progress from recreational to compulsive use, this can happen within days to weeks with crack" (Rosecan, Spitz, and Gross 1987: 299).

Interviews with crack users in drug treatment programs revealed the apparent power of this substance (Frank et al. 1987: 12):

> Despite the many years of using other drugs, the experience with Crack was quite different. Most respondents had been in control of their drug use, even those who had been using very heavily. The majority (63 percent) had never needed treatment for their drug use before using Crack. The experience with Crack, however, was very much a jolt, for which these users were not prepared in spite of their past experience. For many it was a very frightening experience. Respondents remembered feelings and behaviors under the influence of Crack that they had never experienced before—the irritability, rage, and aggression. Most of the clients had held jobs and valued the money they earned. Now, in retrospect, the loss of so much spent on Crack was incomprehensible to them.

Females who become compulsive users frequently exchange sex for the drug.

That crack is smoked rather than injected has increased its appeal. Indeed, it constitutes the first psychoactive drug experience of many young abusers, who try it even before alcohol and marijuana (Rosecan, Spitz, and Gross 1987). Unfortunately, "because of the large, concentrated doses that reach the brain, seizures are more likely to occur from smoking cocaine than from snorting it, and smoking can lead more easily to respiratory failure and/or cardiac arrest" (Washton 1989: 16). It was crack that led to the death of college basketball star Len Bias, age 22 years, and professional football player Don Rogers, age 23 years.

Reports—some would say hysteria—about the power of crack to produce dependence have subsided, and today it is rarely mentioned in the media. Although crack is admittedly a strongly dependence-producing substance, recent research indicates that it is not the all-powerful drug the media had portrayed. Crack appears to be less addictive than nicotine, though more addictive than alcohol (Kolata 1989b; Egan 1999a). A study of seventy-nine crack users in Toronto revealed a "lack of strong evidence to support the view that use of the drug is necessarily compulsive. Over half of the respondents had never or rarely experienced a craving to take crack" (Cheung, Erickson, and Landau 1991: 133). There has been a dramatic change in the crack-using population, as adolescents began to reject the substance and "crackheads," no longer considered "cool," became outcasts. Crack users today are more likely to be older (in their late twenties or early thirties) males.

Cocaine Tolerance

After frequent and high doses of cocaine, the failure to continue ingestion produces a withdrawal syndrome characterized by psychological depression, irritability, extreme fatigue, and prolonged periods of restless sleep. Roger

Weiss and Steven Mirin report a form of reverse tolerance: "long-term users may experience more excitatory effects from the same, or even smaller, doses of the drug," a phenomenon referred to as **kindling** (1987: 48).

Many researchers have reported that tolerance to the euphoric effects occurs with repeated use, although the biological basis underlying sensitization or tolerance to cocaine is not yet fully understood (O'Brien and Cohen 1984; Grinspoon and Bakalar 1985; Zahniser et al. 1988; Izenwasser and Unterwald 1994). This tolerance causes the abuser to increase the dosage. "Chronic users often find themselves caught in a futile, obsessive chase to recapture the original cocaine 'high,' but as dosages and frequency increase, so does the user's tolerance to the euphoric effects" (Washton, Stone, and Henrickson 1988: 367). And "in face of dose escalation, one might eventually achieve blood levels of cocaine high enough to induce toxic local anesthetic effects" that include panic attacks and the risk of seizures (Post and Weiss 1988: 232). However, Steven Karch (1996), a medical examiner, reports that because of tolerance, chronic cocaine users can consume massive amounts without apparent ill effects. There is evidence of cocaine tolerance in binge-type ingestion (Kreek 1997).

Cocaine Withdrawal

After frequent and high doses of cocaine the failure to continue ingestion produces a withdrawal syndrome characterized by psychological depression, irritability, extreme fatigue, and prolonged periods of restless sleep. James Inciardi (1986: 79) states that this syndrome is not necessarily physiological; it might simply be the result of an emotional letdown that results when heavy abusers try to discontinue the drug: "they *think* they have a physical need for cocaine."

Strong cravings for the substance and the malaise that follows cessation are possibly brain-mediated behavioral changes indicating physical dependence, and the elevation in reward thresholds as a result of cocaine use could trigger a withdrawal effect after use is discontinued (Koob et al. 1994). "When the cocaine- or amphetamine-dependent person is not taking one of these drugs, dopamine release will be diminished to levels lower than normal, which could contribute to the anhedonia [inability to enjoy routine pleasures], dysphoria [chronic discontent], and other symptoms of withdrawal that motivate repeated drug taking" (Hyman and Nestler 1996: 158). Chronic overstimulation of postsynaptic DA receptors could lead to a new adaptive state, so continued use of the drug would be required to maintain homeostasis (Bolla, Cadet, and London 1998). Despite the lack of signs of physical dependence, animals that are given free access to cocaine will continue to self-administer the drug until death, something they will not do for opiates (Geary 1987). The *Merck Manual* (Berkow 1982: 1427) refers to cocaine as "probably the best example of a drug to which neither tolerance nor physical dependence develops, but to which psychic dependence develops that can lead to addiction." While the cocaine withdrawal syndrome does not generally require medical treatment or pharmacotherapy, the risk of relapse is highest during withdrawal (McCance 1997).

"Withdrawal in [cocaine-] dependent subjects is not characterized by the obvious physical signs like those observed with opiates or sedative-hypnotics" (Koob et al. 1994: 7). Indeed, "there is no withdrawal syndrome after abruptly stopping cocaine. That is, the body has never developed a need for cocaine to maintain homeostasis" (Washton and Stone-Washton 1993: 17). "The absence of a clear-cut withdrawal syndrome and serious medical risk following abrupt cessation of the drug use obviates the need either for switching the cocaine-dependent patient to a substitute drug or for having to detoxify the patient by means of a gradual withdrawal procedure, as is routinely done in the treatment of heroin addicts and severe alcoholics" (Washton, Stone, and Henrickson 1988: 376). However, one study found evidence of cardiac and mood-related symptoms during short-term abstinence from chronic crack use that could indicate specific withdrawal phenomena (Kajdasz et al. 1999).

Although tolerance can mask sensitization to cocaine-induced euphoria, craving persists. During early abstinence, persisting tolerance masks sensitization, but as tolerance wears off, sensitization becomes manifest as craving based on environmental cues increase (Bonson et al. 2002). Thus, abstinent cocaine users who are no longer experiencing withdrawal symptoms develop craving on returning to environments linked to the use of cocaine (discussed in Chapter 3). Research has revealed that cocaine-addicted patients respond to these cues "as if they were stressful situations, with the release of adrenaline and other hormones that increase pulse rate and blood pressure," and these responses take a long time to normalize, indicating that cocaine heightens sensitivity to stress (Whitten 2005: 1).

Medical Use of Cocaine

In addition to its anesthetizing qualities, cocaine constricts blood vessels when applied topically. It is the only local anesthetic that has this effect, and cocaine was the anesthetic of choice for eye surgery because of this ability to limit the flow of blood. However, when it was discovered that the reduced flow could damage the surface of the eye, cocaine was no longer recommended for use in ophthalmology. It continues to be used in surgery of the mucous membranes of the ear, nose, and throat and for procedures that require passing a tube through the nose or throat (Van Dyke and Byck 1982), about 200,000 operations a year (P. White 1989). Plastic surgeons use it for nose alterations.

Dangers of Cocaine Use

In "very small and occasional doses," argues Inciardi, "cocaine is no more harmful than equally moderate doses of alcohol or marijuana" (1986: 79). One research effort found that "experimental use of cocaine during adolescence has benign consequences over a one-year period," although the researchers could not deny the possibility of long-term negative consequences (Newcomb and Bentler 1986: 273). Large doses of cocaine, however, intensify each of the drug's reactions and can sometimes cause irrational behavior. In heavy abusers the euphoria is often accompanied by intensified heartbeat, sweating, dilation of pupils, and a rise in body temperature. After the initial euphoria, depression, irritability, insomnia, and, in more serious instances, paranoia may result. Extreme reactions, such as delirium, hallucinations, muscle spasms, and chest pain, may appear. In a small of number of people—the risk appears to be genetically determined—high levels of cocaine ingestion leads to a psychosis syndrome characterized by bizarre, paranoid agitation that frequently ends in death (Karch 1998).

Research indicates that cocaine users are four times more likely to develop a coronary aneurysm than are nonusers. Although coronary aneurysms rarely burst, they could set up cocaine users for a heart attack. The reasons are unclear, but researchers suspect that cocaine weakens the artery wall by causing sharp spikes in blood pressure and damaging cells in the inner walls of the heart's arteries (Altman 2005).

Chronic users can also suffer from "cocaine bugs" (**formication**, known as Magnon's syndrome), a sensation similar to that of bugs crawling under the skin. In extreme cases, the sensation can become so great that the user will cut open his or her skin to get at "them." Less extreme reactions cause the user to scratch and pick at the "bugs," causing sores.

When people mix cocaine and alcohol consumption, they are compounding the danger each drug poses and unknowingly performing a complex chemical experiment within their bodies. Researchers have found that the human liver combines cocaine and alcohol and manufactures a third substance, cocaethylene, which intensifies cocaine's euphoric effects while possibly increasing the risk of sudden death (National Institute on Drug Abuse 2001a).

Cardiac and Circulatory Dangers   Cocaine causes blood vessels to constrict and increases heart rate and blood pressure. As a result, the heart requires more oxygen-rich blood to nourish its muscle cells (Karch 1996). In people whose coronary arteries are narrowed by atherosclerosis, reactions can range from mild angina to a fatal heart attack. Even in people with normal coronary arteries, the ingesting of cocaine has resulted in angina and heart attacks that are believed to be consequences of spasms that reduce or shut off the flow of the oxygenated blood that nourishes the heart.

There is also evidence that cocaine can painlessly and permanently damage heart muscles: "Cocaine causes vascular disease. Vessels throughout the body can be involved, but the brunt of the injury is borne by the heart" (Karch 1996: 83). Several thousand people a year die as the result of sudden cardiac death induced by cocaine; the exact number is unknown because diagnosing the cause of death in such cases is quite difficult and the mechanism causing this fatal outcome is unknown (Karch 1996). Using advanced brain-scanning techniques, researchers have found that the temporary narrowing of blood vessels caused by cocaine results in a cumulative effect: More cocaine use leads to more narrowing of the arteries. This suggests that heavy cocaine users are susceptible to strokes, bleeding inside the brain, thinking and memory deficits, and other brain disorders (Bolla, Cadet, and London 1998; National Institute on Drug Abuse 1998d). The American Heart Association (1999) reports that cocaine use can lead to the development of aneurysms—ballooning-out of the wall of an artery—in heart arteries. An aneurysm in a heart artery can lead to a heart attack; an aneurysm in an artery of the brain could burst and trigger a stroke. Some aneurysms do not cause symptoms; others may cause chest pain and other coronary artery disease symptoms. The lack of judgment, unreliability, poor foresight, difficulty making decisions, disinhibition, apathy, euphoria, and irritability exhibited by chronic cocaine abusers appear to be related to damage the drug causes in the part of the brain (the prefrontal lobe) that controls or modifies these behaviors (Bolla, Cadet, and London 1998).

Crack Babies   Cocaine use by pregnant women has been linked to various abnormalities in their infants because the substance reduces the supply of blood and oxygen to the fetus (e.g., Mayes 1992; Woods 1993). Children born to crack-abusing mothers exhibit serious emotional difficulties that can hinder their psychological and social development (Blakeslee 1989).

But these difficulties are more likely caused by poor prenatal nutrition and health than by the pharmacology of cocaine. Researchers have had difficulty isolating maternal drug use from the typically negative environment in which the children are raised: "If you grow up in such a lousy environment, things are so bad already that cocaine exposure doesn't seem to make much difference" (Barry Lester quoted in Begley 1999: 62). More recent research has revealed that "snow babies" are neither the emotional and cognitive cripples that many predicted nor the perfectly normal kids that others have claimed. "Worries that 'crack babies' would never be able to function in society have turned out to be unfounded for the great majority" (Leshner 1999b: 3).

Crack or cocaine exposure in utero has not been demonstrated to affect physical growth and does not appear to independently affect developmental scores in the first six years of life (although there are insufficient data to assess this for infants born preterm). Findings are mixed regarding early motor development, but any effect appears to be transient and might, in fact, reflect tobacco exposure (Chavkin 2001). Preschool children of crack-using mothers do not appear to suffer any language or cognitive development problems. However, in one controlled study, they exhibited higher rates of emotional and behavioral problems than did children from similar backgrounds whose mothers did not use cocaine. It was not determined whether this is a function of the drug or the postnatal environment (Hawley, Halle, Drasin, and Thomas 1995). "The 'crack baby' became a convenient symbol for an aggressive war on drug users because of the implication that anyone who is selfish enough to irreparably damage an innocent child for the sake of a quick high deserves retribution. This image, promoted by the mass media, makes it easier to advocate a simplistic punitive response than to address the complex causes of drug use" (Chavkin 2001: 1627).

Because cocaine causes blood vessels to constrict, snorting can cause the cartilage in the middle of the nose to be deprived of oxygen. When the drug wears off, the tissue swells, which is why cocaine users frequently have stuffy, runny noses. Eventually, gradual deterioration of the nasal cartilage can cause the nose to collapse. The constriction of blood vessels in the nose also means a delay in the absorption of cocaine. Thus, intravenous injection of the drug is more efficient and quickly produces a powerful rush; it can also cause abscesses on the skin. This form of ingestion "produces the more debilitating effects of psychoses and paranoid delusions" (Inciardi 1986: 81) and is more likely than other forms of ingestion to have fatal results.

Cocaine and Sex   Although cocaine has the reputation of being an aphrodisiac, heavy use can cause male abusers to become impotent or incapable of ejaculation, and females can experience difficulty in reaching an orgasm. Freebasing and intravenous use increase sexual desire but not performance. In fact, cocaine may produce spontaneous ejaculation without sexual activity and can replace the sex partner of either gender (M. Gold et al. 1986).[3] Arnold Washton and Nanette Stone-Washton (1993) report that cocaine produced hypersexuality and sexual compulsivity in their patients, and "sexual feelings and fantasies often trigger powerful urges and cravings for cocaine." Crack cocaine has been associated with the spread of sexually transmitted diseases, especially AIDS, often the result of young women having unsafe sex with multiple partners in exchange for crack (Chitwood, Rivera, and Inciardi 1996).

Cognition   The detrimental effects of heavy cocaine use—two or more grams a week—on an individual's manual dexterity, problem solving, and other critical skills can last for up to a month after the drug was taken last. In one study, heavy cocaine users were outperformed by moderate users and nonusers on most tests measuring verbal memory, manual dexterity, and other cognitive skills. Although the intensity (measured in grams per week) of cocaine use was more closely associated with decreased performance than was duration of use, all cocaine users studied experienced reduced cognitive function. Dose-related effects were seen primarily on tasks involving the prefrontal cortex, which is the area of the brain most responsible for attention/concentration, planning, and reasoning. The heaviest cocaine users showed slower median reaction times and poorer attention and concentration (National Institute on Drug Abuse 1999g).

---

[3] Cocaine has anesthetic properties, however, and is sometimes applied directly to the head of the penis or to the clitoris to anesthetize the tissues, prolonging intercourse by retarding orgasm.

AMPHETAMINES

"Among the commonly used psychoactive drugs," note Grinspoon and Peter Hedblom (1975: 258), "the amphetamines have one of the most formidable potentials for psychological, physical, and social harm." Unlike cocaine, amphetamines are products of the laboratory—they are synthetic drugs. Although their chemical structures are distinctly different (Snyder 1986) and amphetamine has no anesthetic properties, the effects of cocaine and amphetamines are similar. In fact, experienced intravenous cocaine users frequently identified amphetamine incorrectly as cocaine. In animal studies, cocaine and amphetamines often substitute for one another and have similar reinforcing patterns of self-administration (Balster 1988).

Legally produced amphetamine is taken in the form of tablets or capsules. Some abusers will crush the substance, dissolve it in water, and ingest it intravenously. There are three basic types of amphetamine, the methyl-amphetamines having the greatest potential for abuse because they are fast acting and produce a rush. There are three types of methyl-amphetamine: dextro-methamphetamine (D-methamphetamine), dextro-levo-methamphetamine (D,L-methamphetamine), and levo-methamphetamine (L-methamphetamine). D-Methamphetamine is the most potent and widely abused form of methamphetamine in the United States today. It is a white, odorless, bitter-tasting crystalline powder that easily dissolves in water or alcohol (National Institute on Drug Abuse 1998a).

According to the World Health Organization, methamphetamine is second only to marijuana as the most abused drug in the world. Methamphetamine is known by many street names, such as "speed," "crank, "go," "crystal," "crystal meth," and "poor man's cocaine." It can be used by all of the common routes of illicit drug administration (inhalation, intranasal snorting, intravenous injection, or orally) but must be purified before it can be smoked. *Ice* is a purified form that is frequently sold as large crystals (rocks) that are smoked. Like rock salt in size and appearance, ice produces a high that is reputed to last from seven to twenty-four hours. Because of its purity, ice exaggerates all of the effects of methamphetamine. Overdoses are more common with ice because it is difficult for smokers to control the amount being inhaled. The substance could easily substitute for crack.

Ice rocks are made by melting methamphetamine crystals using a variety of techniques; "the turkey bag method" is the most popular: Dry methamphetamine crystals are placed in an aluminum turkey-roasting bag, which is then closed and dipped into boiling water until the methamphetamine melts. The melted material is then placed in cool water or in the refrigerator until it solidifies as a large crystal. The crystal is then cut into rocks that fit the various glass pipes that are used for smoking ice. Methamphetamine is usually smoked by inhaling it from a sheet of aluminum foil or through a glass pipe. When foil is used, the drug is heated in a crease of the foil until it vaporizes; it is then inhaled via a straw. Pipes for smoking D-methamphetamine differ from those used for smoking crack; methamphetamine vaporizes at a much lower temperature than crack does, so smoking it in a crack pipe at high heat would destroy it. Methamphetamine pipes have a large glass ball at the end for holding the methamphetamine, and a lighter is held under the ball to vaporize the drug. Airflow is regulated by a finger placed over a hole on the top of the pipe. Some users reportedly prefer glass pipes for smoking methamphetamine because they fear developing Alzheimer's disease from using aluminum foil (Lukas 1996).

With $500 worth of chemicals, laboratory glassware, and a rudimentary knowledge of chemistry, an outlaw chemist can easily produce a pound of methamphetamine worth $20,000 to $30,000. As a result, hundreds of clandestine laboratories have sprung up in remote regions throughout the United States. Recipes for manufacturing methamphetamine are widely available through pamphlets and the Internet. The clandestine manufacturing process has undergone substantial changes over the years. Phenyl-2-propanone (P2P), which was originally used in illegal manufacturing, is now controlled by the Drug Enforcement Administration as a bulk "immediate precursor" of methamphetamine. Accordingly, lab operators shifted to ephedrine, an ingredient that was common in over-the-counter cold and allergy remedies. Subsequent regulatory efforts led manufacturers to switch to the use of pseudoephedrine tablets. The yield from both methods is typically 70 percent of the precursor. Thus, one kilogram of ephedrine yields 700 grams of methamphetamine. The federal Combat Methamphetamine Epidemic Act of 2005 requires that over-the-counter pseudoephedrine products such as nasal decongestants be kept behind the counter. Purchasers must show a photo ID and can buy only a limited supply. Purchases are logged so that law enforcement agencies can monitor the amount of pseudoephedrine being purchased at a particular location.

During the 1980s, clandestine manufacturers using the precursor chemical pseudoephedrine created D-methamphetamine. For the user, D-methamphetamine not only is significantly more potent than other forms, but also has fewer adverse side effects. D-Methamphetamine eventually became the predominant form of methamphetamine illegally manufactured in the so-called superlabs in the Central Valley of California or by Mexican polydrug trafficking organizations (discussed in Chapter 11). The rest, about 20 percent, is produced in the small labs of rural America (Butterfield 2005).

D-Methamphetamine is clandestinely manufactured by using the ephedrine or pseudoephedrine reduction method, producing quantities of up to 200 pounds at a time. The manufacturing process is fairly simple, though quite dangerous, and almost all the necessary ingredients are easily attainable either through commercial sources or by producing the chemicals clandestinely. Some chemists die as a result of the toxic fumes produced or from explosions that can easily be ignited by a tiny spark or even the flip of a light switch. Illegal methamphetamine production also poses a serious environmental problem, because outlaws dump the chemical wastes into local streams or lakes or bury it in ditches. Methamphetamine labs are so contaminated that they pose a risk to the law enforcement officers who seize them. Home-based labs present a danger to all who live anywhere in the house, particularly children (Butterfield 2004a).

Amphetamine/Methamphetamine: Uses and Effects

Classification: Stimulant

CSA Schedule: Schedule II

Trade or Other Names: Biphetamine, Desoxyn, Dexedrine, Obetrol, ice

Medical Uses: Attention–deficit/hyperactivity disorder, narcolepsy, weight control

Physical Dependence: Possible

Psychological Dependence: High

Tolerance: Yes

Duration (hours): 2–4

Usual Method: Oral, injected, smoked

Possible Effects: Increased alertness, excitation, euphoria, increased pulse rate and blood pressure, insomnia, loss of appetite

Effects of Overdose: Agitation, increased body temperature, hallucinations, convulsions, possible death

Withdrawal Syndrome: Apathy, long periods of sleep, irritability, depression, disorientation

Source: Drug Enforcement Administration.

Effects of Amphetamines

Methamphetamine accelerates the body's metabolism and produces euphoria, increases alertness, and gives the abuser a sense of increased energy. It can enable a shy person to become more outgoing and a tired person to become energized. Its ability to produce intensified feelings of sexual desire can, at least in part, explain it popularity. Although methamphetamine can impair the ability to operate a motor vehicle, truck drivers often abuse it to keep them awake during long hauls. The driver risks suddenly being rendered unconscious during the "crash" stage of methamphetamine use (discussed later).

Experiments have shown that when given a choice, animals will readily operate pumps that inject them with amphetamine and will work hard to get more of the drug. Rhesus monkeys that are given unlimited access to amphetamine will continually ingest the substance day and night, going almost completely without water, food, or sleep for six to eight days, until they collapse into exhausted sleep for two days. On waking, they show an immediate interest in food and water and then embark on another week-long binge of amphetamine. When access to the drug is discontinued for a few weeks and the monkeys are returned to their cages, they will push the (now nonoperative) buttons for amphetamine an average of 4,000 times, indicating that a significant level of craving exists even in the absence of physiological dependence. When the substance is heroin, the monkeys will press the nonoperative buttons an average of 2,000 times, indicating that the craving for amphetamine is higher than that for heroin (Grinspoon and Hedblom 1975).

Methamphetamine stimulates by triggering the release of dopamine, serotonin, and norepinephrine while inhibiting their reuptake (Selden et al. 1993). Thus, like cocaine, methamphetamine mimics naturally occurring substances and causes a biochemical arousal—a "turn on"—without the presence of sensory input requiring such arousal. The body becomes physiologically activated, but it is a false alarm. Because reuptake is blocked, the depletion of the body's stimulating neurotransmitters is believed to be responsible for the crash that results after the ingestion of high doses of amphetamine. The abuser becomes almost lifeless for one or more days, and the body uses the crash to replenish its depleted supply.

As with cocaine, in small doses methamphetamine results in illusions of increased mental and sensory alertness and physical strength, an indifference to pain, and a "rush" or "flash" that lasts a few minutes and is described as extremely pleasurable. The rush is the initial response the user feels when smoking or injecting methamphetamine and is the aspect of the drug that low-intensity users do not experience when snorting or swallowing the drug. During the rush, the user's heartbeat races and metabolism, blood pressure, and pulse soar, and the user can experience feelings that have been described in terms of multiple orgasms. Unlike the rush associated with crack cocaine, which lasts for approximately two to five minutes, the methamphetamine rush can continue for five to thirty minutes. The rush is a result of methamphetamine triggering the adrenal gland to release epinephrine (adrenaline), a hormone that puts the body in a fight-or-flight mode. As with cocaine, the body feels the chemistry of fright, tension, and anxiety, but the brain gives the message that everything is better than fine because methamphetamine causes the explosive release of dopamine in the pleasure center of the brain. After the rush, a high ensues, during which the user feels euphoric, energized, and aggressively smarter; he or she may become argumentative, often interrupting other people and finishing their sentences. The high can last four to sixteen hours. Snorting or oral ingestion produces a high but not an intense rush. Snorting produces effects within three to five minutes, and oral ingestion produces effects within fifteen to twenty minutes.

Booty-Bumping

Anal insertion of methamphetamine, known in the gay community as "booty-bumping," results in the substance passing quickly though anal tissue, causing physical and psychological stimulation that leads to a likelihood of hypersexual anal activity (Halkitis, Parsons, and Wilton 2003).

Taken episodically and in low doses, amphetamine can enhance sexual drive and performance; used habitually at high dosage, it can impair sexual functioning. In some abusers it provides a substitute for sex (D. E. Smith 1979). Grinspoon and Hedblom (1975: 103) state that although some people experience improved sexual performance, which might be an important reason for its popularity, "amphetamines are particularly dangerous in the hands of people whose sexuality is abnormal or overtly perverse" because the drugs appear to obliterate conventional restraints. The "crystal meth" version has proven popular in the gay community and is associated with the transmission of HIV/AIDS among gay males who take it with Viagra or similar drugs and engage in unprotected sex with multiple partners. The substance is also thought to cripple immune system functioning (A. O'Connor 2005).

Methamphetamine Tolerance and Withdrawal

Tolerance does not develop to all effects of methamphetamine at the same rate; indeed, there may be increased sensitivity to some of them. For the high-intensity user, each successive rush becomes less euphoric, and it takes more methamphetamine to achieve it. Likewise, each high is not quite as strong as the one before, and the user needs more methamphetamine more often to get a high that is not as good as the last one. "Because tolerance for methamphetamine occurs within minutes—meaning that the pleasurable effects disappear even before the drug concentration in the blood falls significantly—users try to maintain the high by binging on the drug" (National Institute on Drug Abuse 1999b: 3–4).

The most common symptoms of withdrawal among heavy amphetamine users are fatigue, long but troubled sleep, irritability, intense hunger, and moderate to severe depression, which can lead to suicidal behavior. Fits of violence may also occur. These disturbances can be temporarily reversed if the drug is taken again. Less systematic users experience no acute, immediate symptoms of physical distress during methamphetamine withdrawal, a stage that the abuser might enter slowly. Often, thirty to ninety days must pass after the last drug use before the abuser realizes that he or she is in withdrawal. First, without really noticing, the individual becomes depressed, loses the ability to experience pleasure, becomes lethargic, and has no energy. Then the craving for more methamphetamine hits.

Medical Use of Amphetamines

Because amphetamines appear to act on the hypothalamus to suppress the appetite—although other CNS or metabolic effects may be involved—at one time the drugs were widely prescribed to treat obesity. In contrast to more natural forms of dieting, however, the appetite returns with greater intensity after withdrawal from the drug, and it is only as a last resort that methamphetamine hydrochloride (Desoxyn) is used to treat obesity as one component of a weight reduction regimen; even then, the treatment is limited to only a few weeks.

As it became known that most of the benefits from treating many ailments with amphetamine were due to the drug's ability to elevate mood, medically accepted uses declined. Besides obesity, there are only two such uses in the United States: for treating narcolepsy, a sleeping disorder that affects about 250,000 Americans and is usually treated with Dexedrine, and certain types of hyperactivity—hyperkinetic syndrome—in children with minimal brain damage or adolescent attention deficit/hyperactivity disorder (ADHD) when other remedies have proven insufficient. About 3 to 5 percent of the general population has ADHD, which is characterized by agitated behavior and an inability to focus on tasks. Paradoxically, in children with ADHD these drugs produce a calming effect, and tolerance does not develop; these children have no exceptional risk for drug abuse problems in later life.

Ritalin (methylphenidate), which has effects similar to those of amphetamines but is less potent, is often the preferred drug for treating ADHD.

Methamphetamine Versus Cocaine

Methamphetamine is structurally similar to the neurotransmitter dopamine, but it is quite different from cocaine. Although these stimulants have similar behavioral and physiological effects, there are some major differences in the basic mechanisms of how they work at the level of the nerve cell. However, the bottom line is that methamphetamine, like cocaine, results in an accumulation of the neurotransmitter dopamine, and this excessive dopamine concentration appears to produce the stimulation and feelings of euphoria that the user experiences. In contrast to cocaine, which is quickly removed and almost completely metabolized in the body, methamphetamine has a much longer duration of action, and a larger percentage of the drug remains unchanged in the body. This results in methamphetamine being present in the brain for a longer time, which ultimately leads to prolonged stimulant effects (National Institute on Drug Abuse 2002a).

Researchers speculate that methylphenidate amplifies the release of dopamine, thereby improving attention and focus in individuals who have dopamine signals that are weak, such as individuals with ADHD. When taken as prescribed, methylphenidate is a valuable medicine. Research shows that people with ADHD do not become addicted to stimulant medications when they are taken in the form prescribed and at treatment dosages. Another study found that boys with ADHD who are treated with stimulants such as methylphenidate are significantly less likely to abuse drugs and alcohol when they are older than are nontreated boys with ADHD ("Methylphenidate" 2001).

Because of its stimulant properties, however, in recent years there have been reports of abuse of methylphenidate by people for whom it is not a medication. Some individuals abuse it for its stimulant effects: appetite suppression, wakefulness, increased focus/attentiveness, and euphoria. When abused, the tablets are either taken orally or crushed and snorted. Some abusers dissolve the tablets in water and inject the mixture; complications can arise from this because insoluble fillers in the tablets can block small blood vessels (National Institute on Drug Abuse 2001e). There are reports of Ritalin being used illegally by college students, often as an aid in staying awake for late night studying during exam week (Zielbauer 2000).

Amphetamine continues to have military uses; for instance, the U.S. Air Force provided it to air crews during the Persian Gulf War. "More that sixty percent of the pilots who used the drug said it was 'essential' to accomplishing their mission" (Groopman 2001: 53; Rosenkranz 2003).

Dangers of Methamphetamine Use

A small amount of methamphetamine can increase breathing and heart rates, cause heart palpitations, and provoke anxiety or nervousness. Higher doses can make these effects more intense. Headaches, dizziness, and a rapid or

Ritalin: Uses and Effects

Classification: Stimulant

CSA Schedule: Schedule II

Trade or Other Names: Methylphenidate

Medical Uses: Attention-deficit/hyperactivity disorder, narcolepsy

Physical Dependence: Possible

Psychological Dependence: High

Tolerance: Yes

Duration (hours): 2–4

Usual Method: Oral, injected

Possible Effects: Increased alertness, excitation, euphoria, increased pulse rate and blood pressure, insomnia, loss of appetite

Effects of Overdose: Agitation, increased body temperature, hallucinations, convulsions, possible death

Withdrawal Syndrome: Apathy, long periods of sleep, irritability, depression, disorientation

Source: U.S. Drug Enforcement Administration.

irregular heartbeat can occur. Some users become hostile and aggressive. Methamphetamine often causes hypothermia with renal failure that can be fatal. Although less commonly than with cocaine, methamphetamine use can lead to heart failure (Karch 1996). Using amphetamines over a long period of time can cause some health problems. With increased doses, users may become talkative, restless, and excited and may feel a sense of power and superiority. With prolonged use, the short-term effects are exaggerated.

Because methamphetamine suppresses appetite, chronic heavy users generally fail to eat properly and thus develop various illnesses related to vitamin deficiencies and malnutrition. They may also be more prone to illness because they are generally run down, lack sleep, and live in an unhealthy environment. Chronic heavy users may also develop a drug-induced psychosis, a mental disturbance that is very similar to paranoid schizophrenia. The condition is an exaggeration of the short-term effects of high doses. Symptoms include hearing voices and paranoia—delusions that other people are threatening or persecuting the person. Heavy users may be prone to sudden, violent, and irrational acts. Herbert Meltzer (1979: 156) notes that "normal volunteers screened to exclude any subjects with schizophrenic symptoms will become psychotic within 1 day if given repeated doses of amphetamine totaling several hundred milligrams." Symptoms of psychosis at an abated level can persist for some time after the drug is discontinued (Institute for the Study of Drug Dependence 1987).

"Meth Mouth"

In rural America, where methamphetamine has had a significant impact, dentists have been treating the ravaged teeth of the drug's abusers. Although it is not clear what is causing this condition, there are hypotheses: The substance causes dry mouth, and the lack of saliva promotes the growth of bacteria; the drug causes thirst, and users crave a constant supply of sugary drinks that spur decay; caustic ingredients used in the drug's manufacture contribute to the damage when "meth" users tend to grind and clench their teeth nervously, aggravating already damaged gums and teeth (Davey 2005).

The heightened feelings of energy combined with a significant lowering of social restraints on unconventional or aggressive behavior can, in some people and/or in some situations, lead to extremely violent behavior: "Under the influence of speed even the most normally lethargic person *must* do something, even if it is as boring and repetitive as stringing beads for hours. When such a deep and insistent need to do *something* is thought to be disapproved or blocked, the speed abuser may attack the perceived thwarter with murderous rage" (Grinspoon and Hedblom 1975: 204). The symptoms usually disappear within a few days or weeks after drug use is stopped. Methamphetamine increases the libido and is associated with rougher sex that might lead to bleeding and abrasions, increasing the danger of HIV/AIDS transmission (National Institute on Drug Abuse 1998a).

Methamphetamine poisoning or overdose can cause brain hemorrhage, heart attack, high fever, coma, and occasionally death; however, most methamphetamine-associated deaths are due to accidents while the person is under the influence of the drug. Methamphetamine may contain substances that do not easily dissolve in water. When users inject the drug, these particles can pass into the body and block small blood vessels or weaken the blood vessel walls. Kidney damage, lung problems, strokes, or other tissue injury can result. There is also the danger of acute lead poisoning because a common method of production uses lead acetate as a reagent (National Institute on Drug Abuse 1998a).

Methamphetamine at doses abused by humans leads to dopamine transporter reductions in the brain, and this reduction is associated with the functional impairment experienced by those with Parkinson's disease (Volkow et al. 2001). Research indicates that methamphetamine also causes damage to nerve endings of dopamine-containing cells and persists for years after drug use has stopped. The damage is similar to that caused by Parkinson's disease but less extensive.

In laboratory experiments, a single exposure to methamphetamine at high doses or prolonged use at low doses destroyed up to 50 percent of the brain cells that use dopamine. Although this damage might not be immediately apparent, scientists believe that with aging or exposure to other toxic agents,

Parkinson symptoms may eventually emerge. These symptoms begin with lack of coordination and tremors and may eventually result in a form of paralysis. Methamphetamine users risk long-term brain damage, since methamphetamine amplifies a process known as *apoptosis*, by which the brain culls defective cells, to the point at which healthy cells are also eliminated (Mathias 2000; Zickler 2000a). These results provide evidence that methamphetamine at dose levels taken by human abusers of the drug leads to dopamine transporter reduction that is associated with motor and cognitive impairment (Volkow et al. 2001).

Little research has been done in humans into the effects of amphetamine use on pregnancy and fetal growth, although experiments with animals suggest that use during pregnancy might produce adverse behavioral effects.

NICOTINE

Nicotine is one of more than 4,000 chemicals found in the smoke from tobacco; smokeless tobacco also contains a high level of nicotine (National Institute on Drug Abuse 1998b). About 1 percent of the weight of tobacco leaf is nicotine, and if all the nicotine in one cigarette were absorbed quickly into the body, the effect would be toxic and even fatal (A. Goldstein 2001). Most American cigarettes contain at least ten milligrams of nicotine, and the average smoker, through inhalation, takes in one to two milligrams per cigarette. Nicotine is absorbed through the skin and mucosal lining of the mouth and nose by inhalation into the lungs (National Institute on Drug Abuse 2001d).

Effects of Nicotine

After each inhalation from a cigarette, within ten seconds the brain is swamped by a new drug spike (A. Goldstein 2001). Immediately after ingestion there is a "kick" that results in part from stimulation of the adrenal glands and resulting discharge of epinephrine (adrenaline). Depending on the level of CNS arousal and the dose of nicotine taken, as with alcohol, the nicotine can also exert a sedative effect (National Institute on Drug Abuse 2001d).

The manner in which nicotine produces behavioral and cognitive effects is quite complex (see, e.g., McGehee et al. 1995). Like other stimulants, particular CNS receptors have an affinity for nicotine. As is the case with other psychoactive drugs, nicotine attaches to these (nicotinic cholinergic) receptors located on the surface of neurons, triggering the release of stimulating neurotransmitters such as acetylcholine and glutamate. In addition, nicotine indirectly causes a release of dopamine in the brain regions that control pleasure and motivation. This reaction is similar to that seen with other drugs of abuse, such as cocaine and heroin, and is thought to underlie the pleasurable sensations that many smokers experience.

Immediately after exposure to nicotine, there is a "kick" that is caused in part by the drug's stimulation of the adrenal glands and resulting discharge of epinephrine (adrenaline). The rush of adrenaline stimulates the body and causes a sudden release of glucose as well as an increase in blood pressure, respiration, and heart rate. Nicotine also suppresses insulin output from the pancreas, which means that smokers are always slightly hyperglycemic. "In addition, nicotine indirectly causes a release of dopamine in the brain regions that control pleasure and motivation" (Society for Neuroscience 2002: 33). Nicotine also acts on a group of regulatory cells whose job is to control the dopamine response. When these mechanisms are disabled, the reward system continues to operate long after it should normally have shut down, causing a high that can last an hour (Kotulak 2002a). Furthermore, some tobacco smoke ingredient other than nicotine, decreases levels of the MAO enzyme, which exists in forms A and B. Cigarette smokers have a 40 percent MAO-B deficiency, causing the dopamine triggered by nicotine to remain active and thus enhancing its impact (National Institute on Drug Abuse 2001d).

This characteristic of smoking cigarettes indicates that it might be a **gateway drug** leading to addiction to other drugs of abuse (Glassman and Koob 1996). Cigarette use typically precedes the use of illegal substances (Clymer 1994), and people who abuse heroin and cocaine are more likely to also be tobacco smokers than is the rest of the population (Zickler 2000b). Research has revealed that children who have never smoked are certain not to use heroin or cocaine, while a significant proportion of children who smoke heavily have used these drugs, and many have become drug-dependent (Center on Addiction and Substance Abuse 1994). The stimulating effects of nicotine are followed by depression and fatigue, leading the user to seek more nicotine, an explanation for chain-smoking (National Institute on Drug Abuse 2004).

As with other psychoactive substances, research has revealed that the use of nicotine might be a form of self-medication, smokers using nicotine to ward off depression; antidepressants can often help hardcore depressed smokers to quit (Brody 1997). And as is the case with alcohol, discussed in Chapter 4, genetics seem to play a role in the predisposition to nicotine dependence: "People with a gene variant in a particular enzyme metabolize or break down nicotine in the body more slowly and are significantly less likely to become addicted to nicotine than people without the variant" (Mathias 1999: 5; see also Zickler 2003). Research has discovered that prenatal exposure to tobacco is a significant risk factor for early substance abuse among preadolescents (National Institute on Drug Abuse 1997c).

Smoking is also a hazard to those who are exposed to secondhand smoke, a 1986 finding by the U.S. Surgeon General that was confirmed in 2006:

- There is no safe level of secondhand smoke, and even brief exposure can be harmful, especially to children, pregnant women, and those with respiratory diseases.
- For nonsmoking adults exposure to secondhand smoke raises the risk of heart disease by 25 percent and the risk of cancer by 20 to 30 percent (O'Neil 2006).

Craving and Brain Injury

In 2007, researchers revealed that the craving for nicotine appears to be contained in the insula, a prune-size region under the frontal lobs of the brain near the ear. Chronic smokers who have suffered a stroke that injured the insula no longer have any desire to smoke cigarettes (Carey 2007). Injury to the insula can also lead to apathy and loss of libido. The insula is important for anticipating events and becomes activated when an addict experiences stimuli associated with drug use (Blakeslee 2007).

In contrast to cocaine and amphetamine, nicotine can also exert a sedative effect, depending on the level of the smoker's nervous system arousal and the dose of nicotine taken. At high doses there is evidence that nicotine might actually block cholinergic transmission, preventing the release of the neurotransmitter acetylcholine and producing sedation. Many users report a calming effect; this might be related to nicotine's ability to activate cells in the spinal cord that reduce muscle tone and thus serves as a muscle relaxant. It also reduces appetite, although this might be at least partially offset by a decrease in metabolic rate.

Cigarette smoking "produces a rapid distribution of nicotine to the brain, with drug levels peaking with 10 seconds of inhalation. The acute effects of nicotine dissipate in a few minutes, causing the smoker to continue dosing frequently throughout the day to maintain the drug's pleasurable effects and prevent withdrawal" A typical smoker "will take 10 puffs on a cigarette over a period of 5 minutes that the cigarette is lit. Thus, a person who smokes about 1.5 packs (30 cigarettes) daily, gets 300 'hits' of nicotine to the brain each day" (National Institute on Drug Abuse 2001d: 2).

The addictive nature of nicotine is highlighted by the difficulty smokers exhibit in attempting abstinence. Fewer than 7 percent of smokers who try to quit on their own achieve more than one year of abstinence, and most relapse within a few days of attempting to quit. As humorist Will Rogers (1879–1935) quipped: "Quitting smoking is easy; I've done it hundreds of times." Chronic use of nicotine products such as cigarettes produces physiological and/or psychological dependence. These smokers experience heightened stress between cigarettes, and smoking briefly restores their stress levels to normal; the apparent mood benefits reflect relief of withdrawal symptoms (Parrott 1999). An estimated 62 million Americans smoke, and an additional 6.8 million use smokeless tobacco (National Institute on Drug Abuse 2001d).

Addiction to nicotine is influenced by gender. For men, the "compulsion to smoke is driven more strongly by nicotine's pharmacological effects on the brain, while women's addiction owes more to the visual, tactile, taste, and olfactory sensations" (G. R. Hanson 2002a: 4).

Chewing Tobacco
He was one of the world's best saddle bronc riders on the rodeo circuit. When he died at age 47, his throat cancer was so bad that it had wrapped around his jugular vein and got into his brain. His family brought a lawsuit against the nation's leading manufacturer of chewing tobacco, which is also the oldest sponsor of the rodeo (Egan 2004).

Nicotine Tolerance and Withdrawal

Repeated exposure to nicotine results in the development of tolerance, and higher doses of the drug are required to produce the same initial stimulation. Nicotine is metabolized fairly rapidly, disappearing from the body in a few hours. Although some tolerance is lost overnight, smokers often report that the first cigarette of the day is the strongest and/or the "best," indicating that it relieves the discomfort of withdrawal. As the day progresses, acute tolerance develops, and later cigarettes have less effect. Tolerance produces withdrawal symptoms when the consumption of nicotine ceases: slowing of brain activity, restless sleep, decreased heart rate and thyroid functioning, anxiety, anger, cognitive and attentional deficits, and increased appetite (J. R. Hughes 1990).

Withdrawal may begin within a few hours after the last cigarette, and symptoms peak within the first few days and may subside within a few weeks. For some people, however, symptoms persist for months or longer (National Institute on Drug Abuse 1997c). "Dramatic changes in the brain's pleasure circuits during withdrawal from chronic nicotine use rival the magnitude and duration of similar changes observed during withdrawal from other abused drugs such as cocaine, opiates, amphetamines, and alcohol" (National Institute on Drug Abuse 1998c: 1). Failure to continue the ingestion of nicotine causes severe craving, which can last for six months or longer—a major reason for relapse (National Institute on Drug Abuse 1998b).

The craving for nicotine is an important but poorly understood component of the withdrawal syndrome that has been described as a major obstacle to successful abstinence. Although the withdrawal syndrome is related to the pharmacological effects of nicotine, many behavioral factors also can affect the severity of withdrawal symptoms. For some people the feel, smell, and sight of a cigarette and the ritual of obtaining, handling, lighting, and smoking the cigarette are associated with the pleasurable effects of smoking and can make withdrawal or craving worse. Although nicotine gum and patches may alleviate the pharmacological aspects of withdrawal, cravings often persist.

Dangers of Nicotine Use

The medical consequences of nicotine exposure result from effects of both the nicotine itself and how it is taken. The most deleterious effects of nicotine addiction are the result of smoking cigarettes, which accounts for one third of all cancers, particularly lung cancer. Cigarette smoking has been linked to about 90 percent of all lung cancer cases, and lung cancer is the nation's single leading cause of death and disability (Brody 2001). Smoking also causes lung diseases such as chronic bronchitis and emphysema, and it has been found to exacerbate asthma symptoms in adults and children. Smoking is also associated with cancers of the mouth, pharynx, larynx, esophagus, stomach, pancreas, cervix, kidney, ureter, and bladder. About 440,000 people die annually from the deadly effects of tobacco smoke.

Environmental Tobacco Smoke

According to the American Lung Association, environmental tobacco smoke, or ETS (sometimes referred to as secondhand smoke), is believed responsible for 35,500 nonsmoker deaths a year from heart disease. ETS can cause irritation of the eyes, nose, throat, and lungs, which can lead to coughing, an achiness in the chest, and excessive phlegm production. People who are exposed to secondhand smoke are more likely to have serious health problems, including lung cancer, cardio-vascular disease, low birth weight, sudden infant death syndrome, asthma, bronchitis, pneumonia, middle ear infections, and nasal and eye irritation.

Children whose bodies are still developing are especially vulnerable to ETS; effects include ear infections, croup, bronchitis, tonsillitis, and even cancers and leukemias. ETS is a risk factor for child behavior problems, such as acting out, hyperactivity, and disruptive types of behaviors. Children who are exposed to higher levels of ETS exhibited more depression, withdrawal, and anxiety-type behaviors. Exposure to secondhand smoke was also found to negatively affect a child's reading and math skills (Kirkey 2006).

In 1999 it was revealed that cigar smokers are twice as likely to get cancer of the mouth, throat, and lungs, as nonsmokers are (Associated Press 1999d). The overall rates of death from cancer are twice as high among smokers as among nonsmokers, heavy smokers having rates that are four times greater than those of nonsmokers (National Institute on Drug Abuse 2004).

Preliminary research has linked cigarette smoking by fathers to an increased risk of brain cancer and leukemia in their offspring, and children whose parents smoke are three to four times more likely to develop serious infectious diseases. An estimated 5,600 infant deaths are caused by smoking among pregnant women (Associated Press 1995). Nicotine affects the blood vessels in the placenta, interfering with oxygen supply to the fetus (A. Goldstein 2001). According to a study by Laurence Namur, newborns whose mothers smoke during pregnancy have the same nicotine level as adult smokers and spend the first few days of life going through withdrawal (Associated Press 1997a). In addition, research in 2001 found that prenatal exposure to smoke could predispose children to early smoking experimentation. The researchers speculate that maternal smoking during pregnancy causes disturbances in the neurophysiological functioning of the fetus (Thomas 2001). There is also considerable research indicating that children whose mothers smoke during pregnancy are at much greater risk than other children for drug abuse and conduct disorder (Varisco 2000). The toxic effects of prenatal exposure to nicotine has been found to include lower IQ and increased risk of developing ADHD (Williams 2004).

In addition to the ability of smoking to cause cancer, a relationship between cigarette smoking and coronary heart disease was first reported in the 1940s. Since that time, it has been well documented that smoking substantially

"Soft" on Smoking

Smoking affects erectile performance. Men who smoke a pack or more per day have a 40 percent greater risk of erectile dysfunction. Nicotine is a vasoconstrictor (i.e., it tightens blood vessels and restricts blood flow) that has been shown to cause permanent damage to arteries. Because a man's erection depends on blood flow, researchers theorized that smoking would affect erections, and studies have confirmed this. Although young smokers might not notice negative effects, their sexual futures could be limp.

increases the risk of heart disease, including stroke, heart attack, vascular disease, and aneurysm. It is estimated that nearly one fifth of deaths from heart disease are attributable to smoking (National Institute on Drug Abuse 2004). There is also the problem of passive or secondhand smoke, which is a major source of indoor air contaminants.

Nicotine causes blood vessels in the skin to constrict, reducing blood and oxygen supplies to the extremities—an obvious detriment in high-energy sports—and might be the reason why the skin of cigarette smokers tends to be more wrinkled than that of nonsmokers of the same age. As with heroin, nicotine stimulates centers of the brain cell that control vomiting, and new smokers may experience nausea.

According to researchers at the Centers for Disease Control and Prevention, because cigarette smoke makes it harder for the lungs to expel foreign material and easier for bacteria to stick, smokers are four times more likely than nonsmokers to get life-threatening blood infections or meningitis from bacteria that usually causes pneumonia. And the more cigarettes a person smokes, the higher is the risk of an infection. The researchers noted that former smokers have an increased risk of the infection for at least ten years after they quit (McConnaughey 2000).

HERBAL STIMULANTS

So-called herbal stimulants, particularly **ephedra** (also known by its Chinese name *ma huang*), are sold in the form of pills in many health food stores under a variety of brand names. Ephedra contains **ephedrine**, which is an amphetamine precursor and is produced as a stimulant in nonprescription asthma and some cold and allergy medicine. Sometimes other ephedra derivatives and caffeine are added to increase its stimulating properties. Within twenty minutes of taking the substance, there is a jump in the heart rate and blood pressure. One popular brand is called Herbal Ecstasy, although it is not related to MDMA (ecstasy) (discussed in Chapter 6).

Herbal substances are used by young people as a "safe" alternative to illegal drugs. Ephedra products are promoted as health and exercise supplements and have been linked to athlete deaths (Hobson 2002). Because it is classified as a dietary supplement, not a drug, ephedra is not subject to Food and Drug Administration (FDA) regulation, although some states have passed restrictions because of reports of deaths that were believed related to herbal products containing ephedrine. The 1994 Dietary Supplement Health and Education Act was passed as the result of an effective lobbying campaign by the food supplement industry. The statute deregulated the industry and now permits the marketing of any supplement until the FDA is able to prove that it is unsafe. The law also enables companies to make unrestrained and unjustified health claims. Adverse physical reactions to herbal supplements include liver failure, elevated blood pressure, heart palpitations, and strokes (Burros and Jay 1996; G. Crowley 1996; Kolata 1996; Lambert 1996).

CAFFEINE

Caffeine—found in tea, coffee, many cola drinks, cocoa products, and pain relievers—is the most widely used psychoactive drug; about 90 percent of the adult North American population ingests caffeine regularly. After ingestion of caffeine, the chemical's compounds dissolve in the bloodstream and travel to the brain. Caffeine molecules are almost identical to those of the neurotransmitter adenosine, which controls the release of other chemicals that excite the central nervous system and thus acts as a natural "sleeping pill" (Reid 2005). Caffeine occupies adenosine receptor sites in the brain, neutralizing its hypnotic function.

The result is an elevation of mood, a decrease in fatigue, and, in high doses, insomnia and a racing heart. Abrupt withdrawal of caffeine can result in headaches, lethargy, and depressionlike symptoms (Griffiths 1990; Griffiths et al. 1990; Blakeslee 1991, 1994; "Quitting Caffeine Can Bring on the Blahs" 1991)—hence a person's *need* for that first cup of coffee in the morning. Withdrawal symptoms disappear in two to four days but can last up to a week (Reid 2005). Research has revealed that drinking two cups of coffee a day has some health benefits for adults.

Caffeine is routinely served to children as an ingredient in sodas and chocolate bars. "In fact, most babies in the developed world enter the universe with traces of caffeine in their bodies, a transfer through the umbilical cord from the mother's latte or Snapple." There is no evidence, however, that caffeine in small doses is unsafe for children (Reid 2005: 13).

SUMMARY

In moderation stimulants enhance mood, increase alertness, and relieve fatigue. Short-term euphoria may result in a desire to ingest again. Powerful stimulants, such as cocaine and methamphetamine, have limited medical use and in large doses can produce irrational behavior and paranoia. Discontinuing their use can cause depression as a result of a dopamine depletion. Cocaine is a blood vessel constrictor, and heavy use can lead to heart failure.

Although chemically quite different than cocaine, amphetamine has similar effects. Methamphetamine is easy but dangerous to produce; the chemicals are toxic and highly combustible. In addition to use for the euphoric effects, amphetamines have been used as diet aids and by long-haul truck drivers to ward off sleepiness. Methamphetamine poisoning or overdose can cause brain hemorrhage, heart attack, high fever, coma, and occasionally death.

Nicotine is a highly addictive substance whose methods of ingestion—smoking and chewing—are associated with secondary dangers such as cancer and emphysema. Smoking serves as a gateway drug for heroin and cocaine. As with other psychoactive chemicals, use of nicotine may be a form of self-medication to ward off depression. In contrast to cocaine and amphetamine, nicotine can also exert a sedative effect, depending on the level of the smoker's nervous system arousal and the dose of nicotine taken. Tolerance develops to nicotine, and those who are addicted must start each day with a cigarette to ward off withdrawal symptoms.

Caffeine is the most widely used stimulant and has all of the characteristics of other stimulants but in much milder form. There do not appear to be any long-term dangers to its use.

REVIEW QUESTIONS

1. What impact do stimulants have on a user?
2. How can dependence on cocaine be explained by a neurotransmitter deficiency?
3. What naturally occurring phenomena does cocaine imitate?
4. What is the typical reaction to small doses of cocaine?
5. What are the possible negative reactions to heavy use of cocaine?
6. Why do some cocaine users prefer crack?
7. What are the possible effects of cocaine on sexual activity?
8. What are the differences between the effects of cocaine hydrochloride and those of crack?
9. In what ways are the effects of methamphetamine and cocaine similar?
10. Why is the use of methamphetamine by certain people dangerous?
11. How does nicotine differ from other CNS stimulants?
12. What are herbal stimulants?
13. How is caffeine similar to other CNS stimulants?

Hallucinogens, Club Drugs, Marijuana, and Inhalants

Hallucination: Perception of visual, auditory, tactile, olfactory, or gustatory experiences without an external stimulus and with a compelling sense of their reality.

American Heritage Dictionary (2000: 782)

"A hallucinogen is a drug that changes a person's state of awareness by modifying sensory inputs, loosening cognitive and creative restraints, and providing access to material normally hidden in memory or material of an unconscious nature" (Jacob and Shulgin 1994: 74). Hallucinogens can change a person's perception, making the person see or hear things that do not exist. They can also produce changes in thought, sense of time, and mood. According to Erich Goode (1972), the term *hallucinogen* implies something undesirable and suggests being "crazy." Supporters of the use of such chemicals prefer the term **psychedelic**.[1] "Under the influence of hallucinogens, people see images, hear sounds, and feel sensations that seem real but do not exist" (National Institute on Drug Abuse 1999a: 1).

Hallucinogenic substances occur both naturally and synthetically. They excite the central nervous system (CNS), overwhelming its ability to modulate sensory input. Autonomic hyperactivity results in distortions of the perception of objective reality. These include:

- *Depersonalization*: "Out-of-body" experiences or misperceptions of reality
- *Synesthesia*: "Seeing" sound and "hearing" visual input
- *Hallucinations*: Perceiving sounds, odors, tactile sensations, or visual images that arise from within the person, not the environment

The sensory illusions produced by hallucinogens are often accompanied by mood alterations that are usually euphoric but sometimes severely depressive (Drug Enforcement Administration 1989) and that mimic severe mental illness (National Institute on Drug Abuse 1987). Marked impairment of judgment can lead to poor decision making and serious accidents (Berkow 1982). A number of hallucinogens produce cross-tolerance. Unlike depressants and stimulants, hallucinogens do not function as reinforcers in animals (Winter 1994). Hallucinogens apparently have their own receptors ($5\text{-}HT_2$) in the CNS (Lin and Glennon 1994).

LYSERGIC ACID DIETHYLAMIDE (LSD)

Lysergic acid diethylamide (LSD) was synthesized in 1938. The first LSD "trip" was recorded by its discoverer, Albert Hofmann, a research chemist in Basel, Switzerland. In 1943 Hofmann accidentally ingested a minute quantity of the drug through the skin of his fingers (Grinspoon 1979). About this experience, Hofmann relates:

> I had to leave my work in the laboratory and go home because I felt strangely restless and dizzy. Once there, I lay down and sank into a not unpleasant delirium which was marked by an extreme degree of fantasy. In sort of a trance with closed eyes . . . fantastic visions of extraordinary vividness accompanied by a kaleidoscopic play of intense coloration continuously swirled around me. After two hours this condition subsided. (quoted in Goode 1972: 98–99)

---

[1] The term *psychedelic* was coined by research psychiatrist Humphrey Osmand in 1957.

Three days later Hofmann experimented by swallowing 250 micrograms of LSD, not realizing that this was an extremely high dose. He soon became terrified, fearing that he would lose his mind or perhaps die (Grinspoon 1979).

In 1949 LSD was introduced into the United States as an experimental drug for treating psychiatric illnesses, but until 1954 it remained relatively rare and expensive because the ergot fungus from which it was derived was difficult to cultivate. In that year the Eli Lily Company announced that it had succeeded in creating a totally synthetic version of LSD (J. Stevens 1987). So had outlaw chemists.

Pure, high-potency LSD is a clear or white odorless crystalline material that is soluble in water. It is mixed with binding agents, such as spray-dried skim milk, for producing tablets or is dissolved and diluted in a solvent for application onto paper or other materials. Variations in the manufacturing process or the presence of precursors or by-products can cause LSD to range in color from clear or white, in its purest form, to tan or even black, indicating poor quality or degradation. To mask product deficiencies and disguise discoloration, distributors often apply LSD to off-white, tan, or yellow paper.

LSD has a slightly bitter taste and is usually taken by mouth. Commonly referred to as "acid," LSD is sold on the street in tablet, capsules and, occasionally, liquid form. LSD is often added to absorbent paper ("blotter acid") and divided into small decorated squares, each square representing one dose. It may be mixed with any number of substances, sugar, or gelatin sheets ("window panes"). It takes only 0.01 milligram for LSD to have an effect.

Just how LSD works in not completely understood. "The molecular structure of LSD is similar to that of the neurotransmitter serotonin. LSD therefore has a high affinity for serotonin receptors and interferes with the normal functioning of these receptors" (Henderson 1994a: 42). Stimulation of serotonin receptors by agonists such as LSD and the hallucinogen psilocybin inhibits the activity of a mechanism (a neural system called the raphe) that modulates sensory input into the brain stem. This mechanism would normally integrate sensory inflow and the emotional and ideational state of the organism and suppress irrelevant information. Serotonin agonists occupy serotonin receptor sites in the brain and thereby cause a backup of serotonin that exceeds the ability of MAO to control serotonin. Serotonin overloads the sensory input systems of the CNS, so normal stimuli take on distorted images—the size of the signal delivered to the cerebral cortex is greatly enlarged. This combination—inhibition of control mechanisms and increasing signal size—overloads the brain (Ray 1978). The result is actually a serotonin, rather than LSD, trip and consists of intoxication for several hours (Palfai and Jankiewicz 1991).

Effects of LSD

LSD is absorbed easily from the gastrointestinal tract and rapidly reaches a high concentration in the blood. It is circulated throughout the body and subsequently to the brain. LSD is metabolized in the liver and is excreted in the urine in about twenty-four hours. The effects of LSD range from blurred vision to a visual field filled with strange objects. Three-dimensional space appears to contract and enlarge, and light appears to fluctuate in intensity. Auditory effects also occur but to a lesser degree. All of these changes are episodic. Temperature sensitivity is altered, the environment being perceived as abnormally cold or hot. Body images are altered (out of-body experiences), and body parts appear to float. Time is sometimes perceived as running fast forward or backward. "Perceptually," notes Grinspoon (1979: 12), "LSD produces an especially brilliant and intense impact of sensory stimuli on consciousness. Normally unnoticed aspects of the environment capture the attention: ordinary objects are seen as if for the first time and with a sense of fascination or entrancement, as though they had unimagined depths of significance." There is apparently selective recall of some aspects of the LSD experience: "During the period of drug activity the subject may report that he feels less friendly, more aggressive or agitated, or depressed. Much later, he will recall the experience as illuminating and pleasurable. He will rarely recall psychotic symptoms" (Meltzer 1979: 162).

A trip begins between thirty to sixty minutes after ingestion, peaks after two to six hours, and fades out after about 129 hours. There are "good acid trips" and "bad acid trips." They appear to be controlled by the user's attitude, mood, and expectations and often depend on suggestions of those around the user at the time of the trip. Favorable expectations produce good trips, and excessive apprehension is likely to produce the opposite. Because the substance appears to intensify feelings, the user might feel a magnified sense of love, lust, and joy or anger, terror, and despair: "The extraordinary sensations and feelings may bring on fear of losing control, paranoia, and panic, or they may cause euphoria and even bliss" (Grinspoon 1979: 13). According to James MacDonald and Michael Agar (1994: 12), a good trip, when everything is touched by magic but the user remains aware that reality will return when the drug wears off, turns into a bad trip when the user "loses sight of this fact [that reality will return] for too long." The bad trip is the result of a failure to comprehend that reality has not changed, merely its perception while under the influence of LSD. Sensations and feelings change much more dramatically than do the physical signs, which are as varied as the psychological ones and include dilation of the pupils (almost always); increased heart rate, blood pressure, and body temperature; mild dizziness or nausea; chills; trembling; slow, deep breathing; loss of appetite; and insomnia (Grinspoon 1979).

The user might feel several different emotions at once or swing rapidly from one emotion to another. If taken in a large enough dose, the drug produces delusions and visual hallucinations. The user's sense of time and self changes. Sensations might seem to "cross over," giving the user the feeling of hearing colors and seeing sounds. These changes can be frightening and can cause panic. Although LSD has been used experimentally to treat a variety of psychological illnesses, it currently has no accepted medical use.

A Bad Trip

A **bad trip** is an acute anxiety or panic reaction following the ingestion of LSD. On a bad trip, painful or frightening feelings are intensified, just as pleasurable sensations are on a good trip. Distortion of the sense of time can cause this experience to seem almost unbearably long. The person might feel that he or she has lost control of the drug and that the trip will never end; he or she might exhibit paranoia or attempt to flee. A bad trip is an acute reaction to LSD, however, and dissipates as the effects of the drug wear off (Henderson 1994b: 58).

LSD: Uses and Effects

Classification: Hallucinogen

CSA Schedule: Schedule I

Trade or Other Names: Acid, microdot

Medical Uses: None

Physical Dependence: None

Psychological Dependence: Unknown

Tolerance: Yes

Duration (hours): 8–12

Usual Method: Oral

Possible Effects: Illusions and hallucinations, altered perception of time and distance

Effects of Overdose: Longer, more intense "trip" episodes; psychosis; possible death

Withdrawal Syndrome: Unknown

Source: U.S. Drug Enforcement Administration.

LSD Tolerance and Withdrawal

Tolerance develops rapidly; repeated doses become completely ineffective after a few days of continuous use, and there is cross-tolerance to other hallucinogens. LSD is not addicting; there are no physical withdrawal symptoms (Institute for the Study of Drug Dependence 1987).

Dangers of LSD Use

LSD use can produce mydriasis (prolonged dilation of the pupil of the eye), raised body temperature, rapid heartbeat, elevated blood pressure, increased blood sugar, salivation, tingling in fingers and toes, weakness, tremors, palpitations, facial flushing, chills, gooseflesh, profuse perspiration, nausea, dizziness, inappropriate speech, blurred vision, and intense anxiety. Death caused by the direct effect of LSD on the body is virtually impossible. However, death related to LSD abuse has occurred as a result of the panic reactions, hallucinations, delusions, and paranoia experienced by users (Drug Enforcement Administration n.d.).

There are no known physical dangers in long-term use, although psychosis has been reported in a few instances. Some users report experiencing severe, terrifying thoughts and feelings; fear of losing control; fear of insanity and death; and despair while using LSD. For those who knowingly ingest LSD at low doses, there is usually mild euphoria and a loosening of inhibitions (Grinspoon 1979). Ingesting LSD unknowingly, however, can result in a highly traumatic experience as the victim might feel that he or she has suddenly "gone crazy" (Brecher 1972). Fatal accidents have occurred during states of LSD intoxication.

Some LSD users, fewer than 25 percent (Abrahart 1998), report recurring low-intensity trips—"flashbacks"—without having ingested the substance recently. This might be caused by LSD stored in and eventually released from fatty tissue. A flashback occurs suddenly, often without warning, and may occur within a few days or more than a year after the last use of LSD. Flashbacks usually occur in people who have used hallucinogens chronically or have an underlying personality problem; however, otherwise healthy people who use LSD occasionally may also have flashbacks. In normal (i.e., nonpsychotic) populations more than half of those who experience flashbacks report them as pleasant (Abrahart 1998). However, it remains to be established whether there are any causal links between flashbacks and LSD use; the link could be explained by the lack of control over what an LSD user is actually ingesting. Like other illegally produced drugs, LSD may contain any variety of additives, including methamphetamine, which appears to increase the likelihood of a bad trip (Ray 1978). Medically supervised LSD research would use pharmaceutically pure LSD, but because LSD use was prohibited in 1966, most research on adverse effects involved individuals who had obtained black-market LSD, the real composition, purity, and strength of which would be unknown (Abrahart 1998).

Most users of LSD voluntarily decrease or stop its use over time. LSD is not considered an addictive drug, since it does not produce compulsive drug-seeking behavior. But because tolerance develops rapidly, some users take progressively higher doses to achieve the state of intoxication that they had previously achieved—a dangerous practice, given the unpredictability of the substance.

PHENCYCLIDINE (PCP)

Phencyclidine (PCP) was initially developed as a general anesthetic for surgery. Although it produces distortions of sight and sound and feelings of dissociation from the environment and self, these mind-altering effects are technically not hallucinations and more properly known as "dissociative anesthetics" (National Institute on Drug Abuse 1999a). The drug is reported to have received the name PCP (or "peace pill") on the streets of San Francisco, where the drug was reputed to give illusions of everlasting peace. PCP is a white crystalline powder that has a distinctive bitter chemical taste. It is readily soluble in water or alcohol, and more than 100 variations (analogs) are produced easily and cheaply in clandestine laboratories (Lerner 1980). PCP can be mixed easily with dyes and turns up on the illicit drug market in liquid form and a variety of tablets, capsules, and colored powders. Like any drug sold on the street, PCP is often mixed with other psychoactive substances. It is sometimes sold as LSD. Although it can be snorted or eaten, PCP is most commonly applied to a leafy material such as mint, parsley, oregano, or marijuana ("killer joints" or "crystal supergrass") and smoked.

PCP is typically made by mixing ingredients in three buckets for several hours. This is often accomplished in the back of a van that is moving to disperse the fumes that are produced. The ingredients must be poured from one bucket to the other, leading to the term "bucket chemists." PCP is sold on the street by such names as "angel dust," "ozone," "whack," and "rocket fuel." The variety of street names for PCP reflects its bizarre and volatile effects.

Effects of PCP

PCP was first synthesized in 1956 and was found to be an effective surgical anesthetic when tested on monkeys. As a **dissociative anesthetic** it induces a lack of responsive awareness not only of pain, but also of the general environment, without a corresponding depression of the autonomic nervous system (Dotson, Ackerman, and West 1995). Experiments on humans were carried out in 1957, and although PCP proved to work as an anesthetic, it had serious side effects. Some patients manifested agitation, excitement, and disorientation during the recovery period. Some male surgical patients became violent, and some females appeared to experience simple intoxication (Linder, Lerner, and Burns 1981). "When PCP was subsequently given to normal volunteers in smaller doses, it induced a psychotic-like state resembling schizophrenia. Volunteers experienced body image changes, depersonalization, and feelings of loneliness, isolation, and dependency. Their thinking was observed to become progressively disorganized" (Lerner 1980: 14).

There is evidence of PCP receptors in the brain, suggesting that an "important relationship exists between the chemical structure of the 'phencyclidines' and receptors in the CNS related to neurotransmitters" (Burns and Done 1980: 100). Exactly how PCP acts on the body is not completely known, although it appears that the release of dopamine is a critical piece of the puzzle (French, Levenson, and Ceci 1990). In contrast to other anesthetics, PCP increases respiration, heart rate, and blood pressure, qualities that make it useful for patients who are endangered by a depressed heart rate or low blood pressure. In the 1960s PCP became commercially available for use in veterinary medicine as an analgesic and anesthetic, but diversion to street use led the manufacturer to discontinue production in 1978.

Within thirty to sixty minutes of ingesting a moderate amount of PCP, the user experiences a sense of detachment, distance, and estrangement from his or her surroundings. Numbness, slurred speech, and a loss of coordination also occur. These symptoms, which last up to five hours, are often accompanied by feelings of invulnerability. "A blank stare, rapid and involuntary eye movements, and an exaggerated gait are among the more common observable effects" (Drug Enforcement Administration 1989: 50). Under laboratory conditions a subject might experience a feeling of "flying with angels" and "peace and tranquility" (R. Siegel 1989: 220). At low to moderate doses, the physiological effects of PCP include a slight increase in breathing rate and a

Phencyclidine: Uses and Effects

Classification: Hallucinogen

CSA Schedule: Schedule I, II

Trade or Other Names: PCE, PCPy, TCP, PCP, hog, loveboat, angel dust

Medical Uses: None

Physical Dependence: Unknown

Psychological Dependence: High

Tolerance: Yes

Duration (hours): Days

Usual Method: Oral, smoked

Possible Effects: Illusions and hallucinations, altered perception of time and distance

Effects of Overdose: Longer, more intense "trip" episodes, psychosis, possible death

Withdrawal Syndrome: Unknown

Source: U.S. Drug Enforcement Administration.

more pronounced rise in blood pressure and pulse rate. Respiration becomes shallow, and flushing and profuse sweating occur. Generalized numbness of the extremities and muscular incoordination may also occur. Psychological effects include distinct changes in body awareness, similar to those associated with alcohol intoxication.

PCP Tolerance and Withdrawal

PCP use does not seem to result in any significant tolerance or withdrawal symptoms (National Institute on Drug Abuse 1991). "Generally 24–48 hours are required until the person again feels completely normal" (Lerner 1980: 16).

Dangers of PCP Use

PCP can result in mood disorders, acute anxiety, paranoia, and violent behavior. PCP-intoxicated individuals can present severe management problems to treatment staff and law enforcement personnel because the drug activates stress hormones that allow users to demonstrate remarkable strength. Some reactions are similar to those in LSD intoxication: auditory hallucinations and image distortion similar to fun house mirror images. "PCP is unique among popular drugs of abuse in its power to produce psychoses indistinguishable from schizophrenia" (National Institute on Drug Abuse 1989: 50). As a result, "the phencyclidine intoxicated patient is often improperly diagnosed and treated by well-meaning uninformed personnel" (Lerner 1980: 13).

Use of PCP among adolescents can interfere with hormones related to normal growth and development as well as with the learning process. At high doses of PCP there is a drop in blood pressure, pulse rate, and respiration. This may be accompanied by nausea, vomiting, blurred vision, flicking up and down of the eyes, drooling, loss of balance, and dizziness. High doses of PCP can also cause seizures, coma, and death (though death more often results from accidental injury or suicide during PCP intoxication). Speech is often sparse and garbled. People who use PCP for long periods report memory loss, difficulties with speech and thinking, depression, and weight loss. These symptoms can persist up to a year after cessation of PCP use. Mood disorders also have been reported. PCP has sedative effects, and interactions with other CNS depressants, such as alcohol and benzodiazepines, can lead to coma or accidental overdose.

MUSHROOMS AND CACTUS

Some natural substances produce effects similar to those of the synthetic hallucinogens. **Mescaline** is the primary hallucinogenic ingredient of the fleshy part of the small spineless peyote cactus, referred to as *buttons*, which are the size of a quarter to several inches across. Indians in Northern Mexico have used mescaline as part of their religious rites since prehistoric times. The Native American Church, which has about 250,000 members, continues to use peyote as part of religious ceremonies for which the church has been exempted from certain provisions of the federal Controlled Substances Act. Twenty-three states also exempt the sacramental use of peyote from criminal penalties.[2] Six people are licensed by the state and federal governments to harvest peyote that grows wild (cultivation is illegal) in South Texas thirty miles east of Laredo (Milloy 2002).

Although the buttons may be chewed or boiled in water to produce a tea, peyote is usually ground into a powder and taken orally. Mescaline can also be produced synthetically. A typical dose of 350–500 milligrams produces illusions and hallucinations that last anywhere from five to twelve hours (National Institute on Drug Abuse 1989). In healthy volunteers half a gram of mescaline produced symptoms of psychosis that were indistinguishable from those of schizophrenia (Karch 1996). There have been no reports of fatal overdoses of mescaline.

Psilocybe mushrooms have also been used for centuries in Native American religious ceremonies. The sacred or magic mushroom is typically eaten. Its active ingredients—**psilocybin** and psilocyn—are chemically similar to LSD and can be produced synthetically. Like mescaline and LSD, they affect

---

[2] In 1990 the Supreme Court, in an Oregon case, ruled 6-3 that states can prohibit the use of peyote by members of the American Indian Church, the First Amendment notwithstanding (Greenhouse 1990). In the wake of this decision, Congress enacted a statute providing a defense for people who use the substance "with good faith practice of a religious belief."

Mescaline and Peyote: Uses and Effects

Classification: Hallucinogen

CSA Schedule: Schedule I

Trade or Other Names: Mescal, buttons, cactus

Medical Uses: None

Physical Dependence: None

Psychological Dependence: Unknown

Tolerance: Yes

Duration (hours): 8–12

Usual Method: Oral

Possible Effects: Illusions and hallucinations, altered perception of time and distance

Effects of Overdose: Longer, more intense "trip" episodes; psychosis; possible death

Withdrawal Syndrome: Unknown

Source: U.S. Drug Enforcement Administration.

perceptions and mood (National Institute on Drug Abuse 1989), and users cannot distinguish between psilocybin and LSD. There has been little research into this substance and virtually none on human subjects (Karch 1996).

Dimethyltryptamine (DMT) is a hallucinogenic substance that occurs naturally in many plants and is used by Caribbean and Latin American Indians; it is also found in Ololiuqui, the seeds of the morning glory plant that are used by Indian priests in Latin America to produce delirium.

Another hallucinogen is the "magic mushroom": *Amanita muscaria*. In the past it had religious significance in the culture of Siberia, and in Scandinavia it was reputedly used by Vikings to increase their ferocity in battle (Ray 1978), although Richard Blum (1969) disputes this legend. A brownish solid material that smells like mothballs, the mushroom must be smoked or injected; it is not activated when taken orally. It is typically placed at the end of a tobacco or marijuana cigarette. A single inhalation will produce a five- to ten-minute trip. There has been little research into the substance, and it is not known whether the mushroom has toxic effects (Karch 1996).

CLUB DRUGS

Club drugs is a general term for a number of illicit drugs, primarily synthetic, that are most commonly encountered at nightclubs and "raves." The drugs include MDMA (ecstasy), ketamine, GHB, GBL, and Rohypnol.

Raves

Raves emerged in the late 1980s, starting in the party atmosphere of a Mediter-ranean island frequented by British youths on vacation. Rave music originated in the United States, mainly in Detroit, Chicago, and New York. The rave scene soon spread to other European countries, Australia, New Zealand, and elsewhere around the world. Raves vary in size; some draw a few hundred people, while others draw tens of thousands. They are commonly advertised in flyers distributed in clubs and music stores and on Internet websites.

Raves usually start late at night and continue into the morning. A well-known disk jockey is often the rave's main attraction. Ravers often wear or carry glow sticks or other brightly lit accessories and eat lollipops and candy necklaces. Some wear painters' masks with mentholated vapor rub applied to the inside to enhance ecstasy's effects. Rave culture has become increasingly commercialized since its early days and today accounts for a large part of the youth entertainment industry. So-called energy drinks (nonalcoholic beverages laced with amino acids) are often marketed at rave clubs. Bottled water is also prevalent at raves, since participants drink a lot of water to keep their bodies hydrated and their body temperatures down (Scott 2002: 20–21).

Ecstasy

Ecstasy, the common name for MDMA (3,4-*m*ethylene*d*ioxy-N-*m*eth*a*mphetamine), is a synthetic drug that has stimulant and hallucinogenic properties. Although MDMA does not cause overt hallucinations, many people report distorted time and exaggerated sensory perception while under the influence of the drug (Hanson 2001). Developed in Germany in 1914 as an appetite suppressant and for some psychiatric research (Nichols and Oberlender 1989; McNeil 2002), MDMA is but one of about 200 amphetamine analogs of the methylenedioxyamphetamine (MDA) type. Accordingly, *ecstasy* is frequently used as a generic term for this family of substances.[3] In the 1970s it was used by some therapists to help patients explore their feelings for each other. In a controlled setting it was reputed to promote trust between patients and physicians (Karch 1996).

Ecstasy (or "X-TC") proved popular among white professionals—earning its nickname as a "yuppie drug"—and individuals who consider themselves part of the New Age spiritual movement (Beck and Rosenbaum 1994). MDMA is usually ingested orally in tablet or capsule form. It is also available as a powder and is sometimes snorted and occasionally smoked but rarely injected.

MDMA is reported to be popular on college campuses in the United States and at dance parties known as **raves**.

---

[3] GHB (gamma-hydroxybutyrate), discussed later, and its precursor GBL (gamma-butyrolactone) are sometimes sold as "liquid ecstasy."

Rave culture has become increasingly commercialized since its early days, and today accounts for a large part of the youth entertainment industry. MDMA is a popular drug at raves—the drug can produce stimulant effects such as an enhanced sense of pleasure and self-confidence and increased energy. Its psychedelic effects include feelings of peacefulness, acceptance, and empathy. Users claim they experience feelings of closeness with others and a desire to touch them.

©Brand X Pictures/Alamy

Effects of Ecstasy   MDMA has a chemical structure similar to those of the stimulant methamphetamine and the hallucinogen mescaline. MDMA increases the activity levels of at least three neurotransmitters: serotonin, dopamine, and norepinephrine; this is a likely cause of the increased heart rate and blood pressure that can accompany MDMA use (National Institute on Drug Abuse 2006). Compared to the very potent stimulant methamphetamine, MDMA causes greater serotonin release and somewhat less dopamine release (Hanson 2001). During the 1950s, along with other hallucinogens, MDMA was used—unsuccessfully—by the military as a "truth serum." It was not until its "rediscovery" in the late 1970s that ecstasy received a great deal of attention because of its purported ability to produce profound pleasurable effects: acute euphoria and long-lasting positive changes in attitude and self-confidence, some symptoms resembling those caused by LSD but without the severe side effects typically associated with methamphetamine.

The effects of MDMA usually become apparent twenty to sixty minutes following oral ingestion of an average dose (100–125 milligrams) on an empty stomach. The sudden and intense onset of the high experienced by many users is commonly

MDMA: Uses and Effects

Classification: Hallucinogen

CSA Schedule: Schedule I

Trade or Other Names: 2,5-DMA, STP, MDA, MDMA, ecstasy, DOM, DOB

Medical Uses: None

Physical Dependence: Unknown

Psychological Dependence: Unknown

Tolerance: Yes

Duration (hours): Variable

Usual Method: Oral, injected

Possible Effects: Illusions and hallucinations, altered perception of time and distance

Effects of Overdose: Longer, more intense "trip" episodes; psychosis; possible death

Withdrawal Syndrome: Unknown

Source: U.S. Drug Enforcement Administration.

referred to as the "rush" (also the "wave" or "weird period"). This phase was often (particularly during initial use) experienced with a certain degree of trepidation, tension, stomach tightness, and/or mild nausea. This discomfort was generally transitory and melted away into a more relaxed state of being. Although novice users occasionally experienced some apprehension during this initial onset, anxiety levels typically decreased with subsequent use, allowing for increased enjoyment. (Beck and Rosenbaum 1994: 63)

The total effects of MDMA last from three to six hours.

The drug's rewarding effects vary with the individual taking it, the dose and purity, and the environment in which it is taken. MDMA can produce stimulant effects such as an enhanced sense of pleasure and self-confidence and increased energy; as with amphetamines, it increases heart rate and blood pressure. Its psychedelic effects include feelings of peacefulness, acceptance, and empathy. Users claim that they experience feelings of closeness with others and a desire to touch them. Because MDMA engenders feelings of closeness and trust and has a short duration of action, some clinicians claim that the drug is potentially valuable as a psychotherapeutic agent.

The mechanism by which the drug exerts its unique effects in humans is not well understood (Tancer and Schuster 1997). It is known that, like amphetamine, MDMA increases serotonin in the synapses, but it inhibits reuptake several times as much as amphetamine does. To a lesser degree, MDMA inhibits dopamine reuptake. Research indicates that ecstasy destroys serotonin-producing neurons, which play a direct role in regulating aggression, mood, sexual activity, sleep, and sensitivity to pain. It is probably this action on the serotonin system that gives it the purported properties of heightened sexual experience, tranquility, and conviviality.

Ecstasy Tolerance and Withdrawal   Although tolerance to ecstasy develops, withdrawal symptoms, if any, are not known.

Dangers of MDMA   Ecstasy causes large increases in blood pressure, heart rate, and myocardial oxygen consumption that can increase the risk of a cardiovascular catastrophe in people with preexisting heart disease (Mathias and Zickler 2001). Additional adverse effects include muscle tension, involuntary teeth clenching, nausea, blurred vision, feeling faint, tremors, rapid eye movement, and sweating or chills (Office of National Drug Control Policy 2002d). Because many users of MDMA use other drugs at the same time and because a dose of ecstasy may contain other drugs, it is difficult to isolate out the effects of MDMA.

In 1985 MDMA was placed in the Drug Enforcement Administration (DEA)'s Schedule I, although some medical supporters argue for its experimental use in psychotherapy. Indeed, the DEA has been criticized for placing MDMA in Schedule I, thereby precluding its use clinically, without methodical study of the substance (Shenk 1999). Scheduling hearings on MDMA were conducted in 1985, and the administrative law judge expressed his view that there was sufficient evidence for safe utilization under medical supervision and recommended Schedule III status. He was overruled by the director of the DEA, who in 1988 placed MDMA in Schedule I—high potential for abuse, no medically accepted use. Nevertheless, there is continued interest in testing the drug for such disorders as posttraumatic stress disorder (PTSD), and in 2005 the Food and Drug Administration (FDA) approved clinical trials of the drug to treat anxiety in terminally ill cancer patients and hospital patients suffering from PTSD (McNeil 2002; Conant 2005). The consensus among drug researchers is that there is no proof that ecstasy causes any permanent damage (McNeil 2003).

In small doses MDMA can greatly reduce the body's ability to metabolize the drug, so it remains active in the body for longer periods. When users take multiple doses over a brief period, the increased toxic effects can lead to dehydration, hypothermia, and seizures (Mathias and Zickler 2001). In high doses ecstasy may cause the body's temperature to increase markedly (malignant hyperthermia), leading to muscle breakdown and kidney and cardiovascular system failure, which in some cases has proven fatal. Although drinking water does not reduce the effects of ecstasy, it prevents dehydration. Drinking too much water, however, can lead to serious health complications in some people. Ecstasy can also produce a hangover effect: loss of appetite, insomnia, depression, and muscle aches. It can also make concentration difficult, particularly on the day after ecstasy is taken. Higher doses of ecstasy can produce hallucinations, irrational behavior, vomiting, and convulsions. Some evidence

The Danger

"MDMA gives you tons of energy to dance for five straight hours, raises your body temperature and causes dehydration. Though you are not hallucinating, you're so swept up in that terrific sense of wellbeing that you don't feel as though you're overheating, even when you are. And if you drink too much water to quench that terrific thirst," it can be fatal (Klam 2001: 43). During intense expenditures of energy the kidneys cannot excrete excess water, causing hyponatremia. The extra water eventually moves into neurons and causes them to swell. With no room to expand, neurons press against the skull and compress the brain stem, which controls such vital functions as breathing.

suggests that long-term use of ecstasy might cause damage to the brain, heart, and liver. "Ecstasy users at clubs and raves dance energetically in stuffy quarters, increasing the risk of exhaustion, which can result in dangerous dehydration leading to convulsions and, on occasion, death" (Stryker 2001: D5).

Paramethoxyamphetamine (PMA), an illegal synthetic hallucinogen that has stimulant effects similar to those of MDMA, is sometimes sold as ecstasy. When users take PMA thinking that they are really ingesting MDMA, they often conclude that they have taken weak ecstasy because PMA's effects take longer to appear. "They then ingest more of the substance to attain a better high, which can result in overdose and death" (Office of National Drug Control Policy 2002a: 2).

Ketamine

Ketamine is a dissociative anesthetic similar to PCP but produces less confusion, irrationality, and violence. Developed in the 1960s, ketamine is used as a surgical anesthetic for children who are typically able to avoid unpleasant reactions, for battlefield injuries in which rapid onset is critical, and for repeated procedures such as chemotherapy and treatment of burns. It is also used in veterinary medicine, primarily to immobilize cats or monkeys. Its use in human surgery has declined with introduction of safer, more effective products.

The synthesis of ketamine is complicated, and at this time diversion of the legitimate product—particularly from burglary of veterinary facilities—is the only known source on the street. Street users often refer to the drug as "K" or "special K," and it is sold in powder, capsule, tablet, solution, and some injectable forms. Ketamine powder can be snorted like cocaine, mixed into drinks, or smoked. The liquid is injected, applied to smokable materials, or consumed in drinks. Its illegal use is associated with "acid house" music, which also makes references to other hallucinogens, such as LSD and MDMA. Less is known about the extent of the abuse and dangers of ketamine, although habituation can result in significant mental and emotional problems (Dotson, Ackerman, and West 1995).

A pharmaceutical vial of liquid contains the equivalent of about one gram of powder. A smaller quantity, called a "bump," is about 0.2 gram and costs about $20. Ketamine can produce a very wide range of effects, and users adjust the dosage depending on the desired effect. The drug's effect can be influenced by body size, tolerance, the presence of alcohol or other drugs, the method of administration, and the setting in which the drug is consumed. In the past several years law enforcement has encountered ketamine powder packaged in small plastic bags, folded paper, aluminum foil, and capsules. These packets commonly contain 0.2 gram and more recently 0.07 gram. Some users inhale about 0.02 gram in each nostril, repeated at five- to ten-minute intervals until the desired state is reached. A dose of 0.07 gram may produce intoxication. A larger dose of 0.2 gram may result in "kland," a "mellow, colorful wonder-world." A dose of 0.5 gram can produce a so-called "K-hole," or out-of-body, near-death experience. With repeated daily exposure users can develop tolerance and psychological dependence. In 1999 ketamine was placed in Schedule III of the Controlled Substances Act.

Rohypnol

The benzodiazepine **Rohypnol** (flunitrazepam), although not approved for use in the United States, where it is classified as a Schedule III drug, is prescribed in about seventy countries for the short-term (four weeks or less) treatment of insomnia; it is the most widely prescribed sedative in Europe (Office of National Drug Control Policy 1998). It is ten times as potent as Valium. The effects begin within twenty minutes of administration and, depending on the amount ingested, may persist for more than twelve hours. The drug can be detected in urine for up to seventy-two hours (Office of National Drug Control Policy 2002c).

Rohypnol is known on the street as "rophies," "roofies," "rope," "ruffies," "R2," "roofenol, "roche," and "roachies." The illegal flunitrazepam that is sold in the United States is typically diverted from legal sources in Mexico and South America. Usually sold here in the original bubble packs of one- or two-milligram tablets, the drug is taken with alcohol or marijuana to enhance intoxication and is popular in some adolescent and young adult crowds. Heroin abusers use flunitrazepam to enhance the effects of low-quality heroin, and cocaine abusers have reported using Rohypnol to ease themselves down from a cocaine or crack binge. "Like other benzodiazepines, when taken alone, it is unlikely to cause problems. But, if combined even with a small amount of alcohol, the intoxication effects may be extreme, leading to severely impaired judgment and motor skills" (Fields 2001: 57). Eight to twenty-four hours might be required for recovery, and the person might have no memory of any events that transpired while under the influence.

Lethal overdose is unlikely. As is the case with other benzodiazepines, prolonged use will result in physical dependence. Withdrawal symptoms include headache, muscle pain, and confusion. Severe withdrawal involving hallucinations and convulsions can occur. Seizures have been reported a week or more after last use. The substance, which can be ingested orally, snorted, or injected, induces muscle relaxation, short-term amnesia, and sleep. Rohypnol takes about fifteen to twenty minutes to affect the CNS, lasts more than eight hours, and induces tolerance (Navarro 1995). Adverse effects include drowsiness, hangover, dizziness, gastrointestinal upsets, confusion, and headaches.

Because Rohypnol is colorless, odorless, and tasteless, it has been implicated in cases of "date rape": People may unknowingly be given the drug, which, when mixed with alcohol, can incapacitate a victim and prevent the person from resisting sexual assault. It can also cause a blackout and little if any memory of the assault. In response, in 1996 Congress passed the Drug-Induced Rape Prevention and Punishment Act, which provides for severe punishment for distribution of a controlled substance to an individual without that person's knowledge or consent and with the intent to commit a crime of violence, including rape (Navarro 1995; Seligmann and King 1996). Rohypnol can be lethal when mixed with alcohol and/or other depressants.

GHB and GBL

Similar to Rohypnol, **GHB** (gamma-hydroxybutyrate) and its precursor **GBL** (gamma-butyrolactone) are colorless, odorless, and virtually tasteless. They are typically sold as a white powder or a clear liquid; both have a salty taste. Since about 1990 GHB has been abused in the United States for euphoric, sedative, and anabolic (bodybuilding) effects. Like Rohypnol, GHB has been associated with sexual assault (National Institute on Drug Abuse 1999c).

In very low doses these drugs are CNS depressants; in higher doses they can produce unconsciousness and even respiratory failure. GBL was widely available as a dietary supplement in health food stores until an FDA recall in 1999. GBL is used as an industrial solvent, and tens of thousands of metric tons are produced each year and sold by its chemical name, 2(3H)-furanone dihydro (E. Brown 1999). Ingredients in GBL and GHB are found in a number of dietary supplements sold in health food stores, where they are promoted to induce sleep, build muscles, and enhance sexual performance. More than two dozen states have outlawed GHB, and at the beginning of 2000 it was placed in Schedule I of the Controlled Substances Act. It is typically manufactured from caustic chemicals such as paint or furniture polish remover, and when poorly prepared, it can cause severe chemical burns of the user's throat. An error in dosage of a tiny fraction of a gram can result in coma and death. GHB has been used by sexual predators because in addition to being rendered unconscious, victims are often unable to recall what happened. Mixing GHB or GBL with alcohol is particularly dangerous, since it enhances the drug's depressant effects.

GHB has a withdrawal syndrome that has aspects of alcohol withdrawal (delirium tremens) and benzodiazepine withdrawal (long duration of symptoms). The syndrome appears to manifest itself in patients who have self-administered GHB in an around-the-clock dosing schedule; that is, users who take GHB every two to three hours are at increased risk for the emergence

Encounter with GHB

In a Detroit suburb, Samantha, an outgoing 15-year-old known as "Hammy Sammy," and two of her girlfriends were with several boys from her high school. Samantha and a girlfriend unknowingly drank Mountain Dew that the boys had spiked with GHB. Both girls were soon unconscious. Samantha never regained consciousness (Christian 2000). Three of the young men were convicted of involuntary manslaughter, and a fourth was convicted of a lesser charge.

of severe symptoms. GHB withdrawal can occur after several months of around-the-clock use. Because of the drug's short duration of action and rapid elimination, the signs and symptoms of GHB abstinence syndrome appear rapidly, generally within one to six hours after the last dose.

Withdrawal symptoms begin with anxiety, insomnia, tremor, and episodes of tachycardia. Symptoms may rapidly progress to a state of uncontrolled delirium and agitation (Zickler 2006). Despite its apparent dangers, GHB has been useful in treating an illness experienced by about 50,000 people who also suffer narcolepsy, a serious sleeping disorder that afflicts more than 200,000 people in the United States. That illness, cataplexy, results in muscle weakness that can cause victims to collapse without warning. Under the brand name Xyrem, GHB has been approved by the FDA for treatment of cataplexy and is sold under severe restrictions (J. Reese 2000; "FDA: Date-Rape Drug has Medical Use" 2002).

CANNABIS

Marijuana does not fit easily into any of the categories we have already discussed, so we will consider it separately. Its scientific name, *Cannabis sativa*, Latin for "cultivated hemp," was given by the Swedish scientist Linnaeus, which accounts for the "*L*." that is sometimes added to the term. The plant grows wild throughout most of the tropical and temperate regions of the world, including parts of the United States. It has been cultivated for the tough fiber of its stem, and its seed is used in feed mixtures and its oil in paint. The psychoactive part of the plant is an isomer of tetrahydrocannabinol, delta9-tetrahydrocannabinol (THC), which is most highly concentrated in the leaves and resinous flowering tops.

The THC level of marijuana cigarettes varies considerably: Domestic marijuana has typically had less than 0.5 percent, although more recently cultivated plants have considerably higher levels. Indeed, the domestic cultivation of marijuana has spawned a significant market in horticultural equipment. These suppliers advertise in *High Times,* a magazine devoted to marijuana use. Much of the cultivation in the United States is accomplished indoors. The plant grows best under the same conditions that favor corn. The amount of THC in Jamaican, Colombian, and Mexican marijuana ranges from 0.5 to 4 percent; and the most select product, sinsemilla (from the Spanish *sin semilla*, "without seed"), has been found to have as much as 8 percent THC. Male plants are killed so that the female plant, in seeking to trap pollen, produces more and more of the sticky resin that covers the buds. These buds can grow as large as a man's arm from the fingertips to the elbow. Growers concentrate on sinsemilla, selling these flowering tops; indeed, nowadays the leaves of the cannabis plant ("shake") are typically discarded. Indoor cultivation has been aided by miniaturization ("marijuana bonsai") of plants with an abundance of THC-rich buds (Pollan 1995).

Marijuana: Uses and Effects

Classification: Cannabis

CSA Schedule: Schedule I

Trade or Other Names: Pot, Acapulco Gold, grass, reefer, sinsemilla, Thai sticks

Medical Uses: None

Physical Dependence: Unknown

Psychological Dependence: Moderate

Tolerance: Yes

Duration (hours): 2–4

Usual Method: Smoked, oral

Possible Effects: Euphoria, relaxed inhibitions, increased appetite, disorientation

Effects of Overdose: Fatigue, paranoia, possible psychosis

Withdrawal Syndrome: Occasional reports of insomnia, hyperactivity, decreased appetite

Source: U.S. Drug Enforcement Administration.

Hashish, usually from the Middle East, contains the drug-rich resinous secretions of the cannabis plant, which are collected, dried, and then compressed into a variety of forms: balls, cakes, or cookielike sheets. Hashish has a potency as high as 10 percent THC. It is usually mixed with tobacco and smoked in a pipe. Hashish oil—a misnomer—is simply the result of repeated extractions of cannabis plant materials to yield a dark, viscous liquid with a THC level as high as 20 percent. A drop or two on a tobacco cigarette has the effect of a single marijuana cigarette. Marijuana prepared for street sale may be diluted with oregano, catnip, or other ingredients and may also contain psychoactive substances such as LSD. Marijuana from Vietnam often contained opium.

Effects of Cannabis

Cannabis preparations can be eaten or drunk in mixtures of resin and water or milk, a form known as in India as *bhang*. In the United States marijuana is usually rolled in paper or inserted into a hollowed-out cigar ("blunting") and smoked, the user typically inhaling the smoke deeply and holding it in the lungs for as long as possible. This tends to maximize the absorption of THC, about one half of which is lost during smoking. THC appears to act as a dopamine agonist while also having an opiatelike effect on the brain's receptor system (M. Gold 1994). The psychoactive reaction occurs in one to ten minutes and peaks in about ten to thirty minutes, with a total duration of about three to four hours.

Exactly how marijuana affects the central nervous system is not entirely known. In 1990, researchers discovered **cannabinoid receptors** discretely

Hashish: Uses and Effects

Classification: Cannabis

CSA Schedule: Schedule I

Trade or Other Names: Hash, hash oil

Medical Uses: None

Physical Dependence: Unknown

Psychological Dependence: Moderate

Tolerance: Yes

Duration (hours): 2–4

Usual Method: Smoked; Oral

Possible Effects: Euphoria, relaxed inhibitions, increased appetite, disorientation

Effects of Overdose: Fatigue, paranoia, possible psychosis

Withdrawal Syndrome: Occasional reports of insomnia, hyperactivity, decreased appetite

Source: U.S. Drug Enforcement Administration.

located throughout the brain. These brain receptors are stimulated by the drug, indicating that there could be a naturally occurring THC neurotransmitter (Hilts 1990; B. R. Martin et al. 1994). It was subsequently discovered that, in fact, humans produce a cannabinoid: **anandamide** (Harris 1999). Brain receptors react to anandamide as well as to compounds in cannabis, triggering similar effects. In 1997 researchers found that marijuana triggers the release of dopamine, which stimulates pleasure centers of the brain and a craving for more marijuana (Blakeslee 1997; Carroll 2002).

The most important variables with respect to the drug's impact are the individual's experiences and expectations and the strength of the marijuana. Thus, the first-time user might not experience any significant reaction. In general, low doses tend to induce restlessness, an increasing sense of well-being, and gregariousness, followed by a dreamy state of relaxation and frequently hunger, especially for sweets. Higher doses may induce changes in sensory perception, resulting in a more vivid sense of smell, sight, hearing, and taste, which may be accompanied by subtle alterations in thought formation and expression.

The Medical Controversy

Although marijuana has some use in medicine—for example, to relieve the pressure on the eyes of glaucoma patients, to control the nausea and vomiting that accompany cancer chemotherapy, and to control the muscle spasms of multiple sclerosis patients—its use remains illegal. Since 1982, however, there has been a legally available pharmaceutical for physicians in ophthalmology and cancer treatment: **Marinol** (dronabinol), which is 98.8 percent pure THC. There is some dispute as to whether or not oral THC is as effective as smoking marijuana (see, for example, Grinspoon [1987] and a response from Jourbert [1987]; also in opposition to smoking marijuana, see Nahas and Pace [1993]). In 1989 an administrative law judge for the DEA recommended that marijuana be placed on a less restricted schedule, one that would make it available by medical prescription. The judge called marijuana "one of the safest therapeutically active substances known to man." The DEA rejected the judge's recommendation ("U.S. Resists Easing Curb on Marijuana" 1989). In 1999 a federally commissioned report by the Institute of Medicine stated that the active ingredient in marijuana is useful for treating pain, nausea, and the severe weight loss experienced by victims of AIDS. Because the smoke emitted by marijuana is even more toxic than tobacco smoke, the report recommended use of the drug only on a short-term basis, under close supervision, for patients who failed to respond to other therapies (Stolberg 1999).

In 1997 voters in Arizona and California approved referendums permitting the use of marijuana for medical purposes by seriously ill patients suffering from chronic pain. San Francisco has about thirty outlets serving some 25,000 patients and caregivers; they sell cannabis to patients with a doctor's note. Residents in some neighborhoods have opposed the "marijuana clubs," complaining of crime and the reselling or marijuana (McKinley 2006).

The federal government responded to these referendums by threatening to punish doctors who advise patients that marijuana might ease some of their symptoms by revoking their DEA registration to prescribe controlled substances. Ten doctors and six patients brought a class-action lawsuit challenging

Dana May walks between rows of marijuana plants that he is growing in the basement of his home in Aurora, Colorado. May, who suffers from a nerve disease, counts himself as one of the 668 Coloradans who hold a certificate allowing them to use and grow marijuana for pain relief under a constitutional amendment voters approved in 2000. But it remains a violation of federal law.

©AP Photo/David Zalubowski

that policy, and in 2002 the U.S. Court of Appeals for the Ninth Circuit ruled that the federal policy violated both the free speech of doctors and the principles of federalism. In 2003 the U.S. Supreme Court refused to consider a government appeal of the Ninth Circuit decision. Seven of the nine states in that circuit have laws permitting medical use of marijuana that nevertheless is illegal under federal law. In 2005 the Court (*Gonzales* v. *Raich*, No. 03-1454) upheld an appeals court decision (*Gonzales* v. *Raich* 352 F.3d 1222) that affirmed the power of the federal government to enforce federal prohibitions against possession and use of marijuana for medical purposes even in the eleven states that permit its use.

In 2003 five jurors in a federal trial in California that convicted a medicinal marijuana advocate issued a public apology to him and demanded that the judge grant him a new trial. The jurors said that they had been unaware that the defendant, Ed Rosenthal, was growing marijuana for medical purposes when they convicted him on three federal counts of cultivation and conspiracy. The reason for Rosenthal's marijuana cultivation was ruled inadmissible at trial (Murphy 2003). Although the government sought a two-year sentence, the judge sentenced him to only one day. The government appealed the sentence, and in 2006 the conviction was overturned for juror misconduct.

In 2006, in a controversial statement, the FDA denied that any medical benefits result from the use of marijuana. The FDA statement was criticized for being more ideological than scientific; it did not provide any research data and ignored a report by the prestigious National Academy of Science (Joy, Watson, and Benson 1999) that the substance does provide some benefits to certain patients suffering from AIDS and chemotherapy-related nausea and vomiting (Zernike 2006b). An editorial in the *New York Times* ("Politics of Pot" 2006: 14) argued that the "Food and Drug Administration, for no compelling reason, unexpectedly issued a brief, poorly documented statement disputing the therapeutic value of marijuana." In response Henry Miller, a physician and former head of the FDA's Office of Biotechnology, wrote in support of the FDA that marijuana smoking cannot be subjected to clinical trials because it does not come in standardized doses and therefore cannot meet the accepted standards for purity, potency, and quality (H. Miller 2006).

Marijuana Tolerance and Withdrawal

Animal and human studies conducted since the 1970s have revealed a marijuana withdrawal syndrome, which, though less severe than that for alcohol, heroin, or cocaine, is characterized by insomnia, restlessness, loss of appetite, irritability, anger, and aggression (Carroll 2002). In 1999 a study found that people who have smoked marijuana daily for many years display more aggressive behavior when they stop smoking the drug (National Institute on Drug Abuse 1999a). However, THC has a very long half-life, working its way out of the body slowly over many days and thereby obviating severe withdrawal symptoms (Markel 2002). In fact, marijuana withdrawal is similar to that experienced by cigarette smokers when they quit (Carroll 2002; Zickler 2002).

Dangers of Marijuana Use

The negative short-term effects of marijuana seem quite limited; there is loss of inhibition, and some users also experience a loss of self-confidence, aggressiveness, and even auditory hallucinations. High doses impair learning, short-term memory, and reaction time (Misner and Sullivan 1999). The more potent marijuana ingested by users today, compared to that of the heady days of Woodstock and the 1960s, is more likely to bring on paranoia in some users (Markel 2002).

Marijuana causes a significant increase in heart rate; however, this increase is no more dangerous than that caused by using caffeine or nicotine. Casual use of marijuana results in the same impairments that one would expect from equal amounts of alcohol (Abel 1978). The long-range effects are more controversial, some claiming no significant physical or psychological damage and others finding the opposite. Although most marijuana users are able to quit, there appears to a small portion of that population, 10–14 percent, who become strongly dependent (Carroll 2002).

Marijuana is frequently referred to (by government and "drug warrior" sources) as a *gateway drug*. In other words, the "road to drug hell" (abuse of heroin and cocaine) begins with marijuana. Although many if not most users of hard drugs did at one time use marijuana (e.g., Office of National Drug Control Policy 2004), they also smoked cigarettes and used alcohol as well as caffeine. The most obvious connection is via the retail dealer, who is often a "walking drug store." Because marijuana is illegal, enterprising outlaws selling the substance might have a smorgasbord of products available to tempt marijuana users, possibly when their preferred substance is unavailable or from a desire for novelty.

INHALANTS

Commonly abused inhalants are usually **volatile substances** such as hydrocarbon solvents produced from petroleum and natural gas; the two main exceptions are **amyl nitrite** and **nitrous oxide**. (*Volatile* means that the hydrocarbons evaporate when exposed to air; *solvents* refers to their capacity, in liquid form, to dissolve many other substances.) Inhalants include a variety of readily available products that are often kept in the home. They can be divided into four classes:

1. *Volatile solvents*, such as glue, paint thinner, cleaning fluid, nail polish remover, and gasoline
2. *Aerosols*, such as hair spray, spray paint, frying pan lubricants, and deodorants
3. *Anesthetics*, such as nitrous oxide ("laughing gas" used as a whipped cream propellant) and ether
4. *Volatile nitrates*, such as amyl nitrate, a prescription drug used to treat angina, and butyl nitrate, formerly used in room deodorizers but now illegal

Toluene (methyl benzene), a common ingredient of most solvents, has the greatest abuse potential, and some industries have added mustard oil to their toluene-rich products so that the nasal irritation it causes will deter abusers. For a long time the mechanism by which toluene attracts users was not known. In 2003 researchers at the University of Arizona discovered that the substance enhances dopamine activity in the brain's pleasure center. In other words, toluene is in the same category as other drugs that are subject to abuse (Sherman 2005).

Effects of Inhalants and Solvents

With some exceptions inhalants and solvents are not usually produced for their psychoactive qualities, but when used for mind-altering purposes, they are drugs. Although different in makeup, nearly all abused inhalants produce effects similar to those of anesthetics: They slow down the body's functions (National Institute on Drug Abuse 2001b). In general, these chemicals are abused by young (preadolescent and adolescent) males, although some, such as the volatile nitrites, are popular among aficionados of anal sex because they relax the sphincter muscles; they are also reputed to increase the intensity of orgasm. Inhaled vapors from solvents and propellants enter the bloodstream directly from the lungs and are then rapidly distributed to the brain and liver, the organs with the largest blood supply. Most volatile hydrocarbons are fat-soluble and are thus absorbed quickly into the central nervous system.

Immediate effects are very similar to those of alcohol and include feeling less inhibited, disoriented, and uncoordinated. After inhaling, there is a euphoric feeling, characterized by lightheadedness and exhilaration. The effects of the first brief inhalation fade after several minutes. The experienced user may prolong the effects for up to twelve hours, increasing the dose by concentrating the drug inside a plastic bag and continuing to sniff. For the majority of users most effects disappear within an hour after sniffing is stopped, although hangovers and headaches can last several days.

Although some volatile hydrocarbons are metabolized and then excreted through the kidneys, many are eliminated from the body unchanged, primarily through the lungs. The odor of solvents may therefore remain on the breath for several hours following inhalation. The complete elimination of volatile hydrocarbons can take some time, since they are released slowly from fatty tissues back into the blood.

Inhalant Tolerance and Withdrawal

Regular users can become dependent on volatile substances, as the substances become important in their daily lives. But even with extended use, the possibility of developing tolerance is very small. It is also rare for withdrawal symptoms to occur when a person stops using (Hormes, Filley, and Rosenberg 1986). Very heavy users, however, may experience headaches, muscular cramps, and abdominal pain.

Dangers of Inhalant Use

Research evidence suggests that short-term use of volatile substances rarely causes permanent damage, and effects are reversible if the person stops using inhalants. The dangers of inhalants have often been exaggerated, but long-term use of aerosols and cleaning fluids can damage the kidneys, liver, and brain, though this is rare. Perception and coordination become impaired, and heavy use can cause unconsciousness. The "high" may be accompanied by sedation, hallucinations, and delusions. High dosage can result in vomiting, paralysis, and coma. A common method of use, a plastic bag covering the head, can lead to unconsciousness and death by suffocation.

The long-term inhaling of leaded gasoline can cause leukemia and various types of cancers, because the lead accumulates in the body. Other physical effects of gasoline sniffing can include anorexia, seizure, and "sudden sniffing syndrome." This syndrome is caused by heart failure that can happen if a person does strenuous exercise or has a sudden fright immediately after sniffing. However, this is rare and is usually associated with aerosols, butane gas, and cleaning fluid. The harms that are most associated with volatile substances are in how and where they are sniffed. Deaths or accidents can occur as a result of sniffing in unsafe place, such as on a roof or by a railroad line (information from the Centre for Education and Information on Drugs and Alcohol in New South Wales).

Research sponsored by the National Institute on Drug Abuse (Mathias 2002) revealed that chronic inhalant abuse is associated with brain abnormalities and cognitive impairment at a considerably higher rate than that experienced by cocaine abusers.

SUMMARY

Hallucinogens, which occur both naturally and synthetically, overwhelm the ability of the CNS to modulate sensory input, changing a person's perception so that he or she sees images, hears sounds, and feels sensations that seem real but do not exist. LSD, the best-known hallucinogen, is an odorless and tasteless substance whose impact depends largely on the user's expectations. LSD has no accepted medical use. Tolerance develops rapidly, and there are no withdrawal symptoms.

PCP was developed as a surgical anesthetic but produces extreme distortions of reality that mimic mental illness, and some people become violent under its influence. There is a lack of tolerance or withdrawal symptoms.

Certain mushrooms and plants have hallucinogenic qualities. Peyote (from cactus) continues to be used by the Native American Church in its religious rituals.

Club drugs include MDMA (ecstasy), ketamine, GHB, GBL, and Rohypnol. MDMA, which has both stimulant and hallucinogenic properties, is associated with dance parties. It has no lawful uses in the United States, and there is controversy over its long-term effects. Rohypnol combined with alcohol causes impaired judgment, and the user might have no memory of what transpired; rohypnol is sometimes referred to as the "date rape drug."

Marijuana has stimulant, depressant, and hallucinogenic properties and, like other psychoactive drugs, has specific receptor sites in the brain. Depending on the environment and how much is ingested, marijuana can produce a sense of well-being and a dreamy state of intoxication. High doses produce hallucinogenic effects. The active chemical in cannabis, THC, is available by prescription for limited medical use, although products using the cannabis leaf are illegal. THC has a long half-life and therefore a relatively mild withdrawal, similar to that of cigarette smoking. Although short-term effects are limited, there is controversy over long-term effects. Impairments are similar to those of nicotine and alcohol.

Inhalants are nondrug products that are usually abused by youngsters for their intoxicating effects. Short-term use does not cause permanent damage, although long-term use is associated with certain cancers and cognitive impairment.

REVIEW QUESTIONS

1. How do hallucinogens affect the central nervous system?
2. What determines whether an LSD trip will be a good one or a bad one?
3. How does PCP affect the user?
4. What are the dangers of PCP use?
5. What is ketamine? What are its effects?
6. How is mescaline produced?
7. What are the effects of peyote?
8. What is MDMA? What are its dangers?
9. What are the effects of smoking cannabis?
10. What are the effects of inhalants and solvents?
11. What are the dangers involved in using inhalants and solvents?
12. What are the issues surrounding medical use of marijuana?
13. Why is calling marijuana a gateway drug problematic?

The Sociology of Drug Abuse

In order to be motivated to continue to experiment with the use of any drug, the individual must learn to use the drug appropriately and to experience its effects as pleasurable. This may depend partly on genetic predisposition, which influences whether drug use is pleasurable, and to a large degree on contact with a peer/user network already socialized into these practices and understandings.

Advisory Council on the Misuse of Drugs (1998: 31)

Since the discovery of drugs as a social problem (discussed in Chapter 2) attempts have been made to explain why some people become dependent on chemicals while others, even those who use the same substances, do not. These explanations go beyond simply labeling abusers as "bad" or "weak" people who are oriented toward a harmful vice: "Some believe it is a medical disease,[1] while others believe it is a behavioral problem. Some consider it to have genetic origins; others consider it to be primarily environmentally determined. Some examine it within a cultural context, others consider it to be an individual adjustment reaction. Some view it as a personality disorder, while others view it as a psychosocial problem" (Pickens and Thompson 1984: 53). In the bio-psychosocial model, drug dependence is seen as being determined by the interaction of psychological, environmental, and physiological factors (Donovan 1988).

Theories of drug use typically depend on the discipline of the observer: neurology and pharmacology (discussed in Chapters 3, 4, 5, and 6), psychology (discussed in Chapter 8), and sociology, discussed in this chapter. Although many theories of drug use presented by these disciplines might seem competitive or even conflicting, our examination will emphasize their complementary nature: Each provides a partial explanation for drug use and has important treatment and policy implications. Indeed, the "real" explanation could involve a combination of factors. For example, although we know that certain types of drug abuse are concentrated in areas of relative deprivation, most people in such areas do not abuse drugs. So perhaps what promotes drug abuse in this situation is a biologically vulnerable person (having an endorphin deficiency) living in deprived social circumstances who is exposed to heroin.

SOCIOLOGICAL THEORY

Because the social or behavioral sciences are concerned with behavior that is peculiarly human, the amount of ethically based testing that can be done is limited. We can subject rats to extreme levels of physical stress and then study their reaction to morphine, but we cannot subject human beings to similar levels of stress, expose them to morphine, and then find out whether they become drug addicts. The social or behavioral sciences have to study the etiology of drug addiction in a more circuitous manner.

Sociological theory is concerned with social structures and social behavior, so it examines drug use in its social context. A sociological perspective often views drug use as the product of social conditions and relationships that cause

---

[1] "Moving etiological and rehabilitative issues from the context of morals to that of medicine offered many advantages. The legitimacy bestowed on substance abuse by treating it as a disease opened the way for more humane and effective treatment of patients. In addition, this view provided the impetus for scientific research into the condition" (Siegal et al. 1995: 67).

Summary of Risk Factors for Drug Use

Culture and Society

- Laws favorable to drug use
- Social norms favorable to drug use
- Availability of drugs
- Extreme economic deprivations
- Neighborhood disorganization

Interpersonal

- Parent and family drug use
- Positive family attitudes toward drug use
- Poor/inconsistent family management practices
- Family conflict and disruption
- Peer rejection
- Association with drug-using peers

Psychobehavioral

- Early/persistent problem behavior
- Academic failure
- Low commitment to school
- Alienation
- Rebelliousness
- Favorable attitudes toward drug use
- Early onset of drug use

Biogenetic

- Inherited susceptibility to drug abuse
- Psychophysiological vulnerability to drug effects

Source: Newcomb (1995: 17).

despair, frustration, hopelessness, and general feelings of alienation in the most disadvantaged segments of the population (Biernacki 1986). The National Institute on Drug Abuse (1987) outlines factors that are associated positively with adolescent substance abuse, factors that are frequently found in deprived socioeconomic environments (most arrested cocaine and heroin users reside in disadvantaged neighborhoods [Lo 2003]):

1. Families whose members have a history of alcohol abuse and/or histories of antisocial behavior or criminality
2. Inconsistent parental supervision, with reactions that swing from permissiveness to severity
3. Parental approval or use of dangerous substances
4. Friends who abuse drugs

5. Children who fail in school during the late elementary years and show a lack of interest in school during early adolescence
6. Children who are alienated and rebellious
7. Children who exhibit antisocial behavior, particularly aggressive behavior, during early adolescence

There is also a strong link between childhood sexual and physical abuse and substance abuse (Brems et al. 2004).

Many sociological studies have found that drug use among adolescents is motivated by intermittent feelings of boredom and depression and that, like other aspects of adolescence, drug use is typically abandoned when the person reaches adulthood. Furthermore, contrary to conventional wisdom, research has found that drug use is typically a group activity of socially well-integrated youngsters (Glassner and Loughlin 1989). That is, contrary to some psychological views, the adolescent drug user is socially competent (or ego sufficient). Sociological studies often challenge the conflicting views of the adolescent drug user as either a deviant isolate or a peer-driven conformist. Sociology also cautions us to separate drug use that is situational and transitional from drug dependence or addiction, which is compulsive and dysfunctional. In England the much smaller number of adolescents who use illicit drugs regularly, in contrast to those who have tried illicit drugs, "reminds us that because a young person has tried an illicit drugs does not mean that they will necessarily develop a pattern of long term misuse" (Advisory Council on the Misuse of Drugs 1998: xii). This has important policy implications, and treatment approaches based on sociological theories usually "stress resocialization, the adopting of prosocial values, and/or submission to a peer culture that is strongly opposed to drug use." Thus, "according to a social stress model, adolescents initiate substance use as a means of coping with a variety of stressors and influences that may arise from within the family, the school, the peer group, or the community." And adolescents "will be more resilient and, as such, less likely to engage in problematic early usage as a means of coping with these stressors if they are members of prosocial, supportive social networks" (Rhodes and Jason 1990: 396).

STAGES OF DRUG ADDICTION

Sociologists have studied and labeled the stages that alcohol, heroin, and cocaine users go through on the path to addiction.

Alcohol

The alcoholic typically passes through several stages on the way to becoming addicted to alcohol (Catanzarite 1992):

- *Social drinking*: In this initial pattern alcohol is used to enhance pleasant social situations. The drug is taken for relaxation and entertainment. For some individuals drinking alcohol has a ritualistic dimension—a glass of wine or beer or a drink with a meal or as part of a religious ritual. Others may have an alcoholic beverage after work with colleagues—"a beer with the boys." The social drinker imbibes small amounts and does not experience harmful effects such as loss of control or impaired judgment. Although social drinkers view alcohol as generating positive feelings, they do not need the substance for enjoyment. The social drinker observes societal conventions about when, where, and how much to drink.

- *Heavy drinking*: The heavy drinker uses alcohol to escape. For one type of drinker this critical step involves a circular problem: He or she experiences constantly high levels of stress and seeks relief by drinking alcohol, which creates additional stress that must be relieved by more alcohol. Another type of person resorts to heavy alcohol use when particular stressful problems are encountered and reduces drinking in the absence of stressors. By becoming intoxicated, both types of drinkers violate social conventions about the use of alcohol and suffer negative side effects with respect to family, friends, and employment. They become defensive about their drinking and deny the influence of alcohol on their lives.

- *Dependent drinking*: The person is now addicted to alcohol and suffers from many consequences, in particular an inability to function normally either socially, intellectually, or physically. He or she is not able to control drinking behavior and becomes obsessed and preoccupied with alcohol. Indeed, the person needs alcohol to "feel normal."

While many college students are focused on academics, others are learning to abuse alcohol and other drugs. The overindulgence of alcohol has become a social norm at college fraternities across America.

©Michael Jang/Getty Images

Heroin and Cocaine

Heroin and cocaine addiction have been studied extensively, with two general conclusions (Gerstein and Harwood 1990):

1. Initial use is experimental in nature and begins during adolescence
2. Very few people begin using drugs after reaching age 25 (unless drugs were not previously available).

The pattern has a familiar sequence: from tobacco and alcohol to marijuana and then to other illegal psychoactive substances such as heroin and cocaine. Although most new users do not progress very far, the earlier the onset of use, the more likely is dependence. "Individuals who do not initiate the use of alcohol or tobacco tend not to initiate the use of marijuana. Similarly, those who do not initiate the use of marijuana tend not to progress to hard drug use" (Golub and Johnson 1994: 404).

Heroin   The life of a heroin addict can be conceived of as a "career" with a number of stages:

1. *Experimentation.* The individual, usually an adolescent, experiments with a variety of substances, including alcohol, cigarettes, marijuana, and perhaps barbiturates and amphetamines, and might snort heroin or inject it subcutaneously.
2. *Initiation.* The drug abuser is initiated into intravenous use of heroin. Although the first use is often accompanied by unpleasant side effects such as vomiting, the user learns to enjoy subsequent injections. Heroin use begins to be a center of existence.
3. *Commitment.* The user is now an addict and takes on the social identity associated with the drug subculture, orienting his or her life toward the maintenance of a heroin habit.
4. *Disjunction.* The addict's life is now characterized by crime, arrest, and imprisonment, interspersed with participation in drug-treatment programs in response to court direction (to avoid imprisonment), to reduce an expensive habit to manageable size, or to deal with severe physical ailments.
5. *Maturation.* At some point, usually when the addict is closer to age 40 than to 20, he or she typically begins to use only sporadically, gives up drugs completely as a result of treatment, or simply experiences spontaneous remission—or he or she dies. Although there are relatively few addicts over the age of 50 in the heroin-using population, one California study found that among hard-core addicts, by age 50 to 60 years, half of the 242 subjects tested positive for heroin (Hser et al. 2001). The "aging out" phenomenon is also found in other types of deviant behavior, such as crime in general.

"The addict lifestyle," notes Marsha Rosenbaum (1981: 14), "rotates around taking heroin for the purposes of alleviating withdrawal symptoms and/or getting high." Heroin is quite costly and too expensive for most addicts to secure with only legitimate sources of income. Nevertheless, a habit requires intravenous use three, four, or five times daily, and the addict also requires funds for minimal life-support items such as food, clothing, and housing. The addict who is also a dealer or is sufficiently organized is able to start the day with a fix. Few addicts, however, are able to plan even for the immediate future, so they rarely keep enough heroin in reserve to begin the day with a "wake-up fix." Without funds or drugs the addict must begin the day hustling for money to get the first fix.

After a "connection" has been made and the heroin has been purchased, the drug must be ingested as part of an almost ritualistic process. A safe place must be found where the addict, often in the company of other addicts, can inject the substance using a hypodermic syringe. The addict typically allows the solution to mix with blood by bringing blood back and forth between the vein and the syringe ("booting"), an act that some researchers see as analogous to sexual intercourse and that many users describe as more pleasurable and intense than sexual orgasm. In any event, as the short-term heightened feeling of euphoria that follows ingestion—the rush—subsides, the addict begins to experience the high, a feeling of general well-being that lasts about four hours. The cycle then needs to be repeated. "This is the 'addict's cycle'—an existence almost literally from fix to fix—with the necessary heroin-related activities in between" (M. Rosenbaum 1981: 15).

The heroin user recognizes the dangers of addiction, but "it is typical of the early experience of the addict-to-be that he knows or knows of people who use narcotics and who get away with it" (Duster 1970: 192). He sees himself as indestructible: "the tendency of the ego to treat the self as exempt from the experience of personal disaster."

Some heroin users, particularly postadolescents, are attracted to unconventional media images that romanticize the "traffic beauty" of heroin users. For some, if their favorite musicians can use heroin and still maintain or even excel in their careers, a positive light is cast on heroin use. Others are attracted to "heroin chic," the thin, wan look promulgated by the fashion industry (Duterte et al. 2003).

Cocaine   Here are some typical steps involved in becoming a cocaine abuser (based on D. E. Smith 1986):

1. *Experimental use.* The individual begins his or her initiation out of curiosity in a social situation in which some friends offer a "taste" of cocaine. Most of the person's friends are nonusers, and the person uses cocaine only when it is offered to enhance feelings. Relationships remain normal, and no significant health or financial problems appear. There might even be an improvement in work performance and social functioning—gregariousness or extroversion.

2. *Compulsive use.* The person begins to buy cocaine and increases the number of friends who are users. Solitary use of cocaine follows, and use to

enhance moods and performance and to ward off depression associated with the "crash" of coming down off cocaine continues to increase. Social disruptions appear, particularly mood swings, as well as health problems due to a lack of proper nutrition and sleep. Work performance begins to deteriorate steadily, and the user avoids non-drug-using friends. The user begins to encounter financial problems that result from supporting a growing cocaine habit.

3. *Dysfunctional use*. The abuser is preoccupied with drug use and associates only with cocaine-using friends. The abuser might begin to deal in cocaine and/or to engage in other illegal or financially damaging activities to support the dependence on cocaine. Severe disruption of social life follows, possibly including marital violence and divorce. Serious medical pathology appears, with a risk of seizure and toxic psychosis, paranoia, delusions, and hallucinations. The abuser has chronic sleep and nutritional problems as well. His or her physical appearance deteriorates; this is usually accompanied by a lack of concern about personal hygiene and dress. Compulsion, a loss of control, and an inability to stop despite adverse consequences might lead the abuser to seek treatment, often because of pressure from family, friends, and/or employer and/or because of serious legal entanglements.

Early research (e.g., Washton and Gold 1987) and journalistic sources reported that addiction to crack cocaine appeared to present a different progression because the speed with which this substance acts can lead to chronic habituation or addiction very quickly. In their research, however, Jeffrey Fagan and Ko-lin Chin (1991) found no significant difference between the addictive qualities of crack and those of powdered cocaine. However, crack users more often reported an inability to stop using it. For reasons that have not yet been determined, crack has proven to be more popular among women than heroin is, leading to a significant increase in child neglect and abuse as well as to increasing numbers of newborn children with cocaine in their urine and syphilis resulting from the rampant sexual activity of their crack-abusing mothers. A seller describes a crack house as "full of young girls—fourteen, fifteen, sixteen years old. Some of these girls stayed for days at a time, getting high and having sex with these guys," any guy who offered drugs (T. Williams 1989: 108). Smoking crack reduces inhibitions while creating a desire for more drugs, leading female users to unprotected sexual behavior and the risk of sexually transmitted diseases, including AIDS. In their research Fagan and Chin (1991: 327) found "no significant differences among those involved in crack, cocaine HCL [powdered cocaine], heroin or other drugs in the location, motivation or methods of introduction to their new drug." Most users (90 percent) were introduced to the new drug by family or friends, and most (71 percent) got it free. In their study Andrew Golub and Bruce Johnson (1994) found that older crack users were nearly all former heroin injectors or cocaine snorters, while crack tended to be the first hard drug for younger users.

Let us now examine some of the major sociological theories that help to explain drug abuse.

Substance Abuser Characteristics

"Regardless of social class differences, substance abusers share important similarities. All reveal some problems in socialization, cognitive/emotional skills, and overall psychological development, which is evident in their immaturity, poor self-esteem, conduct and character disorders, or antisocial characteristics. Typical features include low tolerance for all forms of discomfort and delay of gratification; inability to manage feelings (particularly hostility, guilt, and anxiety); poor impulse control (particularly sexual or aggressive); poor judgment and reality testing concerning consequences of actions; unrealistic self-appraisal in terms of a discrepancy between personal resources and aspirations; prominence of lying, manipulation, and deception as coping behaviors; and problems with authority and personal and social irresponsibility (i.e., inconsistency or failures in completing expected obligations and persistent difficulties in managing guilt)." (De Leon 1994: 19–20)

ANOMIE

Derived from the Greek meaning "lack of law," the term *anomie* was used by sociologist Émile Durkheim (1858–1917) to describe an abnormal social condition wherein the cohesion of society is weakened by some crisis, such as an economic depression, that causes each individual to pursue his or her own solitary interests without concern for the wider society. In 1938 Robert Merton Americanized the concept, arguing that no other society comes so close to viewing economic success as such an absolute value that the pressure to succeed tends to eliminate social constraint over the means employed to achieve success. In the United States, in this view, "good" (ambition) causes "evil" (deviance). According to Merton (1964: 218), anomie results when people, confronted by the contradiction between goals and means, "become estranged from a society that promises them in principle what they are denied in reality [economic opportunity]." This sense of strain is particularly strong among the disadvantaged segments of our population, whose use of drugs is endemic.

Response to Anomie

Strain leads to anomie, suffering to which people respond in one of four ways:

1. *Conformity*. Most people scale down their aspirations and conform to conventional social norms.
2. *Rebellion*. Some people rebel, rejecting the conventional social structure and seeking instead to establish a new social order through political action or alternative lifestyles.
3. *Innovation*. Some people turn to innovation, which Merton defines as the use of illegitimate means to gain success, in particular professional and organized criminality, including drug trafficking.

4. *Retreatism*. The final response, retreatism, explains drug abuse: The individual abandons all attempts to reach conventional social goals in favor of a deviant adaptation.

The retreat into drug abuse allows the addict to expend time and energy on achieving an attainable goal: getting high. Dan Waldorf (1973: 10) notes:

> The need for heroin requires an active life. The addict *may* be, as psychologists have claimed, depressed, he may be psychopathic, and he may use drugs to escape some reality in his life, but he is active in pursuit of a demanding life that requires considerable skill and ability to sustain. Addiction is *not* some aberrant, part-time leisure activity that one indulges in from time to time but that never engages one's life. On the contrary, addiction does engage the addict in an active life that has a precise purpose and satisfies a specific physical need. Whatever the individual's motives for using heroin or the ways in which a specific addict approaches his heroin use, he most certainly experiences an absorbing or engrossing drive, lives an active life, and is very much part of a social group.

Edward Preble and John Casey (1995: 121) argue that the behavior of the heroin addict is anything but an escape: "They are actively engaged in meaningful activities and relationships seven days a week. The brief moments of euphoria after each administration of a small amount of heroin constitute a small fraction of their daily lives. The rest of the time they are aggressively pursuing a career that is exacting, challenging, adventurous, and rewarding. They are always on the move and must be alert, flexible, and resourceful."

Some heroin addicts view life as an adventure. As a San Francisco addict explained to John Irwin (1970: 19): "Cowboys and Indians at the Saturday matinee didn't have a life that was any more exciting than this. The cops are the bad guys, you are the glorious bandit. . . . The chase is on all day long. You awaken in the morning to shoot the dope you saved to be well enough to go out and get some more. First you have to get some money. To steal you have to outwit those you steal from, plus the police. It is very exciting." The typical heroin addict, note Bertram Sackman and his colleagues (1978: 433), "exhibits as much pride in his heroin-getting skills as does the licit craftsman. He thinks about hustling and heroin, he talks about his exploits to other addicts, and his righteousness about heroin is rewarded by his women in the admiration and respect they accord him and his skills." Being "in the life" is reinforcing (see Chapter 8).

According to Richard Cloward and Lloyd Ohlin (1960), however, the heroin addict is actually a double failure, unsuccessful at both legitimate and illegitimate enterprises, since his or her crimes are typically high-risk, low-yield activities. In this case the first response to anomie is *innovation*; when that fails to reduce the anomic condition, the addict moves to *retreatism*.

Problems with the Theory

Chein and his colleagues (1964) used a questionnaire to examine anomic attitudes. The questionnaires were administered to classes of male eighth-grade public school students in three neighborhoods with varying rates of delinquency: low, medium, and high (though even the "low" neighborhood had a relatively high rate of delinquency). Anomie was highly correlated with heroin use. But, as was noted in Chapter 1, the drug-to-crime sequence is not at all certain. According to Cloward and Ohlin's (1960) thesis, delinquency or crime precedes drug dependence, but research has not clearly supported this contention. In any event the successful and skilled (innovative) criminal is so rare that the double failure thesis must be questioned (Lindesmith and Gagnon 1964).

Of course, anomie does not explain cocaine use by people who are not retreatists and who have achieved notable social and economic success in either criminal or noncriminal enterprises. Nor does it satisfactorily explain the relatively high rate of drug abuse among physicians, whose use of drugs is better explained by access than by anomie. Access, not anomie, is also put forth as an explanation for the high concentration of drug use in ghetto areas: Lack of viable economic opportunity induces more people to take the risks associated with drug trafficking, resulting in greater availability of illegal substances (Lindesmith and Gagnon 1964). Of course, greater access can be the result of anomie, drug trafficking being an innovative response to the anomic condition.

Working from a psychoanalytical model, Frederic Schiffer (1988) found retreatism motivating cocaine abuse in the patients he treated, the drug taken because of a fear of failure: "Unconsciously, despair seemed familiar and inevitable, and success seemed foreign and unattainable" (1988: 134). In contrast to these views, Erich Goode declares that "anomie theory seems to explain no significant feature of drug use, abuse, or addiction" (1989: 64). For Elliott Currie (1993: 145), however, the breeding conditions for anomie are connected to drug abuse, and these conditions have grown more severe: "It is not just that material prospects have dimmed for the relatively young and poor, but that they have dimmed just when there has been an explosion of affluence and a growing celebration of material consumption at the other end." This is exacerbated by the increasing gap between this country's wealthiest citizens and its poorest: Of the sixteen most industrialized nations the United States has the widest gap between rich and poor, and its poor children are the worst off (Bradsher 1995a, 1995b, 1995c).

The Adaptive Model of Anomie

Bruce Alexander sees drug dependence (compulsive as opposed to casual or recreational use) as functional. The addict's behavior is an attempt to deal with a failure to integrate, that is, "failure to achieve the kinds of social acceptance, competence, self-confidence, and personal autonomy that are the minimal expectation of individuals and society" (1990: 39). In the *adaptive model*, as in the retreatist perspective, the addict perceives the identity and life of an addict, with its attendant misery, ill health, and social stigma, to be less painful than the void of no identity at all. According to Alexander, people who have not failed at integration and can form social strong bonds are not in danger of drug dependence. (This view is an important part of social control theory, discussed later in the chapter.)

Drug dependence serves "as a strategy to remove the individual [a retreat] from competitive situations in which defeat is almost certain" (Alexander 1990: 45). This model contrasts with the *disease model* of drug dependence because it sees the addict as a healthy person who is a social, not biological or psychological, failure. The addict is not under the control of a drug, nor is his or her drug use "out of control"; the behavior is self-directed and purposeful, though not necessarily on a conscious level.

DIFFERENTIAL ASSOCIATION

As proposed by Edwin Sutherland (1973), differential association explains how criminal behavior is transmitted. *Differential association* complements learning theory (discussed in Chapter 8): Criminal behavior is learned, and the principal learning occurs in intimate personal groups. The effectiveness of learning depends on the degree of intensity, frequency, and duration of the association. With respect to drug use, differential association can be conceived of as a scale in balance. On each side of the scale deviant and prosocial associations accumulate; at some theoretical point drug use will be initiated when there is an excess of deviant associations (drug abusers) over nondeviant or prosocial associations.

Robert Burgess and Ronald Akers (1969) reformulated Sutherland's central premise into a differential association reinforcement theory: A person becomes delinquent if social norms or laws do not actually reinforce conforming legal behavior. Because behavior is shaped by positive reinforcement, if lawful behavior does not result in reinforcement, the strength of that lawful behavior is weakened, and a state of reinforcement deprivation results. This deprivation increases the probability that other—deviant—behaviors will be reinforced and strengthened. Members of the person's social a group also make social reinforcement, such as social approval, esteem, and status, contingent on the new deviant behavior.

In fact, initiation into drug use appears to be completely dependent on peer associations. "The first source of contact with the drug [heroin] was usually a friend," notes Troy Duster (1970: 180). The typical user receives his or her first "taste" free from relatively new users who do not have expensive habits and will therefore share their drugs. Most frequently, the user is introduced to heroin as a result of meeting a friend who was on his way to "cop" or was preparing a "fix"; "he rarely sought out the drug the first time. Thus, initiation depended more on fortuitous circumstances than on a willful act by the new user" (P. H. Hughes 1977: 84).

In their study of heroin addicts in San Antonio, James Maddux and David Desmond (1981) found that only 4 percent obtained their first heroin directly from a dealer. Similar scenarios of heroin initiation are reported by Richard Rettig, Manual Torres, and Gerald Garrett (1977) and by Chein and his colleagues (1964). Waldorf (1973: 31) found a similar pattern and notes that heroin use is a social, not solitary, phenomenon: "Persons are initiated in a group situation among friends and acquaintances." The first experience with drugs, notes Duster (1970: 183), "is usually in a group situation." In England the situation is the same; Geoffrey Pearson (1987: 9) found that "the first time someone is offered heroin it will be by a friend. Or maybe by a brother or a sister. But always by someone well known, liked and even loved."

The relationship between initiation and friendship or kinship presents a problem for preventing the first use of drugs: "In light of the decisive role of friendship networks in disseminating drugs, it is difficult to conceive of any effective form of conventionally conceived drug enforcement policy to control access at this level—quite simply, how might one be expected to police friendship?" (Advisory Council on the Misuse of Drugs 1998: 30).

What of the relationship between parental use of psychoactive substances and the use of these substances by their children? (Peer relationships might simply serve as a mediating or intervening variable.) According to the theory of differential association, parental influence is responsible for generating the type of behavior that parents explicitly condemn in their children. However, in her research Denise Kandel (1974: 235) found that "parental influence is relatively small, especially when compared with the influence of peers." Peers provide social acceptance or reinforcement for the rules governing acceptance or conforming behavior valued by the peer group. To the adolescent, this reinforcement is typically more relevant than that provided by parents. Kandel concludes, however, that parents can enhance differential association: "When their friends use illegal drugs, children of nondrug-using parents are somewhat *less* likely to use illegal drugs, whereas children of drug-using parents are *more* likely to use drugs" (1974: 235).

According to Coryl Jones and Robert Battjes (1987: 15), the use of certain drugs allows adolescents to emulate adults while at the same time rebelling against parental standards: "In emulation of their elders, adolescents use drugs to assuage immediate or anticipated discomfort, and, in rejection of their elders, they seize upon certain drugs of which their elders would disapprove. The use of illicit substances offers young adolescents the unique opportunity simultaneously to rebel against the rules their elders set down and to conform with the underlying attitudes which parental behavior manifests."

However, an extensive study found that favorable parent-adolescent relationships can offset personality risk factors for drug use and enhance personality protective factors against drug use. The study also found that peer drug use during adolescence was not a strong predictor of initiation into drug use during early adulthood (Morojele and Brook 2001).

Anomie and differential association help to explain what Patrick Hughes (1977: 88) referred to as a heroin epidemic. In a Chicago-based study he posited a theory of heroin contagion in the form of microepidemics and macroepidemics: "The multiple drug using friendship group served as fertile soil for the growth of heroin addiction" into microepidemics, while "macroepidemics generally occurred in neighborhoods that had recently undergone rapid population change, leading to a breakdown in community stability and established mechanisms of social control [anomie]. In other words, not only had heroin addiction become rampant in these neighborhoods, but so had other forms of deviance as well." Hughes states that intensive treatment and outreach efforts can nip a new heroin-using network before it burgeons into an epidemic.

Identifying oneself as a "doper," "pothead," or "cokehead" typically results from being enmeshed in a social network that includes others who are similarly situated. For some this becomes the primary reference group, and they might spend most of their time with other dopers, potheads, or cokeheads, withdrawing from non-drug-using social contacts. The substance becomes a symbol of group cohesion and unity and provides a sense of belonging, thus offering strong support for continued use (Roffman and George 1988).

SOCIAL CONTROL THEORY

Social control theorists focus on why only relatively few people engage in deviant behavior such as crime and drug abuse, and their answer is that the strength of an individual's bond to society is the determining factor. Youths who maintain strong attachments with and commitment toward parents and school are less likely to engage in deviant behavior. According to control theorists, deviance "results when an individual's bond to society is weak or broken" (Hirschi 1969: 16). The strength of this social bond is determined by internal and external restraints. In other words, internal and external restraints determine whether people move in the direction of deviance or law-abiding behavior.

Internal restraints include what psychoanalytic theory (discussed in Chapter 8) refers to as the *superego*—they provide a sense of guilt. Dysfunction during early stages of childhood development or parental influences that are not normative can result in an adult who has no prosocial internal constraints—sociopathology. (There is also evidence tying sociopathology to brain defects.) Criminal behavior, devoid of any genuine remorse, can be explained by this theory. According to social control theory, deviants are poorly socialized, and the family is the basic unit for socialization. Thus, whether they are conceived of in terms of psychology or sociology, internal constraints are linked to the influence of the family (Hirschi 1969). Adolescent involvement with drugs and/or crime is therefore "highly correlated with family estrangement" (Brounstein et al. 1990: 10), an influence that can be supported or weakened by the presence or absence of significant external restraints.

External restraints include social disapproval linked to public shame and/ or social ostracism and fear of punishment. In other words, people are typically deterred from criminal behavior by the possibility of being caught and the punishment that can result, ranging from public shame to imprisonment (and in extreme cases capital punishment). However, the strength of official deterrence— force of law—is measured according to two dimensions: risk versus reward. Risk involves the criminal justice system's ability to detect, apprehend, and convict the offender. The amount of risk is weighed against the potential rewards. Both risk and reward, however, are relative to one's socioeconomic situation. In other words, the less one has to lose, the greater is the willingness to engage in risk; and the greater the reward, the greater is the willingness to engage in risk. This theory explains why people in deprived economic circumstances would be more willing to engage in certain criminal behavior. However, the potential rewards and a perception of relatively low risk can also explain why individuals in more advantaged economic circumstances would engage in remunerative criminal behavior such as corporate crime.

Social control theory does not argue that only people with weak societal ties will engage in drug use. Instead, it is the persistence of drug use that indicates a lack of societal bonds. Instead of conforming to conventional norms, through differential association some people organize their behavior according to the norms of a delinquent or criminal group with which they identify or to which they belong. This is most likely to occur in environments that are characterized by relative social disorganization, in which familial and communal controls are ineffective in exerting a conforming influence. "A similar process also helps explain why drugs are sometimes rampant in more affluent communities. Just as strong families and cultures can shield the materially deprived from drugs, so weakened families, the absence of available or concerned adults, and the pervasiveness of an insistent consumer culture can make the affluent more vulnerable" (Currie 1993: 103).

Another study revealed that family monitoring and rules, family conflict, and family bonding predict an adolescent's risk of illicit drug initiation. The researchers found that a warm and supportive family environment characterized by a strong bond to family members and a low level of family conflict predicted a lower risk for illicit drug initiation during adolescence. Thus, good parental control and supervision characterized by close parental monitoring and clear family rules for children's behavior may significantly reduce the risk of illicit drug initiation throughout adolescence by affecting children's association with peers. These findings regarding family influences are consistent with findings from previous studies (Guo et al. 2002).

In a major study of the strength of family ties and risky behavior (involving cigarettes, marijuana, and sex) by adolescents, researchers found that lower risk was closely related to a close-knit family. Family ties were found to be more important than peer relations (S. Gilbert 1997). In a longitudinal study designed to test social control theory, in particular that element relating poor interpersonal relations with deviance (in this case drug abuse), Denise Kandel and Mark Davies (1991: 459) found no relationship between integration failure and drug abuse. In fact, they found illicit drug use to be "positively associated with intimacy among members of male friendship networks, whether intimacy refers to confiding or to interacting with friends. Further, the structure of the networks of illicit users is similar to that of nonusers. To the extent that some differences occurred, they tended to indicate closer friendships for drug users than nonusers."

The researchers note that their findings tend to support subcultural (or cultural deviance) theory rather than control theory. George Vaillant (1983), a research psychiatrist, found that culture plays an important role in the genesis of alcoholism and that family practices—drinking habits into which a child is socialized, rather than a lack of social control (or even social distress)—are a dominant factor. The idea that drug abuse, in particular alcoholism, is the result of a habit learned in accord with the same principles that govern other learning experiences is consistent with the behavior/learning theory of drug abuse (Bandura 1969, 1974).

SUBCULTURES AND CULTURAL DEVIANCE THEORY

Some sociologists explain deviant behavior as the result of people conforming to subcultures to which they belong. "Subcultures are patterns of values, norms, and behavior which have become traditional among certain groups." They are "important frames of reference through which individuals and groups see the world and interpret it" (Short 1968: 11). A person without important bonds to conventional society but with strong ties to a drug-using subculture would be more likely to abuse drugs. Members of a drug subculture promote its values and norms to people who are attracted to "the life" (socialization). The person who joins must reorder his or her life in conformity with the new subculture to be accepted by the others and to remain a member in good standing. The subculture provides rewards and punishments along the lines proposed by operant conditioning theory to retain the member's loyalty.

Albert Cohen (1965) argues that certain lower-class subcultures negate middle-class values, and this negation is a severe handicap because middle-class cultural characteristics are necessary to succeed in our society. These characteristics include:

1. Ambition
2. A sense of individual responsibility
3. Skills for achievement
4. Ability to postpone gratification
5. Industry and thrift
6. Rational planning, such as budgeting time and money
7. Cultivation of manners and politeness
8. Control of physical aggression
9. Respect for property
10. A sense of wholesome recreation

The norms of some lower-class subcultures, according to James Short (1968) and Walter Miller (1958), are simply not conducive to conventional types of achievement. The members of an adolescent street group adhere to the norms of a lower-class subculture, whose focal concerns are (Miller 1958):

- *Trouble*: law-violating behavior
- *Toughness*: physical prowess, daring
- *Smartness*: ability to con others, shrewdness
- *Excitement*: thrills, risk, danger

- *Fate*: being lucky
- *Autonomy*: independence of external restraint

Trouble often involves fighting or sexual adventures while drinking; troublesome behavior for women frequently means sexual involvement with disadvantageous consequences. Trouble-producing behavior is a source of status. Toughness evolves out of the significant proportion of lower-class males reared in female-dominated households and the resulting concern over homosexuality that Miller contends runs through lower-class culture.

Gambling, also prevalent in lower-class culture, is rooted in the belief that life is subject to a set of forces over which there is little or no control—fate. Autonomy is often expressed in statements such as "No one is going to push me around" and "I'm going to tell him to take this job and shove it." Such sentiments, however, often contrast with actual patterns of behavior; in other words, according to Miller, many lower-class individuals desire highly restrictive social environments such as the armed forces, prison, and drug treatment programs: "Being controlled is equated with being cared for" (1958: 13).

Chein and his colleagues note that "boys who become addicts are clearly related to the delinquent subculture. Even before they started using drugs regularly, most users have had friends who have been in jail, reformatory, or on probation" (1964: 13). Without exception they found that addicts come from homes that are devoid of a father or strong father figure—female-dominated households. These individuals are identified with what others have dubbed the *criminal underclass subculture* (B. D. Johnson et al. 1990), of which the drug subculture is an important component.

The concept of a drug subculture, notes John O'Donnell (1969: 84), implies that addicts are in contact with each other (differential association):

> In this contact, learning takes place. The learning can be of facts and techniques. For example, the neophyte can learn from more experienced addicts that his withdrawal symptoms are the result of not having his usual dose of narcotics, and will be relieved by a dose; that the intravenous route enhances the drug effect; how to obtain narcotics, or money for narcotics; new sources of narcotics; how to prepare narcotics for administration, and other knowledge of this kind. He will usually learn new attitudes too. He may learn to define himself as an addict, learn new justifications for his drug use, and new and negative attitudes toward the laws that try to prevent drug use.

As the drug user comes to define himself or herself as an addict, the wider society perceives him or her as such, in a process known as *labeling* (see the next section).

Drug cultures come in many different types. Some are linked to the use of particular substances; others seem to be part of a larger subculture. Using participant observation, Patricia Adler provides an insider's look at a marijuana- and cocaine-smuggling subculture centered in the middle- and upper-class environs of the coastal communities of Southern California. She states: "This subculture provides guidelines for their dealing and smuggling, outlining members' rules, roles, and reputation. Their social life is deviant as well, as evidenced by their abundant drug consumption, extravagant spending, uninhibited sexual mores, and focus on immediate gratification" (1985: 1).

In general, cocaine abusers do not appear to present any clearly discernible subculture. Surveys of cocaine users have revealed that there is apparently no "typical" cocaine user (President's Commission on Organized Crime 1986). Heavy cocaine users fit no easy stereotype of drug abuse:

> A large proportion are successful, well-educated, upwardly mobile professionals in their early twenties and thirties. They are stockbrokers and lawyers and architects with sufficient disposable income to sink into a diversion that even at "social" use levels can cost $100 or more an evening. Many are, for the most part, otherwise law-abiding citizens who would cringe at being labeled criminals, even though they know what they are doing is illegal. A majority are men, but a growing number are women. And, as cocaine prices fall, more and more are teenagers and others for whom the drug's exorbitant cost once kept it out of reach. (National Institute on Drug Abuse 1985: 1)

Cocaine in the form of crack, however, seems to have produced a drug subculture in poor neighborhoods of urban areas. "The subcultural patterns include an argot of terms that describes the activities having to do with crack, the various crack combinations touted and paraphernalia needed for using, and the institution of base houses [where the substance is smoked] and crack houses [where the substance is purchased]" (Frank et al: 1987: 6). Blanche Frank and her colleagues (1987) point out that the development of this subculture helped to glamorize and thereby spread the use of crack.

Harold Finestone (1964) drew a portrait of the black heroin subculture in Chicago at the beginning of the 1950s. He found that the stereotypical addict eschewed violence, used a deliberately colorful vocabulary, and disdained work. (This contrasted with a small number of white addicts interviewed by Finestone, whose type of adjustment stressed violence.) These addicts, whom Finestone (1964: 284) calls the "cats," had a lifestyle that centered on achieving "kicks." A kick is any act considered taboo by conventional society "that heightens and intensifies the present moment of experience and differentiates it as much as possible from the humdrum routine of daily life." To the cat, heroin abuse provided the ultimate kick. A similar type of stereotypical heroin addict was found by Harvey Feldman (1977), who conducted his research in the late 1960s in a community that he called by the pseudonym "East Highland."

SYMBOLIC INTERACTIONISM/LABELING

Symbolic interactionism is a sociological approach that appears in such perspectives as labeling or societal reaction theory. Its central premise is that people make their own reality:

> Symbolic interactionists suggest that categories which individuals use to render the world meaningful, and even the experience of self, are structured by socially acquired definitions. They argue that individuals, in reaction to group rewards and sanctions, gradually internalize group expectations. These internalized social

definitions allow people to evaluate their own behavior from the standpoint of the group and in doing so provide a lens through which to view oneself as a social object. (Quadagno and Antonio 1975: 33)

Symbolic interactionism does not explain drug abuse because its focus is not on the behavior of the social actor but on how the behavior or person is viewed by others—by society. Thus, Kai Erikson (1966: 6) states: "deviance is not a property *inherent* in any particular kind of behavior; it is a property *conferred* upon that behavior by people who come into direct or indirect contact with it." In Chapter 1 we noted that certain harmful substances—alcohol and tobacco—can be lawfully manufactured, distributed, and possessed, while other chemicals are outlawed and the people who choose to use them are labeled outlaws. In Chapter 2 we noted that at one time the users of certain substances—opiates and cocaine—were not seen as outcasts or criminals. After passage of the Harrison Act what had been lawful behavior became illegal, and a new class of criminals was created, as well as a lucrative new enterprise: drug trafficking. Using this perspective, Thomas Szasz (1974: 11) argues that "before 1914 [and the Harrison Act] there was no 'drug problem' in the United States." Thus, society is inclined to view those who abuse alcohol as suffering from a disease (alcoholism), while those who indulge in illegal chemicals are viewed—stigmatized—as deserving punishment. The societal interactionist view of drug use has important policy implications.

While those who abuse chemicals such as heroin and cocaine are labeled pejoratively, fired from employment, and subjected to law enforcement scrutiny, jail, and prison, the widespread acceptance of the traditional disease concept of alcoholism reduces the stigma associated with that problem. The disease model of alcoholism "provided a way for hundreds of thousands of alcoholics to make sense of their experience, to regain a measure of dignity and self-respect. And to begin to take control of and to rebuilt their shattered lives" (Wallace 1993: 70).

Societal reaction labels—stigmatizes—certain actors, which causes a damaged self-image, deviant identity, and a host of negative social expectations. Furthermore, a damaged self-image can become a self-fulfilling prophecy. Edwin Schur (1973: 124) notes that "once an individual has been branded as a wrong-doer, it becomes extremely difficult for him to shed that new identity." During adolescence "many youths engage in socially disruptive and health-endangering behavior," although "most adolescents who experiment with drugs or other health-compromising and illicit practices do not escalate their worrisome behavior" (Baumrind 1987: 14). This should caution us against unnecessarily labeling people, particularly young people. "Zero tolerance" might be politically viable, but it can significantly limit a young person's social and economic options in a way that does not encourage conforming behavior as an adult.

According to Edwin Lemert, the person who is labeled deviant reorganizes his or her behavior in accordance with the social reaction "and begins to employ his deviant behavior, or role based upon it, as a means of defense,

Labeling

"Young offenders in particular must be confronted with penalties that both deter them from future drug use and embarrass them among their peers. Today, many young offenders boast about their lenient treatment in the hands of the authorities and wear it as a badge of pride; corrections officials must make sure that when juveniles are caught using or selling drugs, their punishment becomes a source of shame. We need a mix of sanctions for juvenile drug use that includes school suspension, parental notification, and postponement of driver's license eligibility, and extends to weekends of 'community service' that involve arduous and unenviable public chores" (Office of National Drug Control Policy 1989: 25).

attack, or adjustment to the overt and covert problems created by the subsequent societal reaction to him" (1951: 76). This *secondary deviance* is best exemplified by drug abusers who are forced to associate with other drug abusers and furthermore must often resort to crime (secondary deviance) in order to support their primary deviance: their drug habits.

SUMMARY

Theories that explain the use of drugs can be biological, psychological, or sociological. Indeed, the explanation may involve a combination of factors because any one factor might not fully explain drug-using behavior. Sociological theory examines drug use in its social context and often views drug use as the product of social conditions and relationships that cause despair, frustration, hopelessness, and general feelings of alienation in society's most disadvantaged segments. Many sociological studies have found that drug use among adolescents is motivated by intermittent feelings of boredom and depression and that, like other aspects of adolescence, drug use is typically abandoned on reaching adulthood.

Sociology has determined that drug users typically pass through several stages on the way to addiction or alcoholism, from social or experimental use to dependency and dysfunction. Anomie explains drug abuse as a form of retreatism by people who are unable to deal with the disconnect between society's economic expectations and an individual's ability to achieve them. Differential association explains that drug use is a learned behavior that is transmitted through intimate personal groups. The effectiveness of learning depends on the degree of intensity, frequency, and duration of the association.

Social control theorists focus on why only relatively few people engage in deviant behavior such as crime and drug abuse. Their answer is the strength of an individual's bond to conventional society.

Subcultures are patterns of values, norms, and behavior that have become traditional among certain groups, and deviant behavior is the result of people conforming to subcultures to which they belong. A person without important bonds to conventional society but with strong ties to a drug-using subculture would be more likely to abuse drugs.

According to labeling theory, people make their own reality, so if a person who uses certain psychoactive substances is labeled—by lawmakers and society—as "bad," he or she will be dealt with accordingly, no matter the reality. Once attached, the label has a strength of its own that can lead to secondary deviance.

In the next chapter we will examine psychological theories that help to explain drug use.

REVIEW QUESTIONS

1. According to the National Institute on Drug Abuse, what seven factors are associated with adolescent drug abuse?
2. What are the three stages to becoming an alcoholic?
3. What stages do heroin users and cocaine users go through on their way to addiction?
4. How does the theory of anomie explain drug abuse?
5. How does differential association explain the spread of drug abuse?
6. How does social control theory explain deviance, including drug abuse?
7. What is the connection between the delinquent subculture and drug abuse?
8. How does symbolic interactionism/labeling explain the "drug problem"?

8 CHAPTER | The Psychology of Drug Abuse

Being a drug abuser becomes a lifestyle. It cannot be treated as an isolated biological or pharmacological problem.

Arnold M. Washton (President's Commission on Organized Crime 1984: 59)

The addictive disorders are complex because they are influenced by genetic, familial, psychological, and sociocultural factors.

American Psychiatric Association (1995: 5)

The sociology of drug use, discussed in Chapter 7, notes that the phenomenon tends to be clustered in environments that are characterized by social conditions and relationships that cause despair, frustration, hopelessness, and general feelings of alienation. However, in these environments drug abusers represent only a small fraction of the populace. Why? Why do people who are exposed to the same physical environment react differently to the use and abuse of drugs? Psychology, a discipline that focuses on the individual, provides some answers. In this chapter, for pedagogical purposes psychological explanations are placed into two broad categories: clinical and behaviorist.

PSYCHOLOGY AND PERSONALITY

Psychology examines individual human behavior, and clinicians attempt to treat abnormal or dysfunctional behavior. Some psychological theories of drug abuse are based on personality: "Drug addiction is primarily a personality disorder. It represents one type of abortive adjustment to life that individuals with certain personality predispositions may choose under appropriate conditions of availability and sociocultural attitudinal tolerance" (Ausubel 1978: 77). Robert Craig (1987: 31) notes that the psychological literature supports such a conclusion: "[D]rug addicts have a paucity of major psychiatric syndromes and neuroses and a plethora of personality disorders and character disorders." An extensive review of the literature on psychological testing of heroin addicts found them to be hostile, demanding, aggressive, rebellious, irresponsible, playful, and impulsive (Craig 1987). But many of these traits are also been found in outstanding athletes. With respect to substance abusers in general, they "are characterized by disregard for established social customs, lack of control and foresight, inability to maintain lasting personal commitments, and the need for unusual and varied experiences" (Cox 1985: 233).

Part of the psychological explanation for drug abuse has been a presumed *addictive personality*, a psychological vulnerability resulting from problematic family relationships, inappropriate reinforcement, the lack of healthy role models, contradictory parental expectations, and/or an absence of love and respect. The psychologically immature drug-dependent personality seeks gratification on a primitive level or, according to the pleasure principle, finds drug use and its attendant behavior reinforcing. He or she ignores the long-term negative consequences of behavior and instead opts for the short-term positive reinforcement that drugs provide.

Unfortunately, the search for the addictive personality—psychological variables that can predict future drug abuse—has not been fruitful (see Lang 1983). Peter Nathan (1988) points out that the search for predictors of drug dependence has discovered a variety of overt acts by prealcoholic and predrug abusers that reveal an unwillingness to accept societal rules. Beyond that, however, few consistent links have been found between other behaviors or personality factors and later abuse of alcohol and drugs. Furthermore,

Nathan (1988) notes that large numbers of abusers have never demonstrated antisocial behavior in childhood and that a substantial number of antisocial or conduct-disordered children never develop alcohol or drug problems as adults.

Psychological theories can be broadly categorized into those that are based on a Freudian or psychoanalytic strain and those that are based on behaviorism or learning theory.

PSYCHOANALYTIC THEORY AND DRUG ABUSE

Psychoanalytic theory was "fathered" by Sigmund Freud (1856–1939). Although it has undergone change over the years, its basic proposition continues to be the influence of unconscious phenomena on human behavior. "Simply put, this concept says that people are not aware of the most important determinants of their behavior" (Cloninger, 1993: 25). According to Freud there are three types of mental phenomena:

1. *Conscious*: what we are currently thinking about
2. *Preconscious*: thoughts and memories that can easily be called into consciousness
3. *Unconscious*: feelings and experiences that have been repressed and that can be made conscious only with a great deal of difficulty and that nevertheless exert a dominant influence over our behavior

The Stages of Psychological Development

Freud posited that unconscious feelings and thoughts relate to stages of psychosexual development from infancy to adulthood. Psychoanalytic theory "conceives of the human being as a dynamic energy system consisting of basic drives and instincts which in interaction with the environment serve to organize and develop the personality through a series of developmental stages. Individuals from birth are pushed by these largely unconscious and irrational drives toward satisfaction of desires which are largely unconscious and irrational" (Compton and Galaway 1979: 90). Although we lack conscious memory of these stages, in later life they serve as a source of anxiety and guilt, psychoneurosis, and psychosis. The stages overlap, and transition from one to the other is gradual, the time spans noted below being approximate and dependent on individual and cultural differences. (See Figure 8.1.)

Oral Stage (Birth to 18 Months)   During the oral stage the infant organizes his or her primitive impulses around the mouth, lips, and tongue, which are the predominant sexual organs during this stage. Desires and gratifications are mainly oral—sucking and biting. The infant is unsocialized, devoid of all self-control, and narcissistic. In the normal infant, the source of pleasure becomes

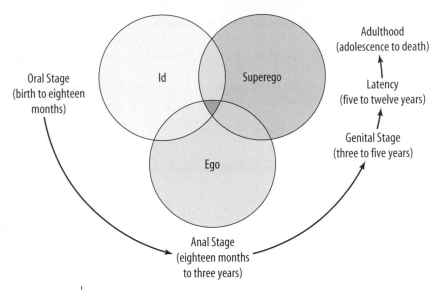

Figure 8.1 | Stages of Psychosexual Development

associated with the touch and warmth of the parent, who gratifies the infant's oral needs. When this gratification is lacking, narcissism remains predominant, and in the narcissistically disturbed adult, drugs become a substitute for maternal warmth and self-esteem.

The infant's physiological balance is precarious, so any environmental change may cause distress. The anxiety that is experienced in the helpless state of infancy is ameliorated by the discovery of a maternal object capable of providing nurture. The absence of warm mother-infant interaction and sensory deprivation during this stage causes the adult to use drugs as a means of reducing anxiety; drugs serve as a substitute for maternal attachment, and drug abuse is a regression back to an unfulfilled oral stage. Experiments conducted on animals reveal that the young of many species experience separation anxiety that can be ameliorated by opiates. "For human species, the experience of social attachments and comfort becomes inevitably bound up with the euphoria of human affection, intimacy, and love." Opiates apparently provide a substitute, albeit an inadequate one, for the absent maternal object (Levinthal 1988: 145).

During this stage the infant attempts to reach a state of homeostatic peacefulness, and this requires a responsive and supportive maternal object. Because of trauma or deficiencies experienced during this stage of development, "the infant may fail to achieve homeostatic balance, in the context of an attachment to a maternal object," and this can lead to drug abuse in the adult. The "substance, be it heroin or some other narcotic or stimulant, works at a physiologic and psychological representational level to facilitate the attainment of this basic homeostatic experience" (Greenspan 1978: 74).

Anal Stage (18 Months to 3 Years) As the infant moves into his or her second year, the "instinctual organization is beginning to organize around the mental representations concerned with anality" (Greenspan 1978: 76). The anus becomes the center of sexual desire and gratification during this stage, with pleasure closely associated with the retention and expulsion of feces. Physiologically, the child is now able to control eliminatory processes. The child typically experiences toilet training and becomes partially social-ized, the beginning of a parental internalizing process that is completed during the genital stage that follows. During the anal stage children may act out destructive urges such as breaking toys or even injuring living organisms, insects, or small animals. A great deal of adult psychopathology, including violent antisocial behavior and sociopathic personality disorders, is traced back to this stage. Depressants such as heroin, alcohol, barbiturates, and tranquilizers can provide a way of managing sadistic and masochistic impulses—self-medication—that were not successfully dealt with during the anal stage. Such people take depressants not for pleasure but to control internal rage. (The policy implications of this theory argue against our cur-rent response to drug use.)

If development is thwarted during this stage, the infant does not succeed in achieving "an internal sense of mastery and delineation of self from the primary other"—the maternal figure. Drugs are used in an effort to obtain a state of mastery and clear demarcation from the maternal figure that is necessary to manage the transition to the genital stage. To gain greater independence, the infant must relinquish the dependent attachment to the maternal object, and if successful, he or she can then move into the genital stage. In those who fail to accomplish this transition, substance abuse "is a defense against separation anxiety and its accompanying depression" (Greenspan 1978: 78).

Genital Stage (3 to 5 Years) In this stage, which anticipates adulthood, the main sexual interest is assumed by the genitals and in normal people is there-after maintained there. During this period boys experience strong attachments to their mothers (*Oedipus complex*) and girls to their fathers (*Electra complex*); both boys and girls have incestuous fantasies, although they do not fully understand the mechanics of adult sexual relations. The child must begin to relinquish the dependent maternal or paternal attachment despite feelings of sadness in doing so. Drugs provide solace to the adult who was unable to deal with the ensuing depression of separation.

As was noted in previous chapters, psychoactive drugs often affect sexual performance—by enhancing or depressing desire and/or performance. Drugs can provide a chemical means of dealing with disturbances experienced during the genital stage of development. Heroin, for example, might serve to suppress the sexual drive that is fixated in the genital stage; that is, the drug helps the person to deal with unconscious (and guilt-provoking) incestuous wishes. Heroin causes a return to the oral stage, enabling the addict to avoid dealing with conflicts that were not adequately resolved.

Adolescence/Adulthood In this stage the individual experiences a dramatic reawakening of genital interest and awareness. The incestuous wish, however, is repressed, and sexual interest is expressed in terms of mature (adult) sexuality. As was noted above, drug use that substitutes for or enhances sexual activity allows the abuser to avoid or overcome the reawakening of incestuous sexual feelings that were never successfully reconciled during the genital stage. Furthermore, each stage is left behind but never completely abandoned. Some amount of psychic energy (*cathexis*) remains attached to earlier objects of psychosexual development. When the strength of the cathexis is particularly strong, it is expressed as a *fixation*. For example, instead of a boy transferring his affection to another woman in the adolescent/adult stage, he might remain fixated on his mother (or a girl on her father):

> At each stage, particular behaviors are important, but as we progress through the stages we use the behaviours associated with stages. So, in early stages, babies gain satisfaction from sucking (for example, at a mother's breast to satisfy the need for food). Later, sucking can also be satisfying—for example, in the use of cigarettes, sweets or in sexual activities. However, adults have a wider range of satisfying activities to choose from. Some people become unconsciously attached to behaviour associated with particular stages (*fixation*). They are driven to seek that form of satisfaction to an unreasonable degree. Consequently they cannot use the full repertoire of behaviour available to them. (Payne 1997: 73)

While the individual is experiencing each of these stages of development, corresponding psychic phenomena develop.

Divisions of the Psyche

Id Each person is born with a mass of powerful drives, wishes, urges, and psychic tensions that are energized in the form of the *libido*. These seek immediate discharge or gratification. These **id** impulses are asocial, operating on the primitive level of pleasure and pain (that is, they are hedonistic), and from about birth to 7 months of age the id is the total psychic apparatus. Id drives are a central component of personality, impelling a person toward activity that leads to cessation of the tension excitement it creates, satisfying the libido. For example, the hunger drive will result in activity that eventually satisfies (gratifies the id of) the person experiencing hunger. A craving for pleasure-producing chemicals will lead the id-driven person to seek drugs at considerable risk in order to satiate his or her desire, and the feelings of omnipotence that drugs can produce reinforce this drive.

Ego Through the environment and training, infants learn to modify their expression of id drives and to delay immediate gratification. Ego development permits them to obtain maximum gratification with a minimum of difficulty; the **ego** tempers the id with reality and is the organism's contact with the real world. In normal development the child learns to relinquish primitive id demands and to adapt behavior to social demands (F. Smart 1970). The stronger the ego, the stronger is the individual's ability to tolerate frustration. Poor ego functioning, manifested by an inability to tolerate the psychological discomfort of frustration or stress, can lead to the abuse of chemicals that lower the discomfort and provide immediate gratification. Furthermore, note Henry Krystal and Herbert Raskin (1970: 31), in the ego-deficient personality "drugs are used to avoid impending psychic trauma in circumstances which would not be potentially traumatic to other persons"; in other words, drug use reflects a dysfunction in reality testing. Through drug use, notes Sandor Rado (1981), stress is alleviated and reality is avoided, but only temporarily; when the chemical reaction subsides, reality returns with renewed vigor, and the subject again seeks relicf through drugs. However, the psyche now finds that the same dosage brings diminished relief—tolerance has developed—leading to increasing dosages.

As a result of disturbances in psychosexual development, a person may remain at the ego level of development; in other words, "the child remains asocial or else behaves as if he had become social without having made actual adjustment to the demands of society. This means that he has not repudiated completely his instinctual wishes but has suppressed them so that they lurk in the background awaiting an opportunity to break through to satisfaction" (Aichhorn 1963: 4). Drug use, a reversion to gratifications associated with the oral stage, is a symptom of such a disturbance. Drug use is also associated with the ego's need to be in control of the source of pleasurable feelings—it is narcissistic (Rado 1981). Edward Khantzian (1980) states that heroin use is caused by the ego's need to control feelings of rage and aggression, emotions that relate to the anal stage of development; a form of self-medication.

The choice of drugs is either ego-constricting or ego-expanding. The weak ego structure of heroin users causes them to seek quiet and lonely lives—a tranquility through ego constriction that is aided by narcotics. Cocaine and amphetamine users, on the other hand, often come from households with warm mothers and fathers who are strong and encouraging. For them, stimulant use grows out of a self-directed and intensely competitive personality: "They take cocaine to expand their egos and their self-confidence" (Spotts and Shontz 1980: 65). The user of stimulants is suffering from anxiety brought on by a lack of stimulation: The ego is disturbed by the absence of stimuli, and intense stimulation is preferred by those using amphetamines and cocaine to ward off boredom and depression (Krystal and Raskin 1970).

In the course of normal development, over time the child integrates outer (social) discipline and imposes it on himself or herself. The instinctual impulses are brought under his or her own control, and we get the beginning of a superego (F. Smart 1970).

Superego Oversimplified as the conscience, the **superego** is a counterforce to the id, exercising a critical influence, a sense of morality that controls behavior. Tied to overcoming the incestuous feelings of the genital stage, the superego serves as an internalized parent, meaning that behavior is no longer exclusively dependent on external forces (the ego level of control). Failures in superego development may leave a person without strong internal controls over id and ego impulses and can result in behavior that is harmful or destructive. The sociopath lacks sufficient superego strength, and the ego is insufficient to control powerful id impulses.

At the other extreme is an overactive superego that cannot make distinctions between *thinking* bad and *doing* bad. Unresolved conflicts of earlier development (e.g., an Oedipus complex) and id impulses that are normally repressed or dealt with through other, less destructive processes (such as reaction formation, discussed below) create a severe sense of guilt. This guilt is experienced (unconsciously) as a compulsive need to be punished; and to alleviate guilt, the person commits acts for which punishment is virtually certain. August Aichhorn (1963) notes that such people are victims of their own personalities. For them drugs accomplish a dual purpose: Drugs reduce the anxiety caused by unresolved inner conflicts, while the deleterious aspects of drug abuse provide external punishment. According to Leon Wurmser (1978), society assists the drug abuser in this quest by imposing shame and punishment.

According to psychoanalytic theory, unconscious forces maintain a delicate balance as the person experiences life's various sociocultural and biological aspects. The balance is easily upset, crossing the very thin line between the normal and the neurotic or between the neurotic and the psychotic. In fact, there is only a difference of degree between the *normal* and the *abnormal*. When repressed material begins to overwhelm the psyche and threatens to enter the person's consciousness, external defense mechanisms come into play in the form of psychoneuroses and, in more serious cases, psychosis. These responses may take the form of phobias—toward heights, insects, or closed spaces, for example. In the paranoid reaction the person projects his or her thoughts onto imagined enemies; in the reaction formation the destructive urges of the anal stage can be channeled into prosocial activities—becoming a surgeon, a veterinarian, or a butcher, for example. The degree to which defense mechanisms cause the person to become dysfunctional provides an objective measurement of abnormality. The psychoneuroses, or the primitive defense mechanism that is drug abuse, allow psychic energy to be discharged without having to confront unconscious material (Wurmser 1978). In his cocaine-abusing patients, Frederic Schiffer (1988) found that drug use was a self-medication aimed at alleviating the pain of early trauma. Cocaine abuse represented an unconscious, symbolic repetition of childhood trauma. Old psychological injuries were reinflicted by the drug, which also allowed the patient to unconsciously gain a (false) sense of control over these early difficulties, providing an opportunity to struggle against them again.

DRUG USE AND ADOLESCENCE

Psychoanalytic theory views drug abuse as a symptom of neuroses that manifest themselves during adolescence. We recognize that adolescents typically undergo periods of boredom, anxiety, anger, frustration, and even short-lived

Adolescents typically undergo periods of boredom, anxiety, anger, frustration, and even short-lived depression; a defining feature of this time is change on many levels. Research has identified these factors as well as the peer group as being associated with drug abuse. Sociopsychological growth and maturity require grappling with reality—drug use reduces social competence and adaptive behaviors, leaving adolescents ill-equipped to become adults.

©Imagesource/Photolibrary

depression. A defining feature of adolescence "is the rapid and far-reaching changes occurring in virtually all aspects of life and the resultant high-level stress" (Newcomb and Bentler 1988: 11). Research has identified these factors as well as the peer group as being associated with drug abuse. The typical adolescent has not had sufficient experience in dealing with feelings of psychosocial stress in a mature—that is, adult—fashion. Psychoactive drugs can be seen as a form of self-medication in response to the stressful conditions of adolescence. These frequently include affective disorders: "Drugs of abuse and medications prescribed for affective disorders have common neurochemical effects that presumably treat the abnormality" (Bukstein, Brent, and Kaminer 1989: 1139).

It is normal for an adolescent to grapple with the problems of physiological and psychological development. The struggle for identity through a progressive process of relationships and experiences enables the person to manage the complexities of adolescence. He or she becomes more competent and eventually moves into young adulthood. "Adolescence is a period of development involving transitions in the major physical, intellectual, psychosocial, and moral processes that make up a person. Transitional stages of development are by definition periods of disequilibration and disruption and, therefore, replete with opportunities for experiences that are both dangerous and growth-enhancing" (Baumrind 1987: 14).

"The adolescent addict, however, sidesteps such growth by at first simply avoiding the situations in which he can gradually acquire competence or by passively going along with the whims and decisions of others and eventually by substituting the anxiety-reducing 'normative' influence of the opiate drugs" (Chein et al. 1964: 202). As Otto Fenichel (1945) points out, euphoric substances protect against painful mental states. However, because of this, the adolescent's reality-testing ability (an ego function) remains primitive, and his or her ability to tolerate stress and frustration remains at an infantile (oral) level. Like the infant during the oral stage, the addict is motivated only by a need to immediately gratify his or her perceived needs. This type of behavior is governed only by the primitive id impulses—the pleasure principle—without any real concern for the results. As a result of their extensive longitudinal research, Michael Newcomb and Peter Bentler (1988: 240) conclude that adolescent drug use, "particularly of cannabis and hard drugs, has measurably negative effects on several critical areas of life functioning as a young adult."

Heroin use typically begins during adolescence, with the drug serving as a means for avoiding psychologically demanding—but healthier—responses to developmental crisis, stress, deprivation, and other forms of emotional pain (Khantzian, Mack, Schatzberg 1974). Sociopsychological growth and maturity require grappling with reality, as exercise aficionados will recognize: "No pain, no gain." Drug use reduces social competence and adaptive behaviors. The therapeutic community, a particular approach to treating drug abusers discussed in Chapter 9, responds to people whose use of drugs is based on an inability to deal with the frustrations of reality.

Unresolved Parental Relationships

According to Freud, "from the time of puberty onward the human individual must devote himself to the great task of freeing himself from the parents; and only after this detachment is accomplished can he cease to be a child and so become a member of the social community" (1961: 345–346). Freud points out that in neurotics, such as addicts, this detachment is not accomplished because the neurotic has a distorted pathological relationship with his or her parents. This relationship is characterized by overdependence and fear of being rejected. Although there is identification with the father (or father figure), it is "at best laden with hostility" (Frazier 1962: 97). Isidor Chein and his colleagues (1964) found that addicts, in contrast to controls from the same environment, came either from single-parent households or from families in which the father was usually distant, presented immoral models of behavior, was primarily concerned with day-to-day gratification of appetites, and impulsive. As would be expected, the fathers had unstable work histories, pessimistic and fatalistic attitudes toward the future, and low aspirations for their sons. The level of interaction between father and son was minimal. A 1999 study at Columbia University found that adolescents who do not get along well with their fathers are much more likely to use nicotine, alcohol, and illegal drugs than are even children from one-parent/mother-only households (Molotsky 1999).

The addict's relationship with his mother includes a long history of emotional deprivation (Frazier 1962: 98):

> Frequently, a tense, dominant, autistic, unhappy mother forced the child into becoming an adjunct to herself rather than allowing him to develop as an independent person. The feeling of hostility toward the mother and the inability to form any close satisfactory relationships date back to these earliest years. The addict's conflicts reflect this oral deprivation in an infantile helplessness, and the drug helps him to regress to "happy" infancy that was never really happy. The effects of the drug handle his hostility and reduce tensions that are symptoms of these lifelong conflicts. The hostility toward the mother generally remains unconscious, but it is expressed through the drug that not only "destroys" the user but also symbolically destroys the mother whom he has incorporated through identification.

Ego Deficiencies

According to Robert Savitt (1963: 45), it is not euphoria that the addict seeks in narcotics but a satiated feeling reminiscent of infancy: "When an infant's basic needs for sustenance and love are fulfilled, he falls asleep." Thus, the purported use of heroin for its euphoric properties is an exaggeration: "It would appear that the elation which the heroin addict experiences has been stressed out of proportion to the sleep or stupor which often soon follows. . . . Like the infant who alternates between hunger and sleep, the addict alternates between hunger for a drug and narcotic stupor" (1963: 44). The adolescent addict suffers from a narcissism (self-love), an infantile level of relating to others that retards the ability to form close, warm, emotional relationships. Other people are simply instruments for the adolescent's own purposes—even his or her own mother, from whom the adolescent has not learned to differentiate as a portion of himself or herself. Interpersonal relationships, even with parents, are shallow. Groups of "junkies" are tied together only by the one thing they share: drugs. It is an easy group, without demands, deliberate structure, or goals beyond those involving continued drug use. Stanley Greenspan (1978: 74) states: "Substance abuse could emanate from the lack of this basic ability of attaching to the human object." A prominent feature of the family situation of the adolescent opiate addict "is the peculiarly close relationship between the addict and his mother. It is not a closeness of warmth or mutual regard so much as it is a clinging and feeling of being bound together" (Chein et al. 1964: 212).

Drug-dependent adolescents suffer from severe ego inadequacies. They have been found to be relatively unresponsive or indifferent to opportunities for education, work, or recreation; they have limited interests and curiosity. They appear to suffer from gross disturbances in early life, leading to a restricted pattern of responsiveness. They have poor reality testing and an inability to delay gratification or accept frustration. They react to criticism by withdrawal, giving up easily in school or employment situations, and they are unable to form realistic goal orientations. While recognizing all of the dangers inherent in heroin use, addicts are unable to exercise restraint. They use heroin to deal with frustrations and pain; they are retreatists for whom heroin relieves anxiety, by changing feelings of tenseness and restlessness into feelings of comfort, relaxation, and peacefulness (Chein et al. 1964). Heroin helps to overcome the usual tensions of adolescence. The heroin addict may also find heroin effective in thwarting feelings of intense destructiveness and sadism associated with a disturbance in the anal stage of development. The drug pacifies such drives, and the negative and punishing results of heroin addiction satisfy the superego's need to punish such feelings (Yorke 1970).

Regression to Infant Sexuality

There are significant sexual implications in drug use, particularly the intravenous use of heroin. "Addicts are persons who have a disposition to react to the effects of alcohol, morphine, or other drugs in such a way that they try to use these effects to satisfy the archaic oral longings which is sexual longing, a need for security, and a need for the maintenance of self-esteem simultaneously" (Fenichel 1945: 376). This pathology has its origins in infantile sexuality, both oral and genital. "The addict uses his addiction to express or act out repressed impulses and needs," and the discharge of psychic energy is pleasurable enough to replace other pleasurable activities, such as sex and eating (Chein et al. 1964: 235). The use of heroin is autoerotic, bypassing genital sex in favor of the infantile or oral-stage eroticism (Yorke 1970).

Psychoanalytic theories of drug abuse have been criticized for their reliance on retrospective self-reports and individual case studies, which are limited methods that lack rigorous empirical grounding. This contrasts with the rigorous experimentation that underlies learning theory.

BEHAVIORISM/LEARNING THEORY

The second major school of psychological thought has its roots in the laboratory of experimental psychology with its dogs, pigeons, rats, monkeys, and mazes (see, e.g., Rachlin 1991). Behaviorists typically reject psychoanalytic theory as unscientific, that is, lacking the rigorous testing to which learning theory has been subjected. Indeed, measurement of objective behavior is intrinsic to **learning theory**, which proceeds on the basis that all forms of behavior are conditioned, the result of learned responses to certain stimuli. Disturbed behavior such as drug abuse results from inappropriate conditioning (London 1964). To the behaviorist a person is simply the sum product of his or her experience or learning, and learning is based on operant conditioning.

Operant Conditioning

The behaviorist stresses—and has been able to prove—that animal behavior can be modified through the proper application of operant conditioning: positive and negative reinforcement. Behavior is *"strengthened* by its consequences, and for that reason the consequences themselves are called

Classical and Operant Conditioning

Behavioral psychology recognizes two basic types of processes associated with learning (Tilson 1993: 2):

Classical conditioning involves the pairing of two stimuli, one of which elicits a reflex and one of which is neutral [food and the sounding of a bell, for example]. With repeated pairing of the two stimuli, the previously neutral stimulus [bell] becomes a conditioned stimulus and elicits the response [salivating, for example] in absence of the original eliciting stimulus [food].

Operant conditioning involves the repeated presentation or removal of a stimulus following a behavior to increase the probability of the behavior (i.e., **reinforcement**). A reinforcer is a stimulus that increases the probability of a behavior. If the probability of a behavior goes up following the presentation of some stimulus, then positive reinforcement has occurred. If the probability of a behavior goes up after the *removal* of a stimulus, then negative reinforcement has occurred.

'reinforcers.'" (Skinner 1974: 40). When some aspect of (animal or human) behavior is followed by a certain type of consequence—a reward—the behavior is more likely to be repeated. The reward is called **positive reinforcement**. If the probability of a behavior goes up after the *removal* of a stimulus, then **negative reinforcement** has occurred. "A negative reinforcer strengthens any behavior that reduces or terminates it" (Skinner 1974: 47). For example, the negative reinforcement that occurs when a heroin addict fails to ingest enough heroin—withdrawal symptoms—strengthens drug-seeking behavior. Both positive and negative reinforcers increase behavioral responses; they differ in their ordering relationship: Positive reinforcers *follow* the behavior they reinforce, while negative reinforcers *precede* the behavior they reinforce. A person *works to receive* a positive reinforcer and *works to escape* a negative reinforcer. Punishment is the third general principle of operant conditioning. *Punishment* decreases the probability or frequency of a behavior (Bozarth 1994).

The noted behaviorist B. F. Skinner states: "Punishment is easily confused with negative reinforcement, sometimes called 'aversive control.' The same stimuli are used, and negative reinforcement might be defined as the punishment of not behaving, but punishment is designed to remove behavior from a repertoire, whereas negative reinforcement generates behavior" (1974: 63). As was noted earlier, a particular psychoactive substance will be reinforcing to some people or to most people under certain conditions—for example, opiates when one is in pain. For most people under ordinary circumstances, the same substance will not provide reinforcement—at least not reinforcement that is sufficiently positive to offset negative consequences—and they do not seek to repeat the behavior.

According to this view, drug use is merely the result of learning directly from others. Chein and his colleagues (1964) note that both the processes involved with the use of heroin, excitement and the actions of the drug itself, become reinforcing, thus shaping—that is, molding—the behavior of the addict. Alfred Lindesmith (1968: 8) argues that a continuation of heroin use is based on negative reinforcement: "persons become addicts when they recognize or perceive the significance of withdrawal distress which they are experiencing" when they cease to use heroin. Lindesmith argues that substances such as cocaine and marijuana, on the other hand, are positive reinforcers because they are taken to enhance mood rather than to stave off withdrawal. From the discussion in Chapter 4 we know that Lindesmith's assertions are questionable: The physiological discomfort of heroin withdrawal is usually no greater than a bout with the flu; discontinuing the use of cocaine can produce depression; and sudden withdrawal from alcohol can be life threatening.

BEHAVIOR MODIFICATION

The abuse of stimulants and depressants can be explained by using learning theory. The use of cocaine, for example, can be quite rewarding: It elevates mood and provides a sense of well-being, strength, and energy, whereas discontinuing use provides negative reinforcement in the form of psychological depression, or the "coke blues." Likewise, heroin use can be quite rewarding to the addict: It significantly reduces perceptions of physical and psychological pain, stress, and anxiety, and provides a sense of euphoria, whereas discontinuing use provides negative reinforcement in the form of uncomfortable physical and psychological withdrawal symptoms. Although chemicals such as cocaine or heroin might initially have been used for social reasons, these substances' ability to provide physiological and psychological rewards explains why addicts seek to continue use even in the face of considerable hardship: Drugs overcome *competing reinforcers*: "The balancing of pleasurable or rewarding experiences and punishing or unpleasant experiences that occurs during the early weeks or months of drug involvement may be of critical importance. If the net impact of those experiences is highly positive, the effect or memory of that 'honeymoon' can remain remarkably strong over time, even as continuing reward diminishes and punishment increases, especially if alternative competitive behaviors are not exercised or reinforced as strongly" (Gerstein and Harwood 1990: 65).

Furthermore, while being known as a "junkie" or a "cokehead" might have negative consequences in conventional society, it often provides positive reinforcement in that it allows entry and acceptance into a small clique that is the drug subculture. Daily activities can now be focused on a clearly identifiable goal: drugs. The sociological dimension of this concept appeared in Chapter 7 in our discussion of anomie and retreatism. Furthermore, the illegal aspects of drug abuse provide a level of excitement that some people find quite rewarding. For drug users who must engage in criminality to support their habits, success in crime also provides an important source of reinforcement, particularly when the users do not possess skills necessary to succeed in noncriminal endeavors that could offer a competing source of reinforcement.

Although a dose of intravenous methamphetamine would probably be physically pleasurable to anyone, Thomas Crowley (1981: 368) points out that not everyone who experiences the pleasure continues to use amphetamines. The person who continues use is more likely to be from an impoverished environment: "Users in impoverished environments, with few other reinforcers available, will probably seek drug reinforcement more actively. Similarly, long experience with disturbed, unloving parents seems to convince many young people that they can never achieve respect or love from others. These young people have not learned to expect reinforcement from their environment, and so they may more actively seek the predictable, regular reinforcement of drug abuse." Most people who find the intake of certain substances rewarding do not become compulsive about continued use. Thus, while some people become obese because of their eating habits, most people do not become compulsive overeaters. While certain foods are pleasing to most people—chocolate or ice cream, for example—relatively few respond by compulsive intake. Large numbers of Americans use alcoholic beverages, but most avoid dependence.

COGNITIVE LEARNING THEORY

Cognition refers to learning and memory, and cognitive processes cannot be observed the way outward behavior can. But many behaviorists believe that cognition plays a crucial role in learning theory in humans.

> An important distinction in learning theory is between observable and unobservable behavior. Many behaviorists use "behavior" only in reference to observable activity, but this is too restrictive. No matter what it is called, unobservable behavior, especially cognitive behavior, is important in people's lives. . . . A cognitive response is simply a thought or feeling, typically in reaction to some stimulus. But a thought or feeling may also serve as a stimulus for a subsequent response. So a cognitive event may act either as a stimulus or as a response, or as both, as these events often do. (Starkweather 1982: 37)

These behaviorists recognize that human behavior is more complex than that of other species—that, for example, human behavior is often mediated by beliefs and symbols. The readiness to fight or die for a cause—symbolized by the cross, the star of David, the crescent, or the red star—illustrates the abstract complexities of human behavior. This recognition has led to *cognitive learning theory*, the major tenets of which are that "human behavior is mediated by unobservables that intervene between a stimulus and a response to that stimulus. Beliefs, sets, strategies, attributions, and expectancies are examples of the types of mediating constructs currently considered crucial to an understanding of emotion and behavior" (S. Gold 1980: 8).

Furthermore, "the way an individual labels or evaluates a situation determines his or her emotional and behavioral responses to it." Thus, based on past learning, a twisted cross (swastika) may have a different meaning to a Jew than to a Navajo Indian (for whom it is a cosmic religious symbol). According to this approach, the drug abuser has difficulty in meeting societal demands or expectations, and this leads to anxiety. Although anxiety is a universal experience, Steven Gold notes (1980: 9), drug abusers' feel that "they cannot alter or control the situation; that they are powerless to affect their environment and decrease or eliminate the sources of stress."

People who face persistent difficulties and anxieties in their lives and who are not prepared to cope with them may resort to analgesic drugs for comfort. "While enabling them to forget their problems and stress, the painkilling experience engendered by such drugs actually *decreases* the ability to cope. This is because such drugs depress the central nervous system and the individual's responsive capacity" (Peele 1980: 143). Heroin or alcohol provides relief from anxiety, and the user also attains temporary euphoria: "Under the influence of the drug the individual temporarily experiences an increased sense of power, control, and well-being." The drug acts as a powerful reinforcer—it can do for the abuser what he or she cannot do for himself or herself. However, these effects are short-lived, and after the drug wears off, the user finds that feelings of powerlessness return with full fury, which leads to further use of the drug and a cycle of continuing drug abuse: "The reliance on drugs to cope with stress therefore creates a vicious cycle; the more drugs are used, the more the individual believes they are necessary. Each drug experience serves to confirm for users the belief that they are powerless to function on their own" (S. Gold 1980: 9). Behaviorists often refer to this state of thinking as *learned helplessness*: Through inappropriate reinforcement, the drug abuser *learns* that he or she can neither escape nor avoid the stimulus leading to drug use.

Stimulants such as amphetamine and cocaine provide not only primary reinforcement as a result of their impact on the central nervous system but also secondary reinforcement as the result of drug-induced behavioral change for those who wish to increase their assertiveness. Amphetamines, for example, can produce a sense of cleverness, clear thinking, energy, alertness, and loquaciousness (Crowley 1981).

Learning theory is difficult to apply in the treatment of drug abusers. As was noted above, drugs are so reinforcing, providing immediate gratification for those who have *learned* to enjoy their use, that finding appropriate reinforcers that can successfully compete is quite difficult. Relapse after treatment can also be explained by learning theory, that is, the classical conditioned response: Certain cues associated with drug-taking behavior trigger a craving (Childress et al. 1993). These cues are discussed in Chapter 9. Agonists and antagonists, also discussed in Chapter 9, can be used to thwart the reinforcing quality of psychoactive substances. That chapter will also examine treatment programs that apply behavior theory.

Psychoanalytic Learning Theory

Stanley Greenspan (1978: 80) explains drug abuse by integrating behaviorism and psychoanalytic theory into a model that defines external experiences in terms of stimuli and reinforcers derived from psychosexual stages of development and the organization of id, ego, and superego. He states, for example, that "a substance abuser who achieves a basic and primitive homeostatic experience by using his addictive drug may be obtaining tremendous and potent reinforcement from the substance abuse. . . . Because of a lack of internalized control and the number of potent internal forces working from within, he tends to be vulnerable to environmental influences in rather dramatic ways and is sensitive to many potentially reinforcing events in his external environment [even though they may be destructive]."

A PSYCHOSOCIOLOGICAL DIMENSION

Drug use has a psychosociological dimension according to which the actor must *learn* that ingesting certain chemicals is desirable; intoxication, for example, is not inherently pleasurable. Expectations are based on learning and influence the direction of drug use. Thus, naive drug users, such as hospitalized patients who are given doses of morphine to relieve pain, do not experience euphoria and do not continue to seek out opiates when the pain subsides (Chein et al. 1964). Chein and his colleagues go so far as to state that opiates "are not inherently attractive, euphoric, or stimulant substances. The danger of addiction to opiates resides in the person, not in the drug" (1964: 348). Edward Brecher (1972: 13) notes that while there is "no doubt that the injection directly into a vein of a substantial dose of morphine or heroin produces a readily identifiable sensation," described by nonaddicts as a sudden flush of warmth and by addicts as a rush, few nonaddicts perceive the rush as particularly pleasurable. R. M. Gilbert (1981: 386) states that just because "a substance *can* have a pharmacological effect, it does not automatically follow that use of the substance is caused by or maintained by that effect." A 16-year-old cigarette smoker reports: "The first time I tried it, last year, I was like, 'This is totally gross.' I was coughing, and I turned green, and I thought I was going to throw up. So I had to *learn* to like it" (Verhovek 1995: 1; emphasis added). In an update of Howard Becker's (1966) work on becoming a marijuana user, however, Michael Hallstone (2002) found that most marijuana users became intoxicated the first time they smoked the substance and did not necessarily have to learn that they were intoxicated through social interaction with other users, and most found the initial experience pleasurable.

People who believe that they are drinking alcohol when actually they have been given nonalcoholic substitutes get more relaxed and outgoing, and a party atmosphere develops (D. Wood 1991). Indeed, levels of sexual arousal increase when people who are given a placebo believe that they have imbibed alcohol, although alcohol reduces sexual performance (Mendelson and Mello 1995).

SUMMARY

The focus of psychology is on the individual and is divided into clinical and behavioral. The first is influenced by Freudian theory, which explains human behavior as being driven through processes that are largely unconscious. Drug abuse is seen as a manifestation of unresolved developmental issues related to oral, anal, or genital stages. While experiencing these stages, the person develops an id, ego, and superego, deficiencies in which can be connected to adult drug use.

Drug abuse in adolescence is explained as an immature response to the stress typical of this period: The adolescent drug user circumvents the demands of maturity. Although users reach chronological adulthood, they remain psychologically preadolescent.

Behaviorism has its roots in the laboratory of experimental psychology and is based on learning theory. All forms of behavior are conditioned, the result of learned responses to certain stimuli. Behavior is strengthened by its consequences and can be modified by operant conditioning: positive and negative reinforcement. Drugs can serve as powerful reinforcers, while withdrawal symptoms provide negative reinforcement.

With these explanations in mind, in the next chapter we will examine the variety of methods that are used to treat drug abusers and prevent drug abuse.

REVIEW QUESTIONS

1. What distinguishes psychological explanations of drug abuse from sociological explanations?
2. What is the basic proposition of psychoanalytic theory?
3. How can problems experienced during the oral stage of development lead to drug abuse in the adult?
4. How can the use of depressants by an adult be connected to the anal stage of development?
5. What is the relationship between difficulty during the genital stage and drug abuse in adulthood?
6. How can drug abuse be explained by id drives?
7. How can drugs compensate for ego deficiencies?
8. How can a deficiency in superego development lead to drug abuse?
9. How can feelings of guilt generated by the superego lead to drug abuse?
10. How does psychoanalytic theory explain drug abuse during adolescence?
11. What basic belief underlies behaviorism/learning theory?
12. How does operant conditioning explain drug abuse?
13. Why is it difficult if not impossible to use psychoanalysis to treat heroin addiction?
14. How does behavior/learning theory explain drug abuse?
15. Why is it difficult to apply behavior theory in the treatment of drug abuse?
16. How do expectations based on learning influence individual drug use?

9 CHAPTER | Drug Abuse Treatment

[T]reatment and prevention programs are frequently required to show that they are cost-effective, a standard never imposed on drug enforcement.

Robert MacCoun and Peter Reuter (1997: 47)

If treatment is conceived of as an ongoing process, rather than as a cure, a different, more optimistic notion of success emerges.

Peggy Orenstein (2002: 74)

That there is no single treatment for drug dependence is most likely a consequence of the multiple factors—physiological, behavioural and social—contributing to the condition.

David Taylor (2002: Internet)

There are probably as many approaches to treating and preventing drug abuse as there are theories explaining the phenomenon. Unfortunately, drug abuse is unlike diseases whose etiology, and therefore treatment and prevention, appears to be clearly physiological. In fact, considering drug dependence a "disease," in the narrow sense of that term, is controversial (see, e.g., Wilbanks 1990; Maltzman 1994). As with other chronic illnesses, the National Institute on Drug Abuse recommends speaking in terms of *remission* and *improvement* rather than *cure* in discussing the treatment of substance abuse (National Institute on Drug Abuse 1987) because the problem has proven to be quite intractable.

Adding to the problem's complexity are the incongruities that were discussed in Chapter 1: The moderate use of any variety of psychoactive substances—from nicotine to cocaine—may be the focus of a treatment response, not because of properties inherent in the chemicals themselves but because of the societal definition of "abuse." Thus, in the United States moderate use of alcohol, tobacco, or coffee is seen as being within the mainstream of acceptable behavior, while even the occasional use of heroin or cocaine is often seen as requiring "treatment" (if not imprisonment). The difficulty is apparent: Patients who do not feel ill, who do not want treatment, and are not dysfunctional are coerced into "treatment" by their families, their employers, or the criminal justice system. And as Dean Gerstein and Henrick Harwood point out, "drug treatment is not designed for the low-intensity user who is readily able to control his or her level of consumption and for whom functional consequences have not yet accumulated" (1990: 69–70).

THE CURE INDUSTRY

Like the quest for an explanation of drug abuse, the search for a cure, particularly a "magic bullet" in the form of a chemical cure, has a history that cautions us to be skeptical. Opiates were once presented as a cure for alcohol dependence; morphine was offered as a cure for opiate addiction; cocaine was offered as a cure for morphine addiction (though patients became dependent on cocaine while remaining addicted to morphine); heroin was proposed as a cure for morphine addiction; and methadone was presented as a cure for heroin addiction. In fact, the "cure industry" has a long and often less than honorable history.

The medical profession "often shared the distaste for drug users that permeated the society" (Morgan 1981: 65). Furthermore, the problem of addiction was only peripheral to the practice of most doctors, who typically sought to avoid association with the failure that was so common to treating drug dependence. This left a fertile field for charlatans, and around the turn of the century the quest for a cure led to the development of an industry similar to that of patent medicines. Unregulated nostrums that were widely advertised as "cures" for drug dependence frequently contained alcohol, cocaine, and opiates. In 1906 these compounds came under regulation by the Pure Food and Drug Administration, which caused a significant decline in sales. In response quacks began to portray themselves as outsiders feared by a medical establishment centered in the eastern United States. This approach had strong appeal, particularly in the South and Midwest, where anti-Eastern feelings ran deep.

Thirteen Principles of Effective Drug Addiction Treatment

More than two decades of scientific research have yielded a set of thirteen fundamental principles that characterize effective drug abuse treatment (National Institute on Drug Abuse 1999d):

1. **No single treatment is appropriate for all individuals.** Matching treatment settings, interventions, and services to each patient's problems and needs is critical.

2. **Treatment needs to be readily available.** Treatment applicants can be lost if treatment is not immediately available or readily accessible.

3. **Effective treatment attends to multiple needs** of the individual, not just his or her drug use. Treatment must address the individual's drug use and associated medical, psychological, social, vocational, and legal problems.

4. **Treatment needs to be flexible** and to provide ongoing assessments of patient needs, which may change during the course of treatment.

5. **Remaining in treatment for an adequate period of time is critical for treatment effectiveness.** The time depends on an individual's needs. For most patients the threshold of significant improvement is reached at about three months in treatment. Additional treatment can produce further progress. Programs should include strategies to prevent patients from leaving treatment prematurely.

6. **Individual and/or group counseling and other behavioral therapies are critical components of effective treatment for addiction.** In therapy patients address motivation, build skills to resist drug use, replace drug-using activities with constructive and rewarding non-drug-using activities, and improve problem-solving abilities. Behavioral therapy also facilitates interpersonal relationships.

7. **Medications are an important element of treatment for many patients**, especially when combined with counseling and other behavioral therapies. Methadone helps people who are addicted to opiates stabilize their lives and reduce their drug use. Naltrexone is effective for some opiate addicts and some patients with co-occurring alcohol dependence. Vivitrol, a reformulated naltrexone, is injected once a month and has shown some success for people who are addicted to alcohol (Hobson 2006). Nicotine patches or gum or an oral medication, such as bupropion,

Any number of self-proclaimed doctors operated clinics for the drug dependent and grew quite wealthy from their "cures." The most famous was Charles B. Towns, a Georgia farm boy, insurance salesman, and stockbroker. David Musto (1973) refers to Towns as the king of the cure proclaimers. After arriving in New York City in 1901, Towns spent several years as a partner in a stock brokerage that failed in 1904. Shortly afterward, he began advertising a secret formula that would cure drug addiction. The medical profession was skeptical, but Towns and his cure were widely accepted and were promoted even by federal agencies; a 1909 article in the *Journal of the American Medical Association* was also favorable. The Charles B. Towns Hospital proclaimed a cure rate between 75 and 90 percent. Determining "success" was rather simple: If the patient never returned, he or she was "cured."[1] Eventually, it was revealed that Towns's secret formula contained three ingredients: prickly ash bark, extract of hyoscyamus (henbane, a poisonous plant), and belladonna (deadly nightshade, a poisonous plant).

There were at the same time, however, sanatoriums whose approach to drug abuse was quite similar, if not identical, to that of many contemporary inpatient programs. The patient was withdrawn from drugs, sometimes with the aid of nonaddicting drugs. Before 1914 treating addiction was all the more difficult

---

[1] Bill Wilson, cofounder of Alcoholics Anonymous (AA), was a patient of the Towns Hospital, where, according to AA publications, he learned that alcoholism was a malady of mind, emotions, and body.

may help some people who are addicted to nicotine, although data indicate that these medications have limited utility in promoting long-term abstinence and are themselves addictive (A. Goldstein 2001; Bartosiewicz 2004). Under the brand name Chantix, varenicline, which is believed to block nicotine receptor sites, has shown promise for controlling smokers' cravings as well as the pleasure that is normally derived from cigarettes (Hobson 2006).

8. **Addicted or drug-abusing individuals with coexisting mental disorders should have both disorders treated in an integrated way.** Because these disorders often occur in the same individual, patients who present for one condition should be assessed and treated for the other.

9. **Medical detoxification is only the first stage of addiction treatment** and by itself does little to change long-term drug use. Medical detoxification manages the acute physical symptoms of withdrawal. For some individuals it is a precursor to effective drug addiction treatment.

10. **Treatment does not need to be voluntary to be effective.** Sanctions or enticements in the family, employment setting, or criminal justice system can significantly increase treatment entry, retention, and success. Research into court-mandated treatment reveals that it does as well as voluntary treatment and that both significantly reduce illegal drug use (Whitten 2006a).

11. **Possible drug use during treatment must be monitored continuously.** Monitoring a patient's drug and alcohol use during treatment, such as through urinalysis, can help the patient to withstand urges to use drugs. Such monitoring also can provide early evidence of drug use so that treatment can be adjusted.

12. **Treatment programs should provide assessment for HIV/AIDS, hepatitis B and C, tuberculosis, and other infectious diseases** and counseling to help patients modify or change behaviors that place them or others at risk of infection. Counseling can help patients to avoid high-risk behavior and help people who are already infected to manage their illness.

13. **Recovery from drug addiction can be a long-term process** and frequently requires multiple episodes of treatment. As with other chronic illnesses, relapses into drug use can occur during or after successful treatment episodes. Participation in self-help support programs during and following treatment often helps to maintain abstinence.

because morphine was usually available in a pure form that made withdrawal particularly painful (Morgan 1981). The patient was given frequent baths, and as soon as he or she began to function more normally, a regimen of nourishing food and exercise was initiated. The patient, now withdrawn from drugs, engaged in such tasks as reading and gardening and was given a great deal of reassurance. The extent of the treatment often depended on a patient's ability to pay (Morgan 1981). More recently, the profit that can accrue from treating certain types of substance abusers—such as those with appropriate health insurance—has led to the expansion of a private cure industry that is often based in health care or hospital settings (Freudenheim 1987). These will be discussed later in the chapter.

Private Treatment Programs

There are approximately 11,000 privately operated substance abuse treatment programs in the United States, of which about 25 percent are for-profit.

For alcoholics there were "inebriate homes" and asylums that operated on the fringes of religion, charity, and law enforcement. The different philosophies and treatment methods tended to merge over time, the medically oriented ones incorporating spiritual and religion-oriented remedies and those operating on moral or religious principles integrating medical and psychological treatments. And as with the profit-making sector of drug addiction treatment, the alcohol cure industry became a business that promoted dubious notions hyped by unsupported claims. Indeed, many organizations claimed success in treating both the drug- and alcohol-addicted (W. L. White 1998). Always pressed for sources of funding, these institutions were abandoned by the temperance movement and met their demise with the onset of Prohibition.

MEDICATION-ASSISTED TREATMENT

A variety of treatment approaches use chemicals, often as a supplement to or in conjunction with some other form of clinical or behavioral therapy. These medications target the pharmacological effect of a particular drug but "do nothing to counteract the effects of craving and overlearned drug-seeking behavioral responses that frequently lead to relapse" (Harwood and Myers 2004: 11).

Opioid Antagonists

As part of the search for a "magic bullet," scientists developed a number of heroin antagonists, substances that block or counteract the effects of opiates. These substances bind with opiate receptor sites, thereby preventing stimulation, or they displace an opiate that is already at the site. Some antagonists, such as cyclazocine and **naloxone**, have significant side effects. While cyclazocine taken orally effectively blocks the effects of heroin for twelve to twenty-four hours, it also produces nausea, sweating, a feeling of intoxication, anxiety, and hallucinations. Users suffer withdrawal symptoms when the substance is discontinued, although they do not develop a craving for it. A dose as small as 0.25 mg of naloxone will block the effects of heroin for ten hours, but it is effective only when administered intravenously. Neither of these substances reduces the "drug hunger" of heroin addicts (DeLong 1972).

Naloxone is recommended for testing for opiate dependence (Narcon test) before admission to a methadone program (Judson and Goldstein 1986). It has no effect on the nondependent person but causes immediate signs of heroin withdrawal in the opiate-dependent person. The substance is administered to people who are seeking methadone because such people might not be opioid-dependent or might have only minimal dependence: "Treatment of these addicts with methadone raises important ethical and legal questions in view of the likelihood of producing physical dependence in previously nondependent persons" (Peachey and Lei 1988: 200). According to federal regulations, admission to methadone treatment is restricted to people who have been addicted to heroin for at least one year. The antagonist nalorphine (Nalline) counters the depression of the central nervous system caused by opiates and is administered as an antidote for heroin overdose.

The National Institute on Drug Abuse was instrumental in developing **naltrexone** hydrochloride, a long-acting orally administered narcotic antagonist first synthesized in 1965 and marketed as Trexan by DuPont. This non-addicting drug defeats the effects of opiates by occupying their receptor sites in the brain. It also displaces any agonists that are present, causing severe precipitated withdrawal in people who are opioid-dependent. Naltrexone users often suffer from nausea and vomiting; less common side effects include headache, anxiety or depression, low energy, skin rashes, and decreased alertness. Discontinuing naltrexone will not cause withdrawal symptoms, but the drug does not ease the craving for heroin (Batki et al. 205).

Like any antagonist, naltrexone is effective only with patients who are motivated to give up the feeling of euphoria that opiates can provide. The manufacturer clearly states that it is recommended for use as an adjunct in the treatment of opioid abusers (Ginzburg 1985: 5): "Treatment failure cannot be blamed on the failure of naltrexone to block opioids nor is treatment success likely to be the consequence of a use of naltrexone alone." About 2,000 people are being treated with naltrexone (Wren 1999c), and preliminary results are promising (K. Carroll et al. 2001).

In 1995 the Food and Drug Administration (FDA) approved naltrexone to prevent alcohol relapse by alcohol-dependent patients, and under the brand name Revia, naltrexone is marketed for use in treating alcoholism. Alcohol causes the release of endorphins, which are believed a major factor in causing a person to continue drinking. Naltrexone blocks the endorphin-mediated rewarding effects of drinking alcohol.

Chemicals for Detoxification

Like those in the past, contemporary treatment programs typically begin with detoxification—"a term left over from an obsolete theory that addicts suffer from an accumulation of toxins" (Dole 1980: 138)—with or without the assistance of drugs. Antagonists are sometimes used as an aid in heroin detoxification. Because of its potency, withdrawal from licit maintenance doses of methadone is generally accomplished by decreasing dosages. The antihypertension drug clonidine has been used to relieve many of the symptoms of opioid withdrawal, particularly those involving autonomic nervous system hyperactivity. The substance is non-addicting (National Institute on Drug Abuse 1987). Some physicians have recommended clonidine for the detoxification of methadone patients who are being maintained on relatively low dosages. Whereas methadone can be found in the patient's system more than a week after the last dose, clonidine has a shorter life. Thus, a clonidine patient can be placed on naltrexone immediately on detoxification, whereas a methadone patient would experience unpleasant withdrawal symptoms under similar treatment (Ginzburg 1985).

Cocaine detoxification presents a serious problem because of the patient's craving for the drug. This may be associated with the depletion of dopamine, which, as was noted in Chapter 5, is essential to maintain life. The extreme depression that occurs during the early days of abstinence, particularly in crack users, can lead to suicide. Withdrawal from opiates and cocaine can be accomplished without using other chemicals, although the patient might feel quite uncomfortable. Detoxification from sedatives can lead to seizures and cardiac arrest and therefore must be accomplished by decreasing dosages of the sedative.

The use of chemicals to facilitate drug withdrawal can serve to attract drug abusers into treatment and increases the probability that they will complete detoxification. However, at least with respect to heroin abusers, the use of chemicals has some troubling aspects: Addicts typically enter treatment when their habit is too expensive to support; at this point the addict has to work quite hard simply to prevent the onset of withdrawal symptoms, while a high level of

Rapid Detox

In a controversial process referred to as "rapid detox," a heroin-addicted patient is strapped to a gurney, anesthetized and breathing through a respirator. He or she then receives intravenous doses of the heroin antagonist naloxone. As naloxone dislodges opiate molecules from their receptor sites, the patient experiences instant withdrawal that is complete in about four hours. Being unconscious, the patient avoids experiencing the usual discomfort that accompanies withdrawal, such as vomiting, shivering, and pain. After a night in intensive care, the patient is able to leave the hospital heroin free. The cost of the procedure can be as high as $8,500. Detoxification, of course, is simply a first step toward abstinence, and rapid detox is criticized for its expense while having no proven benefits in comparison to less costly approaches to withdrawal (Duenwald 2001). Indeed, making withdrawal relatively easy provides little incentive for remaining drug free. As one program points out: "We know that just detoxification is not enough. The highest outcome for success is made up of detoxification followed by continuing care treatment and integration into a lifelong program of recovery such as AA/NA."

Research conducted in 2005 revealed that there is no advantage to rapid detox, which can also be dangerous for individuals with a variety of preexisting conditions, such as diabetes or bipolar disorder. Once awakened from anesthesia, patients in the rapid detox group demonstrated and reported symptoms of discomfort comparable to those experienced by participants who were treated with traditional medical withdrawal methods (buprenorphine or clonidine). The rapid detox patients fared no better on remaining in treatment; only 18 percent remained the full twelve weeks, and the percentage who submitted opiate-positive urine samples during outpatient treatment (63 percent) was the same as with the other methods (Whitten 2006b).

tolerance prevents achieving the high. Under such conditions addiction is no longer fun. "Then he enters a detoxification ward and is comfortably withdrawn from heroin. Detoxification is made so easy, compared to 'cold turkey,'[2] that addicts are not confronted with negatively reinforcing pharmacological and physiological aspects of addiction" (Bellis 1981: 139). Detoxification reduces the addict's tolerance so that the high can be enjoyed once again at an affordable price. Drug program staff "should not be surprised or miffed when addicts leave the detoxification ward and inject heroin within a few minutes or hours" (Bellis 1981: 140).

Opioid Agonists

Certain synthetic substances have a chemical makeup similar to that of opioids. The most widely used agonist, **methadone**, a wholly synthetic narcotic, was developed in Germany (where it was named *Dolophine* in honor of Hitler)

---

[2] A common symptom of withdrawal is piloerection—"goose flesh" (W. L. White 1998).

when access to morphine was cut off during World War II. While it produces virtually the same analgesic and sedative effects as heroin and is no less addictive, orally administered methadone lasts longer. In contrast to the shorter-acting opiates such as heroin, the high it produces is less dramatic. Whereas the effects of heroin wear off in two to three hours, the effects of oral methadone continue for twelve to twenty-four hours. Methadone can be prepared in a way that makes it difficult to inject, rendering it less likely to be diverted into the black market. After World War II methadone was typically used in hospitals to systematically detoxify people addicted to opiates (Dole 1980; Gerstein and Harwood 1990).

The first clinical use of methadone to treat narcotic addiction occurred at the U.S. Public Health Hospital in Lexington, Kentucky, where it was substituted for morphine and heroin to help detoxify addicted patients. Withdrawal from heroin was made relatively painless by first administering doses equivalent to the patient's street use of heroin. The doses were then lowered until the patient was no longer addicted, a process that took seven to ten days (Blackmore 1979). During the early 1960s, when narcotics addiction once again emerged as a major national concern, Vincent Dole and Marie Nyswander of Rockefeller University reported on their successful use of methadone to treat heroin addicts in a dramatically new way: through maintenance.

Methadone: Magic Bullet? In 1964 Doctors Dole and Nyswander gave twenty-two hospitalized heroin addicts increasing doses of methadone until they reached a "stabilized state," meaning that they had neither withdrawal symptoms nor a craving for further increases in the dosage: "With repeated administration of a fixed dose, methadone loses its sedative and analgesic powers. The subject becomes tolerant" (Dole 1980: 146). The patients were then released, but they returned each day for an oral dose of methadone. The following year a research report by Dole and Nyswander (1965) revealed extraordinary results from this approach, which they ascribed to methadone's ability to provide a "pharmacological block" against heroin. Furthermore, it was theorized, heroin abuse in certain addicts results in a metabolic disorder that requires the continued ingestion of narcotics if the person is to remain homeostatic. With such disorders methadone acts like any prescribed medicine, normalizing the patient's functioning.

Continuing research with additional patients provided further support for methadone maintenance: Addict patients refrained from heroin use, secured employment, and avoided criminal activity. In 1966 Dole and Nyswander established a large outpatient methadone program at Beth Israel Hospital in New York City. Other programs followed. Dole and Nyswander (1966) intimated that they had discovered the "magic bullet" because methadone allegedly provides a blockade to the effects of heroin. (See Chambers and Brill [1973] for a review of these early methadone experiments and treatment programs.)

The typical methadone program begins with a period of inpatient care, during which low doses of methadone are substituted for heroin. (The patient is not informed of the dosage he or she receives.) The methadone is usually mixed with orange juice (which helps to reduce its bitter taste) and is consumed in front of a nurse. Slow increases in dosage reduce the high, which disappears once tolerance develops. Addicts subsequently report daily on an outpatient basis and are given take-home doses for weekends. As they progress, less frequent than daily pickups are permitted. Patients usually provide a urine specimen before they are given methadone.

By the late 1960s a few thousand addicts were being maintained on methadone in the United States; by early 1973 there were approximately 73,000 (Danaceau 1974). This change was brought about by the Nixon administration, which was convinced that methadone could help to reduce the crime rate—a cornerstone of the "law-and-order" presidency of Richard Nixon. Experts who knew better, argues Edward Jay Epstein (1974: 22), "chose not to deflate the unrealistic claim that methadone would substantially reduce crime." They hoped that such programs would lure otherwise recalcitrant hard-core heroin addicts into treatment. Eventually, however, the "bad news" came out: Methadone was not the "magic bullet." Indeed, there was no blockade but simply cross-tolerance. The patient who was maintained at significantly high doses of methadone would not experience the high from heroin, but methadone did not affect the euphoric rush. In fact, it was discovered that methadone patients, even those who were on high daily doses, were often abusing heroin as well as other drugs. Furthermore, whereas methadone maintenance was designed for heroin addicts, the problem was often one of polydrug use. In fact, cocaine is a major drug of abuse among methadone patients (C. P. O'Brien et al. 1990). Today, there are about 180,000 methadone users nationally. (Eight states—Idaho, Mississippi, Montana, New Hampshire, North Dakota, South Dakota, Vermont, and West Virginia—prohibit methadone.)

Methadone clinics across the country treat as many as 180,000 ex-heroin users every day. Methadone maintenance appears to be beneficial for certain addicts—it can act as a crutch for those motivated to give up heroin.

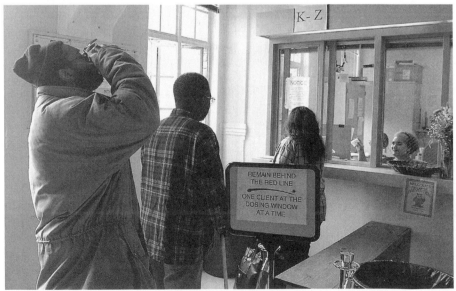

©AP Images

Methadone: Uses and Effects

Classification: Narcotic

CSA Schedule: Schedule I, II

Trade or Other Names: Dolophine, Methadose

Medical Uses: Analgesic, treatment of dependence

Physical Dependence: High

Psychological Dependence: High

Tolerance: Yes

Duration (hours): 12–72

Usual Method: Oral, injected

Possible Effects: Euphoria, drowsiness, respiratory depression, constricted pupils; nausea

Effects of Overdose: Slow and shallow breathing, clammy skin, convulsions, coma, possible death

Withdrawal Syndrome: Watery eyes, runny nose, yawning, loss of appetite, irritability, tremors, panic, cramps, nausea, chills and sweating

Source: Drug Enforcement Administration.

Furthermore, research revealed that the figures given out by Dole and Nyswander were deceptive: The rate of "cure" attributed to methadone was better explained by the screening mechanisms that were used—older and more motivated addicts were preferred—and by the fact that unsuccessful cases were simply dropped from the program and from the final tabulations. Methadone clinics came under severe attack by those associated with the drug-free therapeutic communities (discussed below), and by 1979 they were operating at about 90 percent of capacity (Blackmore 1979). Robert Newman (1977: xx) states that "proponents of specific treatment approaches rarely missed an opportunity to make exaggerated claims for their own modality and to vilify publicly other therapeutic efforts." Residents also strongly opposed the opening of methadone treatment centers in their communities—the NIMBY (not-in-my-backyard) syndrome.

No Magic Bullet, but Methadone Is Still Useful This is not to say that methadone maintenance has no role in treating heroin addiction. Methadone maintenance appears to be quite beneficial to certain heroin abusers (e.g., Byrne 2000). It can act as a crutch for those who are motivated to give up heroin. The programs also attract addicts who are seeking a chemical cure, although the counseling and job assistance that are provided might be the real "cure." Even without such services, notes James DeLong (1972), methadone may have a placebo effect: The addict who believes that methadone is beneficial will find it so. To the extent that heroin addiction is explained by physiology, as discussed in Chapter 3 (e.g., people with abnormal endorphin levels compensating by ingesting heroin), methadone maintenance is the equivalent of providing insulin to diabetics.

If psychoanalytic theory is accurate, methadone might serve as an antiaggression chemical for heroin addicts whose drug use is based on a need to control the rage and aggressive tendencies originating in a problematic anal stage of development (Khantzian 1980). In a review of evaluations of methadone maintenance programs, M. Douglas Anglin and William McGlothlin (1985: 274) conclude that "methadone maintenance has been shown to effectively reduce drug use, dealing, and income-generating crime, and to a lesser extent to increase employment and family responsibility." Furthermore, they note, methadone maintenance "appeals to a portion of the addict population that has not been amenable to other social intervention strategies." And methadone has proven to be effective in suppressing the administration of opiates in laboratory experiments with animals (Winger 1988).

There is some concern that older addicts who might have gone into remission without any intervention are nevertheless maintained on methadone and thus are still addicted. In 2005 New York had ten methadone clients over age 80 years (Marion 2005). On the other hand, "patients who terminate before they have achieved stable social functioning are very unlikely to remain abstinent," and "even patients who terminate under the best of circumstances still may have less than a 50 percent chance of remaining abstinent as long as 3 years" (Hargreaves 1986: 70). Mary Kreek (1987) reports that only 20–30 percent of former "hard-core" heroin addicts remain heroin-free for three years or more following discharge from a methadone maintenance program, which is about the same percentages generally reported for other treatment modalities, including residential drug-free or short-term methadone detoxification programs. Anglin and McGlothlin (1985: 274–275) state that although methadone maintenance has not produced the wonderful results anticipated by early researchers, it makes a "real and beneficial contribution to reducing the social and individual costs associated with addiction."

Critics of New York City's methadone programs argue that they discourage abstinence as an ultimate goal, thus prolonging dependency for those who might be able and willing to give up all drug use. They note that this dependency extends to employment: Fees from methadone patients on welfare are guaranteed, paid for by Medicaid, while patients who are employed can usually afford to pay only a fraction of what Medicaid provides. Few programs offer vocational or job skills training (Massing 1999). Furthermore, methadone maintenance is predicated on the exclusiveness of heroin use, although heroin addicts are usually polydrug users who may continue use of illegal drugs even while being maintained on methadone (Inciardi, McBride, and Surratt 1998). When they enter treatment, methadone patients "frequently bring with them an inclination to experiment with a variety of other drugs and often view themselves as connoisseurs of drug-taking experiences. . . . Thus, continued use of other illicit drugs is frequently a problem in the treatment of a large percentage of methadone patients" (Platt et al. 1998).

The methadone maintenance program that was established by Dole and Nyswander at Beth Israel Medical Center in New York has continued to operate ever since. Beth Israel treats more than 8,000 patients, who make more than 1 million visits annually to the center's twenty-three outpatient clinics. Most patients have been in continuous treatment for more than two years; about half for more than five years. Treatment is voluntary; the program will not take coerced patients. Patients can remain on methadone for as long as they wish, or they can opt for detoxification. For the past decade the program has operated above capacity.

Buprenorphine   Buprenorphine (pronounced "byoo-pre-NOR-feen"), marketed under the brand name Suboxone, is chemically an opioid, but it is only mildly addictive. As was noted in Chapter 4, when an opioid stimulates a particular receptor (the *mu* receptor), neurotransmitters are released, reducing pain sensations and causing feelings of pleasure. Buprenorphine is only a partial agonist and thus yields the same effects as heroin or methadone with less intensity. Because buprenorphine has a great affinity for the *mu* receptor and binds so tightly, taking additional opioids will not produce additional effects because buprenorphine prevents the opioids from locking into the receptor site. Because it detaches from the *mu* receptor site slowly, buprenorphine has a longer duration than methadone: two to three days (A. O'Connor 2004). Since it is a partial agonist, buprenorphine exhibits ceiling effects (i.e., increasing the dose has effects only to a certain level). Partial agonists usually have greater safety profiles than do full agonists because they are less likely to cause respiratory depression, the major toxic effect of opiate drugs (H. E. Jones 2004).

Another benefit of buprenorphine is that the withdrawal syndrome is, at worst, mild to moderate and can often be managed without administration of narcotics. Addicts who are being maintained on high does of methadone, on the other hand, will go through withdrawal symptoms if they are suddenly switched to buprenorphine (Pérez-Peña 2003). However, since buprenorphine is a partial agonist, "in severely addicted people, it may not provide enough opiate agonist activity to treat them adequately" (Mann 2004a: 8).

In 2002 the FDA announced the approval of buprenorphine and buprenorphine-naloxone (a partial opiate agonist with an opiate blocker) under the brand name Subutex. When taken orally, buprenorphine-naloxone does not produce euphoria, and if injected, it makes the user feel sick. Naloxone causes an immediate withdrawal syndrome in opioid addicts. It needs to be taken only every one to three days. As a result of the Drug Addiction Treatment Act of 2000 these drugs can be dispensed in a doctor's office instead of a clinic and are subject to the same restrictions on quantities as methadone. This has the added benefit of avoiding having addicts associating at clinics while they await their methadone. The statute requires doctors to take an eight-hour course on the use of buprenorphine-naloxone, and originally, each doctor or group practice was allowed to treat only thirty patients. Legislation enacted in 2005 allows each qualified doctor within a group medical practice to prescribe Suboxone up to his or her individual physician limit of thirty patients. Group medical practices include large institutions such as hospitals and health maintenance organizations, many of which have numerous doctors who have been certified to treat opioid dependence.

Chemical Responses to Cocaine Abuse

In Chapter 5 we learned that the neurotransmitters dopamine and serotonin appear to play an important role in cocaine abuse. Cocaine agonists and antagonists, which typically affect these neurotransmitters, have been tested as possible treatment agents, but no drug has emerged that effectively treats the cocaine-dependent patient (McCance 1997). Dopamine antagonists are available, but they "can produce serious and permanent motor disorders, unpleasant subjective effects, or increases rather than decreases in cocaine self-administration in experimental animals" (Winger 1988: 125). Medication can be used as an adjunct to treating cocaine abusers either to deal with the deleterious effects of cocaine use itself or to treat the underlying motivations for using cocaine. Medication might be needed by addicts who are at risk of suicide during the postcocaine "crash" period, which is characterized by a lack of energy and an inability to feel pleasure, or by those who exhibit transient psychotic states. Severe delusional states and paranoid reactions from excessive cocaine require medication.

As was noted in Chapters 3 and 5, cocaine use may be a form of self-medication for those who suffer from certain chemical deficiencies, particularly neurotransmitters that affect mood and activity levels. In fact, note Henry Spitz and Jeffrey Rosecan (1987), some cocaine abusers have been successfully treated with prescribed antidepressants, although crack addicts appear to be less amenable to such treatment (Kolata 1989a). Introduced in the 1950s, **tricyclic antidepressants** (TCAs) such as Tofranil (imipramine) treat depression by manipulating the level of several neurotransmitters.[3] They are used to treat cocaine depression, particularly in patients whose cocaine use appears to be a form of self-medication to ward off depression: "[TCAs] appear to reverse some of the neurochemical effects of chronic cocaine administration" (Spitz and Rosecan 1987: 260). It is believed that TCAs could act as cocaine antagonists by displacing or blocking cocaine receptors in the central nervous system and might help to reduce the craving for cocaine.

In 1990 the National Institute of Mental Health won a patent for one TCA, desipramine, a cocaine substitute that is used to wean users off the drug. The substitute does not have any of the dangerous side effects of cocaine and is believed to reduce craving (Andrews 1990). Desipramine has since become the most widely studied medication for dealing with cocaine dependence. In limited clinical trials, it has shown some ability to decrease the reinforcing effects of cocaine and to reduce the craving for it (National Institute on Drug Abuse

---

[3] In many cases TCAs have been replaced by Prozac (fluoxetine), which acts on a single neurotransmitter: serotonin. Fluoxetine has been used experimentally to treat cocaine abuse but with minimal effect (Foltin and Fischman 1994).

1991; Kosten 1993). The substance is most effective with subjects who, in addition to cocaine dependence, suffer from depression (McCance 1997). Lithium, a standard drug for psychotic disorders, particularly depressive states, is used with patients whose cyclothymia (mild mood swings) or bipolar disorder (extreme mood swings) preceded cocaine use.

Chronic cocaine use may deplete the neurotransmitter dopamine, causing a craving in dopamine receptors. Bromocriptine, a dopamine agonist that is used to treat Parkinson's disease, appears to bind to the dopamine receptors, thus reducing the craving for cocaine. It does, however, have serious side effects, including nausea, headaches, dizziness, abnormal involuntary movements, and psychosis. According to Rosecan and Nunes (1987), use of bromocriptine is justified only in treatment-resistant cases in which recovery is hampered by severe craving. And while bromocriptine decreased cocaine use in laboratory monkeys, its chronic administration produced toxic effects including preconvulsive signs (Winger 1988). One study (Eiler, Schaefer, and Salstrom 1995) found little benefit in using bromocriptine to treat cocaine withdrawal, but Elinore McCance (1997) states that it still has potential as a possible treatment agent.

PSYCHOLOGICAL TREATMENTS

Treatment based on psychological theories can be broadly divided into those that are psychoanalytically oriented—sometimes referred to as *dynamic* or *clinical*—and those that utilize some form of behaviorism. Some programs mix the two approaches.

A Psychoanalytic Approach

To the psychoanalyst,[4] symptoms of neurotic behavior, such as drug abuse, are tied to repressed material from early life—the developmental stages examined in Chapter 8. In this view, the symptoms will disappear when the repressed material is exposed under psychoanalytic treatment. Therefore, the psychoanalyst seeks to make unconscious affect and memories available to the patient's consciousness (Holinger 1989). Psychoanalysis and the therapies based on it aim "at inducing the patient to give up the repressions belonging to his early life and to replace them by reactions of a sort that could correspond better to a psychically mature condition." To accomplish this, a psychoanalyst uses interpretation—attempts to get the patient "to recollect certain experiences and emotions called up by them which he has at the moment forgotten or repressed" (Reiff 1963: 274). This is accomplished through dream

---

[4] *Psychoanalyst* is not a restricted title like that enjoyed by psychiatrists, who are physicians, or clinical psychologists, who hold a doctorate in psychology. Although there are certifying bodies for psychoanalysts, they do not enjoy a government-supported monopoly on the use of the title. There is a great deal of acrimony between psychologists and psychiatrists over who is qualified to practice psychoanalysis (Goleman 1988).

interpretation and free association. While in a relaxed state, the patient is asked to say what comes to mind about any given element in a dream, or the therapist might ask the patient to let a proper name or even a number occur to him or her. The train of associations stirred up by the dream, the name, or the number becomes an entry point for the release of repressed material, which the analyst helps the patient to interpret.

To re-create the emotional state that was originally attached to these associations, the therapist takes advantage of transference, the development of an emotional attitude—positive or negative—by the patient toward the therapist. Thus, the psychoanalyst might be emotionally (and unconsciously) perceived by the patient as a paternal or maternal figure in a re-creation of the emotions tied to very early psychic development.

In fact, psychoanalysis is rarely used to treat substance abusers, and there is a paucity of literature on treating substance abusers using this approach. This method requires highly skilled therapists, articulate patients—because psychoanalysis and the therapies based on it are "talk therapies"—and a long period of costly treatment: Psychoanalysis typically involves three to five fifty-minute sessions a week for as long as seven years, at $75 to $200 per session. There are few published reports of successful psychoanalytic treatment of drug-dependent individuals, and those that exist deal almost exclusively with heroin addiction. As Clifford Yorke (1970: 156) has pointed out with respect to heroin addicts, "the number of confirmed addicts seeking psychoanalytic treatment is almost certainly very small, the number of analysts prepared to accept them even smaller, and the number of addicts who pursue their treatment to conclusion smaller still." Freud himself doubted the usefulness of psychoanalysis for treating drug addicts (Byck 1974).

Frederic Schiffer (1988) used short-term therapy based on a psychoanalytic model to treat cocaine addicts in a hospital and subsequently on an outpatient basis. He found their pathology to be based on psychologically abusive conditions covertly carried out by one or both parents during childhood. Patients were filled with a long-standing rage and pain that they could not understand. Therapy allowed the patient to understand and appreciate the cause of his (all patients were male) feelings. Finally, patients were helped to master their traumatic pasts by "reliving, in effect through the patient's memories and transference, the early trauma" (Schiffer 1988: 133). The goal of psychoanalytically oriented therapy is to foster insight and self-awareness, which helps the patient to come to grips with his or her narcissistic disturbance that plays out as drug abuse (narcissistic tranquility). Substance abusers chemically extinguish unpleasant feelings and conflicts; self-awareness enables the patient to understand these emotions and thus learn to use nonchemical responses to them (Forrest 1985).

Psychology, notes James DeLong (1972: 224), has not found a consistent pathology among drug addicts: "No psychiatric diagnosis can be shown to apply to all heroin addicts or even to a majority of them." George E. Woody and his colleagues (1983: 639) argue, however, that "studies indicate that the types of psychiatric problems observed in addicts are similar to illnesses that are often treated with psychotherapy when they occur in nonaddicted populations." In practice, while therapists might be steeped in psychoanalytic theory, they generally avoid the psychoanalytical goal of effecting personality changes in drug abusers. Instead, they focus on improving the ego level of functioning by trying to help patients maintain constructive reality-based relationships, solve problems, and achieve adequate and satisfying social functioning within the existing personality structure. The focus of treatment is on the functions of the ego and its ability to adapt to stress and changes in the environment, despite inadequacies experienced during early stages of development. (For a comparison of the effectiveness of different forms of psychotherapy with opiate addicts, see Woody et al. [1983]; for a discussion of the techniques of psychoanalytically based therapy with addicts, see Kaufman [1994].) This is accomplished through encouragement and moral support, persuasion and suggestion, training and advice, reeducation and counseling—not psychoanalysis. The therapist maintains a substance abuse orientation and typically focuses on identifying specific needs rather than intrapsychic processes. The therapist will deal with impaired self-esteem and ability to form sound interpersonal relationships, characteristics that depend on healthy psychosocial development at early stages of life. While recognizing the unconscious etiology, the therapist focuses on the client's present and future reality. Abstinence, not intrapsychic change, is the goal. For example, at City Roads, a short-term drug treatment program in London,

> the aims of counseling are to clarify *needs* and to build up the residents' motivation to do something about their needs. The first phase involves getting to know the resident, building up confidence and trust in City Roads. The very fact of sitting down and talking to a staff member who takes an interest in the resident is in itself fruitful. The resident starts to feel that someone cares. This was for them a very positive experience, which many drug abusers are not used to.
>
> The next step is "getting to the root of the problem," exploring the personal strengths and weaknesses and their origin, and the needs or problems under investigation are seen as psychological ones. People are seen as being unable to take responsibility, unable to form relationships, depressed, bitter, angry, frustrated, and lacking in trust. The causes of these problems are thought to lie in past experiences, most commonly in an emotionally unstable childhood characterized by lack of parental care, alcoholism in the home, an institutional upbringing, which are thought to lead to deprivation of warmth, care, and stability. (Jamieson, Glanz, and MacGregor 1984: 116–117 [edited])

Behavior Modification

Behavior modification is a treatment approach based on learning theory. The strength of psychoactive substances as positive reinforcers and the negative reinforcement associated with abstinence provide conditioned responses that can explain the key difficulty in treating drug abusers: finding reinforcers that can successfully compete with these substances. Methadone's success in treating some heroin abusers can be explained in terms of behaviorism (Stitzer,

Bigelow, and McCaul 1985). Furthermore, according to operant conditioning, for behavior modification to be effective, reinforcement—negative or positive—must follow immediately after the behavior is exhibited; this instant gratification is what makes drug use so reinforcing and why it is difficult to use behavior modification techniques with chronic drug users.

Aversion Treatment   Behavior modification can also attempt to shape behavior by applying punishment or aversive stimulation. Aversive control was depicted in Stanley Kubrick's motion picture *A Clockwork Orange*. In actual drug treatment Anectine (succinylcholine), a muscle relaxant that causes brief paralysis but leaves the patient conscious, is injected into the subject immediately following the heroin cook-up ritual. The addict-patient remains conscious but is unable to move or breathe voluntarily, conditions that simulate the onset of death. The dangers of heroin use are recited while the patient remains paralyzed.

Drug antagonists can serve a similar function by rendering opiates or other substances ineffective—lacking positive reinforcement—or extremely unpleasant—negative reinforcement or punishment. Disulfiram (Antabuse), metronidazole, or chlorpropamide can serve this purpose for alcohol abusers. **Antabuse**, the best known of these substances, disrupts the liver's metabolism, producing a severe reaction that includes stomach and head pain, extreme nausea, and vomiting. (Milder reactions can be triggered by any number of products that contain alcohol, such as cough medicine, mouthwash, or even skin lotions.) In 1990 a patent was granted for a substance that has the appearance and smell of cocaine and even produces a numbing effect but is not psychoactive. The substance is used in conjunction with an aversive chemical (Andrews 1990). Other behavioral therapies use biofeedback and relaxation training and sometimes assertiveness training to prepare drug abusers to better cope with the stress and anxiety that are believed to be linked to drug use.

Research has discovered a connection between cues and drug use (see Chapter 3). It is believed that the intensity of the drug euphoria burns emotional memories into brain circuits. These memories are encoded into a part of the brain—the amygdala—that operates outside of conscious control to cause intense cravings for re-creating the euphoric experience. These cravings are countered by desensitization treatment: "[P]atients are usually first relaxed, then given repeated exposure to a graded hierarchy of anxiety-producing stimuli (real or imaginal)" to provide a form of immunity (Childress, McLellan, and O'Brien 1985: 957). In voluntary patients electric shocks may be self-administered whenever a craving for the chemical arises. Some researchers report that the use of chemical or electrical stimuli has not proven effective in producing a conditioned aversion in drug abusers, while success has been reported with verbal aversion techniques in which "a patient is asked to *imagine* strongly aversive stimuli (usually vomiting) in association with imaginal drug-related cues, scenes, and/or behavior" (Childress, McLellan, and O'Brien 1985: 951). Thus, imagined aversive stimuli might be superior to real aversive stimuli with the drug-dependent person (although this appears to run

Relapse

Three types of stimulus can trigger intense craving leading to renewed drug use (G. R. Hanson 2002b):

Priming: Just one exposure to a formerly abused substance can precipitate rapid resumption of abuse at previously established levels or greater.

Environmental cues: Exposure to people, places, or things associated with drug use can lead to resumption of abuse.

Stress: Acute and chronic stress can contribute to the establishment, maintenance, and resumption of drug abuse.

contrary to a great deal of research in operant conditioning). In any event, "aversive counterconditioning is not a substitute for support for life-enhancing behavior, rather it suppresses the undesirable behavior while other modalities support positive alternatives" (Frawley and Smith 1990: 21).

In an experiment using both chemical and verbal aversive techniques, cocaine abusers were provided with a nonpsychoactive substitute that smelled like cocaine and numbed the nose. The white substance was set out with a razor blade, a straw, and mirrors for the preparation of "lines." The patient received an injection of nausea-producing drugs. Just before the onset of nausea, the patient snorted the lines of "coke." During the three-hour recovery period the patient was encouraged to dwell on the drug paraphernalia and pictures of cocaine and to pair the use of cocaine with negative consequences. After six months of in-hospital and outpatient booster treatments the abstinence rate was 78 percent. Although a few patients had used cocaine again during the six-month period, the relapses were quite brief (Frawley and Smith 1990).

Social Learning Theory Approach   Social learning theory, a variant of behaviorism, focuses on cognitive mediational processes. According to this view, people are active participants in their operant conditioning processes—they determine what is and what is not reinforcing. For example, as was noted in Chapter 8, the actor must *learn* that ingesting certain chemicals is desirable. In other words, behavior is complex, and reinforcement is often abstract. Thus, notes Albert Bandura (1974: 862), "human beings can cognitively bridge delays between behavior and subsequent reinforcement without impairing the efficacy of incentive operations." People have a unique capacity to use abstractions—symbols, such as the medals and trophies that are so dear to any amateur athlete—as important reinforcers.

The drug abuser is seen as lacking the level of social competence necessary to cope adequately with a variety of situational demands. In using operant conditioning with drug abusers, the social learning theorist stresses patient analysis to discover the variables that are reinforcing. The therapist attempts to discover the situational demands and their related negative emotions that are related to the patient's drug use. The treatment begins with an assessment of the positive and negative aspects of drug use and a self-report on the type, amount, and frequency of drugs used. The assessment includes a focus on the social, physical, and emotional environments in which drug use occurs. After the assessment the role of the therapist is to enable the patient to deal with triggering behavior so that it does not lead to drug use, the patient's own report of the negative aspects of drug use serving as a motivator for adopting more positive coping strategies (Donovan 1988):

- Through a detailed examination of the antecedents and consequences of substance abuse, the therapist attempts to understand why patients might be more likely to use in a given situation and to understand the role that drugs play in their lives. This functional analysis is used to identify the high-risk situations in which they are likely to abuse drugs and thus to provide the basis for learning more effective coping behaviors in those situations.
- The therapist attempts to help patients develop meaningful alternative reinforcers, that is, other activities and involvements (relationships, work, hobbies) that serve as viable alternatives to cocaine abuse and help patients remain abstinent.
- A detailed examination of the consequences, both long-term and short-term, of cocaine and other substance abuse is used as a strategy to build or reinforce the patient's resolve to reduce or cease substance abuse.

Cognitive Behavior Therapy   Cognitive approaches in general tend to focus not on the psychological causes of substance abuse but rather on teaching abusers to understand their cravings and to develop coping skills. This may include detailed planning on how to get from one day to the next without using drugs (Orenstein 2002). Cognitive behavior therapy (CBT) is a short-term (e.g., twelve sessions in twelve weeks) outpatient approach focused on helping patients to recognize, avoid, and cope: *recognize* the situations in which they are most likely to use drugs, *avoid* these situations when appropriate, and *cope* more effectively with a range of problems and problematic behaviors associated with substance abuse (K. Carroll 1998).

In a cognitive approach developed by Anna Rose Childress (1993), the therapist first conducts a study to develop a set of cues that trigger drug cravings. Patients are then taught methods of combating the urges, including a planned delay before acting on a craving, having an alternative behavior planned for this delay period, and systematic relaxation to counter drug arousal. Other techniques include listening to a recording of positive and negative craving consequences, which instructs the addict to list the three most negative consequences of relapsing into drugs and the three most positive consequences of not acting on cravings. Negative imagery is used to encourage patients to remember their worst period of addiction—a type of scare tactic.

Fred Wright and his colleagues (1993) use the Socratic method of challenging questions and answers to stimulate patients to examine and modify their drug-related beliefs. Patients are also taught to keep a log of their cravings;

after each entry they write spontaneous negative thoughts. CBT patients are taught to recognize connections between thoughts, feelings, and actions that undermine attempts to become abstinent. They are taught to avoid specific situations associated with their drug use and to use techniques such as "thought stopping" to cope with cravings. But to benefit, the patient must be intact cognitively (A. Mann 2004b).

Research into CBT with cocaine abusers found a high dropout rate, ranging from 33 percent to 64 percent. The researchers believe that this is related to the impaired attention, learning, memory, reaction time, and cognitive flexibility that are biological consequences of cocaine use. They suggest modifying treatment—a "dumbing down" of the curriculum—in a way that reduces demands on memory and attention (A. Mann 2004b).

Contingency Management and Contingency Contracting Success in modifying behavior using learning theory has been experienced in the controlled setting of a total institution (Goffman 1961) such as a prison or hospital. In such environments, important reinforcers can be manipulated by therapists, often in the form of contingency management and **contingency contracting**.

Sometimes referred to as the *token economy*, contingency management rewards residents for behavior classified as "therapeutic" by providing them with points or tokens that can be redeemed for items the patient values, such as snacks, television time, and weekend passes. Roy Pickens and Travis Thompson (1984) describe the program that is used in a drug-treatment ward at the University of Minnesota Hospital, where staff members record point transactions—added or subtracted—in a small booklet issued to each patient.

Points can be earned for engaging in personal care activities such as cleaning the room or washing clothes, for doing chores such as preparing meals, for participating in ward activities, for attending classes aimed at helping residents to think rationally about themselves, and for assertiveness and problem-solving training that improve interpersonal skills. Extra points can be earned for good-quality participation; these are given to the resident at the end of each activity: "At this time a staff person marks the points earned in the patients' point booklets and briefly describes how the quality of their participation earned them extra points, or how they might improve their participation in the class to earn extra points" (Pickens and Thompson 1984: 55). Points earned are exchangeable for various goods or services, such as snacks, soft drinks, cigarettes, or personal care items. It is obvious that contingency management is not designed to directly affect drug-using behavior but is a means of getting patients to participate in the therapeutic activities that have abstinence as a goal.

The University of Minnesota Hospital uses contingency contracting in the form of "a formalized agreement between a staff person and the patient that specifies the manner in which learning principles are applied to the modification of the patient's behavior" (Pickens and Thompson 1984: 57). The contingency contract is drafted, and the parties sign it. The contract "details the specific behaviors to be changed, how such behaviors are to be monitored, and the contingencies [rewards or punishments] to be placed on the behaviors" (Pickens and Thompson 1984: 57). Contingency contracts are also used with patients during the first several weeks after discharge. The contracts are designed to allow for the implementation of behavioral contingencies in the patient's own home environment to reduce the likelihood of a return to drug use.

Stephen Higgens and Alan Budney (1993) describe a contingency management program for outpatient cocaine abusers that provides points for drug-free urine samples: The number of points multiplies when consecutive negative samples are submitted. The points can be exchanged for a variety of gift items. At the end of three months, patients are shifted from points and gifts to lottery tickets. Methadone clinics have used contingency management to treat patients who ingest opiates and other drugs while on methadone maintenance or methadone withdrawal programs. Rewards for a drug-free urine sample include a cash payment and methadone take-home privileges. Negative contingencies include the loss of cash payments or take-home privileges, daily urinalysis, and counseling (Stitzer et al. 1984; see also Magura et al. 1988; Kidorf and Stitzer 1996). Stephen Magura and his colleagues (1988: 117) report that contingency management utilizing take-home privileges did not have a significant effect on most methadone patients whose polydrug use included cocaine; cocaine was especially attractive to these patients whose drug use was resistant to behavioral modification.

Contingency contracting with negative reinforcement has been used to ensure abstinence in cocaine treatment programs: "For example, a patient participating in such a contract will agree that, in the event of relapse, a previously drafted letter will be sent to his employer informing the latter of the patient's cocaine problem" (Kertzner 1987: 145). Robert Kertzner states that negative contingency contracting has been found to be very effective with patients who agreed to participate. However, he notes, one of the limitations of this strategy is the large number of patients who decline to participate. "Others have modified this technique to include positive sanctions for continued abstinence, such as returning patients' money held in escrow" (Kertzner 1987: 146).

The use of relatively inexpensive reinforcers can improve the outcome of drug treatment. In a study that was conducted at eight community-based treatment programs across the United States, participants who submitted negative drug and alcohol urine samples were immediately able to draw from a container of chips, half with words of encouragement ("good job") and half for prizes valued at between $1 and $200 that were conferred immediately. The number of draws to which they were entitled for being drug free increase by one every week but fell back to just one after a positive sample or a missed appointment. Forty-nine percent of the reinforcement participants and 35 percent of the usual care controls completed twelve weeks of counseling. Reinforcement participants achieved an average abstinence duration of 4.4 consecutive weeks compared to 2.6 weeks for the controls and attended more treatment sessions: nineteen versus sixteen (Whitten 2006c).

Group Treatment

Treatment using psychotherapeutic techniques or behavior modification may utilize casework—one-to-one counseling—or group approaches. "Groups organized around therapeutic goals can enrich members with insight and guidance; and during times of crisis, groups can comfort and guide people who otherwise might be unhappy or lost" (Flores and Georgi 2005: 2). As Helen Northern (1969: 52), points out, one of the advantages of the uses of the group approach "is that stimulation toward improvement arises from a network of interpersonal influences in which all members participate." Philip Flores and Jeffrey Georgi (2005: 2) note the special value of group treatment, since "people who abuse substances often are more likely to remain abstinent and committed to recovery when treatment is provided in groups, apparently because of rewarding and therapeutic forces such as affiliation, confrontation, support, gratifications, and identification."

The basic theory underlying this approach is that peer interactions are more powerful than therapist-patient interactions in the one-to-one situation. In casework the relationship between therapist and patient can remain distant because the therapist typically lacks the all-important personal experience with drug abuse. In the group approach, the group, not the group leader-therapist, is the helping instrument, obviating the therapist's personal experience with drugs. Furthermore, many critical interpersonal behaviors that might not emerge in the casework approach will emerge in a group (Flores 1988). "Group members are more likely to try new forms of behavior if these have been demonstrated effectively by others" (Kauffman, Dore, and Nelson-Zlupko 1995: 365).

Dr. Matthew Hopkins, who now works to help substance abusers overcome their addictions, had to overcome his own addictions.

©AP Photo/Lee Mariner

Summary of Treatment Approaches

Cognitive-behavioral therapy strategies are based on the theory that learning processes play a critical role in the development of maladaptive behavioral patterns. Individuals learn to identify and correct problematic behaviors. Specific techniques include exploring the positive and negative consequences of continued use, self-monitoring to recognize drug cravings early on and to identify high-risk situations for use, and developing strategies for coping with and avoiding high-risk situations and the desire to use. A central element of this treatment is anticipating the problems patients are likely to face and helping them to develop effective coping strategies.

Supportive-expressive psychotherapy is time-limited and has two main components:

1. *Supportive* techniques to help patients feel comfortable in discussing their personal experiences.
2. *Expressive* techniques to help patients identify and work through interpersonal relationship issues.

Special attention is paid to the role of drugs in relation to problem feelings and behaviors and how problems can be solved without recourse to drugs.

Individualized drug counseling focuses directly on reducing or stopping the addict's illicit drug use. It also addresses related areas of impaired functioning such as employment status, illegal activity, and family/social relations as well as the content and structure of the patient's recovery program. Through its emphasis on short-term behavioral goals, individualized drug counseling helps the patient to develop coping strategies and tools for abstaining from drug use and then maintaining abstinence. The addiction counselor encourages twelve-step participation (discussed later) and makes referrals for needed supplemental medical, psychiatric, employment, and other services. Individuals are encouraged to attend sessions one or two times per week.

Motivational enhancement therapy is a client-centered counseling approach for initiating behavior change by helping clients to resolve ambivalence about engaging in treatment and stopping drug use. This approach employs strategies to evoke rapid and internally motivated change in the client rather than guiding the client stepwise through the recovery process. This therapy consists of an initial assessment battery session followed by two to four individual treatment sessions with a therapist. The first treatment session focuses on providing feedback generated from the initial assessment battery to stimulate discussion regarding personal substance use and to elicit self-motivational statements. Motivational interviewing principles are used to strengthen motivation and build a plan for change. Coping strategies for high-risk situations are suggested and discussed with the client. In subsequent sessions the therapist monitors change, reviews cessation strategies being

Source: National Institute of Drug Abuse.

Groups

"Because of our need for human contact is biologically determined, we are, from the start, social creatures. This propensity to congregate is a powerful therapeutic tool" (Flores and Georgi 2005: 2).

Treatment groups are typically formed around one basic trait that all members share and from which the group derives its descriptive label. For example, they might be formed around cocaine abuse, a subtrait being age or gender. In general, notes Henry Spitz (1987), the more heterogeneous the group elements, the greater is the intragroup tension that promotes interaction. The more homogeneous the group elements, the greater is the basis for inter-member trust and group cohesion. Groups may be organized at different points in the treatment process, such as intake, detoxification, inpatient, and outpatient. There may also be groups for parents, siblings, and spouses. Although group approaches have many advantages over casework, considerably fewer therapists are trained in the former than in the latter. Furthermore, "patients whose motivation for change appears highly questionable should not be accepted into a group-oriented treatment program, because they usually have a negative, used, and continues to encourage commitment to change or sustained abstinence. Clients are sometimes encouraged to bring a significant other to sessions. This approach has been used successfully with alcoholics and with marijuana-dependent individuals.

Behavioral therapy for adolescents incorporates the principle that unwanted behavior can be changed by clear demonstration of the desired behavior and consistent reward of incremental steps toward achieving it. Therapeutic activities include fulfilling specific assignments, rehearsing desired behaviors, and recording and reviewing progress, with praise and privileges given for meeting assigned goals. Urine samples are collected regularly to monitor drug use. The therapy aims to equip the patient to gain three types of control:

- *Stimulus control* helps patients to avoid situations associated with drug use and learn to spend more time in activities that are incompatible with drug use.

- *Urge control* helps patients to recognize and change thoughts, feelings, and plans that lead to drug use.

- *Social control* involves family members and other people important in helping patients to avoid drugs. A parent or significant other attends treatment sessions when possible and assists with therapy assignments and reinforcing desired behavior.

Multidimensional family therapy (MDFT) for adolescents is an outpatient family-based drug abuse treatment for teenagers. MDFT views adolescent drug use in terms of a network of influences (i.e., individual, family, peer, community) and suggests that reducing unwanted behavior and increasing desirable behavior occur in multiple ways in different settings. Treatment includes individual and family sessions held in the clinic, in the home, or with family members at the family court, school, or other community locations.

During individual sessions, the therapist and adolescent work on important developmental tasks, such as developing decision-making, negotiation, and problem-solving skills. Teenagers acquire skills in communicating their thoughts and feelings to deal better with life stressors and acquire vocational skills. Parallel sessions are held with family members. Parents examine their particular parenting style, learning to distinguish influence from control and to have a positive and developmentally appropriate influence on their child.

Multisystemic therapy addresses the factors associated with serious antisocial behavior in children and adolescents who abuse drugs. These factors include characteristics of the adolescent (e.g., favorable attitudes toward drug use), the family (poor discipline, family conflict, parental drug abuse), peers (positive attitudes toward drug use), school (dropout, poor performance), and neighborhood (criminal subculture).

demoralizing impact on other patients who may be working hard to remain abstinent" (Washton, Stone, and Hendrickson 1988: 380).

Although group approaches may vary, "most professionals who work with alcoholics and addicts on a sustained basis agree that group therapy offers the chemically dependent individual unique opportunities to (1) share and to identify with others who are going through similar problems; (2) to understand their own attitudes about addiction and their defenses against giving up alcohol and drugs by confronting similar attitudes and defenses in others; and (3) to learn to communicate needs and feelings more directly" (Flores 1988: 7). Support provided by the group enables it to act as a catalyst for abstinence. (This has been the author's experience in working with groups of adolescent drug abusers.) Some researchers, however, advise caution: Group approaches "for youth with histories of antisocial behavior may be counterproductive; participants in a group may tend to validate and legitimize the antisocial behavior of the other group members" (Chavez and Sanchez-Way 1997: 17).

DRUG TREATMENT PROGRAMS

The treatment of drug-dependent people presents an obvious problem: If we do not know the cause, how can we offer the "cure"? This problem is exacerbated by programs that fail to develop theory-centered treatment responses or to incorporate the results of research into their approach to clients. While matching patient needs with specific treatments is the norm in medicine, this approach might be missing even in drug programs that are housed in medical settings (Hester and Miller 1988). The admissions policies of some in-patient programs depend more on financial status than on matching patient needs and program resources. Often, these are relatively new programs looking for middle- and upper-class patients, who are most likely to have third-party or insurance support. Assessment and intake are informal or based on available space. Mounting health-related costs have caused third-party payment organizations to "require treatment organizations to further document and better justify the need for treatment" (Winters and Henly 1988: 4). Indeed, the American Society of Addiction Medicine has established minimum criteria for inpatient drug and alcohol treatment for adults:

- Severe but manageable withdrawal risk
- Need for medical monitoring and a twenty-four-hour structured setting
- High resistance despite negative consequences
- Inability of outpatient treatment to curtail drug use
- Home environment dangerous for recovery

Treatment can be accomplished in a variety of settings: voluntary, involuntary, inpatient, and outpatient. The cost of these programs varies according to whether they are inpatient or outpatient, the qualifications of their staff, and the length of treatment. A particularly vexing problem is community opposition to drug treatment programs. Let us examine the settings and treatments offered by some drug programs.

Treatment Programs in the Criminal Justice System

About half the states have statutory provisions for the civil commitment of drug abusers (Leukefeld and Tims 1988), although few make any regular use of these provisions. Civil commitment, the nonpunitive incarceration of addicts for purposes of treatment, dates back to 1935, when a federal narcotics "farm" was opened in Lexington, Kentucky. A second was opened in 1938 in Fort Worth, Texas. Addict-patients who requested commitment and involuntary patients who had been prosecuted for criminal offenses spent six months at these facilities, which followed a standard course of withdrawal—physical restoration, psychological therapy in the form of individual and group counseling, and vocational counseling—after which patients returned to their communities. The physical structure of these facilities, however, resembled that of a modified prison, and security was strict (H. W. Morgan 1981). Reviews of the program were either mixed or inconclusive, and the federal government chose not to expand civil commitment. Despite this, in 1961 California enacted a program built on the Lexington model.

California Rehabilitation Center   In 1961 the California legislature established within the Department of Corrections the California Rehabilitation Center (CRC) for the compulsory care of individuals addicted to narcotics. In 1962 the U.S. Supreme Court ruled (in *Robinson* v. *California*, 370 U.S. 660) that drug addiction was an illness and that therefore a state could not make this status a crime. In that decision the Court also suggested that the Constitution would not be offended by involuntary civil commitment for the purpose of treating the illness of addiction. A later decision gave further support to the commitment-for-treatment approach, and in 1963 the legislature amended certain sections of the California Rehabilitation Act to emphasize treatment.

California statutes provide four methods of commitment (California Narcotic Addict Evaluation Authority 1994):

1. After a person has been convicted and sentenced to prison for a felony, the judge may suspend the sentence and order the district attorney to file for a narcotic petition. If the judge subsequently determines that the person is addicted or is in imminent danger of becoming addicted, execution of the sentence can be suspended, and the offender is placed in the CRC at Norco. Most residents at the CRC fall into this category.
2. After conviction for a misdemeanor and before or after sentencing, the judge can certify the case to superior court for a commitment petition. After an examination the offender may be sent to the CRC.
3. Any interested party may report to the district attorney under oath his or her belief that another person is addicted to narcotics or is in imminent danger of becoming addicted. If sufficient evidence (probable cause) is present, the district attorney may petition the superior court for a period of commitment not to exceed twelve months.
4. Any person who believes that he or she is addicted or about to become addicted may report such belief to the district attorney, who can then petition the superior court for a period of commitment not to exceed twelve months.

The CRC, which has the capacity for about 4,000 males and 800 females, is a medium-security facility of the Department of Corrections with open dormitories, double fences, and armed officers at the perimeter. It has remedial and high school educational facilities as well as vocational training. Patients may voluntarily join various self-help groups such as Alcoholics Anonymous and Narcotics Anonymous. Leisure activities include organized and individual athletics. Following institutional care, civil commitment patients are released to aftercare: parole supervision that includes regular testing for drug use. Patients who fail to live up to the terms of release can be returned to the CRC. Release to aftercare and return to the CRC are decided by the Narcotic Addict Evaluation Authority. Felony commitment patients on aftercare who remain drug-free for twelve or sixteen months (depending on the length of the commitment) may receive early discharge. Research into the performance of released patients indicates that they did no better than addicts who received drug therapy in California prisons.

Federal Program (NARA)   The federal government has a similar program—the 1966 Narcotic Rehabilitation Act (NARA)—which provides for the commitment of drug users. The act empowers a sentencing judge to commit drug-abusing defendants for a period of evaluation not to exceed ninety days. During that time NARA staff from the Bureau of Prisons evaluate the offender to ascertain his or her suitability for treatment. A report is then submitted to the judge, who can commit the defendant to the custody of the U.S. Surgeon General for treatment that may last up to thirty-six months; convicted offenders may be committed to the Bureau of Prisons for drug treatment for up to ten years (but not to exceed the maximum sentence for their conviction) or placed on probation. Individuals who have not been charged with a federal crime can be committed by means of a petition submitted by a U.S. attorney on their behalf or on behalf of a relative. Involuntary patients have a right to a hearing with counsel to determine whether they are to be civilly committed. Treatment may last up to forty-two months, although the institutional phase may last only six months (Kay 1973). On release from institutional treatment patients can be required to participate in an aftercare program under the Probation Division of the U.S. Courts. A relapse can result in being reinstitutionalized.

Drug Courts

Established as a result of court and prison overcrowding, special "drug courts" have proven popular. In 1989 a special drug court was established by judicial order in Miami, Florida. This high-volume court expands on traditional drug defendant diversion programs by offering a year or more of court-run treatment; defendants who complete this option have their criminal cases dismissed. Between 1991 and 1993 Miami influenced officials in more than twenty other jurisdictions to establish drug courts (National Institute of Justice 1995b).

Although they vary widely, common features of drug courts include a nonadversarial approach to integrating substance abuse treatment with criminal justice case processing. The focus is on early identification of eligible substance abusers and prompt placement in treatment, combined with frequent drug testing (Gebelein 2000).

The Madison County, Illinois, drug court was fueled by a 437 percent increase in drug arrests between 1988 and 1992. The program targets individuals arrested on felony drug charges who have been diagnosed with alcohol or drug dependence that could be treated on an outpatient basis. Those who successfully complete the program have their charges dismissed. The program provides job assistance, which includes vocational training and high school equivalency education. Initially, clients are scheduled for three to five intensive three- to four-hour counseling sessions per week. As the clients progress, the number and length of sessions are reduced. Depending on a client's progress, the program can be completed in about one year or less. Random drug tests are given, and failure to comply with program requirements results in prosecution for the original felony offense (Illinois Criminal Justice Authority 1999).

In Maricopa (Phoenix) County, Arizona, the goal of drug court is considerably different: to increase the number of drug cases entering the system. Using a catchy "do drugs, do time" slogan, law enforcement agencies targeted casual users to enforce a "zero tolerance" policy. Users are "held accountable" for their illegal drug use by a policy of arrest and threatened prosecution; those who accept the treatment option—which includes paying fees—avoid further court action (Hepburn, Johnston, and Rogers 1994).

A study of drug court participants in six U.S. cities found that judicial supervision coupled with treatment is a powerful tool for responding to drug abusers, despite the fact that most participants enrolled to avoid incarceration and not for purposes of rehabilitation. Indeed, the study found that the threat of incarceration and frequent drug testing were essential to program success (National Institute of Justice 2002). A study in New York revealed that drug offenders who complete the court supervised program are less likely to commit crimes than are similar offenders who opt for prison time instead: 29 percent lower over three years (von Zielbauer 2003). Doris Layton MacKenzie (2006) concluded that an examination of research into drug courts reveals that they are effective in reducing participant recidivism.

Treatment Alternative to Street Crime (TASC)

The federally funded Treatment Alternative to Street Crime (TASC) program initiated in 1972 to divert substance-abusing offenders out of the court system and into community treatment, stands somewhere between compulsory and voluntary treatment. Since its inception it has been expanded to include people on probation and parole. TASC identifies, assesses, and refers appropriate drug- and/or alcohol-dependent offenders accused or convicted of nonviolent crimes to community-based substance abuse treatment, as an alternative to or supplement to existing criminal justice sanctions and procedures (Cook and Weinman 1988). TASC monitors the client's progress in drug treatment and reports back to the criminal justice agency that made the referral. Those who fail to conform to program requirements face further criminal justice processing. Research into the effectiveness—reducing recidivism and drug use—of TASC, which operates in about thirty states, have generally been positive (Anglin, Longshore, and Turner 1999).

Coercive treatment, civil or criminal, appears to have a positive outcome (Anglin 1988; Anglin and Hser 1990a; D. Young 2002). Extensive research indicates that "[c]oerced involvement in community-based programs and/or corrections-based treatment can have a substantial impact on the behavior of chronic drug-abusing offenders" (Anglin and Maughr 1992: 76). George Vaillant (1970: 494) found that although the most effective motivation for abstinence is that narcotics are illegal, "the most potent treatment was compulsory supervision. Thus, if the addict is followed over time, external coercion of some kind appears a critical variable in facilitating abstinence."

This was the author's experience when as a parole officer (see Abadinsky 2006) he supervised heroin addicts in New York City. Close personal contact, unannounced home visits and searches, arm checks (for needle marks), and random urinalysis provided the ego and superego strengths for addicts to remain heroin free: "Besides offering addicts compulsory support and an 'external super-ego,' parole itself was probably a substitute for addiction in that it required ex-addicts to remain regularly employed" (Vaillant 1970: 495). The parole officer could redirect the considerable skills and energy that are required to be a successful heroin addict into seeking and maintaining legitimate employment (see also Eaglin 1986). From the behaviorist point of view, the probation or parole officer provides the basis for operant conditioning, applying positive reinforcement for abstinence and negative reinforcement for relapse.

In a study of compulsory treatment—residential treatment or imprisonment for felony offenders—Douglas Young (2002) found that mandatory treatment programs and progressively higher perceived legal pressure can increase treatment retention and that such retention is directly related to a positive treatment outcome for participants. MacKenzie (2006) states that although drug treatment in general is effective in reducing the recidivism of drug-involved offenders, the research literature does not reveal which interventions are most effective.

Therapeutic Community

Therapeutic community (TC) is a generic term for residential, self-help, drug-free treatment programs that have some common characteristics, including concepts adopted from Alcoholics Anonymous (AA): "There is no such thing as an ex-addict, only an addict who is not using at the moment; the emphasis on mutual support and aid; the distrust of mental-health professionals; and the concept of continual confession and catharsis. However, the TC has extended these notions to include the concept of a live-in community with a rigid structure of day-to-day behavior and a complex system of punishment and rewards" (DeLong 1972: 190–191). "The primary aims of the therapeutic community are a global change in lifestyle reflecting abstinence from illicit substances, elimination of antisocial activity, increased employability, and prosocial attitudes and values. A critical assumption in TCs is that stable recovery depends upon a successful integration of these social and psychological goals. The rehabilitative approach, therefore, requires multidimensional influences and training that, for most clients, can only occur after an extended period of living in a 24-hour residential setting" (De Leon 1986b: 69).

The TC "views drug abuse as deviant behavior, reflecting impeded personality development and/or chronic deficits in social, educational and economic skills" (De Leon 1986a: 5; see also DeLeon 2000). "A considerable number of [TC] clients never have acquired conventional lifestyles. Vocational

The Therapeutic Community in Sum

"TCs are drug-free residential settings that use a hierarchical model with treatment stages that reflect increased levels of personal and social responsibility. Peer influence, mediated through a variety of group processes, is used to help individuals learn and assimilate social norms and develop more effective social skills. TCs differ from other treatment approaches principally in their use of the community, comprising treatment staff and those in recovery, as key agents of change" (National Institute on Drug Abuse 2002b: 1).

and educational deficits are marked; mainstream values either are missing or unpursued. Most often, these clients emerge from a socially disadvantaged sector where drug abuse is more a social response than a psychological disturbance. Their TC experience can be termed *habilitation*—the development of a socially productive, conventional lifestyle for the first time in their lives" (De Leon 1994: 19). "According to the TC treatment perspective, drug abuse is a disorder of the whole person; the problem is the person, not the drug, and the *addiction* is only a *symptom* and not the essence of the disorder" (Nielsen and Scarpitti 1997: 280).

TC Models The TC becomes a surrogate family and a communal support group for dealing with alienation and drug abuse that derives from it. Its purpose, notes Mitchell Rosenthal (1973), is to strengthen ego functioning. Therapy, except for the time spent asleep, is total. James DeLong (1972) notes that there is a quasi-evangelistic quality to the "TC movement." The day at a therapeutic community is varied but regimented. A typical day begins at 7:00 A.M. and ends at 11:00 P.M. "and includes morning and evening house meetings, job assignments, groups, seminars, scheduled personal time, recreation, and individual counseling. As employment is considered an important element of successful participation in society, work is a distinctive component of the TC model. In the TC, all activities and interpersonal and social interactions are considered important opportunities to facilitate individual change" (National Institute on Drug Abuse 2002b: 5).

The residences are often similar to the communes that were popular during the late 1960s and 1970s counterculture movement, except that they generally have a strict hierarchy and insist on rigid adherence to norms even more stringent than those of the proverbial middle class. The model of all therapeutic communities, note Jerome Platt and Christina Labate (1976), is Synanon, founded in 1958 by Charles E. Dederich, a former alcoholic who was a participant in and advocate of the Alcoholics Anonymous twelve-step approach to substance abuse. (AA is discussed later in this chapter.) The Synanon Foundation expanded rapidly into several states, with facilities run almost entirely by ex-addicts. Treatment programs based on twelve-step/drug-free approaches frequently have an antimedication bias (Harwood and Myers 2004).

Phoenix House

At Phoenix House in the Bronx, every day begins the same. After a thirty-minute breakfast starting at 7:00 A.M., there is an hour-long meeting that includes inspirational songs and skits written and performed by the residents. The rest of the day consists of seminars, classes to prepare for the general equivalency diploma, rap sessions, job assignments, and more meals and meetings. There is little free time until 9:00 P.M. Lights are out at 11:00 P.M. The 185-word Phoenix House philosophy is recited from memory at least twice a day. The weekend schedule is slightly more relaxed, with rented videos available and highly supervised trips into New York. Most of the residents are between 20 and 40 years old and on welfare, which helps to pay for their stay at the program. They typically have lengthy criminal records (Marriott 1989).

Therapeutic communities such as Odyssey House, however, have been more receptive to using professionals and even medicine-assisted withdrawal. The director of the New York–based Phoenix House, the largest private, nonprofit drug-treatment institution in the country—with ninety programs serving more than 5,000 clients—has long had a psychiatrist, Mitchell Rosenthal, as its executive director, and the program now uses buprenorphine for withdrawing patients from heroin (Horton and McMurphy 2004). David Bellis (1981: 155) is critical of therapeutic communities that resist professional involvement and that instead use untrained staff and residents, "many hardly off heroin themselves," who, under no legal or professional oversight, unleash their own brand of "therapy" on addicts, many of whom are undergoing mandatory treatment because of a plea bargain, probation, or parole status. In his study of a failed therapeutic community Robert Weppner (1983) points out that being a poorly educated ex-addict does not endow one with treatment skills.

Although Synanon requires a lifetime commitment, most TCs have abandoned or modified this aspect of the Synanon model.[5] The TCs frequently offer vocational training and education to prepare residents to live in the community without continuous help from the TC. Indeed, George De Leon describes the TC as "community as method": "*the purposive use of the peer community to facilitate social and psychological change in individuals*" (1995: 9 [italics in original]).

Life in the Therapeutic Community   A prominent feature of the TC has been the stiff entry requirement: a devastating initial interview that tests an applicant's motivation by focusing on his or her inadequacies and lack of

---

[5] Dederich eventually transformed Synanon into a cultlike phenomenon. In 1980 he pled guilty to plotting to murder one of his Synanon critics, a lawyer representing former Synanon members who maintained that they were held against their will. In poor health, Dederich received a sentence of five years' probation and was banned from participating in Synanon. In 1997, at age 83, Dederich died of a heart attack.

■ Odyssey House

Odyssey House operates a TC on New York's Wards' Island for pregnant women and those with young children. Residents include about two dozen women and children. Some of the women are pregnant, and most have been abusing crack. The facility is underfunded and must depend on private donations to make up for inadequate government support. As a result, children's clothing and nursery toys are in short supply. The residents "participate in rigorous therapy, they are given parenting courses including such essentials as how to hold a baby and they must work at jobs. The overbearing and obnoxious scrape plates, while the shy and withdrawn are given pretty clothes and work as front-desk receptionists. But the most prized assignments are in the nursery. . . . Graduation requirements are stiff. Along with conquering addiction, women must complete the equivalent of high school, secure a driver's license and find a full-time job" (D. Martin 1990: 13).

success. Successful applicants must invest completely in the program, which encourages the resident to identify with the former addicts who run it and become resocialized into embracing a drug-free existence. The new resident is isolated from all outside contacts, including family and friends. The withdrawal process is accomplished without drugs but with the support of other residents. Once withdrawal has been accomplished, a program of positive and negative reinforcement is implemented. The resident is assigned menial work projects, such as cleaning toilets, but is given an opportunity to earn more prestigious assignments and greater freedom through conformity with the program. Transgressions are punished by public humiliation such as reprimands, shaved heads, and wearing a sign indicating the nature of the violation. Those who leave, relapse, and return are required to wear a sign announcing their situation. Shame and guilt are constantly used to force the addict to conform and to change his or her view of drugs (Platt and Labate 1976). There is little privacy. Drug use, physical violence, and sexual activity between residents are punished with expulsion.

Residents are kept busy in a highly structured environment that offers little time for idleness or boredom. They are expected to be active in all aspects of the TC program. Failure to do so becomes the subject of criticism at the encounter session, a central feature of the therapeutic process. The encounter is a relatively unstructured, leaderless group session in which members focus on a particular resident (who occupies the "hot seat") and bombard him or her with criticisms about attitude and behavior. The target is encouraged to fight back verbally, although the goal of such sessions is to destroy the rationalizations and defenses that help to perpetuate irresponsible thought patterns and behavior—a resocialization process. "The style of the encounter, with its abrasive attacks and its permitted verbal violence . . . is designed to encourage the spewing out of pent-up hostility and anger, to force the patient to confront his maladaptive emotional response and behavior

Tough Love Is a Reality Check

The ex-addict counselor at San Francisco's Center Point TC addresses one of the residents at a group session: "You like to present yourself as a middle-class white woman with a *little* drug and alcohol problem who some stuff happened to and now you're here to get your life back. . . . [But] you are a homeless dope fiend with no education who chose drugs over your kids" (Orenstein 2002: 37).

patterns" (M. Rosenthal 1973: 91). "TCs are successful because they provide the setting and the mechanisms for clients' learning new roles, attitudes, skills, and definitions of self. The most important mechanism for change is the community of peers who confront the client when old values or behaviors are displayed, who provide positive and negative reinforcements to elicit appropriate behavior, and who serve as role models for lifestyle changes" (Nielson and Scarpitti 1997: 281).

Dan Waldorf (1973) points out that the TC is an exciting, friendly, and highly moral—almost utopian—environment. But, notes Mitchell Rosenthal (1984: 55), it is not for all abusers: "Severe disturbances may be exacerbated by the TC regimen and may have an adverse effect not only on the disturbed client but also on the treatment environment and the progress of others in the treatment population. Also unsuitable for treatment are candidates whose drug involvement is of so limited a nature as to require a less rigorous intervention or who—despite the deleterious effects of drug abuse—are able to function with the help of a positive support network (e.g., family or significant others)."

TCs in Prisons　TCs have been established in prisons in New York, California, and a number of other states (Pendergast et al. 2002). In these so-called "Stay 'N Out" therapeutic communities inmates are recruited at state correctional facilities and housed in units that are segregated from the general prison population, although they eat and attend morning activities with other prisoners. The program, which lasts from six to nine months, is staffed by graduates of community TCs and by ex-offenders with prison experience, who act as role models demonstrating successful rehabilitation.

During the early phase of treatment, the major clinical thrust involves observation and assessment of client needs and problem areas. Orientation to the prison TC procedures occurs through individual counseling, encounter sessions, and seminars. Clients are given low-level jobs and granted little status. During the later phase of treatment, residents are provided opportunities to earn higher-level positions and increased status though sincere involvement in the program and hard work. Encounter groups and counseling sessions are more in-depth and focus on the areas of self-discipline, self-worth, self-awareness, respect for authority, and acceptance of guidance for problem areas. Seminars take on a more intellectual nature. Debate is encouraged to enhance self-expression and to increase self-confidence. (Wexler and Williams 1986: 224)

Chemical Dependency Programs

> Short-term residential programs, often referred to as chemical dependency units, are often based on the Minnesota model of treatment for alcoholism. These programs involve a three- to six-week inpatient treatment phase, followed by extended outpatient therapy or participation in twelve-step self-help groups such as Narcotics Anonymous or Cocaine Anonymous. Chemical dependency programs for drug abuse arose in the private sector in the mid-1980s with insured alcohol and cocaine abusers as their primary patients (National Institute on Drug Abuse 2003: 1).

On release, prison TC graduates are encouraged to become part of the extensive community-based TC network. Research into the effect of the prison TC on parole success found that "Stay 'N Out" reduced recidivism (Wexler, Lipton, and Foster 1985; Wexler, Falkin, and Lipton 1990; Lipton 1995; Wexler et al. 1999).

Do TCs Work?   There has been a great deal of controversy over the success rate of TCs, and most research has been inadequate or inconclusive. Many TCs release statistics that cannot withstand scrutiny by disinterested researchers. The arduous screening process keeps out many drug abusers who would probably fail the program, and an abuser's graduation from a TC does not necessarily mean that the program has succeeded. The TC insists on behavioral change that "is not away from antisocial behavior, that of the street addict, and toward the norms of the larger society, but toward norms accepted in the group alone" (Weppner 1983: xi). Those who need to manage in the community without the continuing support of the group are at risk because they will return to the same environment that led to drug dependence in the first place, and they often bring with them all of the educational and vocational deficiencies they had on entering. Those who enter the TC with a greater degree of mental health, with limited or no attachment to a criminal subculture, and with employment skills are obviously better equipped to deal with post-TC existence.

Chemical Dependency Programs

As was noted at the beginning of this chapter, during the past two decades the number of chemical dependency (CD) programs has increased. Some are for-profit, and others are nonprofit; many call themselves "therapeutic communities," although they differ dramatically from the TCs discussed above. These programs typically share a number of features: They do a great deal of outreach—most employ a marketing person—and often advertise for clients who are likely to have health insurance, such as employed alcohol and cocaine abusers as opposed to heroin addicts, because the costs can run over $1,000 a day for inpatient care. Many CD programs are located in a health care facility, which can increase the cost of treatment. Adding a chemical dependency

Private Hospital Drug Treatment

"Parents are often frightened by media hype or hospital treatment center advertisements that they have seen on television. Insurance coverage and the parents'
willingness to have someone else deal with the 'abuser' are also factors. As a
result, what may be experimental adolescent behavior becomes a reason to place
an adolescent in an inpatient hospital treatment program. Such treatment programs are one of the few large-scale sources of profit for private hospitals. Managers of these programs have become desperate for adolescent admissions
because of the vast overbuilding of these facilities that occurred during the 1980s"
(Lawson 1992: 4).

program to a health care facility can help to reduce the number of otherwise
vacant beds that can be costly to any hospital. The treatment approach usually
includes individual and group counseling, and the model tends to be eclectic
rather than doctrinal.

"Primarily they serve the more socially advantaged substance abusers
whose fee for service is generally covered by insurance, in contrast to the major
modalities whose costs are mostly tax subsidized. The treatment orientation of
these programs is also varied, but mainly reflects a mix of traditional mental
health and 12-Step perspectives [discussed below]. They offer a broad menu of
services such as education, nutrition, relaxation training, recreation, counseling-
psychotherapy, psychopharmacological adjuncts, and self-help groups"
(De Leon 1995: 5). "CD programs do not require patients to perform
housekeeping duties. . . . [and they] are especially attractive to patients with
greater initial functional and social resources who can afford the better
facilities and amenities" (Gerstein 1994: 56).

The typical program is a three- to six-week intensive and highly structured
inpatient regimen:

> Clients begin with an in-depth psychiatric and psychosocial evaluation and
> then follow a general education-oriented program track of daily lectures plus
> two to three meetings per week in small task-oriented groups. Group education
> teaches clients about the disease concept of dependence, focusing on the harmful
> medical and psychosocial effects of illicit drugs and excessive alcohol con-
> sumption. There is also an individual prescriptive track for each client, meetings
> about once a week with a "focal counselor," and appointments with other
> professionals if medical, psychiatric, or family services are needed. (Gerstein and
> Harwood 1990: 171)

Harvey Siegal and his colleagues (1995: 69) are critical: "Since it is the
treatment professional who retains all responsibility for prescribing and
implementing the necessary therapeutic activity, patients may have difficulty
achieving ownership of their recovery program." And **aftercare**—treatment
and services following discharge—is typically meager. "Aftercare is considered
quite important in CD [28-day] treatment, but relatively few program

**There's No Biz Like
Show Biz**
The new class of super-
luxury rehabilitation
centers in California—
ocean-view mansions
where the patients often
come from the world of
show business—charge
from $40,000 to
$100,000 for a thirty-day
stay (J. Adler 2007).

Cost of Care

"The financing and structure of specialty services for addiction treatment have developed idiosyncratically and relatively autonomously from the nation's system for medical care." This reflects a "legacy of poor service for alcohol and drug use disorders in health care and mental health care settings, [and] limited coverage in health plans" exacerbated by efforts to reduce the costs of health care (Harwood and Myers 2004: 26).

resources are devoted to it" (Gerstein 1994: 56). Patients are urged to participate in community twelve-step groups. In fact, virtually all of the many programs that this author has examined throughout the country utilize an Alcoholics Anonymous or Narcotics Anonymous twelve-step approach for both inpatient and outpatient treatment.

ALCOHOLICS ANONYMOUS (AA)

The **Alcoholics Anonymous (AA)** approach of using public confession and commitment and mutual aid concepts can be found in a number of nineteenth century temperance organizations (W. L. White 1998). Alcoholics Anonymous was established during the 1930s by William ("Bill W.") Wilson (1895–1971), a financial investigator and alcoholic, and Robert ("Dr. Bob") Holbrook Smith (1879–1950), a physician and alcoholic. Nan Robertson (1988b) presents a rather unflattering view of the two, particularly of Wilson (see also Cheever 2004), whom she refers to as a Wall Street hustler and compulsive womanizer. Bill W. had joined the Oxford Group (renamed Moral Re-Armament in 1939), an international religious movement, as the result of the influence of another alcoholic whose religious experience appeared to act as a cure. Bill W. was influenced by the work of William James (1842–1910), a psychologist and philosopher, particularly his *Varieties of Religious Experience*, published in 1902.[6] As part of the Oxford Group Bill W. began dedicating his activities to curing alcoholics, an effort that was quite unsuccessful until he met Dr. Bob, also a member of the Oxford Group, in 1935 while on a business trip to Akron, Ohio. He helped Dr. Bob to become abstinent, and the two recognized that success in helping alcoholics was not to be found in preaching abstinence but rather in a fellowship in which each alcoholic simply relates his or her story of drunkenness and conversion to a nonalcoholic lifestyle. The "listening" was as important as the "telling." "There could not have been just one founder of A.A.," notes Robertson (1988b: 34), "because the essence of the process is one person telling his story to another as honestly as he knows how."

---

[6] It is ironic that William James typically found his religious and philosophical insights while intoxicated from nitrous oxide (Tymoczco 1996).

Early in 1939, Bill W. published *Alcoholics Anonymous*, which explained the philosophy and methods—the **twelve steps** of recovery—of his small association of alcoholics and contained case histories of some thirty recovered members. They became known as Alcoholics Anonymous after the title of Wilson's book, which AA members often refer to as "the Big Book" (it was quite bulky when originally published). Wilson, who died in 1971, was supported by the substantial royalties the book eventually generated. His wife, Lois Burnham, who died in 1988 at age 97 years, established **Al-Anon** for the family members of alcoholics. She was a nonalcoholic who patterned her organization on the AA model (Pace 1988). There are now similar groups for the family and friends of cocaine users (Co-Anon) and of users of heroin and other narcotics (Nar-Anon).

The AA Program

The AA program requires an act of surrender—an acknowledgment of being an alcoholic and of the destructiveness that results—a bearing of witness, and an acknowledgement of a higher power. Although AA is nondenominational, there is a strong repent-of-your-sins revivalism; groups begin or end their meetings holding hands in a circle and reciting the Lord's Prayer or the Serenity Prayer: "God grant me the serenity to accept the things I cannot change; courage to change the things I can; and wisdom to know the difference" (DuPont and McGovern 1994: 27). As in Protestant revival meetings, the alcoholic/sinner seeks salvation through personal testimony, public contrition, and submission to a higher authority (Peele 1985; Delbanco and Delbanco 1995). Courts have ruled that Alcoholics Anonymous is a religion for purposes of separation of church and state, thus rendering what transpires at AA meetings subject to the same protection as clergy-parishioner exchanges (Worth 2002). AA also provides "an important social network through which members learn appropriate behavior and coping skills in drinking situations and become involved in various (nondrinking) leisure activities with other recovering alcoholics" (McElrath 1995: 314).

Heavy Price for a "Big Book"

The original version of Bill Wilson's *Alcoholic's Anonymous*, a typewritten manuscript with a multitude of annotations, sold at auction in 2004 for $1.576 million.

According to the organization's publications, AA recognizes the potency of shared honesty and mutual vulnerability openly acknowledged. The AA group supports each member in his or her effort to remain alcohol-free. According to AA literature, "Maintenance of sobriety depends on our sharing of our experiences, strength and hope with each other, thus helping to identify and understand the nature of our disease." AA offers a biological explanation for alcohol addiction, and the AA conceptual model is that alcoholism is a disease, a controllable disability that cannot be cured—thus, there are no ex-alcoholics, only recovering alcoholics. AA members are encouraged to accept the belief that they are powerless over alcohol, that they cannot control their intake, and that total abstinence is required. New members are advised to obtain a sponsor who has remained abstinent and who will help the initiate work through the

"Been There"

> "A man falls into a hole so deep he can't get out. A doctor walks by, and the man calls for help. The doctor writes a prescription, tosses it into the hole, and walks on. A priest walks by, and the man tries again. The priest writes a prayer, tosses it into the hole, and walks on. Finally a friend walks by, and again the man asks for help. To his surprise, the friend jumps in with him. 'Why did you do that?' the man asks. 'Now we're both in the hole.' 'Yes,' the friend responds, 'But I've been in this hole before, and I know the way out'" (Clay 2004: 1).

twelve steps that are the essence of the AA program. Those who are successful "twelfth steppers" carry the AA message and program to other alcoholics—they become "missionaries" for AA.

AA and groups based on the AA approach "attempt to instill the substitution of more adaptive attitudes to replace habitual dysfunctional ones. The extreme use of denial and projection of responsibility for chemical dependency onto other people, circumstances, or conditions outside oneself is an example of a target behavior strongly challenged in the substance abuse self-help group. The familiar opening statement of 'I'm an alcoholic and/or drug addict' epitomizes the concrete representation that defense mechanisms of projection and denial run counter to the group culture and norms" (Spitz 1987: 160).

Because of their fear of losing employment, recovering alcoholics were often unwilling to admit their problem in front of others; therefore, strict anonymity became part of the AA approach. AA never uses surnames at meetings or in its publications. According to an AA publication: "Individual anonymity is paramount. No AA member has the right to divulge the identity or membership of any other member. We must always maintain personal anonymity at the level of press, radio, TV and film" (hence the use of the names "Bill W." and "Dr. Bob"). However, "as a result of AA's popular success and the acceptance of the disease viewpoint," Stanton Peele (1995: 46) notes that "prominent alcoholics today do not place the emphasis on anonymity that AA officially demands of its members: many public figures have described their alcoholism and their treatment before the camera."

AA Organization

More than 50,000 AA groups are registered in the United States (Delbanco and Delbanco 1995). AA has minimal formal organization. The basic AA unit is the local group, which is autonomous except in matters that affect other AA groups or the fellowship as a whole. According to AA literature, "No group has powers over its members and instead of officers with authority, groups rotate leadership." A secretary chosen by the members plans the meetings and sets the agenda. In most local groups the position is rotated every six months. Delegates to the General Service Conference serve two years. There are twenty-one trustees,

Narcotics Anonymous

Nan Robertson (1988b) notes that some AA groups are less than accepting of people who are addicted to substances other than alcohol. Bill Wilson was opposed to allowing heroin addicts to become part of AA. However, there are self-help groups for drug abusers based on the twelve-step approach, such as Narcotics Anonymous (NA) and Cocaine Anonymous (CA). According to its website, NA "sprang from the Alcoholics Anonymous Program of the late 1940s with meetings first emerging in the Los Angeles area of California, USA, in the early Fifties." There are more than 20,000 registered NA groups holding over 30,000 weekly meetings in more than 100 countries.

of whom seven are nonalcoholics who are often professionals in social work or medicine and who may serve for up to nine years; alcoholic trustees may serve only four years.

There are no entry requirements or dues; "the hat is passed" at most meetings to defray costs. Some of this money goes to support a local service committee and the General Service Office in New York. AA does not engage in fund raising, and no one person is permitted to contribute more than $1,000. The sale of publications generates considerable income. The financial affairs of the General Service Office are handled by nonalcoholics: "The reason is that Bill Wilson and the early A.A.'s were afraid that if anybody running A.A. fell off the wagon, that would be bad enough, but if he were handling finances as well, the results could be disastrous" (Robertson 1988a: 57).

AA members typically attend four meetings a week for about five years, after which attendance is less frequent, or they might drop out completely when capable of functioning comfortably without alcohol. "The movement works in quiet and simple ways. Members usually give of themselves without reservation; exchange telephone numbers with newcomers; come to help at any hour when a fellow member is in crisis; are free with tips on how to avoid that first drink" (Robertson 1988a: 47).

The AA approach has been criticized because of its emphasis on total abstinence and its lack of research support: "The erstwhile abstainer who, for whatever reason, takes a drink may in effect be induced to go on a spree by the belief that this is inevitable. Spree drinking could also be induced by the fact that status in A.A. is correlated with length of sobriety. Years of sobriety with their attendant symbols and status can be obliterated by one slip, so the social cost of a single drink is as great as the cost of an all-out binge" (Ogborne and Glaser 1985: 176). Some twelve-step groups "do not consider members 'clean and sober' when they are using any psychoactive medication. Cases of adverse treatment consequences, even suicide, have resulted from well-meaning 12-step members dissuading individuals from taking prescribed medications" (DuPont and McGovern 1994: 56).

Many, if not most, substance abuse treatment programs are based wholly in or part of the twelve-step model.

The Twelve Steps of Narcotics Anonymous

1. We admitted that we were powerless over our addiction, that our lives had become unmanageable.
2. We came to believe that a Power greater than ourselves could restore us to sanity.
3. We made a decision to turn our will and our lives over to the care of God as we understood Him.
4. We made a searching and fearless moral inventory of ourselves.
5. We admitted to God, to ourselves, and to another human being the exact nature of our wrongs.
6. We were entirely ready to have God remove all these defects of character.
7. We humbly asked Him to remove our shortcomings.
8. We made a list of all persons we had harmed, and became willing to make amends to them all.
9. We made direct amends to such people whenever possible, except when to do so would injure them or others.
10. We continued to take personal inventory and when we were wrong promptly admitted it.
11. We sought through prayer and meditation to improve our conscious contact with God as we understood Him, praying only for knowledge of His will for us and the power to carry that out.
12. Having had a spiritual awakening as a result of these steps, we tried to carry this message to addicts, and practice these principles in all our affairs.

NA publishes a monthly journal, *The NA Way*, which is filled with brief personal stories, news, and opinion (available from Narcotics Anonymous World Service Office, PO Box 9999, Van Nuys, CA 91409; telephone: 818-780-3951). Local AA and NA chapters can be found in the telephone book.

The Minnesota Model

One of the best examples of the AA program use in private inpatient chemical dependence treatment is the so-called **Minnesota model,** which integrates the twelve-step approach into the medical treatment of addiction (DuPont and McGovern 1994: xxii). The Hazelden Foundation in Center City, Minnesota, has inspired many similar programs in the United States and England in which substance abuse is seen as an incurable but controllable disease. Total abstinence and lifestyle improvement are the treatment goals. The six- to eight-week program begins with an admissions assessment and detoxification following medical protocol. Individual counseling is provided by abusers who are "in recovery" and professional staff, including physicians, social workers, nurses, and clergy. Therapy groups take various forms, all of which are present and future oriented, including problem solving, personal issues, and decision making related to substance use, family sessions, and confrontations similar in process to those of the therapeutic community. Rounding out the program are lectures and videos on a variety of related topics, including AA/NA, the social and psychological aspects of substance abuse, and techniques for handling substance abuse problems, as well as reading and writing assignments. After-care usually involves attendance at AA or NA meetings (Cook 1988a).

In a review of research on the Minnesota model, Christopher Cook concludes: "Despite exaggerated claims of success, it appears to have a genuinely impressive 'track record' with as many as two-thirds of its patients achieving a 'good' outcome at 1 year after discharge" (1988b: 746). This treatment-rich private sector approach to substance abuse is obviously quite expensive, and patients, who include such luminaries as Betty Ford and Elizabeth Taylor, are therefore representative of the economically successful.

The Minnesota model is used by central Ohio's Maryhaven, whose staff is made up primarily of former twelve-step participants in recovery. "Maryhaven integrates 12-step-related practices and interventions into all of its basic services to assist the patient with the goals of self-diagnosis, acceptance of addiction as an illness, [and] acceptance of abstinence" (Brigham 2003: 46). At Maryhaven substance abuse is viewed as a chronic illness; therefore, treatment is focused on abstinence, not moderation.

Alternatives to AA

The spiritual dimension of AA and its insistence on a disease model of alcoholism—alcoholics cannot help themselves—have encountered opposition and led to the establishment of alternative groups, such as Rational Recovery (RR) and Secular Organization for Sobriety. Although it is a voluntary self-help group in the AA mode, RR rejects the twelve-step approach as fostering dependency and instead argues that alcoholic participants are not powerless but fully capable of overcoming their addiction (T. Hall 1990). According to RR, alcoholism is not a disease but an individual shortcoming. Their approach emphasizes taking personal responsibility for behavior—there isn't any treatment for addiction other than voluntary abstinence.

RR uses "the Big Plan," a commitment never to drink again. It focuses on planning to prevent relapses and attempting to gain insight into how self-defeating beliefs encourage drinking behavior. Various strategies are discussed to deal with high-risk situations in which temptations may run high (Galaif and Sussman 1995).

There are also groups, such as Moderation Management (MM), that reject the total abstinence proviso of AA and instead emphasize sobriety—drinking in moderation. A national support organization, MM is designed for people who want to limit, rather than eliminate, their drinking. While an estimated 30 percent of their members are on abstinence-based programs, most participants seek a way to control but not eliminate their use of alcohol. "An important MM recommendation is to go 30 days without alcohol" (Condor 2002a: Sec. 13: 1, 2002b). A similar program, Drink Wise, suggests two to three weeks without imbibing to reduce tolerance and gain control over the habit. Both programs call for keeping a "drink diary" to become more fully aware of alcohol consumption patterns and temptations (Condor 2002b).

MM and Drink Wise promote tactics that lead to self limits on alcohol consumption (Condor 2002a, 2002b).

- Delay drinking by not having any alcohol until sitting down for dinner
- Stay with beer or wine and avoid mixed drinks
- Alternate between alcoholic drinks and other beverages—club soda with a splash of lemon or lime, for example
- Never drink alcoholic beverages when you are thirsty
- Develop a plan for drinking, such as one or two drinks and leaving after two hours at a party or bar

EVALUATING TREATMENT EFFECTIVENESS

How well do drug treatment programs perform? A straightforward answer to this question is not possible. A variety of programs—hospitals, public health agencies, and independent organizations—offer treatment using an array of methodologies ranging from the twelve steps to drug-free therapeutic communities to methadone maintenance, and the intensity of services and staff qualifications vary significantly. The client population is similarly complex: "They vary in age, social and economic background, number and types of drug abused, health status, and psychological well-being. Some have lengthy histories of addiction and treatment, while others are entering treatment for the first time in the early stages of dependence. Clients may be highly involved in criminal activity or may not have committed any crime other than drug possession" (Hubbard et al. 1989: 9). In general, high-intensity (long-term residential) treatment for high-severity users produces favorable outcomes for at least five years. For low-severity users, brief, low-intensity services have proven adequate and more cost-effective (D. Simpson 2002).

There are additional problems with measuring the effectiveness of treatment for adolescents, as there are with providing them with appropriate programs. Adolescents go through distinctive developmental stages, and their substance abuse patterns differ from those of adults (Hser et al. 2001).

Difficulties in Measuring Effectiveness

Many or most programs that purport to treat specific types of substance abuse are not based on a scientific approach to such problems. They are not organized and structured according to controlled studies with random assignment, and they often are not eager for independent evaluation that could affect their bottom line—their finances. Evaluation requires a measurement of success, such as being drug free for a certain period of time. Tracking individuals who complete treatment is often difficult if not impossible. Programs have different criteria for "completion." Some use length of time; others use number of visits or regularity of attendance. This makes it difficult to compare programs (E. E. Simpson 1989).

Evaluating drug treatment requires a comparison with a similar population that is not being treated or with other programs treating similar populations. In fact, any research efforts that do not include a control group are suspect, because in "the absence of a control group, it is difficult to determine whether unanticipated bias occurred in selecting the subjects for study, and whether the resulting experimental group is sufficiently representative for generalizations to be made about the outcome findings. Furthermore, without comparison groups, behavioral changes during and after treatment that result from the passage of time may wrongly be attributed to program activities" (Anglin and Hser 1990b: 408). However, withholding treatment from control groups has ethical, political, and legal dimensions (De Leon, Inciardi, and Martin 1995; P. J. Cohen 2002).

Some private treatment programs are quite selective. Their patients are required to have financial resources or employment that provide third-party coverage, which are social indicators of a better prognosis. Other programs accept patients with a host of social, psychological, and economic problems that are likely to affect their prognosis. "In the real world of drug abuse treatment," say George De Leon, James Inciardi, and Steven Martin (1995: 88), "program staff choose the clients they feel are ready for treatment and are appropriate for a particular treatment modality."

Patrick Biernacki (1986: 191) notes the serious problems in gauging the success of drug treatment programs. He asks, for example, what a 50 percent rate of success means: Would some, most, or all of the people who were "successful" have abandoned drug addiction without treatment? In fact, he points out, drug treatment programs might be successful only with those individuals who have resolved to stop using drugs: "Once addicts voluntarily have resolved to stop using drugs, treatment programs may then be able to help them realize their resolutions to change" (Biernacki 1986: 191). (For a review of drug treatment outcome research and its methodological shortcomings, see Anglin and Hser 1990b; Moras 1993; De Leon, Inciardi, and Martin 1995.)

Researchers followed 581 male heroin addicts who had been admitted to the California Civil Addict Program (CAP) between 1962 and 1964. The average age of participants on admission to CAP was 25 years. More than 60 percent had started using heroin before age 20. The men were, on average, 57 years old in 1996–1997. Of the 242 subjects who were interviewed at that time, 21 percent tested positive for opiates. A total of 13.8 percent of the original 581 subjects had died by the time of the first interview; 27.7 percent had died by the time of the second interview; and 48.9 percent had died by the time of the latest interview. At the first interview, about 38 percent of the surviving sample had opiate-free urine tests; 41 percent were opiate-free at the second interview; and 56 percent were opiate-free at the last interview. The unanswered question is whether these results were caused by successful programming, aging out, or any combination of the two ("33-Year Study Shows Severe Long Term Effects of Heroin" 2001).

Evaluating Substance Abuse Programs

"Outcome evaluation can prove that treatment works and provides significant financial benefits. Outcome results can be powerful aids in marketing treatment services and persuading health care purchasers to continue to authorize such coverage. They can also be used to position an effective program in a highly competitive marketplace" (from a publication of the American Hospital Association [Hoffmann, Harrison, and Streed 1991: 138]).

And how are we to interpret the effectiveness of adolescent programs when research found that one year after treatment there were favorable reductions in drug use and criminal activity but more than 25 percent of respondents still reported daily use of marijuana and heavy use of alcohol (Hser et al. 2001)?

Measuring AA/Twelve-Step Effectiveness

Evaluations of AA encounter definitional problems from the start. Programs and studies vary in their definitions and measurement of recovery, of success and failure, even of the term *alcoholism* itself (McElrath 1995). William R. Miller and Reid K. Hester (1980: 47), in a review of AA evaluation literature, state:

> Attempts to evaluate the effectiveness of A.A. have met with considerable, if not insurmountable, methodological problems, among them the very anonymity of members, which precludes systematic follow-up evaluation. Most studies have failed to include control groups (a near impossibility because of the availability of A.A. to all who are interested), have relied almost entirely upon self-report (often via mailed questionnaires) and upon abstinence as the sole criteria for success, have been plagued by sizable attrition rates and large selection confounds, and have failed to use single-blind designs, thus remaining open to criticisms of interviewer bias (particularly when the investigators have been "insiders"—members of A.A. themselves).

Although AA contends that upward of 75 percent of its members maintain abstinence, the evidence that is used to make this claim is typically testimonials of long-term, abstinent participants and ignores dropouts, who may be more likely to continue or resume drug and alcohol use. Approximately 50 percent of AA participants will drop out within the first three months of attendance, and only about 13 percent of initial attendees will maintain a long-term relationship with AA (Fiorentine 1999).

In his careful research Geary Alford (1980) found that a residential treatment program for alcoholics that used the AA approach was highly effective. Two years after discharge from the program approximately 50 percent of the patients who had completed inpatient treatment remained largely abstinent, were employed or otherwise functioning productively, and had healthy social relationships. The figure increased to 56 percent if those who drank only very lightly were included. Alford and his colleagues (1991: 122) report that an AA/NA model inpatient treatment program for adolescents whose drug use was primarily alcohol or marijuana was successful: "Some

71% of male treatment completers and 79% of female treatment completers were found to be chemically abstinent or essentially abstinent at 6 months after discharge." However, two years after treatment, the figure for men dropped to 40 percent, while 37 percent of the males who dropped out of the program were also found to be abstinent or essentially abstinent. Thirty percent of female noncompleters were abstinent or essentially abstinent after two years. As with the research reviewed by Miller and Hester (1980), Alford's studies did not utilize a control group. In fact, AA successes appear to be concentrated among middle- and upper-class people who had relatively stable lives before the onset of a drinking problem (Alexander 1990).

In an extensive research effort Robert Fiorentine (1999) reports that any participation in twelve-step programs is associated with lower levels of drug and alcohol use and that the magnitude of the association is about the same for both illicit drug and alcohol use. Less-than-weekly participants, who were more likely to be problematic drinkers, had levels of drug and alcohol use that were no different from those of nonparticipants. Fiorentine's findings suggest that weekly or more frequent twelve-step participation is associated with drug and alcohol abstinence. However, *commitment* to attend a twelve-step program might be a predictor of success; the program itself might actually do little or nothing to generate abstinence. A study comparing the results of AA with those of other forms of treatment found that twelve-step programs were neither more nor less effective than, for example, the cognitive approach discussed earlier (Bakalar 2006).

Despite the paucity of research on its effectiveness, the twelve-step approach is very popular, some arguing that it has become a fad. The rise in the number of twelve-step programs and members and the inclusion of twelve-step philosophy in treatment programs are, of course, evidence only of its popularity, not of its effectiveness (Fiorentine 1999). Groups such as Gamblers Anonymous, Overeaters Anonymous, Debtors Anonymous, and Sex Addicts Anonymous have been formed to address a host of social problems. While they claim inspiration from the AA twelve-step approach, critics see them as groups for whiners who want an audience to dwell on their injured self (Delbanco and Delbanco 1995).

OTHER PROGRAMS

Although treatment at most inpatient chemical dependency programs in the United States is based on a disease model built around an AA twelve-step approach, there is an almost total lack of relevant research data on their effectiveness (Gerstein and Harwood 1990; Galaif and Sussman 1995; Ogborne and Glaser 1985). Furthermore, most of these programs provide no aftercare but refer patients to AA, which deals with the problems of drinking but not with related or contributing problems such as unemployment and interpersonal skills or with drug use as a form of self-medication.

Drug dependence might best be viewed as a career requiring treatment that is similarly oriented. "Many researchers, practitioners, and clinicians have assumed that treatment should occur once and should result in a cure if it is to be termed effective. Substance abuse does not appear to be the kind of problem that makes this orientation pragmatic. When the community in which people live is so strongly pro-intoxication, it is not surprising that treated persons are recruited back into the drug lifestyle." Therefore, "while treatment does not need to be applied forever, repeated episodes of treatment are probably necessary for most who develop serious problems with intoxicants" (Senay 1986: 143).

There is no clear research evidence on the effectiveness of short-term inpatient or outpatient treatment: "Given what is known about the importance of length of stay in treatment and the complexity of the recovery process in addiction, there is little likelihood that twenty-eight-day clinics or short-term modalities (one to six months) will yield positive outcomes" (De Leon 1990: 125). In fact, it might be the availability of legitimate economic opportunity rather than the mode of treatment that predicts posttreatment success. Without such opportunity clients in disadvantaged groups will remain enmeshed in the drug abuse subculture and continue to rely on income-generating crime (Anglin and Hser 1990b). In any event, after noting shortcomings in the research—they question the accuracy of self-reports by drug abusers—the General Accounting Office concludes (1998) that while the effectiveness might be overstated, drug abuse treatment can in fact be effective.

SUMMARY

In the United States moderate use of alcohol, tobacco, or coffee is seen as being within the mainstream of acceptable behavior, while even the occasional use of heroin or cocaine is seen as requiring treatment (if not imprisonment). The difficulty is apparent: People who do not feel ill, who do not want therapy, and who are not dysfunctional, are coerced into "treatment."

Drug antagonists, used for detoxification or as part of a treatment regimen, displace drugs at their receptor sites but do not affect drug craving. Methadone, the best-known agonist for opioid addiction, is a powerful narcotic that lasts much longer in the body than heroin does and is effective if administered orally. It can be used for heroin withdrawal or maintenance. Buprenorphine is a partial agonist approved for use with heroin addicts in medical practice. No drug has emerged as effective for the cocaine-dependent.

Although psychoanalysis is not used to treat drug abuse, there is short-term therapy based on a psychoanalytic model that seeks to aid the patient in dealing with repressed emotions without reverting to drugs.

Behavior modification can be difficult to apply, since the strength of psychoactive substances as positive reinforcers and the negative reinforcement associated with abstinence are difficult to compete with. Some therapists use aversion therapy to reduce the value of drug reinforcement, and because cues can trigger craving, these therapists use techniques that counter or neutralize the cues. Cognitive approaches take advantage of the human ability to bridge delays between behavior and subsequent reinforcement. Contingency management uses point systems for modifying behavior.

The advantage of group treatment is the peer interaction, which is more powerful than therapist-patient interactions in the one-to-one situation. Treatment groups are typically formed around one basic trait that all members share and from which the group derives its descriptive label.

Treatment programs in the criminal justice system have shown an impressive level of success, as have therapeutic communities that provide a resocialization process for particular types of drug abusers. Private chemical dependency programs, some located in health care facilities, depend on clients who have adequate resources, such as medical insurance. These programs often fail to develop theory-centered treatment responses or to incorporate the results of research into their approach to clients.

Many programs use the twelve-step approach developed by Alcoholics Anonymous, according to which alcohol or drug dependence is a disease that can be controlled only by abstinence. Although AA and groups based on this approach are quite popular, conclusive research on effectiveness remains elusive. Evaluation of drug treatment effectiveness, in general, presents difficulties because there is no standard or benchmark.

REVIEW QUESTIONS

1. Why has the medical profession historically avoided dealing with the problem of drug abuse?
2. What are the drawbacks in using heroin antagonists?
3. How have opioid agonists been used to deal with heroin addiction?
4. What are the advantages of using methadone maintenance rather than heroin maintenance?
5. What are the disadvantages of using methadone maintenance?
6. Why is it difficult if not impossible to use psychoanalysis to treat heroin addiction?
7. How is psychoanalytic theory usually operationalized in the treatment of drug abusers?
8. Why is it difficult to apply behavior theory in the treatment of drug abuse?
9. How is contingency management or contingency contracting used in the treatment of drug abuse?
10. What is meant by the civil commitment of drug abusers?
11. What are drug courts?
12. What is the therapeutic community (TC) approach to drug abuse?
13. What are the criticisms of chemical dependency programs?
14. What is the Alcoholics Anonymous (AA) twelve-step approach to dealing with substance abuse?
15. How do moderation management programs differ from AA?
16. Why is it difficult to determine the effectiveness of the AA approach?
17. Why are health care facilities often eager to include a drug rehabilitation program as part of their services?
18. Why is it difficult to determine the success of any drug treatment programs?

Drug Abuse Prevention

Many teachers, parents and politicians believe that drug education will deter young people from using drugs. However, evaluations of all kinds of drug education programmes in this country and all over the developed world show that drug education does not prevent young people from using drugs.

Julian Cohen (1996)

In the early days of prevention education, young people were shown what drugs looked like, with warnings about what evil would befall them if these drugs were taken. In the 1980s, peers and adults were portrayed as vicious culprits exposing innocent children to drugs in the "just say no" campaigns. The more recent focus has been on concurrently teaching refusal skills and bolstering self-esteem with the belief that these will suffice to prevent experimentation with drugs. The problem with all of these prevention approaches is that there is no firm evidence that they work.

J. Kelly Coker (2001: 1)

Efforts at prevention attempt to reduce the supply of or demand for drugs of abuse. The former is the goal of drug law enforcement (which will be examined in Chapter 12); the latter has been the goal of coercive legislation and education. "Considering the difficulty and cost of treating individuals with substance abuse problems, the prospect of developing effective substance abuse prevention programs has long held a great deal of appeal" (National Institute on Drug Abuse 1987: 35). Unfortunately, effective prevention has proven to be as elusive as effective treatment (and effective law enforcement).

MODELS FOR PREVENTION

On the basis of extensive research, the National Institute on Drug Abuse recommends that prevention programs be designed to enhance protective factors and move toward reversing or reducing known risk factors. Protective factors are those associated with reduced potential for drug use; risk factors are those that make the potential for drug use more likely.

Protective factors include strong and positive bonds within a prosocial family; parental monitoring; clear rules of conduct that are consistently enforced within the family; involvement of parents in the lives of their children; success in school performance; strong bonds with other prosocial institutions, such as school and religious organizations; and adoption of conventional norms about drug use.

Risk factors include chaotic home environments, particularly those in which parents abuse substances or suffer from mental illnesses; ineffective parenting, especially with children who have difficult temperaments or conduct disorders; lack of mutual attachments and nurturing; inappropriately shy or aggressive behavior in the classroom; failure in school performance; poor social coping skills; affiliations with deviant peers or peers who display deviant behaviors; and perceptions of approval of drug-using behaviors in family, work, school, peer, and community environments (National Institute on Drug Abuse 2001c: 1).

Most efforts at prevention have focused on schools, and school-based antidrug programs are widespread. These programs have been dominated by three models (Ellickson 1995):

1. *Information model.* Assuming that children and adolescents will avoid drugs when they understand their potential hazards, this model seeks to impart information. Furthermore, the model assumes that students will develop negative attitudes that will deter them from using drugs. "In short, the information model posits a causal sequence leading from knowledge (about drugs) to attitude change (negative) to behavior change (nonuse)" (Ellickson 1995: 100). Sometimes shock or scare tactics are part of this approach, exemplified by hard-hitting antidrug videos, talks by ex-junkies, or TV and billboard campaigns that focus on the horrors of drug use (J. Cohen 1996).

Risk Markers

Addiction-vulnerable people tend to be impulsive, unruly, and easily bored; they are usually outgoing and sociable, rebellious risk-takers more likely to challenge authority. Having a parent with a substance abuse problem increases risk, as does experimenting with alcohol before the age of 15 years. (Legrand, Iancono, and McGue 2005).

Drug Education or Propaganda?

Drug education often is not based on the educational principles that underlie the teaching of other subjects but tends to skew and censor information, to give a narrow view of drug use, and to tell young people what they should think and do. This is propaganda, not education. It often results in young people not being able to talk openly and honestly. Instead, they end up saying what they think their teachers or parents want to hear rather than what they really believe. The gulf between adults and young people widens, open dialogue lessens, and young people with problems or concerns about drugs become less likely to approach adults for support (J. Cohen 1996).

Press release (Washington, D.C., January 23, 2003): "The Office of National Drug Control Policy (ONDCP) today announced the launch of two new sets of advertisements, premiering during the Super Bowl and pre-game show, designed to further educate Americans about the risks of drug use. Two of the ads aimed at teens are a response to research showing that American youth want to be provided with the facts about marijuana. A second pair of ads will follow up on the groundbreaking spots linking drugs, terror and violence that were released during last year's Super Bowl. The ads are part of the ONDCP's National Youth Anti-Drug Media Campaign, which is designed to help America's youth reject illicit drugs."

In 2002 the administration of President George W. Bush initiated an antidrug campaign that featured an attempt to tie terrorism to the use of drugs. Ads on television and the print media depicted people saying: "I helped murder families in Colombia—it was just innocent fun." "I helped a bomber get a false passport—all the kids do it." "I helped blow up buildings—my life, my body." The commercial ends with a tag line: "Drug money supports terror. If you buy drugs, you might too" (A. N. Jones 2002).

2. *Affective model.* Shifting the focus away from education, this model instead seeks to affect personality. The focus is on the individual rather than drugs per se, and it is assumed that young people who have high self-esteem will not use drugs (J. Cohen 1996)."The model assumes that adolescents who turn to drugs do so because of problems within themselves—low self-esteem or inadequate personal skills in communication and decision making" (Ellickson 1995: 101). Affective model programs attempt to improve the affective skills (communication, decision making, self-assertion) that are believed to be related to drug use. In attempting to improve a student's self-image, ability to interact within a group, and problem-solving ability, the model focuses on feelings, values, and self-awareness and, in some programs, on personal values and choices.

3. *Social influence model.* Young people are seen as easy prey to peer pressure and in need of developing the skills to "Say No To Drugs." The approach assumes that young people lack the skills to make rational choices and that if they had these skills, they would not use drugs (Cohen

Scare Tactics

When it became obvious that scare tactics used by college antidrinking programs were not having the desired effect—indeed, it was found that these tactics actually encouraged heavy drinking—the emphasis shifted. Instead of posters showing students covered with vomit and cars wrecked by drunken drivers, the new campaign cites statistics that, in fact, reveal that most students drink in moderation. "Zero to three" read Frisbees handed out at one college, indicating the number of drinks most students have when they are at a party (Zernike 2000).

At the University of Arizona (UA), where it is known as the Social Norms Campaign, the focus is on educating students about accurate drinking norms on campus without the use of scare tactics or admonishments. "The social norms approach mandates that campaign messages consist of accurate majority (normative) statements that address campus drinking misconceptions." According to UA data, students overestimated the amount of alcohol their peers were consuming. To correct this, ads were run in student publications, and appropriate posters were mounted in residence halls, reinforced by bulletin board displays (Johannessen et al. 1999: 5). A study of the social norms approach to curbing college student drinking found it to be ineffective (Schemo 2003).

1996). The social influence model is centered on external influences that push students toward drug use, especially peer pressure, as well as internal influences, such as the desire to be accepted by "the crowd." To deal with adolescent vulnerabilities, the social influence model seeks to familiarize students with the pressures to use drugs, enabling them to develop resistance skills and techniques for saying no in those pressure situations.

Educating people, particularly elementary, high school, and college students (the primary population at risk), about the dangers of drug use would seem at first blush to be devoid of controversy and a sound response to the problem of drug abuse. After all, as Richard Brotman and Frederic Suffet (1975) point out, the thinking behind the idea appears to be quite rational: Provide valid information about the harmful consequences of drug abuse, and most people will elect to avoid drugs. However, as Patricia Wald and Peter Hutt (1972: 18) note, "There is substantial uncertainty and confusion in the area of drug education and prevention" because "there is no real evidence that such educational efforts are successful." Indeed, as research by Isidor Chein and his colleagues (1964) revealed, the youngsters who have the greatest knowledge about drugs are the most likely to use drugs. In addition, there is a substantial drug abuse problem among physicians, who presumably know a great deal about the dangers of drugs (Kennedy 1995; McDougall 2006).

Goodstadt (n.d.: 2) points out that informational programs typically suffer from major weaknesses that might actually encourage drug use: "The unfortunate result is that young people might become more rather than less likely to experiment with drugs." Dan Waldorf (1973) notes that in New York heroin is seemingly everywhere in African-American and Puerto Rican ghettos, where young people are exposed to it at an early age. They know about heroin and drug addicts through firsthand exposure; they witness the drugs being purchased and see addicts nodding on the streets and clustering in doorways, communal washrooms, and rooftops to "get off." They know that addicts steal family belongings to sell for money to buy drugs. The real question, Waldorf states, is not why so many ghetto residents become drug abusers but why a majority avoid becoming addicted to a powerful substance that provides relief from an oppressive environment (1973).

Information Model

The standard educational approach has been to present factual information about the dangers of substance abuse because it was assumed that increased knowledge would serve as an effective deterrent by enabling students to make rational decisions not to use drugs. Unfortunately, this information has been frequently burdened with moral judgments about drug use (Zinberg 1984). The "scare" lecture of physical education teachers or nonschool personnel such as police officers has often been integral to this approach. Although intended to frighten students away from dangerous substances, these lectures often contain so much misinformation or exaggeration that they raise students' skepticism

The standard educational approach has been to present factual information concerning the dangers of substance abuse because it was assumed that increased knowledge would serve as an effective deterrent. While intended to frighten students away from dangerous substances, these lectures often contain so much misinformation or exaggeration that they raise students' skepticism and jeopardize all drug-education efforts.

©Index Stock Imagery

Peers, Volition, and Pleasure

"The emphasis on friendship as 'peer pressure' reflects a major difficulty in so much of the social discourse around drug-related issues—whether mass media, policy formulation, or academic debates—namely the absence of any notion of volition or desire. Health education discourses in particular have often been cleansed of any reference to the possibility that people might use drugs because they find them pleasurable" (Advisory Council on the Misuse of Drugs 1998: 36).

and jeopardize all drug education efforts. Young people have often found, through their own experiences of drug use and what friends tell them, that they have been lied to, and this leads them to mistrust adult sources of information on drugs (J. Cohen 1996; Brotman and Suffet 1975).

The American Social Health Association (1972: 5) states that drug education "must avoid overconcentration on 'the drug problem.' Many youngsters, knowing more about drugs than their parents and teachers, will not accept moralization but will respect realistic, valid information derived from a credible source." A different approach to educating youngsters about certain dangerous chemicals avoids exaggeration and scare tactics, relying instead on a factual presentation about dangerous substances and the body's reaction to them, both the good and the bad. The goal is to provide information so that students can make informed decisions rather than to prevent drug use, which might be too much to expect from any educational program. This approach has some implementation problems:

1. It might be opposed by public officials or parents who believe that schools should teach "proper" behavior, that is, preach on the evils of drug use.
2. A great deal is not known about drugs of abuse.
3. Depending on their ages, students might not be able to understand the information.
4. Providing greater knowledge about drugs might serve the unintended (latent) function of piquing interest in and arousing curiosity about them and might possibly encourage more daring adolescents to seek out drugs (Goodstadt n.d.; Wald and Abrams 1972; Stuart 1974).

Some research indicates that drug addicts are quite familiar with the effects and dangers of the substances they abuse, but they either discount the risks or view them as minor and part of the "game" (see, e.g., Hendler and Stephens 1977). Troy Duster (1970: 192) reports that prospective addicts see themselves as exceptions to the pattern of addiction they see around them: "It is typical of the early experience of the addict-to-be that he knows of people who use narcotics and who get away with it . . . [in that] they are neither addicted nor are they known to the police. This double victory is witnessed by probably every individual who knowingly used heroin illegally for the first time." However, although there is evidence that drug users know much more about

Drug Education in High School

"Young people in this [high school] age group are more likely to be receiving conflicting messages about drugs. They will also be at different levels of knowledge and experience with drugs, even within the same class. Drug education may have lower priority in competition with other curriculum subjects and, whilst teachers also generally support the *principle* of drug education, some may feel that their own drugs knowledge or understanding of cultural issues is deficient. All this at a time when teachers may in any case be losing ground to young people's friends and others in the credibility stakes" (*Drugs Prevention Initiative* 1999: 12).

. . . and College

Considering the high levels of drug use among college students, colleges and universities are important targets for drug information material. Research has revealed that it is frequency of drug use rather than the percentage of drug users per se that increases over time with the college-age population, so emphasis should be on aiming drug information at those who are already drug users. Such information could encourage the formation of less positive attitudes, although there is a need for drug information to be balanced to appear credible (McMillan and Conner 2002).

drugs than do nonusers, "there is no evidence that increases in such knowledge stimulate use" (D. J. Hanson 1980: 273). "Simply providing the child with information about substance abuse would primarily alter the behavior of well-socialized children from cohesive families rather than those most at risk" (Dishion, Patterson, and Reid 1988: 90).

Goodstadt (n.d.: 3) suggests acknowledging the positive reinforcements of drug use: "Drug use consequences are not all negative; if they were, nobody would continue to use drugs. Moderate use of some drugs offers physical, psychological, and social benefits for some people. Drug education programs that do not take into account this important aspect of the decision to start or continue using drugs diminish their credibility and effectiveness." Julian Cohen (1996) concludes that the research evidence shows that appropriate drug education can increase drug knowledge, develop decision-making skills, and make young people more discerning about what they actually do. This does not mean that they will not use either legal or illegal drugs. In other words, drug education can play a role in reducing drug-related harm rather than preventing drug use.

Goodstadt (n.d.: 3) states: "Efforts to prevent drug abuse by reducing the most risky forms of drug use (for example, drinking and driving, cannabis use and gymnastics) need not condone illegal drug use." Information programs should keep in mind that an eight-year study of adolescent drug use revealed that the vast majority of teenagers who occasionally use drugs suffer no long-lasting negative effects and cannot in later years be distinguished from those who abstained from drug use (Blakeslee 1988).

Affective Model

A broad approach to drug abuse prevention involves affective or humanistic education (although the term *humanistic* is likely to trigger negative responses in people who hold certain religious and social views). Public schools have turned away from the "scare 'em" approach toward one that emphasizes the judgment and social skills that are necessary to avoid substance abuse (Berger 1989). Some research indicates that this approach shows promise only with youngsters who are not likely to become problem drug users in the first place. The U.S. Center for Substance Abuse Prevention maintains that a "life skills" approach—problem-solving skills, decision-making skills, resistance skills against adverse peer influences, and social and communication skills—"is associated with short-term reductions in substance abuse among adolescents" and recommends that "life skills curricula should be recognized as an important component of effective substance abuse prevention programs for adolescents" (Chavez and Sanchez-Way 1997: 13, 14).

These affective efforts are designed to enhance self-esteem, to encourage responsible decision making, and to enrich students' personal and social development. The conceptual grounding for this approach was discussed in Chapter 8 as part of behaviorist/learning theory: prevention through the enhancement of social competence. This approach has research support (Pentz 1985).

The bases of this approach are assumptions that (National Institute on Drug Abuse 1987: 35):

1. Substance abuse programs should aim at developing prevention-oriented decision making concerning the use of licit or illicit drugs.
2. Such decisions should result in fewer negative consequences for the individuals.
3. The most effective way of achieving these goals is by increasing self-esteem, interpersonal skills, and participation in alternatives to substance use.

These assumptions are generally implemented through communication training, peer counseling, role-playing, and assertiveness training. In the Los Angeles school system this approach has been implemented through Project D.A.R.E. and Reconnecting Youth, which are discussed below.

Social Influence Model

The *social influence approach* attempts to "inoculate" students against using dangerous substances by making the students aware of the social pressures they are likely to encounter and teaching skills that promote refusal.

Sports and Alcohol

Among white males, but not African American youths, playing sports, particularly football, appears to increase the risk of alcohol use and abuse (Eitle, Turner, and Eitle 2003).

The *social learning approach* views chemical abuse from the perspective of learning theory; that is, like other behavior, it is learned through modeling and reinforcement. Through instruction, demonstration, feedback, reinforcement, behavioral rehearsal (classroom practice), and extended practice through homework assignments, the youngster is taught life-coping skills that have a rather broad range of applications, including drug resistance. There is considerable variation in age groups and length of program. Some groups are led by adults; others use peer leaders (see the discussion of the Preparing for the Drug-Free Years program on page 279).

SAMPLE PROGRAMS

Project D.A.R.E.

D.A.R.E. (Drug Abuse Resistance Education) has proven popular with police departments throughout the United States. Any number of departments advertise the program on their police vehicles. The Los Angeles Police Department (LAPD) and the Los Angeles Unified School District jointly sponsor Project D.A.R.E., which is designed to equip fifth, sixth, and seventh graders with the skills and motivation they need to resist peer pressure to use drugs, alcohol, and tobacco. D.A.R.E.'s instructors are uniformed police officers on full-time duty with the project. All are veteran officers and volunteers who are carefully selected by D.A.R.E. supervisory staff and fully trained by officers and specialists from the school district.

> A D.A.R.E. police officer is assigned to teach in every elementary school under the LAPD's jurisdiction, offering the 17-session core curriculum to either fifth- or sixth-grade students. A junior-high program for seventh-graders, which includes early intervention with students deemed at risk, is also at full implementation in 58 junior high schools.
>
> In bringing the core curriculum to the elementary schools, D.A.R.E. officers are assigned to five schools per semester, and they visit each classroom once a week. Beyond this, the officers conduct one-day visits at other schools for an assembly program and follow-up visits in individual classrooms; hold formal training sessions on drug abuse for teachers; and conduct evening parent meetings. (DeJong 1987a: 4)

The use of uniformed police officers as instructors is seen as a key element in the program's success: "Police have knowledge of the drug scene and its impact on both individuals and society as a whole that regular classroom teachers cannot match. Indeed, many classroom teachers frankly admit their discomfiture in teaching lessons on drug abuse. For children this age, police hold a mystique. Kids respond to them" (DeJong 1987a: 7). And because the program "involves police officers in positive, nonpunitive roles, students are more likely to develop positive attitudes toward police officers and greater respect for the law" (1987a: 17). The D.A.R.E. curriculum ends with a schoolwide assembly that includes the reading of the winning "D.A.R.E. Pledges." Each student who completes the program receives a certificate of achievement signed by the chief of police and the superintendent of schools.

Reconnecting Youth

Reconnecting Youth is a peer group approach to building life skills for high school students who are at risk for dropping out. Designed to build resiliency, the program is presented in the form of a personal growth class, typically delivered in daily fifty- to sixty-minute sessions during regular school hours by specifically trained school personnel (e.g., teachers, counselors, nurses) who work with students in a small-group format with a ratio of 1:12 per class. An important component is the enhancement of learning skills: "One of the most important risk factors for substance abuse is academic failure" (National Institute on Drug Abuse 1997a: 17).

During the first two weeks students are given an overview of the course as well as rules and expectations for working together as a group. Students learn about concepts such as inner strength, self-praise, and group praise, and they set goals for their participation in the class. This overview is followed by four life skills training units:

1. *Self-esteem enhancement* provides the basis for training in the other units and includes visualization, relaxation techniques, self-praise, group praise, and liberal praise of others in the group. Students are encouraged to generate more and more positive self-portraits and, as these develop, to be able to make positive lifestyle changes.

2. *Decision making* is designed to help students enhance personal empowerment by learning to exercise greater freedom of choice and personal control over decisions. The benefits—increased self-esteem and improved mood—are emphasized. Participants examine how to make decisions in a group by reaching agreement and resolving conflicts: stopping an impulsive response, thinking of options, evaluating options in terms of whether each is helpful or hurtful, putting into action the most helpful option, and self-praise for taking these steps.

3. *Personal control* over stress, depression, and anger. Students probe for what triggers feelings of depression and destructiveness, and they explore the effect of uncontrolled aggression on themselves and others. They practice strategies for dealing with stress, anger, and depression, with an emphasis on developing a repertoire of strategies that emphasize giving and receiving support from friends and others in their social network.

4. *Interpersonal communication* focuses on skills for communicating more effectively, and students practice ways of expressing concern for and developing healthy relationships with others at school.

As they develop, issues that are raised in the group become the basis for introducing and working on specific skills. At the beginning of a personal growth class, for example, the group leader might start with a check-in to monitor all members of the group to assess how they are doing with respect to mood, school, and substance abuse control. The group works on setting the agenda for the day. The leader asks whether anyone has individual issues for which they want group support and problem-solving time. Using group work and discussion skills, the leader is able to relate the students' issues to the planned skills-training session and activities. "The challenge for the leader is to balance the students' daily needs with related skills building, skills application, and group problemsolving applied to the students' current concerns and real-life issues" (National Institute on Drug Abuse 1997a: 61).

The program provides students with opportunities for prosocial recreation and school volunteer activities, which are designed to enhance self-esteem and school bonding. During the final two weeks of the class, students review what they have learned and celebrate their experiences.

Effective Prevention Strategies

Prevention strategies targeting youths have evolved over the past twenty years as evaluation research has revealed more about what works. Several strategies are used effectively, especially in combination:

- *Information dissemination.* This strategy provides awareness and knowledge of the nature and extent of alcohol, tobacco, and other drug use, abuse, and addiction and their effects on individuals, families, and communities as well as information to increase perceptions of risk. It also provides knowledge and awareness of prevention policies, programs, and services. It helps to set and reinforce norms (e.g., a policy that underage drinking and drug dealers will not be tolerated in this neighborhood).
- *Prevention education.* This strategy aims to affect critical life and social skills, including decision making, refusal skills, critical analysis (e.g., of media messages), and systematic and judgmental abilities.
- *Alternatives.* This strategy provides for the participation of targeted populations in activities that exclude alcohol, tobacco, and other drug use by youths. Constructive and healthy activities offset the attraction to, or otherwise meet the needs that are usually filled by, alcohol, tobacco, and other drug use.
- *Problem identification and referral.* This strategy calls for identification, education, and counseling for youths who have indulged in age-inappropriate use of tobacco products or alcohol or who have indulged in the first use of illicit drugs. Activities under this strategy would include screening for tendencies toward substance abuse and referral for preventive treatment for curbing such tendencies.
- *Community-based process.* This strategy aims to enhance the community's ability to provide prevention and treatment services to alcohol, tobacco, and other drug use disorders more effectively. Activities include organizing, planning, enhancing efficiency and effectiveness of services implementation, interagency collaboration, coalition building, and networking. Building healthy communities encourages healthy lifestyle choices.
- *Environmental approach.* This strategy sets up or changes written and unwritten community standards, codes, and attitudes, influencing the incidence and prevalence of alcohol, tobacco, and other drug use problems in the general population. Included are laws to restrict availability and access, price increases, and communitywide actions.

Source: Indiana Prevention Resource Center at Indiana University.

Preparing for the Drug-Free Years (PDFY)

"The goal of PDFY is to empower parents of children ages 8 to 14 years to reduce risks that their children will abuse drugs and alcohol or develop other common adolescent problems" (Haggerty et al. 1999: 1). PDFY is based on extensive research on factors that increase risk:

- Little parental supervision and monitoring
- Low degree of parent-child communication and interaction
- Poorly defined and communicated rules and expectations for children's behavior
- Inconsistent and excessively severe discipline
- Parental alcohol and drug use

Parents are recruited through public service announcements and advertisements. Since establishment of the program in 1987, more than 120,000 families have been trained in five two-hour sessions or ten one-hour sessions in more than thirty states and Canada. The focus is on strengthening family bonding (see social control theory in Chapter 7), and children join their parents for a session that focuses on risk factors, including friends who use drugs, and how to resist peer pressure to use alcohol or other drugs. Sessions are typically conducted by two trained workshop leaders from the community aided by a curriculum kit that includes videos and family activity books.

Strengthening Families Program

This seven-week curriculum is designed for parents and youths ages 10–14 years. It aims at reducing substance abuse and other problem behavior during adolescence. "Intermediate objectives include improved parental nurturing and limit-setting skills, improved communication skills for both parents and youth, and youth prosocial skills development" (Molgaard, Spoth, and Redmond 2000: 2). Participants are recruited by a local family services agency that identifies a core of groups of parents and motivates them to recruit other families to the program. Recruitment material includes a motivational video and incentives such as $5 grocery certificates and fast-food coupons for youths.

There are separate skill-building sessions for parents and youths for the first hour, followed by a second hour together in supervised family activities, during which facilitators offer assistance and model appropriate skills. The separate sessions contain parallel content; for example, while parents are learning how to use consequences when youths break rules, youths are learning about the importance of following rules. In small- and large-group discussions the youth sessions "focus on strengthening goals for the future, dealing with stress and strong emotions, appreciating parents and other elders, increasing the desire to be responsible, and building skills to deal with peer pressure" (Molgaard, Spoth, and Redmond 2000: 2). Topics are presented in gamelike activities that are designed to keep participants engaged and sustain their interest while they are learning.

Parent sessions focus on understanding the developmental characteristics of young people, providing nurturing support, and dealing effectively with youths in everyday interactions. The need to set appropriate limits and to follow through with reasonable and respectful consequences is emphasized, as well as the sharing of beliefs and expectations regarding alcohol and drug use. The sessions include didactic presentations, role-playing, group discussions, and the use of videotapes. "Two-thirds of each family session is spent within individual family units in which parents and youth participate in discussions on projects. The remaining time is spent in large-group skill building activities and games" (Molgaard, Spoth, and Redmond 2000: 2).

Child Development Project (CDP)

Although billed as a substance abuse prevention effort, the Child Development Project (CDP) did not address this issue. Instead, the program focused on developing a strong sense of community in twelve elementary schools in six districts across the country as an indirect way of reducing involvement in drug use and other problem behaviors. The effort to develop this sense of community included training school staff in revised teaching practices that used cooperative learning activities, cross-grade buddy programs, and schoolwide events and activities that involved parents with their children. "Students' sense of the school as a community was associated with a wide range of positive outcomes, including increased liking for the school" and "reduced involvement in drug use and delinquent behaviors" (Brounstein and Zweig n.d.: 22).

PREVENTION RESEARCH

A well-designed research effort found that a program based on a social influence model of prevention (Project ALERT) that seeks to motivate young people to resist drugs and helps them develop the skills to do so can be effective in preventing or reducing adolescent use of cigarettes and marijuana. Students develop reasons for not using drugs and responses to internal and external pressures to use them. The research effort involved randomly selected seventh- and eighth-grade students across geographic, racial, and socioeconomic lines. ALERT had clearly positive results with respect to cigarette and marijuana use with both low-risk and high-risk students. The impact on alcohol consumption was negligible; and a "boomerang effect"—increased use of tobacco—was found for confirmed smokers (Ellickson and Bell 1990; Ellickson et al. 2003).

In Kansas City, Kansas, and Indianapolis, Indiana, beginning in the sixth and seventh grades, students were exposed to information about the dangers of drug use at school, at home, and in the community. Parents were trained to reinforce the antidrug message at home, and public service announcements were carried by news organizations throughout the community. Of the high school students who participated in the program, 1.6 percent said that they had used cocaine in the last month, whereas 3.7 percent of the control group did. With respect to marijuana the figures were 14.2 percent versus 20.2 percent; for alcohol they were 36 percent versus 50 percent; and for cigarettes they were 24 percent versus 32 percent (C. Johnson et al. 1990; Treaster 1990a).

Research into eight programs that used different prevention strategies found that each of them, in its own setting and in its own manner, promoted supportive

Project Alert

This two-year classroom program starts with eleven lessons in seventh grade that specifically target alcohol, cigarettes, and marijuana, substances that middle-school youths are likely to try first. The seventh-grade lessons are reinforced with three more in the eighth grade. Program activities—videos, guided classroom discussions, small-group activities, intensive role-playing, and parent-involved homework assignments—are designed to help students identify and resist pro-drug pressures and understand the social, emotional, and physical consequences of using harmful substances.

and caring relationships between youth and members of their families, their communities, and their peer groups. And each program implemented multi-faceted interventions targeting the specific needs of its audiences. Each of the programs was successful either in increasing the time before first alcohol, tobacco, and drug use; in reducing the frequency of alcohol, tobacco, and drug use; or in effectively reducing risk factors and/or enhancing protective factors related to the development of substance use (Substance Abuse and Mental Health Services Administration 2001). Research into LifeSkills Training (LST), a school-based life skills (discussed earlier) prevention program, found that its positive effects extended beyond the typical low-risk youths to those who were at higher than average risk: LST "significantly reduced initiation of drug use among urban, middle school students who were doing poorly academically and had substance-abusing friends." After one year, "these youths reported lower rates of cigarette, alcohol, and inhalant use than a comparable group of nonparticipating students" (Mathias 2003: 12).

The Child Development Project (CDP) discussed earlier revealed positive results in a research design that paired program schools to similar ones that did not utilize the CDP. Over a four-year period, use of alcohol by students declined from 48 percent to 37 percent, while in the matched schools it rose from 36 to 38 percent; cigarette use declined in the program schools from 25 percent to 17 percent and declined in the comparison schools from 17 percent to 14 percent; marijuana use declined in the program schools from 7 to 5 percent and rose in the matched schools from 4 percent to 6 percent (Brounstein and Zweig n.d.).

Two short-term reviews of Project D.A.R.E. (Nyre 1985; Aniskiewicz and Wysong 1990) have been positive: The program enhanced antidrug attitudes and knowledge while strengthening the social skills that are believed to be important in resisting drug use. A third evaluation (DeJong 1987b) contradicted these findings but nevertheless found that the D.A.R.E. students showed significantly less drug use. A subsequent analysis by Earl Wysong, Richard Aniskiewicz, and David Wright (1994: 467), which tracked a D.A.R.E. program for five years, found "no long-term effects for the program in preventing or reducing adolescent drug use." In their review of eight D.A.R.E. studies, Susan Ennett and her colleagues (1994) did not find encouraging results. They also questioned the use of law enforcement personnel as teachers in the program, noting that there have been no studies on whether or not this is an effective use of police personnel. A controlled study of D.A.R.E. in Houston, Texas, found that drug, alcohol, and tobacco use increased among students who had been exposed to the program (Gay 1999). Nevertheless, on July 8, 1999, White House Drug Czar Barry R. McCaffrey gave the keynote address at the 12th Annual National D.A.R.E. Officers Association Training Conference. He praised D.A.R.E. both as a tool and as an important message to children about the positive role of police in the community.

Criticism of the program continued to grow. In an editorial, the conservative *Chicago Tribune* advised (August 11, 1999: 18): "It's time to show D.A.R.E. the door. Year after year, about 80 percent of the elementary schools in the country allocate resources and classroom time for a curriculum that simply doesn't work, and few of them seem to care." In response to the increasing criticism, in 2001 the leaders of D.A.R.E. acknowledged its shortcomings and proposed changing the program accordingly. A new curriculum was developed, focusing exclusively on middle and high schools, and the role of police officers was significantly reduced (Zernike 2001). Nevertheless, research-based reports continued to criticize the program, and by 2003 state funding began to dry up, and more and more resource-starved police departments and school districts began dropping D.A.R.E. (Vogt 2003).

Harith Swadi and Harry Zeitlin (1987: 745) state: "It must be our conclusion that the available methods of drug education that aim at preventing drug abuse are at least ineffective, if not counterproductive." The National Institute on Drug Abuse (1987: 50) notes that "[s]ubstance abuse prevention research remains in its infancy" and that "we are still far from having a range of prevention strategies whose long-term efficacy is in little doubt." The General Accounting Office (1987) reported to Congress that drug prevention efforts have been unevaluated or have shown little or no impact, and in 1990 William Bennett, the federal drug policy director, stated before a congressional committee that drug education was not effective and that children were more likely to respond to law enforcement efforts and punishment (Berke 1990). Research has revealed that "simply giving information and training the child in self-control techniques would probably not be effective for the subset of children most at risk for later substance abuse. Even at age 10, this subset of most-at-risk children are already difficult to change, whether by family, teachers, or therapist" (Dishion, Patterson, and Reid 1988: 90).

Research has found that although it is relatively easy to increase knowledge and change attitudes, it is more difficult to bring about long-term sustained behavior change. "However, long-term changes can be achieved. The most persuasive support for this view comes from cigarette smoking. In 1972, about 46% of the British population smoked cigarettes and by 1992 this had been reduced to 30%. These gains were not won by one simple strategy nor by any interventions applied only in the short term. . . . Effecting health behaviour change through education is difficult but not impossible. It is likely to require perseverance, multiple approaches, and a long-term view" (Advisory Council

| **Prevention at the Community Level**

> The largest-ever study of community-based antidrug partnerships found that male residents served by Community Anti-Drug Partnerships funded by the Center for Substance Abuse Prevention had slightly lower rates—by an average of about 3 percent—of alcohol and illicit drug use than their counterparts in nonpartnership communities. The study compared rates of alcohol and other drug use in twenty-four communities that had antidrug partnership programs to those in twenty-four similar communities without such partnerships. Use rates were measured in 1994 and 1996 through a survey of 83,473 adults plus eighth- and tenth-grade students. Results for females were not nearly as encouraging: Past-month and past-year alcohol and other drug use rates were unchanged among women and girls between 1994 and 1996, and use of illicit drugs among eighth-grade girls in the partnership communities actually increased during that time period (Substance Abuse Resource Center 1999).

on the Misuse of Drugs 1993: 16). Michael Goodstadt (n.d.: 1–2) states that in the United States there is promising evidence of the impact of educational programs, based on smoking prevention studies "that offer approaches that can be applied to education about other drugs." In fact, "Americans are smoking and drinking less . . . not because the Army imprisoned North Carolina tobacco farmers or bombed stills in Scotland, but because attitudes have been changing with the help of education and treatment programs" (May 1988a: 12). The smoking rate among younger adolescents in the United States is half of what it was during the 1990s (Associated Press 2004a). And increased public awareness of the dangers of alcohol abuse, coupled with an emphasis on physical fitness and nutrition, has dramatically reduced alcohol consumption in the United States.

Smoking among adolescents has been declining, but the explanation has little to do with school-based antismoking campaigns. "A review of school programs that have been tested with randomized controlled trials shows no evidence of long-term effectiveness in any of them" (Bakalar 2005: F7). Instead, "[i]t has been shown over and over that kids are especially sensitive to tax increases" (Sarah Weiss quoted in Bakalar 2005: F7).

TECHNICAL PROBLEMS AND CRITICISMS

The difficulty in producing and implementing effective drug abuse prevention programs could be related to some of the technical aspects of these programs. It might be—and there is evidence to support such a hypothesis—that instead of intervention models based on firm theoretical and empirical foundations, drug abuse prevention programs are too often put together and implemented by well-meaning but otherwise limited people, a method that results in a naive or simplistic approach to a complex problem. For example, Patricia Bush and

Knowing and Doing

"Student orientation, alcohol awareness weeks, and curriculum infusion are typical interventions found on high school and college campuses. The assumption guiding these efforts is that people make wise choices if they know the facts about alcohol. Although this may be true, information alone is usually insufficient to change behavior. Evaluations of these stand-alone programs have found no effect on alcohol use or alcohol-related consequences" (K. D. Johnson 2004: 43).

Ronald Iannotti (1987) note that programs designed to educate elementary school children about drug abuse often fail to consider cognitive development theory (originally developed by Jean Piaget) and therefore might be inappropriate for the children's developmental stage and thus a waste of resources. The U.S. Department of Education has attempted to deal with this problem by preparing a curriculum model that is grade-level specific: *Learning to Live Drug Free: A Curriculum Model for Prevention.*

School drug education staff are often more enthusiastic about their programs' effectiveness than the empirical data warrant. An evaluation of junior high school antidrug programs in the Kansas City, Missouri, area, for example, found that although school staff viewed the programs as beneficial and successful, outcome measurements did not support their optimism (Gilham, Lucas, and Siverwright 1997). In fact, support for drug prevention programs, as Aniskiewicz and Wysong (1990) note, might have more to do with politics than research. Such programs appear to rest less on clear-cut evidence of effectiveness than on their popularity as symbolic action against the "drug crisis." Being associated with such efforts can enhance the public standing of elected, police, and school officials.

Furthermore, "strategies which are adequate for preventing experimentation among those at low risk of engaging in serious antisocial behaviors may be wholly inadequate for preventing initiation and use by those who exhibit a 'deviance syndrome.' On the other hand, well-founded strategies for preventing drug abuse among those at highest risk for abuse may be inappropriate for those at risk of only becoming experimental users" (Hawkins, Lishner, and Catalano 1987: 78). Thus, a rational prevention program needs to establish and explicate its goals. "If the goal of prevention is to prevent serious maladaptive behavior associated with drug abuse in adolescence, then it may be desirable from an etiological perspective to focus prevention efforts on those youth who manifest behavior problems, including aggressive and other antisocial behaviors during the elementary grades. On the other hand, if the goal is to prevent experimentation with drugs, or to delay the age of experimentation in the general population, such highly focused efforts may by inappropriate" (Hawkins, Lishner, and Catalano 1987: 80).

Diana Baumrind (1987: 32) cautions that "when socially deviant youths are required to participate in the school setting in peer-led denunciation of activities they value, they are more likely to become alienated than

Gimmicks, Gadgets, and Drugs

Television audiences have been exposed to a variety of (purportedly) antidrug messages geared to adolescents. Some are questionable. For example, drugs "fry your brain like an egg" (yet people use drugs and live quite well) or cause monkeys to give up food and sex (the stuff must be really great!). Now even cereal boxes, toys, and school notebooks contain antidrug messages.

converted." An eight-year study revealed that once an adolescent decides to use drugs in response to internal problems, peer-based prevention programs will not work (Blakeslee 1988). Michael Newcomb and Peter Bentler (1989: 246) recommend that prevention and intervention "focus on the misuse, abuse, problem use, and heavy use of drugs to meet internal needs, cope with distress, and avoid responsibility and important life decisions and difficulties. The youngsters facing these tasks are in need of help, education, and intervention." Newcomb and Bentler argue that it "is misleading to bask in the success of some peer programs that have reduced the number of youngsters who experiment with drugs (but would probably never have become regular users, let alone abusers) and ignore the tougher problems of those youngsters who are at high risk for drug abuse as well as other serious difficulties" (1989: 246).

An examination of the potential impact of a universal school-based prevention effort concludes that "it would not dramatically affect the course of drug use and the benefits would take years to accrue" (Caulkins et al. 1999: xxxi). However, "implementing model prevention programs seems to be justifiable in the sense that the benefits would likely outweigh the costs of the resources used" (Caulkins et al 1999: xxxii). Best estimates are that prevention reduces lifetime consumption of cigarettes by 2.1 percent, of alcohol by 2.2 percent, and of cocaine by 3.0 percent. Although these numbers might seem relatively low, even small reductions in use can cause large decreases in social costs. With only thirty hours of programming, small reductions might be all that anyone should expect from prevention. ("What Kind of Drug Use Does School-Based Prevention Prevent?" 2002).

SUMMARY

Effective prevention has proven to be as elusive as effective treatment. Prevention programs should be designed to enhance protective factors and move toward reversing or reducing known risk factors. School-based efforts at prevention have been dominated by three models: information, affective, and social influence.

Research has found that although it is relatively easy to increase knowledge and change attitudes, it is difficult to bring about long-term sustained behavior change. Drug education efforts can sometimes actually be thinly disguised propaganda, and since there is a correlation between knowledge and use, poorly designed drug education could encourage use.

One very popular but discredited program (D.A.R.E.) used police officers to lead elementary school classes using a "scare 'em" format. The social influence model instituted through Project ALERT has proven effective in reducing cigarette and marijuana use in select groups, and a variety of programs are successful in prevention efforts for specific substances among specific populations. Successful prevention strategies must be appropriate for the specific audience: low-risk or high-risk.

REVIEW QUESTIONS

1. What drawbacks are inherent in educating youngsters about the dangers of drug abuse?
2. What is the affective or humanistic approach to drug education?
3. What is the social influence approach to drug abuse prevention?
4. What are the dangers of the "scare" approach to drug prevention?
5. What general conclusion have researchers reached about the usefulness of drug education programs?
6. Why is it crucial to aim a prevention program at a specific audience?
7. What technical problems are encountered in implementing and evaluating drug prevention efforts?

11 CHAPTER | The Business of Drugs and the Drug-Terrorism Connection

Regardless of what we think we are trying to do, when we make it illegal to traffic in commodities for which there is an inelastic demand, the effect is to secure a kind of monopoly profit to the entrepreneur who is willing to break the law. In effect, we say to him: "We will set up a barrier to entry into this line of commerce by making it illegal and, therefore, risky; if you are willing to take the risk, you will be sheltered from the competition of those who are unwilling to do so. Of course, if we catch you, you may possibly (although not necessarily) be put out of business; but meanwhile you are free to gather the fruits that grow in the hothouse atmosphere we are providing for you.

Herbert L. Packer (1968: 279)

Inside Operation

In 2003 federal officials broke up a ring of twenty-five cargo handlers at Kennedy International Airport who had been smuggling drugs for a decade. The men, who had unrestricted access to the tarmac and airplanes, worked together to unload drug shipments and move them to safe areas for pickup and distribution. Their knowledge of airport security allowed them to bypass surveillance cameras and all forms of border inspection (Worth 2003). In 2005 all were convicted (Marzulli 2005).

This chapter examines the international and domestic traffic in illegal drugs, which, by any estimate, is a multibillion-dollar-a-year industry with enormous profit-to-cost ratios. For example, heroin can be purchased in 700-gram units in Bangkok, Thailand, for between $7,500 and $9,500 and can be sold in the United States for $60,000–70,000. Because the product is illegal but nevertheless in great demand, drug trafficking is characterized by a level of free enterprise that Adam Smith never envisioned. It is a market that is totally devoid of legal constraints in which prices and profits are governed only by the law of supply and demand.

The business of illegal drugs shares some elements with the business of selling legal products: "It requires lots of working capital, steady supplies of raw materials, sophisticated manufacturing facilities, reliable shipping contractors and wholesale distributors, the all-important marketing arms and access to retail franchises for maximum market penetration" (Brzezinski 2002: 26).

As in any major industry there are various functional levels: manufacturers, importers, wholesalers, distributors, retailers, and consumers. Workers in the drug business range from leaders of powerful international cartels to street dealers whose activities support a personal drug habit. At the manufacturing and importation levels, the drug business is usually concentrated among a relatively few people who head major trafficking organizations; at the retail level, it is filled with a large, fluctuating, and open-ended number of dealers and consumers. Because people at the highest levels of the drug trade are often connected by kinship and ethnicity, we will frequently refer to the ethnicity of criminal organizations in this chapter.

Drugs are smuggled into the United States from both source and transshipment countries. Traffickers may use circuitous routes to avoid the suspicion that is normally generated by shipments from source countries. For example, cocaine might be shipped from Colombia to Africa and move from there to the United States as part of legitimate maritime cargo. Indeed, "traffickers are increasingly using Africa, both east and west, to smuggle cocaine from Latin America into Europe" (Lacey 2006: 4). Pleasure crafts and fishing vessels blend in with normal maritime traffic, and low-profile vessels made of wood or fiberglass and measuring up to 40 feet in length are difficult to spot and do not readily appear on radar. Smugglers also use aircraft, landing on isolated runways and even highways or dropping their cargo from the air. Motor vehicles

Young Mule

In 2002 a 12-year-old boy landed at Kennedy International Airport from Nigeria but became ill on the cab ride to Brooklyn. After the cab driver took him to a hospital in Queens, the boy told officials that he had swallowed condoms filled with heroin, for which he was promised $1,900. The boy's father is in a federal prison in Virginia for drug offenses involving the use of students in their late teens and early twenties as drug couriers (Baker 2002).

use land routes across Canada and Mexico and onto Indian reservations bordering the United States. The traffickers then move the drugs across national borders into the United States for distribution (Kershaw 2006).

INTERNATIONAL DRUG TRAFFICKING[1]

For decades heroin trafficking in the United States was controlled principally by traditional organized crime groups that lived and operated inside the country. In a drug-trafficking network that became known as the French Connection, New York City–based Mafia "Families" purchased heroin from Corsican sources working with French sailors operating from Marseilles to transship the drug directly to the United States. The heroin was distributed throughout the United States by other Mafia Families to street-level dealers working in low-income, minority communities. However, in 1972 French and U.S. drug agents effectively dismantled the French Connection, ending the domestic Mafia's monopoly on heroin distribution in the United States.

The demise of the French Connection coupled with the subsequent emergence of criminal syndicates based in Colombia marked a significant evolution in the international drug trade. These new traffickers introduced cocaine into the United States on a massive scale, launching unparalleled waves of drug crimes and violence. Throughout the 1980s and 1990s the international crime syndicates continued to increase their wealth and dominance over the U.S. drug trade, overshadowing the domestic Mafia Families.

Today, traffic in illegal drugs at the highest wholesale levels is controlled by international organized crime syndicates from Colombia, Mexico, and other countries. From their headquarters overseas, foreign drug lords produce and distribute unprecedented volumes of cocaine, methamphetamine, and heroin. The international nature of the drug business is highlighted by the 2006 seizure by Colombian authorities of tons of potassium permanganate, a chemical that is necessary for producing cocaine, that was being smuggled from the Republic of Korea to Colombia by Korean nationals.

---

[1] Unless otherwise cited, information in this section is from the Drug Enforcement Administration.

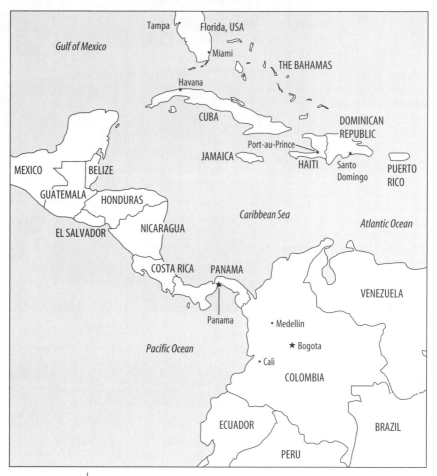

Figure 11.1   Colombia, Center of the World's Cocaine Trafficking

These traffickers maintain tight control of their workers through highly compartmentalized cell structures that separate production, shipment, distribution, money laundering, communications, security, and recruitment. Traffickers have at their disposal the most technologically advanced airplanes, boats, vehicles, radar, communications equipment, and weapons that money can buy. They have also established vast counterintelligence capabilities and transportation networks.

Colombia

Control of most of the world's cocaine industry remains in the hands of Colombian organizations. A nation of about 26 million, Colombia is the only South American country that has both Pacific and Caribbean coastlines (see Figure 11.1). It is a nation that has been torn by political strife, with civil wars

Cocaine lab uncovered by the Colombian military. Refining laboratories have relocated to cities far from cultivation sites to be closer to sources of precursor chemicals and also because improved law enforcement methods facilitate the detection of jungle laboratories. Precursor chemicals are usually manufactured in the United States and Germany, and Panama and Mexico serve as major transit sources.

©Greg Smith/Corbis

in 1902 and 1948. *La Violencia*, as the civil war of 1948–1958 is known, cost the lives of about 300,000 people (Riding 1987). It ended when the Liberals and the Conservatives formed the National Front, but several Marxist insurgencies continued to threaten the stability of the central government. Not only was murder frequent, but the methods that were used were often sadistic, such as the *corte de corbata*—the infamous "Colombian necktie"—in which the throat is cut longitudinally and the tongue is pulled through to hang like a tie. Another practice, *no dejar la semilla* ("don't leave the seed"), includes the castration of male victims and the execution of women and children (Wolfgang and Ferracuti 1967).

La Violencia: **The Violence That Never Ended** In Colombia drug traffickers exemplify a lack of belief in the legitimacy of the country's political and economic institutions. "Breaking the law—any law—is justified, and not just for the usual economic reasons that criminals favor. For traffickers, the law, law-enforcement officials, U.S. drug operatives, and drug-control organizations all represent the traditional elite, international imperialism, or other international competitive economic interests, none of which has any historical moral standing in their eyes. Therefore, moralistic arguments about restraining violent behavior do not capture these people's attention . . . [and] allows traffickers to garner enthusiastic support in some areas" (Tullis 1995: 66).

"At the root of Colombia's easy violence is an extraordinary indifference toward death" (Romoli 1941: 37). The homicide rate is ten times higher than that of the United States (Rohter 2000a, 200b). Murder is the leading cause of death for Colombian males aged 15 to 44 years (Schemo 1997). The country has the highest child murder rates in the world; street children kill each other, and hundreds are murdered by vigilante groups as part of their campaign of "social cleansing" (Luft 1995).

In this sociopolitical atmosphere bandits have roamed freely, engaging in a combination of brigandage, terrorism, and revolution. In a country where drug barons act as a state within a state, dozens of armed paramilitary groups "ply their murderous trade in the cities and countryside, sometimes selling themselves to the highest bidder as outmanned and intimidated judges and government officials feel helpless to stop them" (de Lama 1988: 5; Duzán 1994). These paramilitaries are sometimes allied with—and sometimes fighting against—the drug traffickers, and they receive financial backing from wealthy landowners. In coca-growing regions "guerilla and paramilitary groups substitute for the state in imposing a very authoritarian regime, defining and applying their own laws and regulations, and providing education, police, and civil justice to solve conflicts among the population. In exchange, these groups charge coca production and cocaine export taxes" (Thoumi 2002: 106).

For many decades coca leaf was converted to cocaine base in Bolivia and Peru and smuggled by small aircraft or boats into Colombia, where it was refined into cocaine in jungle laboratories. Laboratories have relocated to cities far from cultivation sites to be closer to sources of precursor chemicals and because improved law enforcement methods have facilitated the detection of jungle laboratories. Precursor chemicals are usually manufactured in the United States and Germany; Panama and Mexico serve as major transit sources. Colombian cartels, using dummy companies and multiple suppliers, pay up to ten times the normal prices for these chemicals. Traffickers have also been stealing precursor shipments in transit from the point of entry into Colombia en route to a legitimate end-user.

Some Colombian traffickers set up laboratories in other Latin American countries and even the United States in response to increased law enforcement in Colombia and the increasing cost of ether, sulfuric acid, and acetone in Colombia. Acetone, sulfuric acid, and ether are widely available for commercial purposes in the United States. While sulfuric acid and acetone have wide industrial use in Colombia, ether does not, and each kilo of cocaine requires 17 liters of ether. The cost of these chemicals has increased as a result of controls imposed by the Colombian government on their importation and sale and of U.S. Drug Enforcement Administration efforts to disrupt the supply of chemicals that are essential in the cocaine refinement process (Hall 2000).

In the past because Colombian coca was significantly lower in quality than that grown in Peru and Bolivia, Colombia had not been a major coca producer. Success in eradicating coca in Bolivia and Peru led to a major increase in Colombian coca cultivation, and in 1998 Colombia became the world's leading coca producer (Goering 1998; Krauss 2000). Colombian traffickers achieved extraordinary levels of efficiency in extracting cocaine from their coca crops (*International Narcotics Control Strategy Report* 2000). By 2002, however, coca was making a comeback in Peru, driven by a combination of poverty and soaring prices for coca. In Bolivia coca production shot up in 2005, the result of a backlash against U.S.-financed eradication programs that had helped to destabilize the country and topple several governments (Forero 2002, 2005).

About three quarters of the coca that is grown in Colombia comes from six rural provinces about the size of Kansas, with a population of about 6 million, southwest of the capital, Bogotá. The area is desperately poor and plagued by left- and right-wing paramilitary groups (Forero 2001a). Indeed, Colombia is the only country in Latin America that is still fighting a major guerilla insurgency (Howe 2000).

The Colombian government has conceded to the main Marxist guerilla group, the Revolutionary Armed Forces of Colombia (FARC), with about 18,000 fighters, an area in central Colombia about the size of Switzerland. FARC acts as a "labor organizer in the coca fields, keeping the price of a bushel up while taking a hefty percentage from the farmers" (Howe 2000: 38). In FARC-controlled areas, the economy is built on coca, and coca paste often serves as the local currency. Because paper currency is in short supply, "it is not unusual for people to be paid for their work in coca. They, in turn, pay for the necessities with the paste, which is soft and powdery like flour" (Forero 2001b: 12). The traffickers buy the paste, process it into cocaine, and ship it by the ton to the United States, while FARC taxes the trade. "To prevent narcotraffickers from ripping off farmers, the rebels set a minimum price for a kilo of coca paste. They also tax the traffickers for protection of smuggling routes, the use of clandestine runways, the importation of cocaine-processing chemicals, and the export of every kilo of refined cocaine shipped from the region" (Semple 2001: 61; Guillermoprieto 2002).

Contesting the FARC and other leftist militias are right-wing paramilitaries that often receive assistance from wealthy landowners, ranchers, and the Colombian military (Forero 2001c; Romero 2007). They are part of a loose-knit coalition, the United Self-Defense Forces of Colombia, about 11,000 strong, that is fighting Marxist guerillas for control of poppy- and coca-producing regions. Ranchers who had been under siege from the guerillas helped to transform this group of outlaws into a formidable army (Forero 2001c; Guillermoprieto 2002). The militias have proven to be more effective against the guerillas than government forces are, and this has endeared them to elements of the population that is at risk. The militias have reinforced this support by building roads and schools in the areas from which they have driven the guerillas (Forero 2001c; Guillermoprieto 2002).

Growing and Trafficking Cocaine in Colombia The economic modernization of Colombia failed to bring about a corresponding respect for government. Delegitimization of government and *La Violencia* "left legacies which have worked to permit, if not encourage, the development of the

---

Unique
Colombia is the only country in the world where the three main plant-based illegal drugs—cocaine, heroin, and marijuana—are produced in significant amounts (Thoumi 2002).

cocaine industry" (Thoumi 1995: 84). Delegitimization spurred the development of smuggling, particularly export of cattle, emeralds, and coffee out of Colombia and into Venezuela and Ecuador, providing experience in contraband trade and money laundering. The propensity to use violence led to domination of potential Bolivian and Peruvian rivals in the cocaine business. "Aside from their disdain for Colombian institutions and their long criminal records, Colombian traffickers share other characteristics. They appear to be great believers in fate and providence and seem unmoved by normal considerations of personal danger. It is a perspective unaltered by normal law-enforcement efforts and one that makes dealing with or trying to control them such a dangerous enterprise" (Tullis 1995: 67). Speculative capitalism with a focus on very high short-term profits, a feature of Colombia's financial elite, provided the resources for development of a cocaine industry (Thoumi 1995).

Colombia is a relatively large country, and many regions have only a weak federal presence. "While Colombian authorities built suburbs and major highways between cities, they ignored vast sections of the country; much of rural Colombia is isolated by hilly, trackless terrain" (Duzán 1994: 63). Three steep mountain ranges run the length of Colombia, and impenetrable jungle covers the south: "The government didn't lose control of this half of Colombia; it never had it" (Robinson 1998a: 39). The vacuum left by the central government has proved ideal for coca cultivation and cocaine manufacture because it left areas where only local officials had to be bribed, a cheaper and less risky action than bribery at the federal level (Thoumi 1995). In 1998 Colombia became the world's leading coca producer; Peru had fallen to second place (Goering 1998). However, Colombian coca is significantly lower in quality than that grown in Peru and Bolivia. In response, traffickers have imported the type of coca that is native to Peru and, with the help of agronomists, have grafted it onto the weaker Colombian species to create a powerful hybrid (Rohter 1999a).

In the remote jungle areas where coca is cultivated, powerful Marxist guerrilla forces protect the crops and levy taxes on the drug business. They have been effective against Colombia's mostly poorly trained and motivated conscript military (Robinson 1998b; Rohter 1999b). Furthermore, the involvement in widespread human rights abuses by members of the Colombian military, often those trained by the United States, often generates support for the rebels and drug traffickers (Schemo and Golden 1998). Attempts to eradicate the crop have encountered stiff opposition from the subsistence farmers, for whom it is an economic lifeline ("Anti-Drug Efforts Encounter Resistance in Colombia" 1995).

Although it originated as a Marxist militia, in more recent years FARC has resembled organized banditry, operating its own coca farms and laboratories in rural Colombia (Brooke 1995). FARC has also collected taxes from traffickers and has permitted them to operate in jungle areas that FARC controls. In 1996 there were mass protests against the government's campaign to eradicate both coca and poppy crops in response to U.S. pressure.

Colombia has been spraying herbicides from the air in several rural provinces. In support of these protests, FARC launched an attack on military and police installations, destroying two police stations and killing and abducting dozens of soldiers and police officers. At the end of 1998 in an effort to advance peace negotiations with FARC guerrillas, the Colombian government evacuated its security forces from a swath of Colombia as big as Switzerland (Schemo 1999).

Cells and Cartels   Colombia-based cocaine trafficking groups in the United States continue to be organized around "cells" that operate within a given geographic area. Because these cells are based on family relationships or close friendships, outsiders who attempt to penetrate the cell run a high risk of arousing suspicion. Some cells specialize in a particular facet of the drug trade, such as cocaine transport, storage, wholesale distribution, or money laundering. Each cell, which may comprise ten or more individuals, operates with little or no knowledge about the other cells. In this way, should one of the cells be compromised, the operations of the other cells would not be endangered.

A rigid top-down command and control structure is characteristic of these groups. The head of each cell reports to a regional director, who is responsible for the overall management of several cells. The regional director, in turn, reports directly to one of the top drug lords or his designate, based in Colombia. Trusted lieutenants of the organization in the United States have discretion in day-to-day operations, but ultimate authority rests with the leadership in Colombia (Ledwith 2000).

Traffickers from Colombia are increasingly using state-of-the-art encryption devices to translate their communications into indecipherable code. This evolving technology presents a significant impediment to law enforcement investigations of criminal activities. In the past the necessity for frequent communication between drug lords in Colombia and their surrogates in the United States made the drug-trafficking organizations vulnerable to law enforcement wiretaps. Now, however, through the use of encryption technology, the traffickers can protect their electronic business communications from law enforcement interception and hide information that could be used to build criminal cases against them.

Colombian managers dispatched to Puerto Rico[2] and the Dominican Republic operate these command and control centers and are responsible for overseeing drug trafficking in the region. These groups also direct networks of transporters that oversee the importation, storage, exportation, and wholesale distribution of cocaine destined for the continental United States. They have franchised to criminals from the Dominican Republic a portion of the midlevel wholesale cocaine and heroin trade on the East Coast of the United

---

[2] Puerto Rico, a 110-mile-long island with the third busiest seaport in North America, is ideal for smugglers, who have fewer problems getting their goods to the United States because shipments from Puerto Rico are not searched by customs agents.

States. The Dominican trafficking groups, already firmly entrenched as low-level cocaine and heroin wholesalers in the larger northeastern cities, were uniquely placed to assume a far more significant role in this multi-billion-dollar business. However, the Colombian groups remain in control of the sources of supply.

The Dominican traffickers operating in the United States, not the Colombians, are now the ones who are subject to arrest, while the top-level Colombians control the organization with sophisticated telecommunications. This change in operations reduces profits somewhat for the syndicate leaders but reduces their exposure to U.S. law enforcement. If arrested, the Dominicans will have little damaging information that can be used against their Colombian masters. Reducing their exposure, together with sophisticated communications, puts the Colombian bosses closer to their goal of operating from a political, legal, and electronic sanctuary.

Heroin Trafficking in Colombia   Since the 1980s Colombia has become a leading poppy grower, and Colombians have become major heroin wholesalers. At the end of 1991 police raids in Colombia disclosed thousands of acres of poppy plants ("Colombian Heroin May Be Increasing" 1991). On the mountain slopes of Colombia's Andean rain forests guerrillas and drug traffickers grow significant crops. On the hillsides of a reservation in the southern Colombian state of Cauca, at an altitude of 9,000 feet, Guambiano Indians cultivate their most precious crop. Gum from their poppies brings about $115 a pound and represents the difference between food and hunger. Nine other states are known to have poppy plantations (Tamayo 2001).

By 1998 Colombian heroin accounted for more than 50 percent of the drug smuggled into the United States. The high purity level of Colombian heroin—it passes through fewer hands from "the farm to the arm" than the Asian variety—enables ingestion by sniffing and smoking, methods that are much safer than injection, which is the only way to get a potent high with weaker versions of the drug. By 1999 Colombia was believed the source of 70 percent of the heroin sold on the East Coast. In New York Colombians caused a glut on the heroin market, with declining prices and street-sale purity as high as 90 percent, whereas in the early (pre-Colombian) 1980s the purity was barely 5 percent (Wren 1999a).

During the 1980s the Colombian drug lords relied heavily on organized groups from Mexico to transport cocaine into the United States after it was delivered to Mexico from Colombia. Currently, the greatest proportion of cocaine available in the United States is still entering the United States through Mexico. Using their skills as seasoned drug traffickers with a long tradition of polydrug smuggling, crime lords from Mexico soon established cocaine-trafficking routes and contacts. In the late 1980s Colombia-based organizations, which had paid transporters from Mexico cash for their services, began to pay them in cocaine—in many cases up to half of the shipment. As a result the organizations from Mexico evolved from mere transporters of cocaine to major cocaine traffickers in their own right, and today they pose a grave threat to the United States. Mexican organized crime syndicates now control the wholesale distribution of cocaine in the western half and the Midwest of the United States (Ledwith 2000).

Mexico

Mexico is a nation of about 95 million people, 75 percent of whom live in urban areas. Independence from Spanish rule in 1821 was followed by a series of revolutions, rigged elections, and general turmoil. There was a war with the United States in 1848 and a French invasion and occupation from 1863 to 1867. In still another violent overthrow, Porfirio Diaz came to power in 1876 and ruled Mexico for thirty-five years. Out of the revolution that ousted Diaz emerged Mexico's dominant political party, known today as the PRI (Partido Revolucionario Institucional).

For decades after its founding, the PRI "was a tool of successive presidents using authoritarian methods to insure one-party rule" (Dillon 1999b: 1). The police forces—federal, state, and local—that evolved out of this atmosphere have been deployed not to protect but to control the population. Furthermore, police officers have been poorly paid, and it is understood that they can supplement their pittance with bribes as long as they remain loyal to the government (Dillon 1996). The PRI ruled Mexico for more than seventy years without any strong opposition, during which time corruption became endemic.

From Heroin to Cocaine   The popular culture is infused with songs and ballads—known as *narcocorridos*—glamorizing drug trafficking. Major *narcotraficantes* are celebrated, along with their subculture of violence. Many songs contain references to an outlaw code of behavior, and *narcocorrido* music videos depict violence, including torture and the murder of police officers (Dillon 1999a). Mexicans distrust the police while fearing the traffickers, who have resorted to beheadings to terrorize the public. "Along with the widespread fear comes a certain respect. Big-time mobsters are treated like folk heroes in their home regions, their stories told and retold in popular songs" (J. C. McKinley 2007: 10).

Mexico is the source of "brown" or "black tar" heroin, a less refined form of the substance that gained a foothold in the U.S. drug market after the demise of the French Connection. Whereas white heroin from the Golden Triangle and the Golden Crescent in Southwest Asia can approach 100 percent purity, Mexican brown generally ranges from 65 to 85 percent pure.

The poppy is not native to Mexico but was brought into the country at the turn of the twentieth century by Chinese laborers who were helping to build the railroad system. Chinese immigrants dominated heroin trafficking until anti-Chinese riots and property confiscations during the 1930s caused the trade to pass into Mexican hands (Lupsha 1991). Poppy fields are generally small and difficult to detect, although larger fields cultivated by more sophisticated

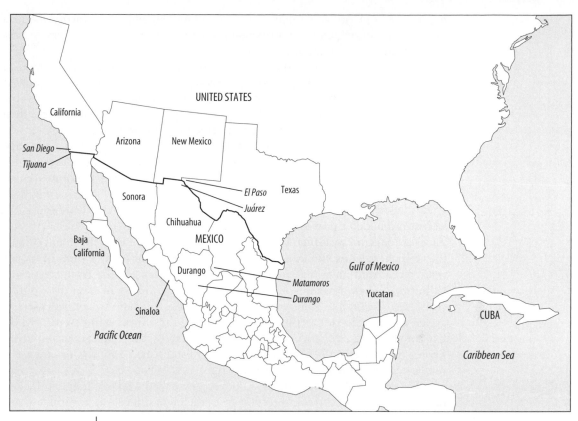

Figure 11.2 | Mexico and the States That Border It

growers have been discovered. The poppies are grown in remote areas of the Sierra Madre states of Durango, Sinaloa, and Chihuahua as well as in Sonora (the Mexican state just south of Arizona) (see Figure 11.2). Opium gum is then transported to nearby villages. *Acaparadores* (gatherers) travel around the countryside buying large quantities of opium gum, which is flown to secret laboratories that are owned and operated by major heroin organizations. The conversion process takes about three days (although with special equipment and trained personnel it can be accomplished in one day). Once the chemists are finished, the heroin is moved to large population centers. From there Mexican couriers transport the heroin to members of the trafficking organization in the United States.

In the early 1990s the Mexicans struck a deal with the Colombians whose cocaine they were moving from Mexico into the United States on a contract basis: For every 2 kilograms of smuggled cocaine the Mexicans would keep 1 kilogram as payment in kind (O'Brien and Greenburg 1996; Wren 1996). Both sides benefited. The Colombians had an abundance of cocaine, and the Mexicans had a distribution network in the United States that they had previously used for heroin. This arrangement was aided by the North American Free Trade Act, which further opened the already porous borders between the United States and Mexico.

The relationship with the Colombians also led to structural changes as some Mexican drug groups modeled their organizations along Colombian lines: compartmentalized units operating independently of each other but controlled hierarchically. They have also copied the Colombians in their attacks on journalists. The new arrangement had significant benefits to the Mexican traffickers: Profits increased five to ten times. It also led to a dramatic increase in payments to public officials to protect the lucrative business (Golden 1997). This arrangement also had a certain logic for the Colombia-based traffickers, who in 1989 had been stunned by four costly cocaine seizures. Under the new payment plan, if a shipment was seized in a U.S. warehouse, the losses to the Colombia-based traffickers would be cut by half.

The markups for drug sales were so great that the new arrangement offered the traffickers from Mexico an opportunity to make far greater sums of money than they could have made being mere transporters for the traffickers from Colombia. More revenues meant more profits to invest in new distribution strategies. Eventually, the United States became divided into two marketing areas: the Mexico-based traffickers controlling the Midwest and West and the Colombia-based traffickers controlling the East. As a result organized crime figures from Mexico began using their long-established contacts to emerge as major cocaine traffickers in their own right.

The drug trade is big business in poverty-wracked Mexico. Large traffickers have traditionally received protection from the highest levels of government and law enforcement. Indeed, some important traffickers have backgrounds in law enforcement. As Peter Lupsha notes, "For some of Mexico's top enforcement officials entrance into drug trafficking has simply been a lateral transfer" (1990: 12). This ugly facet of the drug trade was dramatically revealed when several Mexican law enforcement officers were implicated in the torture-murder of a U.S. drug agent. They were acting on orders from drug kingpin Rafael Caro Quintero. When Quintero and other members of his Guadalajara cartel were arrested, they were carrying credentials identifying them as agents of the Dirección Federal de Seguridad, the Mexican equivalent of the FBI. Sicilia Falcón, another leading Mexican trafficker, carried similar credentials (Lupsha 1991). In Rafael Quintero's hometown of Sinaloa, just south of Arizona, he and other members of the Caro Quintero clan are revered and are even the subjects of songs and legends (Bowden 1991). Drug-related corruption and violence that includes the murder (sometimes by beheading) of police officers continues to plague Mexico (J. C. McKinley 2006). As was noted earlier in the chapter, Mexican organizations are now transporting cocaine into the United States for Colombian traffickers.

The length and remoteness of the 1,933-mile-long border between Mexico and the United States make patrolling very difficult and facilitate the transportation of drugs into Texas, California, Arizona, and New Mexico. Drugs are also secreted in a variety of motor vehicles and smuggled past official border entry points. Private aircraft make use of hundreds of small airstrips that dot the

U.S.-Mexican border and dozens of larger airstrips on the Yucatán Peninsula to move heroin north. On the Mexican side of the border across from Laredo, Texas, the city of Nuevo Laredo has been turned into a "Little Baghdad" by warring drug cartels attempting to control this critical distribution center. Victims include journalists and police officers (G. Thompson 2005).

Methamphetamine   Although they are latecomers to the trade, Mexican drug organizations have become dominant in the manufacture and distribution of methamphetamine. They import precursor chemicals from Asia and Europe and convert them into "speed" in Mexico-based laboratories. The drugs are then smuggled into the United States (Dillon 1995). Methamphetamine provides Mexican organizations an opportunity for profit that does not have to be shared with others, as do the profits from cocaine with Colombians, for example. And the profits from methamphetamine are substantial, usually a tenfold return on investment (Arax and Gorman 1995).

Better organization and an extensive drug portfolio have enabled Mexican organizations to diversify by dividing operations into heroin, cocaine, marijuana, and now methamphetamine units. Mexican involvement with methamphetamine apparently began when the Hells Angels motorcycle club turned to Mexicans to avoid the hazards posed by methamphetamine manufacture: It is explosive, the chemicals are caustic, inhalation can be fatal, and the strong odor can alert law enforcement. Eventually, the Mexicans improved on the methods learned from the bikers, and now it is the bikers who typically buy for distribution from the Mexicans (Arax and Gorman 1995).

Although major international trafficking organizations have traditionally specialized in one substance—heroin or cocaine—in several cases commodity lines have become blurred: Colombians, historically cocaine traffickers, have become involved in the heroin business, while Mexicans, traditionally heroin traffickers, have become major cocaine dealers.

Golden Triangle

The Golden Triangle of Southeast Asia encompasses approximately 150,000 square miles of forested highlands, including the western fringe of Laos, the four northern provinces of Thailand, and the northeastern parts of Myanmar, formerly Burma (see Figure 11.3). Myanmar accounts for about 90 percent of the total heroin production of the Golden Triangle[3] and is the world's second largest source of heroin and opium. Myanmar is also a major producer of methamphetamine (Mydans 2003). These countries emerged from colonial rule with relatively weak central governments. Their rural areas were inhabited by bandits and paramilitary organizations such as the Shan United Army. Colonial officials, particularly the French, used these organizations and indigenous

---

[3] Drug traffickers in Myanmar have diversified into methamphetamine, which is being smuggled into other Asian countries.

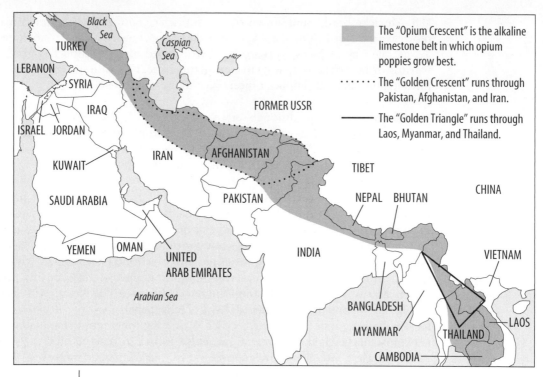

Figure 11.3 | Major Asian Opium Regions

tribes against various insurgent groups, particularly those that followed a Marxist ideology. As support for overseas colonies dwindled at home, French officials in Southeast Asia utilized the drug trade to finance their anti-insurgent efforts. Golden Triangle opium was shipped to Marseilles, where the Corsican underworld processed it into heroin for distribution in the United States. The French withdrew from Southeast Asia in 1955, and several years later the United States took up the struggle against Marxist groups there. The Vietnam War is part of this legacy. The U.S. Central Intelligence Agency (CIA) waged its own clandestine war. Again, heroin played a role, for many of the indigenous tribal groups that were organized by the CIA cultivated opium. In Laos and South Vietnam corrupt governments were heavily involved in heroin trafficking, making the substance easily available to U.S. soldiers (A. W. McCoy 1972, 1991). This long-standing tradition of using drugs to help finance military efforts continues in that part of the world.

Shan United Army The Shan States, an area somewhat larger than England, lie on a rugged, hilly plateau in the eastern part of central Burma, flanking the western border of China's Yunnan Province. The Shan States contain an array of tribal and linguistic groupings. The largest group is the Shans, who speak Thai and therefore have more in common with their neighbors in

Thailand than with Burma. The Shans are lowland rice cultivators, but hill tribes on the mountain ridges around them cultivate opium. During British colonial rule (1886–1948) the Shan States were administered independently from Burma, and the Shan princes enjoyed a great deal of autonomy. When Burma won independence in 1948, the Shans, with great misgivings, agreed to join the Union of Burma in return for statehood and guarantees of a number of ministry posts. As a final incentive the Shans were given the right to secede after 1957. Since a coup in 1962, Burma has been dominated by a repressive military dictatorship. In 1989 the country changed its name to Myanmar. Brutality against ethnic minorities and collaboration with drug trafficking continue.

The Burmese government's heavy-handed approach to the Shan States set the stage for revolution. Official Burmese financial policies were devastating to many hill farmers, who turned more and more to poppy cultivation as a cash crop outside of central government control (Delaney 1977). Shan princes (known as *sawbwas*) "had been encouraged to introduce the opium poppy to their fiefdoms by the British as far back as 1866 and opium shops had been opened throughout Burma to retail the narcotics to licensed addicts" (Bresler 1980: 67). In later years the British made a number of efforts to abolish opium cultivation in the Shan States, although they were never completely successful (A. W. McCoy 1972). In any event many Shans blamed their princes for accommodating the central government, and traditional systems of authority deteriorated.

Mong Tai Army   Originally known as the Shan United Army, the Mong Tai Army (MTA), under the leadership of Chang Chifu, who is half-Chinese, half-Shan and better known as Khun Sa, resorted to opium trafficking to purchase arms and support its independence movement (Delaney 1977). The MTA came to dominate the opium trade along the Thai-Burmese border, where about 400,000 hill tribesmen had no source of income other than heroin (Permanent Subcommittee on Investigations 1981a). The MTA was able to control both the shipments of opium and the production of heroin in its laboratories.

In the 1980s the Thai government succeeded in driving the MTA out of Thailand and back into Burma, but the group continued to dominate opium traffic, taxing drug caravans crossing their territory. In 1990 the Shans suffered significant setbacks: A U.S. federal grand jury indicted Khun Sa for drug trafficking, and the United States offered a $3 million reward for his capture and conviction in a U.S. court. Also, his Mong Tai Army suffered defeats by the primitive but ferocious Wa tribesmen (Schmetzer 1990).

In 1994 a joint U.S.-Thai operation ("Tiger Trap") closed the Thai-Myanmar border in areas where the MTA operates. This cut off Khun Sa's ability to move heroin into Thailand and curtailed purchase of supplies for his forces. Later that year, Thai police arrested thirteen major MTA brokers who had been indicted by a federal grand jury in New York. The squeeze was complete in 1995 when the Myanmar army moved against Khun Sa, whose

Heroin's Long Journey

In the mist-shrouded mountains along the border between China and Myanmar, where the monsoon washes away roads linking villages without electricity or running water, heroin begins its long journey to North America. By the time it reaches the streets of America's cities, the heroin will have traveled through half a dozen countries, soared at least 5,000-fold in price, and changed hands a hundred times. A kilo that will ultimately sell for more than $200,000 wholesale in New York City costs as little as $2,500 in Myanmar. The real profits in heroin are all downstream, in transportation and distribution. The first fingers to touch it, though, belong to people such as a certain 36-year-old mother of seven. She and her husband begin the harvest by scoring each poppy pod with a needlelike knife. A creamy gum oozes from the cuts, and once it turns black, it is scraped off with a crescent-shaped tool that has been in her family for as long as she can remember. It is painstaking work, and for their labor they earn $600 annually, barely enough to feed their children. Brokers come from the valley in early March to purchase the raw opium gum, which sells for about $135 a kilogram (Brzezinski 2002).

forces were low on food, ammunition, and medical treatment for their wounded. Shortly afterward, ethnic strife broke out. The rank-and-file ethnic Shans mutinied against the MTA, whose top officers are ethnic Chinese (Shenon 1996). Khun Sa began secret negotiations with Myanmar, and in 1996 a deal was made. In front of reporters from Thailand the 61-year-old Khun Sa submitted his resignation—he was retiring to raise chickens, he told them—and disbanded the MTA. The Myanmar government refuses to extradite him, and until his health deteriorated, Khun Sa regularly golfed with the generals against whom he had fought a protracted guerrilla war (Wren 1998a). As a result of Khun Sa's retirement the amount of Southeast Asian heroin entering the United States dropped dramatically (replaced by heroin from Colombia).

United Wa State Army   Until 1989 another formidable private army in the Golden Triangle served the Burmese Communist Party (BCP). The BCP force had in the past received support from the People's Republic of China. After Beijing cut off this aid to improve relations with Myanmar, the BCP, following a long-established precedent in the region, went into the opium business. The BCP controlled much of the poppy-producing area and received opium as a form of tax and tribute from local farmers, which the BCP then refined into heroin in its own laboratories.

In 1989 its ethnic rank-and-file Wa tribesmen—fierce warriors whose ancestors were headhunters—rebelled, and the BCP folded as an armed force (Haley 1990). Most Wa political groups reached an accommodation with the Myanmar ruling junta, but one faction of the Wa organized as the United Wa State Army (UWSA). Headquartered on the border of China's Yunnan Province, the UWSA uses trafficking in heroin—and more recently methamphetamine—as a means of funding efforts against Burmese control (Witkin and Griffin 1994). Nearly one million Wa straddle the border between Myanmar and China, and the UWSA has an estimated strength of 15,000–20,000 men, well armed with ground-to-air missiles and modern communications equipment. In 1997 a Myanmar military patrol of thirty men stumbled onto a Wa drug caravan smuggling methamphetamine into Thailand and was wiped out. For the Wa profits from methamphetamine production and smuggling have surpassed those from heroin. Ironically, the Wa routinely executes anyone who is caught dealing heroin for local use (Wren 1998b). "Since the surrender of the SUA/MTA, the UWSA has reigned supreme in narcotics production in Burma," the world's largest producer of heroin (National Narcotics Intelligence Consumers Committee 1998: 50).

Thailand

 Whatever its source, Southeast Asian opium in the form of morphine base or of almost pure heroin is usually brokered in Thailand, which has modern communications and transportation systems. A nation of 50 million people, Thailand is almost as large as France. A staunch anti-Communist ally of the United States, Thailand sent troops to fight alongside U.S. soldiers in Korea and Vietnam. In addition to its role in drug trafficking, Thailand, with an estimated 50,000 active brothels, has the reputation of being the world's biggest whorehouse (Schmetzer 1991). Thailand is also a major consumer of methamphetamine smuggled in from Myanmar (Mydans 2003). In 1991 a military coup—one of seventeen since 1932—overthrew the democratically elected Thai government, as did another coup in 2006.

> In Southeast Asia, not only did the British and French opium monopolies create massive addict populations, but they also inadvertently formed a smuggling network that was crucial to the post–World War II heroin epidemic. Although the colonial administrations reaped huge profits, they never became involved in the drug's distribution and sale. That work was left to each colony's licensed opium merchant. Invariably they were Chinese. (Posner 1988: 66)

Bangkok has a large population of Thai-born Chinese, called Haw, who are known by Thai names but maintain close ties with Chinese in Hong Kong, Yunnan province,[4] Amsterdam, and British Columbia. From Bangkok Chinese criminal organizations have flooded their China White into major cities of Europe, Canada, and the United States. At the center of much of this drug trafficking are the Triads.

---

[4] Because it is located next to the Golden Triangle, China's Yunnan ("south of the clouds") province, with a population that includes twenty of the country's minority groups, has been a center for drug trafficking. High-quality heroin passes easily over borders that were opened for trade more than a decade ago, supported by rampant corruption among the police and other officials. The traffickers are well armed, gunfights are frequent, and the army has been used extensively to combat the drug gangs (Tyler 1995).

Triads

Secret societies have a long history in China; some date back to the beginning of the common era (Fong 1981; Chin 1990). An important part of these societies are the Triads and their American offshoots: tongs and Chinatown gangs. They draw their strength from the unique cultural dynamics of Chinese society, in which loyalty to family and friends is a moral imperative (J. Liu et al. 1998). "Chinese are born into a hierarchically organized society in which they never see themselves or others as free individuals, but as bound to others in an ever expanding web of social relations bearing mutual obligate bonds of varying strength" (W. Myers 1995: 3).

In this cultural setting, as Willard Myers (1995) notes, law is marginalized, relegated to a position well below mediative mechanisms within a particularistic social order of human relationships. These cultural manifestations, while not ipso facto criminal, facilitate criminal organization. Of particular interest are people of Cantonese and Fukienese heritage,[5] who as immigrants throughout the world were subjected to pernicious discrimination, to which they responded by relying on cultural attributes that provided great advantages in business, both legal and illegal. And the cultural concept of *guanxi* (personal networks involving a system of favors or services) is global, providing a dynamic for international business, both legal and illegal. The Triad phenomenon is a natural extension of these cultural attributes.

The term *Triad* refers to the Chinese societies' common symbol: an equilateral triangle representing the three basic Chinese concepts of heaven, earth, and man. These groups, based in Hong Kong and Taiwan, wear distinctive dress and engage in highly ritualized behavior; secret hand signs, passwords, and blood oaths are used in elaborate initiation ceremonies (Carter 1991).

The Triad phenomenon is believed to have originated in opposition to the Ch'ing dynasty that was established by the conquering Manchus in 1644 (Fong 1981). The Ch'ing dynasty ended in 1911 with the success of Dr. Sun Yat-sen (1866–1925), who had been a Triad member. Many Triad members turned to criminal activities: gambling, loan-sharking, extortion, and trafficking in opium from the Golden Triangle of Southeast Asia. This trade was strengthened considerably by the activities of Chinese Nationalist forces in the Golden Triangle. Chiang Kai-shek, himself a Triad member, is reputed to have used Triads in his war against the Communists and labor unions. Triads were suppressed with a great deal of violence on the mainland by Mao Zedong when his Communist forces defeated Chiang's Nationalist Army in 1947. Triad members who fled to Taiwan with Chiang Kai-shek were tightly controlled by the Kuomintang (the Nationalist Party) and were unable to expand their criminal operations on the island (Chin 1990).

Thousands of other Triad members fled into the British colony of Hong Kong, which already had locally organized Triads that dated back to the early twentieth

---

[5] Competition between members of these two groups, in both licit and illicit spheres, has led to violence in a number of U.S. cities (W. Myers 1995).

century. The indigenous Hong Kong Triads had begun as guilds and benevolent societies. They extended into criminal activities and actively collaborated with the Japanese during Japan's occupation of the colony during World War II. In the postwar era they emerged as powerful criminal societies (Chin 1995).

The drug-trafficking Triads expanded their operations during the Vietnam War, when thousands of U.S. soldiers were attracted to the potent heroin of Southeast Asia. When the Americans withdrew from Vietnam, the Triads followed the market and internationalized their drug operations. Because many soldiers were stationed in Europe, a major Triad marketplace developed there, with operations headquartered in Amsterdam.

Heroin manufactured in the Golden Triangle is smuggled into China's Yunnan Province and transported eastward to the coast and beyond. It is also smuggled through the Lao People's Democratic Republic and Vietnam into the Guangxi Autonomous Region and Guangdong Province of China. Other important transit routes bring heroin from the Golden Triangle to major cities on the southeast Asian peninsula, where it is sold in the illicit markets there or transported to other parts of the world.

Korean Kingpins
According to U.S. officials, North Korea produces about forty tons of opium a year and tons of high-quality methamphetamine that are smuggled into East Asia. This is allegedly accomplished by using Korean diplomatic and trade missions ("Far East Sopranos" 2003).

Golden Crescent

The Golden Crescent of Southwest Asia includes Afghanistan, Pakistan, and parts of Iran (see Figure 11.3 on page 302). The region has limestone-rich soil, a climate and altitude that are ideal for poppy cultivation, and, like the Golden Triangle, a ready abundance of cheap labor for the labor-intensive production of opium.

Afghan "Oil"
"What crude oil is to the Middle East, poppies are to Afghanistan" (Powell 2007: 31).

Unlike Southeast Asia, Afghanistan's rugged terrain and the martial tradition of its tribes kept it free of colonialism. Western interest in this nation of about 27 million was limited until the Soviet invasion. The Pashtuns, a tribal group that populates Pakistan's Northwest Frontier Province, make up about 40 percent of the inhabitants of Afghanistan. The border dividing Pashtuns in Pakistan from their tribal brethren in Afghanistan was drawn by the British more than a century ago and is generally ignored; there are few border patrols in the region (Ahmed-Ullah 2001).

In the wake of the September 11, 2001, terrorist attacks, and U.S. military action against the Taliban government, the poppy once again became an indispensable crop in parts of Afghanistan. "There is no other way to survive," notes one farmer. A pound of raw opium can be sold for $100 or more, over one hundred times what a pound of fruits or vegetables will bring. By 2004 Afghanistan was producing more than three fourths of the world's opium—more than 4,000 tons. That same year, the rush to grow poppy caused a glut on the market and a steep decline in its price (Gall 2004; Rohde 2004). Opium is so critical to the Afghan economy—roughly one third of the country's total gross national product—that U.S. officials have been reluctant to engage in an antidrug war that could conflict with efforts to combat terrorism (Ives 2004; Schmitt 2004; Waldman 2004). High-ranking members of the government are reportedly profiting from the drug trade, as are terrorist groups (Gall 2003).

Wealth from the drug trade has increased the power of regional local warlords, whose militias are a threat to the central government (Schmitt 2004). In 2005 the United States criticized the Afghan leadership for the government's failure to curtail poppy cultivation. Antidrug efforts are hampered by a lack of alternative crops for impoverished farmers, and Taliban fighters have joined forces with drug smugglers against the government and Western troops (Cloud and Gall 2005; Schmitt 2006). "Poppy growing is so uncontrolled that despite millions of aid dollars spent to train anti-drug forces and to help farmers grow other crops, Afghanistan is showing no signs of leaving its position as the world's biggest producer of opium." (Gall 2006a: 4). It now accounts for more than 90 percent of global opium production as farmers in every province of Afghanistan cultivate opium poppies (Gall 2006b; Hafvenstein 2006). Afghan opium is processed into heroin in local laboratories or shipped to processing plants in Pakistan.

In Pakistan the typical poppy farmer lives in a semiautonomous northern tribal area outside the direct control of the central government in Islamabad. The Pakistani authorities have little control in these areas and must appeal to tribal leaders to move against the region's dozens of illegal opium-processing laboratories. In northwest Pakistan's Karakoram Mountains an acre of poppies yields about a dozen kilos of opium gum; ten kilos of opium gum can be converted into one kilo of base morphine. The wholesaling is accomplished in lawless border towns such as Landi Kotal, which is about three miles from the Afghan border.

The United States has pressured Pakistan to move against poppy cultivation, but the infusion of hundreds of thousands of Afghan tribesmen into Pakistan has made this difficult if not impossible. Tribesmen in Pakistan are now armed with rocket-propelled grenade launchers and automatic weapons to protect miles of poppy plants, pledging to die fighting rather than give up their best cash crop. Furthermore, there is a growing domestic market for heroin in Pakistan. While most poppies now grow on the Afghan side of the border and are shipped to Europe and North America in the form of powdered heroin, Pakistan's heroin-smoking population has grown, with estimates as high as 1 million users.

Iran has been fighting a deadly battle against heavily armed Afghan traffickers and has lost several thousand men in the effort. The traffickers, equipped with antiaircraft missiles, night-vision goggles, and satellite telephones, are better armed than are their opponents in Iranian law enforcement (M. Moore 2001). Turkey, which serves as a land bridge to markets in the West for heroin from the Golden Crescent, is fighting a similar battle. Kurdish separatists and Turkish criminal groups (*babas*) have important connections in the Western drug market. They move heroin across the highways of Turkey and into Europe, where other criminal organizations, in particular Mafia and Camorra groups, distribute the drug throughout the European market.

The nations of Central Asia that surround Afghanistan, such as Tajikistan, have a predominantly young, rapidly growing, and poverty-stricken population. Add heroin to this mix, and you get an expanding addict population and drug

Poppyland

In southern Afghanistan's Helmand Province, which borders on Pakistan, schools closed in 2006 because teachers and students were busy with opium-poppy harvesting, as were the driver and bodyguard of the provincial prosecutor (Rubin 2006).

Though Pakistani officials have little control in the prevention of drug exportation, they do manage to seize some heroin destined for the United States. Most heroin trade in Pakistan is controlled by the Quetta Alliance.

©Francoise de Mulder/Corbis

organizations taking advantage of porous borders and easily bribed officials. "The drug business sustains up to 50 percent of the Tajik economy and props up its currency, if only because of the great number of people it employs" (Orth 2002: 168). For many of the warlords who are part of the post-Taliban Afghan government, heroin was the way they supported their armed followers. Islamic terrorist groups also operate in this region, and heroin provides then with an invaluable source of funds. And the connection between drugs and corruption reaches into the highest ranks of the Russian military (Orth 2002).

THE TERRORISM CONNECTION

Any number of terrorist groups use drug trafficking to further political ends: overthrowing governments and imposing their world view. "It is not particularly uncommon for terrorist groups to recruit some of their members among criminal elements, particularly among individuals who may have special skills or common criminals who contribute to its goals in instrumental, training, and other matters" (Préfontaine and Dandurand 2004: 16). Terrorist and drug-trafficking groups share some attributes, in particular organizational structure such as compartmentalization. Terrorist groups and criminal organizations often have similar requirements for moving people, money, material, and weapons across borders and often operate under a similar set of contingencies. The distinction between drug trafficking and terrorism is becoming increasingly blurred, and we see an overlapping, symbiotic relationship between terrorism, drugs, and organized crime (Perl 2000). Leftist guerillas in Colombia benefit from dealing cocaine, as do their right-wing paramilitary enemies.

Terrorism

As defined by the U.S. Department of State, *terrorism* is premeditated, politically motivated violence perpetrated against noncombatant targets by subnational groups or clandestine agents, usually intended to influence an audience.

Taliban insurgents in Afghanistan have been using heroin to finance their efforts. In 2005 Afghan drug lord Baz Mohammad, age 47, was extradited to the United States, where he is accused of heading an organization that controlled poppy fields in Afghanistan, heroin-processing plants in Pakistan, and a trafficking network that smuggled millions of dollars worth of drugs into the United States. In a partnership with the Taliban Mohammad told supporters that they would be committing jihad by selling heroin to Americans (McFadden 2005; Zambito 2005).

In Southeast Asia's Golden Triangle there is a long-standing tradition of using heroin trafficking to support insurgencies. According to John Walters, Director of the Office of National Drug Control Policy, "Almost half of the State Department's list of known terrorist organizations are known to have, at one point or another, trafficked in drugs" (2003: 9). This gives rise to the term *narcoterrorism*—terrorist acts carried out by groups that are directly or indirectly involved in cultivating, manufacturing, transporting, or distributing illegal drugs.

The links between terrorist organizations and drug traffickers can take many forms, ranging from facilitation—protection, transportation, and taxation—to direct trafficking by the terrorist organization itself to finance its activities. Traffickers and terrorists have similar logistical needs in terms of materiel and the covert movement of goods, people, and money. Relationships between drug traffickers and terrorists are mutually beneficial. Drug traffickers gain from access to terrorists' military skills and weapons supply; terrorists gain a source of revenue and expertise in illicit transfer and laundering of proceeds. Both bring corrupt officials whose services provide mutual benefits, such as greater access to fraudulent documents, including passports and customs papers. Drug traffickers can also gain considerable freedom of movement when they operate in conjunction with terrorists who control large amounts of territory (Beers and Taylor 2002).

DOMESTIC DRUG TRAFFICKING

The enormous profits that accrue in the drug business are part of a criminal underworld in which violence is always an attendant reality. Drug transactions must be accomplished without recourse to the formal mechanisms of dispute resolution that are usually available in the world of legitimate business. This reality leads to the creation of private mechanisms of enforcement. The drug world is filled with heavily armed and dangerous individuals in the employ of the larger cartels, although even street-level operatives are often armed. These private resources for violence serve to limit market entry, to ward off competitors and predatory criminals, and to maintain internal discipline and security within an organization.

In several areas of the United States, particularly in New York City and Los Angeles, the relatively stable neighborhood criminal organizations that once dominated the heroin and cocaine trade have found new competitors: youthful

Barbaric Violence, Rational Violence

"Regular displays of violence are essential for preventing rip-offs by colleagues, customers, and professional holdup artists. Indeed, upward mobility in the underground economy of the street-dealing world requires a systematic and effective use of violence against one's colleagues, one's neighbors, and, to a certain extent, against oneself. Behavior that appears irrationally violent, 'barbaric,' and ultimately self-destructive to the outsider, can be reinterpreted according to the logic of the underground economy as judicious public relations and long-term investment in one's 'human capital development'" (Bourgeois 1995: 24).

crack dealers. Entry into the crack trade requires only a small investment, since an ounce of cocaine can be converted to 2,500 milligrams of crack. Street gangs or groups of friends and relatives have entered the market, often resulting in competition that touches off explosive violence involving the use of high-powered handguns and automatic weapons.

The dramatic drop in homicides during the 1990s has been linked to the decline of crack (Butterfield 1997). In New York City "in communities that used to have more open-air crack markets than grocery stores, where children grew up dodging crack vials and gunfire, the change from a decade ago is startling. On the surface, crack has disappeared from much of New York, taking with it the ragged and violent vignettes that were a routine part of street life" (Egan 1999c: 1). New York's experience has been replicated in other major cities that had been plagued by the crack epidemic. In a dramatic change in attitude toward crack, "crackheads" became community pariahs. The remaining crack market has moved indoors, or dealers use cellular phones to arrange sales, typically to users who are considerably older than the adolescents who once made up the core of the crack scene.

Dominicans

The Dominican Republic, with a population of 8 million, occupies about two thirds of the Caribbean island of Hispaniola, which it shares with Haiti. Although the Dominican Republic is not as depressed as Haiti, in the mid-1960s political unrest and economic upheavals caused many residents to seek their fortunes by going north. In New York City Dominicans who have legally entered the United States number about 350,000; thousands more are illegal aliens. Some of these immigrants, legal and illegal, have entered the drug trade. Known as Dominican-Yorks, the traffickers keep a low profile in the United States, returning their profits to cities in the Dominican Republic such as San Francisco de Macoris, a city that is conspicuous for its wealth in a country where the per capita income is less than $900 a year (French 1991). The structure of Dominican drug-trafficking organizations is based on familial or regional loyalties.

The center of the Dominican wholesale trade in crack is the uptown Manhattan neighborhood of Washington Heights. In recent years some of the leaders have slipped out of New York and are running operations from their homeland, where corruption is endemic among airport officials and law enforcement. Until 1998 the Dominican Republic refused to extradite its citizens for crimes committed in the United States. In that year two notorious traffickers were sent to New York, where they were wanted for drug trafficking and murder.

Dominicans have demonstrated the necessary talent for moving large amounts of heroin, crack cocaine, and, more recently, ecstasy at the street level. They purchase heroin and cocaine directly from Asian and Colombian importers, sharing a common language and entrepreneurial values with the latter. Ecstasy is purchased in the Netherlands. Dominicans have apparently applied their well-known skills as traders and merchants to become New York City's top traffickers and have captured markets in Pennsylvania. They also control a significant portion of the cocaine trafficking in New England. Dominicans generally provide top-quality uncut drugs at competitive prices, avoiding the common practice of diluting the product as it passes through the distribution chain. Often operating out of grocery stores, bars, and restaurants in Latino neighborhoods, they employ a variety of marketing gimmicks to move their product. In Philadelphia they sold heroin packets with lottery tickets attached that a winner could use to claim an additional twelve packets.

Dominicans developed a reputation as reliable dealers who pay their suppliers promptly and avoid using violence to muscle in on others or maintain exclusive control of a particular market. Instead, they competed on the basis of efficiency and pricing, allowing them to avoid high-profile violence (Pennsylvania Crime Commission 1990). However, while "early Dominican gangs were known for keen marketing techniques . . . their successors in the 1990s mark out their territories" and use violence to maintain hegemony (Kleinknecht 1996: 260–261). Several Dominican groups have become noted for their excessive violence, both to maintain discipline and to deal with competitors. In one instance The Company, a Brooklyn-based gang, even lured a police officer to his death (Wren 1998c).

Dominicans have come to dominate the middle echelon between the Colombians and the street dealers of cocaine and heroin in the New York City area and into New England (Wren 1998a; Rohter and Krauss 1998b). In part this is a result of Colombian dissatisfaction with their Mexican counterparts. By 1995 major Colombian organizations had established themselves in the Dominican Republic to coordinate activities with their Dominican partners. "While the bulk of Colombian cocaine and heroin continues to move through Mexico, the Colombian traffickers have in the last few years come full circle, returning to the Caribbean as a base of operations" (Rohter and Krauss 1998a: 6). The influence of drug money on the island has been pervasive: "Office buildings, hotels and shopping centers are springing up in Santo Domingo, Santiago, and San Francisco de Macoris—often in the gaudy style that some describe as narcodeco" (Rohter and Krauss 1998a: 6). Police corruption is widespread and often coordinated with law enforcement counterparts in Colombia.

Drug traffickers take advantage of the fact that the region of Central America and the Caribbean is located between major drug-producing areas and significant illicit drug markets, that there are hundreds of relatively small islands in the Caribbean with multitudes of cays, and that the socioeconomic situation in most of the countries in the region is difficult. The relatively weak institutional and political situations in some of the countries and the large number of political entities in the Caribbean pose challenges to efforts to ensure strategic coordination in the fight against illicit drug trafficking and abuse.

In the Caribbean a common practice is to airdrop illicit drug consignments into coastal waters and then have them picked up by speedboat. Private vessels, fishing boats, cruisers, and pleasure ships are also increasingly being used in maritime drug trafficking. Because of the increased efforts by the authorities of some countries to combat drug-related crime, drug traffickers have turned to moving their operations quickly to weaker jurisdictions. In addition, illicit drug stockpiling in isolated locations has become more common.

The Dominicans and their Colombian partners have made Haiti, which (along with the Dominican Republic) lies roughly between Colombia and Florida, the fastest-growing transit point for cocaine being shipped to the United States. Haiti has proven attractive to the traffickers because it is the poorest country in the hemisphere, making it relatively cheap to find criminal labor and bribe officials. The police force had to be created from scratch after the old force was abolished in the wake of the U.S. troop landing in 1994, and the police have limited training and resources.

Street-Level Drug Business

Below the wholesale level, selling cocaine or heroin is an easy-entry business, requiring only a source and funds. Any variety of groups can come together to deal heroin, such as street gangs in many urban areas. A variety of black criminal groups exist throughout the United States. Some are homegrown, such as the Gangster Disciples; others, such as Jamaican posses, are imported. There are important black criminal organizations in the heroin business, particularly in New York, Detroit, Chicago, Philadelphia, and Washington, D.C. Whereas African Americans have traditionally been locked out of many activities associated with organized crime (e.g., labor racketeering and loan-sharking) by prejudice, dope is an equal opportunity employer. African American criminal groups made important strides in the heroin business when the Vietnam War exposed many black soldiers to the heroin markets of the Golden Triangle; previously, black drug-trafficking groups had depended on organized crime Families for their heroin. As a result of their overseas experience, black organizations were able to bypass traditional organized crime and buy directly from suppliers in Thailand.

Some street gangs have also been expanding their organizations and drug markets to other states. Los Angeles gangs, in particular the Crips, have moved into Seattle, Denver, Minneapolis, Oklahoma City, St. Louis, and Kansas City as well as smaller cities throughout California. Along with their smaller rival group, the Bloods, the Crips moved east with startling speed. "Neither gang is rigidly hierarchical. Both are broken up into loosely affiliated neighborhood groups called 'sets,' each with 30 to 100 members. Many gang members initially left Southern California to evade police. Others simply expanded the reach of crack by setting up branch operations in places where they visited friends or family members and discovered that the market was ripe" (Witkin 1991: 51).

Thomas Mieczkowski (1986) studied the activities of The Young Boys, Inc., a loosely organized retail heroin group in Detroit. At the center of their activities is a *crew boss*, who receives his supply of heroin from a drug syndicate lieutenant. The crew boss gives a consignment of heroin to each of his seven to twenty *runners*, young (16- to 23-year-old) African American males whom he recruits. Each runner then takes his station on a street adjacent to a public roadway to facilitate purchases from vehicles. To avoid rip-offs and robberies, each crew is guarded by armed men, including the crew boss himself. Runners reported earning about $160 for a 10 1/2 hour workday.

> Participants in these drug networks tend to be the most serious drug delinquents who are frequently hired by adult or older adolescent street drug sellers as runners. Loosely organized into crews of 3 to 12, each boy generally handles small quantities of drugs—for example, two or three packets or bags of heroin. They receive these units "on credit," "up front," or "on loan" from a supplier and are expected to return about 50 to 70 percent of the drug's street value.
>
> In addition to distributing drugs, these youngsters may act as lookouts, recruit customers, and guard street sellers from customer-robbers. They typically are users of marijuana and cocaine, but not heroin. Moreover, in some cities, dealers and suppliers prefer to hire distributors who do not "get high" during an operation. But their employment as runners is not generally steady; it is interspersed with other crimes including robbery, burglary, and theft.
>
> A relatively small number of youngsters who sell drugs develop excellent entrepreneurial skills. Their older contacts come to trust them, and they parlay this trust to advance in the drug business. By the time they are 18 or 19 they can have several years of experience in drug sales, be bosses of their own crews, and handle more than $500,000 a year. (Chaiken and Johnson 1988: 12)

The net profits in heroin for most participants at the street level, however, are rather modest. While dealers typically work long hours and subject themselves to substantial risk of violence and incarceration, their incomes generally range from $1,000 to $2,000 a month. Less successful participants eke out a living that rivals that of minimum wage. Many get involved to support their own drug habits, to supplement earnings from legitimate employment, or both. The sale of cocaine and crack is carried out by thousands of small-time operators who may dominate particular local markets—a public housing complex, city blocks, or simply street corners. Control is exercised through violence.

Income is modest considering the dangers of death or imprisonment, and the sellers often work for less than minimum wage—for example, $30 a day for acting as a lookout, or 50 cents for each vial of crack sold. These may add up to $100 to $200 per week for long hours under unpleasant conditions without unemployment compensation, medical insurance, or any of the usual benefits of legitimate employment. A study in Washington, D.C., found that a majority of drug sellers in the sample did not sell drugs on a daily basis. Their median annual income was about $10,000. Those who sold daily earned about $3,600 a month (Reuter, MacCoun, and Murphy 1990).

The domestic business of cocaine requires only a connection to a Colombian source and sufficient financing to initiate the first buy. Any variety of people several steps removed from the Colombian source are involved in the domestic cocaine business. Because the cocaine clientele is traditionally at least middle-income, distributors likewise tend to come from the (otherwise) respectable middle class. The popularity of crack, however, dramatically altered the drug market at the consumer level, in particular the age of many retailers. James Inciardi and Anne Pottieger, experienced drug researchers, were shocked by the youthfulness of crack dealers compared with those involved in the heroin business: "While both patterns ensnare youth in their formative years, crack dealers are astonishingly more involved in a drug-crime lifestyle at an alarmingly younger age" (1991: 269).

At the retail level, sellers frequently deal several different drugs. Heroin dealers added cocaine to their portfolio when that substance started becoming popular at the end of the 1970s. More recently, crack dealers have reflected a shift in the market by also selling heroin (Chitwood, Comerford, and Weatherby 1998). It is common for long-term users of cocaine to use a depressant to "mellow out." Alcohol is frequently used for this purpose, but cocaine users with access to it prefer heroin.

Marcia Chaiken and Bruce Johnson (1988) state that small drug sales are common among adult users and that some adolescents distribute drugs without being involved in more serious criminal activity. These dealers sell drugs to adolescent friends and relatives less than once a month to support their own drug use, and "most of these adolescents do not consider these activities 'serious' crimes" (Chaiken and Johnson 1988: 10). They rarely have contact with criminal justice agencies: "Since these youths conceal their illicit behavior from most adults, and are likely to participate in many conventional activities with children their age, criminal justice practitioners can take little direct action to prevent occasional adolescent sellers from distributing drugs and recruiting new users" (Chaiken and Johnson 1988: 11).

Street-Level Drug Market

At the retail end of the drug trade, there are two market systems: those that are *person-specific*, relying on personal and/or social networks for information about vendors and potential customers, location, and prices, and those that

Prescription Abuse
In 2007 five people in New Jersey, including a medical doctor and a pharmacist, were charged with having sold one million OxyContin and Percocet (an acetaminophen and Oxycontin compound) tablets for street distribution (Chen 2007).

are *place-specific*, often open-air drug markets that operate in geographically well-defined areas and at identifiable times so that informed buyers can locate a source with relative ease. While open-air markets maximize customer opportunity, participants are more vulnerable to law enforcement efforts. In response open-air may become transformed into closed markets, in which sellers do business only with people they know or those introduced by another trusted person (Hough 2005).

Like more conventional consumer items, drugs sold at the street level often carry a name and/or logo to promote "brand loyalty." "Among the more important marketing techniques are attractive packaging (stamps), name recognition (brand names), and consumer involvement and camaraderie around drug-consuming activities (product name contests). Moreover, product names . . . reflect strong, positive attributes and notions of success, strength, power, excitement, and wealth, encourage consumers to make symbolic connections with these products" (Waterston 1993: 117).

As in other stages of the drug trade, the street-level drug business is filled with violence. Paul Goldstein (1985: 497) reports that violence in the drug trade is sometimes the result of brand deception:

> Dealers mark an inferior quality heroin with a currently popular brand name. Users purchase the good heroin, use it, then repackage the bag with milk sugar for resale. The popular brand is purchased, the bag is "tapped," and further diluted for resale.
>
> These practices get the real dealers of the popular brand very upset. Their heroin starts to get a bad reputation on the streets and they lose sales. Purchasers of the phony bags may accost the real dealers, complaining about the poor quality and demanding their money back. The real dealers then seek out the purveyors of the phony bags. Threats, assaults, and/or homicides may ensue.

In the drug business, as Goldstein (1985) notes, norm violations—for example, a street-level dealer failing to return enough money to his superior in a drug network—often result in violence. Violence almost invariably results from the robbery of a drug dealer. No dealer who wants to remain in the business can allow himself to be robbed without exacting vengeance. Death is also the punishment for a norm violation that, although serious, is nevertheless widespread in the drug business: informing. Informing can be the means of eliminating competition or exacting vengeance for the sale of poor-quality dope, but more often, informing results from an attempt to gain leniency from the criminal justice system.

Occasionally, distinct patterns of injury can be recognized. For example, drug runners—teenagers who carry drugs and money between sellers and buyers—are seen in the emergency room with gunshot wounds to the legs and knees. A more vicious drug-related injury has emerged in the western part of the United States. In this injury, known as "pithing," the victim's spinal cord is cut, and he or she is left alive but paraplegic (De La Rosa, Lambert, and Gropper 1990).

Marijuana and Methamphetamine

The business of drugs involves products other than cocaine and heroin. Substances such as PCP, LSD, methamphetamine, and barbiturates are produced in domestic laboratories; marijuana is also grown in the United States and Canada. The people and groups that manufacture and traffic in these drugs are quite varied. They fit into no particular ethnic pattern; white, rural, working- and middle-class individuals are as likely to be involved as any identifiable racial or ethnic group. For example, there is little or no pattern to marijuana trafficking in the United States. It is an easy-entry business, and a number of relatives, friendship groups, and former military veterans have come together to "do marijuana."

In rugged rural western North Carolina, for example, the same county that historically produced moonshine whiskey now has extensive marijuana cultivation. Patches of marijuana can be grown undetected in remote areas, where it blends with legitimate crops or vegetation. For an illicit farmer a single marijuana plant will bring hundreds if not thousands of dollars on the street. During the July 2002 harvesting season law enforcement officers seized more than 2,000 plants with an estimate street value of $4 million (Cantrell 2002).

The September 11, 2001, terrorist attacks led to substantial tightening of the U.S.-Mexican border that affected marijuana smuggling routes. As a result Mexican organizations have been increasing their presence in the United States, where they grow and harvest marijuana in national forests. In March and April growers are driven to planting spots that were scouted during the winter. The growers move into the forest with seedlings and lightweight irrigation systems and live there until autumn, when the crop is harvested (Verini 2007).

Canadian marijuana known as "B.C. bud," a highly potent form named for British Columbia, where it is grown, is smuggled into Washington State and points east as far as Michigan. The trade is often two-way, with cocaine flowing north in exchange for marijuana flowing south. Criminal organizations that are involved in the trade include outlaw motorcycle clubs, Asian gangs, and Indo-Canadians, whose knowledge of the terrain gives them an advantage in transportation.

B.C. bud sells for about $3,000 to $3,500 a pound and is usually grown indoors. By way of contrast, marijuana smuggled across the southern border sells for about $400 to $1,000 a pound. The violence associated with the drug trade on the Mexican border has also become part of the Canadian scene. In 2005, for example, four officers of the Royal Canadian Mounted Police were murdered while searching for a marijuana-growing operation (Kershaw 2005).

Fewer than a dozen chemists are believed to be manufacturing nearly all of the LSD that is available in the United States. Some have probably been operating since the 1960s. LSD manufacturers and traffickers can be separated into two groups. The first group, located in northern California, is composed of chemists (commonly referred to as "cooks") and traffickers who work together in close association; typically, they are major producers who are capable of distributing LSD nationwide. The second group is made up of independent producers who, operating on a comparatively limited scale, can be found throughout the country; their production is intended for local consumption (Drug Enforcement Administration n.d.a).

LSD chemists and top-echelon traffickers form an insiders' fraternity of sorts. They have remained at large because there are so few of them. Their exclusivity is not surprising, given that LSD synthesis is a difficult process to master. Although cooks need not be formally trained chemists, they must adhere to precise and complex production procedures. In instances in which the cook is not a chemist, the production recipe most likely was passed on by personal instruction from a formally trained chemist. At the highest levels of the traffic, at which LSD crystal is purchased in gram or multiple-gram quantities from wholesale sources of supply, it rarely is diluted with adulterants, a common practice with cocaine, heroin, and other illicit drugs. However, to prepare the crystal for production in retail dosage units, it must be diluted with binding agents or be dissolved and diluted in liquids. The dilution of LSD crystal typically follows a standard, predetermined recipe to ensure uniformity of the final product. Excessive dilution yields less potent dosage units that soon become unmarketable (Drug Enforcement Administration n.d.).

Production of methamphetamine has blossomed in parts of rural America. "In Texas, most of the labs are located in rural areas and are reportedly set up and run by local residents. The predominant pattern for methamphetamine lab operations in the plains of West Texas and in heavily wooded East Texas is similar to the operation of small-scale production and distribution of moonshine whiskey during the prohibition era; individually owned and operated, with networks of local users, but also with connections for export to urban population centers" (Spence 1989: 6). In Arkansas outlaw chemists have been stealing ammonia normally used for fertilizer to use instead for conversion to methamphetamine by the "Nazi method," so called because German troops used anhydrous ammonia in World War II (Parker 1999). In 2002 in the state of Washington's rural Snohomish County there were more methamphetamine lab seizures than in New York, Pennsylvania, and New England combined (Egan 2002). In farming communities isolation and the easy availability of one of the drug's main ingredients, anhydrous ammonia, a fertilizer, have spawned methamphetamine production (Butterfield 2004b).

The number of meth labs seized in North Carolina has increased dramatically, from eighteen in 2000 to thirty-four in 2001 and forty-eight in the first six months of 2002. About half of these seizures have been in the rural mountain area in the western part of the state. Similar activity has been reported in rural communities in Tennessee and Georgia. The labs are inexpensive for dealers to set up, but the cost to the taxpayers for cleanup ranges from $2,000 to $20,000 per lab and is accomplished by crews wearing hazardous material suits for protection from fumes and deadly liquids. These suits, which range in cost from $700 to $2,000, frequently need to be disposed of after one use (Brevorka 2002).

As was noted earlier, in recent years there has been an increase in the involvement of Mexican gangs operating in southern California, where they produce methamphetamine in unpopulated desert areas. "Once the domain of outlaw biker gangs, the nation's meth trade has been taken over by Mexican drug families in the rural belt from San Diego County to Redding. Operating from Sinaloa and other states deep inside Mexico, these families oversee teams of cookers dispatched to orchards, cotton fields, chicken ranches, and abandoned dairies north of the border" (Arax and Goirman 1995: 1).

Although the vast majority of MDMA (ecstasy) that is consumed in the Unites States is produced in Europe—primarily the Netherlands and Belgium—a limited number of MDMA labs operate here. In recent years Israeli crime syndicates, some composed of Russian émigrés associated with Russian organized crime syndicates, have forged relationships with Western European traffickers and gained control over a significant share of the European market. The Israeli syndicates are currently the primary source for U.S. distribution groups.

Overseas ecstasy-trafficking organizations smuggle the drug in shipments of 10,000 or more tablets via express mail services, couriers aboard commercial airline flights, or air freight shipments from several major European cities to cities in the United States. While ecstasy costs as little as 25 cents per pill to produce, wholesale prices range from $5 to $20, and retail prices range from $10 to $50 a dose. Traffickers in ecstasy use brand names and logos as marketing tools and to distinguish their product from those of competitors. The logos are produced to coincide with holidays or special events. Among the more popular logos are butterflies, lightning bolts, and four-leaf clovers (Office of National Drug Control Policy 2004e).

MONEY LAUNDERING

Drug traffickers operating at the upper levels of the business have a serious problem: What to do with the large amounts of cash the business is continually generating? Ever since Al Capone was imprisoned for income tax evasion, successful criminals have sought to launder their illegally secured money. Further complicating the problem is that this cash is frequently in small denominations. In some cases "laundering" may simply be an effort to secure hundred-dollar bills so that the sums of money are more easily handled (500 bills weigh about one pound; $1 million in twenties weighs about 100 pounds) or to convert them into one or more cashier's checks.

To avoid Internal Revenue Service (IRS) reporting requirements under the Bank Secrecy Act, transfers of cash to cashier's checks or hundred-dollar bills must take place in amounts under $10,000 or through banking officials who, for a fee (generally 5 percent), agree not to fill out a Currency Transaction Report (CTR). A CTR is required for each deposit, withdrawal, or exchange of currency or monetary instruments in excess of $10,000. It must be submitted to the IRS within fifteen days of the transaction. In 1984 tax amendments extended the reporting requirements to anyone who receives more than $10,000 in cash in the course of a trade or business. A CMIR (Currency and Monetary

Modern Money Laundering

"Modern financial systems permit criminals to transfer instantly millions of dollars through personal computers and satellite dishes. Money is laundered through currency exchange houses, stock brokerage houses, gold dealers, casinos, automobile dealerships, insurance companies, and trading companies. The use of private banking facilities, offshore banking, free trade zones, wire systems, shell corporations, and trade financing all have the ability to mask illegal activities. The criminal's choice of money laundering vehicles is limited only by his or her creativity" (U.S. Department of State 1999: 3). The international trade in gold has proven to be an excellent vehicle for concealing the source of funds. Drug profits are used to buy gold, which is then legally exported for the jewelry trade and sold, the money returning to the original sources, that is, "laundered" (D. Kaplan 1999).

Instrument Report) must be filed for cash or certain monetary instruments exceeding $10,000 in value that enter or leave the United States. Federal Reserve regulations require banks to file suspicious-activity reports when they suspect possible criminal wrongdoing in transactions. Attempts to strengthen these regulations have met vigorous opposition from the banking industry (Wahl 1999).

Currency exchanges (*casas de cambio*) have sprouted up along the Texas-Mexico border. These poorly regulated enterprises accept (illegally) large amounts of cash. They pool many customers' funds into one account and deposit the money in a domestic or foreign bank, keeping records on what is owed to each customer. When a foreign drug trafficker wants to send money to his own country, the *casa* operator wires the funds from the bank to the trafficker's foreign account or accounts. Even when a U.S. bank completes a CTR, it names the *casa* as the owner of the funds, not the actual owner. In the Houston area, in addition to *casas* there are *giro* (wire) houses. In general, the *giros* move drug money to Colombia, while the *casas* move Mexican drug money (Webster and McCampbell 1992).

In some schemes money launderers use dozens of people (known as "smurfs") to convert cash into money orders and cashier's checks that do not specify payees or that are made out to fictitious individuals. Each transaction is held to less than $10,000 to avoid the need for a CTR. One ring operating out of Forest Hills, New York, employed dozens of people who used about thirty banks in New York and New Jersey to launder about $100 million a year for the Cali cartel. The checks were pasted between the pages of magazines and shipped to Cali, Colombia; from there the money was transferred to banks in Panama. In 1989 sixteen people were indicted when one of the banks became suspicious of the unusual number of cash transactions and reported them to federal authorities (Morgan 1989). "Smurfing" has now been made a federal crime, and increased bank scrutiny has made tellers suspicious of cash transactions just under $10,000. In response, smurfs have reduced transactions to as low as $5,000 and often make dozens of transactions in a day, typically in banks that do not usually have long lines (Walter 1990).

Advances in banking technology have greatly facilitated money laundering. It has become increasingly difficult for the government to effectively monitor banking transactions. "An alternative to physically removing money from the country is to deposit the cash, then transfer the funds electronically to other domestic and foreign banks, financial institutions, or securities accounts. Swiss law enforcement officials report that when money is transferred by wire to Switzerland, it seldom comes directly from the country of origin, rather it is 'prewashed' in a third country such as Panama, the Bahamas, the Cayman Islands, or Luxembourg" (Webster and McCampbell 1992: 4). The sheer volume of wire transfers makes accounting difficult; one major bank in New York handles about 40,000 wire transfers each business day.

A customer can instruct his or her personal computer to direct a bank's computer to transfer money from a U.S. account to one in a foreign bank. The bank's computer then tells a banking clearinghouse that assists in the transfer; no human talks to another. Although depositing more than $10,000 in cash into an account requires the filing of a CTR, the government receives more than 7 million such reports annually and is hopelessly behind in reviewing them. The daily average volume of U.S. transactions is about $7 billion. On one day it actually amounted to $1.25 trillion (Labaton 1989).

As part of an overseas laundering scheme a lawyer acting on behalf of a client creates a "paper" (or "boilerplate") company in any one of a number of countries that have strict privacy statutes, such as Panama, which has over 200,000 companies registered. The funds to be laundered are transferred physically or wired to the company's account in a local bank. The company then transfers the money to the local branch of a large international bank. The paper company is then able to borrow money from the United States (or any other) branch of this bank, using the overseas deposit as security (Walter 1990). An employment contract can also be set up between the launderer and his or her "paper" company for an imaginary service for which payments are made to the launderer. In some cases the lawyer may also establish a "boilerplate bank"; like the company, this is a shell. Not only does the criminal get the money laundered, but he or she also earns a tax write-off for the interest on the loan. Under the Bank Secrecy Act, wiring or physically transporting cash or other financial instruments out of the country in excess of $10,000 must be reported to U.S. customs officials. Once the money is out of the United States, however, it can be impossible for the IRS to trace it. Liechtenstein, with a population of 32,000, has 80,000 trust companies and associated banks whose transactions are protected by bank secrecy laws; the tiny principality has been a favorite for money laundering by the Sicilian Mafia, Colombian drug cartels, and Russian organized crime (Tagliabue 2000).

Another method of laundering funds without actually moving cash out of the country involves otherwise legitimate companies that import goods from the United States. Representatives of the Cali cartel in the United States paid for imported goods with dollars that went to the exporters. In return, the participating companies paid the cartel in Colombia at slightly less than the true exchange rate (C. Krauss and Frantz 1995). Instead of shipping currency, drug proceeds can also be used to purchase easily sold goods such as expensive liquor or electronic products. These are shipped to Colombia and sold at a 20–30 percent discount (Sanger 1995).

SUMMARY

Trafficking in illegal drugs at the highest wholesale levels is controlled by international organized crime syndicates from Colombia, Mexico, and other countries. Headquartered in a foreign country, leaders maintain tight control of their workers through highly compartmentalized cell structures.

Control of most of the world's cocaine industry remains in the hands of Colombian organizations, which have expanded into heroin. Colombia, a nation of 26 million, has a violent history with a culture to match. The country is wracked by leftist insurgencies and right-wing militias, both using drug trafficking to finance their efforts. For distribution in the United States Colombian organizations are aligned with Mexican and Dominican organizations.

Mexico, an urbanized nation of about 95 million, has a long history of political corruption that has affected law enforcement, and leading drug traffickers are publicly celebrated. Mexican drug organizations have cells operating in the United States; in addition to dealing Mexican-produced heroin, they have partnered with Colombians to distribute cocaine. Although they are latecomers to the trade, Mexican drug organizations have also become dominant in the manufacture and distribution of methamphetamine.

The Golden Triangle of Southeast Asia encompasses parts of Laos Thailand, and Myanmar (formerly Burma). Myanmar accounts for about 90 percent of the total heroin production of the Golden Triangle, is the world's second largest source of opium and heroin, and is also a major producer of methamphetamine. The region has a history of colonialism, opium production, and the use the heroin trade to finance political efforts. At the center of much of the traffic in Southeast Asian heroin are Chinese Triads, which have extensive connections in overseas Chinese communities throughout the world.

The Golden Triangle of Southwest Asia includes Iran, Afghanistan, and Pakistan. Tribal groups in Afghanistan, which extend across the border into Pakistan, have a long martial history supported by opium production. As in the Golden Triangle, politics intersects with opium and hampers efforts to deal effectively with drug trafficking.

Drug trafficking has connections to terrorism. Terrorists may use the business to finance their efforts and/or personnel in drug and terrorist groups may overlap. Terrorists can offer military skills and weapons, while traffickers provide a source of revenue and expertise in illicit transfer and laundering of proceeds.

The profit potential in a business in which transactions must be accomplished without recourse to the formal mechanisms of dispute resolution leads to the creation of private mechanisms of enforcement and boundless violence. Drugs have provided lucrative opportunities to African American criminals who had been locked out of other areas of criminal success by the same prejudice that their legitimate counterparts endured.

Below the wholesale level, selling drugs is an easy-entry business, requiring only a source and funds, leading a variety of groups to enter the trade, such as street gangs in many urban areas. At the lowest retail levels are people who, while taking significant risks from law enforcement and other criminals, barely eke out a living. There is less specialization farther down the "food chain," and at the lowest levels of the drug trade can be found the "walking drugstore," who retails a variety of substances.

Methamphetamine production has blossomed in rural parts of the United States, where in farming communities there is easy access to anhydrous ammonia, a fertilizer. Meth labs contain toxic chemicals, and cleanup of a seized lab can cost government thousands of dollars.

At the wholesale levels, drugs generate large amounts of cash whose source must be disguised—hence the term *money laundering*. There are many schemes to accomplish this, some relatively simple and others involving complex overseas financial transactions.

Our examination of the business of illegal drugs provides a framework for understanding the problems that confront law enforcement officials who are trying to constrain trafficking in dangerous drugs, the topic of the next chapter.

REVIEW QUESTIONS

1. What is meant by "compartmentalization" in the drug business?
2. How did the demise of the French Connection change the drug business?
3. Why has it been so difficult for the Colombian government to wipe out the growing of coca?
4. What is the relationship between Colombian and Mexican drug organizations?
5. How has the popularity of crack cocaine affected the business of drugs?
6. What are the major heroin-producing areas of the world?
7. What is the link between politics and the production of heroin in the Golden Triangle?
8. What is the link between politics and the production of heroin in the Golden Crescent?
9. What has been the traditional role of Chinese organizations in drug trafficking?
10. Why is it impossible to control the production of opium in the Golden Crescent?
11. Why is the drug business typically violent?
12. Why is the street-level drug business an easy-entry enterprise?
13. What is the purpose of money laundering?
14. What are the various ways in which money laundering can be accomplished?

12 CHAPTER | Drug Laws and Law Enforcement

Drug laws reflect the decision of some persons that other persons who wish to consume certain substances should not be permitted to act on their preferences. Nor should anyone be permitted to satisfy the desires of drug consumers by making and selling the prohibited drug. . . . [The] most important characteristic of the legal approach to drug use is that these consumptive and commercial activities are being regulated by force.

Randy Barnett (1987: 73)

"The most important precipitating factor in narcotic addiction is degree of access to narcotic drugs" (Ausubel 1980: 4), an assertion that is supported by research into heroin consumption (Anglin 1988). This is why narcotic use is higher in the inner city than in the suburbs and why the incidence of narcotic addiction in the United States approached the zero level during World War II. This also helps explain the relatively high level of drug abuse among physicians, in particular, anesthesiologists whose specialty offers ready access to fentanyl (McDougall 2006). "Thus, no matter how great the cultural attitudinal tolerance for addictive practices is, or how strong individual personality predispositions are, nobody can become addicted to narcotic drugs without access to them. Hence the logic of a law enforcement component in prevention" (Ausubel 1980: 4).

If drug abuse is seen as based on some combination of susceptibility and availability—"that drug abuse occurs when a prone individual is exposed to a high level of availability" (R. S. Smart 1980: 46)—it follows that a considerable reduction in availability can reduce drug abuse.[1] Availability also involves questions of cost; at some point the cost of purchasing a drug can reduce to near zero its availability to potential abusers, and law enforcement efforts can affect the cost of illegal drugs.

Before we can examine the strategies and techniques that law enforcement agencies use to deal with drug trafficking and to reduce the availability of drugs of abuse, we need to consider three issues that severely constrain law enforcement in general and drug law enforcement in particular: constitutional limitations, jurisdictional limitations, and corruption.

CONSTITUTIONAL CONSTRAINTS

Law enforcement agencies in the United States operate under significant constitutional constraints, generally referred to as *due process*—literally meaning the *process that is due* a person before something disadvantageous can be done to him or her. Due process restrains government from arbitrarily depriving a person of life, liberty, or property. There is an inherent tension between society's desire for security and safety and the value we place on liberty. Herbert Packer (1968) refers to this as a conflict between two conceptual models of criminal justice: crime control and due process. (A conceptual model is a way of representing an idea that facilitates discussion and understanding of the reality represented by the model.)

Conceptual Models of Criminal Justice

The *crime control model* "is based on the proposition that the repression of criminal conduct is by far the most important function to be performed by the criminal justice process" (Packer 1968: 158). The stress is on achieving the

---

[1] That is, of course, if we discount the abuse of alcohol and the possibility—or probability—that people who are unable to secure their preferred drug will switch to alcohol.

greatest amount of societal security and safety. Effective crime control requires a high level of efficiency; the system must be able to investigate, apprehend, prosecute, and convict a large proportion of criminal offenders. However, the system must respond to these cases with only limited resources. Consequently, efficiency demands that cases be handled speedily, with a minimum of formality and without time-consuming challenges. This efficiency can be accomplished only by a presumption of guilt: "The supposition is that the screening processes operated by the police and prosecutors are reliable indicators of probable guilt" (p. 160). To maximize crime control after this screening, the system must move expeditiously to conviction and sentencing. The crime control model is characterized by a high level of confidence in the ability of police and prosecutors to separate the guilty from the innocent. It conflicts with the due process model.

The *due process model* stresses the need for protecting individual freedoms. It assumes that the criminal justice system is deficient and stresses the possibility of error: "People are notoriously poor observers of disturbing events—the more emotion-arousing the context, the greater the possibility that recollection will be incorrect; confessions and admissions by persons in police custody may be induced by physical or psychological coercion so that the police end up hearing what the suspect thinks they want to hear rather than the truth; witnesses may be animated by a bias or interest that no one would trouble to discover except one specially charged with protecting the interests of the accused (as the police are not)" (Packer 1968: 163).

Due process confronts crime control and its need for efficiency and speed with an obstacle course of formalities, technicalities, and civil rights: "Power is always subject to abuse—sometimes subtle, other times, as in the criminal justice process, open and ugly. Precisely because of its potency in subjecting the individual to the coercive power of the state, the criminal justice process must . . . be subjected to controls that prevent it from operating with maximal efficiency" (Packer 1968: 166). The due process model requires the system to slow down until it "resembles a factory that has to devote a substantial part of its input to quality control" (Packer 1968: 165)—due process guarantees.

Due process, while it protects individual liberty, also benefits the criminal population by guaranteeing the right to remain silent (Fifth Amendment), the right to counsel (Sixth Amendment), the right to be tried speedily by an impartial jury (Sixth Amendment), and the right to confront witnesses (Sixth Amendment). The Fourth Amendment and the exclusionary rule are particularly important for drug law enforcement.

The Fourth Amendment and the Exclusionary Rule

The Fourth Amendment guarantees that "the right of the people to be secure in their persons, houses, papers and effects, against unreasonable searches and seizures shall not be violated, and no Warrants shall issue, but upon probable

Figure 12.1 | Crime Control versus Due Process

cause, supported by Oath or affirmation, and particularly describing the place to be searched, and the persons or things to be seized." In practice, information sufficient to justify a search warrant in drug cases is difficult to obtain; in contrast to such conventional crimes as robbery and burglary, there is an absence of innocent victims who will report the crime in drug cases. The exclusionary rule is the court's way of enforcing the Fourth Amendment; it provides that evidence that is obtained in violation of the Fourth Amendment cannot be entered as evidence in a criminal trial (*Weeks v. United States*, 232 U.S. 383, 1914; *Mapp v. Ohio*, 357 U.S. 643, 1961), although there are a number of exceptions that are beyond the scope of this book. The purpose of the exclusionary rule is to control the behavior of law enforcement agents, for example, making drug enforcement efforts that violate the Constitution not worth the effort. (See Figure 12.1.)

To respond effectively to drug trafficking, law enforcement officials require information about the activities of suspected traffickers. The Fourth Amendment and Title III of the Omnibus Crime Control and Safe Streets Act of 1968 (18 U.S.C. Section 2510-520) place restraints on how the government can secure this information. Thus, to surreptitiously intercept conversations by wiretapping telephones or using electronic devices ("bugging"), officials must secure a court order that, like a search warrant, must be based on information that is sufficient to meet the legal standard of probable cause. When an order to intercept electronic communications is secured (generally referred to as a "Title III"), it is quite limited, requires extensive documentation, and demands that the people whose communications are being intercepted be notified after the order expires. These requirements make electronic surveillance expensive, in terms of personnel hours expended, and difficult to accomplish properly.

The supervision of drug law enforcement agents is also difficult, because they typically operate covertly or undercover. This means that "legal control over agents is problematic, and the circumstances of arrest are often such that there is a great temptation to perjury, violation of the exclusionary rule, misuse of informants, discretionary dropping, overlooking and altering charges, and other violations of procedural and/or legal rules" (J. Williams, Redlinger, and Manning 1979: 6). The greater the pressure on law enforcement officers "to do something about drugs," the greater is the temptation to avoid the significant constraints of due process and take unlawful (though often effective) shortcuts.

JURISDICTIONAL LIMITATIONS

The U.S. Constitution provides for a form of government in which powers are diffused horizontally and vertically. This is accomplished by three branches—legislative, judicial, and executive—and four levels of government within each branch: federal, state, county, and municipal (Figure 12.2). Although each level of government has responsibilities for responding to drug abuse and drug trafficking, there is little or no coordination among them. Each level responds to the problem of drugs independently of the others. Federalism was part of a deliberate design to help protect us against tyranny; unfortunately, it also provides us with a level of inefficiency that significantly handicaps efforts to curtail drug trafficking.

On the federal level, a host of executive branch agencies (to be examined later), ranging from the military to the Federal Bureau of Investigation, are responsible for combating drug trafficking. The separate federal judicial system is responsible for trying drug cases, and the legislative branch is responsible for enacting drug legislation and allocating funds for federal drug law enforcement efforts. At the local level are about 20,000 police agencies. Each state has state-level drug law enforcement agents, a state police or similar agency, and agencies that manage prisons and the parole system (if one exists). County government is usually responsible for prosecuting defendants, and a county-level agency, usually the sheriff, is responsible for operating jails. The county may also have a police department with drug law enforcement responsibilities under, or independent of, the sheriff's office, and almost every municipality has a police department whose officers enforce drug laws. Each of these levels of government has taxing authority and allocates resources with little or no consultation with other levels of government. The sum total is a degree of inefficiency surpassing that of most other democratic nations.

U.S. efforts against drug abuse are also limited by national boundaries: Cocaine and heroin originate where U.S. law enforcement has no jurisdiction. The Bureau of International Narcotics Matters within the Department of State has primary responsibility for coordinating international programs and gaining the cooperation of foreign governments in antidrug efforts. But the bureau has no authority to force governments to act in a manner that is beneficial to U.S.

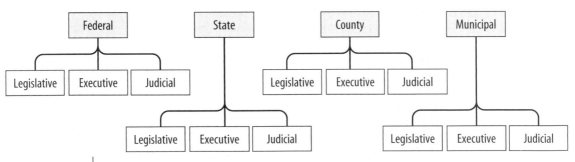

Figure 12.2 | Governmental Complexity

efforts in dealing with cocaine or heroin. Elaine Sciolino (1988: E3) reports that the bureau "has little influence even within the department [of State]. Foreign Service officers," she states, "readily admit that they try to avoid drug-enforcement assignments because they generally do not result in promotions." The State Department also collects intelligence on policy-level international narcotics developments, while the Central Intelligence Agency (CIA) collects strategic narcotics intelligence and is responsible for coordinating foreign intelligence on narcotics. The CIA, however, has often protected drug traffickers who have provided useful foreign intelligence. U.S. efforts against drug trafficking are often sacrificed to foreign policy (Sciolino and Engelberg 1988).

International Efforts

In 1988 the International Convention Against Illicit Traffic in Narcotic Drugs and Psychotropic Substances was adopted in Vienna, with two main purposes:

> First, to establish an internationally recognized set of offenses relating to drug trafficking that are to be criminalized under the domestic law of the parties to the convention; and second, to create a framework for international cooperation to enhance the prospect that traffickers and others who profit from trafficking will be brought to justice. . . .
>
> The Convention focuses on the eradication of drugs and drug-producing laboratories; the international transportation of precursor chemicals used to produce illegal drugs; the tracing of laundered drug trade profits back to the drug cartels; and the worldwide extradition of drug criminals so that they can have no safe havens. Significantly, the Convention obligates parties to make money laundering an extraditable offense, to afford the widest measure of international mutual legal assistance in judicial proceedings, and to cooperate closely to enhance the effectiveness of law enforcement actions to suppress narcotics trafficking and related offenses. (Thornburgh 1989: 59)

In 1994 President Bill Clinton signed legislation authorizing the president to provide assistance for the prevention and suppression of international drug trafficking and money laundering. While international law (multinational treaties) provides the basis for eradicating illicit poppy and coca cultivation, adherence to treaties depends on a level of cooperation that is often sacrificed on the altar of domestic economic and political realities (discussed in Chapter 13). Under treaties coca- and poppy-producing countries are to limit their cultivation acreage to a level that is in line with legitimate world needs. Strict controls over growers require them to deliver their crops to a government monopoly to prevent diversion to the black market. Crops growing wild are to be destroyed. The price paid by the government, however, is not competitive with that offered by traffickers, and the illegal diversion of coca or opium is the only significant source of cash for many peasant growers, whose standard of living is already marginal. Attempts to substitute other cash crops have met with only limited success because such programs cannot challenge the reality of the marketplace. As was noted in Chapter 11, coca and poppies are grown in regions where governments often have only nominal control.

On Being Tough on Drugs

He was famous in the Texas panhandle, an area overrun with methamphetamines, for his unyielding prosecution of drug offenders. In 2005 Richard James Roach, the outspoken and hot-tempered Republican prosecutor for five counties, was arrested by Federal Bureau of Investigation (FBI) agents for stealing meth-amphetamine and other drugs from police seizures. Before his arrest he had been injecting himself with methamphetamine (Blumenthal 2005). In 2005 the former district attorney was sentenced to five years in a federal prison.

Jurisdictional limitations, however, can sometimes overcome constitu-tional restrictions. For example, because the Bill of Rights applies only to actions of the U.S. government, the Fourth Amendment and exclusionary rule do not govern seizures in foreign countries by those nations' police. This holds even when the evidence that is seized is from U.S. citizens; thus, it would be admissible in a U.S. court (Anderson 1992). Furthermore, the Supreme Court has held that constitutional protections do not obtain in U.S. government actions against foreign nationals on foreign soil. In *United States v. Verdugo-Urquidez* (110 S.Ct. 1056 1990) a Mexican national who was suspected in the 1985 torture-murder of a Drug Enforcement Administration (DEA) agent was apprehended by Mexican police on a U.S. warrant and turned over to U.S. marshals at the California border. At the request of the DEA, Mexican police, without a warrant, searched the fugitive's two residences and seized in-criminating documents, which were turned over to the DEA. The evidence was ruled admissible.

In a 1992 ruling on another case involving the DEA agent's murder, the Supreme Court ruled that kidnapping a suspect on foreign soil does not prevent the suspect from being tried in the United States. In this case (*United States v. Alvarez Machain*, 504 U.S.) Mexican bounty hunters kidnapped a medical doctor and took him to El Paso; they were paid $20,000 and given the right to settle with their families in the United States. The Mexican government reacted with outrage to the decision.

CORRUPTION

In Chapter 11 we examined the complex world of drug trafficking and the enormous profits that accrue to many of those involved. The easy availability of large sums of money and the clandestine nature of the business make drug law enforcement vulnerable to corruption. Two basic strategies are available to law enforcement agencies—reactive and proactive—and many use a combination of both.

Reactive law enforcement has its parallel in firefighting: Firefighters remain in their fire stations, equipment at the ready, until they get a call for service. Reactive law enforcement encourages citizens to report crimes; the agency will then respond to the reports. This type of law enforcement is used for dealing with such conventional criminal behavior as murder, rape, assault, robbery,

On Being Shocked

We should be shocked not that there are police officers on the take but that there are police officers who are not on the take. Making $35,000 a year, they arrest people who are driving cars worth several times that (Boaz 1990). The French Connection heroin case, the subject of a best-selling book and an Academy Award–winning movie (Best Picture and Best Actor in 1971) is an example.

In 1962 Detectives Eddie "Popeye" Egan (played in the movie by Gene Hackman) and his partner Sonny Grosso (played by Roy Scheider) smashed an international drug ring that was smuggling Turkish heroin into New York from Marseilles. That same year, the drugs that were seized in connection with the case—fifty-seven pounds of almost pure heroin—were vouchered with the police property clerk by Detectives Egan and Grosso. In 1972 the Police Commissioner of the City of New York held a news conference: The French Connection heroin, he announced, had been stolen and replaced with white flour. Several days later, an inventory of the property clerk's office revealed that additional heroin was missing: A total of nearly 400 pounds had been stolen—*by police officers* (Wallance 1981). In 1989 a DEA supervisory agent who had worked on the French Connection case was indicted for transporting more than sixty-two pounds of cocaine from Miami to Boston (Berke 1989).

burglary, and theft, which are likely to be reported to the police. (It should be noted, however, that with the exception of murder and auto theft, studies indicate that most crimes of these types are *not* reported to the police.) *Proactive law enforcement* requires officers or agents to seek out indications of criminal behavior, always a necessity when the criminal violation includes victim participation (e.g., gambling, prostitution, and drugs). These crimes are often described as consensual or "victimless," although they clearly have victims who are unlikely to report the crime to the police. The problem of corruption is in part tied to the proactive strategy.

Exposure to Temptation

To seek out criminal activity in the most efficient manner possible, proactive law enforcement officers must conceal their identities and otherwise deceive the criminals they are stalking. As James Q. Wilson (1978: 59) points out, both reactive and proactive law enforcement officers are exposed to opportunities for graft, but the latter are more severely tested: The reactive officer, "were he to accept money or favors to act other than as his duty required, would have to conceal or alter information about a crime already known to his organization." The proactive agent, however, "can easily agree to overlook offenses known to him but to no one else or to participate in illegal transactions (buying or selling drugs) for his own rather than for the organization's advantage." Undercover officers pretending to be criminals are difficult to supervise; the agency they work often for knows only what the agents tell it.

Mexican Drug Czar Sentenced

A Mexican court sentenced an army general, who also happened to be the national antidrug chief, to thirty-two years and forty years for taking bribes from the Juarez cartel to aid its operations while cracking down on those of its rivals. A codefendant, the state police chief in the western state of Jalisco, was sentenced to twenty-one years (Associated Press 2000a).

Cops versus Soldiers
In 2006, eight Colombian soldiers were arrested for killing ten antinarcotics police officers. The soldiers were reported to be in the employ of right-wing paramilitary militias that were seeking to protect their cocaine-smuggling operations (Reuters 2006).

There is also corruption in foreign countries that grow, process, or serve as transshipment stations for illegal substances.[2] In fact, the corrupt official is an essential ingredient in the drug business, according to the President's Commission on Organized Crime (1986). The commission concluded that "[c]orruption linked to drug trafficking is a widespread phenomenon among political and military leaders, police and other authorities in virtually every country touched by the drug trade. The easily available and enormous amounts of money generated through drug transactions present a temptation too great for many in positions of authority to resist" (p. 178). In addition to corruption, there is the problem of brutality. The militaries in many drug source and transshipment countries have earned widespread condemnation for violating basic human rights.

Informants

Corruption is often intertwined with the problem of informants. Informants come in two basic categories; the "good citizen" and the "criminal." The former is such a rarity, particularly in drug law enforcement, that we will deal only with the criminal informant, the individual who helps law enforcement in order to further his or her own personal ends. These include vengeance, efforts to drive competition out of business, and/or financial rewards, but most frequently the information is given to "work off a beef"—to secure leniency for his or her own criminal activities that have become known to the authorities. Jerald Cloyd (1982: 188n) found that one federal district had a specified menu for every "beef": For each arrest resulting from informant assistance and yielding approximately the same amount of drugs that the defendant is being charged with, there is "a reduction of charges by one count. Being charged with two counts (one count of possession, one of possession with intent to sell), one arrest would get her a reduction of one count (felony possession) in exchange for an expedient plea of guilty. One good arrest and a guilty plea would reduce the charge to misdemeanor possession. Two good arrests would get her case dismissed."

Despite law enforcement agency regulations, often "while serving as informers, suspects are allowed to engage in illegal activity" notes Joseph Goldstein (1982: 37). "Continued use of narcotics is condoned; the narcotics

---

[2] For an examination of corruption in Mexico, see Gomez-Cespedes (1999) and O'Day and Venecia (1999).

From the Newspapers

- "[NYPD] Detectives Called Drug Couriers." *New York Times* (October 26, 2000): C20.
- "10 Cops Arrested on Federal Charges of Aiding Traffickers." *Chicago Tribune* (March 23, 2001): 8.
- "Ex-Cops Sentenced in Huge Drug Sting." *Chicago Tribune* (August 10, 2002): 12.
- "Sting Snags Cop in Drug Cash Theft." *Chicago Tribune* (September 7, 2002): 15.
- "Indicted Police Officer Tests Positive for Cocaine." *Chicago Tribune* (January 30, 2003): Sec. 2: 3.
- "Ex-Cop Held in Drug Theft, Sale: Cocaine Evidence Fueled a Lavish Lifestyle." *Chicago Tribune* (February 7, 2003): Sec. 2: 1, 7.
- "Hunt Rogues in Blue: Bust of 2 Narcs in Drug Cash Theft Sparks Widening Corruption Probe." *New York Daily News* (December 14, 2003): 3.
- "Cop Used Drug Cash for Home." *New York Daily News* (April 29, 2004): 2.
- "2 Newark [NJ] Officers Indicted in Drug Thefts." *New York Times* (October 2, 2004): B4.
- "Bust Bronx Cop in Drug-Heist Plot." *New York Daily News* (December 11, 2004): 6.
- "Retired Detective Pleads Guilty in Drug Case." *New York Times* (June 26, 2005): B3.
- "Cop is Indicted in Scheme to Rob Drug Dealers." *New York Daily News* (May 19, 2006): 4.
- "Six [New Jersey] Police Officers Charged with Protecting Drug Ring." *New York Times* (July 12, 2006): B3.
- "New Jersey Ex-Trooper Gets 24-Year Sentence for Involvement with Drug Gang." *New York Times* (July 15, 2006): B5.
- "Boston Officers Arrested on Drug Charges," *New York Times* (July 22, 2006): 11.
- "Ex-Detective Turned Drug Dealer Gets 6-Year Prison Sentence." *New York Times* (October 6, 2006): B3.
- "Ex-Police Lieutenant Gets Prison Term in Drug Money Case." *New York Times* (October 13, 2006): B2.
- "A Virginia Sheriff is Charged With Selling Drug Evidence." *New York Times* (November 3, 2006): 24.
- "Virginia: Ex-Officers Plead Guilty in Drug Scheme." *New York Times* (December 29, 2006): 23.

detective generally is not concerned with the problem of informants who make buys and use some of the evidence themselves." Goldstein points out that although "informers are usually warned that their status does not give them a 'license to peddle,' possession of a substantial amount of narcotics may be excused" (1982: 37).

Informing for Profit . . .

While the behavior of criminal informants is usually motivated by a desire to avoid or ameliorate imprisonment, informing can also be quite profitable, as the case of Philip Han reveals. Between 1987 and 1990 the stylishly dressed 35-year-old member of the Ghost Shadows gang in New York's Chinatown received more than $400,000 for aiding the DEA. Before that, Han served a four-year term for conspiracy to commit murder. "DEA informants, working on commission, were kept so busy [during the 1980s] that at times the 300 registered informers outearned investigators, annually pulling down $50,000 to $75,000 in their constant quest to bring us information" (Stutman and Esposito 1992: 42).

. . . and for Freedom

In an effort to convict Manuel Noriega, federal prosecutors dropped three life terms and reduced the sentences of four convicted high-level drug traffickers by 546 years. The men testified against the former Panamanian strongman, and two were freed in 1991. Each was given a new identity and government financial support worth hundreds of thousands of dollars. Some of the informants did not need government largesse—they were allowed to keep the profits of their drug dealings (millions of dollars) in return for testifying against Noriega. (Lubasch 1990; Richey 1991).

Obviously, the more involved in criminal activity the informer—"snitch" or CI (confidential informant)—is, the more useful is his or her assistance. This raises serious ethical and policy questions. Should the informant be given immunity from lawful punishment in exchange for cooperation? If so, who is to make that determination? The agent who becomes aware of the informant's activities? The agent's supervisor? The prosecutor who is informed of the situation? A trial judge? Should a murderer be permitted to remain free because he or she is valuable to law enforcement efforts against drug trafficking? Should a drug addict-informant be allowed to continue his or her abuse in order to keep in touch with traffickers? If so, doesn't this contradict the goal of drug statutes, which is to curtail drug abuse? Should the government encourage informants even if they face serious physical danger (and they usually do)? Most drug agents would argue, however, that without informants there can be no effective drug law enforcement. The issues are complex and without definitive answers.

There are other dangers. In south Florida, for example, given the number of law enforcement agencies and "given their heavy dependence on intelligence, it is inevitable that there are informants who inform on other informants, who are probably informing on them. A consequence of that is selective prosecution:

Other Dangers

Special agents from the U.S. Customs Service and Drug Enforcement Agency used a battering ram to enter a posh California residence, and they responded with automatic weapons when the occupant fired on them. The agents thought they were raiding the headquarters of a heavily armed drug gang who protected the house with vicious rottweilers; the badly wounded computer executive thought he was defending his house against home invaders. No drugs, dogs, or weapons were found. Information leading to the raid had been provided by a confidential informant, who was subsequently convicted of perjury (Katel 1995).

On the basis of information supplied by a confidential informant, New York City police officers broke down the door of a Brooklyn apartment and tossed in a stun grenade. The residents, including an 18-year-old retarded girl who was being bathed, were handcuffed. There were no guns and no drugs—but there soon was a multimillion-dollar lawsuit (M. Cooper 1998).

In 1998, in Houston, Texas, six police officers, acting on an informant's tip, burst into the apartment of a Mexican immigrant and shot him twelve times. No drugs or evidence of illegal activity was found (Lyman 1998).

---

arbitrary decisions made by police officers and agents as to who will go to jail and who will be allowed to remain on the street. Given the vast amounts of money at stake in the drug business, selective prosecution raises the specter of corruption" (Eddy, Sabogal, and Walden 1988: 85).

Working closely with informants is potentially corrupting. The informant helps the agent to enter an underworld that is filled with danger—as well as great financial rewards. There is always concern that the law enforcement agent might become something else to the informer—a friend, an employee, an employer, or a partner. The rewards can be considerable: Agents can confiscate money and drugs from other traffickers or receive payment for not arresting traffickers; at the same time they can improve their work record by arresting competing dealers. It is often only a small step from using drug traffickers as informants to going into business with them.

STATUTES AND LEGAL REQUIREMENTS

The legal foundation for federal drug law violations is Title II of the Comprehensive Drug Abuse Prevention and Control Act of 1970, as amended (usually referred to as the Controlled Substances Act [CSA]). Among the provisions of the CSA is a set of criteria for placing a substance in one of five schedules (Table 12.1). Following the federal model, most states have established the five-schedule system, but many "have chosen to reclassify particular substances within those five schedules. Variation also exists in the number of

Table 12.1 | Schedule of Controlled Substances

Schedule I

A. The drug or other substance has a high potential for abuse.

B. The drug or other substance has no currently accepted medical use in treatment in the United States.

C. There is a lack of accepted safety for use of the drug or other substance under medical supervision.

Schedule II

A. The drug or other substance has a high potential for abuse.

B. The drug or other substance has a currently accepted medical use in treatment in the United States or a currently accepted medical use with severe restrictions.

C. Abuse of the drug or other substances may lead to severe psychological or physical dependence.

Schedule III

A. The drug or other substance has a potential for abuse less than the drugs or other substances in Schedules I and II.

B. The drug or other substance has a currently accepted medical use in treatment in the United States.

C. Abuse of the drug or other substance may lead to moderate or low physical dependence or high psychological dependence.

Schedule IV

A. The drug or other substance has a low potential for abuse relative to the drugs or other substances in Schedule III.

B. The drug or other substance has a currently accepted medical use in treatment in the United States.

C. Abuse of the drug or other substance may lead to limited physical dependence or psychological dependence relative to the drugs or other substances in Schedule III.

Schedule V

A. The drug or other substance has a low potential for abuse relative to the drugs or other substances in Schedule IV.

B. The drug or other substance has a currently accepted medical use in treatment in the United States.

C. Abuse of the drug or other substance may lead to limited physical dependence or psychological dependence relative to the drugs or other substances in Schedule IV.

Source: Drug Enforcement Administration.

schedules employed by the states [North Carolina, for example, uses six] and in the purpose of these schedules" (*Illicit Drug Policies* 2002: 8). Massachusetts categorizes drugs on the basis of the penalty rather than using the federal scheme of potential for abuse and medical use. Like federal law, state statutes refer to the drug involved (e.g., cocaine or heroin), the action involved (e.g., simple possession, possession with the intent to sell, sale, distribution, or trafficking), and the number of prior offenses. Across states there is significant variation in the penalties for cocaine-, marijuana-, methamphetamine-, and ecstasy-related offenses (*Illicit Drug Policies* 2002).

People who are involved in the illegal drug business can be arrested and prosecuted for a number of different offenses: manufacture, importation, distribution, possession, or sale; conspiracy to manufacture, import, distribute, possess, or sell; or failure to pay the required income taxes on illegal income. Possession of drugs may be *actual*—for example, actually on the person, in pockets, or in a package that the person is holding; or *constructive*—not actually on the person but under his or her control, directly or through other people. Possession must be proven by a legal search, which usually requires a search warrant as per the Fourth Amendment (an important exception is at ports of entry). A search warrant requires the establishment of probable cause—providing a judge with sufficient evidence of a crime to justify a warrant. Drugs can easily be secreted in any variety of places, including inside the human body. Federal trafficking penalties are shown in Table 12.2.

In response to the Ecstasy Anti-Proliferation Act of 2000, the U.S. Sentencing Commission raised the guideline for judges' sentences for trafficking MDMA. For 800 pills, about 200 grams, the sentence increased from fifteen months to five years; for 8,000 pills, the sentence increased from forty-one months to ten years.

Enacted in 2003, the Illicit Drug Anti-Proliferation Act (sometimes known as the "Rave Act") prohibits "knowingly opening, maintaining, managing, controlling, renting, leasing, making available for use, or profiting from any place for the purpose of manufacturing, distributing or using any controlled substance." Penalties include imprisonment for up to twenty years, criminal fines of $500,000, and civil penalties of $250,000.

CONSPIRACY

Conspiracy is an agreement between two or more individuals to commit a criminal act; the agreement becomes the *corpus* (body) of the crime. Conspiracy requires proof (beyond a reasonable doubt) that two or more individuals planned to violate drug laws and that at least one overt act in furtherance of the conspiracy was made by a conspirator (e.g., the purchase of materials to aid in the transportation or dilution of illicit drugs). Conspiracy statutes are valuable tools for prosecuting drug offenders because:

1. Intervention can occur before the commission of a substantive offense.
2. A conspirator cannot shield himself or herself from prosecution because of a lack of knowledge of the details of the conspiracy or the identity of coconspirators and their contributions.
3. An act or declaration by one conspirator committed in furtherance of the conspiracy is admissible against each coconspirator (an exception to the hearsay rule).
4. Each conspirator is responsible for the substantive crimes of coconspirators; even late joiners can be held liable for prior acts of coconspirators if the latecomer's agreement is given with full knowledge of the conspiracy's objective.

Table 12.2 | Federal Trafficking Penalties: Narcotic Penalties and Enforcement Act of 1986

CSA Schedule	Drug/Quantity	Penalty
I and II	Heroin, 1 kg mixture Cocaine, 5 kg mixture Cocaine Base, 50 gram mixture PCP, 100 gram or 1 kg mixture LSD, 10 gram mixture Fentanyl, 400 gram mixture Fentanyl Analog, 100 gram mixture	**First Offense:** Not less than 10 years. Not more than life. If death or serious injury, not less than 20 years, not more than life. Fine of not more than $4 million individual, $10 million other than individual. **Second Offense:** Not less than 20 years. Not more than life. If death or serious injury, not less than life. Fine of not more than $8 million individual, $20 million other than individual.
	Heroin, 100 gram mixture Cocaine, 500 gram mixture Cocaine Base, 5 gram mixture PCP, 10 gram or 100 gram mixture LSD, 1 gram mixture Fentanyl, 40 gram mixture Fentanyl Analog, 10 gram mixture	**First Offense:** Not less than 5 years. Not more than 40 years. If death or serious injury, not less than 20 years, not more than life. Fine of not more than $2 million individual, $5 million other than individual. **Second Offense:** Not less than 10 years. Not more than life. If death or serious injury, not less than life. Fine of not more than $4 million individual, $10 million other than individual.
	Others*/Any Amount	**First Offense:** Not more than 20 years. If death or serious injury, not less than 20 years, not more than life. Fine $1 million individual, $5 million not individual. **Second Offense:** Not more than 30 years. If death or serious injury, life. Fine $2 million individual, $10 million not individual.
III	All/Any Amount	**First Offense:** Not more than 5 years, fine not more than $250,000 individual, $1 million not individual. **Second Offense:** Not more than 10 years, fine $500,000 individual, $2 million not individual.
IV	All/Any Amount	**First Offense:** Not more than 3 years, fine not more than $250,000 individual, $1 million not individual. **Second Offense:** Not more than 6 years, fine not more than $500,000 individual, $2 million not individual.
V	All/Any Amount	**First Offense:** Not more than 1 year, fine not more than $100,000 individual, $250,000 not individual. **Second Offense:** Not more than 2 years, fine not more than $200,000 individual, $500,000 not individual.

*Does not include marijuana, hashish, or hash oil.

Source: Drug Enforcement Administration.

There are three basic types of conspiracy:

1. *Wheel conspiracies.* One person at the "hub" conspires individually with two or more people, who make up the "spokes" of the wheel. For the conspiracy to be (legally) complete, the wheel needs a "rim": Each spoke must be aware of and agree with the others in pursuit of one objective.

2. *Chain conspiracies.* Like the lights on a Christmas tree, each conspirator depends on the successful participation of every other member. Each member is a "link" who, to complete the conspiracy, must understand that the success of the scheme depends on everyone in the chain.

3. *Enterprise conspiracies.* Part of the RICO (Racketeer Influenced and Corrupt Organizations) statute of the Organized Crime Control Act of 1970, the enterprise conspiracy avoids the practical limitations inherent in proving wheel and chain conspiracies. The statute makes it a separate crime to conspire to violate drug laws as part of an agreement to participate in an enterprise by engaging in a pattern of racketeering activity. Members of the conspiracy need not know each other or even be aware of each other's criminal activities. All that needs to be shown is each member's agreement to participate in the organization—the "enterprise"—by committing two or more acts of racketeering, such as gambling or drug violations, within a ten-year period. The enterprise conspiracy facilitates mass trials, with each member of the enterprise subject to the significant penalties—twenty years imprisonment on each count—that can result from a conviction.

The *Continuing Criminal Enterprise* (CCE) statute is similar in purpose to RICO but targets only illegal drug activity. The statute makes it a crime to commit or conspire to commit a continuing series of felony violations of the 1970 Drug Abuse Prevention and Control Act when the violations are undertaken in concert with five or more individuals. The courts have ruled that a "series" requires three or more violations. "For conviction under this statute, the offender must have been an organizer, manager, or supervisor of the continuing operation and have obtained substantial income or resources from the drug violations" (Carlson and Finn 1993: 2). In 1999 the Supreme Court ruled (*Richardson v. United States* No. 526 U.S. 813) that juries must agree on which specific illegal acts were committed by a defendant rather than simply finding that he or she committed a series of drug violations without specifying which ones. The 6–3 decision will make it harder to convict people for violating the CCE.

TAX VIOLATIONS

In 1927 the Supreme Court decided the case of *United States v. Sullivan* (274 U.S. 259), which denied the claim of self-incrimination as an excuse for failure to file income tax on illegally gained earnings. This decision enabled the federal government to successfully prosecute Al Capone and members of his organization. Drug entrepreneurs have devised ways to successfully evade taxes by, for example, dealing in cash, keeping minimal records, and setting up fronts. This is countered by the indirect method known as the *net worth theory*: "The government establishes a taxpayer's net worth at the commencement of the taxing period [which requires substantial accuracy], deducts that from his or her net worth at the end of the period, and proves that the net gain in net worth exceeds the income reported by the taxpayer" (E. Johnson 1963: 17–18). In effect, the Internal Revenue Service (IRS) reconstructs the total expenditures of the taxpayer by examining his or her standard of living and comparing it with reported income. The government can then maintain that the taxpayer did not report his or her entire income; the government does not have to show a probable source of the excess unreported gain in net worth.

MONEY LAUNDERING ACT

The Attorney General of the United States has pointed out that so much cash is involved in large, illicit drug-trafficking operations that tracking the money from these drug activities is often a more fruitful investigative endeavor than is tracking the underlying criminal activities (Thornburgh 1989). Before passage of the Money Laundering Control Act of 1986 (Title 18 U.S.C. Sections 1956 and 1957), money laundering was not a federal crime, although the Department of Justice had used a variety of federal statutes to successfully prosecute money-laundering cases. The act consolidated these statutes with the goal of increasing prosecutions for this offense. Money laundering was made a separate federal offense punishable by a fine of $500,000 or twice the value of the property involved, whichever is greater, and twenty years imprisonment. Title 18 U.S.C. Section 981 provides for the civil confiscation of any property related to a money laundering scheme. Legislation enacted in 1988 allows the government to file a suit claiming ownership of all cash funneled through operations intended to disguise its illegal source. The courts can issue an order freezing all contested funds until the case is adjudicated (Weinstein 1988). A person is guilty of money laundering if he or she, knowing that the property involved represents the proceeds of an illegal activity, attempts to conceal or disguise the nature, location, source, ownership, or control of the proceeds or attempts to avoid a transaction-reporting requirement. Furthermore, whoever transports or attempts to transport a monetary instrument or funds out of the United States in an attempt to conceal or disguise the nature, location, source, ownership, or control of the proceeds to avoid a transaction-reporting requirement with the intent to promote an unlawful activity or with the knowledge that the monetary instrument or funds represent the proceeds of an unlawful activity shall be guilty of money laundering. For a conviction under section 1957 the prosecutor must prove:

1. That the defendant engaged in a monetary transaction in excess of $10,000,
2. That the defendant knew the money to be the fruit of criminal activity, and
3. That the money was in fact the fruit of a specified unlawful activity (Weinstein 1988).

Until 1988 the act permitted the Department of Justice to prosecute attorneys and seize fees obtained from tainted sources. Defense attorneys argued that this created a situation "in which a defendant cannot retain an attorney because of the government's threat of criminal and civil sanctions against any attorney who takes the case" (Weinstein 1988: 381). The defendant is left without a free choice of attorneys and therefore must depend on a public defender who might not be familiar with the complexities of RICO prosecutions. Supporters of this legislation argue that criminals who have grown wealthy from crime are not entitled to any greater consideration with respect to legal representation than are their less successful criminal colleagues, who are often represented by public defenders. On November 18, 1988, President Ronald Reagan signed the antidrug abuse bill, which contains an amendment to 18 U.S.C. Section 1957, effectively excepting defense attorneys' fees from the criminal money-laundering provisions. Thus, while criminal defense fees could still be subject to forfeiture, the attorney who accepts tainted fees is exempt from criminal prosecution. In 1989 the Supreme Court, in a 5–4 decision, ruled that the government, under the Comprehensive Forfeiture Act, can freeze the assets of criminal defendants before trial (*Caplin and Drysdale v. United States*, 491 U.S. 616; *United States v. Monsanto*, 491 U.S. 600).

SEIZURE AND FORFEITURE OF ASSETS

Federal and state statutes provide for the forfeiture of property that is used in criminal activity or secured with the fruits of criminal activity. Forfeiture has proved particularly useful in dealing with drug traffickers. There are four types of forfeitable items:

1. *Contraband*, such as controlled substances, are illegal to possess and may be seized and destroyed without a court order.
2. *Derivative contraband* includes conveyances that are used to transport contraband, such as aircraft, vessels, and motor vehicles. While not illegal in themselves, they are classified as contraband when used in furtherance of a criminal act.
3. *Direct proceeds* are usually cash.
4. *Derivative proceeds* include real estate and stock.

In practice, vehicles and cash are the most frequently seized assets, because the pursuit of real property requires extensive financial investigation. "The investigative expense may be cost effective," however, if "the property is valuable and the potential for disrupting the criminal organization is high" (Stellwagen 1985: 5).

There are two types of forfeiture proceedings: criminal and civil. *Criminal forfeiture* is applicable only as part of a successful criminal prosecution. "The defendant in the criminal case must be convicted of the crime involving the property, or the property cannot be subject to forfeiture" (Poethig 1988: 11).

Thus, the government can use criminal forfeiture to seize the home of a *convicted* drug dealer who used the home to store drugs. *Civil forfeiture*, on the other hand, does not require criminal charges; civil forfeiture can proceed even in the absence of a criminal prosecution and has certain advantages over criminal forfeiture: The level of evidence required is considerably less than that in a criminal action, and the considerable due process guarantees accruing to a criminal defendant are not applicable in a civil action. Interestingly, civil forfeiture proceedings are brought against property that is involved in a criminal offense, not against a person. "Possession of the property in and of itself may not be illegal, but the property may be subject to seizure and forfeiture because of the way it was used. No criminal charge or conviction need exist against the owner of the property for the civil case to occur" (Poethig 1988: 11). Thus, the government can use civil forfeiture to seize an automobile that is used to transport drugs even if no conviction resulted from this activity.

RICO and the 1984 Comprehensive Forfeiture Act (CFA) provide for the seizure of assets under certain conditions. The CFA "creates a rebuttable presumption that any property of a person convicted of a drug felony is subject to forfeiture if the government establishes by a preponderance of evidence that the defendant acquired the property during the period of violation or within a reasonably short period thereafter, *and* there was no likely source for the property other than the violation" (President's Commission on Organized Crime 1986: 274). Much of the money that is taken in forfeitures goes toward state and local law enforcement efforts. To stop commuter customers from driving into New York City to purchase drugs, law enforcement officials have been seizing the cars of those making drug purchases. Some vehicles have been returned to their owners when the owners were not the ones arrested; hundreds of others have been auctioned off.

In any number of jurisdictions, disputes have arisen over how to allocate the fruits of seized assets. Because these funds do not incur a political cost—not being linked to taxes—they are highly valued. However, "once the money reaches the local police, it often can become a political football with law enforcement and politicians squabbling over how to spend it" (Soble 1991: 23). In several California communities, for example, police officials wanted to put the money into drug law enforcement, but elected officials insisted instead on increasing the uniformed police force. There is also concern that pressure to produce revenue will encourage legally questionable activity and even alter the basic goal of drug law enforcement.

Intertwined with this concern is that expressed over the seizure of property owned by innocent third parties. Three fraternity houses that were seized at the University of Virginia in 1991, for example, were owned by alumni, not the current occupants, some of whom were arrested for drug violations. (Two houses were returned before the 1991–1992 school year began.) Innocent parties can be deprived of a residence, vehicle, business, or cash until they are able to prove they were not involved in law-violating activity—a reversal of the normal presumption of innocence. To get back seized property, the owner needs an attorney, and litigation can take several months without any guarantee of success. For people who make the "mistake" of traveling with large amounts of cash—particularly if they are black, Hispanic, or Asian—the results can be more than an inconvenience. A study by the *Pittsburgh Press* revealed several cases in which the cash of innocent people was seized at airports and kept for years without any criminal charges being filed (Schneider and Flaherty 1991). "Overcoming the burden of proof can be hard even for the most upright citizens. How does a mother prove she didn't know her son was using the family car to transport drugs? How does a landlord prove he didn't know a tenant was a drug dealer? . . . The effort is also expensive, and even if you win, you're still out the money to pay your lawyer, which can be more than the value of the property you've recovered" (Chapman 1992: 23). In 1996 the Supreme Court determined that property can be seized even when the owner was innocent of any wrongdoing. In this case, *Bennis v. Michigan* (517 U.S. 1163), a jointly owned car was impounded after the husband used it to solicit a prostitute. In response to these criticisms, in 2000 the 1984 statute was revised to require the government to prove that confiscated property either had been used for illegal activity or was purchased with the proceeds of criminal activity.

Forfeiture has also been criticized as a plea-bargaining device for drug kingpins. They negotiate lighter sentences by promising to reveal hidden assets and not put up court challenges to their seizure. Law enforcement agencies, eager for additional funds, promote leniency for those at the top of the drug-trafficking ladder while those down below, without substantial hidden assets, face significant penalties (Navarro 1996).

GRAND JURY

A grand jury comprises fifteen to twenty-three citizens who have been selected to hear evidence against accused individuals and to determine whether sufficient evidence exists to bring these individuals to trial—to *indict* them. Although not all states use grand juries to indict defendants, all states and the federal government empower the grand jury to conduct investigations of criminal activity, usually pertaining to official corruption. The Organized Crime Control Act of 1970 requires that a special grand jury be convened at least every eighteen months in federal districts of more than one million people; it may also be convened at the request of a federal prosecutor, and its life may be extended to thirty-six months. The special grand jury is often used to investigate drug law violations.

The broad investigative powers of the grand jury permit jurors to consider tips and rumors as well as more substantial evidence offered by the prosecutor. Even illegally secured evidence may be used as a basis for questioning witnesses. A grand jury can issue subpoenas for documents and individuals. Federal (and most state) grand juries do not permit witnesses to be accompanied by counsel (although defendants are free to leave the grand jury room to consult with their attorneys). Testimony before a grand jury is given under oath and recorded, although the proceedings are secret until released by the court. Witnesses who

Levels of Drug Law Enforcement

There are five levels of drug law enforcement (Kleiman 1985):

1. *Source control*. This comprises actions aimed at limiting cultivation and production of poppies and opium, coca and cocaine, and marijuana. Both the State Department and the Drug Enforcement Administration have agents assigned to foreign countries.
2. *Interdiction*. The interception of drugs being smuggled into the United States is primarily the role of the Coast Guard and Customs Service and Border Protection. (Since 2002 these two agencies have been in the Department of Homeland Security.)
3. *Domestic distribution*. The disruption of high-level trafficking is usually the responsibility of the Drug Enforcement Administration and the Federal Bureau of Investigation.
4. *Wholesaling*. The focus on midlevel dealing is usually the role of state and local law enforcement.
5. *Street sales*. Low-level dealing, often by addicts supporting their own drug habits, is usually left to local law enforcement.

invoke their constitutional right to remain silent can be granted immunity, which requires that they testify or suffer summary incarceration for the remainder of the life of the grand jury.

LAW ENFORCEMENT AGENCIES

As was noted earlier, local efforts against drug trafficking are usually directed at midlevel dealers, although most frequently, it is the low-level street dealer who is arrested and prosecuted at the local level. Federal drug law enforcement seeks to disrupt illicit trafficking organizations and to reduce the availability of drugs for illicit use. This is accomplished in three ways (Comptroller General 1983: 3):

- Arrest, prosecution, and incarceration of traffickers and the immobilization of trafficking organizations eliminate some capacities for supplying illicit drugs.
- Removal of drugs from the distribution networks directly reduces supply.
- Seizure of equipment and operating resources leaves the drug networks at least inconvenienced, at best crippled.

On the federal level, because the United States, unlike most other democratic nations, does not have a national police force, the job of carrying out these objectives falls on a confusing number of agencies in several departments—Transportation, Justice, Treasury, Defense—whose responsibilities for

DEA Antecedent Agencies

1973–Present: Drug Enforcement Administration

1968–1973: Bureau of Narcotics and Dangerous Drugs

1930–1968: Federal Bureau of Narcotics

1927–1930: Bureau of Prohibition

1915–1927: Bureau of Internal Revenue

enforcing drug laws often overlap. This fragmentation is the result of the ad hoc creation of law enforcement agencies at the national level; each time a particular problem arose, an agency was established without significant attention to the problem of coordination. We will discuss the agencies in the order listed in Table 12.3.

Drug Enforcement Administration (DEA)

The DEA evolved out of several predecessor agencies, particularly the Federal Bureau of Narcotics (see Chapter 2). It is a single-mission agency that is responsible for enforcing federal statutes dealing with controlled substances by investigating alleged or suspected major drug traffickers. The DEA is also

Table 12.3 | Federal Drug Law Enforcement Agencies

Department of Justice

Drug Enforcement Administration

Federal Bureau of Investigation

Bureau of Alcohol, Tobacco, Firearms and Explosives

U.S. Marshals Service

Department of Homeland Security

Immigration and Customs Enforcement

Customs Service and Border Protection

Secret Service

Coast Guard

Department of the Treasury

Internal Revenue Service

Postal Service

Postal Inspection Service

Mule Skinning

DEA special agents, working with state and local police agencies, monitor airports at key junctions for drugs entering the United States. In addition to such primary ports of entry as south Florida, Los Angeles, and New York City, they cover such secondary locations as Atlanta and Chicago, where travelers frequently change planes. Using a drug courier profile developed over the past fifteen years, the agents look for specific clues—primary and secondary characteristics—that have been proven to characterize individuals ("mules") who are most likely to be carrying wholesale quantities of illegal substances. The clues that a person might be a mule include arrival from or departure to an identified foreign source country such as Colombia or domestic source city such as Miami or unusual travel patterns—for example, short turnaround times for lengthy airplane trips.

While these primary and secondary characteristics may be consistent with lawful behavior, they also indicate a person who should be questioned. Passengers who have enough profile characteristics may be approached and questioned—asked for identification and travel documentation. Agents are particularly interested in signs of excessive nervousness. If such signs are observed, agents will ask the passenger to consent to a drug search, which can include a cavity search. The rare refusal can result in detention and the securing of a drug-sniffing dog and/or a search warrant. At times agents discover large amounts of cash that cannot be accounted for. This is seized until its "lawful" owner appears to claim it—a highly unlikely event. If a courier is arrested, efforts are made to "flip" the mule to implicate the person who is supposed to be picking up the drugs.

Although its use is controversial, the profile permits drug agents to act in the absence of specific information (the sort that is usually provided by

Sources: Elsasser (1989); Greenhouse (1989); Hedgepath (1989); Belkin (1990); Crank and Rehm (1992).

responsible for regulating the legal trade in such controlled substances as morphine, methadone, and barbiturates. Diversion agents conduct accountability investigations of drug wholesalers, suppliers, and manufacturers. They inspect the records and facilities of major drug manufacturers and distributors, and special agents investigate instances in which drugs have been illegally diverted from legitimate sources. DEA special agents are also stationed in sixty-five countries (Thornburgh 1989), where their mission is to gain cooperation in international efforts against drug trafficking and to help train foreign enforcement officials.

The basic approach to DEA drug law enforcement is the *buy and bust* or the *controlled buy*. Typically, a drug agent is introduced to a seller by an informant. The agent arranges to buy a relatively small amount of drugs and then attempts to move farther up the organizational ladder by increasing the amount purchased. When arrests are made, DEA agents attempt to "flip" the suspect, convincing him or her to become an informant, particularly if the person has knowledge of the entire operation, so that a conspiracy case can be effected. As was discussed above, the use of informants is problematic.

The DEA's mission is to enforce the controlled substances laws and regulations and to bring to justice the organizations and principal members that are involved in the growing, manufacture, or distribution of controlled substances appearing in or destined for illicit traffic in the United States and to recommend and support nonenforcement programs aimed at reducing the availability of illicit controlled substances in the domestic and international criminal informants). The use of the profile and the seizure of any evidence that is discovered have been upheld by the courts as legitimate law enforcement tools, the Fourth Amendment notwithstanding. In 1989 the Supreme Court, in a 7–2 decision, ruled that the profile provides a "reasonable basis" to suspect that a person is transporting drugs. The case involved Andrew Sokolow, who in July 1984 flew from Honolulu to Miami and returned to Hawaii forty-eight hours later. Sokolow, dressed in a black jumpsuit and gold jewelry, purchased two airline tickets in Miami for $2,100 in cash taken from a roll of twenty-dollar bills containing about twice that amount. He was traveling under a name that did not match his telephone listing. Sokolow did not check any luggage and appeared very nervous. After stopping him in Honolulu, drug agents used a drug-sniffing dog, which led them to 1,063 grams of cocaine in Sokolow's carry-on luggage. Writing for the Court, Chief Justice William H. Rehnquist stated that "while a trip from Honolulu to Miami,

standing alone, is not a cause for any sort of suspicion, here there was more: surely few residents of Honolulu travel from that city for 20 hours to spend 48 hours in Miami during the month of July." The Court, however, did not base its decision on the existence or use of the DEA drug profile; according to the decision, agents must justify their decision to stop a suspect on the basis of their own observations and experience.

While the profile has proven useful in interdiction efforts, it is not without controversy because its use appears to relate to ethnicity and race; the darker a person's skin, the more likely it is that he or she will be targeted. A stop can involve several hours of detention and accompanying humiliation. Nevertheless, the practice has been extended to highways, where vehicles and their occupants, if they fit certain profiles, are subjected to a stop and interrogation.

markets. According to the DEA's website, the agency's primary responsibilities include:

1. Investigation and preparation for the prosecution of major violators of controlled substance laws operating at interstate and international levels.
2. Management of a national drug intelligence program in cooperation with federal, state, local, and foreign officials to collect, analyze, and disseminate strategic and operational drug intelligence information.
3. Seizure and forfeiture of assets derived from, traceable to, or intended to be used for illicit drug trafficking.
4. Coordination and cooperation with federal, state, and local law enforcement officials on mutual drug enforcement efforts and enhancement of such efforts through exploitation of potential interstate and international investigations beyond local or limited federal jurisdictions and resources.
5. Coordination and cooperation with federal, state, and local agencies and with foreign governments in programs designed to reduce the availability of illicit abuse–type drugs on the U.S. market through nonenforcement methods such as crop eradication, crop substitution, and training of foreign officials.
6. Responsibility, under the policy guidance of the Secretary of State and U.S. ambassadors, for all programs associated with drug law enforcement counterparts in foreign countries.
7. Liaison with the United Nations, Interpol, and other organizations on matters relating to international drug control programs.

Federal Bureau of Investigation (FBI)

The FBI is as close to a federal police force as exists in the United States. Its broad investigative mandate was expanded in 1982, when the FBI was given concurrent jurisdiction with the DEA for drug law enforcement and investigation. In addition, the administrator of the DEA is now required to report to the director of the FBI, who has overall responsibility for supervising drug law enforcement efforts and policies. Despite its increased mandate, the primary role of the FBI is to deal with domestic espionage; it is the only law enforcement agency having jurisdiction over this activity. The dramatic changes in what was known as the Eastern (Communist) bloc have led to the reassignment of hundreds of FBI agents from counterespionage to more conventional criminal activity, such as drug trafficking.

Immigration and Customs Enforcement (ICE)

Immigration and Customs Enforcement (ICE) is the result of a post-9/11 restructuring of the Immigration and Naturalization Service and the Customs Service. The primary role of the immigration enforcement arm of ICE is to prevent illegal entry into the United States and to apprehend people who have entered illegally. Border Patrol officers check suspicious individuals within 100 miles of border areas that are likely to be used as illegal crossing points, and they often arrest people who are transporting drugs.

The Customs Service was established in 1789 to collect duties on various imports. Inspectors examine cargoes and baggage; articles worn or carried by individuals; and vessels, vehicles, and aircraft entering or leaving the

Special teams of U.S. Customs inspectors and canine enforcement officers examine cargo imported into the United States. Agents don't need probable cause or warrants to search for drugs at ports of entry.

©Amy C. Etra/PhotoEdit

Drug-Smuggling Interceptions

- A light gray spray-painted bust of Jesus composed of molded cocaine
- 5 pounds of cocaine packed in condoms surgically implanted in a sheepdog
- 37 pounds of cocaine packed in condoms and inserted in the rectums of live boa constrictors
- 1,000 pounds of cocaine packed in hollow plaster shells shaped and painted to resemble yams
- 6,000 pounds of cocaine packed in kilo bricks inside ice-packed cases of broccoli
- 2,000 pounds of cocaine in the soles of a shipment of sneakers
- 16 tons of cocaine inside concrete fence posts
- 3,000 pounds of cocaine hidden beneath a shipment of iced fish fillets
- Mexican drug organizations were found to have smuggled cocaine into the United States secreted in tombstones engraved with the Virgin Mary.
- 12 pounds of heroin were discovered by customs officials at Newark Airport; they were in more than 100 candy bars that had been individually wrapped and packaged.

Sources: Speart (1995), Associated Press (1999c), Lambert (2006); Associated Press (2007).

United States. The frontiers of the United States, to the north and the south, "are the longest undisputed, undefended borders on earth" (T. Weiner 2002: 14).

Special teams of inspectors and canine enforcement officers concentrate on cargo and conveyances that are considered to be at high risk. In 1981 the Customs Service established the Office of Intelligence to better manage information and target suspects; it participates in several multiagency programs designed to combat organized criminal activities in drug trafficking. The service works with commercial carriers, often signing cooperative agreements, to enhance the carriers' ability to prevent their equipment from being used to smuggle drugs. Special agents are responsible for carrying out investigations into drug smuggling and currency violations as part of money-laundering schemes.

ICE is not bound by Fourth Amendment protections that typically restrain domestic law enforcement. Agents do not need probable cause or warrants to engage in search and seizure at ports of entry; certain degrees of suspicion will suffice. The typical case is a "cold border bust," the result of an entry checkpoint search. Because it is impractical if not impossible to thoroughly search most vehicles and individuals entering the United States, agents have developed certain techniques for minimizing inconvenience to legitimate travelers and shippers while targeting those who are most likely to be involved in smuggling activity. Besides being alert to various cues that act as tip-offs, the officials at border-crossing points have computers containing information such as license plate numbers and names of known or suspected smugglers. People arrested by ICE become targets for offers of plea bargaining in efforts to gain their

(Almost) Undetectable Cocaine

In 1991 federal agents raided several houses in south Florida, where they discovered a rather unique method of disguising cocaine for smuggling purposes. Agents found hundreds of pounds of harmless-looking black plastic molds into which cocaine had been blended, making detection using routine methods impossible. In fact, only the discovery of chemicals used in cocaine processing alerted agents to the blend. The drug is extracted from the plastic in much the same way that it is removed from the coca plant. The plastic is about one-quarter cocaine and can be made into any shape, allowing cocaine to be smuggled in the form of toys, glasses, camera lenses, or any plastic product (Rhor 1991).

cooperation in follow-up enforcement efforts by the Drug Enforcement Administration; they are pressured to become informants in return for some form of leniency. As the result of the 9/11 attacks, ICE priorities have shifted to intercepting potential terrorists seeking to enter the United States.

ICE is hampered by the need to patrol more than 12,000 miles of international boundary, which more than 420 billion tons of goods and 270 million people cross each year. About half the drugs entering the United States come through commercial ports, where they are secreted in tightly sealed steel containers, twenty or forty feet long, twelve feet high, and eight feet wide, millions of which enter the country every year. Officials can inspect only a small number (about 10 percent) of these containers; and without advance information, the drugs typically pass right through the ports. Drugs that are intercepted are easily replaced.

Coast Guard

A Fishy Haul

In 2004 naval frigates with Coast Guard officers aboard intercepted two ships from Colombia 300 miles west of the Galapagos Islands. The first had 30,000 pounds of cocaine hidden in a sealed ballast tank; the second contained 26,000 pounds of cocaine hidden under fish and ice in the cargo hold ("A Fishy Haul" 2004).

The Coast Guard, formerly part of the Department of Transportation and now part of the Department of Homeland Security, is responsible for drug interdiction at sea. Coast Guard personnel do not have to establish probable cause before boarding a vessel at sea. "Responsible in large part for U.S. drug interdiction efforts, the Coast Guard's strategy has been mainly directed toward intercepting mother ships as they transit the major passes of the Caribbean. To effect this 'choke point' strategy, the Coast Guard conducts both continuous surface patrols and frequent surveillance flights over waters of interest, and boards and inspects vessels at sea" (President's Commission on Organized Crime 1986: 313).

Smugglers bringing drugs from Colombia across the Caribbean to the Florida coast carry extra fuel for the 700-mile round trip in boats that are thirty to forty-five feet long, are capable of carrying 3,000 pounds of cocaine, and travel at nearly seventy miles per hour. In response, in 1999 the Coast Guard modernized a tactic that had last been employed during Prohibition: Helicopter-borne sharpshooters disable the engines of speedboats that refuse to follow the orders of Coast Guard vessels (Stout 1999).

Internal Revenue Service (IRS)

The mission of the IRS is to encourage and achieve the highest possible degree of voluntary compliance with tax laws and regulations. When such compliance is not forthcoming or not feasible, as in the case of drug traffickers, the Criminal Investigation Division receives the case. Agents examine bank records, canceled checks, brokerage accounts, property transactions, and purchases, compiling a financial biography of the subject's lifestyle to prove that proper taxes have not been paid. As a result of the excesses that were revealed in the wake of the Watergate scandal, Congress enacted the Tax Reform Act of 1976, which reduced the law enforcement role of the IRS and made it difficult for law enforcement agencies (other than the IRS) to gain access to income tax returns. Amendments in 1982 reduced the requirements and permits the IRS to better cooperate with the efforts of other federal law enforcement agencies that are investigating drug traffickers.

U.S. Marshals Service

The U.S. Marshals Service is the oldest federal law enforcement agency, dating back to 1789. During the period of westward expansion the U.S. marshal played a significant role in the "Wild West." Today, marshals provide security for federal court facilities, transport federal prisoners, serve civil writs issued by federal courts, and investigate and apprehend certain federal fugitives. Marshals are responsible for seizing, managing, and disposing of forfeited properties and assets from major drug cases. The Marshals Service's most important task relative to drug trafficking is its responsibility for administering the Witness Protection Program.

Because of the potentially undesirable consequences for a witness who testifies in a drug trafficking case, efforts have been made to protect such witnesses from retribution. The *Witness Protection Program* was authorized by the Organized Crime Control Act of 1970:

> The Attorney General of the United States is authorized to rent, purchase, modify, or remodel protected housing facilities and to otherwise offer to provide for the health, safety, and welfare of witnesses and persons intended to be called as Government witnesses, and the families of witnesses and persons intended to be called as Government witnesses in legal proceedings instituted against any person alleged to have participated in an organized criminal activity whenever in his judgment testimony from, or a willingness to testify by, such a witness would place his life or person, or the life or person of a member of his family or household, in jeopardy. Any person availing himself of such an offer by the Attorney General to use such facilities may continue to use such facilities for as long as the Attorney General determines the jeopardy to his life or person continues.

The program was given over to the Marshals Service to administer. There was logic behind this arrangement (Permanent Subcommittee on Investigations

1981b: 54): "Law enforcement officers wanted the protecting and relocating agency to be in the criminal justice system but to be as far removed as possible from both investigating agents and prosecution. That way the Government could more readily counter the charge that cooperating witnesses were being paid or otherwise unjustifiably compensated in return for their testimony."

Bureau of Alcohol, Tobacco, Firearms and Explosives (ATF)

The Bureau of Alcohol, Tobacco, Firearms and Explosives (ATF) dates back to 1791, when a tax was placed on alcoholic spirits. It eventually evolved into the Prohibition Bureau, which, with the repeal of Prohibition, became known as the Alcohol Tax Unit. The bureau was given jurisdiction over federal firearms statutes in 1942 and over arson and explosives in 1970. ATF agents often encounter drug traffickers during their investigation of firearms and explosives violations. They have been particularly active in efforts against outlaw motorcycle clubs, which typically traffic in firearms and drugs.

The Military

The most controversial federal agency involved in drug law enforcement is the Department of Defense (DOD). In 1878 congressional Democrats enacted the Posse Comitatus (literally "force of the county") Act to stop Republican presidents from using the army to further Reconstruction in the states of the erstwhile Confederacy. The act (as amended) makes it a crime to use the military as a domestic police force: "Whoever, except in cases and under circumstances expressly authorized by the Constitution or Act of Congress willfully uses any part of the Army or Air Force as a posse comitatus or otherwise to execute the laws shall be fined not more than $10,000 or imprisoned not more than two years or both" (18 USCA Section 1385 (1984). In 1956 Congress added the Air Force to the Posse Comitatus Act, while the Navy and Marines promulgated administrative restrictions.

Until 1981 DOD limited its involvement in drug law enforcement to lending equipment and training civilian enforcement personnel in the use of military equipment. In that year, as part of a new "War on Drugs," Congress amended the Posse Comitatus Act, authorizing a greater level of military involvement in civilian drug law enforcement, particularly the tracking of suspect ships and planes and the use of military pilots and naval ships to transport civilian enforcement personnel. As a result of this legislation, DOD provided surveillance and support services, using aircraft to search for smugglers and Navy ships to tow or escort vessels seized by the Coast Guard to the nearest U.S. port. The legislation authorized the military services to share information collected during routine military operations with law enforcement officials and to make facilities and equipment available to law enforcement officials.

Further amendments to the 1981 legislation led to the use of military equipment and personnel in efforts against cocaine traffickers in Bolivia, Colombia, and Peru. These amendments permit the use of such personnel and

Corrupting the Navy . . .

In 1996 twenty-one U.S. sailors were arrested in Italy by the Naval Criminal Investigative Service, whose agents were able to infiltrate a Nigerian drug ring that paid the defendants to carry bags of cocaine and heroin across European borders. A lieutenant commander was the highest-ranking member of the group ("Navy Holds 21 Sailors in Italy in Smuggling Case" 1996).

. . . and the Marines . . .

In 2002, at the Camp Lejeune Marine base in North Carolina the Naval Criminal Investigation Service arrested eighty-four marines and sailors and ninety-nine civilians and seized $1.4 million in drugs. The suspects were accused of trafficking in ecstasy, cocaine, LSD, and methamphetamine (Kilian and Mendell 2002). The eighty-four military personnel were convicted and sentenced to prison terms ranging from three to nineteen years ("84 Military Personnel Convicted. . . ." 2002).

. . . and the Air National Guard

In 2006 a captain and a master sergeant in the Air National Guard pled guilty to importing 290,000 ecstasy pills from Germany on a military aircraft. When the captain was arrested, $700,000 in cash was found in his Bronx apartment (Preston 2005).

Department of Defense

DOD has extraordinary technical capabilities developed from its long experience in monitoring the skies and the waters for incoming Soviet or other hostile military aircraft, warships, and missiles. DOD adds the ability to alert law enforcement agencies to the presence of suspected drug smugglers to an existing detection system along the southern U.S. border and in the Caribbean basin (Mabry 1995).

equipment if the Secretary of State or the Secretary of Defense and the Attorney General jointly determine that an emergency exists in that the scope of specific criminal activity poses a serious threat to the interests of the United States. Combined operations involving U.S. Army Special Forces, DEA agents, U.S. Border Patrol officers, and Bolivian police and military officers have been successful in destroying hundreds of coca paste laboratories in the coca-growing Champare region of Bolivia. In 1999 a U.S. spy plane crashed in an isolated region of Colombia, killing five U.S. soldiers and revealing their controversial role in antidrug efforts. As FARC guerrillas continue to finance their revolution through trafficking in cocaine and heroin, the U.S. struggle against drug trafficking and the fight against Marxist insurgencies have become blurred.

The 1981 statute and subsequent amendments maintain the prohibition against the involvement of U.S. military personnel in arrest and seizure activities. This prohibition was based on the fear that further DOD involvement in drug law enforcement could:

- Compromise U.S. security by exposing military personnel to the potentially corrupting environment of drug trafficking (Sciolino and Engelberg 1988);
- Impair the strategic role of the military; and
- Present a threat to civil liberties.

DOD and Dope

U.S. Army Colonel James Hiett was in command of 200 U.S. military personnel waging a campaign against drug trafficking in Colombia. In 1999 a criminal complaint filed in Brooklyn federal court accused his wife of using the special mail service at the U.S. embassy in Bogotá to smuggle drugs into the United States (Watson 1999). Mrs. Hiett pled guilty. In 2000 the colonel was implicated in the case; he also pled guilty (Feuer 2000; Hays 2000).

Despite this fear, in 1988 legislation was overwhelmingly approved to dramatically expand the role of the military and allow the arrest of civilians under certain circumstances.

The U.S. Department of State uses former military pilots to fly helicopter gunships, transport planes, and crop dusters used by U.S. and foreign drug agents in countries where U.S. military operations are barred. Early in 1990 and again in 2006 National Guardsmen, who as members of state militias are not governed by the Posse Comitatus Act, were deployed to search for drugs and illegal immigrants along the border with Mexico and at ports of entry. U.S. military officials have traditionally opposed the involvement of the armed forces in law enforcement.

Postal Inspection Service

The Postal Inspection Service, among its several responsibilities, investigates the use of the U.S. mail to transport drugs.

Strike Forces and Task Forces

To overcome the inefficient competitive efforts and turf-protecting proclivities of enforcement agencies, since 1966 the federal government has utilized task forces in response to organized crime. That year, the Department of Justice established the "Buffalo Project" in upstate New York, bringing together personnel from a number of federal enforcement agencies. The success of the project led to the establishment of a strike force in every city that is known to have organized crime (Mafia) groups. In his 1982 "War on Drugs" speech, President Ronald Reagan announced the creation of regional Organized Crime Drug Enforcement Task Forces, and by the end of 1983 twelve such task forces were located in such core cities as New York, Los Angeles, and Detroit. In 1984 a thirteenth, the Florida/Caribbean task force, was added.

"The Task Force Program relies largely on the Continuing Criminal Enterprise statutory provision and the Racketeer Influenced and Corrupt Organizations (RICO) statutes. The conviction rate in cases reaching disposition is approximately 95 percent. State and local officers participate in nearly one-half of the Task Force investigations" (President's Commission on Organized Crime 1985: 319). Local enforcement officers may be sworn in as special U.S.

marshals, allowing them to enforce federal statutes and to cross jurisdictional boundaries that typically inhibit local enforcement agencies. Guidelines for the Organized Crime Drug Enforcement Task Force specify that a case is appropriate for Task Force adoption if it:

- appears to involve major drug trafficking figures;
- requires the resources and expertise of another agency because of possible violations other than those involving narcotics;
- has serious investigative ramifications extending to other geographical jurisdictions; and/or
- requires the assistance of an assistant U.S. attorney during the early stages of an investigation.

INTERPOL

The International Police Organization, known by its telegraphic designation INTERPOL, assists law enforcement agencies with investigative activities that transcend international boundaries. INTERPOL meant very little to the U.S. law enforcement community until 1968, when Iran announced that it was going to end its ban on opium production. At the same time there appeared to be an epidemic of drug use in the United States. A U.S. INTERPOL National Central Bureau (NCB) was quickly activated in Washington, D.C.

As of 2005, there were 186 INTERPOL members; a country becomes a member merely by announcing its intention to join. In each member country there is an NCB that acts as a point of contact and coordination with the General Secretariat, which is headquartered in Lyon, France. The General Secretariat has a staff of around 500 people, some of whom are law enforcement officers, from more than eighty different countries. INTERPOL is under the day-to-day direction of a secretary general; it is a coordinating body and has no investigators or law enforcement agents of its own.

The U.S. NCB receives about 12,000 requests for assistance from federal, state, and local law enforcement agencies each year. These are checked and coded by technical staff and entered into the INTERPOL Case Tracking System (ICTS), a computer-controlled index of people, organizations, and other crime information items. The ICTS conducts automatic searches of new entries, retrieving those that correlate with international crime. The requests are forwarded to senior staff members, who serve as INTERPOL case investigators. These are usually veteran agents from a federal agency whose experience includes work with foreign police forces. Each investigator is on loan from his or her principal agency.

Requests for investigative assistance include a whole range of criminal activity—murder, drug violations, illicit firearms traffic—and often involve locating fugitives for arrest and extradition. The bureau also receives investigative requests for criminal histories, license checks, and other ID verifications (Fooner 1985). The Financial and Economic Crime Unit at INTERPOL headquarters facilitates the exchange of information about offshore banking and money-laundering schemes. Monitoring this type of activity can sometimes lead to identifying suspects involved in drug trafficking who had previously escaped detection.

STREET-LEVEL LAW ENFORCEMENT

Efficient street-level enforcement, argues Mark Moore (1977), is a strategy worth pursuing, even if there is *displacement*—sellers moving to new locations and becoming more cautious. Jonathan Caulkins (1992) agrees that even when there is complete displacement, benefits to society accrue. Because street-level enforcement makes sellers more cautious and therefore more difficult to find, the buyer is forced to spend more time searching for a connection and less time searching for money (criminal opportunity) or actually using drugs. Under such conditions many users might be motivated to seek treatment, although there is often a shortage of available treatment programs. New users in particular will have difficulty "scoring." If this situation becomes widespread, profits from drug wholesaling will drop as if there were a drop in consumer demand.

In Lynn, Massachusetts, a drug task force made up of six state police officers and a city detective was deployed to decrease the flagrant selling of heroin in the city's High Rock area. Open drug dealing poses special threats. "Some neighborhood residents, particularly children, may become users; and . . . the behavior of buyers and sellers will be disruptive or worse. In poor neighborhoods, the opportunity for quick money offered by the illicit market may compete with entry-level licit jobs and divert labor-market entrants from legitimate careers. When the drug sold is heroin, residents are likely to be bothered by users 'nodding' in doorways and heroin-using prostitutes soliciting" (Kleiman 1988: 10). The goal was achieved, and drugs were harder to purchase in the area. This led to an increase in the number of people seeking treatment for drug abuse. A significant reduction in street crime was also reported for the area (Kleiman 1988). The drying up of immediate sources of heroin can potentially reduce experimentation, although long-term users will merely be inconvenienced. The time and energy required to establish new sources, however, might otherwise be spent on drug use and criminality. If treatment is available, the crackdown might serve as an incentive for entering a treatment program.

In New York City a 1984 street-level enforcement effort known as Operation Pressure Point (OPP) was designed to improve the quality of life and reduce drug-related crime in an area of the city's Lower East Side. Drug trafficking in the area had become so blatant that residents and their political representatives demanded police action. OPP instituted aggressive patrolling by uniformed officers, cleared abandoned buildings and parks of drug users, and sent out detectives to make "buy-and-bust" arrests. The risk of arrest increased dramatically for both buyers and sellers, and most of them abandoned the area and others resorted to low-profile trafficking. OPP followed up these activities with programs designed to strengthen the community and increase cooperation with and support for the police. The program achieved its goals and

Drug-Sniffing Dogs

In 2000 the Supreme Court ruled (*Indianapolis v. Edmond, et al.* 531 U.S. 32, 2000) that in the absence of any suspicion, police checkpoints that briefly detain drivers and use drug-sniffing dogs violate the Fourth Amendment. Checkpoints are permitted, however, for discovering and taking intoxicated drivers off the road because that protects public safety. In 2005, however, the Court ruled (*Illinois v. Caballes*, 543 U.S. 405) that during a routine traffic stop police may use a trained dog to sniff the car for drugs. Such drug-sniffing activity had already been ruled permissible for luggage at airports.

neighborhood residents reported being very satisfied. Similar operations in other parts of New York City, however, have not been as successful (Zimmer 1990). Mike Hough (2005) cautions that this type of drug enforcement can have the unintended consequence of increased revenue for remaining dealers, who face less competition.

Street-level enforcement is expensive and, if it is to be more than briefly effective, must be combined with sufficient prison space to accommodate the increase in population. In an attempt to stem the 1985 crack epidemic in New York City, police initiated a street-level crackdown with impressive results: Crack arrests and jailings reached record levels; felony drug arrests went up 21 percent the first year and 70 percent the next. Total jail sentences for drug felonies increased by 60 percent in 1987. Nevertheless, the street price of crack dropped steadily. And in response to the stepped-up police activity, crack dealers began recruiting thousands of young addicts to make street sales, overwhelming a number of city neighborhoods as well as the city's overextended police force. Placing unusually large resources in one area also raises the possibility that the problem will be displaced into areas where law enforcement efforts are less concentrated. Furthermore, the reduction of crime in Lynn, Massachusetts, discussed earlier was short-lived, and a similar crackdown in Lawrence, Massachusetts, actually resulted in an increase in crime, particularly burglary and robbery (A. Barnett 1988; Bouza 1990: 47).

In New York, in response to intensive police efforts against street dealing, sellers moved away from high-profile and vulnerable street sales to mobile delivery services using pagers and/or cellular telephones. As a result of the extra costs associated with this type of drug trafficking, in terms of both the equipment and time spent making deliveries, sellers began dealing only with those who could purchase large amounts at once, with the attendant risk of increased consumption. These buyers may become dealers to their friends. This strategy can also move drug selling from urban areas into the suburbs, making drugs more accessible to those who were reluctant to purchase in neighborhoods with which they are not familiar.

Street-level enforcement efforts bring with them the specter of corruption and related abuses: "Bribery, perjured testimony, faked evidence and abused rights in the past have accompanied street-level narcotics enforcement. Indeed,

"Buy-and-Bust" Is a Bust

"[I]t is unlikely that buy-bust operations aimed specifically at street dealers will significantly disrupt the distribution system. Sellers operating at this level are easily replaced and while buy-bust operations may result in large number of arrests, convictions rarely lead to lengthy sentences" (Hough 2005: 25).

The 100-to-1 Ratio: Crack Penalties and Race

Cocaine in the form of crack is most likely to be used and sold by African Americans, while powdered cocaine is often used and sold by whites. Under federal statutes, "It takes one hundred times the amount of powder cocaine to equal the same sentence as crack cocaine" (*Illicit Drug Policies*, 2002: 134). A cocaine dealer would have to sell $75,000 worth of the drug in powdered form to get the same mandatory five-year federal sentence that a crack dealer would receive for selling $750 worth. And "crack is the only drug that carries a mandatory prison term for possession, whether or not the intent is to distribute" (C. Jones 1995: 9).

it was partly to avoid such abuses that many police departments began concentrating on higher-level traffickers and restricted drug efforts to special units" (Moore and Kleiman 1989: 8). These special units have brought problems of their own. New York provides an example. In 1971, to centralize drugs, vice, and organized crime enforcement and to prevent corruption through stricter supervision, the city established the Organized Crime Bureau. Early in 1992 the police department's chief of inspectional services submitted a confidential report citing recent cases in which the bureau's narcotic officers were accused of lying to strengthen cases and to obtain search warrants; there were no accusations of corruption. The report noted: "Of all units in the department, the greatest integrity hazards and vulnerability exist in narcotics" (Raab 1992).

ISSUES IN DRUG LAW ENFORCEMENT

Besides those discussed at the beginning of this chapter, several perplexing issues complicate drug law enforcement. The first involves measuring success: How can we determine whether drug law enforcement in general or specific activities in particular are successful? What criteria can provide a standard for measuring success? The number of people arrested, convicted, or imprisoned? The amount of drugs seized? The level of purity or price of the product sold on the streets? The number of people admitted to hospital emergency rooms for drug overdoses? The number of people seeking admission to drug treatment programs? In practice, we use all of these, with often confusing results. For example, increased arrests and drug seizures have often been accompanied by declining prices and greater levels of purity. A 1983 report by the Comptroller General points out that while enhanced federal resources increased the amount of illegal drugs seized, purity at the retail level increased while prices fell. The Comptroller General also revealed that some drug seizures are counted several times by different agencies that are eager to claim credit and improve their statistics. Sometimes there is triple-counting: The Coast Guard typically turns its interdicted drugs over to Customs, while the seizure may be the result of intelligence information developed by DEA, and all three agencies include the amount in their totals.

Successful law enforcement efforts, at least in theory, should reduce the available supply of drugs while driving up the price and reducing purity. When the level of purity dips below some hypothetical level but the price remains high, the abuser will supposedly no longer find it worth his or her while to make a purchase. The abuser will either switch to a more readily available chemical—perhaps alcohol—or abandon drug use completely. In fact, successful law enforcement efforts may cause a switch from a less dangerous substance—for example, marijuana—to a more dangerous substance, such as heroin, a situation that apparently occurred when Operation Intercept at the Mexican border effectively choked off supplies of marijuana in 1969. "There was an upsurge in heroin use among urban, white, middle-class high school students shortly after Operation Intercept" (Zinberg and Robertson 1972: 210). More recent successful campaigns against marijuana might be causing an increase in the use of alcohol, particularly among adolescents. Increases in law enforcement do not necessarily translate into reductions in supply; a widely heralded (by politicians) 1986 $1.7 billion federal antidrug law resulted in an increase in drug seizures and arrests with no discernible impact on supply (J. Johnson 1987).

The structure of the drug market, as was noted in Chapter 11, makes it the last refuge of laissez-faire capitalism. The Drug Enforcement Administration (2003: 7) argues that the "element of risk created by strong enforcement policies raises the price of drugs, and therefore lowers the demand." But how does law enforcement affect the price and use of illegal drugs? Mark Kleiman (1985: 69) states that the key to analyzing this question "is the response of drug purchasers to increasing drug prices." If there is a reduction in supply and a corresponding increase in price, will the amount of drug consumption remain unchanged? Is demand relatively inelastic to price? If demand is relatively elastic, consumption will decrease as price goes up. This will cause a decrease in the profits of drug traffickers. If demand is inelastic, however, drug law enforcement may actually increase the profits of traffickers, since those who elude arrest and prosecution will reap higher prices. With respect to heroin, Kleiman notes, consumption is likely to decrease in the long run as addicts, unable to keep up with the increase in price, enter drug treatment or find alternative drugs. The issue with respect to cocaine is more difficult. Cocaine has typically been relatively expensive, although the introduction of crack altered the market. Nevertheless, Kleiman argues, an increase in price as a result of law enforcement efforts is likely to increase the profits of cocaine traffickers; it is a market that is relatively impervious to price.

At the domestic distribution level, successful law enforcement efforts whittle down the number of people involved in drug trafficking. This may leave a void at certain levels of distribution that, in a seller's market, will simply attract new entrepreneurs. Furthermore, the better-organized groups resist and survive law enforcement efforts. Thus, the level of law enforcement vigor and ability determines whether or not certain groups will come to dominate the drug trade and bring a concomitant increase in profits by virtue of oligopolistic (scarcity of sellers) market circumstances. On the other hand, reduced law enforcement allows more groups to remain in business, with a corresponding reduction in profits, resulting from a more competitive market. Under such conditions organizations that are equipped with resources for violence may be tempted to use force to reduce competition.

Steven Wisotsky (1987) argues that, at least in theory, combating cocaine abuse should be significantly easier than battling heroin abuse. The major traffickers operate out of Colombia with major supply lines that are more restrictive than those for heroin (which comes from several continents). However, there are analogs for many popular drugs of abuse. Successful interdiction might reduce the amount of heroin and cocaine entering the United States, but if demand remains unchanged, underground chemists will be inspired to greater creativity. Indeed, experienced cocaine users cannot tell the difference between cocaine and synthetic substances that mimic cocaine, and heroin addicts often prefer the synthetic opiate fentanyl to the diluted heroin typically available on the streets.

Another issue is the argument that the substantial investment in drug law enforcement increases criminality—drug abusers committing crimes to support habits—and diverts resources that could be better utilized to deal with more serious criminality. Police, prosecutors, and judges are occupied with drug law enforcement, and U.S. jails, prisons, and probation and parole systems are overcrowded. Our drug enforcement agents are exposed to great danger, both from a most violent class of criminals and from being around the drugs themselves.

Our "war" on drugs is really a fight against socioeconomic dynamics that are reputed to be unconquerable: the profit motive and the law of supply and demand.

SUMMARY

Drug abuse is a combination of susceptibility and availability, and law enforcement can affect availability. Law enforcement efforts are constrained by constitutional due process, in particular the Fourth Amendment, jurisdictional limitations, and corruption, both domestic and foreign. The necessary use of informants and undercover work in the fight against drug trafficking is particularly prone to corruption.

The legal foundation for federal drug law violations is the Controlled Substances Act, which places a substance in one of five schedules, and states have largely followed the federal model. People who are involved in the illegal drug business can be arrested and prosecuted for such offenses as manufacture, importation, distribution, possession, and sale. Particularly useful are conspiracy statutes that obviate the need for proving a substantive crime and permit the prosecution of an entire organization. Since money laundering is a crucial element in wholesale drug dealing, there is a specific statute that outlaws efforts to conceal the source of funds. More controversial are civil forfeiture statutes because of the possibility of harming innocent third parties.

Local law enforcement efforts are typically directed against midlevel or street-level dealers; federal efforts focus on large-scale wholesalers, many of whom operate on a transnational basis. While several federal agencies have some responsibility for drug enforcement, it is the DEA and Immigration and Customs Enforcement that have the largest roles. Military involvement in drug law enforcement is limited by the Posse Comitatus Act, and military officials have traditionally opposed even a supportive role.

Street-level drug law enforcement can result in displacement but disrupts connections between retailers and consumers. Intensive street-level operations are expensive and can have the effect of reducing competition and increasing profits of remaining dealers. The increased arrests can also overburden the justice system.

Measuring "success" in drug law enforcement is elusive because of a lack of standards regarding arrests, seizures, and purity levels. Law enforcement that reduces the available supply of a particular drug may cause substitution, and the profits that can result with such market conditions may encourage new players to get involved.

In the next chapter, we will examine our policy for responding to drug abuse.

REVIEW QUESTIONS

1. In terms of reducing drug use, how do cost and availability explain the purpose of drug law enforcement?
2. What is the relationship between drug law enforcement and the two models of criminal justice—crime control and due process?
3. How do constitutional and jurisdictional limitations constrain drug law enforcement?
4. How does the exclusionary rule restrain drug law enforcement agents?
5. Why is the supervision of law enforcement agents particularly difficult in drug law enforcement?
6. What are the two main purposes of the 1988 International Convention Against Illicit Traffic in Narcotic Drugs and Psychotropic Substances?
7. Why is corruption more of a problem in drug law enforcement than in other areas of law enforcement?
8. What problems arise in using criminal informants in drug law enforcement?
9. What are the offenses for which people involved in drug trafficking may be prosecuted?
10. What is the difference between actual and constructive possession of dangerous drugs?
11. What two legal elements are necessary to support a charge of conspiracy?
12. What is the advantage of using conspiracy statutes in dealing with drug-trafficking organizations?

13. What is the difference between criminal and civil forfeiture?
14. Why is civil forfeiture controversial?
15. What powers of a grand jury make it a useful tool in drug investigations?
16. Why is federal drug law enforcement so fragmented in the United States?
17. Why is the use of the military in drug law enforcement so controversial in the United States?
18. What are some of the unintended negative consequences of successful drug law enforcement?
19. What are the responsibilities of each of the following federal agencies with respect to drug law enforcement?
    (a) Coast Guard
    (b) Immigrations and Customs Enforcement
    (c) Drug Enforcement Administration
    (d) Federal Bureau of Investigation
    (e) Internal Revenue Service
    (f) Military
    (g) U.S. Marshals Service
20. What is a controlled buy?
21. What is the strike force/task force concept, and what is its purpose?
22. Why is it difficult to measure success in drug law enforcement?
23. How can drug law enforcement actually increase the profits of some traffickers?
24. What are the advantages and disadvantages of concentrating drug law enforcement efforts at the street level?

Drug Abuse Policy

Five years and $3 billion into the most aggressive counter narcotics operation ever here, American and Colombian officials say they have eradicated a record-breaking million acres of coca plants; yet cocaine remains as available as ever on American streets, perhaps more so.

Joel Brinkley (2005: 3)

America is not going to be the world's first drug-free society.

Jonathan Caulkins, Peter Reuter, Martin Iguchi, and James Chiesa (2005: 35)

Out of the history that we explored in Chapter 2 developed two basic models for responding to the use of dangerous substances. The first is a *disease model*: The abuser is "helpless" and "blameless," analogous to the cancer or coronary patient. This model defines substance abuse as a disease to be prevented or treated, just like any other public health problem. The second is a *moral-legal model* that defines alcohol and other psychoactive drugs as either legal or illegal and attempts to control availability through penalties. The moral-legal model utilizes three methods to control potentially dangerous drugs in the United States:

1. *Regulation.* Certain substances that may be harmful to their consumers can be sold with only minimal restrictions. These substances are heavily taxed, providing government with an important source of revenue. Alcoholic beverages and tobacco products are subjected to disproportionate taxation, and their sale is restricted to people above a certain age. Special licenses are usually required for the manufacture, distribution, and sale of regulated substances.

2. *Medical auspices.* The use of certain potentially harmful substances is permitted under medical supervision. The medical profession is given control over legal access to specific substances that have medical uses because when the substances are taken under the direction of a physician, their value outweighs their danger (J. Kaplan 1983a). In this category are barbiturates, amphetamines, certain opiates (morphine and codeine), and heroin substitutes such as methadone.

3. *Criminalization.* Statutory limitations make the manufacture or possession of certain dangerous substances a crime and empower specific public officials to enforce these statutes. Certain other substances are permitted under medical auspices, but punishment is specified for individuals who possess these substances outside of accepted medical practice. Thus, heroin has no permissible use in the United States—an absolute prohibition—while other psychoactive substances, such as morphine and Seconal (secobarbital sodium), are permissible for medical use but are illegal under any other circumstances.

Revisionist History

"Only when the negative consequences of cocaine addiction were recognized and publicized did perceptions change. Drug abuse was condemned, and new laws were passed producing a healthier nation with a lower crime rate" (Office of National Drug Control Policy 2001: 3).

The official response to a particular substance—regulation or law enforcement—determines the manner in which the user of that substance will be treated. Thus, the alcoholic is typically viewed according to the disease model, while the user of illegal drugs has the criminal label attached. From the Civil War to the 1920s the U.S. response to dangerous drugs moved from permissiveness to one of rigid law enforcement—from the public health model to the moral-legal model. The practical effect of this change was "to define the addict as a criminal offender" (Schur 1965: 130), leading to the creation of a vast black market in which drug entrepreneurs quickly filled the void left by the withdrawal of lawful sources: "In the 1920s this country had a large number of addicts, but they were not regarded as criminals by the law; in general, they did not commit crimes and conducted their lives much the same way as the nonaddict population did. Clinics and private physicians were free

Symbiosis

"Drug treatment . . . is demonstratively effective in reducing crime. Law enforcement helps 'divert' users into treatment and makes the treatment system work more efficiently by giving treatment providers needed leverage over the clients they serve. Treatment programs narrow the problem for law enforcement by shrinking the market for illegal drugs" (Office of National Drug Control Policy 2002b: 4).

to prescribe maintenance doses. It was the outlawing of the addictive drug that gave rise to an illegal market controlled by organized crime; and it is the exorbitant cost of the outlawed drug that has driven addicts into criminal activity to support their habit" (National Council on Crime and Delinquency 1974: 4).

Drug policy in the United States has been guided by "commonly shared simplifications"—in particular, the belief that "drug problems are largely attributable to morally compromised or pathological individuals who were not properly inculcated in childhood with normal American values such as self-control and respect for the law. These individuals must be disciplined and punished by authorities to deter them from involvement (for pleasure or profit) with inherently dangerous, addicting drugs" (Gerstein and Harwood 1990: 41).

Drug use, notes Gresham Sykes, "became defined as a fundamental affront, part of a larger pattern challenging society with an alternative view of a meaningful life." The wrongdoing of the drug user was "moved into the category of the most serious offense—treason—where the individual forsakes his society for an enemy allegiance" (Sykes 1967: 77). A "clearer case of misapplication of the criminal sanction," writes Herbert Packer (1968: 333), "would be difficult to imagine." Post–Harrison Act efforts against certain psychoactive chemicals were based on their potential to harm users. Policy has now come full circle, and it is the user who is the target of vigorous enforcement efforts: "We must focus responsibility and sanctions on illegal drug users" (White House Conference for a Drug Free America 1988: 9).

INCONGRUITIES BETWEEN FACTS AND POLICIES

Before examining the current policy, we need to return to the first chapter and recall some of the incongruities. Of the most widely used psychoactive drugs, heroin and cocaine (except for limited topical use) are banned; barbiturates, tranquilizers, and amphetamines are restricted; and alcohol, caffeine, and nicotine products are freely available. These inconsistencies make any response to the problem of substance abuse very difficult. How do you tell the progeny of cigarette-smoking, coffee- and alcohol-drinking, sedative-using parents that drugs should not be used for recreational purposes? "Someone who smokes tobacco is a *smoker*, but someone who smokes marijuana is a *drug user*" (Whiteacre 2005: 9). Therefore, "a major step toward developing sounder policy with respect to drugs would be to use that label for alcohol and nicotine (as the scientific literature already does), and to make an augmented Office of Drug Control Policy responsible for coordinating federal policy toward alcohol and nicotine as part of the overall national drug control strategy" (Reuter and Caulkins 1995: 1061).

Liquor and the Media

The U.S. liquor industry has adhered to a voluntary ban on advertising on radio since 1936 and on network television since 1948. Early in the twenty-first century, while the major networks continued their own ban, liquor ads began appearing on cable TV's hundreds of local broadcast stations (Elliott 2003).

To what extent does knowledge actually affect drug policy? Although nicotine and alcohol are clearly dangerous psychoactive chemicals—*drugs*—semantic fiction portrays them otherwise. Statutory vocabulary and social folklore have established the fiction that alcohol and nicotine are not really

Accomplices to Terror

In the wake of the September 11, 2001, terrorist attacks, the administration of President George W. Bush initiated a television campaign linking drugs to terrorism. Buying drugs, the splashy commercials announced, meant handing money to the 9/11 terrorists and their ilk. As part of this multimillion-dollar campaign, supporting ads were run in more than 200 newspapers. Problems with this approach are obvious. The most widely used illegal drug in the United States is marijuana, a domestic product. And, of course, U.S. allies, such as Afghanistan's Northern Alliance, have a long history of drug trafficking (Bendavid 2002).

Setting a National Example

When the citywide ban on smoking in the workplace took place in the nation's capital in 2006, Congress was exempt from its reach. Standing ashtrays, usually filled with cigar and cigarette butts, are still in the corridors, and the reception areas where lawmakers gather remain a smoke-filled environment (Kornblut 2006).

drugs at all (National Commission on Marijuana and Drug Abuse 1973). Furthermore, as the National Commission on Marijuana and Drug Abuse points out, to do otherwise would be inconsistent with our stated policy goal of eliminating drug abuse—an admission that we can never eliminate the drug use problem. Joseph Gusfield (1975) suggests that we distinguish between *scientific* knowledge—the body of facts and theories related to drug use—and *political* knowledge, which concerns public attitudes toward drug use, including scientific knowledge. Norman Zinberg (1984: 200) states that in the field of drug use, the truth will not necessarily set one free. The scientific truth he notes, is that not all psychoactive drug use is misuse; but because this concept contravenes formal social policy, those who present this message run the risk that "their work will be interpreted as condoning use."

Our response to easily abused substances is not based on the degree of danger inherent in their use. Indeed, measured on any dimension, alcohol is a more serious drug of abuse than marijuana, though this is not reflected in the U.S. legal system. And while marijuana smokers are subject to arrest and prosecution, people who smoke tobacco are left free of restraint save for the inconvenience posed by smoking-related cancer and emphysema. In 2006, it was determined that for some unknown reason, smoking marijuana does not increase the risk of lung cancer (Bloomberg News 2006). Furthermore, many dangerous substances, such as amphetamines, barbiturates, and a variety of sedatives, were actively promoted for use in dealing with anxiety, stress, obesity, or insomnia. Famous abusers of these substances, such as Marilyn Monroe and Elvis Presley, who have been commemorated on our postage stamps, are representative of a large abusing population that is not subjected to arrest and imprisonment. The pushers of these substances—the drug companies and their willing partners in the medical profession—are not arrested or prosecuted.

That some drugs are outlawed while others are legally and widely available is better understood in terms other than those of science or medicine: in terms of the tobacco industry, the alcoholic-beverage industry, the drug-manufacturing industry, and the dietary supplements industry. The 1994 Dietary Supplement Health and Education Act allows manufacturers to market an array of products, many of them ephedra-based, with claims that these products will boost energy

■ | Voice of Reason

Dealing appropriately with raves is difficult for police. On the one hand, police often face substantial pressure from mainstream society to put an end to raves, usually through aggressive law enforcement. On the other hand, raves are enormously popular among a significant minority of teenagers and young adults, most of whom are generally law-abiding and responsible. Strict enforcement efforts can alienate a key segment of this population from government in general and the police in particular. To be sure, raves can pose genuine risks, but these are frequently exaggerated in the public's mind (Scott 2002: 1–2).

levels, improve your sex drive and performance, help you to lose weight, and cause you to gain muscle. "The law states that you don't have to prove natural supplements are safe or effective before you market them; the government has to prove that they aren't after the fact" (O'Keefe and Quinn 2005: 88). Ironically, one of the major purveyors of these products is a multimillionaire and convicted drug dealer.

In addition to political contributions, the purveyors of legal psychoactive substances are able to protect their interests through advertising and employment of media specialists. In fact, the public's knowledge of and response to the "drug problem" is mediated through newspapers and television. Frightening news stories create pressure for more vigorous drug enforcement, which increases drug-fighting budgets, which yield more arrests (L. G. Hunt 1977). The resulting statistics are then viewed as proof of a growing drug problem. "Evidence," in fact, "has little bearing on the kind of moral beliefs many people hold: that the use of psychoactive drugs is wrong, and their sale more wrong; or that government intrusion into the drug use decision is wrong, and harsh sanctions against possession are also wrong" (Caulkins, Reuter, Iguchi, and Chiesa 2005: 2).

The "volume of attention generated when the national press converges on a story, like drugs, virtually demands a political response. In their haste, these [politicians'] reactions may not always be carefully considered" (Merriam 1989: 31). Convergence occurs when media sources discover an issue and respond to each other "in a cycle of peaking coverage, before largely dismissing the issues" (Reese and Danielian 1989: 30n). In 1989, for example, President George H. W. Bush made a major television address during which he "declared war" on drugs. For the next week, network news averaged four stories each evening on drugs, and an opinion poll indicated that 64 percent of the public viewed drugs as America's most important problem. A year later, that figure had fallen to 10 percent as new problems received presidential and media attention (Oreskes 1990).

On November 17, 1985, crack cocaine was mentioned for the first time in the major media, in the *New York Times*. In less than eleven months, every major news source had stories about crack—more than 1,000 of them—capped

One DEA Agent's Lament

"It is both sobering and painful to realize, after twenty-five years of undercover work, having personally accounted for at least three thousand criminals serving fifteen thousand years in jail, and having seized several tons of illegal substances, that my career was meaningless and had absolutely no effect whatsoever in the so-called war on drugs" (Levine 1990: 11).

by specials on CBS and NBC (Inciardi, Surratt, Chitwood, and McCoy 1996). This set off an ill-conceived and, some argue, racist legislative response. Under federal law, for purposes of punishment a given amount of crack is equivalent to 100 times that amount of powdered cocaine.

In 1991 the Minnesota Supreme Court found unconstitutional and discriminatory against African Americans a state law providing twenty years in prison for crack possession but only five years for possession of powdered cocaine. In 1988, of the people charged with crack possession in Minnesota 96.6 percent were black, while those charged with possessing cocaine hydrochloride were 79.6 percent white (*State v. Russell* 477 N.W.2d 886). In the twenty-first century it would be difficult to find mention of crack in the major media.

With these incongruities serving as a backdrop, let us critically examine U.S. drug policy on reducing the supply of drugs and reducing demand for them.

SUPPLY REDUCTION THROUGH THE CRIMINAL SANCTION

In a free-market economy, in theory, reducing the supply of a product will drive up the price and thus reduce demand and consumption. But in the drug economy an increase in price might just raise the revenue for traffickers because there is no significant decrease in consumption. The evidence is that there is not a single documented instance in which one or a succession of high-level drug cases coincided with a substantial reduction in consumption in a city (Kleiman 1989). John DiNardo (1993: 63) failed to find "any significant effects of law enforcement on the price of cocaine faced by users." (See also Caulkins, Crawford, and Reuter 1993.) Thus, enforcement to reduce the supply of drugs might simply eliminate the less-organized criminal distributors, resulting in an increase in the profits of criminal organizations that are strong enough and ruthless enough to survive (Kleiman 1989).

Overflowing Prisons

An alternative strategy, focusing on lower-level dealers, presents two additional problems: the political problem of going after small wrongdoers while largely ignoring the big ones (Kleiman 1985) and the practical problem of the

A Racist Drug War?

A study conducted by *USA Today* revealed that African Americans are four times as likely as whites to be arrested on drug charges, even though both groups use drugs at about the same rate; and African Americans are more likely to be imprisoned for drug charges than are non-Hispanic whites (Meddis 1993).

The war on drugs also exacerbates racial disparities related to health and well-being in minority communities: (1) Federal law prohibits ex-prison inmates from receiving any federal benefits for five years if their conviction was for drug possession or drug trafficking; (2) they are also barred from Temporary Assistance to Needy Families and food stamps; (3) and they become ineligible for one year after conviction, two years after a second conviction, and indefinitely after a third for federal education assistance ("How the War on Drugs Influences the Health and Well-Being of Minority Communities" 2001).

cost of arresting, prosecuting, and imprisoning large numbers of people. However, this approach was the mainstay of the so-called (Governor) Rockefeller Laws in New York during the 1970s. As a result, the time needed to dispose of drug cases nearly doubled between 1973 and 1976, and by mid-1976 the system was approaching collapse. Research indicates that the use of drugs increased during this time, as did drug-related crimes such as burglary, robbery, and theft (Joint Committee on New York Drug Law Evaluation 1977).

In 1987 the strategy recommended by Kleiman caused New York City to establish special courts to rapidly dispose of felony drug cases through plea bargaining because the regular criminal courts were being flooded with arrests of street-level drug dealers. Because of the volume, it was taking six to twelve months to dispose of a case, which created a chaotically overcrowded situation on Riker's Island, the city jail for people awaiting trial (Raab 1987). In the decade from 1981 to 1991 the average daily jail population in New York City increased 170 percent. The *New York Times* concluded that "New York City's war on drugs has resulted in so many arrests that there are simply not enough prosecutors, judges, Legal Aid lawyers or probation officers to give adequate attention to each of the thousands of cases, let alone courtrooms to try the suspects in or jail cells to hold the convicts" ("Drug Arrests and the Courts' Pleas for Help" 1989: E6).

Other states followed New York's lead, with similar results. The number of people who were convicted of drug felonies in state courts increased almost 70 percent in the two-year period from 1988 to 1990. In Cook County (Chicago), Illinois, the chief criminal court judge stated that drug cases were overwhelming the county's court system (O'Connor 1990). In the federal courts the number of drug arrests has so backed up the system that judges are unable to attend to civil cases, increasing delays despite a drop in the number of civil filings in the past few years. By 2004 federal prisions were operating at 140 percent of capacity, and state prisons were operating

Hypocrisy?

- In 1997 Texas Governor George W. Bush signed a bill authorizing judges to imprison people convicted of possessing one-twenty-eighth of an ounce of cocaine. In 1999, as a Republican presidential candidate, Governor Bush was asked by reporters whether he had ever used cocaine. He refused to answer the question.
- In 2006 Rush Limbaugh admitted to illegally securing OxyContin. The conservative radio host, who had advocated imprisoning drug users, avoided this fate by paying a fine and agreeing to drug testing.

at 115 percent of capacity (*Prisoners in 2004*, 2005). Jails throughout the United States are already being operated severely over capacity, and any strategy that causes a significant increase in the inmate population could be disastrous.

The General Accounting Office (1991) found that overcrowded jails and prisons, the result of increased drug arrests and prosecutions, resulted in more offenders being placed in the probation and parole systems, which, in turn, has generally decreased the level of supervision of probationers and parolees as a result of excessive caseloads. It has also led to emergency prison release programs and an increase in plea bargaining—signs of a system that is spinning its wheels. Jails and prisons are scarce resources because of their exorbitant cost: The annual per-inmate cost of imprisonment ranges as high as $30,000, and the cost of building a prison is as high as $100,000 per cell. Are scarce tax dollars being spent wisely in the "war" on drugs? A report by the RAND Drug Policy Research Center concluded that mandatory minimum prison sentences for low-level drug violators are "not justifiable on the basis of cost-effectiveness at reducing cocaine consumption, cocaine expenditures, or drug-related crime" (Caulkins, Rydell, Schwabe, and Chiesa 1997: xvi). A study of similar convicted drug offenders found that those "placed on probation had substantially lower recidivism rates than those who were sentenced to prison" (Spohn and Holleran 2002: 351).

Manhattan district attorney Robert M. Morgenthau (1988: 27) has noted that "we are putting more drug dealers in jail for longer terms than ever before." But "not only have we not 'conquered drugs,' but drugs are more available on the streets of our cities than ever before." "Long sentences for serious crimes have intuitive appeal. They respond to deeply held beliefs about punishment for evil actions, and in many cases ensure that, by removing a criminal from the streets, further crimes that would have been committed will not be. But in the case of black-market crimes like drug dealing, a jailed supplier is often replaced by another supplier if demand remains" (Caulkins 1997: xxv). In 1996 and again in 1998 Arizona voters took matters into their own hands and enacted propositions that mandate treatment instead of imprisonment for drug offenders (Egan 1999b).

Marijuana Policy

The cannabis policy debate "has often been represented as a forced choice between two positions: Doves who argue that cannabis use is harmless, and hence it should be legalized; and Hawks who argue that cannabis use is harmful to health, and hence should continue to be prohibited. This false antithesis has prevented a realistic appraisal of the adverse health effects of cannabis. It has meant that the public has been exposed to two polarized views of the adverse health effects of cannabis dictated by their proponents' views on the legal status of cannabis. The Doves focus on the modest health risks of intermittent cannabis use; the Hawks emphasize the worst-case interpretation of the evidence on the risks of chronic cannabis use. There seems to be an implicit agreement between Doves and Hawks that the acute health effects of intermittent cannabis use provide at best a weak justification for prohibition. The Doves stress that there is no risk of overdose from cannabis. The Hawks respond by pointing to the possibility of death or serious injury in a motor vehicle accident if cannabis users drive, and to the social consequences of engaging in risky sexual and other behavior while intoxicated by cannabis" (Hall 1999: 1).

Would Changing the Penalties Help?

Seldom?

"Seldom does anyone in this country go to prison for nothing more than smoking pot" (Office of National Drug Control Policy n.d.: 31).

What about a policy of incarceration for only the most serious criminal offenders, such as robbers, among the drug-abusing population? Unfortunately, this is not feasible. "Existing criminal justice practices would fail to detect most persons who actually are robber-dealers" (B. Johnson, Lipton, and Wish 1986a: 187). In their study, Bruce Johnson and his colleagues found that none of the high-rate addict-robbers were ever arrested for robbery. In fact, "less than 1 percent of self-reported crimes by cocaine-heroin abusers result in an arrest; the higher the crime rate, the lower the possibility of arrest per thousand crimes" (1986b: 4).

In a report to the Ford Foundation, Patricia Wald and Peter Hutt (1972: 37) recommended reducing penalties to a fine or abolishing them completely for those possessing drugs for personal use: "If this were done, drug users—but not drug traffickers—could then be handled on a public health and social-welfare basis. . . . Law-enforcement efforts would, and in our opinion should, continue, but they would be directed at illegal distribution. And illegal drugs would remain subject to confiscation wherever found." In Switzerland and the Netherlands (as will be discussed in Chapter 14) there has been an unofficial policy of tolerating small-time drug sellers and their customers, as long as they do not become public nuisances. At best, states Kleiman (1989: xviii), law enforcement efforts can prevent the "effective decriminalization" of drugs, the point at which trafficking "is so open and flagrant that demand increases because the apparent social disapproval is reduced."

Increasing penalties for drug trafficking seems an unrealistic strategy because sentences for trafficking are already high—forty years for a second

Winning the War by Getting Tough

- The 32-year-old real estate attorney and Harvard Law School graduate was sentenced to fifteen years in prison for possession of cocaine. The police had discovered 36 grams (28.35 grams equals 1 ounce) of diluted cocaine in a raid on the attorney's home in Hoffman Estates, Illinois. Authorities had been tipped off by a boarder, who was seeking leniency for a drug conviction of his own.

- A 49-year-old dockworker was flagged down by an acquaintance and for five dollars agreed to drive him to a hamburger stand. Once there, the acquaintance was arrested by federal agents for dealing drugs. The dockworker, who had no criminal record, was convicted of conspiracy and received a ten-year sentence as mandated by the 1986 Anti-Drug Abuse Act. He will be eligible for release after serving 8.5 years.

- In St. Louis a 24-year-old mother of three young children received a mandatory 11.5-year federal prison sentence without possibility of parole for her minor role in a cocaine deal. It was her first offense, and evidence indicates that her involvement was the result of a combination of fear and ignorance.

- In California a 36-year-old Mexican American field worker, who does not speak English and who is the mother of five daughters, was found guilty of transporting several hundred pounds of cocaine and heroin into the United States. She claimed that she did not know that the van, which was not hers, contained drugs; at trial it was not proven that she did know. Her ten-year sentence does not permit parole but does allow about sixteen months off for good behavior.

Sources: "New Drug Law Leaves No Room for Mercy" (1989); Tackett (1990); Chapman (1991b).

offense—and because capital punishment (for drug-transaction-related murders) has now become part of the federal effort against drugs. (Severe penalties encourage in traffickers the mindset that they have little or nothing to lose by using violence in their attempts to avoid arrest and prosecution.)

Penalties in Other Nations

Some third-world countries execute drug dealers, but the impact of this policy is questionable. For example, although Malaysia imposes the death penalty for anyone who is found trafficking in heroin or marijuana, the substances are readily available even to foreigners traveling through that country. The U.S. Drug Enforcement Administration (DEA) points out that "despite severe penalties, no significant diminution of trafficking or production occurred" (1991: 9). Draconian attempts to deal with opium and heroin abuse in Iran have proven unsuccessful. Smugglers and traffickers have been hanged there at a rate of about six hundred a year since 1988 (Ghazi 1991). (The U.S. State

Drug Justice

Under a Michigan "get tough on drugs" law the mandatory term for possession of more than 650 grams (about 23 ounces) of an illegal drug exceeds that for either rape or second-degree murder. By 1992 more than 160 people were serving life sentences without parole in Michigan for drug offenses. One was Gary Fannon. Fannon had just completed high school and was planning a career as an auto mechanic when he was approached by an undercover Michigan police officer. The officer, who was later fired for drug use, paid Fannon to purchase drugs for him, the amounts getting larger and larger until he bought 2.2 pounds for $32,000. Although he had no prior criminal record, Fannon was sentenced to life without parole. Although the Michigan law was upheld by the U.S. Supreme Court (*Harmelin v. Michigan*, 111 S.Ct. 2680, 1991), in 1992 the state supreme court ruled it unconstitutional: The justices found the denial of parole to be unconstitutionally harsh—it is the penalty for first-degree murder—and ordered those sentenced under the law to be considered for parole after ten years.

Sources: Associated Press (1991, 1992); Cauchon (1992).

Department has accused Iran of executing political prisoners under the guise of drug trafficking cases [Tyler 1991].)

The People's Republic of China routinely executes drug traffickers who are found in possession of a pound or more of heroin; in 1994 more than 466 were killed in Yunnan Province alone (Tyler 1995). On one day in 1999 China executed at least seventy-one people as part of its antidrug campaign (Associated Press 1999b). Despite the executions drug trafficking continues to thrive, particularly in Yunnan and Guangdong provinces in southern China, and the country has become a transshipment point for Golden Triangle and Golden Crescent heroin (French 2004).

Centralizing Federal Drug Law Enforcement

Increasing the government's drug law enforcement ability—for example, by improving enforcement resources and centralizing the operational command structure of the executive branch—can bring its own dangers. These are stressed by Edward Jay Epstein (1977: 8), who argues that President Richard Nixon used the "war on heroin" to "set up a series of special units which, it was hoped, would conduct clandestine surveillance of both government officials and newsmen during his first administration." On the basis of an executive order, the Office of Drug Abuse Law Enforcement (ODALE) was established with agents requisitioned from the Bureau of Narcotics and Dangerous Drugs, Customs, the Internal Revenue Service, and the Bureau of Alcohol, Tobacco and Firearms. This strike force was funded by the executive branch (Law Enforcement Assistance Administration), thus bypassing the need for congressional

A Sting Hurts

> U.S. DEA agents hid 100 pounds of cocaine on a Belize Air International Flight going from Miami to Honduras. Hoping to track and capture drug smugglers, the DEA did not inform the three crew members, the three passengers, or Honduran officials. In Honduras the cocaine was discovered, and the passengers and crew were detained and subjected (they allege in a lawsuit) to twelve days of electric shock treatment and rubber hose beatings. The six were released when U.S. officials acknowledged the sting ("Victims of Botched U.S. Drug Sting Sue" 1995).

approval. A special-action office was set up in the White House to work with ODALE; it included Watergate participants Egil Krogh, G. Gordon Liddy, and E. Howard Hunt (McWilliams 1992). Had the Watergate scandal not intervened, Epstein (1977: 252) argues, the drug superagency proposed by the administration "might have served as the strong investigative arm for domestic surveillance that President Nixon had long quested after." As was noted in Chapter 12, inefficient law enforcement is the price we pay for our constitutional form of government.

In theory, if at some point the price of drugs rises significantly and/or the amount available for consumption falls off considerably, abusers will seek treatment or give up their drug-using habits. Indeed, research has found that the amount of heroin use is related to price (Bach and Lantos 1999). But experience reveals that when drug abusers are unable to secure their preferred substance, they frequently switch to other substances that could be even more harmful. We have already seen that heroin and cocaine have analogs that are produced in the United States. As long as demand remains strong, successful interdiction will encourage the production of domestic inorganic (agonists) depressants and stimulants. However, with respect to heroin, increases in cost lead to more addicts seeking methadone treatment (Bach and Lantos 1999).

Enforcement Results

Richard Cowan (1986: 27) argues that federal efforts against cocaine led to the development of crack: "*The iron law of drug prohibition is that the more intense the law enforcement, the more potent the drug will become.* The latest stage of this cycle has brought us the crack epidemic." Free-market conditions provide an incentive for traffickers to improve the attractiveness of their product. Jeffrey Fagan and Ko-Lin Chin (1991) point out that crack was the subject of an ingenious production and marketing strategy (see also Witkin 1991). A glut of cocaine forced prices down in 1983, but even lower prices did not keep up with production: "At this point, a new product was introduced which offered the chance to expand the market in ways never before possible: crack, packaged in small quantities and selling for $5 and sometimes even less—a fraction of the usual minimum for powder—allowed dealers to attract

Winning Battles, Losing Wars

> Reducing the market for illegal drugs can have unpleasant outcomes because "competition will increase among dealers, perhaps violently. In addition, because selling cocaine has been the primary source of earnings for poor adult males dependent on cocaine, these individuals may turn to other forms of crime to finance their continued consumption, relying more on muggings, burglary, and shoplifting for income, just as heroin users/dealers have done for many years" (RAND Drug Policy Research Center 1992).

an entirely new class of consumers. Once it took hold this change was very swift and very sweeping" (T. Williams 1989: 7).

Crack never became a mainstream drug, and by 1990 the epidemic had peaked, but heroin use increased. Because heroin had lost its dominant market position to cocaine, heroin purity levels increased substantially, drawing in new users who can snort or smoke the substance instead of injecting it intravenously in the more traditional manner. But the "crack scare" of the 1980s left in its wake new laws and greater use of imprisonment, adding significantly to an already overcrowded prison system (Egan 1999a). As David Musto notes: "History shows that excessive use of a drug at one time does not mean that such a high rate will continue indefinitely; the drug may fade in esteem and usage, even to the vanishing point. Reasonable drug policies must take into account the long-term perspective. We should avoid hastily surrendering to defeat at a time of extensive use nor declare victory after a long and deep decline in drug use" (1998: 58).

Insofar as drug abuse is caused by societal deficiencies in education, housing, and other quality-of-life-variables, the more we expend on law enforcement, the less we have available to deal with these social ills, which continue to foster greater drug abuse. Not only are we spinning our wheels in the mud, but the faster we go, the deeper the hole becomes. Furthermore, "when criminals are the most successful people in a community, the effect on that community's natural order is devastating. The authority of parents, schools, religious leaders, and (legal) businesspeople is undermined, and violent criminals become role models" (Boaz 1990: 3).

Conclusion

Wisotsky (1987) argues that our law enforcement efforts have failed and will continue to do so. He certainly has the lessons of history and classical economics on his side. "Stop talking about winning drug wars," states Trebach (1987: 383). "In the broadest sense, there is no way to win because we cannot make the drugs or their abusers go away. They will always be with us. We have never run a successful drug war and never will." Nevertheless, more extreme measures are being considered, such as shooting down aircraft that are suspected of transporting drugs. Legislation to accomplish this was introduced in

The Law of Unintended Consequences

In 2005 Iowa, like nearly thirty other states, enacted a law restricting the sale of cold medicines whose pseudoephedrine can be used to make methamphetamine. As a result, during the first seven months there was a significant decrease in home-cooked methamphetamine; lab seizures went from 120 to 20, and whereas $2.8 million dollars had been spent in 2004 on treating people at the University of Iowa Burn Center whose skin had been scorched by toxic chemicals, there was a virtual absence of victims in 2005.

But the bad news was that more methamphetamine-dependent patients were under treatment and the seizure of the drug increased as the home-made powdered version was replaced by the more powerful Mexican crystal methamphetamine (Zernike 2006a).

Voice of Experience
Cali Cartel leader Gilberto Rodriguez Orejuela has been quoted as saying, "Economics has a natural law: Supply is determined by the demand. When cocaine stops being consumed, when there's no demand for it . . . that will be the end of the business" (Moody 1991: 36).

---

the Senate in 1989 but ran into a storm of opposition from pilots who feared possible mistakes. The Mexican government reports, however, that they have shot down aircraft that are suspected of carrying drugs when the planes refuse to respond to warnings. Peru has done the same, and this has cost the lives of innocent travelers on commercial airliners.

We must recognize a troubling aspect of drug trafficking: It operates according to the powerful forces of free-market capitalism. It is paradoxical that politicians who argue that capitalism defeated Communism in Eastern Europe also talk of defeating the business of drugs. They fail to recognize that these same forces are operating in the drug trade—and that government cannot compete effectively with the free market.

SUPPLY REDUCTION BY CONTROLLING DRUGS AT THEIR SOURCE

The current U.S. policy of attempting to control drugs at their source has had unintended consequences: displacement of production and human rights violations.

The "Balloon Effect" and Human Rights Violations

The successful effort to force Turkey to curtail its production of opium in the 1970s resulted in a concomitant rise in opium production in Mexico and Southeast Asia. Mexican antidrug efforts have led to a rise in poppy production in neighboring Guatemala, whose government is ill equipped to respond to the problem (Sheppard 1990). Crackdowns in Colombia succeeded in displacing the problem into other countries: Ecuador and Brazil now have cocaine-processing laboratories; Argentina, Uruguay, and Chile have emerged as major money-laundering centers; and drug-related corruption scandals have hit

Argentina and Venezuela, which, along with Chile, serve as major cocaine transshipment centers (Nash 1992).

Bolivia reduced coca cultivation by more than half, but at a price: According to the Human Rights Watch, pressure on the government of Bolivia to deal with coca cultivation has led to widespread trampling of civil rights and physical abuse of citizenry (Vivanco 1995). Using similar methods, Peru has also cut coca cultivation by more than half. "Peru leads the world in documented cases of disappearances of people taken prisoner by security forces" (Brooke 1991: 6). In response to declines in these source countries, the Colombian wholesalers who bought Bolivian and Peruvian coca increased domestic production (Krauss 1999a).

Coca production in Colombia has more than doubled from 1995 to 2000; the country is now the source of more than 500 tons of cocaine a year, 90 percent of the world's supply. The breakup of the powerful Medellín and Cali drug cartels spurred coca cultivation in more remote regions of the country and resulted in alliances between new drug gangs and leftist guerillas. Added to this volatile mix are right-wing paramilitary forces who, like their left-wing enemies, are supported by the drug trade. "Feeling relatively safe on their native soil, native coca-growing syndicates have invested heavily in developing more potent strains, some of which can be harvested in as little as 60 days" (Rohter 2000b). Colombian syndicates have achieved extraordinary levels of efficiency in extracting cocaine from their coca crops. Higher-yielding varieties of coca are being grown in parts of Colombia. Likewise, Colombian laboratory operators are more efficient in processing coca leaf into cocaine base than they had been previously (U.S. Department of State 2000).

After Congress approved a Clinton administration allocation of $1.6 billion to help the Colombian government fight drug traffickers an editorial in the *Chicago Tribune* (March 12, 2000: 18) argued: "This policy threatens to entangle the U.S. in a decade-old foreign guerilla war while doing nothing to dampen the engine that ultimately drives narcotrafficking: America's roughly $50 billion a year appetite for illicit drugs." The editorial, after noting the involvement of the Colombian army and its right-wing paramilitary allies in massive human rights violations, stated: "It would be repugnant to funnel American aid to a foreign army with such bloody credentials."

With financial support from the United States, Colombia is using more than eighty planes to spray herbicide on more than 1 million acres of coca and poppy plants—five planes have been shot down. Nevertheless, cocaine prices in the United States have remained stable, and purity has improved (Brinkley 2005).

Economic Importance of the Coca Crop in Peru and Bolivia

In Peru and Bolivia inhabitants of coca-growing areas are strongly opposed to U.S.-inspired efforts to eradicate their most important cash crop, and both countries face Marxist insurgencies that are particularly strong in these remote regions. Unfortunately, in addition to providing a livelihood for impoverished Bolivian farmers, cocaine brings into Bolivia more money than all legal exports combined.

Coca

"Not only is coca fully integrated into Andean society but it is also an integral part of the region's ecosystem—a stubborn and dismaying biological fact impeding those who would like to make it disappear. As a cultivated plant, coca is nearly ideal. It has few predators and pests. . . . The plant will grow in soils too poor and on slopes too steep to support other crops, will live for forty years or more, and will tolerate many harvests a year" (Weil 1995: 72).

Balloon Effect

There is one immutable rule in the drug business: As long as demand remains strong, successful efforts against it at the source level will shift cultivation to a new location. This is what happened in Peru in 2002. In addition to shifting much production to Colombia, a tightened supply has tempted poor farmers in virgin areas to begin cultivating coca (Forero 2002).

In Peru's Upper Huallaga Valley, which extends for 200 miles along the Huallaga River, an estimated 60,000 families depend on coca as a cash crop for their survival. Large-scale eradication, notes Alan Riding (1988: 6), could "provoke a social convulsion, forcing thousands of families to leave the area" and creating deep resentment that Marxist guerrillas exploit. And "coca is Peru's largest export, earning more than one billion dollars a year. As many as one million of the country's twenty-one million citizens are involved in the trade" (Massing 1990: 26). Under President Alberto K. Fujimori, Peruvian armed forces shot down planes suspected of transporting drugs—about twenty-five aircraft have met this fate. This strategy succeeded in breaking the "air bridge," and when the price of coca leaf dropped more than 60 percent in 1995, farmers began abandoning the crop. With U.S. help, Peruvian officials began teaching farmers to raise coffee instead of coca. By 1999, however, traffickers had reopened some air routes and had replaced others with river, road, and sea channels, once again making coca profitable, and the crop rebounded (Krauss 1999b). Government anti-coca efforts in Bolivia left thousands of Indian farmers without a source of income and helped to generate violent protests that left several soldiers, police officers, and farmers dead (Associated Press 2000b).

Wisotsky (1987: 57) states that "in both Peru and Bolivia, the failure of coca control is not a temporary aberration but a function of culture, tradition, and the weakness and poverty of underdevelopment. These basic social conditions render effective enforcement against coca impossible. Widespread corruption in the enforcement agencies, the judiciary, and elsewhere in government is endemic. Indeed, the central governments do not necessarily control major portions of the coca-growing countryside, where the traffickers rule like feudal lords." Participation in the illicit cocaine economy, writes Edmundo

A View from Latin America

Thirteen people, including jurists, doctors, artists, religious leaders, and three former Latin American presidents—Belisario Betancur of Colombia, Violeta Chamorro of Nicaragua, and Nobel Peace Prize Laureate Oscar Arias of Costa Rica—signed a letter stating that the U.S.-led military-style war on drugs has failed and should be changed to focus more on ending the demand for drugs and drug money. "The escalation of a militarized drug war in Colombia and elsewhere in the Americas threatens regional stability, undermines efforts towards demilitarization and democracy and has put U.S. arms and money into the hands of corrupt officials and military . . . units involved in human rights abuses. It is time to admit that after two decades, the U.S. war on drugs—both in Latin America and in the United States—is a failure." Despite tens of billions of dollars spent for raids on drug labs, crop eradication, and arrests and imprisonment at home, "today in the U.S., illicit drugs are cheaper, more potent and more easily available than two decades ago" (Jelinek 1999).

"Plan Colombia"

"The latest chapter in America's long war on drugs—a six-year, $4.7 billion effort to slash Colombia's coca crop—has left the price, quality and availability of cocaine on American streets virtually unchanged" (Forero 2006).

Morales (1986: 157), "is inevitable. Not only is the natives' traditional way of life intertwined with coca, but their best cash crop is the underground economy for which no substitute has yet been provided."

In 2002 President George W. Bush met with the Bolivian president at the White House. The Bolivian leader promised President Bush that he would press ahead in his campaign to eradicate the coca crop but needed more U.S. assistance to help ease the impact on farmers. Otherwise, Gonzalo Sánchez de Lozado stated, "I may be back here in a year seeking political asylum." Mr. Bush laughed and wished him luck. The following year, Mr. Lozado was living in exile in the United States after having been ousted by a popular uprising (Rohter 2003).

Crop Eradication or Substitution

Crop substitution programs have been part of our effort to control drugs at their source but have met with only limited success. As long as demand remains high, the price offered for poppy or coca will be many times that received for conventional crops. There are other problems: In 1991 the leader of a Peruvian coca growers association who had agreed to a crop substitution program was murdered, reputedly by corrupt government officials who earned money from the cocaine business (Strong 1992).

Attempts to eradicate the crop by cutting or burning result in healthier and more bountiful growth, and uprooting coca plants causes the soil to become unproductive for as long as eight to ten years (Morales 1989). An eradication program in the Upper Huallaga Valley was established with U.S. funding in 1982, but about forty of its workers were eventually murdered. The United States subsequently suspended the program (Massing 1990).

Cost at the Source

"It costs cocaine refiners only 30 cents to purchase the coca leaf needed to produce a gram of cocaine, which sells for about $150 in the United States. Even if the price of the leaves needed for that gram of the finished produce doubled, it would be negligible. And if retail prices don't rise, then consumption in the United States will not decline" (Reuter 2000: 29).

An alternative is the use of aerial herbicides that are either sprayed or dropped as pellets and that melt into the soil when it rains. The United States has been conducting research on a variety of environmentally safe herbicides. The most successful herbicides, however, kill many species of plants, including crop plants, and remain in the soil, affecting future plantings. Environmentalists have raised objections to the use of herbicides, and the companies that produce them are concerned about potential liability and fear that their employees in South America could become targets of retribution by trafficking organizations (Riding 1988). Furthermore, Lee McIntosh (1988: 26) has found that a "single genetic mutation can give rise to complete resistance in a similar herbicide. This implies it may be necessary continually to spray different classes of herbicides in the future." The human and political dangers inherent in this approach to drug control should serve as a restraining influence.

Successful eradication and interdiction efforts can affect both availability and price. However, because of the pattern of price markups in the cocaine business, efforts to eradicate crops or supply routes that increase the cost of the coca leaf tenfold add only 5 percent to the retail consumer price, and doubling seizures from importers increases consumer cost by only 10 percent (Passell 1990).

If all of the coca that the producing countries of Latin America have publicly committed themselves to eradicate were actually eradicated, the effect in the United States would be minimal. It is likely that African, Middle Eastern, and Southeast Asian areas would be able to cultivate enough to meet consumer demand in coca indefinitely (as they have done with opium). It should be noted that coca leaf has been grown commercially in Indonesia, Malaysia, Nigeria, Sri Lanka, and Taiwan. Indeed, the crop that is grown in Java and Taiwan contains more than twice the cocaine of the varieties grown in Latin America (Karch 1998). Epstein (1988: 25) points out that "the entire cocaine market in the United States can be supplied for a year by a single cargo plane." Furthermore, as was noted in previous chapters, curtailing importation without affecting demand provides an incentive for greater domestic efforts: the production of synthetic analogs for cocaine and heroin and stronger strains of marijuana.

The highly inventive marijuana horticulturists of California are using a new, faster-growing, highly potent strain that matures in three months (older strains require four months). Cultivation of this new strain has been discovered in the national forests of Northern California. (Growing marijuana

Crop Eradication
"Forcible crop eradication moves the problem around, enriches traffickers by raising the price of their holdings, and creates turmoil in rural areas" *New York Times* editorial (May 27, 2005: 22).

"BC Bud"

Indoor cultivation of very powerful strains of marijuana has blossomed in the western Canadian province of British Columbia (B.C.). Although Canadian law is similar to the United States with respect to marijuana, attitudes in British Columbia reflect a different mindset; even wholesale growers receive light penalties, often just fines. Much of the B.C. crop is smuggled into the United States, where it fetches premium prices owing to the high level of its THC.

on federal lands was made a felony in 1987, punishable by a prison term of up to ten years.)

In response to law enforcement efforts against imported marijuana, some innovative growers have established elaborate underground farms equipped with diesel-powered lights and ventilation systems. Their use of hydroponic technology—growing plants in water to which nutrients have been added—has helped to make marijuana the number one cash crop in the United States. In response the DEA has been subpoenaing the records of businesses that sell hydroponic equipment in order to discover indoor marijuana growers. These records contain the names of mostly legitimate growers paying by check or credit card—marijuana traffickers usually pay cash—who may be subjected to DEA inquiries (Bishop 1991).

Aerial marijuana searches continue to locate illegal farms, but as this photo shows, clever cultivators have gone underground. Innovations can include diesel-powered lights, ventilation systems, and hydroponic technology.

©Owen Franken/Getty Images

Drug Enforcement and Foreign Policy

There is evidence that U.S. efforts against drug trafficking are often secondary to foreign policy considerations. The Anti-Drug Abuse Act of 1986, for example, requires the president to certify to Congress that producer and transshipment nations have made adequate progress in attacking drug production and trafficking. Without certification a country can lose aid, loans, and trade preferences. Elaine Sciolino (1988) reports that the law has numerous loopholes that have allowed several nations to be certified despite their failure to cooperate in the war against drugs. In 1990, of the twenty-four major drug-producing and drug-transiting countries only four—Afghanistan, Myanmar, Iran, and Syria—were denied certification.

At the other extreme the United States turned to the military in Guatemala, a major producer of opium and a leading transshipment point for Colombian cocaine, to take the lead in efforts against trafficking. The Guatemalan military has been responsible for human rights abuses that have plagued the country (Gruson 1990).

For many years the United States tolerated the drug-trafficking activities of Central American ally General Manuel Noriega. When his politics took on a decidedly anti-U.S. tone, in 1988 the general was indicted and apprehended, following the "Operation Just Cause" invasion of Panama by the U.S. military. (For a discussion of Noriega, his relationship with the United States, and drug dealing, see Dinges [1990] and Kempe [1990].) According to Thomas A. Constantine, retired director of the DEA, the Clinton administration was more concerned about trade and other economic issues in its relationship with Mexico than with corruption and drug trafficking (Golden 1999).

Peter Andreas and his colleagues (1991–1992: 107) note that "after more than a decade of U.S. efforts to reduce the cocaine supply, more cocaine is produced in more places than ever before. Curiously, the U.S. response to failure has been to escalate rather than reevaluate." Andreas and colleagues state: "The logic of escalation in the drug war is in fact strikingly similar to the arguments advanced when U.S. counterinsurgency strategies, undercut by ineffective and uncommitted governments and security forces, were failing in Vietnam: 'We've just begun to fight.' 'We're turning the corner.'" Andreas and his colleagues argue that "since failure can so easily be used to justify further escalation, how do we know whether we are really turning the corner or simply running around in a vicious circle?"

DEMAND REDUCTION BY DRUG TESTING

The President's Commission on Organized Crime (1986), in what has become its most controversial recommendation, suggested extensive drug testing as a device for reducing consumer demand (see Table 13.1). Public and private employers began testing new and existing employees, generating criticism and lawsuits. Drug testing of prospective employees has become almost routine at many large corporations. About 61 percent of major U.S. companies administer pre-employment drug tests, and more than 500 school districts have screening programs (D. Hawkins 2002).[1] The military has extended its program of drug testing, and various levels of government have initiated the testing of employees in critical areas involving public safety, particularly law enforcement and transportation. Some states have reacted to increasing protests about the practice by enacting legislation barring random testing of employees, and in a number of states the practice is thwarted by constitutional provisions guaranteeing individuals the right to privacy.

Case Law Results

For an intrusive act such as mandatory drug testing to be constitutional, there must be a "compelling interest." In a 1987 case a computer programmer who had been dismissed from her job for refusing to take a drug test on the grounds of personal privacy was awarded $485,000; the San Francisco jury failed to find "compelling interest." That city subsequently enacted an ordinance prohibiting mandatory testing except when an employer has reason to believe ("reasonable suspicion") that an employee is impaired because of drug use (Bishop 1987).

In 1989 the Supreme Court upheld the testing of railroad employees for drugs after an accident and ruled that personnel of the U.S. Customs Service in sensitive positions must submit to drug testing even in the absence of "individualized suspicion" (*Skinner v. Railway Labor Executives' Association*, 109 S.Ct. 1402; *National Treasury Employees Union v. von Raab*, 109 S.Ct. 1384). In a six-month study completed in 1990, slightly more than 3 percent of 65,000 U.S. transportation workers tested positive for drugs—mostly marijuana and cocaine—as did 4.2 percent of applicants for such positions (Cawley 1990). Lower federal courts have rejected the testing of *public* employees who are suspected of using drugs in a manner that does not affect job performance; the U.S. Constitution does not similarly protect *private* employees. In an Oregon case the U.S. Supreme Court (6–3) approved of the random urinalysis of public school athletes as a condition of their continued participation in sports (*Vernonia School District v. Acton*, 515 U.S. 646 [1995]).

In 2002 the Supreme Court, in a 5–4 decision (*Board of Education v. Earls*, 536 U.S. 822), extended *Vernonia* by upholding an Oklahoma school district's policy of requiring students engaged in virtually all extracurricular school activities to submit to random drug testing. The majority opinion written by Justice Clarence Thomas stated that given the epidemic of drug use by youngsters and the schools' "custodial responsibilities," drug testing was entirely reasonable. That led hundreds of school boards across the country, mostly in smaller districts, to consider proposals for testing students (Lewin 2002).

---

[1] In Alabama, where the legal age for smoking tobacco products is 19 years, about a dozen school districts test for nicotine in addition to alcohol and illegal drugs (Giuffrida 2002).

Table 13.1 | Pros and Cons of Various Drug Testing Methods

Type of Test	Pros	Cons	Window of Detection
Urine	• Highest assurance of reliable results. • Least expensive. • Most flexibility in testing different drugs, including alcohol and nicotine. • Most likely of all drug-testing methods to withstand legal challenge.	• Specimen can be adulterated, substituted, or diluted. • Limited window of detection. • Test sometimes viewed as invasive or embarrassing. • Biological hazard for specimen handling and shipping to lab.	• Typically 1 to 5 days.
Hair	• Longer window of detection. • Greater stability (does not deteriorate). • Can measure chronic drug use. • Convenient shipping and storage (no need to refrigerate). • Collection procedure not considered invasive or embarrassing. • More difficult to adulterate than urine. • Detects alcohol/cocaine combination use.	• More expensive. • Test usually limited to basic 5-drug panel. • Cannot detect alcohol use. • Will not detect very recent drug use (1 to 7 days prior to test).	• Depends on the length of hair in the sample. Hair grows about a half-inch per month, so a 1 1/2-inch specimen would show a 3-month history.
Oral Fluids	• Sample obtained under direct observation. • Minimal risk of tampering. • Noninvasive. • Samples can be collected easily in virtually any environment. • Can detect alcohol use. • Reflects recent drug use.	• Drugs and drug metabolites do not remain in oral fluids as long as they do in urine. • Less efficient than other testing methods in detecting marijuana use.	• Approximately 10 to 24 hours.
Sweat Patch	• Noninvasive. • Variable removal date (generally 1 to 7 days). • Quick application and removal. • Longer window of detection than urine. • No sample substitution possible.	• Limited number of labs able to process results. • People with skin eruptions, excessive hair, or cuts and abrasions cannot wear the patch. • Passive exposure to drugs may contaminate patch and affect results.	• Patch retains evidence of drug use for at least 7 days, and can detect even low levels of drugs 2 to 5 hours after last use.

Source: Office of National Drug Control Policy (2002a).

Drug-Testing Process

Drug testing has spawned a growth industry. The National Institute on Drug Abuse (NIDA) certifies drug-testing firms, a necessity for securing federal contracts. NIDA has certified about fifty labs, which must maintain stringent standards in areas such as sample collection, storage, personnel, laboratory controls, and testing procedures and accuracy. Various testing methods are used, but the most common is urinalysis.

Urinalysis Primarily because of its low cost, about five dollars a test, the enzyme-multiplied immune test is the most frequently used urinalysis (Wish n.d.: 2): "These tests depend on a chemical reaction between the specimen and an antibody designed to react to a specific drug. The chemical reaction causes a change in the specimen's transmission of light, which is measured by a machine. If the reading is higher than a given standard, the specimen is positive for the drug." Eric Wish (n.d.: 2) notes that there have been complaints of relatively high rates of false positives using this test, sometimes as a result of commonly used licit drugs cross-reacting with the test's antibody. "Sloppy recording procedures by laboratory staff and failure to maintain careful controls over the chain of custody of the specimen can also produce serious test errors."

The most accurate test, gas chromatography/mass spectroscopy (GC-MS), notes Wish (n.d.), is relatively expensive, about $100 per specimen for screening and confirmation, but so is the cost of firing or not hiring someone because of a false positive. Drug-testing programs often use the enzyme-multiplied immune test for an initial screening and then submit all positives for GC-MS. But GC-MS is not perfect. "The test works by extracting and heating molecules from a sample and using an electric field to separate and identify them." At best, however, this is 95–99 percent accurate. Furthermore, some labs, as a cost saving device, "look for only a few fragments of the drug

The President's Commission on Organized Crime suggested extensive drug testing as a device for reducing consumer demand. Drug testing of prospective employees has become almost routine at many major corporations. About 61 percent of major U.S. companies administer pre-employment drug tests, and more than 500 school districts have screening programs.

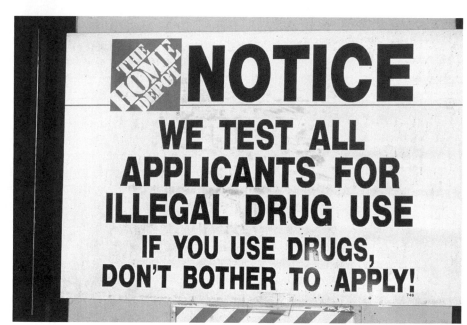

Drug Testing as Failed Policy

A federally financed study of 76,000 students found that drug testing had no effect on drug use—it does not change "hearts and minds" (G. Winter 2003).

molecules which raises the risk of mistaking legitimate medicines, herbs, and foods like poppy seeds for illegal drugs" (Hawkins 2002: 47).

Hair Analysis   Collecting hair samples is easy and is not subject to evasive actions designed to produce false negatives; shampooing, for example, has no effect. Hair analysis has been used for some time to detect exposure to such toxic metals as mercury and lead. In a process similar to that of urinalysis, dissolved hair shafts reveal whether drugs are in the blood. Because of the unique qualities of hair growth—about one-half inch a month—it may be possible to determine the amount of drug use over a period of several months and whether it is increasing or decreasing. There are complications, however. The test can also be positive for those who come into contact with drugs via touching the skin or sweat of a user or through exposure to air where the substance has been smoked (Baumgartner, Hill, and Blahd 1989), and these contaminants can be discriminatory in their impact: "drug molecules, whether ingested or picked up from the environment, have an affinity for the pigment melanin and bind more strongly to dark hair than light" (Hawkins 2002: 48). Hair analysis has been suggested as an initial screening method for drug use, positives to be corroborated by urinalysis or GC-MS (Magura, Kang, and Shapiro 1995; Mieczkowski 1995; Hawkins 2002).

Sweat Patch   For this type of test, a Band-Aid®-like patch is attached to the skin to collect sweat for up to seven days and is subsequently lab-tested for drug residue. If the patch is removed, it cannot be reattached. This test is often used by probation and parole agencies. However, drug molecules from clothes or other people can penetrate the patch and trigger a false positive (Hawkins 2002).

Drug Residues   Portable devices that detect drug residues are used in the workplace and schools. They can identify vapors from minuscule particles of heroin, cocaine, and methamphetamines. Samples are gathered at such critical areas as doorknobs or desktops by cloth or vacuum cleaners and are analyzed through gas chromatography, a process that separates out compounds according to their boiling points; a readout indicates the type of substance that is detected. The DrugWipe®, which detects drug residues left on surfaces from contact with the skin or sweat of users, has been used in some schools to check locker handles, computer keyboards, vending machines, and sports equipment. Residue can be detected for up to eight weeks. There is a version for cocaine and opiates and another for marijuana and amphetamines and their derivatives.

Testing Problems

At best, drug testing can determine only that the subject has used a drug recently; it cannot determine when or how much. Tests cannot distinguish the casual user from a chronic one. There is also concern over the inadequacy of

"Oops"

"A Delta Air Lines flight attendant who was fired after a drug-testing laboratory incorrectly said that she had cheated on a drug test will receive $400,000 from the lab" (Associated Press 2001).

testing—false positives that could destroy the careers of innocent employees. In 2000 the U.S. Department of Health and Human Services revealed that the shortcomings of drug-testing laboratories were jeopardizing the jobs of innocent employees (Zuckerman 2000).

The rationale behind drug testing is confused and ironic: Employers are interested in having a drug-free workplace because controlled substances are presumed to be detrimental to job performance. If this is so, then monitoring job performance—a rather routine managerial task—makes more sense than drug testing, since some people will perform quite well even though their urine reveals drugs. People who lawfully come into contact with cocaine, such as plastic surgeons and drug law enforcement officers, will test positive for the substance, as will anyone who is exposed to crack cocaine fumes, even though the dose is far too low to produce symptoms (Karch 1996).

Another standard explanation is that impaired workers represent a workplace hazard. This might be indeed be true, but drug testing does not reveal impairment, and impaired workers are most likely to be alcohol abusers. There is a lack of documentation proving that workers who test positive for illegal drugs have a higher rate of accidents (Noble 1992). Sound public relations might better explain workplace drug testing than sound public policy does.

The criminal justice system uses drug testing in making bail or pretrial release decisions and in probation and parole supervision.

DEMAND REDUCTION BY CRIMINAL PROSECUTION FOR FETAL LIABILITY

The prosecution of drug-using pregnant women for fetal endangerment, delivering drugs to a minor, or child abuse dates back to the end of the 1980s, when drug abuse was high in the political consciousness of elected officials and an increasing number of "drug babies" were being reported. It is estimated that about 350,000 infants annually are exposed prenatally to some form of illegal drug (Nolan 1990). Prosecution is sometimes used to coerce women into drug treatment, although drug treatment programs might not be readily available and those that are might be unwilling or unable to provide for pregnant clients.

The first woman convicted for delivering a controlled substance to her fetus, in Florida in 1990, was sentenced to a year in a drug treatment program and fourteen years probation; her conviction was upheld by a state appeals court the following year but was later voided by the Florida Supreme Court (Lewin 1991, 1992). In 1991 the Michigan Court of Appeals ruled that a woman who took crack hours before giving birth could not be charged with delivering cocaine to her son through the umbilical cord. In response to the ruling, the Muskegon County prosecutor defended his decision to charge the woman: "This is a major health care crisis and we must use whatever means we can to reach a solution" (Wilkerson 1991: 13). Health care officials who supported the woman expressed fear that prosecuting drug-using pregnant women will drive them away from prenatal care. Courts have dismissed similar cases in North Carolina, Ohio, and Florida (Lewin 1991).

Despite considerable concern about the high rate of cocaine use among pregnant women, studies have failed to find a homogeneous pattern of fetal effects, and there is little consensus on the adverse effects of the drug (Finnegan et al. 1994). In a study of birth outcomes and developmental growth of children who were exposed to drugs in utero, infants varied in their birth outcomes, a majority evidencing no significant problems (Cosden, Peerson, and Elliott 1997). An overwhelming majority of women who use cocaine also ingest other drugs, including nicotine, alcohol, marijuana, and opiates, and many suffer from sexual and physical abuse (Finnegan 1993). It is difficult to separate the effects of cocaine from other potential hazards to the fetus. "Women who use cocaine during pregnancy also engage in other behaviors, such as alcohol and tobacco use, that are risk factors for poor pregnancy outcome. In addition, they often live in circumstances that, in themselves, create an environment that fosters poor developmental outcome. To understand the unique or independent effects of cocaine exposure during pregnancy, it is critical to separate factors that correlate with prenatal cocaine use and with the outcome, both at birth and during the postpartum period" (Richardson and Day 1999: 234).

Although we know that women who abuse heroin during pregnancy frequently give birth to infants suffering from neonatal abstinence syndrome—the newborn suffers withdrawal symptoms—we do not know whether there are long-range effects that are directly attributable to the use of drugs; as with cocaine, it is difficult, if not impossible, to separate the effects of drugs from those of poverty and poor prenatal care. Furthermore, the fetus can be endangered by any number of maternal behaviors that are not related to illegal drug use, for example, "too much or too little exercise, an inadequate or harmful diet, or use of cigarettes, alcohol [6,000 to 8,000 born annually with fetal alcohol syndrome], and other [lawful] drugs" (Nolan 1990: 13–14). Other risks include the general environment and specific workplace exposures.

Research has revealed that infants (about 750,000 per year) who are exposed to a high level of cigarette smoke (one pack or more per day) in utero suffer from decreased birth weight, head circumference, and body length; there are also increased rates of spontaneous abortions and bleeding during pregnancy. An estimated 5,600 infants die each year as a result of smoking by their pregnant mothers. A study in 1994 revealed that mothers who smoke as few as ten cigarettes a day cause their children under age five years to test positive for cancer-causing compounds (Hilts 1994). A study of 4,400 youngsters ages six to sixteen by Kimberly Yoltan of the Cincinnati Children's Medical Center revealed that, after controlling for factors such as race, income, and parents' educational levels, children exposed to high-levels of second-hand smoke have significantly lower test scores in reading, math, and problem-solving than those with the low-levels of exposure as determined by the presence of a nicotine by-product (cotinine) in their blood (Szabo 2005).

And what of the liability of the father who is using illegal drugs or alcohol or tobacco? Recent research suggests that psychoactive substances are hazardous to spermatozoa (Finnegan 1993), and secondhand smoke has been proven to seriously harm the health of children. Furthermore, what of the societal responsibility to provide adequate prenatal care for all pregnant women? The nonmedical use of controlled substances is only one facet of a significantly greater social problem that will not be resolved by a simplistic recourse to criminal law.

An equally pressing problem is the cost of providing for infants of drug-abusing mothers: Foster care for one child ranges from $15,000 to $20,000 a year. New York City has responded to this problem by permitting drug-abusing mothers to keep their children at home under the intensive supervision of a social worker (Treaster 1991). A study in Illinois found that although white and African American women show similar rates of illegal drug use during pregnancy, "the black women are more likely to be reported to authorities" (Olen 1991: Sec. 3: 14). Illinois is one of a number of states where medical personnel are required to report suspected prenatal drug use to authorities. But there are few places in the state to care for babies born with drugs in their bloodstream, so the babies are usually sent home with their mother with some type of outpatient help and monitoring (Poe and Searcey 1996).

DEMAND REDUCTION BY EXPANDING TREATMENT

The core of the U.S. response to drug use has centered on enforcement, but expanding the availability of treatment might be more productive for reducing demand. There is almost universal agreement that without reduced demand, antidrug efforts will remain ineffective.

Justifying Treatment
"Treatment and prevention programs are frequently required to show that they are cost-effective, a standard never imposed on drug enforcement" (MacCoun and Reuter 1997: 47).

The cost-effectiveness of treatment versus law enforcement is emphasized by Peter Rydell and Susan Everingham (1994: xv). They argue that $246 million would have to be spent on domestic law enforcement to achieve the same reduction in drug use that could be achieved by spending $34 million on treatment. And no assumption is made about the long-range effect of treatment—abstinence—on the individual abuser: "The cost advantage is so large that even if the after-treatment effect is ignored, treatment is still more cost-effective than law enforcement."

It is the possession of controlled substances that constitutes a crime; an addict is not a criminal by virtue of his or her addiction. In *Robinson v. California* 370 U.S. 660 (1962) the Supreme Court ruled that individuals cannot be prosecuted for "being under the influence" or for "internal possession" of illegal drugs. In that same decision the Court upheld the civil commitment of drug addicts for purposes of treatment (similar to commitment of the mentally ill): "A state might determine that the general health and welfare require that the victims of these and other human afflictions might be dealt with by compulsory treatment, involving quarantine, confinement, or

View from the Right

> "Treatment is not now available for almost half of those who would benefit from it. Yet we are willing to build more and more jails in which to isolate drug users even though at one-seventh the cost of building and maintaining jail space and pursuing, detaining, and prosecuting the drug user, we could subsidize commensurately effective medical care and psychological treatment" (William F. Buckley et al. 1996: 37).

sequestration." Some twenty-seven states have made such a determination and enacted legislation that permits the civil commitment of drug addicts (J. Kaplan 1983b). Only California and New York, however, have made extensive use of such statutes.

As was noted in Chapter 9, in 1961 the California legislature passed comprehensive legislation raising the penalties for drug violations and providing for the compulsory civil commitment of narcotic addicts. In its first twelve years the California Civic Addict Program admitted more than 18,000 addicts for treatment. Most of those who were committed to the program, however, were people who had been convicted of felony crimes, with a much smaller number convicted of misdemeanors and an even smaller number committed without any criminal charges at all (R. Wood 1973). The California program continues to operate, but the New York program was discontinued in 1974 after an enormous expenditure of tax dollars with, at best, questionable results.

Bruce Johnson and his colleagues (1986a, 1986b) argue in favor of mandatory treatment because almost all objective evidence suggests that drug treatment has an important impact on the criminality of heroin and cocaine abusers. The cost of such a policy, they note, would be prohibitive unless treatment were on an outpatient basis, a method that they support. Because most heroin and cocaine abusers have come into contact with the criminal justice system, all criminal defendants should be subjected to drug tests, which, if positive, should require mandatory treatment. Johnson and colleagues argue that drug treatment should be part of any sentence for convicted drug abusers and that postrelease treatment should be a condition of probation or parole supervision, with careful monitoring of urine for at least one year (see, for example, Benedict, Huff-Corzine, and Corzine 1998). This writer has supervised heroin addicts on parole in New York, and their careful monitoring by a parole officer does ensure a high rate of abstinence, at least during the period of supervision. But in any number of jurisdictions supervision in the community is superficial, with caseloads so large that clients cannot be monitored adequately. Offenders who violate the conditions of supervision by using drugs often go unnoticed or unpunished, remaining at liberty until they are arrested again for another drug offense (Abadinsky 2006).

MEASURING THE RESULT OF POLICY CHANGES

A major problem with instituting any changes in policy is measurement of results. Increases or decreases in the number of people using illegal substances cannot be measured with any accuracy, and the statistics that are often presented as "data" are usually meaningless. There are no direct measures of the incidence or prevalence of drug use in the general population; all estimates are inferences derived from various data gathered by law enforcement or medical sources.

Patrick Biernacki (1986: 189) points out that "it cannot be determined with any degree of certainty what effect U.S. drug policy has had on the addict population. What we do know is that the indicators used to estimate the size of the addict population at any one time are unreliable. For example, if the number of hospital emergency room admissions for heroin overdoses drops, does this indicate the effectiveness of police control methods, or the successful treatment of addicts? Or can the drop in admissions be attributed to a change in drug preference? Or to an increase in the number of natural recoveries?" Natural recovery, or the abandoning of heroin use, was discovered among returning Vietnam veterans on a relatively large scale (Robins 1973, 1974; Robins, Helzer, Hesselbrock, and Wish 1980).[2] To the extent to which we have been able to measure the effect of U.S. drug policy, the results, though not necessarily the claims, have been unclear. The question remains: Should we be punishing people "simply because we are unable to demonstrate the benefits of *not* punishing them"? (Husak and de Marneffe 2005: 26). The next chapter will explore issues relating to that question.

SUMMARY

The United States has two basic models of responding to the use of dangerous substances: the disease model and the moral-legal model, which utilizes three methods: regulation, medical auspices, and law enforcement. The response—regulation or law enforcement—determines the manner in which the user is viewed: the alcoholic according to the disease model, the user of illegal drugs as criminal. These responses are not based on the relative dangers inherent in psychoactive substances, and drug *use* is not necessarily drug *abuse*.

Although reducing the supply of drugs should, in theory, drive up the price and reduce consumption, there is an absence of support for this proposition. Increasing enforcement does increase the profits of the more resilient drug organizations and contributes to a problem with prison overcrowding. When drug abusers are unable to secure their preferred substance, they frequently switch to other substances that might be even more harmful. Insofar as drug

---

[2] On natural recovery among middle-class addicts, see Granfield and Cloud (1996).

abuse is caused by societal deficiencies in education, housing, and other quality-of-life-variables, the more we expend on law enforcement, the less we have available to deal with these social ills.

Efforts against drugs at their source can generate a balloon effect and citizen antagonism when carried out by governments with human rights violations, and poppy and coca crops are often important economic assets in areas of extreme poverty. Crop eradication and substitution programs have met with only limited success, and U.S. efforts against drug trafficking are often secondary to foreign policy considerations.

Efforts to reduce drug use include drug testing and prosecution for fetal liability, but most promising is the expansion of treatment programs. Mandatory treatment has shown success with drug abusers.

Because there is no way to accurately determine changes in the number of people using illegal drugs, evaluating policy changes is difficult.

Now that we have examined drug policy in the United States, in the next chapter we will consider more radical changes, some of which are being or have been adopted by European countries.

REVIEW QUESTIONS

1. What are the differences between *scientific* knowledge and *political* knowledge?
2. Why have some psychoactive drugs been outlawed while others are legally and widely available?
3. What are the disadvantages of focusing law enforcement on low-level dealers?
4. What are some of the unanticipated results of drug law enforcement?
5. How does the iron law of capitalism work against effective drug law enforcement?
6. Why is criminal prosecution for fetal liability a questionable policy?
7. What are the drawbacks in controlling such drugs as cocaine and heroin at their source countries?
8. What are the various ways to conduct drug use testing?
9. Why is drug treatment more cost-effective than drug law enforcement?
10. Why is it difficult, if not impossible, to measure the success of any change in drug policy?

Drug Decriminalization and Harm Reduction[1]

The easy cynicism that has grown up around the drug issue is no accident. Sowing it has been the deliberate aim of a decades-long campaign by proponents of legalization, critics whose mantra is "nothing works," and whose central insight appears to be that they can avoid having to propose the unmentionable—a world where drugs are ubiquitous—if they can hide behind the bland management critique that drug control efforts are "unworkable."

National Drug Control Strategy (2002b: 3)

Considerable evidence suggests that the legalization of drugs would create behavioral and public health problems to a degree that would far outweigh the current consequences of the drug prohibition.

James A. Inciardi (2002: 281)

U.S. drug policies are punitive (in both rhetoric and reality), divisive (certainly by race, probably by age and perhaps by class), intrusive (in small ways for many and in large ways for some), and expensive ($30 billion to 35 billion annually). Yet the nation has a drug problem more severe than that of any other rich Western society, whether measured in terms of extent of drug use, drug-related AIDS cases, or the level of violence and corruption associated with these drugs.

Peter Reuter (2001: 15)

---

[1] Harm reduction is a component of a more global effort known as *harm minimization* that comprises three major strategies: supply reduction, demand reduction, and harm reduction.

The question I believe should be asked—Should drug use be criminalized?—and the question that is generally asked—Should drug use be decriminalized?—are different, and the difference is important. The right question demands a justification for our existing policy.

Douglas Husak (in Husak and de Marneffe 2005: 26)

What should we as a nation do about drug use? What are our options beyond enforcement? In this chapter we look at some other possibilities.

DECRIMINALIZATION OF DRUG ABUSE

Decriminalization refers to the absence of laws punishing people for using drugs, as is the case with alcohol and tobacco, drugs restricted only to those below a certain chronological age. Decriminalization exists when the state allows people to be free to use drugs and, if viewed along a continuum, would include authorizing registered persons to use drugs, as would be the case with heroin maintenance or marijuana prescription programs. Reducing penalties for the possession of small amounts of marijuana, as some states have done, is not decriminalization. Private sector employment contracts, club rules, such as those of the Boy Scouts, and tenant leases prohibiting use of certain drugs are not incompatible with decriminalization (Husak and de Marneffe 2005).

John Kaplan (1983b: 101) poses a policy question: "Could we not lower the total social costs of heroin use and the government response to it by allowing the drug to be freely and cheaply available in liquor stores, or as an over-the-counter drug?" Such policy would be consistent with the U.S. approach to other unhealthy habits, such as cigarette smoking, drinking alcohol, and overeating, or the approach to sports such as mountain climbing, skydiving, bull riding, football, and boxing—an acknowledgment of an individual's freedom to enjoy himself or herself or to earn money, even through activities that might be injurious to that person's health. In fact, deliberately engaging in dangerous pursuits can be explained by these activities causing release of potentially reinforcing neurotransmitters such as dopamine or endorphins.

Edward Brecher (1972: 528) notes that most of the harmful aspects of heroin use are the result of its being illegal: "Many American morphine and heroin addicts before 1914 led long, healthy, respectable, productive lives despite addiction—and so do a few addicts today. The sorry plight of most heroin addicts in the United States results primarily from the high price of heroin, the contamination and adulteration of the heroin available on the black market, the mainlining of the drug instead of safer modes of use, the laws against heroin and the ways in which they are enforced, the imprisonment of addicts, society's attitudes toward addicts, and other nonpharmacological factors." Expressing historical ignorance, Barry McCaffrey, Director of the Office of National Drug Control Policy in the Clinton administration, argued that "addictive drugs were criminalized because they are harmful; they are not harmful because they were criminalized," but he avoided any reference to nicotine and alcohol (Office of National Drug Control Policy 1999). "Our attempt to protect drug users from themselves," notes James Ostrowski (Committee on Law Reform of the New York County Lawyers Association 1987: 6), "has backfired, as it did during the prohibition of alcohol. We have only succeeded in making drug use much more dangerous and driving it underground, out of the reach of moderating social influences." Furthermore, imprisonment serves as a form of networking and recruitment for drug dealers and their clients (Currie 1993).

The Pros

The practical advantages of a drug decriminalization policy are impressive:

1. There would be a reduction in the resources necessary for drug law enforcement. Federal, state, and local governments spend billions of tax dollars annually for drug law enforcement; additional billions are spent on imprisonment and probation and parole supervision of drug users. These resources could be shifted to other areas of crime control and for drug treatment and prevention. Jonathan Caulkins and his colleagues caution that if the money that is saved from not having to enforce drug prohibition were used to fund drug prevention, "even by our most optimistic estimates of prevention's effectiveness" it would not offset any increase in use resulting from relaxation of controls (1999: xxx).
2. The low cost of psychoactive substances would curtail secondary criminality—that needed to support an expensive drug habit. It would obviate the need to trade sex for drugs, a practice that has helped to spread AIDS.
3. Criminal organizations that are supported by drug trafficking would no longer remain viable unless, of course, they moved into other criminal activities.
4. The aggressive marketing by traffickers aimed at expanding their customer bases would no longer be operative. This type of marketing resulted in the widespread use of crack cocaine.
5. Those who are dependent on heroin, cocaine, or other currently illegal psychoactive substances could lead more normal lives; the time and energy needed to maintain the habit could be channeled into more constructive pursuits; and abusers would have an opportunity to become contributing members of society. For example, it is not the drug but the law that makes heroin hazardous to the addict. Opiates, like widely prescribed sedatives, provide relief from anxiety, distress, and insomnia to people who would have difficulty functioning normally in the absence of such substances. Similar arguments can be made for cocaine and other substances. For those who

The "So What?" Problem

"People use drugs because they are pleasurable, and because they are an effective antidote to anxiety, frustration, and feelings of inadequacy. Were drugs legal, they would be socially destigmatized and they would become easier to acquire, cheaper to purchase [unless, of course, they were heavily taxed], and safer to use. Given the genuine psychological benefits of drug use, we can be sure that it would increase were drugs legalized" (de Marneffe 2003: 34). But, while the number of users might increase, society could ultimately benefit if the average harm caused by each was reduced (Husak and deMarneffe 2005).

accept the disease theory of addiction—the idea that some people take heroin or cocaine to compensate for a physiological deficiency—decriminalization is a reasonable suggestion. Allowing these people to access drugs is analogous to the diabetic's need for insulin. Some researchers have found a strong correlation between poor mental health and drug abuse. People frequently self-prescribe drugs to deal with their mental problems, and psychoactive drugs do alleviate psychological discomfort, at least temporarily, enabling the person to relax and/or function more effectively.

6. Intravenous use of heroin would not necessarily involve the danger of hepatitis or AIDS because each user would have his or her own hypodermic kit. In the United States, while the incidence of AIDS among the homosexual population has stabilized, the disease is spreading quickly among drug addicts. Decriminalization would also make many drugs available in liquid form for oral ingestion. Under government oversight drugs would be distributed in precisely measured doses, free of any dangerous contaminants. The chance of a drug overdose would thus be reduced.

7. Decriminalization would enable the use of social controls that inhibit antisocial, albeit lawful, behavior. Because drugs are illegal, users avoid detection and are shielded from social pressure. "Therefore, illicit drug users generally escape the potent forms of social control that are applied to smokers and drunk drivers" (Alexander 1990: 8).

The Cons

There are, of course, important disadvantages:

1. Cocaine, amphetamines, and heroin freely available to adults could be abused by youngsters as easily as cigarettes and alcohol are. Restrictions on these items have not proven effective in keeping the substances away from young people (see, e.g., Feder 1996a). Adolescents who are motivated toward drug use are unlikely to be thwarted by legislative acts and law enforcement efforts. As Zimring and Hawkins (1992: 121) point out, however: "To the extent that prohibition policies make drugs more

U.S. Policy on Legalization

"Those who would legalize the use of illicit drugs tend to fall back on familiar arguments, perhaps the most common of which is that we should treat illegal drugs 'like we treat alcohol or cigarettes.' They neglect to point out that there are 120 million regular drinkers in the United States and some 61 million smokers. The comparable figure for illegal drugs is about 20 million—a large number to be sure, but far smaller than would be the case if drugs were legal" (Office of National Drug Control Policy 2004c: 8).

difficult or more expensive for adults to acquire, the same policies will mean that young persons will encounter a prohibited drug less often and will often be unable to afford the purchase even when a source is located." Of course, taxing policies—"sin taxes"—could make legalized substances unaffordable to most young people as long as the taxes were not so high as to generate a black market (Miron 2001).

2. More people would be tempted to try legalized controlled substances, and abuse-related problems might increase accordingly. As was noted in an earlier chapter, because of easier access, medical practitioners have a higher rate of drug use than among the general population. According to the President's Commission on Organized Crime (1986: 331) "legalization would almost certainly increase demand, and therefore spread this destruction." The American Academy of Psychiatrists in Alcoholism and Addictions argues against legalization of drugs because "increased availability will lead to increased use, abuse and addiction to illegal substances, and . . . there is no rational plan for distribution of these drugs that would not be hazardous and full of ethical problems" (American Academy of Psychiatrists in Alcoholism and Addictions Board of Directors 1990). Robert Peterson (1991) argues that drug prohibition, as contrasted with the devastation caused by a lack of similar controls over alcohol, saves billions of dollars and thousands of lives each year. Chanoch Jacobsen and Robert Hanneman (1992) state that the illegitimacy of drug abuse allows for the activation of informal social controls through families, peers, and community that restrain drug abuse. Of course, some people find the outlaw nature of illegal drugs part of the allure. However, opiates are not seductive substances that "hook" the unsuspecting and the innocent. A study of 11,882 hospital patients who had been treated with pain-killing drugs revealed that only four became addicted. A study of more than 10,000 burn victims who received injections of narcotics for weeks or months found not a single case of addiction attributed to this treatment (Melzack 1990). Russell Portnoy, M.D., director of analgesic studies in the Pain Service at Sloan-Kettering Memorial Hospital, points out, "Just as the vast majority of people who drink do not become alcoholics, those who are treated with opioid for pain do not become addicts" (Goleman 1987: 10;

Bipartisan Insanity?

Former police chief of San Diego Joseph McNamara has been quoted as saying, "If the drug war worked, I'd be all for it, but it doesn't. And when you look at what politicians say to get elected, you realize there's this bipartisan insanity. They say let's get tougher on drugs and more and more of what hasn't worked for the past 80 years" (Horowitz 1996: 28).

Brownlee and Schrof 1997). While two out of every three Americans consume alcohol, 10 percent of the drinkers account for half of all the alcohol consumed in the United States. Because some users of psychoactive substances will become dysfunctional as a result, is that sufficient to ban their use? "It is very hard to see why one's freedoms should be held hostage this way"—why individual rights should be held hostage to the person who is most irresponsible (Shapiro 2003: 43).

3. Legalizing all psychoactive substances would signal an acceptance of their use similar to the acceptance of alcohol and tobacco. Most users of alcohol do not become addicted, but Kaplan (1983b) argues that we do not know whether this would hold true for such drugs as heroin. Studies indicate that rats and monkeys perform considerable amounts of work to earn injections of heroin or cocaine but do not respond so eagerly to alcohol. However, as was noted previously, many people have used opiates without becoming addicted: hospital patients experiencing pain, "chippers" and "weekenders" who use heroin much as a social drinker uses alcohol, and soldiers returning to the United States who used high-quality heroin while in Vietnam but discontinued use when they were no longer confronted by the anxiety and depression of the war experience and when the cheap, high-quality heroin to which they had grown accustomed was no longer available (Robins 1973, 1974; Robins et al. 1980). The availability of cheap heroin in the United States, argues Wilson (1990), might have kept these veterans addicted. And the availability of cheap drugs could lead to greater use by pregnant women.

4. The easy availability of legal heroin, cocaine, and other currently illegal psychoactive substances would reduce the incentive for those who are already addicted or habituated to enter drug treatment or otherwise to seek a drug-free existence. Of course, there is no reason to believe that a drug-free existence would facilitate a constructive, crime-free lifestyle in most people who are currently using psychoactive substances. Most heroin addicts, for example, go right on using heroin despite the threat or actuality of imprisonment and often despite efforts to cure the affliction.

The legal availability of heroin, however, could prolong heroin addiction beyond the age (35 to 40 years) at which spontaneous remission typically occurs. Recall that the availability of cheap high-grade heroin in Vietnam helps to explain its widespread use by U.S. servicemen (Zinberg

The Free Speech Problem

"Free speech and open expression are time-honored institutions on the college campus. Unfortunately, the same openness that fosters intellectual growth can also make students vulnerable to the misguided and destructive messages of groups pushing for relaxing drug laws" (Office of National Drug Control Policy 2004c: 45).

Sending the Wrong Message

Some argue that decriminalization would send the wrong message, that drug use is acceptable. However, many activities that are wrong—breaking promises, lying to friends, cheating on a spouse or a boy- or girlfriend should not be punished by law. Only in the context of drug use is failure to punish is viewed pro-drug (Husak and de Marneffe 2005).

1984). Indeed, by 1999 it was apparent that the increasing use of heroin in the United States was the result of the drug's becoming purer, cheaper, and more readily available for intravenous use or sniffing and smoking. New users are often white and from more affluent backgrounds than was typical of heroin addicts in the past (Wren 1999a).

POLICY ISSUES

Focus on Causes

To develop a policy that answers these serious concerns, we need to understand the cause(s) of drug use. Are some people more vulnerable than others? As we saw in earlier chapters, we do not know why some people use or abuse drugs while others who have similar access do not. We do not know why some people who experiment with certain drugs become dependent while others do not. Any discussion of drug policy is conditioned on views of drug abuse and on the particular theory that one adopts:

- Drug abuse is a disease with a physiological basis.
- Drug abuse is a psychological condition or personality disorder.
- Drug abuse is a response to oppressive social conditions.
- Drug abuse is simply the pleasure-seeking activity of hedonistic individuals.

We know that there is a very high correlation between urban poverty and heroin and cocaine use. A great deal of drug use, it seems, feeds on human misery. "Britain first came to experience widespread and serious problems of drug misuse amidst the economic downturn of the early 1980s which devastated the local economies of many local industrial working class communities. Subsequently, chronic drug-related problems have become established as a common feature of the social landscape in many neighborhoods in this condition. Under such circumstances, local efforts to curb drug misuse are likely to be severely handicapped unless supported by wider schemes of urban regeneration, access to jobs and training, and other initiatives to combat social exclusion" (Advisory Council on the Misuse of Drugs 1998: 40). Similarly, a serious effort to deal logically with drugs in the United States would require greater efforts to reduce the ills of urban America. The policy of "drug warriors" seldom reflects on social conditions as a source of drug misuse.

No Loans for Student Drug Offenders

U.S. Department of Education regulations, based on a law enacted in 1998, bar students who have been convicted of drug offenses from receiving federal college tuition aid. A first possession conviction bars aid for a year, and a sales conviction will bar aid for two years. Students who are convicted for a second time of possessing drugs will lose aid for two years; those who are convicted a third time lose it permanently. A student who has been convicted twice of selling drugs will lose aid permanently. Some students will be able to retain eligibility by completing a drug rehabilitation program. Students must report any drug convictions on federal financial aid forms, including Pell grants and student loans. Students who lie will have to return any aid that they have received and may be prosecuted (McQueen 1999).

Mexico Decriminalizes Possession of Small Amounts of Drugs

In 2006 Mexico enacted legislation decriminalizing possession of 25 milligrams of heroin, half a gram of cocaine, or a fifth of an once of marijuana. Small amounts of amphetamines and hallucinogens were also decriminalized.

Chein and his colleagues (1964: 381) extend this argument further: "Is a society which cannot or will not do anything to alleviate the miseries which are, at least subjectively, alleviated by drugs better off if it simply prevents the victims of these miseries from finding any relief?" Furthermore, remember that much of the damage that is inflicted by drugs is the result of their illicit status and not from their pharmacology.

Among those who are strongly opposed to drug decriminalization, however, are many leaders of the African American community. They have expressed the view that such programs are merely schemes designed to tranquilize members of the minority community who would be attracted by the availability of cheap drugs to alleviate their social and psychological frustrations. Some members of the minority community would abandon protest and political activity for the "easy fix," and such programs would saddle the community with lifelong abusers who have been robbed of the incentive to give up drugs.

Congressman Charles B. Rangel of New York, whose district includes Harlem, while chairman of the House Select Committee on Narcotics Abuse and Control vigorously opposed any type of drug maintenance program or decriminalization. He states that while "illegal drug-trafficking violence would end under decriminalization, a new crime source would be created by the influx of new addicts," and "hyperactive reactions to such drugs as cocaine will spur criminal behavior" (1990: 14).

EMERGENCE OF DECRIMINALIZATION AS A POLICY ISSUE

Until 1988 the debate over drug decriminalization remained basically academic; that is, it was discussed seriously only by a few university educators and liberal or libertarian political ideologues. In that year drugs became a—possibly *the*—major political issue of the presidential campaign. In response to the obvious—that antidrug efforts have not had any significant effect—*Time*

Models of Drug Decriminalization

1. Dangerous drugs can be dispensed only through government-controlled clinics or specially licensed medical personnel and only for short-term treatment purposes; unauthorized sale or possession entails criminal penalties. Long-term maintenance is limited to the use of methadone. This is basically the approach that is currently used in England.
2. Dangerous drugs can be prescribed by an authorized medical practitioner for treatment or maintenance; criminal penalties are imposed for sale or possession outside medical auspices. This is the old British system.
3. Dangerous drugs can be sold and used as tobacco and alcohol products are; that is, nonprescription use by adults is permitted. This was the case in the United States before the Harrison Act.

Pat O'Malley and Stephen Mugford (1991) argue for a more limited version:

1. Providing safer options by, for example, making coca tea readily available but significantly limiting cocaine and severely restricting crack, which, along with morphine and heroin, would be available only through prescription or licensing arrangements. There would be no incentives to attract new users.
2. Offering and encouraging safer ingestion. For example, smoking opium would be readily available, but intravenous drug use would be severely restricted.
3. Permitting cultivation and possession of small amounts of marijuana and criminalizing large-scale operations.
4. Banning prodrug advertising—including that for tobacco and alcohol products—while encouraging education and antidrug advertising, which would be financed through drug-related tax revenues.

magazine (30 May 1988) presented a cover article on the issue: "Should Drugs Be Made Legal?" In a balanced presentation *Time* outlined the benefits and disadvantages of such a proposal and concluded that "even though corner drug shops are not going to pop up anytime soon, nor should they, the hot new debate over legalization is a significant one. It reflects the widespread and understandable dismay over anti-drug efforts that have gone to such discomforting lengths as to call in the military without noticeably making a dent in the crime and abuse problem."

The following year, the *New York Times* reported that while popular opinion still opposed decriminalization, debate over the issue had intensified: "It has become a staple of editorial pages, letters to the editor, talk shows on television and radio and public lectures. And many who do not go as far as advocating legalization show a new interest in the subject" (Corcoran 1989: 9). The discussion of decriminalization brought a hostile response from William Bennett, then the "drug czar" (actually, federal director of drug policy). He argued that any public discussion of the issue only worsens the problem and undermines efforts to combat drug abuse (Sly 1989).

MEDICAL MAINTENANCE

Heroin

Kaplan (1983b) argues that our inability to predict the consequences of making heroin freely available raises doubts about a policy of drug legalization. Nadelmann (1988: 91) responds: "The case for legalization [of heroin, cocaine, and marijuana] is particularly convincing when the risks inherent in alcohol and tobacco use are compared with those associated with illicit drug use." Chein and colleagues (1964) and Trebach (1982) recommend a more modest policy: placing greater trust in the medical profession and allowing physicians to treat addicts with a variety of drugs, including heroin. They recommend that clinics be established to implement this policy. (Such clinics have never been popular with community residents, however, and it would be difficult to open them in most neighborhoods.)

Any person who is shown to be addicted to heroin could receive prescriptions for the drug. Determining whether or not a person is addicted and how much heroin he or she should be given would be left to the medical profession. Trebach notes that some drugs would be diverted into the black market, but the black market in illegal heroin is already considerable.

Legalization would, of course, reduce the price of heroin, thereby reducing the incentive for dealing in the substance. This policy, Trebach argues, would attract heroin addicts in large numbers and cause significant decreases in crime. Such clinics would also offer a wide variety of social services, including help in becoming drug-free (which would be encouraged but not imposed by clinic staff).

In 2005 Canada initiated a clinical trial providing heroin to about ninety addicts with a comparison group receiving methadone. It is too soon to judge its effectiveness.

Cocaine

Although cocaine abuse is a major problem, fewer researchers are calling for its decriminalization (Wisotsky 1987; O'Malley and Mugford 1991). Kaplan (1983b) notes that monkeys who become addicted to heroin will increase their dosage to a relatively high level and then stabilize the amount and work to earn food or other rewards; laboratory animals that are given unlimited access to cocaine, by contrast, will continue to increase self-injected doses of the substance until the supply is cut off or they die from debilitation (see Dworkin et al. 1987). Of course, monkeys do many things that humans do not, and this might be one of them. However, while satiety for heroin can be satisfied by substituting methadone, cocaine might induce greater craving. Thus, providing clinic doses of cocaine could stimulate rather than reduce the demand for street cocaine (National Institute on Drug Abuse 1997b). Interestingly, Brecher and the editors of Consumer Reports (1972) advocate legalizing heroin for addicts but take no similar position with respect to cocaine (or amphetamines).

Comparison to Legal Substances

Wisotsky (1987) argues that we have continuously focused on the negatives of substances whose nonmedical use is subjected to criminal sanctions. Yet these substances provide relief from anxiety, euphoria, a sense of enhanced well-being, and experiences that the user obviously finds pleasing. Although these substances carry some dangers, so do a host of other substances, such as tobacco, alcohol, and even certain foods whose abuse can lead to obesity and high blood pressure, not to mention firearms, extreme martial arts, and any number of dangerous pastimes that people find pleasurable—that produce a "high." Why pick on chemicals, or rather on the specific chemicals we have chosen to control with criminal sanctions? To the person whose appetite appears insatiable, certain food (sometimes referred to as "junk food") is addicting, yet we do not restrict the intake of potentially harmful foods that have little, if any, nutritional value.

The noted economist Ludwig von Mises (1949: 728–729), a favorite of many political conservatives, argues:

> Opium and morphine are certainly dangerous, habit-forming drugs. But once the principle is admitted that it is the duty of government to protect the individual against his own foolishness, no serious objections can be advanced against further encroachments. A good case could be made out in favor of the prohibition of alcohol and nicotine. And why limit the government's benevolent providence to the protection of the individual's body only? Is not the harm a man can inflict on his mind and soul even more disastrous than any bodily evils? Why not prevent him from reading bad books and seeing bad plays? The mischief done by bad ideologies surely, is much more pernicious, both for the individual and for the whole society, than that done by narcotic drugs.

Nadelmann (1988: 97) adds: "There is little question that if the production, sale, and possession of alcohol and tobacco were criminalized, the health costs associated with their use and abuse could be reduced. But most Americans do not believe that criminalizing the alcohol and tobacco markets would be a good idea. Their opposition stems largely from two beliefs: that adult Americans have the right to choose what substances they will consume and what risks they will take, and that the economic costs of trying to coerce so many Americans into abstaining from those substances would be enormous and the social costs disastrous."

"Most people," states Wisotsky (1987: 207), "will not *permit* themselves to become addicted, just as most people will not consistently overeat to the point of obesity." With respect to heroin and cocaine the "dominant pattern consists of controlled recreational use or social use, not chronic, compulsive, or obsessive use." Zinberg (1984) points out that our policies have failed to distinguish between the controlled user of psychoactive substances and the one for whom drug use has become dysfunctional. The use of drugs in the United States is widespread, and most of those who ingest psychoactive chemicals, from alcohol and marijuana to heroin and cocaine, do not become dysfunctional. However, the President's Commission on Organized Crime (1986: 483) recommended that "[n]o Federal,

Dangers of Drug Law Enforcement

In response to New York City's intensified war against drug sellers, dealers have adopted more perilous tactics: "Five or six times each month, undercover investigators are now forced to use cocaine or heroin at gunpoint, to prove to dealers that they can be trusted. At least twice a month, an officer is shot or otherwise wounded during a staged purchase" (Kocieniewski 1998: 18).

State, or local government funds should go directly or indirectly to programs that counsel 'responsible' drug use or condone illicit drug use in any way."

It appears irrational to give the dysfunctional alcoholic a "legal pass" while subjecting the occasional user of marijuana, heroin, or cocaine to criminal sanctions—sanctions that can result in labeling that, in itself, may be socially, psychologically, and economically debilitating. In fact, much of what society decries about drug abuse is the result of our policy of criminal sanctions. With a redefinition of the problem Wisotsky (1987: 214) asserts, "drug abuse would become like any other health problem, managed by research, prevention, education and treatment," an approach that could be funded by the considerable amount of money now spent on drug law enforcement. This approach would help to destroy heroin and cocaine cartels that threaten the integrity and stability of a number of nations faced with Marxist insurgencies while reducing the everyday dangers to which we expose the public and our drug law enforcement agents. Two models of drug decriminalization are presented in the box on p. 401.

EFFORTS TO DECRIMINALIZE MARIJUANA

There has been some movement toward decriminalization with respect to marijuana. Possession of marijuana for personal use has been decriminalized in some states, and some authorities have proposed legalization and taxation. Although the state supreme court in Alaska decriminalized the possession of small amounts of marijuana in 1975, fifteen years later voters passed a ballot initiative making it illegal once again. (Marijuana was also recriminalized in Oregon.) There is no evidence to indicate that legal changes have resulted in a marijuana abuse problem in these states. European countries such as the Netherlands and Spain have similarly decriminalized the possession of marijuana for personal use. In the Netherlands thousands of "coffee shops" sell marijuana and hashish under government regulation (discussed later in the chapter).

In 2002 England established a policy of not arresting people for possessing small amounts of marijuana for personal use. This was apparently based on a six-month experiment in South London's Brixton area, where people who were caught smoking marijuana were given warnings rather than being arrested. The policy is not without its critics; residents complained of the openness of

Maturing Out

In Australia, where most young people have used cannabis at some time in their lives, use decreases with age, marriage, and parenthood, and "only a small proportion use the drug for several years or more." Heavy users regularly use alcohol and are likely to have experimented with a variety of illegal drugs (Hall, Degenhardt, and Lynskey 2001: xviii).

marijuana smoking and the fact that sellers often peddle an array of illegal substances, not just marijuana. In response Parliament increased penalties for drug selling, particularly of heroin and cocaine (Lyall 2002). A government reclassification of cannabis downward resulted in a 30 percent drop in arrests, enabling the police to increase efforts against Class A drugs such as heroin and cocaine (Home Office 2004).

In the United States the decriminalization of marijuana appears to have considerable opposition. Polls show that most Americans oppose decriminalization and that the adverse effects of alcohol and tobacco are not seen as justifying decriminalization of marijuana. The President's Commission on Organized Crime (1986: 483) suggested that laws in certain states that decriminalized the possession of marijuana are equivalent to condoning the use of drugs and should be reconsidered.

In 1992 the U.S. Public Health Service rescinded approval of marijuana for a handful of carefully screened patients suffering from AIDS, cancer, or glaucoma. In an editorial the *Chicago Tribune* (March 16, 1992: 20) argued that "apparently the federal government just wants to have nothing more to do with marijuana, no matter who might benefit." The alleged reason was that "[i]t doesn't want to be embarrassed politically by having to admit that marijuana might not be all bad, that it may have some benign uses after all." In 1999 residents of the nation's capital voted overwhelmingly to permit the medical use of marijuana, but the referendum was effectively nullified by Congress. About a dozen states have decriminalized marijuana possession, and eight states have laws allowing patients to use marijuana with a doctor's recommendation, but federal law prohibits the practice (Adams 2002; Haynes 2002). The vehemence of government opposition is characterized by a statement issued by the U.S. Office of Narcotics and Drug Control with respect to the cultivation of hemp for its fiber, particularly in the American apparel and paper industries: "Legalizing hemp production would send a confusing message to our youth concerning marijuana. Also, it may lead to the *de facto* legalization of marijuana cultivation" (July 29, 1997).

CONTAINMENT IN ZURICH

A somewhat ambiguous middle position was adopted in Zurich, Switzerland: a policy of containment. Vigorous police action drove hard-core users into a park near the heart of the city, where open drug sale and use were tolerated. "Needle

Pot Docs in California

Voters in California passed a referendum (Compassionate Use Act) in 1996 granting physicians authority to recommend marijuana for any illness for which it would provide relief. For about eight years about 30,000 gravely ill patients were able to consume marijuana. A subsequent referendum protecting doctors was passed and an estimated 250,000 new patients have been given medically authorized access to marijuana for ailments such as insomnia and headaches—one doctor recommended it to treat stuttering, writer's cramps, and corns (Kenneally 2007).

Park" accommodated about 400 hard-core users of heroin and cocaine and about 3,000 others who passed through daily. An AIDS prevention program was established in the park, and free needles were distributed as part of the effort. Social workers attempted to guide users into treatment programs, and volunteers provided free lunches. Because of the number of drug overdoses—an average of twelve a day—five doctors had to be stationed in the park. Urination killed off all the trees and flowers.

Drug users were drawn to the park from throughout Europe, an important factor in the park's demise: In 1992 the park was shut, and it remains sealed behind a ten-foot iron fence (Treaster 1990b; R. Cohen 1992). The drug market in Zurich did not end with the closing of the park; it moved a half-mile away to a little-used railway station. There, a policy of tolerance again ensued until increasing violence, including the murder of four dealers, led to a 1995 government crackdown, and the area was closed off with razor wire and steel fencing (Cowell 1995).

Switzerland, with a population of about seven million, has about 30,000 drug addicts. In 1997 the Swiss public voted to continue a program that permits hard-core heroin addicts to receive their drugs from the government. Three times a day, enrolled addicts visit authorized centers, where they pay a modest fee and receive heroin that they inject at antiseptic clinic tables. As part of the program, participants are enrolled in health, social, and psychological services, and abstinence programming is available (Olson 1997; Associated Press 1997b). In a review of the program, research found criminal activity among participants—drug- and non-drug related-crimes—decreased markedly, while daily ties to the drug scene were broken and lives were stabilized; however, participants had difficulties securing and maintaining employment (Güttinger et al. 2003; Ribeaud 2004).

NEEDLE-EXCHANGE PROGRAMS

It was discovered that intravenous drug abusers who are also diabetic do not get AIDS. At first this appeared to be connected to their diabetes, but it was subsequently explained by their legal access to hypodermic needles (Chapman

1991a). As a result, needle-exchange programs began to gain support. In these programs intravenous drug users present their used needles, which are exchanged for unused sterile ones. In an effort to reduce the spread of AIDS among intravenous drug users and to reduce AIDS among infants of addict mothers, in 1988 a service agency in the city of Portland, Oregon, became the first to distribute free needles as part of a pilot project involving 125 addicts. Oregon has no law restricting the distribution of hypodermic needles, but addicts frequently do not have the necessary funds to purchase them. In 1992 Connecticut changed its law to permit the purchase and possession of hypodermic needles without a prescription. As a result the number of AIDS cases fell by 40 percent (G. Judson 1995). By 1992 eight U.S. cities had needle-exchange programs, half of them in the state of Washington (Navarro 1992). Opponents among law enforcement, political, religious, and drug treatment officials contend that free needles promote drug use—that making needles available suggests that the government is condoning drug use. (Similar arguments have been made about distributing condoms.) Nevertheless, at the end of 2006, New Jersey, which has one of the highest rates of HIV in the nation, became the last of the fifty states to approve legislation permitting needle-exchange programs.

Switzerland and the Netherlands distribute hypodermic needles to reduce the spread of AIDS (Bollag 1989), as does almost every other country in Western Europe. Australia has a needle- and syringe-exchange program, which has been operating in the state of New South Wales since 1986. While Australia has a relatively high number of AIDS cases and intravenous drug users, there are very few intravenous drug users with AIDS (Wodak 1990; Wodak and Lurie 1997).

As a harm reduction measure, needle exchange programs are considered a small but important step in curbing HIV, which can spread through shared and dirty needles.

The "Why" of Needle-Exchange Programs

According to an editorial in the *New York Times* in support of needle-exchange programs, "Intravenous-drug users who spread disease by sharing dirty needles and engaging in unprotected sex are responsible for more than a third of all the AIDS cases in the United States and more than half of the new cases of hepatitis C" (September 24, 2004: 26).

In 1995 a report by the National Academy of Sciences commissioned by Congress found that programs that encourage drug abusers to exchange used needles for new ones greatly reduce the spread of AIDS (Leary 1995). In 1997 the American Medical Association endorsed the concept of using needle-exchange programs to combat AIDS. Nevertheless, in 1998 President Clinton, fearing criticism from congressional Republicans, refused to lift a 1989 federal ban on financing for programs that distribute clean needles to drug addicts even though government scientists reported that such programs do not encourage drug use and could save lives by reducing the spread of AIDS (Stolberg 1998).

HARM REDUCTION[2]

Informal Harm Reduction

European Union countries frequently practice what can be called *unofficial harm reduction*; that is, they utilize informal police and prosecutorial practices to eliminate punishments for obtaining or possessing small amounts of illegal drug (Böllinger 2004).

Like Switzerland, a number of other European countries have been exploring a third model of response to drug abuse: **harm reduction**. Harm reduction is offered as an alternative to the *supply reduction* strategy—aggressive law enforcement and pressure on producer nations—and the *demand reduction* strategy—treatment and prevention. This alternative recognizes that while abstinence is desirable, it is not a realistic goal. Instead, this approach examines harm from two points of view: harm to the community and harm to the drug user. The focus, then, is on lowering the amount of harm to each. "Each policy or programmatic decision is assessed for its expected impact on society. If a policy or program is expected to reduce aggregate harm, it should be accepted; if it is expected to increase aggregate harm, it should be rejected. The prevalence of drug use should play no special and separate role" (Reuter and Caulkins 1995: 1060). As Jonathan Caulkins (1996: 232) notes, however, "attempting to translate the concept of harm reduction into formal terms brings out key philosophical questions that must be addressed. How does one measure harm? How does one aggregate and compare different types of harm? Which (whose) harms count?"

---

[2]For a general discussion of the role of law enforcement in harm reduction, see Caulkins and Heinz (2002).

Example: Harm Reduction Information on Methamphetamine

Speed has the ability to make you feel good. You can have intense feelings of pleasure and well-being and be able to function at top speed, getting lots of work or studying done or dancing all night. Of course, with the up comes the down. There are not-so-pleasurable effects of using speed too. As with other drugs, the more you use speed, the more of it your body needs. This is called tolerance. Tolerance occurs more rapidly when speed is injected or smoked. Speed tells your body that you do not need food or sleep, so you are extremely tired and depleted when you take a break. Depression, nightmares, and insomnia are also side effects of using speed. Then there is the crash. To avoid crashing, people often take more speed, which intensifies the negative effects of the crash when it does come—and the crash always comes (Harm Reduction Coalition 1998).

Principles of Harm Reduction

At present there is no agreement in the addiction literature or among practitioners as to the definition of harm reduction (Tammi 2004), but in harm reduction approaches, the use of drugs is accepted as a fact, and focus is placed on reducing harm while use continues. The main characteristics or principles of harm reduction are as follows (Conley et al. n.d.):

- *Pragmatism*: Harm reduction accepts that some use of mind-altering substances is a common feature of human experience. It acknowledges that while carrying risks, drug use also provides the user with benefits that must be taken into account if drug-using behavior is to be understood. From a community perspective containment and amelioration of drug-related harms may be a more pragmatic or feasible option than efforts to eliminate drug use entirely.
- *Humanistic values*: The drug user's decision to use drugs is accepted as fact. This does not mean approval. No moralistic judgment is made either to condemn or to support use of drugs, regardless of level of use or mode of intake. The dignity and rights of the drug user are respected.
- *Focus on harms*: The fact or extent of a person's drug use per se is of secondary importance to the risk of harms consequent to use. Harms that are addressed are related to health, social, economic, and other factors affecting the individual, the community, and society as a whole. Therefore, the first priority is to decrease the negative consequences of drug use to the user and to others rather than focusing on decreasing the drug use itself. Harm reduction neither excludes nor presumes the long-term treatment goal of abstinence. In some cases reduction of level of use may be one of the most effective forms of harm reduction. In others alteration to the mode of use may be more effective.
- *Balancing costs and benefits*: A pragmatic process of identifying, measuring, and assessing the relative importance of drug-related problems, their associated harms, and costs and benefits of intervention is carried out in order to

Figure 14.1 | Risk Continuum

focus resources on priority issues. The analysis extends beyond the immediate interests of users to include broader community and societal interests. Because of this rational approach, harm reduction approaches theoretically lend themselves to evaluation of impacts in comparison to some other, or no, intervention. In practice, however, such evaluations are complicated because of the number of variables to be examined in both the short and the long term.

- *Priority of immediate goals*: Most harm-reduction programs have a hierarchy of goals, with the immediate focus on proactively engaging individuals, target groups, and communities to address their most pressing needs. Achieving the most immediate and realistic goals is usually viewed as first steps toward risk-free use or, if appropriate, abstinence.

Reducing the Risky Consequences of Drug Use

In the view of Alan Marlatt, Julian Somers, and Susan Tapert (1993), harm reduction seeks to avoid marginalizing drug users because more can be done to control the often destructive behavior of drug abusers when they are "normalized." While abstinence is an ultimate objective, in the continuum shown in Figure 14.1, Marlatt and colleagues posit that *any* steps that decrease risk are worthwhile goals.

The focus is on reducing the risky consequences of drug use rather than on reducing drug use per se. In place of the "war" analogy and "total victory" rhetoric, Marlatt and colleagues support even small steps that reduce harm. For example, intravenous use would be made safer through needle-exchange programs. The next step would be to encourage safer methods of ingestion. Risk would be further reduced by substituting methadone for heroin or other legal substances for cocaine and then by moderating the use of drugs—including nicotine and alcohol—en route to abstinence when this is possible. Related risk-taking behavior would also be targeted in an effort to deal with AIDS and other sexually transmitted diseases; in this case the focus of harm reduction would be on reducing the frequency of high-risk sexual activity by promoting less risky sexual practices, monogamous sex, and the use of birth control.

HARM REDUCTION IN THE UNITED KINGDOM

The harm reduction approach is more easily achieved in England, where controlled substances can be prescribed for those dependent on them and local governments have some flexibility in their approach to drug use. In the province of Merseyside, a severely disadvantaged region whose largest city is Liverpool, vestiges of the "old British system" remain, with addicts taking home injectable

The British Response: Old and New Systems

The first British drug control laws (passed in 1916) dealt with cocaine, a substance that was being used by soldiers on leave from World War I. The government had difficulty interpreting the statute for action, and in response the Ministry of Health formed a committee of physicians that moved the problem of drug abuse toward a medical response (Stimson and Oppenheimer 1982). The committee noted that some medical experts favored a program of providing diminishing doses until the patient became drug-free. Other physicians argued that some addicts will never be able to live drug-free, and for them, after all other treatment had proven unsuccessful, heroin maintenance was suggested—if not cure, then care. Most important, the committee report stated that drug abuse is a disease, not an indulgence (Trebach 1982). The British system that resulted from the committee's report gave the medical profession almost unhindered freedom to treat drug addicts by means of providing drugs.

Problems grew in the 1950s when a substantial market in heroin tablets grew in London. Most of the new addicts were young recreational users whose lifestyles were more deviant than those of the older class of addicts. A 1966 report concluded that the problem was caused by a handful of doctors who were over-prescribing heroin, which was being diverted into a black market. As a result, the use of opiates and cocaine to treat addiction was restricted to specially licensed physicians and drug treatment clinics. Between the late 1970s and the early 1980s there was a large growth in the volume of smokable and injectable heroin in all parts of the United Kingdom. This problem continued throughout the 1980s, during which there was a growth in the acid house music culture, with major media coverage of MDMA (ecstasy) and other hallucinogenic drugs. In 1999 cocaine was determined to be overtaking heroin in popularity (Murray and Tendler 1999). Today, specially licensed doctors can provide heroin or cocaine for drug treatment, but this has become rare. Instead of heroin most licensed physicians and clinics prescribe methadone for oral ingestion, although any medical doctor can provide heroin as an analgesic for physical pain.

The modern British system involves two barely compatible policies operating at the same time: a political policy whose focus is on supply reduction and penal policies in the belief that elimination of drug use is possible, and a services policy whose focus is on local prevention campaigns and providing a variety of local services, including needle-exchange schemes, advice and counseling services, and a variety of prescribing options from short-term outpatient detoxification to long-term prescribing and rehabilitation. "At the heart of this approach is the view that drug use cannot be eliminated, but its most harmful consequences for the individual, society, and public health can be moderated" (Turner 1991: 184–185).

opiates. But Merseyside has also introduced a comprehensive harm reduction (see the box entitled "The Merseyside Model"). "By no means soft on drugs, the Drug Squad of the Merseyside police force arrest and charge a greater number of people for drug offenses than all other provincial forces."

The Merseyside Model

At present the only truly comprehensive harm reduction program is in Merseyside, England; it involves needle exchange, counseling, prescription of drugs including heroin, and employment and housing services. Many levels of service and a wide variety of agencies are involved, and services are integrated to provide drug users with help when they need it. Pharmacists play a vital role in the workings of the Merseyside system. Some fill prescriptions for smokable drugs in the form of "reefers," which provide an alternative to injection and produce the "buzz" that some intravenous users crave. To prepare reefers, drugs such as heroin and methadone are injected into either herbal or regular cigarettes. Clients who have received injectable prescriptions for more than ten years are now voluntarily switching to reefers in an attempt to stop injecting. In addition to reefers, pharmacists dispense drugs in the form of ampoules, liquid, and aerosols.

The Merseyside police have become national leaders in developing a cooperative harm reduction strategy with the regional health authority. The police sit on health authority drug advisory committees and employ health authority officers in police training courses involving the issue of drugs and HIV. The police have also agreed not to conduct surveillance on treatment centers, to refer arrested drug offenders to services, not to charge for possession of syringes to be exchanged, and to publicly support syringe exchange.

A key feature of the Merseyside police strategy has been to use resources to deal with drug traffickers while operating a cautioning policy toward drug users. Cautioning involves confiscating the drug, taking an offender to a police station, recording the incident, and formally warning the offender that any further unlawful possession of drugs will result in prosecution. The offender must also meet certain conditions, such as not having a previous drug conviction and not having an extensive criminal record. He or she is given information about treatment services in the area, including syringe exchanges. On the second and third occasions the user is sent to court and fined for possession of small quantities or sentenced for possession of large amounts. If an addict becomes registered by getting in touch with service agencies, then he or she is legally entitled to carry drugs for personal use. The overall effect of this policy is to steer users away from crime and possible imprisonment (Riley, n.d.).

Nevertheless, their focus on harm reduction means that first offenders who are found in possession of any drug are cautioned. Harm reduction aims at "avoiding the amplification of a drug-using career that may stem from a first conviction" (O'Hare 1992: xiv).

As part of a harm reduction approach to battle an alarming number of AIDS cases, physicians in Edinburgh, Scotland, are permitted to prescribe oral doses of nearly any drug craved by abusers. And there is indeed harm reduction: Great Britain has the lowest rate of AIDS in Europe (Schmidt 1993). In Britain harm reduction principles are not seen as incompatible with vigorous street policing; "indeed in many circumstances they actually require it" (Advisory

Council on the Misuse of Drugs 1994: 2). While U.S. "drug warriors" have frequently denounced the harm reduction approach as capitulation (or worse), the British Advisory Council on the Misuse of Drugs, whose membership includes police executives, recommends "the wider adoption of harm reduction principles in developing law enforcement strategies" (1994: 83). Although the United Kingdom has demonstrated greater flexibility than has the United States, basic U.K. drug policy is prohibitionary with a heavy emphasis on law enforcement (Home Office 2004). There is also extensive use of the criminal justice system to identify and treat drug users. Working out of police or custodial facilities, "Arrest Referral" counselors, many of whom are trained ex-addicts, interview and offer assistance to drug users (O'Shea and Powis 2003).

The harm reduction approach is popular throughout Europe, where officials generally avoid the "drug warrior" approach. Since 1990 the International Harm Reduction Association has been holding an annual conference in various cities—not in the United States—throughout the world. The U.S.-based Harm Reduction Coalition has been holding annual conferences since 1996 (for information, phone 212-213-6376 or 510-444-6969 or go to the organization's website at www.harmreduction.org). The country that is most identified with a national policy of harm reduction is the Netherlands.

DUTCH DRUG POLICY

The Netherlands is one of the most densely populated countries in the world, a largely urban population of about 16 million people in an area about the size of South Carolina. The Dutch have a strong belief in individual freedom, and government is expected to avoid becoming involved in matters of morality and religion. At the same time there is a strong sense of responsibility for the well-being of the community. The Netherlands has a very extensive system of social security, while health care and education are accessible to everyone (Barnard 1998; Bullington 1999). Accordingly, drug treatment programs are readily available (de Kort and Cramer 1999). In contrast to the U.S. experience discussed in Chapter 2, drugs in the Netherlands have not been strongly associated with marginalized groups (Uitermark 2004).

Dutch policy is based on the idea that drug use is a fact of life and needs to be discouraged in as practical a manner as possible (Barnard 1998). In place of prohibitionism's "war on drugs" and "user accountability," the Dutch have implemented a pragmatic and nonmoralistic approach whose main objective is to minimize the risks associated with drug use, both for users themselves and for those around them. The Dutch distinguish between "soft" drugs such as marijuana and "hard" drugs such as heroin, cocaine, and ecstasy. The idea is to separate the market so that users of soft drugs are less likely to come into contact with hard drugs and will not suffer the negative consequences of labeling (discussed in Chapter 8), since young people who become stigmatized are more likely to start using more dangerous drugs (de Kort and Cramer 1999; von Solinge 2004).

During the 1970s possession or sale of small amounts of marijuana (30 grams, reduced to 5 grams in 1995) was virtually decriminalized, and the substance remains widely available in so-called coffee shops (MacCoun and Reuter 1997); by contrast, trafficking in hard drugs can bring a twelve-year sentence. Although drug users are rarely arrested, those involved in secondary criminality are prosecuted, and drugs are not a mitigating circumstance (Silvas 1994). "Criminalization of the consumer is considered a harmful way of discouraging drug use" (Wever 1994: 64). The "coffee shops must follow specific rules: no advertising, no nuisance, no minors (under age 18 years), no hard drugs, and total stock not exceeding 500 grams (von Solinge 2004).

The Dutch response to ecstasy was similarly laissez faire, and MDMA was not outlawed until 1988, the result of international concern that the Netherlands might become a production site. This fear has materialized; The Netherlands reportedly produces 80 percent of the world supply of ecstasy. Nevertheless, officials do not consider the substance a major health issue, and the government provides facilities where pills can be tested, providing greater safety for the user and data for monitoring the drug market (Uitermark 2004).

Policy Change to Harm Reduction

Extensive social services in the Netherlands provide aid to drug abusers that is not available in many other countries, including the United States. Nevertheless, in the early 1980s downtown areas of larger Dutch cities became increasingly dominated by a highly visible population of untreated drug users. This fostered a change in approach, which had previously focused almost exclusively on promoting abstinence. Treatment was expanded to deal with the host of social and physical problems that abusers experience. Harm reduction became the focus: If abstinence is not possible, then safer use of drugs and safer sex practices should be the near-term goals. Drug abusers are now provided with health-related education and a wide variety of treatment programs are readily available, including methadone maintenance (Wever 1994), and there are sites in social service facilities where drugs may be safely ingested. This arrangement reduces neighborhood nuisances and exposes addicts to available services and drug treatment (Wolf, Linssen, and de Graaf 2003; van de Mheen and Gruter 2004).

Drug abuse prevention efforts in the Netherlands treat alcohol and tobacco, as well as heroin and cocaine, as dangerous drugs; legal versus illegal is not considered a sound basis for differentiation. This avoids the double standard that provokes cynicism in young people. The focus is on risky behavior, which also includes eating disorders. The policy seeks to deglamorize drugs and stresses individual responsibility for the consequences of substance abuse. People are cautioned against using dangerous substances while being provided with information on how to reduce the risks for those who insist on experimenting with drugs (Marshall and Marshall 1994). As was noted earlier, there are extensive treatment programs for those who become drug dependent.

Ineke Marshall and Chris Marshall note the differences between the Dutch and U.S. approaches to drugs (1994: 226): "The American mass media, public,

As a component of the harm reduction approach in The Netherlands, a safe house outside a rave provides a safer venue for the use of drugs and will analyze controlled substances so that users will know what type and how much of a substance they will be ingesting.

politicians, and educators appear to devote considerably more resources and energy to issues related to drug prevention than is the case in Holland. Differences in intensity of prevention efforts reflect fundamental differences in the definition of drugs as a social problem in the U.S. and Netherlands: In the U.S., drugs are viewed as a terrible evil to be fought with heavy arms (both in terms of prevention and repression); in the Netherlands, from a policymaker's viewpoint, drugs are viewed as a 'normal' social and health risk controlled by minimal measures or even ignored (e.g., cannabis, XTC)." Marshall and Marshall conclude that the "Dutch pragmatic approach has prevented the use of radical measures such as forced treatment, drug testing at the workplace, and fear-inducing information campaigns—'solutions' which may give the appearance of a tough approach, but which frequently cause more problems than they solve" (1994: 226).

Problems Over the Past Twenty Years

The Dutch approach has had problems. From 1979 to 1983 Amsterdam permitted drug use rooms where drugs could be consumed. It eventually became obvious that drug dealers were in charge and that the group norm within these centers was aimed at maintaining high levels of drug use and criminality. In 1983 the centers were closed, and more emphasis was given to police interventions and public order problems. By the early 1990s the coffee shops were becoming increasingly commercial and multiplying rapidly. Since they operated on the margins of society, there was the very real prospect of the coffee shops becoming centers of criminal activity—receiving stolen goods, for example—and they were attracting increasing numbers of foreigners. In response new restrictions were announced: no more than

5 grams per transaction and, owing to an increase in marijuana among school-children, a ban on those under age 18 years. Local authorities were given the power to ban or close coffee shops, and their numbers began to fall. Their regulation is now largely a local affair (de Kort and Cramer 1999).

Drug policy led to an influx of heroin users from other countries. In part, this appears to have been the unanticipated result of success in lowering the use of heroin—since methadone maintenance is readily available—which caused a decrease in price and attracted users from elsewhere (Korf, Riper, and Bullington 1999). In defending the Dutch approach, Herbert Barnard (1998), counselor for health and welfare at the Netherlands Embassy in Washington, D.C., stated that the Dutch policy has kept the number of heroin addicts relatively low in comparison with the number in many countries and that the addict population is rather stable and rapidly aging. Furthermore, the number of addicts who are infected with HIV is exceptionally low. He argues that despite the fact that marijuana is readily available, the rate of cannabis use in the Netherlands is lower than that in the United States (see also von Solinge 2004). A situation that is often encountered in other nations, in which the user—in most cases a minor—runs the risk of getting into trouble with the police is seen as highly undesirable in the Netherlands.

Larry Collins (1999) disputes this view. He states that marijuana use is a serious problem in the Netherlands. However, on the basis of the figures he presents, marijuana use is actually greater in the United States. Collins argues that because of the Netherlands' liberal attitude, that country has become a Mecca for drug traffickers and drug trafficking. The Dutch have the world's biggest seaport (Rotterdam), making it attractive to shippers of unlawful goods as well as lawful ones. Its central geographical position makes it a hub for European commerce. That the liberal Dutch attitude toward drugs attracts drug traffickers is an argument "built on the assumption that (potential) drug traffickers rationally consider and compare countries in order to decide from which to operate. The reality, however, is that professional drug traffickers do not expect to be caught" (von Solinge 2004: 134). As was noted in Chapter 13, even the death penalty has not stopped drug dealing.

Collins notes that much of the ecstasy entering other European countries originates in the Netherlands. The Dutch have recognized this problem and responded by setting up a special national unit to deal combat synthetic drugs. But MDA-type synthetic drugs such as MDMA remain a problem to which the Dutch have responded with a public campaign on their dangers and, in line with the harm reduction approach, by providing first-aid resources where the substance is most likely to be used. Indeed, since certain chemical configurations of MDA are more dangerous than others, Dutch policy provides pill testing for potential consumers. Crack cocaine has also been a problem in the Netherlands, although its use is primarily among a stable subset of polydrug users who also abuse heroin and methadone (de Kort and Cramer 1999). But despite greater visibility of drug users and the ready availability of drugs in the Netherlands, this "has not led to high(er) domestic drug use" (von Solinge 2004: 107).

CANADA CHANGES DIRECTION

Despite opposition from the United States, Canada is slowly moving in the Western European direction of harm reduction. Part of a larger concern with the issue of what behavior constitutes a crime, the Law Commission of Canada (2003) is examining the effects criminalizing drug use. Meanwhile, Canada, which has already decriminalized marijuana use for medical purposes, is considering permitting possession of small amounts of marijuana for personal use. Following the lead of Switzerland, a project is underway in Toronto, Vancouver, and Montreal to determine whether crime and health problems can be reduced by giving hard-core heroin addicts prescriptions (C. Krauss 2003).

Vancouver, a port city that serves as an entry point for Asian drugs, has an active and open drug subculture. In a drug-infested neighborhood a window sign in a long-abandoned storefront announces "Safer Injection Site," a place where about twenty-five heroin and cocaine addicts arrive every night to inject their drugs. A registered nurse dispenses fresh needles, sterile water, and advice on how to maintain veins. While technically illegal, the operation is condoned by the mayor, who was elected by a landslide on a platform of more treatment for addicts and regulated injection sites (C. Krauss 2003).

HARM REDUCTION: A NEW APPROACH TO EDUCATION[3]

Harm reduction is a relatively new and controversial approach to drug education. Instead of focusing on preventing *use*, harm reduction attempts to prevent *abuse* (J. Cohen 1996). This paradigm recognizes that people will always use psychoactive substances whether they are legal or illegal and attempts to minimize the hazards of use as a more realistic goal (Duncan et al. 1994). Supporters of this approach are critical of school and media drug education programs that present information that is intended to demonstrate the adverse consequences of drug use because of the tendency to exaggerate the dangers and to perpetuate certain convenient stereotypes. In addition, the "just say no" approach assumes, against evidence to the contrary, that a child's decision not to use drugs becomes much easier once he or she is acquainted with the consequences. In fact, evaluations have shown that information has little or no impact on whether young people use drugs. Indeed, some studies suggest that excessive use of primary prevention might actually encourage drug use by creating a sense of mystique around the subject, which appeals to children's natural curiosity.

Primary prevention approaches stress drug use as abnormal and views drug users as deficient in knowledge, self-esteem, or skills. Yet, as was noted earlier, some studies show that individuals with high self-esteem actually are more likely to experiment with drugs. Moreover, research indicates that experimentation is an extremely poor predictor of long-term use or abuse. Primary

---

[3] Unless otherwise noted, this section is based on Riley (n.d.).

prevention approaches also ignore the pleasure and other benefits of drug use and fail to acknowledge that decisions to try drugs are often expressions of independence. "Deviancy amplification" divides users and nonusers and works against meaningful dialogue with adults. The harm reduction approach to education instead focuses on nonjudgmental information about different drugs, their properties and effects, the law and legal rights, how to reduce risks, and where to get help if needed. It helps youths to develop a wide range of skills in assessment, judgment, communication, assertiveness, conflict resolution, decision making, and safer use. Teaching begins in early years about familiar substances other than drugs and emphasizes that most of the things we consume have the potential for both harm and benefit depending on the way we use them.

Norman Zinberg (1984: 207), a psychiatrist and well-known researcher on drug use, recommends educational programs that parallel the approach that is often used to deal with adolescent sexual behavior: "although our society does not condone teenage sexual activity, it has decided that those who are unwilling to follow its precepts should be given the basic information needed to avoid disease and unwanted pregnancy." Accordingly, drug education "should provide information on how to avoid the effects of destructive drug combinations (for example, barbiturates and alcohol), the unpleasant consequences of using drugs of unknown purity, the hazards of using drugs with a high dependence liability, the dangers of certain modes of administration, and the unexpected effects of various dose levels and various settings" (Zinberg 1984: 207).

The harm reduction approach contrasts markedly with U.S. policy toward another potentially addictive behavior: gambling. The United States went from outlawing most forms of gambling to aggressively promoting the behavior in search of tax revenue. Some critics might even be tempted to use the term *hypocrisy*.

CONCLUSION

Suggesting a comprehensive policy that is acceptable to mainstream America does not take a great deal of imagination, but it would take a great deal of money. The level of funding that would be required to institute most of these recommendations makes them unrealistic in the present United States. We already spend about $4 billion a year on controlling illegal drugs, more than half of that going for drug law enforcement.

Reducing the consumption of drugs by increasing law enforcement and large-scale treatment programs does not solve such significant sociological problems as lack of educational and employment opportunity and residential instability. We know that drug abuse is not randomly dispersed over the population but is concentrated in areas of poverty. Insofar as drug abuse is the result of despair, frustration, hopelessness, and alienation, programs directed only at the symptom—drug abuse—cannot succeed. Elliott Currie (1993) points out that drug abuse is not an isolated problem within stricken inner-city

A Comprehensive Program for Responding to Drug Abuse

1. Institute educational programs at the elementary, high school, and college levels that fully present all aspects of the use of psychoactive chemicals, including moderation and controlled use. Unfortunately, to date there has been little evidence to indicate that educational efforts actually reduce the use of drugs, although they might encourage a more rational or controlled use.

2. Decriminalize marijuana for personal use to conserve valuable resources and to avoid stigmatizing persons unnecessarily. Breaking the connection between marijuana and hard drugs might also help to keep young people away from hard drugs. Furthermore, notes Richard Cowan (1986), effective law enforcement against marijuana drives up the price and might move users toward more readily available crack cocaine.

3. Reduce the supply of drugs by enhancing domestic law enforcement; that is, significantly increase personnel and equipment for the Coast Guard, Customs, and Drug Enforcement Administration (the Federal Bureau of Investigation should not have drug law enforcement responsibilities, because this merely increases interagency conflict and detracts from that agency's major law enforcement role, which includes combating espionage and terrorism).

4. Reduce the supply of drugs at source countries; that is, provide more technical support and equipment and greater financing for crop substitution and eradication programs.

5. Reduce the consumer market by expanding local law enforcement efforts and place all convicted drug abusers on intensive probation supervision or incarceration followed by intensive parole supervision. This would require a significant increase in local law enforcement personnel assigned to drug law enforcement, an expansion of correctional facilities (which are already overtaxed), and a significant increase in probation and parole personnel.

6. Drastically expand the availability of treatment programs, enabling every substance abuser—including those addicted to nicotine and alcohol—to have access to treatment. Continue research efforts into the causes of substance abuse and the effectiveness of various approaches to treatment.

7. Provide educational and vocational programs for drug abusers who have enrolled in treatment programs. In addition to the problem of financing such efforts, there is the problem of equity: Should only drug abusers be entitled to receive educational and vocational services, or should these be made available to all disadvantaged individuals?

8. Enact and enforce legislation prohibiting employment discrimination against former substance abusers.

This comprehensive program would require a significant expenditure of tax dollars. A *Newsweek* poll (September 18, 1989) revealed that while Americans were in favor of increasing penalties and additional funding for treatment and law enforcement, 63 percent opposed an increase in personal income taxes to support these goals.

How the Swedes Do It

The rate of people who are dependent on psychoactive substances in the United States is between 20 and 40 percent higher than that in Sweden. This translates into significantly more expenditures for law enforcement and imprisonment.

Although Swedish drug policy, like that of the United States, has been consistently repressive, not only on trafficking but also on the use of drugs, prevention of drug abuse is part of a wider social policy that strives to reduce relative deprivation. Active government job programming to keep down unemployment and a high progressive taxation system provides for poverty-reducing programs, readily available high-quality health care, and affordable and comfortable housing for the most disadvantaged socioeconomic and ethnic groups (Segre 2003; von Solinge 2004).

communities but part of a syndrome that includes family disintegration, child abuse and neglect, delinquency, and alcohol abuse. Successful treatment of individual drug abusers would not stem the tide of new entries generated by unchanged social conditions that serve as a fertile breeding ground. "Even the best, most comprehensive programs to help addicts transform their lives will inevitably be compromised if we do not simultaneously address the powerful social forces that are destroying the communities to which they must return" (Currie 1993: 279).

No author enjoys ending a book on a note of pessimism. Defeatism is anathema to the American culture. We like to believe that Yankee ingenuity can overcome any problem, just as we have overcome the Nazis, the Communists, and a host of diseases. But reality indicates that some problems, particularly social ones like crime and poverty, can be intractable. The United States has the widest gap between rich and poor in the industrialized world, and that gap is growing (Bradsher 1995b, 1995c; Segre 2003). David Bellis (1981: xiv) states that "resolving issues like poverty, crime and addiction, especially in isolation from one another, and unmediated by economic, social and political factors may be impossible."

That our current strategies in response to drug abuse have failed is obvious. Despite the posturing and dramatic pronouncements of several administrations, we have been unable to stem the flow of heroin and cocaine into the United States and are unlikely to do so in the future. Our success against foreign marijuana has led to improvements in domestic cultivation, so pot connoisseurs now prefer the homegrown crop. There is every reason to believe that if efforts to eradicate coca and poppy cultivation in source countries and/or to improve antismuggling techniques ever succeeded, it would simply spur the domestic production of cocaine and heroin substitutes. Furthermore, as was indicated in Chapters 9 and 10, there is no evidence that widespread educational efforts have significantly reduced the number of persons using drugs, or ever will, or that treatment programs will be any more successful. There also remains the problem of widespread deprivation: "We are far from suggesting that all types

Medicating a Social Problem

"A person who is ill-educated, whose skills are not in demand, who does not feel admired or respected by society, who has no clear path to social success or financial security, is likely to feel self-doubt and frustration in large measure. Such feelings can be relieved by heroin" (de Marneffe 2003: 34).

and levels of drug use are at all times and in all circumstances deprivation-related. What we do, however, feel confident in asserting is that deprivation relates statistically to types and intensities of drug use which are problematic" (Advisory Council on the Misuse of Drugs 1998: 111).

Our current policy of "shared simplifications" (Gerstein and Harwood 1990) appears to reflect the popular will: allowing the majority of society to be against drug abuse while remaining free to abuse alcohol and tobacco. In other words, laws and law enforcement efforts against substances that are desired by a substantial minority of our citizenry provide symbolic opposition for the majority without actually impairing their own freedom to enjoy dangerous substances and activities—a policy that most Americans would be pleased to "drink to."

SUMMARY

Most of the harmful aspects of heroin use are the result of its being illegal. We permit a wide assortment of dangerous behaviors such as cigarette smoking, drinking alcohol, skydiving, and football, acknowledging freedom to enjoy activities that may be injurious to health. Why do we single out psychoactive chemicals—but only some of them?

Decriminalization would allow drug criminal justice resources to be used elsewhere, curtail secondary criminality, weaken or destroy drug-trafficking organizations, and allow drug users to lead healthier and more normal lives by using pharmaceutical-quality substances.

Greater availability would mean that more people would be tempted to use drugs and would signal a societal acceptance of drug use. There would be no incentive for addicts to enter drug treatment, and drug use might continue beyond the typical age of remission.

Offering intelligent policy alternatives requires understanding the cause(s) of drug use: biological, psychological, sociological, or a combination. Although medical maintenance using opiates or methadone has been suggested for heroin addicts, cocaine is more problematic.

A number of countries have decriminalized marijuana, but even its medical use is a federal crime in the United States.

In Western Europe harm reduction policies, official and unofficial, have become popular, most notably in the Netherlands. Dutch drug abuse prevention efforts treat alcohol and tobacco, as well as heroin and cocaine, as dangerous drugs; legal versus illegal is not considered a sound basis for differentiation. Despite U.S. objections, Canada has been experimenting with harm reduction.

REVIEW QUESTIONS

1. What are the arguments for decriminalizing drugs in the United States?
2. What are the possible drawbacks of decriminalizing drugs in the United States?

3. If drug use is related to a physiological condition—an endorphin deficiency, for example—what policy implications are suggested?
4. What is the harm reduction approach to drug abuse?
5. Why is it easier to institute a harm reduction approach in England than in the United States?
6. What is the Merseyside model?
7. What are the advantages of a needle-exchange program?
8. How does Dutch drug policy differ from that of the United States?

Glossary

absorption Process by which elements from the outside move inside the body

abstinence Non-use of psychoactive substances

acetaldehyde A byproduct of the metabolism of alcohol

acetylcholine Neurotransmitter found in the brain where it regulates memory and in the peripheral nervous system where it regulates skeletal and smooth muscle

acute Intense and/or rapid onset

additive Two drugs that have similar actions are ingested, and the effect is cumulative $(1 + 1 = 2)$

adenosine Neurotransmitter regulating sleep for which caffeine is an antagonist

addiction A preoccupation with the use of psychoactive substances characterized by neurochemical and molecular changes in the brain

adrenaline Epinephrine; hormone secreted by the adrenal gland that arouses the sympathetic nervous system

affective processes Govern mood, feelings, and emotions

aftercare Treatment that follows discharge from a residential treatment program

agonist A substance that stimulates receptor sites

Al-Anon Mutual self-help organization for the families of alcoholics affiliated with Alcoholic Anonymous

alcohol Complex psychoactive substance that has both stimulating and depressing characteristics

Alcoholics Anonymous (AA) Original twelve-step mutual self-help organization

Amanita muscaria Hallucinogenic mushroom; fly agaric

amino acid transmitters The most prevalent neurotransmitters in the brain, these include glutamate and aspartate, which have excitatory actions, and glycine and gamma-amino butyric acid (GABA) which have inhibitory actions

amphetamine Artificially produced central nervous system stimulant

amygdala Part of forebrain that plays a role in emotional learning

amyl nitrate Volatile inhalant muscle relaxant

analgesic Substance that has the ability to reduce feelings of pain without loss of consciousness

analog Chemical compound that is similar to another drug in its effects but differs slightly in its chemical structure

anandamide Neurotransmitter that binds to cannabinoid receptors

423

angel dust Phencyclidine (PCP), an stimulant and hallucinogen

anhedonia Inability to feel pleasure

anomie A condition characterized by estrangement from society, the result of being unable to achieve financial success through legitimate avenues

Antabuse A drug that produces unpleasant reactions when used with alcohol

antagonist A drug that counters or blocks the effects of another drug

antagonistic Two or more drugs are taken together, and one counteracts the effects of the other(s) $(1 + 1 = 0)$

antidepressant Psychoactive drug prescribed for depressive disorders

arousal theory The theory that those whose central nervous system quickly habituates to incoming stimuli owing to a neurotransmitter malfunction are most apt to be reinforced for engaging in antisocial behavior and less likely to learn alternative behavior patterns

autonomic nervous system Part of the peripheral nervous system responsible for regulating the activity of involuntary bodily functions such as that of the heart and lungs. It includes the sympathetic and parasympathetic nervous systems

axon The fiberlike extension of a neuron by which the cell sends information to target cells

bad trip Slang for negative effects of hallucinogen ingestion

barbiturates CNS depressants

behavior modification Treatment approach based on learning theory

behavior processes These include voluntary movements such as walking and talking, and the

autonomic bodily functions (such as those of the heart, lungs, and digestive system) are involuntary functions that are regulated by the **autonomic nervous system**

benzodiazepines Drugs that relieve anxiety or are prescribed as sedatives; among the most widely prescribed medications, including valium and librium

bind The attaching of a neurotransmitter to a receptor

blood alcohol level (BAL) Amount of alcohol in the blood: .08 or .10 is legal standard by intoxication as measured by a breathalyzer test

blood-brain barrier System that filters blood for toxins before it can enter the brain

brain stem The major route by which the forebrain sends information to and receives information from the spinal cord and peripheral nerves. It controls, among other things, respiration and regulation of heart rhythms

buprenorphine Drug that blocks the action of opiates by occupying their receptor sites

caffeine Mild stimulant found in coffee and also used in some beverages

cannabinoid receptor Binding site for active ingredients in cannabis

cannabis Marijuana

catecholamines The neurotransmitters dopamine, epinephrine and norepinephrine active in the brain and sympathetic nervous system

cell body (soma) Central structure of a neuron

central nervous system (CNS) Brain and the spinal vertebrae which carry information to the brain; CNS

cerebral cortex The outermost layer of the cerebral hemispheres of the brain. It is responsible for all forms of conscious experience, including perception, emotion, thought, and planning

chasing the dragon Slang for smoking heroin

China White Southeast Asian heroin of high purity

chipper Occasional user of heroin

chronic Condition that persists over time

cirrhosis Scarring of the liver, the result of alcohol abuse

classical conditioning Learning in which a primary stimulus that naturally produces a specific response is repeatedly paired with a neutral stimulus. With repeated pairing, the neutral stimulus becomes a conditioned stimulus that can evoke a response similar to that of the primary stimulus

Clonidine An antihypertension drug used to relieve many of the symptoms of opioid withdrawal, particularly those involving autonomic nervous system hyperactivity

club drug A term used to characterize psychoactive substances associated with dance parties or *raves*, in particular MDMA, known as ecstasy

CNS See *central nervous system*

cocaine Powerful stimulant derived from the coca plant

coca paste Product of the first step in extracting cocaine from coca leaves

cognition Process by which organism gains knowledge and uses that knowledge for comprehension and problem-solving

cold turkey slang term for giving up drug use without use of chemicals

contingency contracting Treatment using a mutually agreed upon contract providing privileges for compliance and negative contingencies for violations

crack Smokable form of cocaine

crank Methamphetamine

crash Slang for depression that occurs when high levels of stimulant ingestion are discontinued

craving Powerful and sometimes uncontrollable desire for psychoactive substances

cross-tolerance Tolerance to one substance that carries over to another

decriminalization Policy of not using criminal sanctions against drug users

delirium tremens (DTs) A severe symptom of alcohol withdrawal

demand reduction strategies that reduce consumption of drugs as opposed to those that reduce supply

dendrite A treelike extension of the neuron cell body. Along with the cell body, it receives information from other neurons

depressants Sedating drugs that depress the central nervous system

depression Mental disorder characterized by depressed mood and abnormalities in sleep, appetite, and energy level

designer drugs Analog of a restricted drug that has psychoactive properties

detoxification Process of allowing the body to rid itself of a drug while managing the symptoms of withdrawal

dependence Stage of physical adaptation characterized by

physical and/or psychological withdrawal symptoms when a substance is discontinued

Dextromethorphan (DMX) Active ingredient in many over-the-counter cough medicines that has hallucinogenic properties

diagnosis Classification of the nature and severity of a medical problem

dimethyltryptamine (DMT) A hallucinogenic substance that occurs naturally in many plants

disease model Explanation for drug use based on deficiencies or abnormalities in a person's physical or psychological make-up

dissociative anesthetics Anesthetics that distort perceptions of sight and sound and produce feelings of detachment

distillation Process used to extract alcohol from fermented grains or fruit

diversion Unauthorized distribution of a controlled substance from lawful sources

DMT Abbreviation for dimethyltryptamine

dopamine A stimulating (catecholamine) neurotransmitter present in regions of the brain that regulate movement, emotion, motivation, and feelings of pleasure; its absence results in Parkinson's disease

drug abuse Excessive use of psychoactive substances

ecstasy 3, 4-methylenedioxy-methamphetamine (MDMA); designer drug having hallucinogenic and amphetamine-like characteristics

ego Psyche's contact with reality that maximizes gratification with a minimum of difficulties

electroencephalogram (EEG) Graphic record of electrical brain activity

EMIT Commonly used drug test

emphysema Lung disease, often caused by smoking, in which tissue deterioration results in difficult breathing and shortness of breadth

employee assistance program (EAP) Help provided by employers to aid workers dealing with substance abuse

endogenous Produced by the body

endorphins Neurotransmitters produced in the brain that generate cellular and behavioral effects similar to morphine

ephedra Plant species with stimulant properties

ephedrine Stimulant used in treating allergies and cold symptoms

epinephrine A hormone, released by the adrenal medulla and the brain, that acts with norepinephrine to activate the sympathetic division of the autonomic nervous system; sometimes called adrenaline

enkephalins Neurotransmitter; endogenous opioid

fentanyl Potent opiate agonist

fermentation Process by which yeast interacts with plant sugars to produce alcohol

forebrain The largest part of the brain, which includes the cerebral cortex and basal ganglia. It is credited with the highest intellectual functions

formication Sensations caused by cocaine and amphetamine that insects are crawling under the skin

freebase Cocaine hydrochloride whose crystalline base is separated to enable smoking

GABA Gamma-aminobutyric acid; inhibitory neurotransmitter

gamma-amino butyric acid (GABA) An amino acid transmitter in the brain whose primary function is to inhibit the firing of neurons

gateway drug Substances that presage use of other psychoactive drugs; e.g., nicotine leading to marijuana leading to heroin

GBL (gamma-butyrolactone) a GHB precursor, colorless, odorless, virtually tasteless, and in very low doses CNS depressant; in higher doses can produce unconsciousness and even respiratory failure. GBL was widely available as a dietary supplement in "health food" stores until an FDA recall in 1999. GBL is used as an industrial solvent and tens of thousands of metric tons are produced each year

GHB Similar to Rohypnol, GHB (gamma-hydroxybutyrate) is colorless, odorless, virtually tasteless, and in very low doses a CNS depressant; in higher doses, can produce unconsciousness and even respiratory failure. Ingredients in GHB are found in a number of dietary supplements sold in health food stores. GHB has been used by sexual predators since in addition to rendering victims unconscious, they are often unable to recall what happened

glutamate amino acid Neurotransmitter that acts to excite neurons

half-life The time it takes for one-half of a drug to be eliminated from the body

halfway house Drug treatment residence

hallucinogens Natural or artificial chemicals that can produce distortions of reality

harm reduction Policy that seeks to reduce the harm of using drugs without requiring abstinence

hashish More potent form of marijuana

hepatitis C Liver disease spread through sexual intercourse and sharing of hypodermic needles

heroin Opiate produced from and more powerful than morphine

high Euphoria or feeling of well-being enjoyed by a substance user

hippocampus Section of the brain dealing with emotions, learning, and memory

homeostasis A state of equilibrium or balance achieved through the self-adjusting characteristics of the body

hypothalamus Brain structure that integrates information from a variety of sources and is the control center of the central nervous system

id Mass of powerful drives, wishes, urges that are energized in the form of the libido

inhalant Volatile psychoactive chemical produced for nondrug purposes

intravenous Ingestion of a drug into a vein

ions Electrically charged atoms or molecules

khat Stimulant leaves of an African plant

ketamine Surgical anesthetic related to phencyclidine (PCP)

kindling Recurring drug reaction that occurs without continued ingestion

Korsakoff's syndrome A disease associated with chronic alcoholism

characterized by memory loss and psychotic behavior

LAMM Levo-alpha-acetylmethadol; synthetic opiate

learning theory Concept that behavior is shaped by its consequences

levo-alpha-acetylmethadol Opiate agonist similar to methadone used to treat heroin addiction

LSD Lysergic acid diethylamide; an hallucinogen

lysergic acid diethylamide Hallucinogen that can be produced artificially or from ergot; LSD

magnetic resonance imaging (MRI) Imaging technique for pictures of the brain

marijuana Cannabis

Marinol Trade name for pharmaceutical delta-9 tetrahydrocannabinol (THC), the active ingredient in marijuana that is used in medicine

MDMA Ecstasy

medial forebrain bundle Brain pathway that produces pleasure when stimulated

mescaline Hallucinogen found in the peyote cactus

mesolimbic system Section of the brain that generates feelings, emotions, and motivations; also important for learning and memory

metabolism Process by which the body breaks down matter into more simple components and for elimination as waste

methadone Opiate agonist used to treat heroin addiction

methamphetamine Powerful CNS stimulant

monoamine oxidase (MAO) Chemicals in the presynaptic

terminals that control the level of neurotransmitters

MAO inhibitors Drugs used to treat depression by controlling the reuptake of serotonin

Minnesota model Private inpatient treatment using a twelve-step approach

morphine Opiate derivative used to relieve pain

naloxone Short-acting opiate antagonist

naltrexone Opiate agonist that is longer lasting than naloxone

narcotic CNS depressant derived from opiates

nativism Hostility toward foreigners

needle exchange Program that provides intravenous drug users with sterile needles

negative reinforcement Removal of a stimulus that increases the likelihood of a behavior

neuroadaption After repeated ingestion of a psychoactive drug, the CNS adjusts to its effects; tolerance

neuron Nerve cell for the transmission of information and characterized by long fibrous projections called axons, and shorter, branch-like projections called dendrites

neurotransmitter A chemical released by neurons at a synapse for the purpose of relaying information via receptors

nicotine Tobacco plant alkaloid responsible for smoking's psychoactive and addictive effects

nitrous oxide "Laughing gas" used as an anesthetic and abused for its intoxicating effects

norepinephrine A neurotransmitter produced in the brain and in

the peripheral nervous system that governs arousal and elevates mood

nucleus accumbens Located in the limbic system, provides feelings of pleasure when stimulated

operant conditioning Repeated presentation or removal of a stimulus (reinforcer) following a behavior to increase the probability of the behavior. If the probability of a behavior increases after removal, negative reinforcement has occurred

opiates Drugs derived from opium

opium Psychoactive sap of the poppy plant

overdose Ingestion of a psychoactive substance way above the level of tolerance; can be fatal

OxyContin Class II prescription opioid often diverted and abused

parasympathetic nervous system A branch of the autonomic nervous system concerned with the conservation of the body's energy and resources during relaxed states

Parkinson's disease Neurological disorder caused by a dopamine deficiency and characterized by muscular rigidity and difficulty starting movements, tremors, and loss of balance

passive smoke Product of tobacco or cannabis use—second-hand smoke—causing involuntary exposure

patent medicines Secret formulas that carried no patent and often contained coca or opiates

PCP phencyclidine, a dissociative drug

performance-enhancing drugs Chemicals used by athletes to improve physical abilities

peripheral nervous system A division of the nervous system consisting of all nerves not part of the brain or spinal cord

peyote Cactus plant whose "buttons" have hallucinogenic properties

phencyclidine (PCP) Anesthetic, dissociative drug

physical dependence Physiological states that results from a pattern of regular drug use as tolerance builds and results in withdrawal symptoms if the drug is discontinued

polydrug use Use of more than one psychoactive drug

poppy Flowering plant from which opium is derived

positive reinforcement A stimulus that increases the likelihood that a behavior will be repeated

positron emission tomography (PET scan) Brain imaging technique

potentiating Two drugs have different actions but when taken together each enhances the effect of the other

precursor Chemical that is critical to the manufacturing process and becomes part of the final drug

Prohibition Period between 1920 and 1933 when alcohol as a beverage was outlawed

psilocybin Hallucinogen found in certain mushrooms

psychedelic Hallucinogen

psychoactive Referring to a substance that affects the central nervous system

psychoanalytic theory Belief that unconscious material controls conscious behavior

psychosis Severe symptom of mental illness characterized by being out of contact with reality

psychotherapy Talk-based treatment

rave Late-night dance party at which club drugs are often used

receptor sites Sites consisting of molecules on the surface or inside cells where neurotransmitters attach and exert their effects

reinforcement Consequence of a behavior that increases the likelihood that it will reoccur

relapse Reversion to drug use after abstinence and/or treatment

remission Absence of symptoms even though the underlying condition has not been cured

reuptake A process by which released neurotransmitters are absorbed for subsequent reuse

reverse tolerance Increase in the reaction to a drug that develops after chronic use; sensitization

Ritalin (methylphenidate) Stimulant used for treating attention deficit hyperactivity disorder

reward Process that reinforces behavior

Rohypnol A benzodiazepine (sedative) widely prescribed in Europe but not approved for use in the United States. Known to abusers as "roofies" or "rope," it is often ingested with alcohol or marijuana

rush How drug users describe a surge of pleasure that follows the intake of a psychoactive substance

sedative CNS depressant that can produce calm and induce sleep

selective tolerance Tolerance to one aspect of a drug's effect

self-medicating Nonmedical use of psychoactive substances in response to physiological and/or psychological difficulties

sensitization Increase in a drug's effect with repeated administration, the change being in the opposite direction of tolerance

serotonin A neurotransmitter that elevates mood; antidepressant drugs often stimulate the release of serotonin

social norms Explicit or implicit rules that guide social behavior in a given community

soma See *cell body*

speed Methamphetamine

spontaneous remission Discontinuing drug use without treatment intervention

stimulant Psychoactive chemical that activates the central nervous system and elevates mood

subcutaneous Ingesting a drug under the skin

substance abuse Harmful use of one or more psychoactive substances

superego Psychic mechanism exercising a critical influence; a sense of morality that controls behavior

symbolic interactionism Sociological perspective whose focus is on how particular people or behaviors are labeled

sympathetic nervous system A branch of the autonomic nervous system responsible for mobilizing the body's energy and resources during times of stress and arousal

synapse A gap between two neurons that functions as the site of information transfer from one neuron to another

synergistic Two drugs have similar actions but their combined effect is more than cumulative

tetrahydrocannabinol (THC) Active ingredient in marijuana

thalamus Structure deep within the brain serving as a filter and relay station for information

theory Building block for scientific knowledge that organizes events, explains past events, and predicts future events

therapeutic community Residential drug treatment program based on Alcoholics Anonymous emphasizing addicts helping one another to become socially conforming persons

thought processes Involve the ability to reason, categorize, organize, abstract, and pay attention

tobacco Dried plant leaves containing nicotine

tolerance Progressive ability of the body to adopt to the effects of a drug used at regular and frequent intervals, making the drug less effective; higher doses of a drug are required to produce the same effect

toluene Ingredient in solvents that causes intoxication when inhaled; methyl benzene

tranquilizer Prescribed drugs having a sedating effect

transporter Neuron chemical that carries a neurotransmitter back to its presynaptic terminal

tricyclic antidepressants Used to treat depression by manipulating the level of several neurotransmitters

twelve steps Principles on which Alcoholics Anonymous and similar programs are based

unconscious According to psychoanalytic theory, repressed feelings and experiences that exert an influence over conscious behavior

ventral tegmental area (VTA) Neurons containing dopamine

volatile substance nondrug chemical inhaled for its psychoactive effects

Volstead Act Federal statute for enforcing the Eighteenth (Prohibition) Amendment

withdrawal Unpleasant symptoms that result when an addicted person fails to ingest a sufficient amount of addictive substance

References

Abadinsky, Howard
2007a   *Organized Crime,* 8th ed. Belmont, CA: Wadsworth.
2007b   *Law and Justice: An Introduction to the American Legal System,* 6th ed. Upper Saddle River, NJ: Prentice Hall.
2006   *Probation and Parole: Theory and Practice,* 9th ed. Upper Saddle River, NJ: Prentice Hall.
Abel, Ernest L., ed.
1978   *The Scientific Study of Marijuana.* Chicago: Nelson-Hall.
Abrahart, David
1998   "Concerning Lysergic Acid Diethylamide (LSD) and Mental Health." Master of Arts thesis, Department of Mental Health Studies, University of Portsmouth, England.
Acker, Caroline Jean
2002   *Creating the American Junkie: Addiction Research in the Classic Era of Narcotic Control.* Baltimore: Johns Hopkins University Press.
Adams, Jane Meredith
2002   "Medical Marijuana Users Sue U.S. Officials." *Chicago Tribune* (October 10): 12.
Addiction Research Unit
1998   *Dopamine.* Internet. Buffalo: State University of New York at Buffalo.
Adler, Jerry
2007   "Rehab Reality Check." *Newsweek* (February 19): 44–46.

2003   "In the Grip of a Deeper Pain." *Newsweek* (October 20): 48–49.
Adler, Patricia A.
1985   *Wheeling and Dealing: An Ethnography of an Upper-Level Drug-Dealing and Smuggling Community.* New York: Columbia University Press.
Adrade, Xavier, Stephen J. Sifaneck, and Alan Neaigus
1999   "Dope Sniffers in New York City: An Ethnography of Heroin Markets and Patterns of Use." *Journal of Drug Issues* 22 (2): 271–98.
Advisory Council on the Misuse of Drugs
1998   *Drug Misuse and the Environment.* London, England: Home Office.
1994   *Police, Drug Misusers and the Community.* London, England: Home Office.
1993   *Drug Education in Schools: The Need for New Impetus.* London, England: Home Office.
"A Fishy Haul"
2004   *New York Daily News* (September 28): 5.
Agar, Michael
1973   *Ripping and Running: A Formal Ethnography of Urban Heroin Addicts.* New York: Seminar Press.
Ahmed-Ullah, Noreen S.
2001   "Pashtun Identity Defies Colonial Line." *Chicago Tribune* (November 6): 15.
Aicchorn, August
1963   *Wayward Youth.* New York: Viking.

Alexander, Bruce K.
1990   "Alternatives to the War on Drugs." *Journal of Drug Issues* 20 (1): 1–27.

Alford, Geary S.
1980   "Alcoholics Anonymous: An Empirical Outcome Study." *Addictive Behaviors* 5: 359–70.

Alford, Geary S., Roger A. Koehler, and James Leonard
1991   "Alcoholics Anonymous-Narcotics Anonymous Model Inpatient Treatment of Chemically Dependent Adolescents: A 2-Year Outcome Study." *Journal of Studies on Alcohol* 52 (March): 118–26.

Allen, Frederick
1998   "American Spirit." *American Heritage* (May/June): 82–92.

Altman, Lawrence K.
2005   "Cocaine Users Face Greater Risk of Aneurysm." *New York Times* (May 10): F6.

Alvarez, A.
2001   "Drugs and Inspiration." *Social Research* 68 (Fall): 779–95.

American Heart Association
1999   "More Bad News for Cocaine Users: Drug Can Triple Risk of Aneurysm." (November 9): Internet.

American Heritage Dictionary
2000   Boston: Houghton Mifflin.

American Psychiatric Association (APA)
1995   *Psychiatric Services for Addicted Patients.* Washington, DC: APA.

1994   *Diagnostic and Statistical Manual of Mental Disorders,* 4th ed. (DSM-IV). Washington DC: APA.

American Social Health Association
1972   *Guidelines: A Comprehensive Community Program to Reduce Drug Abuse.* Overview I. NY: Amcrican Social Health Association.

Anderson, Austin A.
1992   "Transnational Crimes: A Global Approach." *FBI Law Enforcement Bulletin* (March): 26–32.

Andrews, Edmund L.
1990   "2 Treatments for Cocaine Addiction." *New York Times* (July 21): 18.

Angier, Natalie
1995   "Variant Gene Tied to a Love of New Thrills." *New York Times* (January 2): 1, B9.

1991   "Moderate Drinking Cuts Risk of Heart Disease, Study Says." *New York Times* (August 24): 10.

Anglin, M. Douglas
1988   "The Efficacy of Civil Commitment in Treating Narcotic Addiction." Pages 8–34 in *Compulsory Treatment of Drug Abuse: Research and Clinical Practice.* Rockville, MD: National Institute on Drug Abuse.

Anglin, M. Douglas and George Speckart
1988   "Narcotics Use and Crime: A Multisample, Multimethod Analysis." *Criminology* 26 (May): 197–233.

Anglin, M. Douglas and Thomas H. Maughr II
1992   "Ensuring Success in Interventions with Drug-Using Offenders." *Annals* 521 (May): 66–90.

Anglin, M. Douglas and William McGlothlin
1985   "Methadone Maintenance in California: A Decade's Experience." Pages 219–80 in *The Year Book of Substance Use and Abuse,* edited by Leon Brill and Charles Winick. New York: Human Services Press.

Anglin, M. Douglas and Yih-lng Hser
1990a   "Legal Coercion and Drug Abuse Treatment: Research Findings and Social Policy Implications." Pages 151–76 in *Handbook of Drug Control in the United States,* edited by James A. Inciardi. Westport, CT: Greenwood.

1990b   "Treatment of Drug Abuse." Pages 393–460 in *Drugs and Crime,* edited by Michael Tonry and James Q. Wilson. Chicago: University of Chicago Press.

Anglin, M. Douglas, Douglas Longshore, and Susan Turner
1999   "Treatment Alternative to Street Crime: An Evaluation of Five Programs." *Criminal Justice and Behavior* 26 (June): 168–95.

Aniskiewicz, Rick and Earl Wysong
1990   "Evaluating DARE Drug Education and the Multiple Meanings of Success." *Policy Studies Review* 9 (Summer): 727–47.

Anonymous
2006   "To Quit Heroin Cold Turkey." *Esquire* (August): 126.

Anslinger, Harry J. and William F. Tompkins
1953   *The Traffic in Narcotics.* New York: Funk and Wagnalls.

Anthony, James C. and Valerie Forman
2000   "At the Intersection of Public Health and Criminal Justice Research on Drugs and Crime." Draft of a paper for the Drugs and Crime Research Forum.

"Anti-Drug Efforts Encounter Resistance in Colombia"
1995   *New York Times* (December 12): 4.

Arax, Mark and Tom Gorman
1995   "The State's Illicit Farm Belt Export." *Los Angeles Times* (March 13): 1, 16, 17.

Asbury, Herbert
1950   *The Great Illusion: An Informal History of Prohibition.* Garden City, NY: Knopf.

Ashley, Richard
1975   *Cocaine: Its History, Use and Effects.* New York: St. Martin's Press.

Associated Press
2007   "Feds Seize Candy Bars Filled with 5M in Heroin." *New York Daily News* (February 24): 10.

2006   "A Deadly Heroin Mix is Claiming Dozens of Lives." *New York Times* (May 28): 27.

2005   "Pregnancy Warning on Antidepressants." *New York Times* (May 18): 21.

2004a   "Smoking and Drug Use by Teenagers Drops Again." *New York Times* (December 22): B8.

2004b   "Two Drinks Can Kill Brain Cells in a Fetus, Studies Suggest." *New York Times* (February 15): 21.

2002   "Doctor I Sentenced for OxyContin Deaths." *New York Times* (March 23): 11.

2001   "Jury Awards Flight Attendant $400,000 in Drug Test Case." *New Jersey Online* (July 6): Internet.

2000a   "Ex-Mexico Drug Czar Gets More Jail" (February 22): Internet.

2000b   "Economic Protests Disrupt Bolivia." *Chicago Tribune* (April 10): 11.

1999a   "Alcohol-Linked Road Death at Low." Internet.

1999b   "China Executes at Least 71 in a Day." Internet.

1999c   "Cocaine Seized in Fish Shipment." Internet.

1999d   "Study Links Cigars to High Risk of Cancer." *New York Times* (June 10): 24.

1998   "Alcohol, Violence Link Still Strong, U.S. Says." *Chicago Tribune* (April 6): 5.

1997a   "High Nicotine Levels Found in Smoking Moms' Babies." *Chicago Tribune* (March 20): 13.

1997b   "Swiss Back Heroin Project." *New York Times* (September 29): 1.

1995   "5,600 Infant Deaths Tied to Mothers' Smoking." *New York Times* (April 13): 11.

Ausubel, David P.

1980   "An Interactional Approach to Narcotic Addiction." Pages 4–7 in *Theories on Drug Abuse: Selected Contemporary Perspectives,* edited by Dan J. Lettieri, Mollie Sayers, and Helen Wallenstein Pearson. Rockville, MD: National Institute on Drug Abuse.

1978   *What Every Well-Informed Person Should Know About Drug Addiction.* Chicago: Nelson-Hall.

Avants, S. Kelly, Arthur Margolin, Thomas R. Kosten, and Ned L. Cooney

1995   "Differences Between Responders and Nonresponders to Cocaine Cues in the Laboratory." *Addictive Behaviors* 20 (March/April): 214–24.

Bach, Peter B. and John Lantos

1999   "Methadone Dosing, Heroin Affordability, and the Severity of Addiction." *American Journal of Public Health* 5 (May): 662–65.

Baer, John S.

2002   "Student Factors: Understanding Individual Variation in College Drinking." *Journal of Studies on Alcohol* 14 (March): 40–53.

Bailey, Pearce

1974   "The Heroin Habit." Pages 171–76 in *Yesterday's Addicts; American Society and Drug Abuse, 1865–1920,* edited by Howard Wayne Morgan. Norman: University of Oklahoma Press.

Bakalar, Nicholas

2006   "Review Sees No Advantage in 12-Step Programs." *New York Times* (July 25): F6.

2005   "When the Smoke Doesn't Clear." *New York Times* (March 22): F7.

Baker, Al

2002   "Boy, 12, Flies Into U.S. After Swallowing Heroin in Condoms." *New York Times* (April 12): 24.

Ball, John C., Lawrence Rosen, Ellen G. Friedman, and David N. Nurco

1979   "The Impact of Heroin Addiction upon Criminality." Pages 163–69 in *Problems of Drug Dependence 1979,* edited by Louis S. Harris. Rockville, MD: National Institute on Drug Abuse.

Balster, Robert L.

1988   "Pharmacological Effects of Cocaine Relevant to Its Abuse." Pages 1–13 in *Mechanisms of Cocaine Abuse and Toxicity,* edited by Doris Clouet, Khursheed Asghar, and Roger Brown. Rockville, MD: National Institute on Drug Abuse.

Balter, Mitchell B.

1974   "Drug Abuse: A Conceptual Analysis and Overview of the Current Situation." Pages 3–21 in *Drug Use: Epidemiological and Sociological Approaches,* edited by Eric Josephson and Eleanor E. Carroll. New York: Wiley.

Bandura, Albert

1974   "Behavior Theory and the Models of Man." *American Psychologist* 29 (December): 860–66.

1969   *Principles of Behavior Modification.* New York: Holt, Rinehart and Winston.

Barnard, Herbert P.

1998   *The Netherlands' Drug Policy: 20 Years of Experience.* Internet. Washington, DC: Royal Netherlands Embassy.

Barnett, Arnold

1988   "Drug Crackdowns and Crime Rates: A Comment on the Kleiman Paper." Pages 35–42 in *Street-Level Drug Enforcement: Examining the Issues,* edited by Marcia R. Chaiken. Washington, DC: U.S. Government Printing Office.

Barnett, Randy E.

1987   "Curing the Drug-Law Addiction: The Harmful Side Effects of Legal Prohibition." Pages 73–102 in *Dealing with Drugs: Consequences of Government Control,* edited by Ronald Hamowy. Lexington, MA: D.C. Heath.

Bartosiewicz, Petra

2004   "A Quitter's Dilemma: Hooked on the Cure." *New York Times* (May 2): BU8.

Batki, Steven L., Janice F. Kauffman, Ira Marion, Mark W. Parrino, and George E. Woody

2005   *Medication-Assisted Treatment for Opioid Addiction in Opioid Treatment Programs.* Rockville, MD: U.S. Substance Abuse and Mental Health Services Administration.

Baumeister, S.E. and P. Tossmann

2005   "Association Between Early Onset of Cigarette, Alcohol and Cannabis Use and Later Drug Use Patterns: An Analysis of a Survey in European Metropolises." *European Addiction Research* 11: 92–99.

Baumgartner, Werner A., Virginia Hill, and William H. Blahd

1989   "Hair Analysis for Drugs of Abuse." *Journal of Forensic Sciences* 34 (November): 1433–53.

Baumrind, Diana

1987   "Familial Antecedents of Adolescent Drug Use: A Developmental Perspective." Pages 13–44 in *Etiology of Drug Abuse: Implications for*

Prevention, edited by Coryl LaRue Jones and Robert J. Battjes. Rockville, MD: National Institute on Drug Abuse.

Beck, Jerome and Marsha Rosenbaum
1994   *Pursuit of Ecstasy: The MDMA Experience.* Albany, NY: State University of New York Press.

Becker, Howard S.
1977   "Knowledge, Power, and Drug Effects." Pages 167–90 in *Drugs and Politics,* edited by Paul E. Rock. New Brunswick, NJ: Transaction Books.
1967   "History, Culture, and Subjective Experience: An Exploration of the Social Bases of Drug-Induced Experiences." *Journal of Health and Social Behavior* 8: 163–76.
1966   *Outsiders: Studies in the Sociology of Deviance.* New York: Free Press.

Beeching, Jack
1975   *The Chinese Opium Wars.* New York: Harcourt Brace Jovanovich.

Beers, Rand and Francis X. Taylor
2002   "The Worldwide Connection Between Drugs and Terror." Testimony Before Senate Committee on the Judiciary Subcommittee on Technology, Terrorism and Government Information (March 13): Internet.

Begley, Sharon
1999   "Hope for Snow Babies." *Pressweek* (September 29): 62–63.

Belenko, Steven
1993   *Crack and the Evolution of Anti-Drug Policy.* Westport, CT: Greenwood.

Belenko, Steven and Ko-lin Chin
1989   "Typologies of Criminal Careers Among Crack Arrestees." Paper presented at the annual meeting of the American Society of Criminology, Reno, NV, November.

Belkin, Lisa
1990   "Airport Anti-Drug Nets Snare Many People Fitting 'Profiles.'" *New York Times* (March 20): 1, 11.

Bellis, David J.
1981   *Heroin and Politicians: The Failure of Public Policy to Control Addiction in America.* Westport, CT: Greenwood.

Bendavid, Naftali
2002   "Critics Decry Ads Linking Drugs, Terror." *Chicago Tribune* (March 24): 1, 17.

Benedict, William Reed, Lin Huff-Corzine, and Jay Corzine
1998   "'Clean Up and Go Straight': Effects of Drug Treatment on Recidivism Among Felony Probationers." *American Journal of Criminal Justice* 22 (2): 169–87.

Bennett, David H.
1988   *The Party of Fear: From Nativist Movements to the New Right in American History.* Chapel Hill: University of North Carolina Press.

Bennett, William Ira
1988   "Patterns of Addiction." *New York Times Magazine* (April 10): 60–61.

Berger, Joseph
1989   "Judgment Replaces Fear in Drug Lessons." *New York Times* (October 30): 1, 8.

Berke, Richard L.
1990   "Bennett Doubts Value of Drug Education." *New York Times* (February 3): 1, 9.
1989   "Corruption in Drug Agency Called a Crippler of Inquiries and Morale." *New York Times* (December 17): 1, 22.

Berkow, Robert, ed.
1982   *The Merck Manual of Diagnosis and Therapy.* Rahway, NJ: Merck Sharp and Dohme.

Biernacki, Patrick
1986   *Pathways from Heroin Addiction: Recovery Without Treatment.* Philadelphia: Temple University Press.

Binder, Arnold and Gilbert Geis
1983   *Methods of Research in Criminology and Criminal Justice.* New York: McGraw-Hill.

Bishop, Katherine
1991   "Business Data Is Sought in Marijuana Crackdown." *New York Times* (May 24): B9.
1987   "Ex-Employee Wins Drug Testing Case." *New York Times* (October 31): 18.

Blackmore, John
1979   "Diagnosis: Heroin Addiction. Prescription: Methadone." *Corrections Magazine* 5 (December): 24–31.

Blakeslee, Sandra
2007   "A Small Part of the Brain and Its Profound Effects." *New York Times* (February 6): F6.
1998   "Two Studies Shed New Light on Cocaine's Effect on Brain." *New York Times* (May 14): 18.
1997   "Studies of Brain Find Marijuana Can Have the Same Effect as Other Drugs." *New York Times* (June 27): 13.
1994   "Yes, People Are Right. Caffeine Is Addictive." *New York Times* (October 5): B9.
1991   "Finding the Secrets of Caffeine, the Drug." *New York Times* (August 7): B6.
1989   "Crack's Toll Among Babies: A Joyless View of Even Toys." *New York Times* (September 18): 1, 12.
1988   "8-Year Study Finds 2 Sides to Teen-Age Drug Use." *New York Times* (July 21): 1, 13.

Bloom, Floyd E.
1993   "Brain Research for Today and Tomorrow: Recent Advances and Research Frontiers." Pages 9–26 in *International Research Conference on Biomedical Approaches to Illicit Drug Demand Reduction,* edited by Christine R. Hartel. Washington, DC: U.S. Government Printing Office.

Bloomberg News
2006   "Pot-Cancer Link up in Smoke—Study." *New York Daily News* (May 24): 10.

Bluhm, Judy
1987   *When You Face the Chemically Dependent Patient: A Practical Guide for Nurses.* St. Louis, MO: Ishiyaku EuroAmerica.

Blum, Kenneth, Ernest P. Noble, Peter J. Sheridan, Anne Montgomery, Terry Ritchie, Puduer Jagadeeswaran, Harou Nogami, Arthur H. Briggs, and Jay B. Cohn
1990   "Allec Association of Human Dopamine D2 Receptor Gene in Alcoholism." *Journal of the American Medical Association* 263 (April 8): 2055–60.

Blum, Richard H. and Associates
1969   *Society and Drugs.* San Francisco: Jossey-Bass.

Boaz, David, ed.
1990   *The Crisis in Drug Prohibition.* Washington, DC: Cato Institute.

Bolla, Karen I., Jean-Lud Cadet, and Edythe D. London
1998   "The Neuropsychiatry of Chronic Cocaine Abuse." *Journal of Neuropsychiatry* 1 (Summer): 280–89.

Bollag, Burton
1989   "Swiss-Dutch Drug Stance: Tolerance." *New York Times* (December 1): 4.

Böllinger, Lorenz
2004   "Drug Law and Policy in Germany and the European Community: Recent Developments." *Journal of Drug Issues* 34 (Summer): 419–420.

Bonnie, Richard J. and Charles H. Whitebread II
1970   "The Forbidden Fruit and the Tree of Knowledge: An Inquiry into the Legal History of American Marijuana Prohibition." *Virginia Law Review* 56 (October): 971–1203.

Bonson, Katherine R., Steven J. Grant, Carlo S. Contoreggi, Jonathan M. Links, Janet Metcalfe, Lloyd Weyl, Varughese Kurian, Monique Ernst, and Edythe D. London
2002   "Neural Systems and Cue-Induced Cocaine Craving." *Neuropsychopharmacology* 26 (3): 376–86.

Bourgois, Philippe
1995   *In Search of Respect: Selling Crack in El Barrio.* Cambridge, England: Cambridge University Press.

Bouza, Anthony
1990   *The Police Mystique: An Insider's Look at Cops, Crime, and the Criminal Justice System.* New York: Plenum.

Bowden, Charles
1991   "La Virgen and the Drug Lord." *Phoenix* (March): 96–103.

Bowman, Rex
2005   "Prescription for Crime." *Time* (March 28): 50–51.

Bozarth, Michael A.
1994   "Pleasure Systems in the Brain." Pages 5–16 in *Pleasure: The Politics and the Reality*, edited by D. M. Warburton. New York: John Wiley & Sons.

Bradsher, Keith
1995a   "Low Ranking for Poor American Children." *New York Times* (August 14): 7.
1995b   "Gap in Wealth in U.S. Called Widest in West." *New York Times* (April 17): 1, C4.
1995c   "Widest Gap in Incomes? Research Points to U.S." *New York Times* (October 27): C2.

Brecher, Edward M. and the Editors of Consumer Reports
1972   *Licit and Illicit Drugs.* Boston: Little, Brown.

Brems, Christiane, Mark E. Johnson, David Neal, and Melinda Freemon
2004   "Childhood Abuse History and Substance Use Among Men and Women Receiving Detoxification Services." *American Journal of Drug and Alcohol Abuse* 30 (November): 799–822.

Bresler, Fenton
1980   *The Chinese Mafia.* New York: Stein and Day.

Brevorka, Jennifer
2002   "Meth Lab Seizures on Rise in North Carolina." *Asheville Citizen-Times* (July 22): 1, 5.

Brewington, Vincent, Michael Smith, and Douglas Lipton
1994   "Acupuncture as a Detoxification Treatment: An Analysis of Controlled Research." *Journal of Substance Abuse Treatment* 11 (4): 289–307.

Brigham, Gregory S.
2003   "12-Step Participation as a Pathway to Recovery: The Maryhaven Experience and Implications for Treatment and Research." *Perspectives* 2 (August): 43–51.

Brinkley, Joel
2005   "Anti-Drug Gains in Colombia Don't Reduce Flow to U.S." *New York Times* (April 28): 3.

Brody, Jane E.
2003   "Addiction: A Brain Ailment, Not a Moral Lapse." *New York Times* (September 30): F8.
2001   "An Old Enemy, Smoking, Hangs Tough." *New York Times* (December 11): D7.
1997   "Many Smokers Who Can't Quite Are Mentally Ill, a Study Shows." *New York Times* (August 27): B10.
1995   "Tourette Syndrome Can't Be Cured, but Knowledge Often Reduces Suffering." *New York Times* (March 1): B8.
1988   "Personal Health." *New York Times* (April 21): 24.
1987   "Role of Heredity in Alcoholism." *New York Times* (August 14): 14.

Brooke, James
1995   "Colombia's Rebels Grow Rich from Banditry." *New York Times* (July 2): 1, 4.
1991   "Marxist Revolt Grows Strong in the Shantytowns of Peru." *New York Times* (November 11): 1, 6.

Brotman, Richard and Frederic Suffet
1975   "The Concept of Prevention and Its Limitations." *Annals* 417 (January): 53–65.

Brounstein, Paul J. and Janine M. Zweig
n.d.   *Understanding Substance Abuse Prevention. Toward the 21st Century: A Primer on Effective Programs.* Washington, DC: Substance Abuse and Mental Health Services Administration.

Brounstein, Paul J., Harry P. Hatry, David M. Altschuler, and Louis H. Blair
1990   *Substance Use and Delinquency Among Inner City Adolescent Males.* Washington, DC: Urban Institute.

Brown, Ethan
1999   "Clear and Present Danger." *New York* (November 22): 43–45.

Brownlee, Shanon
1999   "Inside the Teen Brain." *U.S. Press and World Report* (August 9): 44–53.
Brownlee, Shanon and Joannie M. Schrof
1997   "The Quality of Mercy." *U.S. Press and World Report* (March 17): 54–62, 65–67.
Brzezinski, Matthew
2002   "Re-Engineering the Drug Business." *New York Times Magazine* (June 23): 24–29, 46, 54, 56.
Buckley, William F., et al.
1996   "War on Drugs Is Lost." *National Review* (February 12): 34–48.
Buchanan, David R.
1992   "Social History of American Drug Use." *Journal of Drug Issues* 22 (Winter): 31–52.
Bukstein, Oscar, David A. Brent, and Yifrah Kaminer
1989   "Comorbidity of Substance Abuse and Other Psychiatric Disorders in Adolescents." *American Journal of Psychiatry* 146 (September): 1131–41.
Bullington, Bruce
1999   "Editor's Introduction: The 'Golden Age' of Dutch Drug Policy?" *Journal of Drug Issues* 29 (3): 443–50.
Burgess, Robert L. and Ronald L. Akers
1969   "Differential Association-Reinforcement Theory of Criminal Behavior." Pages 291–320 in *Behavioral Sociology,* edited by Robert L. Burgess and Don Bushell Jr. New York: Columbia University Press.
Burkholz, Herbert
1987   "Pain: Solving the Mystery." *New York Times* (January 15): Internet.
Burns, R. Stanley and Alan Done
1980   "Special Management Procedures for Emergency Medical Staff." Pages 95–120 in *Phencyclidine Abuse Manual,* edited by Mary Tuma McAdams, Ronald L. Linder, Steven E. Lerner, and Richard Stanley Burns. Los Angeles, CA: University of California Extension.
Burros, Marian and Sarah Jay
1996   "Concern Is Growing over an Herb That Promises a Legal High." *New York Times* (April 10): B1, 8.
Bush, Patricia J. and Ronald Iannotti
1987   "The Development of Children's Health Orientations and Behaviors: Lessons for Substance Abuse Prevention." Pages 45–74 in *Etiology of Drug Abuse: Implications for Prevention,* edited by Coryl LaRue Jones. Rockville, MD: National Institute on Drug Abuse.
Butterfield, Fox
2005   "Fighting Illegal Drugs Through Its Legal Source." *New York Times* (January 30): 20.
2004a   "Home Drug-Making Laboratories Expose Children to Toxic Fallout." *New York Times* (February 23): 1, 16.
2004b   "Across Rural America, Drug Casts a Grim Shadow." *New York Times* (January 4): 10.
1997   "Drop in Homicide Rate Linked to Crack's Decline." *New York Times* (October 27): 10.

Byck, Robert, ed.
1974   *Cocaine Papers: Sigmund Freud.* New York: Stonehill.
Byrne, Andrew
2000   "Nine-year Follow-up of 86 Consecutive Patients Treated with Methadone in General Practice, Sydney, Australia." *Drug and Alcohol Review* 19 (June): 153–59.
California Narcotic Addict Evaluation Authority
1994   *All About the Civil Addict Program.* Norco, CA: California Narcotic Addict Evaluation Authority.
"Canadian Study Quantifies Link Between Substance Abuse and Crime: Alcohol Abuse Associated with Violent Offenses"
2002   *Alcoholism and Drug Abuse Weekly* 14 (May 13): 2–5.
Cantrell, Geoffrey
2002   "Valuable Marijuana Crop Found in Madison." *Asheville Citizen-Times* (July 24): B1.
Carey, Benedict
2007   "In Clue to Addictive Behavior, a Brain Injury Halts Smoking." *New York Times* (January 26): 1, 18.
Carlson, Kenneth and Peter Finn
1993   *Prosecuting Criminal Enterprises.* Washington, DC: Bureau of Justice Statistics.
Carpenter, Cheryl, Barry Glassner, Bruce D. Johnson, and Julia Loughlin
1988   *Kids, Drugs, and Crime.* Lexington, MA: D.C. Heath.
Carroll, Kathleen
1998   *A Cognitive-Behavioral Approach: Treating Cocaine Addiction.* Rockville, MD: National Institute on Drug Abuse.
Carroll, Kathleen, Samuel A. Ball, Charla Nich. Patrick G. O'Connor, Dorothy A. Eagan, Tami L. Frankforter, Elisa G. Triffleman, Julia Shi, and Bruce J. Rounsaville
2001   "Targetting Behavioral Therapies to Enhance Naltrexone Treatment of Opioid Dependence." *Archives of General Psychiatry* 58 (August): 755–783.
Carroll, Linda
2003   "Alcohol's Toll on Fetuses: Even Worse Than Thought." *New York Times* (November 4): F1, 6.
2002   "Marijuana's Effects: More Than Munchies." *New York Times* (January 29): D6.
2000   "Genetic Studies Promise a Path to Better Treatment of Addictions." *New York Times* (November 14): D6.
Carter, Hodding IV
1991   "Day of the Triads." *M Inc.* (June): 68–73.
Cashman, Sean D.
1981   *Prohibition.* New York: Free Press.
Catanzarite, Anne M.
1992   *Managing the Chemically Dependent Nurse.* Chicago: American Hospital Publishing.
Cauchon, Dennis
1992   "Michigan Drug Law: No Exceptions, No Mercy." *USA Today* (April 7): 3.

Caulkins, Jonathan P.
1997   "Is Crack Cheaper Than (Powder) Cocaine?"
        Addiction 92: 1437–43.
1996   "What Does Mathematical Modeling Tell Us
        About Harm Reduction?" *Drug and Alcohol
        Review* 15: 231–35.
1994   "What Is the Average Price of an Illicit Drug?"
        Addiction 89 (July): 815–19.
1992   "Thinking About Displacement in Drug Markets:
        Why Observing Change of Venue Isn't Enough."
        Journal of Drug Issues 22 (Winter): 17–30.

Caulkins, Jonathan P. and H. John Heinz III
2002   "Law Enforcement's Role in a Harm Reduction
        Regime." *Contemporary Issues in Crime and
        Justice* 64 (January): 1–12.

Caulkins, Jonathan P., C. Peter Rydell, Susan S.
Everingham, James Chiesa, and Shawn Bushway
1999   *An Ounce of Prevention, a Pound of Uncertainty:
        The Cost-Effectiveness of School-Based Drug
        Prevention Programs.* Santa Monica, CA:
        RAND.

Caulkins, Jonathan P., C. Peter Rydell, William L.
Schwabe, and James S. Chiesa
1997   *Mandatory Minimum Drug Sentences: Throwing
        Away the Key or the Taxpayer's Money?* Santa
        Monica, CA: RAND.

Caulkins, Jonathan P., Gordon Crawford, and
Peter Reuter
1993   "Simulation of Adaptive Response: A Model of
        Drug Interdiction." *Mathematical and Computer
        Modeling* 17 (2): 37–52.

Caulkins, Jonathan P., Patricia A. Ebener, and Daniel F.
McCaffrey
1995   "Describing DAWN's Dominion." *Contemporary
        Drug Problems* 22 (Fall): 547–67.

Caulkins, Jonathan P., Peter Reuter, Martin Y. Iguchi, and
James Chiesa
2005   *How Goes the "War on Drugs"? An Assessment
        of U.S. Drug Policy Problems and Policy.* Santa
        Monica, CA: RAND Drug Policy Research
        Center.

Cawley, Janet
1990   "3% Fail Drug Tests in Transit Industries."
        Chicago Tribune (July 11): 9.

Center on Addiction and Substance Abuse
1994   "Relationship Between Cigarette Smoking and
        Heroin, Cocaine and Crack." Press release,
        March 10.

Chaiken, Jan M. and Marcia R. Chaiken
1990   "Drugs and Predatory Crime." Pages 203–39 in
        Drugs and Crime, edited by Michael Tonry and
        James Q. Wilson. Chicago: University of Chicago
        Press.

Chaiken, Marcia R. and Bruce D. Johnson
1988   *Characteristics of Different Types of Drug-
        Involved Offenders.* Washington, DC: National
        Institute of Justice.

Chambers, Carl D. and Leon Brill
1973   *Methadone: Experiences and Issues.* New York:
        Behavioral Publications.

Chambliss, William
1973   *Functional and Conflict Theories of Crime.* New
        York: MSS Modular Publications.

Chapman, Stephen
1992   "The Awful Price of Fighting the War on Drugs."
        Chicago Tribune (May 21): 23.
1991a   "Do We Want to Save Addicts or Kill Them?"
        Chicago Tribune (February 21): 23.
1991b   "In the Drug War, Bigger Sentences for
        Smaller Crimes." *Chicago Tribune* (June 9):
        Sec. 4: 3.
1991c   "Prohibition—From Alcohol to Drugs—Is a Costly
        Failure." *Chicago Tribune* (September 1): Sec. 4: 3.

Chavez, Nelba and Ruth Sanchez-Way
1997   *Selected Findings in Prevention.* Washington, DC:
        U.S. Substance Abuse and Mental Health Services
        Administration.

Chavkin, Wendy
2001   "Cocaine and Pregnancy: Time to Look at the
        Evidence." *Journal of the American Medical
        Association* 285:1626–28.

Cheever, Susan
2004   *My Name is Bill. Bill Wilson: His Life and the
        Creation of Alcoholics Anonymous.* New York:
        Simon and Schuster.

Chein, Isidor, Donald L. Gerard, Robert S. Lee, and Eva
Rosenfeld
1964   *The Road to H: Narcotics, Delinquency, and
        Social Policy.* New York: Basic Books.

Chen, David W.
2007   "Five Arrested in New Jersey in Illegal Sales
        of Painkillers." *New York Times*
        (January 27): B4.
2006   "No Compromise in Sight on Plan to Fight
        H.I.V." *New York Times* (June 4): 37, 40.

Chermack, Stephen T. and Stuart P. Taylor
1995   "Alcohol and Human Physical Aggression:
        Pharmacological Versus Expectancy Effects."
        Journal of Studies on Alcohol 56 (July):
        449–56.

Cheung, Yuet W., Patricia G. Erickson, and Tammy C.
Landau
1991   "Experience of Crack Use: Findings from a
        Community-Based Sample in Toronto." *Journal
        of Drug Issues* 21 (Winter): 121–40.

Childress, Ann Rose
1993   "Medications in Drug Abuse Treatment." Pages
        73–75 in *NIDA Second National Conference on
        Drug Abuse Research and Practice: An Alliance
        for the 21st Century.* Rockville, MD: National
        Institute on Drug Abuse.

Childress, Anna Rose, A. Thomas McLellan, and Charles P.
O'Brien
1985   "Behavioral Therapies for Substance Abuse."
        International Journal of the Addictions 20:
        947–69.

Childress, Ann Rose, Anita V. Hole, Ronald N. Ehrman, Steven
J. Robbins, A. Thomas McLellan, and Charles P. O'Brien
1993   "Cue Reactivity and Cue Reactivity Interventions
        in Drug Dependence." Pages 73-95 in *Behavioral*

Treatments for Drug Abuse and Dependence, edited by Lisa Simon Onken, John D. Blaine, and John J. Boren. Rockville, MD: National Institute on Drug Abuse.

Childress, Anna Rose, P. David Mozley, William McElgin, Josh Fitzgerald, Martin Reivich, and Charles P. O'Brien
1999   "Limbic Activation During Cue-Induced Cocaine Craving." *American Journal of Psychiatry* 156 (January): 11–18.

Chin, Ko-lin
1995   "Triad Societies in Hong Kong." *Transnational Organized Crime* 1 (Spring): 47–64.
1990   *Chinese Subculture and Criminality: Non-traditional Crime Groups in America.* Westport, CT: Greenwood.

Chitwood, Dale D., James E. Rivers, and James A. Inciardi
1996   *The American Pipe Dream: Crack Cocaine and the Inner City.* Ft. Worth, TX: Harcourt Brace.

Chitwood, Dale D., Mary Comerford, and Norman L. Weatherby
1998   "The Initiation of the Use of Heroin in the Age of Crack." Pages 51–76 in *Heroin in the Age of Crack-Cocaine,* edited by James A. Inciardi and Laura D. Harrison. Thousand Oaks, CA: Sage.

Christian, Sue Ellen
2000   "Teen's Death Sheds Light on a Volatile Party Drug." *Chicago Tribune* (February 7): 1, 34.

Cintron, Myrna
1986   "Coca: Its History and Contemporary Parallels." Pages 25–51 in *Drugs in Latin America,* edited by Edmundo Morales. Williamsburg, VA: College of William and Mary.

Clay, Rebecca A.
2004   "Peer-to-Peer Program Promotes Recovery." *SAMHSA News* 12 (September/October): 1–4.

Clines, Francis X. and Barry Meier
2001   "Cancer Painkillers Pose New Abuse Threat." *New York Times* (February 9): 1, 18.

Cloninger, Susan C.
1993   *Theories of Personality: Understanding Persons.* Upper Saddle River, NJ: Prentice Hall.

Cloud, David S. and Carlota Gall
2005   "U.S. Memo Faults Afghan Leader on Heroin Fight." *New York Times* (May 22); 1, 12.

Cloward, Richard A. and Lloyd E. Ohlin
1960   *Delinquency and Opportunity.* New York: Free Press.

Cloyd, Jerald W.
1982   *Drugs and Information Control: The Role of Men and Manipulation in the Control of Drug Trafficking.* Westport, CT: Greenwood.

Clymer, Adam
1994   "Senate Told That Cigarettes Are Entry into Hard Drugs." *New York Times* (March 11): 12.

Coffey, Thomas A.
1975   *The Long Thirst: Prohibition in America, 1920–1933.* New York: Norton.

Cohen, Albert K.
1965   *Delinquent Boys.* New York: Free Press.

Cohen, Julian
1996   "Drug Education: Politics, Propaganda and Censorship." *The International Journal of Drug Policy* 7 (3): Internet.

Cohen, Peter J.
2002   "Untreated Addiction Imposes an Ethical Bar to Recruiting Addicts for Non-Therapeutic Studies of Addictive Drugs." *Journal of Law, Medicine and Ethics* 30 (Spring): 73–83.

Cohen, Roger
1992   "Amid Growing Crime, Zurich Closes a Park It Reserved for Drug Addicts." *New York Times* (February 11): 11.

Coker, J. Kelly
2001   "Four-fold prevention: strategies to prevent substance abuse among elementary school-aged children." *Professional School Counseling* 5 (October): 70–75.

Collins, James J., Robert L. Hubbard, and J. Valley Rachel
1985   "Expensive Drug Use and Illegal Income: A Test of Explanatory Hypotheses." *Criminology* 23 (November): 743–64.

Collins, Larry
1999   "Holland's Half-Baked Drug Experiment." *Foreign Affairs* 78 (May/June): 82–98.

"Colombian Heroin May Be Increasing"
1991   *New York Times* (October 27): 10.

Colorado Alcohol and Drug Abuse Division
1987   *Drug Use Trends in Colorado.* Denver.

Comings, David E.
1996   "Genetic Factors in Drug Abuse and Dependence." Pages 16–38 in *Individual Differences in the Biobehavioral Etiology of Drug Abuse,* edited by Harold W. Gordon and Meyer D. Glantz. Rockviille, MD: National Institute on Drug Abuse.

Committee on Law Reform of the New York County Lawyers Association
1987   *Advisory Reports. Part I: Why Cocaine and Heroin Should be Decriminalized. Part II: Why Cocaine and Heroin Should Not be Decriminalized.* New York: Photocopied.

Compton, Beaulah and Burt Galaway
1979   *Social Work Processes,* 2nd ed. Homewood, IL: Dorsey Press.

Comptroller General
1988   *Controlling Drug Abuse: A Status Report.* Washington, DC: General Accounting Office.
1983   *Federal Drug Interdiction Efforts Need a Strong Central Oversight.* Washington, DC: General Accounting Office.

Conant, Eve
2005   "Ecstasy: A Possible New Role for a Banned Club Drug." *Newsweek* (May 2): 11.

Condor, Bob
2002a   "Getting a Grip." *Chicago Tribune* (June 30): Sec. 13: 1, 4–5.
2002b   "Learning to Sip: A New Program Helps Problem Drinkers Cut Back on Alcohol" *New York Daily News* (August 12): 42–44.

Conley, Peter, David Hewitt, Wayne Mitic, Christiane Poulin, Diane Riley, Robin Room, Ed Sawka, Eric Single, and John Topp
n.d.   "Harm Reduction: Concepts and Practice: A Policy Discussion Paper." Ottawa: Canadian Centre on Substance Abuse (CCSA) National Working Group on Policy: Internet.

Cook, Christopher C. H.
1988a   "The Minnesota Model in the Management of Drug and Alcohol Dependency: Miracle, Method or Myth? Part I. The Philosophy and the Programme." *British Journal of Addiction* 83: 625–34.
1988b   "The Minnesota Model in the Management of Drug and Alcohol Dependency: Miracle, Method or Myth? Part II. Evidence and Conclusions." *British Journal of Addiction* 83: 735–48.

Cook, L. Foster and Beth A. Weinman
1988   "Treatment Alternatives to Street Crime." Pages 99–105 in *Compulsory Treatment of Drug Abuse: Research and Clinical Practice,* edited by Carl G. Leukefeld and Frank M. Tims. Rockville, MD: National Institute on Drug Abuse.

Coomber, Ross
1999   "The Cutting of Heroin in the United States in the 1990s." *Journal of Drug Issues* 29: 17–36.

Cooper, James
1998   "Statement Presented at the Joint New York Assembly Committee on Alcoholism and Drug Abuse and Committee on Health Hearings, New York City," December 11.

Cooper, Michael
1998   "Police Raid Wrong Apartment in Brooklyn." *New York Times* (May 8): 17.

Corcoran, David
1989   "Legalizing Drugs: Failures Spur Debate." *New York Times* (November 27): 9.

Cosden, Merith, Stacey Peerson, and Katherine Elliott
1997   "Effects of Prenatal Drug Exposure on Birth Outcomes and Early Child Development." *Journal of Drug Issues* 27: 525–39.

Courtwright, David T.
1982   *Dark Paradise: Opiate Addiction in America Before 1940.* Cambridge, MA: Harvard University Press.

Cowan, Richard C.
1986   "A War Against Ourselves: How the Narcs Created Crack." *National Review* (December 5): 26–31.

Cowell, Alan
1995   "Zurich's Open Drug Policy Goes into Withdrawal." *New York Times* (March 12): 3.

Cox, W. Miles
1985   "Personality Correlates of Substance Abuse." Pages 209–46 in *Determinants of Substance Abuse: Biological, Psychological, and Environmental Factors,* edited by Mark Galizio and Stephen A. Maisto. New York: Plenum.

Crabbe, John C.
2002   "Generic Contributions to Addiction." Pages 435–62 in *Annual Review of Psychology,* Vol. 53. Palo Alto, CA: Annual Reviews.

Craig, Robert J.
1987   "The Personality Structure of Heroin Addicts." Pages 25–36 in *Neurobiology of Behavioral Control in Drug Abuse,* edited by Stephen I. Szara. Rockville, MD: National Institute on Drug Abuse.

Crank, John P. and Lee R. Rehm
1992   "From Drug Courier Profiles to Officer Awareness: A Study of a State Drug Interdiction Program." Paper presented at the annual meeting of the Academy of Criminal Justice Sciences, Pittsburg, March.

Crits-Christoph, Paul, Lynne Siqueland, Jack Blaine, Arlene Frank, Lester Luborsky, Lisa S. Onken, Larry R. Muenz, Michael E. Thase, Roger Weiss, David R. Gastfriend, George E. Woody, Jacques P. Barber, Stephen F. Butler, Dennis Daley, Ihsan Salloum, Sarah Bishop, Lisa M. Najavits, Judy Lis, Delinda Mercer, Margaret L. Griffin, Karla Moras, and Aaron T. Beck
1999   "Psychosocial Treatments for Cocaine Dependence." *Archives of General Psychiatry* 56 (June): 493–502.

Crowley, Geoffrey
1996   "Herbal Warning." *Pressweek* (May 6): 60–67.

Crowley, Thomas J.
1981   "The Reinforcers for Drug Abuse: Why People Take Drugs." Pages 367-81 in *Classic Contributions in the Addictions,* edited by Howard Shaffer and Milton Earl Burglass. New York: Brunner/Mazel.

Currie, Elliott
1993   *Reckoning: Drugs, the Cities, and the American Future.* New York: Hill and Wang.

Cushman, Paul Jr.
1974   "Relationship Between Narcotic Addiction and Crime." *Federal Probation* 38 (September): 38–43.

Danaceau, Paul
1974   *Methadone Maintenance Programs: The Experience of Four Programs.* Washington, DC: Drug Abuse Council, Inc.

Davenport-Hines, Richard
2002   *Pursuit of Oblivion: A Global History of Narcotics.* New York: Norton.

Davey, Monica
2005   "Grisly Effect of One Drug: 'Meth Mouth.'" *New York Times* (June 11): 1, 10.

Davis, Joel
1984   *Endorphins: New Waves in Brain Chemistry.* Garden City, NY: Doubleday.

DeJong, William
1987a   *Arresting the Demand for Drugs: Police and School Partnership to Prevent Drug Abuse.* Washington, DC: National Institute of Justice.

1987b   "A Short Term Evaluation of Project DARE: Preliminary Indications of Effectiveness." *Journal of Drug Education* 17: 279–94.

de Kort, Marcel and Ton Cramer
1999   "Pragmatism Versus Ideology: Dutch Drug Policy Continued." *Journal of Drug Issues* 29 (3): 473–92.

De Lama, George
1988   "Besieged Colombia Becoming the Lebanon of Latin America." *Chicago Tribune* (November 20): 5.

Delaney, William P.
1977   "On Capturing an Opium King: The Politics of Law Sik Han's Arrest." Pages 67–88 in *Drugs and Politics,* edited by Paul E. Rock. New Brunswick, NJ: Transaction Books.

De La Rosa, Mario, Elizabeth Y. Lambert, and Bernard Gropper, eds.
1990   *Drugs and Violence: Causes, Correlates, and Consequences.* Rockville, MD: National Institute on Drug Abuse.

Delbanco, Andrew and Thomas Delbanco
1995   "AA at the Crossroads." *New Yorker* (March 20): 50–63.

De Leon, George
2000   *The Therapeutic Community: Theory, Model, and Method.* New York: Springer.
1995   "Residential Therapeutic Communities in the Mainstream: Diversity and Issues." *Journal of Psychoactive Drugs* 27 (1): 3–15.
1994   "The Therapeutic Community: Toward a General Theory and Model." Pages 16–53 in *Therapeutic Community: Advances in Research and Application,* edited by Frank M. Tims, George De Leon, and Nancy Jainchill. Rockville, MD: National Institute on Drug Abuse.
1990   "Treatment Strategies." Pages 115–38 in *Handbook of Drug Control in the United States,* edited by James A. Inciardi. Westport, CT: Greenwood.
1986a   "The Therapeutic Community for Substance Abuse: Perspective and Approach." Pages 5–18 in *Therapeutic Communities for Addictions,* edited by George De Leon and James T. Ziegenfuss Jr. Springfield, IL: Charles C Thomas.
1986b   "Program-Based Evaluation Research in Therapeutic Communities." Pages 69–87 in *Drug Abuse Treatment Evaluation: Strategies, Progress, and Prospects,* edited by Frank M. Tims and Jacqueline P. Ludford. Rockville, MD: National Institute on Drug Abuse.

De Leon, George, James A. Inciardi, and Steven S. Martin
1995   "Residential Drug Abuse Treatment Research: Are Conventional Control Designs Appropriate for Assessing Treatment Effectiveness?" *Journal of Psychoactive Drugs* 27 (1): 85–91.

DeLong, James V.
1972   "Treatment and Rehabilitation." Pages 173–254 in *Dealing with Drug Abuse: A Report to the Ford Foundation.* New York: Praeger.

de Marneffe, Peter
2003   "Against the Legalization of Heroin." *Criminal Justice Ethics* 22 (Winter/Spring): 34–40.

Dembo, Richard, Linda Williams, Alan Getreu, Lisa Genung, James Schmeidler, Estrellita Berry, Eric D. Wish, and Lawrence Voie
1991   "A Longitudinal Study of the Relationship Among Marijuana/Hashish Use, Cocaine Use, and Delinquency in a Cohort of High Risk Youths." *Journal of Drug Issues* 21: 271–312.

De Quincey, Thomas
1952   *The Confessions of an English Opium-Eater.* London: J. M. Dent. Originally published in 1821.

Dettling, Michael, Andreas Heinz, Peter Dufeu, Hans Rommelspacher, Klaus-Jürgen Gräf, and Lutz G. Schmid
1995   "Dopaminergic Responsivity in Alcoholism: Trait, State, or Residual Marker?" *American Journal of Psychiatry* 152 (9): 1317–21.

Dickson, Donald T.
1977   "Bureaucracy and Morality: An Organizational Perspective on a Moral Crusade." Pages 31–52 in *Drugs and Politics,* edited by Paul E. Rock. New Brunswick, NJ: Transaction Books.

Dillon, Sam
1999a   "Mexico's Troubadors Turn from Amor to Drugs." *New York Times* (February 19): 4.
1999b   "Ruling Party, at 70, Tries Hard to Cling to Power in Mexico." *New York Times* (March 4): 1, 12.
1996   "Mexicans Tire of Police Graft as Drug Lords Raise Stakes." *New York Times* (March 21): 3.
1995   "Speed Carries Mexican Drug Dealer to the Top." *New York Times* (December 27): 6.

DiNardo. John
1993   "Law Enforcement, the Price of Cocaine and Cocaine Use." *Mathematical and Computer Modelling* 17 (2): 53–64.

Dinges, John
1990   *Our Man in Panama: How General Noriega Used the United States—and Made Millions in Drugs and Arms.* New York: Random House.

Dishion, Thomas J., Gerald R. Patterson, and John R. Reid
1988   "Parent and Peer Factors Associated with Drug Sampling in Early Adolescence: Implications for Treatment." Pages 69–93 in *Adolescent Drug Abuse: Analyses of Treatment Research,* edited by Elizabeth R. Rahdert and John Grabowski. Rockville, MD: National Institute on Drug Abuse.

Dole, Vincent P.
1980   "Addictive Behavior." *Scientific American* 243: 138–54.

Dole, Vincent P. and Marie F. Nyswander
1966   "Rehabilitation of Heroin Addicts After Blockade with Methadone." *New York State Journal of Medicine* 66 (April): 2011–17.
1965   "A Medical Treatment for Diacetylmorphine (Heroin) Addiction." *Journal of the American Medical Association* 193 (August): 146–50.

Donovan, Dennis M.
1988   "Assessment of Addictive Behaviors: Implications of an Emerging Biopsychosocial Model." Pages 3–48 in *Assessment of Addictive Behaviors,* edited by Dennis M. Donova and G. Alan Marlatt. New York: Guilford.

Dotson, James W., Deborah L. Ackerman, and Louis Jolyon West
1995   "Ketamine Abuse." *Journal of Drug Issues* 25 (Fall): 751–57.

Doyle, A. Conan
1899   *Memoirs of Sherlock Holmes*. New York: Harper and Brothers.

"Drug Arrests and the Courts' Pleas for Help"
1989   *New York Times* (April 9): E6.

Drug Enforcement Administration (DEA)
n.d.a   *LSD Manufacture*. Internet.
n.d.b   *LSD Use and Effects*. Internet.
2003   *Speaking Out Against Drug Legalization*. Washington, DC: DEA.
1994a   *Crack Cocaine*. Washington, DC: DEA.
1994b   *Trends in Heroin*. Washington DC: DEA.
1991   *Worldwide Heroin Situation*. Washington, DC: DEA.
1989   *Drugs of Abuse*. Washington, DC: DEA.

Drugs Prevention Initiative
1999   London, England: Home Office.

Duenwald, Mary
2001   "Fresh Look at a Fast Way to Kick a Heroin Habit." *New York Times* (December 4): D6, 8.

Duncan, David F., Thomas Nicholson, Patrick Clifford, Wesley Hawkins, and Rick Petosa
1994   "Harm Reduction: An Emerging New Paradigm for Drug Education." *Journal of Drug Education* 24 (4): 281–90.

Dunwiddie, Thomas V.
1988   "Mechanisms of Cocaine Abuse and Toxicity: An Overview." Pages 337–53 in *Mechanisms of Cocaine Abuse and Toxicity*, edited by Doris Clouet, Khursheed Asghar, and Roger Brown. Rockville, MD: National Institute on Drug Abuse.

DuPont, Robert L. and John P. McGovern
1994   *A Bridge to Recovery: An Introduction to 12-Step Programs*. Washington DC: American Psychiatric Press.

Duster, Troy
1970   *The Legislation of Morality: Law, Drugs, and Moral Judgment*. New York: Free Press.

Duterte, Micheline, Kristin Hemphill, Terrence Murphy, and Sheigla Murphy
2003   "Tragic Beauties: Heroin Images and Heroin Users." *Contemporary Drug Problems* 30 (Fall): ProQuest.

Duzán, Maria
1994   *Death Beat*. New York: HarperCollins.

Dworkin, Steven I. and Raymond C. Pitts
1994   "Use of Roden Self-Administration Models to Develop Pharmaco-Therapies for Cocaine Abuse." Pages 88–112 in *Neurobiological Models for Evaluating Mechanisms Underlying Cocaine Addiction*, edited by Lynda Erinoff and Roger M. Brown. Rockville, MD: National Institute on Drug Abuse.

Dworkin, Steven I., Nick E. Goeders, John Grabowski, and James E. Smit
1987   "The Effects of 12-Hour Limited Access to Cocaine: Reduction in Drug Intake and Mortality." Pages 221–25 in *Problems of Drug Dependence, 1986*, edited by Louis S. Harris. Rockville, MD: National Institute on Drug Abuse.

Eaglin, James B.
1986   *The Impact of the Federal Drug Aftercare Program*. Washington, DC: Federal Judicial Center.

Eddy, Paul, Hugo Sabogal, and Sara Walden
1988   *The Cocaine Wars*. New York: Norton.

Egan, Timothy
2006   "Youthful Binge Drinking Fueled by Boredom of the Open West." *New York Times* (September 2): 1, 12.
2004   "Taking Aim at the Professional Rodeo Circuit's Drug of Choice." *New York Times* (June 11): 14.
2002   "Meth Building Its Hell's Kitchen in Rural America." *New York Times* (February 6): 14.
1999a   "The War on Crack Retreats, Still Taking Prisoners." *New York Times* (February 28): 1, 20–21.
1999b   "In States' Anti-Drug Fight, A Renewal for Treatment." *New York Times* (June 10): 1, 22.
1999c   "A Drug Ran Its Course, Then Hid with Its Users." *New York Times* (September 19): 1, 27.

"84 Military Personnel Convicted in Drug Case at Camp Lejeune"
2002   *New York Times* (July 4): 8.

Eiler, Kathryn, Melodie R. Schaefer, and Daniel Salstrom
1995   "Double-Blind Comparison of Bromocriptine and Placebo in Cocaine Withdrawal." *American Journal of Drug and Alcohol Abuse* 21 (1): 65–79.

Eitle, David, R. Jay Turner, and Tamela McNulty Eitle
2003   "The Deterrence Hypothesis Reexamined: Sports Participation and Substance Use Among Young Adults." *Journal of Drug Issues* 33 (Winter): 193–222.

Ellickson, Phyllis L.
1995   "Schools." Pages 93–120 in *Handbook on Drug Prevention*, edited by Robert H. Coombs and Douglas Ziedonis. Boston: Allyn and Bacon.

Ellickson, Phyllis L. and Robert M. Bell
1990   "Drug Prevention in Junior High: A Multi-Site Longitudinal Test." *Science* 247 (March 16): 1299–1305.

Ellickson, Phyllis L., Daniel F. McCaffrey, Bonnie Ghosh-Dastidar, and Douglas L. Longshore
2003   "New Inroads in Preventing Adolescent Drug Use: Results from a Large-Scale Trial of Project ALERT in Middle Schools." *American Journal of Public Health*, 93 (11): 1830–36.

Elliott, Stuart
2003   "Thanks to Cable, Liquor Ads Find a TV Audience." *New York Times* (December 15): C1, 11.

Ellis, Lee
1990   "Universal Behavioral and Demographic Correlates of Criminal Behavior: Toward Common Ground in the Assessment of Criminological Theories." Pages 36–49 in *Crime in Biological, Social, and Moral Contexts,* edited by Lee Ellis and Harry Hoffman. Westport, CT: Praeger.

Elsasser, Glen
1989   "Suspicion Is Ruled Ample Basis for Drug Search." *Chicago Tribune* (April 4): 3.

Engel, Madeline H.
1974   *The Drug Scene.* Rochelle Park, NJ: Hayden Book Co.

Ennett, Susan T., Nancy S. Tobler, Christopher L. Ringwalt, and Robert L. Flewelling
1994   "How Effective Is Drug Abuse Resistance Education? A Meta-Analysis of Project DARE Outcome Evaluations." *American Journal of Public Health* 84 (9): 1394–1401.

Epstein, Edward Jay
1988   "The Dope Business." *Manhattan, inc.* (July): 25–27.
1977   *Agency of Fear: Opiates and Political Power in America.* New York: G.P. Putnam's Sons.
1974   "Methadone: The Forlorn Hope." *The Public Interest* 36 (Summer): 3–24.

Epstein, Joan F. and Joseph C. Gfroerer
1997   *Heroin Abuse in the United States.* Substance Abuse and Mental Health Services Administration. Internet.

Erikson, Kai T.
1966   *Wayward Puritans.* New York: Wiley.

Fagan, Jeffrey and Ko-Lin Chin
1991   "Social Processes of Initiation into Crack." *Journal of Drug Issues* 21: 313–43.

Farabee, David, Vandana Joshi, and M. Douglas Anglin
2001   "Addiction Careers and Criminal Specialization." *Crime and Delinquency* 47 (April): 196–220.

"Far East Sopranos"
2003   *U.S. News and World Report* (January 27): 34.

Faupel, Charles E. Carl B. Klockars
1987   "Drugs-Crime Connections: Elaborations from the Life Histories of Hard-Core Heroin Addicts." *Social Problems* 34 (February): 54–68

Fay, Peter Ward
1975   *The Opium War: 1840–1842.* Chapel Hill: University of North Carolina Press.

"FDA: Date-Rape Drug Has Medical Use"
2002   *Chicago Tribune* (July 18): 16.

Feldman, Harvey
1977   "Street Status and Drug Use." Pages 207–22 in *Drugs and Politics,* edited by Paul E. Rock. New Brunswick, NJ: Transaction Books.

Fenichel, Otto
1945   *The Psychoanalytic Theory of Neuroses.* New York: Norton.

Feuer, Alan
2000   "U.S. Colonel Is Implicated in Drug Case." New York Times (April 4): 20.

Fields, Richard
2001   *Drug in Perspective,* 4th ed. New York: McGraw-Hill.

Finestone, Harold
1964   "Cats, Kicks, and Color." Pages 281–97 in *The Other Side,* edited by Howard S. Becker. New York: Free Press.

Finnegan, Loretta
1993   "Discussant and Discussion." Pages 189–207 in *International Research Conference on Biomedical Approaches to Illicit Drug Demand Reduction,* edited by Christine R. Hartel. Washington, DC: U.S. Government Printing Office.

Finnegan, L. P., A. P. Streissguth, G. Koren, D. Neuspiel, and K. Kaltenbach
1994   "The Teratogenicity of the Drugs of Abuse: A Symposium." Pages 51–54 in *Problems of Drug Dependence, 1993.* Vol. I, edited by Louis S. Harris. Rockville, MD: National Institute on Drug Abuse.

Fiorentine, Robert
1999   "After Drug Treatment: Are 12-Step Programs Effective in Maintaining Abstinence?" *American Journal of Drug and Alcohol Abuse* 25 (February): Internet.

Fishbein, Diana H. and Susan E. Pease
1990   "Neurological Links Between Substance Abuse and Crime." Pages 218–43 in *Crime in Biological, Social, and Moral Contexts,* edited by Lee Ellis and Harry Hoffman. Westport, CT: Praeger.

Fishbein, Diana H., David Lozovsky, and Jerome H. Jaffe
1989   "Impulsivity, Aggression, and Neuroendocrine Responses to Serotonergic Stimulation in Substance Abusers." *Biological Psychiatry* 25: 1049–66.

Flores, Philip J.
1988   *Group Psychotherapy with Addicted Populations.* New York: Haworth.

Flores, Phillip J. and Jeffrey M. Georgi
2005   *Substance Abuse Treatment: Group Therapy.* Rockville, MD: Substance Abuse and Mental Health Services Administration.

Foltin, Richard W. and Marian W. Fischman
1994   "Cocaine: Self-Administration Research: Treatment Implications." Pages 139–62 in *Neurobiological Models for Evaluating Mechanisms Underlying Cocaine Addiction,* edited by Lynda Erinoff and Roger M. Brown. Rockville, MD: National Institute on Drug Abuse.

Fong, Mak Lau
1981   *The Sociology of Secret Societies: A Study of Chinese Secret Societies in Singapore and Peninsular Malaysia.* Oxford, England: Oxford University Press.

Fooner, Michael
1985   *A Guide to Interpol.* Washington, DC: U.S. Government Printing Office.

Forero, Juan
2006   "Colombia's Coca Survives U.S. Plan to Uproot It." *New York Times* (August 19): 1, 8.
2005   "Turbulent Bolivia Is Producing More Cocaine, the U.N. Reports." *New York Times* (June 15): 5.
2002   "Farmers in Peru Are Turning Again to Coca Crop." *New York Times* (February 14): 3.
2001a   "New Challenge to the Bogotá Leadership." *New York Times* (May 6): 8.
2001b   "Where a Little Coca Is as Good as Gold." *New York Times* (July 8): Sec. 4: 12.
2001c   "Ranchers in Colombia Bankroll Their Own Militia." *New York Times* (August 8): 1, 6.
Forrest, Gary G.
1985   "Psychodynamically-Oriented Treatment of Alcoholism and Substance Abuse." Pages 307–36 in *Alcoholism and Substance Abuse: Strategies for Clinical Intervention,* edited by Thomas E. Bratter and Gary G. Forrest. New York: Free Press.
Frank, Blanche, Gregory Rainone, Michael Maranda, William Hopkins, Edmundo Morales, and Alan Kott
1987   "A Psycho-Social View of 'Crack' in New York City." Paper presented at the American Psychological Association Convention, New York City, August 28.
Franklin, Stephen
1987   "Detroit Wages All-Out War Against Crack." *Chicago Tribune* (December 13): 29.
Frawley, P. Joseph and James W. Smith
1990   "Chemical Aversion Therapy in the Treatment of Cocaine Dependence as Part of a Multimodal Treatment Program: Treatment Outcome." *Journal of Substance Abuse Treatment* 7: 21–29.
Frazier, Thomas L.
1962   "Treating Young Drug Abusers: A Casework Approach." *Social Work* 7 (July): 94–101.
French, Howard W.
2004   "A Corner of China in the Grip of a Lucrative Heroin Habit." *New York Times* (December 23): 4.
1991   "Filthy Rich with a Drug Connection." New York Times (August 6): 6.
Fredlund, Eric V., Richard T. Spence, Jane C. Maxwell, and Jennifer A. Kavinsky
1990   *Substance Abuse Among Youth Entering Texas Youth Commission Facilities, 1989: Final Report.* Austin: Texas Commission on Alcohol and Drug Abuse.
Friedman, David P.
1993   "Introduction to the Brain: A Primer on Structure and Function of the Brain's Reward Circuitry." Pages 53–62 in *International Research Conference on Biomedical Approaches to Illicit Drug Demand Reduction,* edited by Christine R. Hartel. Washington, DC: U.S. Government Printing Office.
French, Edward D., Stefanie Levenson, and Angelo Ceci
1990   "Characterization of the Actions of Phencyclidine Midbrain Dopamine Neurons." Pages 255–63 in *Problems of Drug Dependence 1989,* edited by

Louis S. Harris. Rockville, MD: National Institute on Drug Abuse.
Freud, Sigmund
1961   *A General Introduction to Psychoanalysis.* New York: Washington Square Press. Originally published in 1924.
Freudenheim, Milt
1987   "Specialty Health Care Booms." *New York Times* (November 24): 25, 26.

Galaif, Elisha and Steve Sussman
1995   "For Whom Does Alcoholics Anonymous Work?" *International Journal of the Addictions* 30 (2): 161–84.
Gall, Carlotta
2006a   "Opium Harvest at Record Level in Afghanistan." *New York Times* (September 3): 1, 30.
2006b   "Another Year of Drug War, and the Poppy Crop Flourishes." *New York Times* (February 17): 4.
2004   "Afghan Poppy Growing Reaches Record Level, U.N. Says." *New York Times* (November 19): 3.
2003   "U.N. Aide Says Afghan Drug Trade Pays for Terrorist Attacks," *New York Times* (September 5): 5.
Gandossy, Robert P., Jay R. Williams, Jo Cohen, and H. J. Harwood
1980   *Drugs and Crime: A Survey and Analysis of the Literature.* Washington, DC: U.S. Government Printing Office.
Gardner, Stephen E., Paul J. Brounstein, and Deborah Stone
2001   *Promising and Proven Substance Abuse Prevention Programs.* Washington, DC: Substance Abuse and Mental Health Administration.
Gawin, Frank H., M. Elena Khalsa, and Everett Elinwod Jr.
1994   "Stimulants." Pages 111–39 in *The American Psychiatric Press Textbook of Substance Abuse Treatment,* edited by Marc Galanter and Herbert D. Kleber. Washington, DC: American Psychiatric Press.
Gay, Bruce
1999   "Drug education programs fail in Houston." *Society* 36 (January–February): Internet.
Geary, Nori
1987   "Cocaine: Animal Research Studies." Pages 19–47 in *Cocaine Abuse: New Directions in Treatment and Research,* edited by Henry I. Spitz and Jeffrey S. Rosecan. New York: Brunner/Mazel.
Gebelein, Richard S.
2000   "The Rebirth of Rehabilitation: Promise and Perils of Drug Courts." *Sentencing and Corrections* 6 (May): 1–7.
Gelernter, Joel, David Goldman, and Neil Risch
1993   "The A1 Allele at the D_2 Dopamine Receptor Gene and Alcoholism." *Journal of the American Medical Association* 269 (April 7): 1673–77.
General Accounting Office (GAO)
1998   *Drug Abuse Treatment Data Limitations Affect the Accuracy of National and State Estimates of Need.* Washington, DC: GAO.

1993   *Drug Use Measurement: Strengths, Limitations, and Recommendations for Improvement.* Washington, DC: GAO.

1991   *The War on Drugs: Arrests Burdening Local Criminal Justice Systems.* Washington, DC: GAO.

1987   *Drug Abuse Prevention: Further Efforts Needed to Identify Programs that Work.* Washington, DC: GAO.

George, William H. and Jeanette Norris
n.d.   "Alcohol, Disinhibition, Sexual Arousal, and Deviant Sexual Behavior." *Health and Research World* posted by the Indiana Prevention Resource Center: Internet.

George, William H. and Susan A. Stoner
2000   "Understanding Acute Alcohol Effects on Sexual Behavior." *Annual Review of Sex Research* 11: 92–122.

Gerstein, Dean R.
1994   "Outcome Research: Drug Abuse." Pages 45–64 in *The American Psychiatric Press Textbook of Substance Abuse Treatment,* edited by Marc Galanter and Herbert D. Kleber. Washington, DC: American Psychiatric Press.

Gerstein, Dean R. and Henrick J. Harwood, eds.
1990   *Treating Drug Problems, Vol. I: A Study of the Evolution, Effectiveness, and Financing of Public and Private Drug Treatment Systems.* Washington, DC: National Academy Press.

Ghazi, Katayon
1991   "Drug Trafficking Is Thriving in Iran." *New York Times* (December 4): 7.

Gilbert, R. M.
1981   "Drug Abuse as Excessive Behavior." Pages 382–95 in *Classic Contributions in the Addictions,* edited by Howard Shaffer and Milton Earl Burglass. New York: Brunner/Mazcl.

Gilbert, Susan
1997   "Youth Study Elevates Family's Role." *New York Times* (September 10): B10.

1996   "Doctors Found to Fail in Diagnosing Addictions." *New York Times* (February 14): B4.

Gilham, Steven A., Wayne L. Lucas, and David Siverwright
1997   "The Impact of Drug Education and Prevention Programs: Disparity Between Impressionistic and Empirical Assessments." *Evaluation Review* 21 (October): 589–613.

Ginzburg, Harold M.
1985   *Naltrexone: Its Clinical Utility.* Rockville, MD: National Institute on Drug Abuse.

Giuffrida, Greg
2002   "Schools Use Testing to Smoke Out Tobacco Use." *Chicago Tribune* (October 8): 8.

Glassman, Alexander H. and George F. Koob
1996   "Psychoactive Smoke." *Nature* 379 (February 22): 677–78.

Glassner, Barry and Julia Loughlin
1989   *Drugs in Adolescent Worlds: Burnouts to Straights.* Houndmills, England: Macmillan.

Goering, Laurie
1998   "In Peru, Battle Against Flow of Drugs Moves to Amazon River Maze." *Chicago Tribune* (June 30): 6.

Goffman, Erving
1961   *Asylums: Essays on the Social Situation of Mental Patients and Other Inmates.* Garden City, NY: Doubleday.

Gold, Mark S.
1994   "Neurobiology of Addiction and Recovery: The Brain, the Drive for the Drug, and the 12-Step Fellowship." *Journal of Substance Abuse Treatment* 11 (2): 99–97.

Gold, Mark S., Charles A. Dackis, A. L. C. Pottash, Irl Extein, and Arnold Washton
1986   "Cocaine Update: from Bench to Bedside." *Advances in Alcohol and Substance Abuse* 5 (Fall/Winter): 35–60.

Gold, Steven
1980   "The CAP Control Theory of Drug Abuse." Pages 8–11 in *Theories on Drug Abuse: Selected Contemporary Perspectives,* edited by Dan J. Lettieri, Mollie Sayers, and Helen Wallenstein Pearson. Rockville, MD: National Institute on Drug Abuse.

Goldberg, Jeff
1988   *Anatomy of a Scientific Discovery.* New York: Bantam.

Golden, Tim
1999   "U.S. Brushed Aside Mexican Role, Former Drug Chief Says." *New York Times* (November 26): 12.

1997   "Mexico and Drugs: Was the U.S. Napping?" *New York Times* (July 11): 1, 10.

Goldstein, Avram
2001   *Addiction: From Biology to Drug Policy,* 2nd ed. New York: Oxford University Press.

Goldstein, Joseph
1982   "Police Discretion Not to Invoke the Criminal Process." Pages 33–42 in *The Invisible Justice System: Discretion and the Law,* 2nd ed., edited by Burton Atkins and Mark Pogrebin. Cincinnati, OH: Anderson.

Goldstein, Paul J.
1985   "The Drugs/Violence Nexus: A Tripartite Conceptual Framework." *Journal of Drug Issues* 15 (Fall): 493–506.

Goldstein, Paul J., Patricia Bellucci, Barry J. Spunt, and Thomas Miller
1991   "Volume of Cocaine Use and Violence: A Comparison Between Men and Women." *Journal of Drug Issues* 21: 345–67.

Goleman, Daniel
1990   "Scientists Pinpoint Brain Irregularities in Drug Addicts." *New York Times* (June 26): B5.

1989   "Lasting Costs for Child Are Found from a Few Early Drinks." *New York Times* (February 16): 20.

1988   "Psychologists and Psychiatrists Clash Over Hospital and Training Barriers." *New York Times* (May 17): 21.

1987   "Physicians Said to Persist in Undertreating Pain and Ignoring the Evidence." *New York Times* (December 31): 10.

Golub, Andrew and Bruce D. Johnson
1994   "Cohort Differences in Drug-Use Pathways to Crack Among Current Crack Abusers in New York City." *Criminal Justice and Behavior* 21 (December): 403–22.

Gomez-Cespedes, Alejandro
1999   "The Federal Law Enforcement Agencies: An Obstacle in the Fight Against Organized Crime in Mexico." *Journal of Contemporary Criminal Justice* 15 (November): 352–69.

Gomez, Linda
1984   "America's 100 Years of Euphoria and Despair." *Life* (May): 57–68.

Goode, Erich
1989   *Drugs in American Society,* 3rd ed. New York: Knopf.
1972   *Drugs in American Society.* New York: Knopf.

Goodstadt, Michael S.
n.d.   *Drug Education.* Rockville, MD: National Institute of Justice.

Grady, Denise
1998   "Hardest Habit to Break: Memories of the High." *New York Times* (October 27): D1, 9.
1996   "Engineered Mice Mimic Drug Use and Mental Illness." *New York Times* (February 20): B5, B8.

Granfield, Robert and William Cloud
1996   "The Elephant That No One Sees: Natural Recovery Among Middle-Class Addicts." *Journal of Drug Issues* 26 (Winter): 45–61.

Greenberg, Brigitte
1999   "Study: Alcohol Cuts Stroke Risk." Associated Press (November 17): Internet.

Greenfeld, Lawrence A.
1998   *Alcohol and Crime.* Washington, DC: Bureau of Justice Statistics.

Greenhouse, Linda
1990   "Use of Illegal Drugs as Part of Religion Can Be Prosecuted, High Court Says." *New York Times* (April 18): 10.
1989   "High Court Backs Airport Detention Based on Profile." *New York Times* (April 4): 1, 10.

Greenspan, Stanley I.
1978   "Substance Abuse: An Understanding from Psychoanalytic Developmental and Learning Theory Perspectives." Pages 73–87 in *Psychodynamics of Drug Dependence,* edited by Jack D. Blaine and Demetrious A. Julius. Rockville, MD: National Institute on Drug Abuse.

Griffiths, Roland R.
1990   "Caffeine Abstinence Effects in Humans." Pages 129–30 in *Problems of Drug Dependence 1990,* edited by Louis S. Harris. Rockville, MD: National Institute on Drug Abuse.

Griffiths, Roland R., Suzette M. Evans, Stephen J. Heisman, Kenzie L. Preston, Christine A. Sannerud, Barbara Wolf, and Phillip P. Woodson
1990   "Low-Dose Caffeine Physical Dependence in Humans." *Journal of Pharmacology and Experimental Therapeutics* 255 (3): 1123–32.

Grinspoon, Lester
1987   "Cancer Patients Should Get Marijuana." *New York Times* (July 28): 23.
1979   *Psychedelic Drugs Reconsidered.* New York: Basic Books.

Grinspoon, Lester and James B. Bakalar
1985   *Cocaine: A Drug and Its Social Evolution: Revised Edition.* New York: Basic Books.
1976   *Cocaine: A Drug and Its Social Evolution.* New York: Basic Books.

Grinspoon, Lester and Peter Hedblom
1975   *The Speed Culture: Amphetamine Use and Abuse in America.* Cambridge, MA: Harvard University Press.

Groopman, Jerome
2001   "Eyes Wide Open." *New Yorker* (December 3): 52–57.

Grosswirth, Marvin
1982   "Medical Menace: Doctors Hooked on Drugs." *Ladies Home Journal* (February): 94, 141–44.

Gruson, Lindsey
1990   "U.S. Pinning Hopes on Guatemalan Army for Stability and War Against Drugs." *New York Times* (July 5): 4.

Guardia, José, Ana M. Catafau, Fanny Batlle, Juan Carlos Martin, Lidia Segura, Begona Gonzalvo, Gemma Prat, Ignasi Carrió, and Miguel Casas
2000   "Striatal Dopaminergic D_2 Receptor Density Measured by [123] Iodobenzamide SPECT in the Prediction of Treatment Outcome of Alcohol-Dependent Patients." *American Journal of Psychiatry* 157 (1): 127–29.

Guillermoprieto, Alma
2002   "Waiting for War." *New Yorker* (May): 48–55.

Gulley, Joshua M., Cecelia McNamara, Thomas J. Barbera, Mary C. Ritz, and Frank R. George
1995   "Selective Serotonin Reuptake Inhibitors on Ethanol-Reinforced Behavior in Mice." *Alcohol* 12 (May/June): 177–81.

Guo, Jie, Karl G. Hill, J. David Hawkins, Richard F. Catalano, and Robert D. Abbott.
2002   "A developmental Analysis of Sociodemographic, Family, and Peer Effects on Adolescent Illicit Drug Initiation." *Journal of the American Academy of Child and Adolescent Psychiatry* 41 (July): 838–46.

Gusfield, Joseph R.
1975   "The (F)Utility of Knowledge? The Relation of Social Science to Public Policy Toward Drugs." *Annals* 417 (January): 1–15.
1963   *Symbolic Crusade: Status Politics and the American Temperance Movement.* Urbana, IL: University of Illinois Press.

Güttinger, Franziska, Patrick Gschwend, Bernd Schulte, and Jürgen Rehm
2003   "Evaluating Long-Term Effects of Heroin-Assisted Treatment: The Results of a 6-Year Follow-Up." *European Addiction Research* 9: 73–79.

Hafvenstein, Joel
2006   "Afghanistan's Drug Habit." *New York Times* (September 30): 27.

Haggerty, Kevin, Rick Kosterman, Richard F. Catalano, and J. David Hawkins
1999   *Preparing for the Drug Free Years*. Washington, DC: Office of Juvenile Justice and Delinquency Programs.

Haley, Bruce
1990   "Burma's Hidden Wars." *U.S. Press and World Report* (December 10): 44–47.

Halkitis, Perry N., Jeffrey T Parsons, Leo Wilton
2003   "An Exploratory Study of Contextual and Situational Factors Related to Methamphetamine Use Among Gay and Bisexual Men in New York City." *Journal of Drug Issues* 33 (Spring): Internet.

Hall, Trish
1990   "New Way to Treat Alcoholism Discards Spiritualism of A.A." *New York Times* (December 24): 1, 10.

Hall, Wayne
1999   "Appraisals of the Adverse Health Effects of Cannabis Use: Ideology and Evidence." *Drug Policy Analysis Bulletin*. Internet.

Hall, Wayne, Louisa Degenhardt, and Michael Lynskey
2001   *The Health and Psychological Effects of Cannabis Use*. Canberra, Australia: Commonwealth Department of Health and Aging.

Hallstone, Michael
2002   "Updating Howard Becker's Theory of Using Marijuana for Pleasure." *Contemporary Drug Problems* 29 (Winter): 821–47.

Hanes, W. Travis and Frank Sanello
2005   *The Opium Wars: The Addiction of One Empire and the Corruption of Another*. New York: Barnes and Noble.

Hanson, David J.
1980   "Drug Education: Does it Work?" Pages 251–82 in *Drugs and the Youth Culture*, edited by Frank S. Scarpitti and Susan K. Datesman. Beverley Hills, CA: Sage.

Hanson, Glen R.
2002a   "Drug Abuse, Gender Matters." *NIDA Notes* 17 (2): 3, 4.

2002b   "New Insights into Relapse." *NIDA Notes* 17 (3): 3–4.

2001   "Looking the Other Way: Rave Promoters and Club Drugs." Hearing before the Senate Caucus on International Narcotics Control (December 4).

Hargreaves, William A.
1986   "Methadone Dosage and Duration for Maintenance Treatment." Pages 19–79 in *Research on the Treatment of Narcotic Addiction: State of the Art*, edited by James R. Cooper, Fred Altman, Barry S. Brown, and Dorynne Czechowicz. Rockville, MD: National Institute on Drug Abuse.

Harm Reduction Coalition
1998   "Effects, Tolerance & Addiction." Internet.

Harris, Gardiner
2007   "Study on Nicotine Levels Stirs Calls for New Controls." *New York Times* (January 19): B1.

Harris, Louis S., ed.
1999   *Problems of Drug Abuse*, 1998. Rockville, MD: National Institute on Drug Abuse.

Harris, Louis S.
1993   "Opiates: A History of Opiates and Their Use in Treatment." Pages 85-90 in *International Research Conference on Biomedical Approaches to Illicit Drug Demand Reduction*, edited by Christine R. Hartel. Washington, DC: U.S. Government Printing Office.

Hartel, Christine R., ed.
1993   *International Research Conference on Biomedical Approaches to Illicit Drug Demand Reduction*. Washington, DC: U.S. Government Printing Office.

Harwood, Henrick J. and Tracy G. Myers, eds.
2004   *New Treatments for Addiction: Behavioral, Ethical, Legal, and Social Questions*. Washington, DC: National Academies Press.

Hawkins, Dana
2002   "Tests on Trial: Jobs and Reputations Ride on Unproven Drug Screens." *U.S. News and World Report* (August 12): 46–48.

Hawkins, J. David, Denise M. Lishner, and Richard F. Catalano
1987   "Childhood Predictors and the Prevention of Adolescent Substance Abuse." Pages 75–126 in *Etiology of Drug Abuse*, edited by Coryl LaRue Jones and Robert J. Battjes. Rockville, MD: National Institute on Drug Abuse.

Hays, Tom
2000   "Army Colonel to Plead Guilty." Associated Press (April 4): Internet.

Hedgepath, William
1989   "'Mule Skinner.'" *Atlanta* (March): 61–62: 93–101.

Heinz, Andreas, Sabine Löber1, Alexander Georgi1, Jana Wrase, Derik Hermann1, Eibe-R. Rey, Stefan Wellek, and Karl Mann
2003   "Reward Craving and Withdrawal Relief: Assessment of Different Motivational Pathways to Alcohol Intake." *Alcohol and Alcoholism* 38 (1): 35–39.

Helmer, John
1975   *Drugs and Minority Oppression*. New York: Seabury Press.

Henderson, Leigh A.
1994a   "About LSD." Pages 37–53 in *LSD: Still with Us After all These Years*, edited by Leigh A. Henderson and William J. Glass. New York: Lexington Books.

1994b   "Adverse Reactions to LSD." Pages 55–75 in *LSD: Still with Us After all These Years*, edited by Leigh A. Henderson and William J. Glass. New York: Lexington Books.

Hendler, Harold I. and Richard C. Stephens
1977   "The Addict Odyssey: From Experimentation to Addiction." *International Journal of the Addictions* 12: 25–42.

Hepburn, John R., C. Wayne Johnston, and Scott Rogers
1994   *Do Drugs. Do Time: An Evaluation of the Maricopa County Demand Reduction Program.* Washington, DC: National Institute of Justice.

Hester, Reid K. and William R. Miller
1988   "Empirical Guidelines for Optimal Client-Treatment Matching." Pages 27–38 in *Adolescent Drug Abuse: Analyses of Treatment Research,* edited by Elizabeth R. Rahdert and John Grabowski. Rockville, MD: National Institute on Drug Abuse.

Higgens, Stephen T. and Alan Budney
1993   "Treatment of Cocaine Dependence Through the Principles of Behavior Analysis and Behavioral Psychology." Pages 97–121 in *Behavioral Treatments for Drug Abuse and Dependence,* edited by Lisa Simon Onken, John D. Blaine, and John J. Boren. Rockville, MD: National Institute on Drug Abuse.

Hilts, Philip J.
1995   "Survey Finds Surge in Smoking by Young." *New York Times* (July 20): C19.
1990   "How the Brain Is Stimulated by Marijuana Is Discovered." *New York Times* (July 21): 1, 5.

Himmelstein, Jerome L.
1983   *The Strange Career of Marijuana: Politics and Ideology of Drug Control in America.* Westport, CT: Greenwood.

Hinson, Riley E.
1985   "Individual Differences in Tolerance and Relapse." Pages 101–24 in *Determinants of Substance Abuse: Biological, Psychological, and Environmental Factors,* edited by Mark Galizio and Stephen A. Maisto. New York: Plenum.

Hirschi, Travis
1969   *Causes of Delinquency.* Berkeley: University of California Press.

Hobson, Katherine
2006   "Conquering Cravings." *U.S. News and World Report* (October 23): 64–66.
2002   "Danger at the Gym." *U.S. News and World Report* (January 21): 59.

Hoffmann, Norman G., Patricia A. Harrison, and Susan G. Streed
1991   "Outcome Evaluation." Pages 137–54 in *Substance Abuse Services: A Guide to Planning and Management,* edited by Joseph Westermeyer and Ronald S. Krug. Chicago: American Hospital Association.

Holinger, Paul C.
1989   "A Developmental Perspective on Psychotherapy and Psychoanalysis." *American Journal of Psychiatry* 146 (November): 1404–12.

Hollon, Tom
2002   "Phenotype Offers New Perception on Cocaine: Researchers Say Glutamate is More Essential to Addiction than Dopamine." *The Scientist* 16 (January 21): 16–17.

Holloway, Marguerite
1991   "Rx for Addiction." *Scientific American* (March): 94–103.

Home Office
2004   *Tackling Drugs Changing Lives. Keeping Communities Safe from Drugs.* London, UK.

Hormes, Joseph T., Christopher M. Filley, and Neil L. Rosenberg
1986   "Neurologic Sequelae of Chronic Solvent Vapor Abuse." *Neurology* 36 (May): 698–702.

Horowitz, Craig
1996   "The No-Win War." *New York* (February 5): 23–33.

Horton, Terry and Suzanne McMurphy
2004   "Phoenix House, A Therapeutic Community." *Perspectives* 2 (August): 27–29.

Hough, Mike
2005   *Drug Dealing in Open-Air Markets.* Washington, DC: U.S. Department of Justice.

Howe, Benjamin Ryder
2000   "Out of the Jungle." *nn* (May): 32–38.

"How the War on Drugs Influences the Health and Well-Being of Minority Communities"
1999   *DPRC* (Drug Police Research Center) *Newsletter* (June): 1–3.

Hser, Yih-Ing, Christine E. Grella, Robert L. Hubbard, Shih-Chao Hsieh, Bennett W. Fletcher, Barry S. Brown, and M. Douglas Anglin
2001   "An Evaluation of Drug Treatments for Adolescents in 4 U.S. Cities." *Archives of General Psychiatry* 58 (July): 689–95.

Hubbard, Robert L., Mary Ellen Marsden, J. Valley, Rachel Henrick, J. Harwood, Elizabeth R. Cavanaugh, and Harold M. Ginsberg
1989   *Drug Abuse Treatment: A National Study of Effectiveness.* Chapel Hill: University of North Carolina Press.

Hughes, John R.
1990   "Nicotine Abstinence Effects." Page 123 in *Problems of Drug Dependence 1989,* edited by Louis S. Harris. Rockville, MD: National Institute on Drug Abuse.

Hughes, Patrick H.
1977   *Behind the Wall of Respect.* Chicago: University of Chicago Press.

Huizinga, David H., Scott Menard, and Delbert S. Elliott
1989   "Delinquency and Drug Use: Temporal and Developmental Patterns." *Justice Quarterly* 6 (September): 419–55.

Humphries, Drew and David F. Greenberg
1981   "The Dialectics of Crime Control." Pages 209–54 in *Crime and Capitalism,* edited by David F. Greenberg. Palo Alto, CA: Mayfield.

Hunt, Leon Gibson
1977   *Assessment of Local Drug Abuse.* Lexington, MA: D.C. Heath.

Hunt, Walter A.
1983   "Ethanol and the Central Nervous System." Pages 133–63 in *Medical and Social Aspects of Alcohol Abuse,* edited by Boris Tabakoff, Patricia B. Sutker, and Carrie L. Randall. New York: Plenum.

Husak, Douglas and Peter de Marneffe
2005   *The Legalization of Drugs.* New York:
        Cambridge University Press.

Ihde, Aaron J.
1982   "Food Controls Under the 1906 Act." Pages 40–50
        in *The Early Years of Federal Food and Drug
        Control,* edited by James Harvey Young. Madison,
        WI: American Institute of the History of Pharmacy.
Ikonomidou, Chrysanthy, Petra Bittigau, Masahiko J.
Ishimaru, David F. Wozniak, Christan Koch, Kerstin Genz,
Madelon T. Price, Vanya Stefovska, Friederlke Hörster,
Tanya Tenkova, Krikor Dikranian, and John W. Olney
2000   "Ethanol-Induced Apoptotic Neurodegeneration
        and Fetal Alcohol Syndrome." *Science* 287
        (February 11): 1056–60.
Illicit Drug Policies: Selected Laws from the 50 States
2002   Chicago, IL: Robert Wood Johnson Foundation.
Illinois Criminal Justice Authority
1999   "Drug Court Provides Treatment Alternative to
        Incarceration." *On Good Authority* 2 (April):
        1–4.
Inciardi, James A.
2002   *The War on Drugs III: The Continuing Saga of
        the Mysteries and Miseries of Intoxication,
        Addiction, Crime, and Public Policy.* Boston:
        Allyn and Bacon.
1986   *The War on Drugs: Heroin, Cocaine, Crime, and
        Public Policy.* Palo Alto, CA: Mayfield.
1981   "Heroin Addiction and Street Crime."
        Pages 53–60 in *International Narcotics
        Trafficking,* hearings before the Permanent
        Subcommittee on Inves-tigations, November 10,
        11, 12, 13, 17, and 18. Washington, DC: U.S.
        Government Printing Office.
Inciardi, James A. and Anne E. Pottieger
1991   "Kids, Crack, and Crime." *Journal of Drug Issues*
        21: 257–70.
Inciardi, James A., Duane McBride, and Hilary L. Surratt
1998   "The Heroin Street Addict: Profiling a National
        Population." Pages 31–50 in *Heroin in the Age of
        Crack-Cocaine,* edited by James A. Inciardi and
        Laura D. Harrison. Thousand Oaks, CA: Sage.
Inciardi, James A., Hilary I. Surratt, Dale D. Chitwood,
Clyde B. McCoy
1996   "The Origins of Crack." Pages 1–14 in *The
        American Dream: Crack Cocaine and the Inner
        City,* edited by Dale D. Chitwood, James E.
        Rivers, and James A. Inciardi. New York:
        Harcourt Brace.
Institute for the Study of Drug Dependence (ISDD)
1987   *Drug Abuse Briefing.* London: ISDD.
Inverarity, James M., Pat Lauderdale, and Barry Field
1983   *Law and Society: Sociological Perspectives on
        Criminal Law.* Boston: Little, Brown.
Irwin, John
1970   *The Felon.* Englewood Cliffs, NJ: Prentice-Hall.
Ives, Nat
2004   "Flavored Kool Cigarettes Are Attracting
        Criticism." *New York Times* (March 9): C11.

Izenwasser, Sari and Ellen M. Unterwald
1994   "Sensitization and Tolerance to Cocaine." Pages
        71–73 in *Problems of Drug Dependence, 1993,*
        edited by Louis S. Harris. Rockville, MD:
        National Institute on Drug Abuse.

Jacob, Peyton III and Alexander Shulgin
1994   "Structure-Activity Relationships of the
        Classic Hallucinogens and Their Analogs."
        Pages 74–91 in *Hallucinogens: An Update,*
        edited by Geraline C. Lin and Richard A.
        Glennon. Rockville, MD: National Institute
        on Drug Abuse.
Jacobsen, Chanoch and Robert A. Hanneman
1992   "Illegal Drugs: Past, Present and Possible Futures."
        Journal of Drug Issues 22 (Winter): 105–20.
Jamieson, Anne, Alan Glanz, and Susanne MacGregor
1984   *Dealing with Drug Misuse: Crisis Intervention in
        the City.* London, England: Tavistock.
Jelinek, Pauline
1999   "Latin Leaders: U.S. Drug War Failed."
        Associated Press (November 3).
Johannessen, Koreen, Carolyn Collins, Beverly Mills-Novoa,
and Peggy Glider
1999   *A Practical Guide to Alcohol Abuse Prevention: A
        Campus Case Study in Implementing Social
        Norms and Environmental Management
        Approaches.* Tucson, AZ: University of Arizona.
Johnson, Bruce D., Andrew Golub, and Jeffrey Fagan
1995   "Careers in Crack, Drug Use, Drug Distribution,
        and Nondrug Criminality." *Crime and
        Delinquency* 41 (July): 275–95.
Johnson, Bruce D., Douglas S. Lipton, and Eric D. Wish
1986a   *Facts About the Criminality of Heroin and
        Cocaine Abusers and Some New Alternatives to
        Incarceration.* New York: Photocopied.
1986b   *Facts About the Criminality of Heroin and
        Cocaine Abusers and Some New Alternatives to
        Incarceration* (Research Summary). New York:
        Narcotic and Drug Research, Inc.
Johnson, Bruce D., Eric C. Wish, James Schmeidler, and
David Huizinga
1991   "Concentration of Delinquent Offending: Serious
        Drug Involvement and High Delinquency Rates."
        Journal of Drug Issues 21: 205–229.
Johnson, Bruce D., Kevin Anderson, and Eric C. Wish
1989   "A Day in the Life of 105 Drug Addicts and Abusers:
        Crimes Committed and How the Money Was
        Spent." *Sociology and Social Research* 72: 185–91.
Johnson, Bruce D., Paul J. Goldstein, Edward Preble, James
Schmeidler, Douglas S. Lipton, Barry Spunt, and Thomas
Miller
1985   *Taking Care of Business: The Economics of Crime
        by Heroin Abusers.* Lexington, MA: D.C. Heath.
Johnson, Bruce D., Terry Williams, Koja A. Dei, and Harry
Sanabria
1990   "Drug Abuse in the Inner City: Impact on Hard-Drug
        Users and the Community." Pages 9–67 in *Drugs and
        Crime,* edited by Michael Tonry and James Q.
        Wilson. Chicago: University of Chicago of Press.

Johnson, C. Anderson, Mary Ann Pentz, Mark D. Weber, James H. Dwyer, Neal Baer, David P. MacKinnon, William B. Hansen, and Brian R. Flay
1990   "Relative Effectiveness of Comprehensive Community Programming for Drug Abuse Prevention with High-Risk and Low-Risk Adolescents." *Journal of Consulting and Clinical Psychology* 58 (August): 447–56.

Johnson, Earl Jr.
1963   "Organized Crime: Challenge to the American Legal System." *Criminal Law, Criminology, and Police Science* 54 (March): 1–29.

Johnson, Julie
1987   "Two Reagan Officials Report Limited Success in Drug War." *New York Times* (December 9): 53.

Johnson, Kelly Dedelo
2004   *Underage Drinking.* Washington, DC: U.S. Department of Justice.

Johnson, Kirk
2006   "Officials Seeking Source of Lethal Heroin Mixture." *New York Times* (June 15): 14.

Johnson, Patrick B., Sharon M. Boles, and Herbert D. Kleber
2000   "The Relationship Between Adolescent Smoking and Drinking and Likelihood Estimates of Illicit Drug Use." *Journal of Addictive Diseases* 19 (2): 75–81.

Joint Committee on New York Drug Law Evaluation
1977   *The Nation's Toughest Drug Law: Evaluation of the New York Experience.* New York: Association of the Bar of the City of New York.

Jones, Allison North
2002   "Strong Views, Pro and Con, on Ads Linking Drug Use to Terrorism." *New York Times* (April 2): C7.

Jones, Charisse
1995   "Crack and Punishment: Is Race the Issue?" *New York Times* (October 16): 1, 9.

Jones, Coryl LaRue and Robert J. Battjes
1987   "The Context and Caveats of Prevention Research on Drug Abuse." Pages 1–12 in *Etiology of Drug Abuse: Implications for Prevention,* edited by Coryl LaRue Jones and Robert J. Battjes. Rockville, MD: National Institute on Drug Abuse.

Jones, Hendrée E.
2004   "Practical Considerations for the Clinical Use of Buprenorpine." *Perspectives* 2 (August): 4–24.

Jones, Kenneth L., Louis W. Shainberg, and Curtis O. Byer
1979   *Drugs and Alcohol,* 3rd ed. New York: Harper and Row.

Jourbert, Lucien
1987   "The Oral Dose Is Safer," Letter to the *New York Times* (August 15): 14.

Joy, Janet E., Stanley J. Watson Jr., and John A. Benson Jr., eds.
1999   *Marijuana and Medicine: Assessing the Science Base.* Washington, DC: National Academy Press.

Judson, Barbara A. and Avram Goldstein
1986   "Uses of Naloxone in the Diagnosis and Treatment of Heroin Addiction." Pages 1–18 in *Research on the Treatment of Narcotic Addiction: State of the Art,* edited by James R. Cooper, Fred Altman, Barry S. Brown, and Dorynne Czechowicz. Rockville, MD: National Institute on Drug Abuse.

Judson, George
1995   "Study Finds AIDS Risk to Addicts Drops if Sale of Syringes is Legal." *New York Times* (August 30): 1, 12.

Kajdasz, D. K., J. W. Moore, H. Donepudi, C. E. Cochrane, and R. J. Malcolm
1999   "Cardiac and Mood-Related Changes during Short-Term Abstinence from Crack Cocaine: The Identification of Possible Withdrawal Phenomena." *American Journal of Drug and Alcohol Abuse* 25(4): 629–37.

Kandel, Denise K.
1974   "Interpersonal Influences on Adolescent Illegal Drug Use." Pages 207–40 in *Drug Use: Epidemiological and Sociological Approaches,* edited by Eric Josephson and Eleanor E. Carroll. New York: Wiley.

Kandel, Denise K. and Mark Davies
1991   "Friendship Networks, Intimacy, and Illicit Use in Young Adulthood: A Comparison of Two Competing Theories." *Criminology* 29 (August): 441–67.

Kaplan, David
1999   "The Golden Age of Crime." *U.S. News & World Report* (November 29): 42–44.

Kaplan, John
1983a   "Drugs and Crime: Legal Aspects." Pages 643–52 in the *Encyclopedia of Crime and Justice,* edited by Sanford H. Kadish. New York: The Free Press.
1983b   *The Hardest Drug: Heroin and Public Policy.* Chicago: University of Chicago Press.

Karch, Steven B.
1998   *A Brief History of Cocaine.* Boca Raton, FL: CRC Press.
1996   *The Pathology of Drug Abuse: Second Edition.* Boca Raton, FL: CRC Press.

Katcher, Leo
1959   *The Big Bankroll: The Life and Times of Arnold Rothstein.* New York: Harper & Brothers.

Katel, Peter
1995   "Justice: The Trouble with Informants." *Pressweek* (January 30): 48.

Kauffman, Eda, Martha Morrison Dore, and Lani Nelson-Zlupko
1995   "The Role of Women's Therapy Groups in the Treatment of Chemical Dependence." *American Journal of Orthopsychiatry* 65 (July): 355–63.

Kaufman, Edward
1994   *Psychotherapy of Addicted Persons.* New York: Guilford Press.

Kay, David C.
1973   "Federal Civil Commitment in the Federal Medical Program for Opiate Addicts." Pages 17–35 in *Yearbook of Drug Abuse,* edited by Leon Brill and Earnest Harms. New York: Behavioral Publications.

Kempe, Frederick
1990 *Divorcing the Dictator: America's Bungled Affair with Noriega.* New York: Putnam's Sons.
Kenneally, Scott
2007 "Use as Directed." *Details* (February): 61–62.
Kennedy, Randy
1995 "Death Highlights Drug's Lethal Allure to Doctors." *New York Times* (November 11): 1, 10.
Kerr, Peter
1988 "Crime Study Finds High Drug Use at Time of Arrest." *New York Times* (January 22): 1, 9.
Kershaw, Sarah
2006 "Through Indian Lands, Drugs' Shadowy Trail." *New York Times* (February 19): 1, 26–27.
2005 "Violent New Front in Drug War Opens on the Canadian Border." *New York Times* (March 5): 1, 8.
Kertzner, Robert M.
1987 "Individual Psychotherapy of Cocaine Abuse." Pages 138–55 in *Cocaine Abuse: New Directions in Treatment and Research,* edited by Henry I. Spitz and Jeffrey S. Rosecan. New York: Brunner/Mazel.
Khantzian, Edward J.
1985 "The Self-Medication Hypothesis of Addictive Disorders: Focus on Heroin and Cocaine Dependence." *American Journal of Psychiatry* 142: 1259–64.
1980 "An Ego/Self Theory of Substance Dependence: A Contemporary Psychoanalytic Perspective," Pages 29–33 in *Theories on Drug Abuse: Selected Contemporary Perspectives,* edited by Dan J. Lettieri, Mollie Sayers, and Helen Wallenstein Pearson. Rockville, MD: National Institute on Drug Abuse.
Khantzian, Edward J., John E. Mack, and Alan F. Schatzberg
1974 "Heroin Use as an Attempt to Cope: Clinical Observations." *American Journal of Psychiatry* 131 (February): 160–64.
Kidorf, Michael and Maxine L. Stitzer
1996 "Contingent Use of Take-Home and Split Dosing to Reduce Illicit Drug Use of Methadone Patients." *Behavior Therapy* 27 (Winter): 41–51.
Kilian, Michael and David Mendell
2002 "$1 Million in Drugs Seized in Base Sting." *Chicago Tribune* (July 3): 10.
King, Rufus
1969 *Gambling and Organized Crime.* Washington, DC: Public Affairs Press.
Kinlock, Timothy W., Thomas E. Hanlon, and David N. Nurco
1998 "Heroin Use in the United States: History and Present Developments." Pages 1–30 in *Heroin in the Age of Crack-Cocaine,* edited by James A. Inciardi and Laura D. Harrison. Thousand Oaks, CA: Sage.
Kirkey, Sharon
2006 "Second-hand Smoke Linked to Behaviour Problems." *Ottawa Citizen* (May 1): Internet.

Kirsebbaum, Susan
2002 "Darling, pass the Xanax: Trading Prescription Painkillers and Sedatives is the Latest Trend at Parties." *Harper's Bazaar* (May): 108–10.
Klam, Matthew
2001 "Experiencing Ecstasy." *New York Times Magazine* (January 21): 38–43, 64, 68, 78–79.
Kleiman, Mark A. R.
1992 *Against Excess: Drug Policy for Results.* New York: Basic Books.
1989 *Marijuana: Costs of Abuse, Costs of Control.* New York: Greenwood Press.
1988 "Crackdowns: The Effects on Intensive Enforcement on Retail Heroin Dealing." Pages 3–18 in *Street-Level Drug Enforcement: Examining the Issues,* edited by Marcia R. Chaiken. Washington, DC: U.S. Government Printing Office.
1985 "Drug Enforcement and Organized Crime." Pages 67–87 in *The Politics and Economics of Organized Crime.* Lexington, MA: D.C. Heath.
Kleinknecht, William
1996 *The New Ethnic Mobs: The Changing Face of Organized Crime in America.* New York: Free Press.
Kocieniewski, David
1998 "In Drug War, Risky Tactic Yields a Fatality." *New York Times* (January 21): 18.
Koerber, Brendan I.
1997 "Extreme." *U.S. Press and World Report* (July 30): 50–60. BW: U.S. New & . . . ?
Kolata, Gina
1996 "The Unwholesome Tale of the Herb Market." *New York Times* (April 21): 6E.
1989a "Medications May Ease Craving for Cocaine." *New York Times* (March 7): 21, 23.
1989b "Experts Finding New Hope on Treating Crack Addicts." *New York Times* (August 24): 1, 9.
Koob, George F., Barak Caine, Athina Markou, Luigi Pulvirenti, and Freidbert Weiss
1994 "Role for the Mesocortical Dopamine System in the Motivating Effects of Cocaine." Pages 1–16 in *Neurobiological Models for Evaluating Mechanisms Underlying Cocaine Addiction,* edited by Lynda Erinoff and Roger M. Brown. Rockville, MD: National Institute on Drug Abuse.
Korf, Dirk J., Heleen Riper, and Bruce Bullington
1999 "Windmills in Their Minds? Drug Policy and Drug Research in the Netherlands." Journal of Drug Issues 29 (3): 451–72.
Kornblut, Anne E.
2006 "All (Puff) in Favor (Puff) Say Aye (Wheeze)." *New York Times* (February 12): WK 3.
Kosten, Thomas R.
1993 "Clinical and Research Perspectives on Cocaine Abuse: The Pharmacology of Cocaine Abuse." Pages 48–56 in *Cocaine Treatment: Research and Clinical Perspectives,* edited by Frank M. Tims and Carl G. Leukefeld. Rockville, MD: National Institute on Drug Abuse.

Kotulak, Ronald
2002a   "Experts Say Love of Nicotine is all in the Mind."
          Chicago Tribune (March 14): 1, 18.
2002b   "Traffic Signal: Red Light, Green Light and
          Booze." *Chicago Tribune* (September 29): Sec 2:
          1, 7.
1997   "Unlocking Secrets of Alcohol's Grip." *Chicago
          Tribune* (August 24): 1, 16.
Krauss, Clifford
2003   "Canada Parts with the U.S. on Drugs." *New
          York Times* (May 19): 9.
2000   "Bolivia Wiping out Coca, at a Price." *New York
          Times* (October 23): 10.
1999a   "Bolivia, at Some Risk, Is Making Big Gains in
          Eradicating Coca." *New York Times*
          (May 9): 6.
1999b   "Peru's Drug Successes Erode as Traffickers
          Adapt." *New York Times* (August 19): 3.
Krauss, Clifford and Douglas Frantz
1995   "Cali Drug Cartel Using U.S. Business to
          Launder Cash." *New York Times* (October 30):
          1, 13.
Kreek, Mary Jeanne
1997   "Goals and Rationale for Pharmacotherapeutic
          Approach in Treating Cocaine Dependence:
          Insights from Basic and Clinical Research."
          Pages 5–35 in *Medication Development for the
          Treatment of Cocaine Dependence: Issues in
          Clinical Efficacy Trials*. Rockville, MD: National
          Institute on Drug Abuse.
1987   "Tolerance and Dependence: Implications for the
          Pharmacological Treatment of Addiction."
          Pages 53–62 in *Problems of Drug Dependence,
          1986*, edited by Louis S. Harris. Rockville, MD:
          National Institute on Drug Abuse.
Kristoff, Nicholas D.
1999   "1492: The Prequel." *New York Times Magazine*
          (June 6): 80–86.
Krystal, Henry and Herbert A. Raskin
1970   *Drug Dependence: Aspects of Ego Function*.
          Detroit: Wayne State University Press.
Kummer, Corby
1999   "Smoky Scotch." *Atlantic Monthly* (December):
          115–19.

Labaton, Stephen
1989   "New Tactics in the War on Drugs Tilt Scales
          of Justice Off Balance." *New York Times*
          (December 29): 1, 14.
Lacey, Marc
2006   "Keystone Kops? No Kenyans, but Often
          Similarly Inept." *New York Times* (April 18): 4.
Lambert, Bruce
2006   "Law Enforcement Agencies Break 2 Major Drug
          Rings." *New York Times* (March 31): B3.
1996   "Fears Prompting Crackdown on Legal Herbal
          Stimulant." *New York Times* (April 23): 12.
Lamour, Catherine and Michael R. Lamberti
1974   *The Second Opium War*. London, England: Allen
          Lane.

Lang, Alan R.
1983   "Addicting Personality: A Viable Construct?"
          Pages 157–235 in *Commonalities in Substance
          Abuse and Habitual Behavior*, edited by Peter K.
          Levison, Dean R. Gerstein, and Deborah R.
          Maloff. Lexington, MA: D.C. Heath.
Latessa, Edward J. and Melissa M. Moon
1992   "The Effectiveness of Acupuncture in an
          Outpatient Drug Treatment Program." *Journal of
          Contemporary Criminal Justice* 8 (December):
          317–31.
Latimer, Dean and Jeff Goldberg
1981   *Flowers in the Blood: The Story of Opium*. New
          York: Franklin Watts.
Law Commission of Canada (LCC)
2003   *What is a Crime? Challenges and Alternatives.
          Discussion Paper*. Quebec, Canada: LCC.
Lawson, Gary W.
1992   "A Biopsychological Model of Adolescent
          Substance Abuse." Pages 3–10 in *Adolescent
          Substance Abuse*, edited by Gary W. Lawson and
          Ann W. Lawson. Gaithersburg, MD: Aspen
          Publications.
Leary, Warren E.
1995   "Report Endorses Needle Exchanges as AIDS
          Strategy." *New York Times* (September 20): 1, 14.
Ledwith, William E. (Chief of International Operations,
Drug Enforcement Administration)
2000   "Statement Before the House Government
          Reform Committee, Subcommittee on Criminal
          Justice, Drug Policy, and Human Resources."
          February 15.
Lee, Rensselaer III
1995   "Drugs in Communist and Former Communist
          Countries." *Transnational Organized Crime* 1
          (Summer): 193–205.
Legrand, Lisa N., William G. Iacono, and Matt McGue
2005   "Predicting Addiction: Behavioral Genetics Uses
          Twins and Time to Decipher the Origins of
          Addiction and Learn Who is Most Vulnerable."
          American Scientist 93 (March–April): 140–48.
Lemert, Edwin M.
1951   *Social Pathology*. New York: McGraw-Hill.
Lerner, Steven E.
1980   "Phencyclidine Abuse in Perspective." Pages
          13–23 in *Phencyclidine Abuse Manual*, edited
          by Mary Tuma McAdams, Ronald L. Linder,
          Steven E. Lerner, and Richard Stanley Burns.
          Los Angeles: University of California
          Extension.
Leshner, Alan I.
1997   "Addiction is a Brain Disease and It Matters."
          Science: 278: 45–47.
1999a   "Editorial: Science is Revolutionizing Our View
          of Addiction—and What to Do About It."
          American Journal of Psychiatry 156 (January):
          1–3.
1999b   "Research Shows Effects of Prenatal Cocaine
          Are Subtle But Significant." *NIDA Notes* 14 (3):
          3–4.

Leukefeld, Carl C. and Frank M. Tims, eds.
1988   *Compulsory Treatment of Drug Abuse: Research and Clinical Practice*. Rockville, MD: National Institute on Drug Abuse.

Levine, Michael
1990   *Deep Cover*. New York: Delacorte.

Levinthal, Charles F.
1988   *Messengers of Paradise: Opiates and the Brain*. Garden City, NY: Doubleday.

Lewin, Tamar
2002   "With Court Nod, Parents Debate School Drug Tests." *New York Times* (September 29): 1, 27.
1992   "Drug Verdict over Infants is Voided." *New York Times* (July 24): B6.
1991   "Guilt Upheld for Drug Delivery by Umbilical Cord." *New York Times* (April 20): 1, 6.

Li, Guohua, Gordon S. Smith, and Susan P. Baker
1994   "Drinking Behavior in Relation to Cause of Death Among US Adults." *American Journal of Public Health* 84 (9): 1402–6.

Lidz, Charles W. and Andrew L. Walker
1980   *Heroin, Deviance and Morality*. Beverley Hills, CA: Sage.

Lin, Geraline and Richard A. Glennon, eds.
1994   *Hallucinogens: An Update*. Rockville, MD: National Institute on Drug Abuse.

Linder, Ronald L., Steven E. Lerner and R. Stanley Burns
1981   *PCP: The Devil's Dust*. Belmont, CA: Wadsworth.

Lindesmith, Alfred C.
1968   *Addiction and Opiates*. Chicago: Aldine.

Lindesmith, Alfred C. and John H. Gagnon
1964   "Anomie and Drug Addiction." Pages 158–88 in *Anomie and Deviant Behavior*, edited by Marshall B. Clinard. New York: Free Press.

Lipton, Douglas S.
1995   *The Effectiveness of Treatment for Drug Abusers Under Criminal Justice Supervision*. Washington, DC: National Institute of Justice.

Liu, Jainhong, Dengke Zhou, Allen E. Liska, Steven F. Messner, Marvin D. Krohn, Lening Zhang, and Zhou Lu
1998   "Status, Power, and Sentencing in China." *Justice Quarterly* 15 (June): 289–300.

Liu, Liang Y.
1994   *Substance Use Among Youths at High Risk of Dropping Out: Grades 7-12 in Texas, 1992*. Austin: Texas Commission on Alcohol and Drug Abuse.

Lo, Celia C.
2003   "An Application of Social Conflict Theory to Arrestees' Use of Cocaine and Opiates." *Journal of Drug Issues* 33 (Winter): 237–67.

London, Perry
1964   *The Modes and Morals of Psychotherapy*. New York: Holt Rinehart and Winston.

Lubasch, Arnold H.
1990   "Trial Shows the Rich Rewards of a Federal Drug Informant." *New York Times* (November 4): 23.

Luft, Kerry
1995   "For Busted Drug Lord, Terror too Crass." *Chicago Tribune* (June 15): 3.

Lukas, Scott E.
1996   *Proceedings of The National Consensus Meeting on the Use, Abuse and Sequelae of Abuse of Methamphetamine with Implications for Prevention, Treatment and Research*. Rockville, MD: U.S. Department of Health and Human Services Substance Abuse and Mental Health Services.

Lupsha, Peter A.
1991   "Drug Lords and Narco-Corruption: The Players Change But the Game Continues." *Crime, Law and Social Change* 16: 41–58.
1990   "The Geopolitics of Organized Crime: Some Comparative Models from Latin American Drug Trafficking Organizations." Paper presented at the annual meeting of the American Society of Criminology, Baltimore, November.

Lyall, Sarah
2002   "Easing to Marijuana Laws Angers Many Britons." *New York Times* (August 12): 3.

Lyman, Rick
1998   "Rights Query on Killing of Immigrant." *New York Times* (October 21): 18.

Mabry, Donald J.
1995   "The U.S. Military and the War on Drugs." Pages 43–60 in *Drug Trafficking in the Americas*, edited by Bruce M. Bagley and William O. Walker III. New Brunswick, NJ: Transaction Publishers.

MacCoun, Robert, Beau Kilmer, and Peter Reuter
2002   "Research on Drug-Crime Linkages: The Next Generation." Drugs and Crime Research forum draft.

MacCoun, Robert and Peter Reuter
1997   "Interpreting Dutch Cannabis Policy: Reasoning by Analogy in the Legalization Debate." *Science* 278 (October): 47–52.

MacDonald, James and Michael Agar
1994   "What Is a Trip—and Why Take One?" Pages 9–36 in *LSD: Still with Us After all These Years*, edited by Leigh A. Henderson and William J. Glass. New York: Lexington Books.

MacKenzie, Doris Layton
2006   *What Works in Corrections: Reducing the Criminal Activities of Offenders and Delinquents*. New York: Cambridge University Press.

Maddux, James F. and David P. Desmond
1981   *Careers of Opioid Users*. New York: Praeger.

Magura, Stephen, Cathy Casriel, Douglas S. Goldsmith, David L. Strug, and Douglas S. Lipton
1988   "Contingency Contracting with Polydrug-Abusing Methadone Patients." *Addictive Behaviors* 13: 113–18.

Magura, Stephen, Sung-Yeon Kang, and Janet L. Shapiro
1995   "Measuring Cocaine Use by Hair Analysis Among Criminally-Involved Youth." *Journal of Drug Issues* 25 (Fall): 683–701.

Males, Mike
2006   "This is Your Brain on Drugs, Dad." *New York Times* (January 3): 21.

Maltzman, Irving
1994   "Why Alcoholism Is a Disease." *Journal of Psychoactive Drugs* 26 (January/March): 13–31.

Manderson, Desmond
1999   "Symbolism and Racism in Drug History." *Drug and Alcohol Review* 18 (2): 179–86.
Mann, Arnold
2004a   "Successful Trial Caps 25-Year Buprenorphine Development Effort." *NIDA Notes* 19 (3): 7–9.
2004b   "Cocaine Abusers' Cognitive Deficits Compromise Treatment Outcomes." *NIDA Notes* 19 (1): 4–5.
Mann, Robert E., Reginald G. Smart, and Richard Govoni
2004   *The Epidemiology of Alcoholic Liver Disease.* Bethesda, MD: National Institute on Alcohol Abuse and Alcoholism.
Mansnerus, Laura
1996   "Timothy Leary, Pied Piper of Psychodelic 60's, Dies at 75." *New York Times* (June 1): 1, 11.
Marion, Ira J.
2005   "Methadone Treatment at Forty." *Science and Practice Perspectives* 3 (December): 25–31.
Markel, Howard
2002   "For Addicts, Relief May Be an Office Visit Away." *New York Times* (October 27): WK 14.
Marlatt, G. Alan, Julian M. Somers, and Susan F. Tapert
1993   "Harm Reduction: Application to Alcohol Abuse Problems." Pages 147–66 in *Behavioral Treatments for Drug Abuse and Dependence,* edited by Lisa Simon Onken, John D. Blaine, and John J. Boren. Rockville, MD: National Institute on Drug Abuse.
Marlowe, Ann
1999   *How to Stop Time: Heroin from A to Z.* New York: Basic Books.
Marriott, Michael
1989   "Struggle and Hope from the Ashes of Drugs." *New York Times* (October 22): 1, 22.
Marshall, Ineke Haen and Chris E. Marshall
1994   "Drug Prevention in the Netherlands: A Low Key Approach." Pages 205–31 in *Between Prohibition and Legalization: The Dutch Experiment in Drug Policy,* edited by Ed. Leuw and I. Haen Marshall. Amsterdam: Kugler Publications.
Martin, B. R., S. Childers, A. Howlett, R. Mechoulam, and R. Pertwee
1994   "Cannabinoid Receptors: Pharmacology, Second Messenger Systems and Endogenous Ligands." Pages 55–60 in *Problems of Drug Dependence, 1993.* Vol. I, edited by Louis S. Harris. Rockville, MD: National Institute on Drug Abuse.
Martin, Douglas
1990   "A Big Bribe Helps Mothers Flee the Seduction of Crack." *New York Times* (March 7): 13.
Martin, Susan E., Christopher D. Maxwell, Helene R. White, and Yan Zhang
2004   "Trends in Alcohol Use, Cocaine Use, and Crime: 1989–1998." *Journal of Drug Issues* 34 (Spring): 333–60.
Marzulli, John
2005   "Jury Convicts 3 in JFK Drug Ring." *New York Daily News* (June 14): XQ 1.

Massing, Michael
1999   "The Real Methadone Problem." *New York* (January 11): 40–43, 102.
1990   "In the Cocaine War, the Jungle Is Winning." *New York Times Magazine* (March 4): 26, 88, 90, 92.
Mathias, Robert
2003   "School Prevention Program Effective with Youths at Risk for Substance Abuse." *NIDA Notes* 18 (5): 12–13.
2002   "Chronic Solvent Abusers Have More Brain Abnormalities and Cognitive Impairments Than Cocaine Abusers." *NIDA Notes* 17 (4): 5–6, 12.
2000   "Methamphetamine Brain Damage in Mice More Extensive Than Previously Thought." *NIDA Notes* 15 (4): 1, 10.
1999   "Study Shows How Genes Can Help Protect from Addiction." *NIDA Notes* 14 (March): 5, 9.
Mathias, Robert and Patrick Zickler
2001   "NIDA Conference Highlights Scientific Findings on MDMA/Ecstasy." *NIDA Notes* 16 (5): 1, 5–8, 12.
Mattison, J. B.
1883   "Opium Addiction Among Medical Men." *Medical Record* 23 (June 9): 621–23. Reproduced in Morgan, 1974, pages 62–66.
May, Clifford D.
1988a   "Drug Enforcement: Once-Lonely Voice Finds an Audience." *New York Times* (June 6): 12.
1988b   "Coca-Cola Discloses an Old Secret." *New York Times* (July 1): 25, 29.
Mayes, Linda G.
1992   "Prenatal Cocaine Exposure and Young Children's Development." *Annals* 521 (May): 11–27.
McBride, Duane C. and Clyde B. McCoy
1981   "Crime and Drug-Abusing Behavior." *Criminology* 19 (August): 281–302.
McCance, Elinore F.
1997   "Overview of Potential Treatment Medications for Cocaine Dependence." Pages 36–72 in *Medication Development for the Treatment of Cocaine Dependence: Issues in Clinical Efficacy Trials,* edited by Betty Tai, Nora Chiang, and Peter Bridge. Rockville, MD: National Institute on Drug Abuse.
McConnaughey, Janet
2000   "Study: Smoking' Dangers Immediate." *Associated Press* (March 9): Internet.
McCoy, Alfred W.
1991   *The Politics of Heroin: CIA Complicity in the Global Heroin Trade.* Brooklyn, NY: Lawrence Hill Books.
1972   *The Politics of Heroin in Southeast Asia.* New York: Harper and Row.
McCoy, H. Virginia, Christine Miles, and James A. Inciardi
1995   "Survival Sex: Inner-City Women and Crack-Cocaine." Pages 172–77 in *The American Drug Scene: An Anthology,* edited by James A. Inciardi and Karen McElrath. Los Angeles: Roxbury.

McDougall, Christopher
2006   "The Junkie in the O. R." *Men's Health*
(November): 186–91; 193.

McElrath, Karen
1995   "Alcoholics Anonymous." Pages 314–17 in *The American Drug Scene: An Anthology,* edited by James A. Inciardi and Karen McElrath. Los Angeles: Roxbury.

McFadden, Robert D.
2005   "Drug Suspect in Afghan Ring is Sent to U.S." *New York Times* (October 25): B1, 2.

McFarland, George C.
1989   *Drug Abuse Indicators Trend Report, District of Columbia.* Washington, DC: Alcohol and Drug Abuse Services Administration.

McGehee, Daniel S., Mark J. S. Heath, Shari Gelber, Piroska Devay, Lorna W. Role
1995   "Nicotine Enhancement of Fast Excitatory Synaptic Transmission in CNS by Presynaptic Receptors." *Science* 269 (September 22): 1692–96.

McGlothlin, William H., M. Douglas Anglin, and B. D. Wilson
1978   "Narcotic Addiction and Crime." *Criminology,* 16: 293–315.

McIntosh, Lee
1988   "Letter to the Editor." *New York Times* (June 39): 26.

McKim, William A.
1991   *Drugs and Behavior: An Introduction to Behavioral Pharmacology,* 2nd ed. Englewood Cliffs, NJ: Prentice-Hall.

McKinley, James C. Jr.
2007   "Mexico's Latest War on Drug Gangs is off to a Rapid Start." *New York Times* (January 27): 10.
2006   "With Beheadings and Attacks, Drug Gangs Terrorize Mexico." *New York Times* (October 26): 1, 12.

McKinley, Jesse
2006   "Marijuana Fight Envelops Wharf in San Francisco." *New York Times* (July 3): 1, 13.

McMillan, Brian and Mark Conner
2002   "Drug Use and Cognitions About Drug Use Amongst Students: Changes Over the University Career." *Journal of Youth and Adolescence* 31 (June): 221–30.

McNeil, Donald G. Jr.
2003   "Research on Ecstasy is Clouded by Errors." *New York Times* (December 2): F1, 4.
2002   "Study in Primate Show Brain Damage from Doses of Ecstasy." *New York Times* (September 27): 26.

McQueen, Anjetta
1999   "No Loans for Student Drug Offenders." Associated Press (October 26). Internet.

McWilliams, John C.
1992   "Through the Past Darkly: The Politics and Policies of America's Drug War." Pages 5–41 in *Drug Control Policy: Essays in Historical and Comparative Perspective,* edited by William O. Walker III. University Park, PA: Pennsylvania State University.

Meddis, Sam
1993   "Is the Drug War Racist?" *USA Today* (July 23): 1, 2.

Meier, Barry
2001   "At Painkiller Trouble Spot, Signs Seen as Alarming Didn't Alarm Drug's Maker." *New York Times* (December 10): 16.

Meier, Barry and Melody Peterson
2001   "Sales of Painkiller Grew Rapidly, but Success Brought a High Cost." *New York Times* (March 5): 1, 15.

Meltzer, Herbert L.
1979   *The Chemistry of Human Behavior.* Chicago: Nelson-Hall.

Melzack, Ronald
1990   "The Tragedy of Needless Pain." *Scientific American* 262 (February): 27–33.

Mendelson, Bruce D. and Linda Harrison
1989   *Drug Use in Denver and Colorado.* Denver: Colorado Alcohol and Drug Use Division.

Mendelson, Jack H. and Nancy K. Mello
1995   "Alcohol, Sex, and Aggression." Pages 50–56 in *The American Drug Scene: An Anthology,* edited by James A. Inciardi and Karen McElrath. Los Angeles: Roxbury.

Merlin, Mark David
1984   *On the Trail of the Ancient Opium Poppy.* Rutherford, NJ: Fairleigh Dickinson University Press.

Merriam, John E.
1989   "National Media Coverage of Drug Issues, 1983–1987." Pages 21–28 in *Communication Campaigns About Drugs: Government, Media, and the Public,* edited by Pamela J. Shoemaker. Hillside, NJ: Lawrence Erlbaum Associates.

Merton, Robert
1964   "Anomie, Anomia, and Social Interaction." Pages 213–42 in *Anomie and Deviant Behavior,* edited by Marshall B. Clinard. New York: Free Press.

Mieczkowski, Thomas
1995   *Hair Analysis as a Drug Detector.* Washington, DC: National Institute of Justice.
1986   "Geeking up and Throwing Down: Heroin Street Life in Detroit." *Criminology* 24 (November): 645–66.

Miller, Henry I.
2006   "Reefer Medicine." *New York Times* (April 28): 23.

Miller, Norman S.
1995   *Addiction Psychiatry: Current Diagnosis and Treatment.* New York: Wiley.

Miller, Norman S. and Mark S. Gold
1990   "Benzodiazepines: Reconsidered." *Advances in Alcohol and Substance Abuse* 8 (3/4): 67–81.

Miller, Walter B.
1958   "Lower Class Culture as a Generating Milieu of Gang Delinquency." *Journal of Social Issues* 14: 5–19.

Miller, William R. and Reid K. Hester
1980   "Treating the Problem Drinker: Modern Approaches." Pages 11–141 in *The Addictive Behaviors,* edited by William R. Miller. New York: Pergamon.

Milloy, Ross E.
2002   "A Forbidding Landscape That's Eden for
        Peyote." *New York Times* (May 7): 14.
Minnesota Department of Human Services
1987   *Chemical Dependency Program Division Biennial
        Report.* St. Paul, MN: Department of Human
        Services.
Mintz, John
1997   "Getting a Financial High from Rope."
        Washington Post National Weekly Edition
        (January 13): 18–19.
Miron, Jeffrey A.
2001   "The Economics of Drug Prohibition and Drug
        Legalization." *Social Research* 68 (Fall): 835–57.
Misner, Dinah L. and Jame M. Sullivan
1999   "Mechanism of Cannabinoid Effects on Long-
        Term Potentiation and Depression in
        Hippocampal CA1 Neurons." *Journal of
        Neuroscience* 19 (August): 6795–6805.
Missouri Division of Alcohol and Drug Abuse (MDADA)
1999   *Status Report on Missouri's Alcohol and Drug
        Abuse Problems.* Jefferson City, MO: MDADA.
Molgaard, Virigina K., Richard L. Spoth, and Cleve
Redmond
2000   *Competency Training.* Washington, DC: Office of
        Juvenile Justice and Delinquency Prevention.
Molotsky, Irvin
1999   "Study Links Teen-Age Substance Abuse and
        Parental Ties." *New York Times* (August 31): 14.
Moody, John
1991   "A Day with the Chess Player." *Time* (July 1):
        34–36.
Moore, Mark H.
1977   *Buy and Bust: The Effective Regulation of an Illicit
        Market in Heroin.* Lexington, MA: D.C. Heath.
Moore, Mark H. and Mark A. R. Kleiman
1989   *The Police and Drugs.* Washington, DC: U.S.
        Government Printing Office.
Moore, Molly
2001   "Iranians Wage War on Afghan Drugs." *Chicago
        Tribune* (July 19): 10.
Morales, Edmundo
1989   *Cocaine: White Gold Rush in Peru.* Tucson:
        University of Arizona Press.
1986   "Coca and Cocaine Economy and Social Change
        in the Andes of Peru." *Economic Development
        and Social Change* 35: 144–61.
Moras, Karla
1993   "Substance Abuse Research: Outcome
        Measurement Conundrums." Pages 217–48 in
        *Behavioral Treatments for Drug Abuse and
        Dependence,* edited by Lisa Simon Onken, John
        D. Blaine, and John J. Boren. Rockville, MD:
        National Institute on Drug Abuse.
Morgan, Howard Wayne
1981   *Drugs in America: A Social History, 1800–1980.*
        Syracuse, NY: Syracuse University Press.
Morgan, Howard Wayne, ed.
1974   *Yesterday's Addicts: American Society and Drug
        Abuse, 1865–1920.* Norman: University of
        Oklahoma Press.

Morgan, Thomas
1989   "16 Charged in Scheme to Launder Millions."
        New York Times (May 14): 24.
Morgenthau, Robert M.
1988   "We Are Losing the War on Drugs." *New York
        Times* (February 16): 27.
Morojele, Neo K. and Judith S. Brook
2001   "Adolescent Precursors of Intensity of Marijuana
        and Other Illicit Drug Use Among Adult
        Initiators." *Journal of Genetic Psychology* 162
        (December): 430–51.
Moss, Andrew
1977   "Methadone's Rise and Fall." Pages 135–53 in
        Drugs and Politics, edited by Paul E. Rock. New
        Brunswick, NJ: Transaction Books.
Murphy, Dean E.
2003   "Jurors Who Convicted Marijuana Grower
        Seek New Trial" *New York Times*
        (February 5): 13.
Murray, Ian and Stewart Tendler
1999   "Cocaine Deaths on the Increase." *London Times*
        (August 9): 6.
Musto, David
1998   "The American Experience with Stimulants and
        Opiates." Pages 51–78 in *Perspectives on Crime
        and Justice: 1997–1998 Lecture Series.*
        Washington, DC: National Institute of Justice.
1987   *The American Disease: Origins of Narcotic
        Control, Expanded Edition.* New York: Oxford.
1973   *The American Disease: Origins of Narcotic
        Control.* New Haven, CT: Yale University Press.
Mydans, Seth
2003   "Thailand Police Crack Down in Deadly Fight
        Against Drugs." *New York Times* (February 17): 6.
Myers, Linnet
1995   "Europe Finds U.S. Drug War Lacking in Results."
        Chicago Tribune (November 2): 1, 24, 25.
Myers, Willard H. III
1995   "Orb Weavers—The Global Webs: The Structure and
        Activities of Transnational Ethnic Chinese Groups."
        Transnational Organized Crime 1 (Winter): 1–36.

Nadelmann, Ethan A.
1988   "U.S. Drug Policy: A Bad Export." *Foreign Policy*
        70 (Spring): 83–108.
Nahas, Gabriel and Nicholas A. Pace
1993   "Marijuana as Chemotherapy Aid Poses
        Hazards." Letter to the *New York Time*
        (December 4): 14.
Nash, Nathaniel C.
1992   "Cocaine Invades Chile, Scorning the Land
        Mines." *New York Times* (January 23): 6.
Nathan Peter E.
1988   "The Addictive Personality is the Behavior of the
        Addict." *Journal of Consulting and Clinical
        Psychology* 56 (April): 183–88.
National Center on Addiction and Substance Abuse
1998   *Behind Bars: Substance Abuse and America's
        Prison Population.* New York: National Center
        on Addiction and Substance Abuse at Columbia
        University.

National Commission on Marijuana and Drug Abuse
1973   *Drug Abuse in America: Problem in Perspective.* Washington, DC: U.S. Government Printing Office.

National Council on Crime and Delinquency
1974   "Drug Addiction: A Medical, Not a Law Enforcement Problem." *Crime and Delinquency* 20 (January): 4–9.

National Institute of Justice.
2002   *An Honest Chance: Perspectives on Drug Courts: Executive Summary.* Internet.
1995a   *Fact Sheet: Drug Related Crime 1994.* Washington, DC: National Institute of Justice.
1995b   *The Drug Court Movement.* Washington, DC: National Institute of Justice.

National Institute on Alcohol Abuse and Alcoholism (NIAAA)
2004   *Alcohol's Damaging Effects on the Brain.* Bethesda, MD: NIAAA.
2003   *Genetics of Alcoholism.* NIAAA 60 (July): Internet.
1997   *Ninth Special Report to the U.S. Congress on Alcohol and Health.* Rockville, MD: NIAAA.

National Institute on Drug Abuse (NIDA)
2006   *MDMA Abuse.* Bethesda, MD: NIDA.
2005   *Prescription Drugs: Abuse and Addiction.* Bethesda, MD: NIDA. Internet.
2004   "Cigarettes and Other Nicotine Products" *National Institute on Drug Abuse Info Facts.* Internet.
2003   *Drug Addiction Treatment Methods.* Rockville, MD: NIDA.
2002a   "Methamphetamine: Abuse and Addiction." NIDA: Internet.
2002b   "Therapeutic Community." *National Institute on Drug Abuse Research Report.* Washington, DC: U.S. Department of Human Services.
2001a   *Crack and Cocaine.* Washington, DC: NIDA.
2001b   *Inhalants.* Internet. Bethesda, MD: NIDA.
2001c   *Lessons from Prevention Research.* Washington, DC: NIAA
2001d   "Nicotine Addiction." *NIDA Research Report.* Rockville, MD: NIDA.
2001e   "Ritalin." NIDA Infofax: Internet.
2000   "Update on Nicotine Addiction and Tobacco Research."*NIDA Notes* 15 (5): 15.
1999a   "Hallucinogens and Dissociative Drugs." *NIDA Research Report.* Rockville, MD: NIDA.
1999b   *Methamphetamine Abuse and Addiction.* Rockville, MD: NIDA.
1999c   *Rohypnol and GHB.* Bethesda, MD: NIDA.
1999d   "Thirteen Principles of Effective Drug Addiction Treatment." *NIDA Notes.* Rockville, MD: NIDA: Internet.
1999e   Press release, June 22.
1999f   Press release, September 1.
1999g   Press release, August 1.
1998a   "Methamphetamine Abuse and Addiction." *Research Report Series.* Washington, DC: NIDA.
1998b   *Nicotine Addiction.* Bethesda, MD: IDA.

1998c   Press release, May 6.
1998d   Press release, February 3.
1997a   *Drug Abuse Prevention for At-Risk Individuals.* Rockville, MD: NIDA.
1997b   *Problems of Drug Dependence 1997.* Rockville, MD: NIDA.
1997c   Press release, June 24.
1991   *Drug Abuse and Drug Abuse Research,* Rockville, MD: NIDA.
1987   *Drug Abuse and Drug Abuse Research.* Rockville, MD: NIDA.
1985   "Cocaine Use in America." *Prevention Networks* (April): 1–10.

National Narcotics Intelligence Consumers Committee
1998   *The Supply of Illicit Drugs to the United States.* Washington, DC: National Narcotics Intelligence Consumers Committee.

Navarro, Mireya
1996   "When Drug Kingpins Fall, Illicit Assets Buy a Cushion." *New York Times* (March 19): 1, C19.
1995   "Drug Sold Abroad by Prescription Becomes Widely Abused in U.S." *New York Times* (December 12): 1, 9.
1992   "New York City Resurrects Plan on Needle Swap." *New York Times* (May 14): 1, B8.

"Navy Holds 21 Sailors in Italy in Smuggling"
1996   *New York Times* (May 29): 13.

Nelson, Jack E., Helen W. Pearson, Mollie Sayers, and Thomas J. Glynn
1982   *Guide to Drug Abuse Research Terminology.* Washington, DC: Government Printing Office.

Nestler, Eric J.
2005   "The Neurobiology of Cocaine Addiction." *Science and Practice Perspectives* 5 (December): 4–10.

Newcomb, Michael D. and Peter M. Bentler
1989   "Substance Use and Abuse Among Children and Teenagers." *American Psychologist* 44 (February): 242–48.
1988   *Consequences of Adolescent Drug Use.* Newbury Park, CA: Sage.
1986   "Cocaine Use Among Adolescents: Longitudinal Associations with Social Context, Psychopathology, and Use of Other Substances." *Addictive Behavior* 11: 263–73.

"New Drug Law Leaves No Room for Mercy"
1989   *Chicago Tribune* (October 5): 28.

"New Hazard of Drinking in Pregnancy Is Found"
1996   *New York Times* (January 3): 9.

Newman, Robert G.
1977   *Methadone Management, Findings, and Prospects for the Future.* New York: Academic Press.

New York State Division of Substance Abuse Services
1986   *Annual Report.* Albany, NY: State Division of Substance Abuse Services.

Nichols, David E. and Robert Oberlender
1989   "Structure-Activity Relationships of MDMA-like Substances." Pages 1–28 in *Pharmacology and Toxicology of Amphetamine and Related Designer Drugs,* edited by Khursheed Asghar and Errol De Souza. Rockville, MD: National Institute on Drug Abuse.

Nielson, Amie L. and Frank R. Scarpitti
1997   "Changing the Behavior of Substance Abusers: Factors Influencing the Effectiveness of Therapeutic Communities." *Journal of Drug Issues* 27 (Spring): 279–98.

Nieves, Evelyn
1991   "Tainted Drug's Death Toll Rises to 10, Officials Say." *New York Times* (February 4): C11.

Noble, Barbara Presley
1992   "Testing Employees for Drugs." *New York Times* (April 12): F27.

Nolan, Kathleen
1990   "Protecting Fetuses from Prenatal Hazards: Whose Crimes? What Punishment?" *Criminal Justice Ethics* 9 (Winter/Spring): 13–23.

Northern, Helen
1969   *Social Work with Groups.* New York: Columbia University Press.

Nunes, Edward V. and Jeffrey S. Rosecan
1987   "Human Neurobiology of Cocaine." Pages 48–94 in *Cocaine Abuse: New Directions in Treatment and Research*, edited by Henry I. Spitz and Jeffrey S. Rosecan. New York: Brunner/Mazel.

Nurco, David N., John C. Ball, John W. Shaffer, and Thomas Hanlon
1985   "The Criminality of Narcotic Addicts." *Journal of Nervous and Mental Disorders* 173: 94–102.

Nyre, George F.
1985   *Final Evaluation Report, 1984–1985: Project DARE.* Los Angeles: Evaluation and Training Institute.

O'Brien, Charles P., Arthur Alterman, Dan Walter, Anna Rose Childress, and A. T. McLellan
1990   "Evaluation of Treatment for Cocaine Dependence." Pages 78–83 in *Problems of Drug Dependence 1989*, edited by Louis S. Harris. Rockville, MD: National Institute on Drug Abuse.

O'Brien, John and Jan Crawford Greenburg
1996   "Raids Reveal How Little Guys Climb the Drug Ladder." *Chicago Tribune* (May 3): 1, 21.

O'Brien, Robert and Sidney Cohen
1984   *Encyclopedia of Drug Abuse.* New York: Facts on File.

O'Connor, Anahad
2005   "Scientists Explore Meth's Role in Immune System." *New York Times* (February 23): F7.

2004   "New Ways to Loosen Addiction's Grip." *New York Times* 9(August 3): F1, 6.

O'Connor, Matt
1990   "Drug Court a Success, but It's Not Enough." *Chicago Tribune* (February 22): 1, 2.

O'Day, Patrick and Rex Venecia
1999   "Cazuelas: An Ethnographic Study of Drug Trafficking in a Small Mexican Border Town." *Journal of Contemporary Criminal Justice* 15 (November): 421–43.

O'Donnell, John A.
1969   *Narcotic Addicts in Kentucky.* Washington, DC: U.S. Government Printing Office.

Oetting, E. R. and Fred Beauvais
1990   "Adolescent Drug Use: Findings of National and Local Surveys." *Journal of Consulting and Clinical Psychology* 58 (August) 385–94.

Office of National Drug Control Policy
n.d.   *Who's Really in Prison for Marijuana?.* Washington, DC: Office of National Drug Control Policy.

2004a   *Pulse Check: Trends in Drug Abuse.* Washington, DC: Office of National Drug Control Policy.

2004b   *Predicting Heavy Drug Use.* Washington, DC: Office of National Drug Control Policy.

2004c   *The Challenge in Higher Education: Confronting and Reducing Substance Abuse on Campus.* Washington, DC: Office of National Drug Control Policy.

2004d   *National Drug Control Strategy.* Washington, DC: Office of National Drug Control Policy.

2004e   *National Synthetic Drugs Action Plan.* Washington, DC: Office of National Drug Control Policy.

2002a   *MDMA (Ecstasy).* Washington, DC: Office of National Drug Control Policy.

2002b   *National Drug Control Strategy.* Washington, DC: Office of National Drug Control Policy.

2002c   *Rohypnol.* Washington, DC: Office of National Drug Control Policy.

2002d   *What You Need to Know About Drug Testing in Schools.* Washington, DC: Office of National Drug Control Policy.

2001   *National Drug Control Strategy: 2001 Report.* Washington, DC: Office of National Drug Control Policy.

2000   *National Drug Control Strategy: 2000 Report.* Washington, DC: Office of National Drug Control Policy.

1998   *Rohypnol.* Washington, DC: Office of National Drug Control Policy.

1995   *Pulse Check: National Trends in Drug Abuse.* Washington, DC: Office of National Drug Control Policy.

1989   *National Drug Strategy.* Washington, DC: Office of National Drug Control Policy.

Ogborne, Alan C. and Frederick B. Glaser
1985   "Evaluating Alcoholics Anonymous." Pages 176–92 in *Alcoholism and Substance Abuse*, edited by Thomas E. Bratter and Gary G. Forrest. New York: Free Press.

O'Hare, P. A.
1992   "Preface: A Note on the Concept of Harm Reducation." Pages xiii–xvii in *The Reduction of Drug Related Harm*, edited by P. A. O'Hare, R. Newcome, A Matthews, E. C. Buning, and E. Drucker. London: Routledge.

O'Keefe, Michael and T. J. Quinn
2005   "Beating the Heat." *New York Daily News* (December 25): 88–91.

Olen, Helaine
1991   "Racial Tinge to Drug Testing of New Moms." *Chicago Tribune* (December 19): 14.

Olson, Elizabeth
1997   "Swiss to Weigh Fate of Clinics Offering Legal Heroin." *New York Times* (September 28): 3.

O'Malley, Pat O. and Stephen Mugford
1991   "The Demand for Intoxicating Commodities: Implications for the 'War on Drugs.'" *Social Justice* 18 (Winter): 49–75.

O'Neil, John
2006   "A Warning on Hazards of Smoke on Others." *New York Times* (June 28): 14.

Orenstein, Peggy
2002   "Staying Clean." *New York Times Magazine* (February 10): 34–39, 50–51, 74–75.

Oreskes, Michael
1990   "Drug War Underlines Fickleness of Public." *New York Times* (September 6): 12.

Orth, Maureen
2002   "Afghanistan's Deadly Habit." *Vanity Fair* (March): 150–52, 165–77.

Oscar-Berman, Marlene and Ksenija Marinkovic
2004   *Alcoholism and the Brain: An Overview.* Bethesda, MD: National Institute on Alcohol Abuse and Alcoholism.

O'Shea, Joanne and Beverly Powis
2003   *Drug Arrest Referral Schemes: A Case Study of Good Practice.* London, UK: Home Office.

Pace, Eric
1988   "Lois Burnham Wilson, a Founder of Al-Anon Groups, Is Dead at 97." *New York Times* (October 4): 15.

Packer, Herbert L.
1968   *The Limits of the Criminal Sanction.* Stanford, CA: Stanford University Press.

Palfai, Tibor and Henry Jankiewicz
1991   *Drugs and Human Behavior.* Dubuque, IA: Wm. C. Brown.

Parker, Suzi
1999   "Ammonia's New Cachet." *U.S. Press & World Report* (September 27): 37.

Parrott, Andy C.
1999   "Does Cigarette-Smoking Cause Stress?" *American Psychologist* 54 (October): 817–20.

Parsons, Loren H., Friedbert Weiss, and George F. Koob
1998   "Serotonin1B Receptor Stimulation Enhances Cocaine Reinforcement." *Journal of Neuroscience* 18 (December): 10078–89.

Passell, Peter
1990   "Cocaine Policy: Gauging Success." *New York Times* (June 6): C2.

Payne, Malcolm
1997   *Modern Social Work Theory,* 2nd ed. Chicago: Lyceum.

Peachey, J. E. and H. Lei
1988   "Assessment of Opioid Dependence with Naloxone." *British Journal of Addiction* 83: 193–201.

Pearson, Geoffrey
1987   *The New Heroin Users.* Oxford, England: Basil Blackwell.

Peele, Stanton
1995   *Diseasing of America.* San Francisco: Jossey-Bass.
1985   *The Meaning of Addiction: Compulsive Experience and Its Interpretation.* Lexington, MA: D.C. Heath.
1980   "Addiction to an Experience: A Social-Psychological Theory of Addiction." Pages 142–44 in *Theories of Drug Abuse: Selected Contemporary Perspectives,* edited by Dan J. Lettieri, Mollie Sayers, and Helen Wallenstein Pearson. Rockville, MD: National Institute on Drug Abuse.

Pennsylvania Crime Commission (PCC)
1990   *Organized Crime in Pennsylvania: A Decade of Change, 1990 Report.* Conshohocken, PA: PCC.

Pérez-Peña, Richard
2003   "New Drug Promises Shift in Treatment." *New York Times* (August 11): 1, B7.

Perl, Raphael
2000   "Organized Crime, Drug Trafficking, and Terrorism in a Changing Global Environment." Statement before the House Judiciary Committee, Subcommittee on Crime, December 13.

Pentz, Mary Ann
1985   "Social Competence and Self-Efficacy as Determinants of Substance Abuse in Adolescence." Pages 117–42 in *Coping and Substance Abuse,* edited by Saul Shiffman and Thomas Ashby Wills. Orlando, FL: Academic Press.

Permanent Subcommittee on Investigation, U.S. Senate
1981a   *International Narcotics Trafficking.* Washington, DC: U.S. Government Printing Office.
1981b   *Witness Security Program.* Washington, DC: U.S. Government Printing Office.

Peterson, Robert C., ed.
1980   *Marijuana Research Findings: 1980.* Rockville, MD: National Institute on Drug Abuse.

Peterson, Robert E.
1991   "Legalization: The Myth Exposed." Pages 324–55 in *Searching for Alternatives: Drug Control Policy in the United States,* edited by Melvyn B. Krauss and Edward P. Lazear. Stanford, CA: Hoover Institution.

"Pharmacy Update: How Addiction Occurs"
2003   *Chemist and Druggist* (December 20): 17.

Physicians' Desk Reference
1988   Oradell, NJ: Medical Economics Company.
1987   Oradell, NJ: Medical Economics Company.

Pickens, Roy W. and Travis Thompson
1984   "Behavioral Treatment of Drug Dependence." Pages 53–67 in *Behavioral Intervention Techniques in Drug Dependence Treatment,* edited by John Grabowski, Maxine L. Stitzer, and Jack E. Henningfield. Rockville, MD: National Institute on Drug Abuse.

Platt, Jerome J. and Christina Labate
1976   *Heroin Addiction: Theory, Research, and Treatment.* New York: John Wiley.

Platt, Jerome J., Mindy Widman, Victor Lidz, and Douglas Marlowe
1998   "Methadone Maintenance Treatment: Its Development and Effectiveness After 30 Years." Pages 160–87 in *Heroin in the Age of Crack-Cocaine,* edited by James A. Inciardi and Laura D. Harrison. Thousand Oaks, CA: Sage.

Poe, Janita and Dionne Searcey
1996   "Few Options Are Open for Drug Babies." *Chicago Tribune* (January 31): Sec. 2: 1, 4.

Poethig, Margaret
1988   "Q & A: Seizing the Assets of Drug Traffickers." *The Compiler* 8 (Winter): 11–12.

"Politics of Pot"
2006   *New York Times* (April 22): 14.

Pollan, Michael
1995   "How Pot Has Grown." *New York Times Magazine* (February 19): 31–35, 44, 50, 56–57.

"Poor Man's Heroin"
2001   *U.S. News and World Report* (February 12): 27.

Posner, Gerald L.
1988   *Warlords of Crime: Chinese Secret Societies—The New Mafia.* New York: McGraw-Hill.

Post, Robert M. and Susan R. B. Weiss
1988   "Psychomotor Stimulant vs. Local Anesthetic Effects of Cocaine: Role of Behavioral Sensitization and Kindling." Pages 217–38 in *Mechanisms of Cocaine Abuse and Toxicity,* edited by Doris Clouet, Khursheed Asghar, and Roger Brown. Rockville, MD: National Institute on Drug Abuse.

Powell, Bill
2007   "Inside the Afghan Drug War." *Time* (February 19): 29–37.

Preble, Edward and John J. Casey
1995   "Taking Care of Business—The Heroin Addict's Life on the Street." Pages 121–32 in *The American Drug Scene: An Anthology,* edited by James A. Inciardi and Karen McElrath. Los Angeles: Roxbury.

Préfontaine, D. C. and Yvon Dandurand
2004   "Terrorism and Organized Crime: Reflections on an Illusive Link and Its Implications for Criminal Law Reform." Paper presented at the annual meeting of the International Society for Criminal Law Reform, Montreal, August 8–12.

Prendergzast, Michael, David Farabee, Jerome Cartier, and Susan Henkin
2002   "Involuntary Treatment Within a Prison Setting: Impact on Psychosocial Change During Treatment." *Criminal Justice and Behavior* 29 (February): 5–26.

Prescott, Carol A. and Kenneth S. Kendler
1999   "Genetic and Environmental Contributions to Alcohol Abuse and Dependence in a Population-Based Sample of Male Twins." *American Journal of Psychiatry* 156 (January): 34–40.

President's Commission on Organized Crime
1986   *America's Habit: Drug Abuse, Drug Trafficking, and Organized Crime.* Washington, DC: U.S. Government Printing Office.
1985   *Organized Crime and Heroin Trafficking.* Washington, DC: U.S. Government Printing Office.
1984   *Organized Crime and Cocaine Trafficking.* Washington, DC: U.S. Government Printing Office.

Preston, Julia
2005   "2 Charged with Smuggling Ecstasy Pills of Military Jet." *New York Times* (April 14): B6.

"Principles of Nerve Cell Communication"
1997   *Alcohol Health and Research World* 21 (2): 107–8.

Prisoners in 2004
2005   Washington, DC: Bureau of Justice Statistics.

Quadagno, Jill S. and Robert J. Antonio
1975   "Labeling Theory as an Oversocialized Conception of Man: The Case of Mental Illness." *Sociology and Social Research* 60 (October): 30–41.

Querna, Elizabeth
2005   "The Newest War on Drugs." *U.S. News and World Report* (February 21): 52–54.

"Quitting Caffeine Can Bring on the Blahs"
1991   *Chicago Tribune* (August 18): 24.

Raab, Selwyn
1992   "Chief Seeks Action on Narcotics Unit." *New York Times* (January 9): B8.
1987   "New York Establishes Special Courts to Hasten Disposal of Drug Cases," *New York Times* (June 7): 17.

Rachlin, Howard
1991   *Introduction to Modern Behaviorism.* New York: W.H. Freeman.

Rado, Sandor
1981   "The Psychoanalysis of Pharmacothymia (Drug Addiction)." Pages 77–94 in *Classic Contributions in the Addictions,* edited by Howard Shaffer and Milton Earl Burglass. New York: Brunner/Mazel.

"Raising Nicotine Doses, on the Sly"
2006   New York Times editorial (August 31): 24.

RAND Drug Policy Research Center
1992   *Cocaine: The First Decade.* Issue Paper 1. Santa Monica, CA: RAND Drug Policy Research Center.

Rangel, Charles B.
1990   "Letter to the Editor: 'What's Wrong with Legalizing Drugs?'" *New York Times* (July 24): 14.

Ray, Oakley
1978   *Drugs, Society, and Human Behavior.* St. Louis: C.V. Mosby.

Reese, Joel
2000   "Problem Drug." *Chicago* (April): 51–60.

Reese, Stephen D. and Lucig H. Danielian
1989   "Intermedia Influence and the Drug Issue: Converging on Cocaine." Pages 29–45 in *Communication Campaigns About Drugs: Government, Media, and the Public,* edited by Pamela J. Shoemaker. Hillsdale, NJ: Lawrence Erlbaum Associates.

Reid, T. R.
2005   "Caffeine." *National Geographic* (January): 2–33.
Reiff, Phillip
1963   *Freud, Therapy and Techniques.* New York: Crowell-Collier.
Rettig, Richard P., Manuel J. Torres, and Gerald R. Garrett
1977   *Manny: A Criminal Addict's Story.* New York: Houghton-Mifflin.
Reuter, Peter
2001   "Supply-Side Drug Control." *Milken Institute Review* (First Quarter): 14–23.
2000   "One Tough Plant." *New York Times* (March 31): 29.
1999   "Drug Use Measures: What Are They Really Telling Us?" *National Institute of Justice Journal* (April): 12–19.
Reuter, Peter and Jonathan P. Caulkins
1995   "Redefining the Goals of National Drug Policy: Recommendations from a Working Group." *American Journal of Public Health* 85 (August): 1059–63.
Reuter, Peter, Robert MacCoun, and Patrick Murphy
1990   *Money from Crime: A Study of the Economics of Drug Dealing in Washington, D.C.* Santa Monica, CA: RAND.
Reuters
2006   "Colombia: Soldiers Arrested in Killing of Policemen." *New York Times* (June 2): 6.
Rhodes, Jean E. and Leonard Jason
1990   "A Social Stress Model of Substance Abuse." *Journal of Consulting and Clinical Psychology* 58 (August): 395–401.
Rhor, Monica
1991   "Nearly Undetectable Cocaine Found." *Chicago Tribune* (June 27): 31.
Ribeaud, Denis
2004   "Long-Term Impacts of the Swiss Heroin Prescription Trials on Crime of Treated Users." *Journal of Drug Issues* 34 (Winter): 163–95.
Richardson, Gale A. and Nancy L. Day
1999   "Studies of Prenatal Cocaine Exposure: Assessing the Influence of Extraneous Variables." *Journal of Drug Issues* 29 (2): 225–36.
Richey, Warren
1991   "Prosecutors' Deal with Criminals: Testify Against Noriega and Go Free." *Chicago Tribune* (November 27): 4.
Riding, Alan
1988   "Dispute Impeding U.S. War on Coca." *New York Times* (June 28): 1, 6.
1987   "Colombia's Drugs and Violent Politics Make Murder a Way of Life." *New York Times* (August 23): E3.
Riley, Diane
n.d.   "The Harm Reduction Model: Pragmatic Approaches to Drug Use from the Area Between Intolerance and Neglect." Canadian Centre on Substance Abuse: Internet.
Roberton, Robert J.
1986   "Designer Drugs: The Analog Game." Pages 91–96 in *Bridging Services: Drug Abuse, Human Services and the Therapeutic Community,* edited by Alfonso Acampora and Ethan Nebelkopf. New York: World Federation of Therapeutic Communities.
Robertson, Nan
1988a   "The Changing World of Alcoholics Anonymous." *New York Times Magazine* (February 21): 40–44, 47, 57, 92.
1988b   *Getting Better: Inside Alcoholics Anonymous.* New York: William Morrow.
Robins, Lee N.
1974   *The Vietnam Drug User Returns.* Washington, DC: U.S. Government Printing Office.
1973   *A Follow-up of Vietnam Drug Users.* Washington, DC: U.S. Government Printing Office.
Robins, Lee N., John E. Helzer, Michi Hesselbrock, and Eric Wish
1980   "Vietnam Veterans Three Years After Vietnam: How Our Study Changed Our View of Heroin." Pages 213–30 in *The Yearbook of Substance Use and Abuse,* Vol. II, edited by Leon Brill and Charles Winick. New York: Human Services Press.
Robinson, Linda
1998a   "Is Colombia Lost to Rebels?" *U.S. News and World Report* (May 11): 38–42.
1998b   "Land for Peace in Colombia." *U.S. News and World Report* (November 23): 37.
Robinson, Terry and Kent C. Berridge
2003   "Addiction." *Annual Review of Psychology:* 25–54.
Rocha, Beatriz, Kimberly Scearce-Levie, José J. Lucas, Noboru Hiroi, Nathalie Castanon, John C. Crabbe, Eric J. Nestler, and René Hen
1998   "Increased Vulnerability to Cocaine in Mice Lacking the Serotonin-1B Receptor." *Nature* 393 (May 14): 175–78.
Roffman, Roger A. and William H. George
1988   "Cannabis Abuse." Pages 325–63 in *Assessment of Addictive Behaviors,* edited by Dennis M. Donovan and G. Alan Marlatt. New York: Guilford.
Rohde, David
2004   "Poppies Flodd Afghanistan: Opium Tide May Yet Turn." *New York Times* (July 1): 13.
Rohter, Larry
2003   "Bolivian Leader's Ouster Seen as a Warning on U.S. Drug Policy." *New York Times* (October 23): 1, 14.
2000a   "Driven by Fear, Colombians Leave in Droves." *New York Times* (March 5): 8.
2000b   "Weave of Drugs and Strife in Colombia." *New York Times* (April 21): 1, 10, 11.
1999a   "Colombia Tries, Yet Cocaine Thrives." *New York Times* (November 20): 6.
1999b   "Colombian Army Hopes to Get Fighting Fit, No Easy Task." *New York Times* (December 5): 17.
Rohter, Larry and Clifford Krauss
1998a   "Dominicans Allow Drugs Easy Sailing." *New York Times* (May 10): 1, 6.

1998b "Dominican Drug Traffickers Tighten Grip on the Northeast." *New York Times* (May 11): 12, 17.

Romach, Myroslava K., Paul Glue, Kyle Kampman, Howard L. Kaplan, Gail R. Somer, Sabrina Poole, Laura Clarke, Vicki Coffin, James Cornish, Charles P. O'Brien, and Edward M. Sellers
1999 "Attenuation of the Euphoric Effects of Cocaine by the Dopamine D1/D5 Antagonist Ecopipam." *Archives of General Psychiatry* 56 (December): 1101–6.

Romero, Simon
2007 "Colombian Government is Ensnared in a Paramilitary Scandal." *New York Times* (January 21): 15.

Romoli, Kathleen
1941 *Colombia.* Garden City, NY: Doubleday, Doran.

Rosecan, Jeffrey S. and Edward V. Nunes
1987 "Pharmacological Management of Cocaine Abuse." Pages 255–70 in *Cocaine Abuse: New Directions in Treatment and Research,* edited by Henry I. Spitz and Jeffrey S. Rosecan. New York: Brunner/Mazel.

Rosecan, Jeffrey S., Henry I. Spitz, and Barbara Gross
1987 "Contemporary Issues in the Treatment of Cocaine Abuse." Pages 299–323 in *Cocaine Abuse: New Directions in Treatment and Research,* edited by Henry I. Spitz and Jeffrey S. Rosecan. New York: Brunner/Mazel.

Rosenbaum, Marsha
1981 *Women on Heroin.* New Brunswick, NJ: Rutgers University Press.

Rosenbaum, Ron
1988 "High Life: The Social Rise of Timothy Leary." *Vanity Fair* (April): 132–44; 154.

Rosenfeld, Richard and Scott H. Decker
1999 "Are Arrest Statistics a Valid Measure of Illicit Drug Use? The Relationship Between Criminal Justice and Public Health Indicators of Cocaine, Heroin, and Marijuana Use." *Justice Quarterly* 16 (September): 685–99.

Rosenkranz, Keith
2003 "High Fliers." *New York Times* (January 23): 27.

Rosenthal, Elisabeth
1993 "Patients in Pain Find Relief, Not Addiction, in Narcotics." *New York Times* (March 28): 1, 11.

Rosenthal, Mitchel
1984 "Therapeutic Communities: A Treatment Alternative for Many but Not all." *Journal of Substance Abuse Treatment* 1: 55–58.

1973 "New York City Phoenix House: A Therapeutic Community for the Treatment of Drug Abusers and Drug Addicts." Pages 83–102 in *Yearbook of Drug Abuse,* edited by Leon Brill and Earnest Harms. New York: Behavioral Publications.

Rothman, Richard B.
1994 "A Review of the Effects of Dopaminergic Agents in Humans: Implications for Medication Development." Pages 67–87 in *Neurobiological Models for Evaluating Mechanisms Underlying*

Cocaine Addiction, edited by Lynda Erinoff and Roger M. Brown. Rockville, MD: National Institute on Drug Abuse.

Rowell, Earle Albert and Robert Rowell
1939 *On the Trail of Marijuana: The Weed of Madness.* Mountain View, CA: Pacific Press.

Royal College of Psychiatrists
1987 *Drug Scenes: A Report on Drug Dependence.* London: Gaskell.

Rubin, Elizabeth
2006 "Inside the Land of the Taliban." *New York Times Magazine* (October 22): 86–97, 172–73, 175.

Russell, Francis
1975 *A City in Terror—1919—The Boston Police Strike.* New York: Viking.

Rydell, C. Peter and Susan S. Everingham
1994 *Controlling Cocaine: Supply Versus Demand Programs.* Santa Monica, CA: RAND.

Sackman, Bertram S., M. Maxine Sackman, and G. G. DeAngelis
1978 "Heroin Addiction as an Occupation: Traditional Addicts and Heroin-Addicted Polydrug Users." *International Journal of the Addictions* 13: 427–41.

SAMHSA News
2006 Vol. 14 (September/October).

Sanger, David E.
1995 "Money Laundering, New and Improved." *New York Times* (December 24): E4.

Santana, Rosa Maria
1996 "Drinking Blamed for Death of Teenager." *Chicago Tribune* (January 3): Sec. 2: 6.

Santora, Marc
2006 "17 Deaths Tied to Resurgence of Deadly Drug Mix in New York." *New York Times* (August 30): B2.

Savitt, Robert A.
1963 "Psychoanalytic Studies on Addiction: Ego Structure in Narcotic Addiction." *Psychoanalytic Quarterly* 32: 43–57.

Sawyers, June
1988 "When Opium Was Really the Opiate of the Masses." *Chicago Tribune Magazine* (January 3): 5.

Schemo, Diana Jean
2003 "A Study of Colleges Critical of Antidrinking Drives." *New York Times* (July 24): 16.

1999 "Bogotá Sees Drug War as Path to Peace." *New York Times* (January 6): 11.

1997 "Players Are Main Danger in Noisy Colombian Game." *New York Times* (December 26): 10.

Schemo, Diana Jean and Tim Golden
1998 "Bogotá Aid: To Fight Drugs or Rebels?" *New York Times* (June 2): 1, 12.

Schiffer, Frederic
1988 "Psychotherapy of Nine Successfully Treated Cocaine Abusers: Techniques and Dynamics." *Journal of Substance Abuse Treatment* 5: 131–37.

Schmetzer, Uli
1991 "Slave Trade Survives, Prospers Across Asia." *Chicago Tribune* (November 15): 1, 18.

1990   "'Prince of Death' Is a Wanted Man." *Chicago Tribune* (March 21): 21.

Schmidt, William E.
1993   "To Battle AIDS, Scots Offer Drugs to Addicts." *New York Times* (February 8): 3.

Schmitt, Eric
2006   "Springtime for Killing in Afghanistan." *New York Times* (May 28): Sec. 4: 1, 3.
2004   "Afghans' Gains Face Big Threat in Drug Traffic." *New York Times* (December 11): 1, 6.

Schneider, Andrew and Mary Pat Flaherty
1991   "Drug Law Leaves Trail of Innocents." *Chicago Tribune* (August 11): 1, 13.

Schnoll, Sidney H.
1979   "Pharmacological Aspects of Youth Drug Abuse." Pages 255–75 in *Youth Drug Abuse*, edited by George M. Beschner and Alfred S. Friedman. Lexington, MA: D.C. Heath.

Schuckit, Marc A.
1985   "Genetics and the Risk for Alcoholism." *Journal of the American Medical Association* 254: 2614–17.

Schur, Edwin H.
1973   *Radical Non-Intervention: Rethinking the Delinquency Problem*. Englewood Cliffs, NJ: Prentice Hall.
1965   *Crimes Without Victims: Deviant Behavior and Public Policy. Abortion, Homosexuality, Drug Addiction*. Englewood Cliffs, NJ: Prentice Hall.

Schuster, Charles R.
1993   "A Natural History of Drug Abuse." Pages 37–51 in *International Reseach Conference on Biomedical Approaches to Illicit Drug Demand Reduction*, edited by Christine R. Hartel. Washington, DC: U.S. Government Printing Office.

Sciolino, Elaine
1988   "Diplomats Do Not Hurry to Enlist in the War on Drugs." *New York Times* (February 21): E3.

Sciolino, Elaine and Stephen Engelberg
1988   "Narcotics Effort Foiled by U.S. Security Goals." *New York Times* (April 10): 1, 10.

Scott, Michael S.
2002   *Rave Parties*. Washington, DC: U.S. Department of Justice.

Segre, Sandro
2003   *Controlling Illegal Drugs: A Comparative Study*. New York: Aldine de Gruyer. Trans. by Nora Stern.

Selden, Lewis W., William L. Woolverton, Stanley A. Lorens, Joseph E. G. Williams, Rebecca L. Corwin, Norio Hata, and Mary Olimski
1993   "Behavioral Consequences of Partial Monoamine Depletion in the CNS After Methamphetamine-Like Drugs: The Conflict Between Pharmacology and Toxicology." Pages 34–51 in *Assessing Neurotoxicity in Drugs of Abuse*, edited by Lynda Erinoff. Rockville, MD: National Institute on Drug Abuse.

Seligmann, Jean and Patricia King
1996   "'Roofies': The Date-Rape Drug." *Pressweek* (February 26): 54.

Semple, Kirk
2001   "Colombia's Cocaine Frontier." *Mother Jones* (November/December): 58–63.

Senay, Edward C.
1986   "Clinical Implications of Drug Abuse Treatment Outcome." Pages 139–50 in *Drug Abuse Treatment Evaluation: Strategies, Progress, and Prospects*, edited by Frank M. Tims and Jacqueline P. Ludford. Rockville, MD: National Institute on Drug Abuse.

"Sexual Dysfunction and Addiction Treatment"
2000   *Addiction Treatment Forum* 9 (Spring): 1, 6–8.

Shapiro, Daniel
2003   "Individual Rights, Drug Policy, and the Worst-Case Scenario." *Criminal Justice Ethics* 22 (Winter/Spring): 41–45.

Shenk, Joshua Wolf
1999   "America's Altered States." *Harper's Magazine* (May): 38–52.

Shenon, Philip
1996   "Opium Baron's Rule May End with Surrender in Myanmar." *New York Times* (January 6): 4.

Sheppard, Nathaniel Jr.
1990   "Guatemalan Climate: Good for Poppy Fields, Drug Traffickers." *Chicago Tribune* (September 23): 12.

Sher, Kenneth J.
1991   *Children of Alcoholics: A Critical Appraisal of Theory and Research*. Chicago: University of Chicago Press.

Sherman, Carl
2005   "Dopamine Enhancement Underlies a Toluene Behavioral Effect." *NIDA Notes* 19 (5): 4–5.

Shiffman, Saul and Mark Balabanis
1995   "Associations Between Alcohol and Tobacco." Pages 17–36 in *Alcohol and Tobacco: From Basic Science to Clinical Practice*. Bethesda, MD: National Institute on Alcohol Abuse and Alcoholism.

Short, James F. Jr.
1968   *Gang Delinquency and Delinquent Subculture*. New York: Harper and Row.

Siegal, Harvey A., Richard C. Rapp, Casey W. Kelliher, James H. Fisher, Joseph H. Wagner, and Phyllis A. Cole
1995   "The Strengths Perspective of Case Management: A Promising Inpatient Substance Abuse Treatment Enhancement." *Journal of Psychoactive Drugs* 27 (1): 67–72.

Siegel, Ronald K.
1989   *Intoxication: Life in Pursuit of Artificial Paradise*. New York: E.F. Dutton.

Silvas, Jos
1994   "Enforcing Drug Laws in the Netherlands." Pages 41–58 in *Between Prohibition and Legalization: The Dutch Experiment in Drug Policy*, edited by Ed. Leuw and I. Haen Marshall. Amsterdam: Kugler Publications.

Simpson, Dwyne
2002   "We Know it Works; Now Let's Make it Better."
        Drugs and Alcohol Findings 7: 7.

Simpson, Edith E.
1989   "Adherence to Cigarette, Marijuana, and Cocaine
        Treatment Programs: A Survival Analysis." Paper
        presented at the annual meeting of the American
        Society of Criminology, Reno, NV, November.

Sinclair, Andrew
1962   *The Era of Excess: A Social History of the
        Prohibition Movement.* Boston: Little, Brown.

Sinclair, Upton
1981   *The Jungle.* New York: Bantam. Originally
        published in 1906.

Skinner, B. F.
1974   *About Behaviorism.* New York: Knopf.

Sly, Liz
1989   "Bennett Attacks Drug Legalization." *Chicago
        Tribune* (December 14): 24.

Smart, Frances
1970   *Neurosis and Crime.* New York: Barnes and
        Noble.

Smart, Reginald G.
1980   "An Availability-Proneness Theory of Illicit Drug
        Abuse." Pages 46–49 in *Theories on Drug Abuse:
        Selected Contemporary Perspectives,* edited by
        Dan J. Lettieri, Mollie Sayers, and Helen
        Wallenstein Pearson. Rockville, MD: National
        Institute on Drug Abuse.

Smith, David E.
1986   "Cocaine-Alcohol Abuse: Epidemiolgical,
        Diagnostic and Treatment Considerations."
        Journal of Psychoactive Drugs 18 (April–June):
        117–29.

Smith, David E., ed.
1979   *Amphetamine Use, Misuse, and Abuse.* Boston,
        MA: G. K. Hall and Co.

Smith, David E. and Donald R. Wesson
1994   "Benzodiazepines and Other Sedative-
        Hypnotics." Pages 179–90 in *The American
        Psychiatric Press Textbook of Substance Abuse
        Treatment,* edited by Marc Galanter and Herbert
        D. Kleber. Washington, DC: American
        Psychiatric Press.

Snyder, Solomon H.
1989   *Brainstorming: The Science of Politics and Opiate
        Research.* Cambridge, MA: Harvard University
        Press.

1986   *Drugs and the Brain.* New York: Scientific
        American.

1977   "Opiate Receptors and Internal Opiates."
        Scientific American (March): 44–56.

Soble, Ronald L.
1991   "Seized Assets Underwrite the War on Drugs."
        Los Angeles Times (April 16): 3, 23.

Society for Neuroscience (SNS)
2002   *Brain Facts: A Primer on the Brain and Nervous
        system.* Washington, DC: SNS.

Speaker, Susan L.
2001   "'The Struggle of Mankind Against Its
        Deadliest Foe': Themes of Counter-Subversion

in Anti-Narcotic Campaigns, 1920-1940."
        Journal of Social History 34 (Spring): Internet.

Speart, Jessica
1995   "The New Drug Mules." *New York Times
        Magazine* (June 11): 44–45.

Speckart, George and M. Douglas Anglin
1987   "Narcotics Use and Crime: An Overview of
        Recent Research Advances." *Contemporary Drug
        Problems* 16 (Winter): 741–69.

1985   "Narcotics and Crime: An Analysis of Existing
        Evidence for a Causal Relationship." *Behavioral
        Sciences and the Law* 3: 259–82.

Spence, Richard T.
1989   *Current Substance Abuse Trends in Texas.* Austin:
        Texas Commission on Alcohol and Drug Abuse.

Spitz, Henry I.
1987   "Cocaine Abuse: Therapeutic Group
        Approaches." Pages 156–201 in *Cocaine Abuse:
        New Directions in Treatment and Research,*
        edited by Henry I. Spitz and Jeffrey S. Rosecan.
        New York: Brunner/Mazel.

Spitz, Henry I. and Jeffrey S. Rosecan
1987   "Overview of Cocaine Abuse Treatment." Pages
        97–118 in *Cocaine Abuse: New Directions in
        Treatment and Research,* edited by Henry I. Spitz
        and Jeffrey S. Rosecan. New York: Brunner/
        Mazel.

Spohn, Cassia and David Holleran
2002   "The Effect of Imprisonment on Recidivism Rates
        of Felony Offenders: A Focus on Drug
        Offenders." *Criminology* 40 (May): 329–357.

Spotts, James V. and Franklin C. Shontz
1980   "A Life-Theme Theory of Chronic Drug Abuse."
        Pages 59–70 in *Theories on Drug Abuse: Selected
        Contemporary Perspectives,* edited by Dan J.
        Lettieri, Mollie Sayers, and Helen Wallenstein
        Pearson. Rockville, MD: National Institute on
        Drug Abuse.

Starkweather, C. Woodruff
1982   "Techniques of Therapy Based on Cognitive
        Learning Theory." Pages 37–47 in
        *Communication Disorders: General Principles of
        Therapy,* edited by William H. Perkins. New
        York: Thieme-Stratton.

Stearns, Peter N.
1998   "Dope Fiends and Degenerates: The Gendering of
        Addiction in the Early Twentieth Century."
        Journal of Social History 31 (Summer): 809–14.

Stellwagen, Lindsey D.
1985   *Use of Forfeiture Sanctions in Drug Cases.*
        Washington, DC: National Institute of Justice.

Stevens, Jay
1987   *Storming Heaven: LSD and the American Dream.*
        New York: Atlantic Monthly Press.

Stimson, Gerry V. and Edna Oppenheimer
1982   *Heroin Addiction: Treatment and Control in
        Britain.* London: Tavistock.

Stitzer, Maxine L., George E. Bigelow, Ira A. Liebson, and
Mary E. McCaul
1984   "Contingency Management of Supplemental
        Drug Use During Methadone Maintenance

Treatment." Pages 84–103 in *Behavioral Intervention Techniques in Drug Abuse Treatment*, edited by John Grabowski, Maxine L. Stitzer, and Jack E. Henningfield. Rockville, MD: National Institute on Drug Abuse.

Stitzer, Maxine L., George E. Bigelow, and Mary McCaul
1985   "Behavior Therapy in Drug Abuse Treatment: Review and Evaluation." Pages 31–50 in *Progress in the Development of Cost-Effective Treatment for Drug Abusers*, edited by Rebecca S. Ashery. Rockville, MD: National Institute on Drug Abuse.

Stocker, Steven
1999   "Studies Link Stress and Drug Addiction." *NIDA Notes* 14 (April): 12–15.

Stolberg, Sheryl Gay
1999   "Government Study of Marijuana Sees Medical Benefits." *New York Times* (March 18): 1, 20.
1998   "President Decides Against Financing Needle Programs." *New York Times* (April 21): 1, 18.

Stout, David
1999   "Coast Guard Using Sharpshooters to Stop Boats." *New York Times* (September 14): 16.

Strong, Simon
1992   "Peru Is Losing More Than the Drug War." *New York Times* (February 17): 11.

Stryker, Jeff
2001   "For Partygoers Who Can't Say No, Experts Try to Reduce the Risks." *New York Times* September 25): D5.

Stuart, Richard B.
1974   "Teaching Facts About Drugs: Pushing or Preventing?" *Journal of Educational Psychology* 66 (April): 189–201.

Stutman, Robert M. and Richard Esposito
1992   *Dead on Delivery: Inside the Drug Wars, Straight from the Street*. New York: Warner.

Substance Abuse and Mental Health Services Administration
2001   *Guide to Science-Based Practices*. Washington, DC: Substance Abuse and Mental Health Services Administration.

Substance Abuse Resource Center
1999   "Study Says Community Partnerships Can Reduce Drug Use" (December 23): Internet.

Sunderwirth, Stanley G.
1985   "Biological Mechanisms: Neurotransmission and Addiction." Pages 11–19 in *The Addictions: Multidisciplinary Perspectives and Treatments*, edited by Harvey B. Milkman and Howard J. Shaffer. Lexington, MA: DC Heath.

Sutherland, Edwin
1973   *On Analyzing Crime*, edited by Karl Schuessler. Chicago: University of Chicago Press.

Swadi, Harith and Harry Zeitlin
1987   "Drug Education for School Children: Does It Really Work?" *British Journal of Addiction* 82: 741–46.

Swan, Neil
n.d.   "Researchers Probe Which Comes First: Drug Abuse or Antisocial Behavior." *Drug Abuse Prevention Research and the Community*. Washington, DC: National Institute on Drug Abuse.

Sykes, Gresham M.
1967   *Crime and Society*, 2nd ed. New York: Random House.

Szabo, Liz
2005   "Study Links Kids' Lower Test Scores to Secondhand Smoke." *USA Today* (January 3): Internet.

Szasz, Thomas
1974   *Ceremonial Justice: The Ritual Persecution of Drugs, Addicts, and Pushers*. Garden City, NY: Doubleday.

Tackett, Michael
1990   "Minor Drug Players Are Paying Big Prices." *Chicago Tribune* (October 15): 1, 9.

Tagliabue, John
2000   "The Prince and His Black Sheep: This is no Liectenstein Fairy Tale." *New York Times* (April 8): 4.

Tamayo, Juan O.
2001   "Colombia's Heroin Trade is Flourishing." *Chicago Tribune* (August 24): 6.

Tammi, Tuuka
2004   "The Harm-Reduction School of Thought: Three Factions." *Contemporary Drug Problems* 31 (Fall): 381–400.

Tancer, Manuel and Charles R. Schuster
1997   "Serotonin and Dopamine System Interactions in the Reinforcing Properties of Psychostimulants: A Research Strategy." *Pressletter of the Multidisciplinary Association for Psychedelic Studies* 7 (Summer): Internet.

Tapper, Andrew R., Sheri L. McKinney, Raad Nashmi, Johannes Schwarz, Purnima Deshpande, Cesar Labarca, Paul Whiteaker, Michael J. Marks, Allan C. Collins, and Henry A. Lester
2004   "Nicotine Activation of [alpha]4* Receptors: Sufficient for Reward, Tolerance, and Sensitization." *Science* 306 (November 5): 1029–33.

Tarter, Ralph E.
1988   "Are There Inherited Behavioral Traits That Predispose to Substance Abuse?" *Journal of Consulting and Clinical Psychology* 56 (April): 189–96.

Tarter, Ralph E., Arthur I. Alterman, and Kathleen L. Edwards
1985   "Vulnerability to Alcoholism in Men: A Behavior-Genetic Perspective." *Journal of Studies on Alcohol* 46 (July): 329–56.

Taylor, David
2002   "Drugs on the Brain." *Meanjean* 61 (June): 138–44.

Terry, Charles E. and Mildred Pellens
1928   *The Opium Problem.* New York: The Committee on Drug Addictions in Collaboration with the Bureau of Social Hygiene, Inc.

"33-Year Study Shows Severe Long-Term Effects of Heroin"
2001   *Brown University Digest of Addiction Theory and Application* 20 (June): 16–20.

Thomas, Josephine
2001   "Maternal Smoking During Pregnancy Associated with Negative Toddler Behavior and Early Smoking Experimentation." *NIDA Notes* 16 (1): 1, 4–5.

Thompson, Ginger
2005   "Drug Violence Paralyzes a City, and Chills the Border." *New York Times* (May 24): 4.

Thornburgh, Dick
1989   *Drug Trafficking: A Report to the President.* Washington, DC: U.S. Government Printing Office.

Thoumi, Francisco E.
2002   "Illegal Drugs in Colombia: From Illegal Economic Boom to Social Crisis." *Annals* 582 (July): 102–116.
1995   "The Size of the Illegal Drug Industry." Pages 77–96 in *Drug Trafficking in the Americas,* edited by Bruce M. Bagley and William O. Walker III. New Brunswick, NJ: Transaction Publishers.

Tilson, Hugh A.
1993   "Neurobehavioral Methods Used in Neurotoxicology." Pages 1–33 in *Assessing Neurotoxicity in Drugs of Abuse,* edited by Lynda Erinoff. Rockville, MD: National Institute on Drug Abuse.

Tindall, George B.
1988   *America: A Narrative History,* Vol. 2. New York: Norton.

Torriero, E. A.
2002   "Afghan Officials Struggle to Stop Opium Bonanza." *Chicago Tribune* (March 3): 6.

Tortora, Gerard J.
1983   *Principles of Human Anatomy,* 3rd ed. New York: Harper and Row.

Treaster, Joseph B.
1991   "Plan Lets Addicted Mothers Take Their Newborns Home." *New York Times* (September 19): 1, 16.
1990a   "Bypassing Borders, More Drugs Flood Ports." *New York Times* (April 29): 1, 18.
1990b   "At City's Heart, Carnival for Haunted." *New York Times* (September 27): 4.

Trebach, Arnold S.
1987   *The Great Drug War: A Radical Proposal That Could Make America Safe Again.* New York: Macmillan.
1982   *The Heroin Solution.* New Haven, CT: Yale University Press.

Tullis, LaMond
1995   *Unintended Consequences: Illegal Drugs and Drug Policies in Nine Countries.* Boulder, CO: Lynne Reinner.

Tuma, Dan J. and Carol A. Casey
2004   *Dangerous Byproducts of Alcohol Breakdown— Focus on Adducts.* Bethesda, MD: National Institute on Alcohol Abuse and Alcoholism.

Tyler, Patrick E.
1995   "China Battles a Spreading Scourge of Illicit Drugs." *New York Times* (November 15): 1, 7.
1991   "Teheran Convicts Nine in Opposition." *New York Times* (September 22): 9.

Tymoczco, Dmitri
1996   "The Nitrous Oxide Philosopher." *Atlantic Monthly* (May): 93–101.

Uelmen, Gerald F. and Victor G. Haddox, eds.
1983   *Drug Abuse and the Law.* New York: Clark Boardman.

Uitermark, Justus
2004   "The Origins and Future of the Dutch Approach Towards Drugs." *Journal of Drug Issues* 34 (Summer): 511–33.

U.S. Department of State
2000   *Policy and Program Overview for 1999.* Washington, DC: Bureau for International Narcotics and Law Enforcement Affairs.
1999   *Money Laundering and Financial Crimes.* Washington, DC: Bureau for International Narcotics and Law Enforcement Affairs.

"U.S. Resists Easing Curb on Marijuana."
1989   *New York Times* (December 31): 14.

Vaillant, George E.
1983   *The Natural History of Alcoholism.* Cambridge, MA: Harvard University Press.
1970   "The Natural History of Narcotic Drug Addiction." *Seminars in Psychiatry* 2 (November): 486–98.

Valenzuela, C. Fernando
1997   "Alcohol and Neurotransmitter Interactions." *Alcohol Health and Research World* 21 (2): 144–48.

van de Mheen, Dike and Paul Gruter
2004   "Interventions on the Supply Side of the Local Hard Drug Market: Towards a Regulated Hard Drug Trade? The Case of the City of Rotterdam." *Journal of Drug Issues* 34 (Winter): 145–62.

Van Dyke, Craig and Robert Byck
1982   "Cocaine." *Scientific American* 246 (March):128–41.

Varisco, Raymond
2000   "Drug Abuse and Conduct Disorder Linked to Maternal Smoking During Pregnancy." *NIDA Notes* 15 (5): 5.

Verhovek, Sam Howe
1995   "Young, Carefree and in Love with Cigarettes." *New York Times* (July 30): 1, 10.

Verini, James
2007   "A Budding Invasion." *Men's Vogue* (March/ April): 71, 74, 78, 80, 86.

Vest, Jason
1997   "DEA to Florists: The Poppies Are Unlovely."
        U.S. Press and World Report (March 17): 49.
"Victims of Botched U.S. Drug Sting Sue"
1995   *Chicago Tribune* (January 24): 7.
Visher, Christy A.
1990   "Linking Criminal Sanctions, Drug Testing, and
        Drug and Drug Abuse Treatment: A Crime
        Control Strategy for the 1990s." *Criminal Justice
        Policy Review* 3: 329–43.
Vivanco, José Miguel
1995   "Letter to the New York Times: 'U.S. Aids Bolivia
        in Trampling Rights.'" *New York Times*
        (July 18): 14.
Vogt, Amanda
2003   "Now Many 'Just Say No' to DARE." *Chicago
        Tribune* (January 26): 1, 14.
Volkow, Nora D.
2006   "NIDA Director's Report to CPDD Meeting:
        Progress, Priorities, and Plans for the Future."
        Pages 70–79 in *Problems of Drug Dependence
        2005*. Bathesda, MD: National Institute on Drug
        Abuse.
Volkow, Nora D., Gene-Jack Wang, Joanna S. Fowler, Jean
Logan, Samuel J. Gatley, Andrew Gifford, Robert
Hitzemann, YuShin Ding, and Naomi Pappas
1999a   "Prediction of Reinforcing Responses to
        Psychostimulants in Humans by Brai Dopamine$_2$
        Receptor Levels." *American Journal of Psychiatry*
        156 (September): 1440–43.
Volkow, Nora D., Gene-Jack Wang, Joanna S. Fowler,
Jean Logan, S. John Gatley, Christopher Wong,
Robert Hitzemann, and Naomi R. Pappas
1999b   "Reinforcing Effects of Psychostimulants in
        Humans Are Associated with Increases in Brain
        Dopamine and Occupancy of D$_2$ Receptors."
        *Journal of Pharmacology and Experimental
        Therapeutics* 291 (October): 409–15.
Volkow, Nora D., L. Chang, Gene-Jack Wang, Joanna S.
Fowler, M. Leonido-Yee, D. Franceschi, M. J. Sedler,
Samuel J. Gatley, Robert Hitzemann, YuShin Ding, Jean
Logan, C. Wong, and E. N. Miller
2001   "Association of Dopamine Transporter
        Reduction with Psychomotor Impairment in
        Methamphetamine Abusers." *American Journal
        of Psychiatry* 158 (March): 377–82.
von Mises, Ludwig
1949   *Human Action: A Treatise on Economics*. New
        Haven, CT: Yale University Press.
von Solinge, Tim Boekhout
2004   *Dealing with Drugs in Europe: An Investigation
        of European Drug Control Experience: France,
        the Netherlands and Sweden*. The Hague: BJu
        Legal Publishers.
von Zielbauer, Paul
2003   "Court Treatment System is Found to Help Drug
        Offenders Stay Clean." *New York Times*
        (November 9): 33.
Vorenberg, James and Irving F. Lukoff
1973   "Addiction, Crime, and the Criminal Justice
        System." *Federal Probation* 37 (December): 3–7.

Wahl, Melissa
1999   "Hitting a Wall of Opposition." *Chicago Tribune*
        (February 4): Sec. 3: 1, 4.
Wald, Matthew
2002   "Hidden Plague of Alcohol Abuse by the
        Elderly." *New York Times* (April 2): D7.
Wald, Patricia M. and Annette Abrams
1972   "Drug Education." Pages 123–72 in *Dealing with
        Drug Abuse: A Report to the Ford Foundation*.
        New York: Praeger.
Wald, Patricia M. and Peter Barton Hutt
1972   "The Drug Abuse Survey Project: Summary of
        Findings, Conclusions, and Recommendations."
        Pages 3–61 in *Dealing with Drug Abuse: A Report
        to the Ford Foundation*. New York: Praeger.
Waldman, Amy
2004   "Afghan Route to Prosperity: Grow Poppies."
        New York Times (April 10): 1, 5.
Waldorf, Dan
1973   *Careers in Dope*. Englewood Cliffs, NJ: Prentice-
        Hall.
Wallace, John
1993   "Modern Disease Models of Alcoholism and
        Other Chemical Dependencies: The New
        Biopsychosocial Models." *Drugs and Society*
        8 (1): 69–87.
Wallance, Gregory
1981   *Papa's Game*. New York: Ballantine.
Walter, Ingo
1990   *Secret Money: The World of International
        Financial Secrecy*. New York: Harper Business.
Walters, John
2003   *Dialogue with John Walters, Director, White
        House Office of National Drug Control Policy*.
        Washington, DC: Center for Strategic and
        International Studies..
Washton, Arnold M
1989   *Cocaine Addiction: Treatment, Recovery, and
        Relapse Prevention*. New York: Norton.
Washton, Arnold M. and Mark S. Gold
1987   "Recent Trends in Cocaine Abuse as Seen from
        the '800-Cocaine Hotline.'" Pages 10–22 in
        Cocaine: A Clinicians Handbook, edited by
        Arnold M. Washton and Mark S. Gold. New
        York: Guilford Press.
Washton, Arnold M., Nannette S. Stone, and Edward
C. Henrickson
1988   "Cocaine Abuse." Pages 364–89 in *Assessment of
        Addictive Behaviors*, edited by Dennis M.
        Donovan and G. Alan Marlatt. New York:
        Guilford.
Washton, Arnold M. and Nanette Stone-Washton
1993   "Outpatient Treatment of Cocaine and Crack
        Addiction: A Clinical Perspective." Pages 15–30
        in *Cocaine Treatment: Research and Clinical
        Perspectives*, edited by Frank M. Tims and Carl
        G. Leukefeld. Rockville, MD: National Institute
        on Drug Abuse.
Waterston, Alisse
1993   *Addicts in the Political Economy*. Philadelphia:
        Temple University Press.

Watlington, Dennis
1987   "Between the Cracks." *Vanity Fair* (December): 146–51, 184.

Watson, Russell
1999   "Coke and Mrs. Colonel." *Pressweek* (August 16): 37.

Webster, Barbara and Michael S. McCampbell
1992   *International Money Laundering: Research and Investigation Join Forces.* Washington, DC: National Institute of Justice.

Weil, Andrew
1995   "The New Politics of Coca." *New Yorker* (May 15): 70–80.

Weiner, Tim
2002   "Border Customs Agents Are Pushed to the Limit." *New York Times* (July 25): 14.

Weinstein, Adam K.
1988   "Prosecuting Attorneys for Money Laundering: A New and Questionable Weapon in the War on Crime." *Law and Contemporary Problems* 51 (Winter): 369–86.

Weisheit, Ralph A.
1990   "Cash Crop: A Study of Illicit Marijuana Growers." Working draft for the National Institute of Justice.

Weiss, Roger D. and Steven M. Mirin
1987   *Cocaine.* Washington, DC: American Psychiatric Press.

Weppner, Robert S.
1983   *The Untherapeutic Community: Organizational Behavior in a Failed Addiction Treatment Program.* Lincoln: University of Nebraska.

Wesson, Donald R. and David E. Smith
1985   "Cocaine: Treatment Perspectives." Pages 193–203 in *Cocaine Use in America: Epidemiologic and Clinical Perspectives,* edited by Nicholas J. Kozel and Edgar H. Adams. Rockville, MD: National Institute on Drug Abuse.
1977   *Barbiturates: Their Use, Misuse, and Abuse.* New York: Human Sciences Press.

Wever, Leon
1994   "Drugs as a Public Health Problem." Pages 59–74 in *Between Prohibition and Legalization: The Dutch Experiment in Drug Policy,* edited by Ed. Leuw and I. Haen Marshall. Amsterdam: Kugler Publications.

Wexler, Harry K., Douglas S. Lipton, and Kenneth Foster
1985   "Outcome Evaluation of a Prison Therapeutic Community for Substance Abuse Treatment: Preliminary Results." Paper presented at the American Society of Criminology, San Diego, CA, November.

Wexler, Harry K., George DeLeon, George Thomas, David Kressel, and Jean Peters
1999   "The Amity Prison TC Evaluation: Reincarceration Outcomes." *Criminal Justice and Behavior* 26 (June): 147–67.

Wexler, Harry K., Gregory P. Falkin, and Douglas S. Lipton
1990   "Outcome Evaluation of a Prison Therapeutic Community for Substance Abuse Treatment." *Criminal Justice and Behavior* 15: 71–92.

Wexler, Harry K. and Ronald Williams
1985   "The Stay 'N Out Therpeutic Community: Prison Treatment for Substance Abusers." *Journal of Psychoactive Drugs* 18 (July-September): 221–30.

"What Kind of Drug Use Does School-Based Prevention Prevent?"
2002   *Drug Policy Research Center Newsletter* (June): Internet.

Wheat, Sue and Philip Withers Green
1999   "Leaf in the Lurch." *Geographical* (September): 42–48.

White, Peter
1989   "Coca–An Ancient Herb Turns Deadly." *National Geographic* (January): 3–47.

White, William L.
1998   *Slaying the Dragon: The History of Addiction Treatment and Recovery in America.* Bloomington, IN: Chestnut Health Systems.

White House Conference for a Drug Free America
1988   *Final Report.* Washington, DC: U.S. Government Printing Office.

Whiteacre, Kevin W.
2005   "Criminal Constructions of Drug Users." Pages 3–13 in *Cocktails and Dreams: Perspectives on Drug and Alcohol Use,* edited by Wilson R. Palacios. Upper Saddle River, NJ: Prentice Hall.

Whiteacre. Kevin W. and Hal Pepinsky
2002   "Controlling Drug Use." *Criminal Justice Policy Review* 13 (March): 21–31.

Whitlock, Rod Van, Howard Collings, and Cathleen Burnett
1990   "Relationship Between Cocaine Use and Severity of Crime." Paper presented at the annual meeting of the American Society of Criminology, Baltimore, November.

Whitten, Lori
2006a   "Court-Mandated Treatment Works as Well as Voluntary." *NIDA Notes* (July): 1, 6.
2006b   "Study Finds Rapid Withdrawal no Easier with Ultrarapid Opiate Detox." *NIDA Notes* (October): 4–5.
2006c   "Low-Cost Incentives Improve Outcomes in Stimulant Abuse Achievement." *NIDA Notes* 21 (October): 1, 6.
2005   "Cocaine-Related Environmental Cues Elicit Physiological Stress Responses." *NIDA Notes* (August): 1, 6–7.

Wicker, Tom
1987   "Drugs and Alcohol." *New York Times* (May 13): 27.

Wilbanks, William
1990   "The Danger in Viewing Addicts as Victims: A Critique of the Disease Model of Addiction." *Criminal Justice Policy Review* 3: 407–22.

Wilkerson, Isabel
1991   "Court Backs Woman in Pregnancy Drug Case." *New York Times* (April 3): 13.

Williams, Jay R., Lawrence J. Redlinger, and Peter K. Manning
1979   *Police Narcotics Control: Patterns and Strategies.* Washington, DC: U.S. Government Printing Office.

Williams, Jill Schlabig
2004   "The Neurobehavioral Legacy of Prenatal
        Tobacco Exposure." *NIDA Notes* 18 (6): 8–9. 13.
Williams, Terry
1989   *The Cocaine Kids: The Inside Story of a Teenage
        Drug Ring.* Reading, MA: Addison-Wesley.
Willoughby, Alan
1988   *The Alcohol Troubled Person: Known and
        Unknown.* Chicago: Nelson-Hall.
Wilson, James Q.
1990   "Against the Legalization of Drugs." *Commentary*
        89 (February): 21–28.
1978   *The Investigators: Managing FBI and Narcotics
        Agents.* New York: Basic Books.
1975   *Thinking About Crime.* New York: Basic Books.
Winerip, Michael
1998   "Binge Nights: The Emergency on Campus."
        New York Times Education Life (January 4):
        28–31, 42
Winger, Gail
1988   "Pharmacological Modifications of Cocaine and
        Opioid Self-Administration." Pages 125–36 in
        Mechanisms of Cocaine Abuse and Toxicity,
        edited by Doris Clouet, Khursheed Asghar, and
        Roger Brown. Rockville, MD: National Institute
        on Drug Abuse.
Winick, Charles
1961   "Physician Narcotic Addicts." *Social Problems* 9:
        174–86.
Winter, Greg
2003   "Study Finds No Sign That Testing Deters Students'
        Drug Use." *New York Times* (May 17): 1, 14.
Winter, Jerrold C.
1994   "The Stimulus Effects of Serotonergic Hallucinogens
        in Animals." Pages 157–82 in *Hallucinogens: An
        Update,* edited by Geraline C. Lin and Richard
        A. Glennon. Rockville, MD: National Institute on
        Drug Abuse.
Winters, Ken C. and George Henly
1988   "Assessing Adolescents Who Abuse Chemicals:
        The Chemical Dependency Adolescent
        Assessment Project." Pages 4–18 in *Adolescent
        Drug Abuse: Analyses of Treatment Research,*
        edited by Elizabeth R. Rahdert and John Grabowski.
        Rockville, MD: National Institute on Drug Abuse.
Wish, Eric
n.d.   *Drug Testing.* Rockville, MD: National Institute
        of Justice.
Wish, Eric D. and Bruce Johnson
1986   "The Impact of Substance Abuse on Criminal
        Careers." Pages 52–88 in *Criminal Careers and
        Career Criminals,* edited by Alfred Blumstein,
        Jacqueline Cohen, Jeffrey A. Roth, and Christy A.
        Visher. Washington, DC: National Academy
        Press.
Wishart, David
1974   "The Opium Poppy: The Forbidden Crop."
        Journal of Geography 73 (January): 14–25.
Wisotsky, Steven
1987   *Breaking the Impasse in the War on Drugs.*
        Westport, CT: Greenwood.

Witkin, Gordon
1991   "The Men Who Created Crack." *U.S. Press and
        World Report* (August 19): 44–53.
Witkin, Gordon and Jennifer Griffin
1994   "The New Opium Wars." *U.S. Press & World
        Report* (October 10): 39–44.
Wodak, Alex
1990   "Needle Exchange Succeeding in Australia."
        Letter to the *New York Times* (March 26):
        14.
Wodak, Alex and Peter Lurie
1997   "A Tale of Two Countries: Attempts to Control
        HIV Among Injecting Drug Users in Australia and
        the United States." *Journal of Drug Issues* 27:
        117–34.
Wolf, Judtih, Loes Linssen, and Ireen de Graaf
2003   "Drug Consumption Facilities in the
        Netherlands." *Journal of Drug Issues* 33
        (Summer): Internet.
Wolfe, Tom
1968   *The Electric Kool-Aid Acid Test.* New York:
        Farrar, Straus and Giroux.
Wolfgang, Marvin E. and Franco Ferracuti
1967   *The Subculture of Violence: Toward an
        Integrated Theory in Criminology.* London:
        Tavistock.
Wood, Roland W.
1973   "18,000 Addicts Later: A Look at California's
        Civil Addict Program." *Federal Probation* 38
        (March): 26–31.
Woodiwiss, Michael
1988   *Crime, Crusades and Corruption: Prohibition in
        the United States, 1900–1987.* Totawa, NJ:
        Barnes and Noble.
Woods, James R. Jr.
1993   "Effects of Drugs of Abuse on Mother and
        Fetus." Pages 179-87 in *International Research
        Conference on Biomedical Approaches to Illicit
        Drug Demand Reduction,* edited by Christine R.
        Hartel. Washington, DC: U.S. Government
        Printing Office.
Woody, George E., Lester Lubrosky, A. Thomas McLellan,
Charles P. O'Brien, Aren T. Beck, Jack Blaine, Ira Herman,
and Anita Hole
1983   "Psychotherapy for Opiate Addicts: Does It
        Help?" *Archives of General Psychiatry* 40 (June):
        639–45.
Worth, Robert F.
2003   "20 Airport Workers Held in Smuggling of Drugs for
        Decade." *New York Times* (November 26): 1, B4.
2002   "Judge's Ruling on Statements to A.A. Is
        Overturned." *New York Times* (July 18): 19.
Wren, Christopher S.
1999a   "A Purer Form of Heroin Lures New Users to a
        Long, Hard Fall." *New York Times* (May 9): 27.
1999b   "Bid for Alcohol in Antidrug Ads Hits Resistance."
        New York Times (May 31): 1, 8.
1999c   "In Battle Against Heroin, Scientists Enlist
        Heroin." *New York Times* (June 8): D1, 6.
1998a   "Road to Riches Starts in the Golden Triangle."
        New York Times (May 11): 8.

1998b   "Afghanistan's Opium Output Drops Sharply, U.N. Survey Shows." *New York Times* (September 27): 11.

1998c   "Drug Officials Sense a Shift in Dominicans." *New York Times* (August 14): 16.

1996   "Mexican Role in Cocaine Is Exposed in U.S. Seizure." *New York Times* (May 3): C19.

Wright, Fred D., Aaron T. Beck, Cory F. Newman, and Bruce S. Liese
1993   "Cognitive Therapy of Substance Abuse: Theoretical Rationale." Pages 123–46 in *Behavioral Treatments for Drug Abuse and Dependence,* edited by Lisa Simon Onken, John D. Blaine, and John J. Boren. Rockville, MD: National Institute on Drug Abuse.

Wurmser, Leon
1978   "Mr. Pecksniff's Horse? (Psychodynamics in Compulsive Drug Use)." Pages 36–72 in *Psychodynamics of Drug Dependence,* edited by Jack D. Blaine and Demetrios A. Julius. Rockville, MD: National Institute on Drug Abuse.

Wysong, Earl, Richard Aniskiewicz, and David Wright
1994   "Truth and DARE: Drug Education to Graduation and as Symbolic Politics." *Social Problems* 41 (August): 448–72.

Ynclan, Nery
2002   "Web Site Gives Addicts Support on the Road." *Chicago Tribune* (October 13): Sec. C10.

Yorke, Clifford
1970   "A Critical Review of Some Psychoanalytic Literature on Drug Addiction." *British Journal of Medical Psychology* 43: 141–59.

Young, Douglas
2002   "Impact of Perceived Legal Pressure on Retention in Drug Treatment." *Criminal Justice and Behavior* 29 (February): 27–55.

Young, James Harvey
1961   *The Toadstool Millionaires: A Social History of Patent Medicines in America Before Federal Regulation.* Princeton, NJ: Princeton University Press.

Zahniser, Nancy R., Joanna Peris, Linda P. Dwoskin, Pamela Curella, Robert P. Yasuda, Laurie O'Keefe, and Sally J. Boyson
1988   "Sensitization to Cocaine in the Nigrostriatal Dopamine System." Pages 55–77 in *Mechanisms of Cocaine Abuse and Toxicity,* edited by Doris Clouet, Khursheed Asghar, and Roger Brown. Rockville, MD: National Institute on Drug Abuse.

Zambito, Thomas
2005   "Afghani Heroin King Denies Rap." *New York Daily News* (October 25): 8.

Zernike, Kate
2006a   "Potent Mexican Meth Floods in as States Curb Domestic Variety." *New York Times* (January 23): 1, 17.

2006b   "F.D.A.'s Report Illuminates Wide Divide on Marijuana." *New York Times* (April 22): 11.

2001   "Antidrug Program Says It Will Adopt a New Strategy." *New York Times* (February 15): 1, 23.

2000   "New Tactic on College Drinking: Play It Down." *New York Times* (October 3): 1, 21.

Zickler, Patrick
2004   "In Chronic Drug Abuse, Acute Dopamine Surge May Erode Resolve to Abstain." *NIDA Notes* 19 (1): 1. 6–7.

2003   "Genetic Variation May Increase Nicotine Craving and Smoking Relapse." *NIDA Notes* 18 (3): 1, 6.

2002   "Study Demonstrates That Marijuana Smokers Experience Significant Withdrawal." *NIDA Notes* 17 (3): 7, 10.

2001   "Cues for Cocaine and Normal Pleasures Activate Common Brain Sites." *NIDA Notes* 16 (2): 1, 5, 7.

2000a   "Brain Imaging Studies Show Long-term Damage from Methamphetamine Abuse." *NIDA Notes* 15 (3): 11, 13.

2000b   "Nicotine Craving and Heavy Smoking May Contribute to Increased Use of Cocaine and Heroin." *NIDA Notes* 15 (5): Internet.

1999   "Twin Studies Help Define the Role of Genes in Vulnerability to Drug Abuse." *NIDA Notes* 14 (4): 1, 5, 8.

Zielbauer, Paul
2000   "New Campus High: Illicit Prescription Drugs." *New York Times* (March 24): 1, 19.

Zimmer, Lynn
1990   "Proactive Policing Against Street-Level Drug Trafficking." *American Journal of Police* 9: 43–74.

Zimring, Franklin E. and Gordon Hawkins
1992   *The Search for Rational Drug Control.* New York: Cambridge University Press.

Zinberg, Norman E.
1984   *Drug, Set, and Setting: The Basis for Controlled Intoxicant Use.* New Haven, CT: Yale University Press.

Zinberg, Norman E. and John A. Robertson
1972   *Drugs and the Public.* New York: Simon and Schuster.

Zinberg, Norman E., Wayne M. Harding, Shirley M. Stelmack, and Robert A. Marblestone
1978   "Patterns of Heroin Abuse." Pages 10–24 in *Recent Developments in Chemotherapy of Narcotic Addiction,* edited by Benjamin Kissin, Joyce H. Lowinson, and Robert B. Millman. New York: New York Academy of Sciences.

Zuckerman, Laurence
2000   "Workers Get Greater Drug Test Protection." *New York Times* (December 15): 20.

Name Index

Subject Index